WHAT'S IT ALL ABOUT?

Michael Caine has starred in over one hundred films, and is one of only two actors to have been nominated for an Academy Award for acting in every decade since the 1960s. He lives in London and Oxfordshire with his wife, Shakira. He has two daughters.

MICHAEL
CAINE

WHAT'S IT ALL ABOUT?

arrow books

Reissued by Arrow Books 2010

13

First published in Great Britain in 1992 by Century
First published in paperback in 1993 by Arrow Books

This edition published in 2010 by
Arrow Books
Random House, 20 Vauxhall Bridge Road,
London SW1V 2SA

www.randomhouse.co.uk

Addresses for companies within The Random House Group Limited can
be found at
www.randomhouse.co.uk offices.htm

The Random House Group Limited Reg. No. 954009

A CIP catalogue record for this book
is available from the British Library

ISBN 9780099553199

Penguin Random House is committed to a sustainable future for
our business, our readers and our planet. This book is made from
Forest Stewardship Council® certified paper.

Printed and bound in Great Britain by Clays Ltd, Elcograf S.p.A.

To Shakira, my wife,
and Dominique and Natasha, my daughters.
All my love forever.

Contents

Foreword

Part One

1	'Mummy's out!'	3
2	'Very flat, Norfolk'	12
3	What I got for a chocolate bar	31
4	Noses Off	43

Part Two

5	'If you can't move it, *paint it*'	63
6	'You never hear the one that gets you'	75
7	'It's only malaria'	91
8	Nowhere to go but up	104
9	'It's only a small part . . .'	120
10	Becoming Michael Caine	127
11	Understudying O'Toole	137
12	Raw steaks through the letter-box	146
13	The first screen test	156

Part Three

14	'When the magic happens . . .'	169
15	$1500 a *week?*	184
16	The two minutes that changed my life	195
17	Butch cooking	205
18	*Alfie*	215
19	Lemon and Micklewhite	224

Part Four

20	*'If* you want to be a star in America . . .'	235

21 The Elephant to Beverly Hills   251
22 Cannes   261
23 Otto's Revenge   269
24 French hours   281
25 Bardot tries it on   287
26 'Oh yes – a Rolls Royce'   298
27 My worst location   307
28 Elizabeth and me   315

Part Five

29 Shakira   337
30 'Call me Larry'   350
31 Natasha   365
32 Gucci shoes   373
33 *The Man Who Would Be King*   389
34 Biting the customers   407
35 *The Swarm* attacks   415

Part Six

36 Welcome to Beverly Hills   425
37 Dressed to kill . . .   437
38 Ma in Beverly Hills   447
39 The Queen and I   463
40 How to lose an Oscar   472
41 Paradise Found   488

Part Seven

42 Working with Woody   503
43 Moving back   518
44 Scoundrels   529
45 In my own write   539
46 A sting in the tail   547
47 David   554
Acknowledgements   559
Picture Credits   561
Index   563

Foreword

Well – what do you think of it so far?

It's not too heavy for you, is it? They told me not to write a long book or it would be too weighty and too expensive, so I've tried to keep the price and the bulk down. But there's still a lot I want to say.

There have been something like 5,000 miles of newsprint and at least seven biographies on me. God knows why. So why add to all this? To set the record straight on my own record player for a change. I have long since stopped reading what is written about me; for the most part it has been wrong or misleading. I am not saying that I am a better or nicer person than I have seen portrayed and, heaven knows, this book is not a work of history or scholarship. But what you will read here is the real me – not for a change, but for the first time.

So what *was* it all about? I'm going to tell you.

PART ONE

1

'Mummy's out!'

I first started to act at the age of three. We were a very poor family and it was my mother's idea to have me help out with her many outstanding bills. She wrote the script and directed the action. The cue to begin my performance was a ring at the door bell. Grasping my small hand, my mother rushed down the three flights of stairs from our small flat and hid behind the front door as I opened it. The unsuspecting third member of the cast – the rent collector – was standing there as I delivered my first lines: 'Mummy's out,' I said, and slammed the door in his face.

I was a painfully shy little boy and terrified at first, but I became accustomed to the role and eventually got to play to a better class of creditor. One day I even played to the local vicar, who was collecting money to repair the church spire. As my mother was Church of England and my father was Roman Catholic, they had not been allowed to marry in either church so they had no reason to go there to thank anybody for anything. My mother was always a firm believer in God, but – like me – never went to church although she did have me christened into the Protestant faith. I asked my father one day why I was Protestant and not Catholic like him and his honest and practical reply was: 'The Protestant church was just around the corner and the Catholic one was a bus ride away and we didn't have the money for the fare.' Of such earth shattering material is one's destiny formed.

I read somewhere in a book on psychiatry that the basis of all our lives is that we become what we are afraid of. For although my performances at the front door continued up to the start of World War Two, I have never got over my initial fear of performing in front of strangers. The rent collector may have become a familiar face but I have never forgotten the time when following the same old rout...e I opened the door and stood there stunned in front of a man I had never seen before with a thick bushy beard – I had never seen a beard before either – shoulder-length hair and terrible piercing eyes. I stood rooted to the spot. He actually reminded me of someone. In the unaccustomed pause, he declared he was a Jehovah's Witness and wanted to speak to my mother. 'Mummy's out,' I mumbled, transfixed by those staring eyes. 'You'll never go to heaven if you tell lies,' he hissed. As I slammed the door, I realised now that I knew who he looked like: the picture of Jesus my mother had shown me. 'Where's heaven, Mum?' I asked as we clambered slowly back up the long flights of stairs. 'I don't know, son,' she replied. 'All I know is that it's not round here.'

In 1985 I was asked by my friend Bob Hoskins to play a small guest part in his movie *Mona Lisa*. I sat in the car on the way to the production office not taking any particular notice of where we were going until we crossed the River Thames. The river divides London not just physically but socially: north of the river is the posh side, the south very definitely isn't. I know this because I come from the south. As the car weaved its way through the grey depressing streets that I had known as a boy, I wondered where the hell we were going. Bob had told me that the film had a very small budget – I knew that from the amount that I was being paid – but how small was it if they had to have an office in such a crummy area? We drove deeper into dark valleys of decaying Dickensian warehouses and finally arrived at a depressingly ugly Victorian building which now housed Bob's production office. As I was led through the long, dark, dank corridors I asked my guide what the place had been before it was converted. 'It was originally built as a hospital years ago,' he replied. 'It was called Saint Olave's.' I stopped dead in my tracks and looked round me. So this was it. I had heard that name all my life but had never known exactly where it was. I was standing in the hospital where I was born.

It turned out that after the hospital was closed down, St Olave's became a lunatic asylum for a while and then a couple of years ago was converted into offices. When I think about it, it seems a cruel joke on the progress of my life – a natural progression from my birth place to lunatic asylum to movie production office. And I bet I'm the only movie actor to have worked out of a production office in the building where he was born.

When I was a young man I used to read a lot of star biographies in movie fan magazines to see if there was anybody like me in them. (There never was.) According to the biographies, all actors had done menial jobs and had a rough life before they became successful. The girls usually claimed to have been waitresses or nurses and the men had dug ditches for a living. No matter what background they actually came from – children of millionaires, relations of the studio boss, boy or girlfriend of the producer or agent – the Hollywood machine would make these stars sound like one of the people.

But in my case it's all true.

I was born in the Charity wing of St Olave's Hospital, Rotherhithe on Tuesday, 14 March 1933 at a few minutes after ten o'clock in the morning. I weighed eight pounds two ounces and my mother later told me that the birth was easy – the last easy thing I was going to do for the next thirty years.

I was born with a mild, non-contagious but incurable eye disease called *Blefora* which makes the eyelids swell. Like many things in my life this problem turned out to be actually in my favour, as by the time I was a young actor my heavy eyelids gave me a rather sleepy and, more importantly, sexy look. Apart from my eyes being a bit dodgy, I'm told I also had ears that stuck out at almost right angles from my head. This time the deformity was curable with the aid of sticking plaster which my mother used to pin them back every time I went to sleep for the first two years of my life. The flattening of my ears was a two-edged sword because they are now so flat against my head that sounds often whiz past without hitting them at all which makes me slightly hard of hearing without being actually deaf.

5

Dodgy eyes and prominent ears. What else? Well, I was born with the vitamin deficiency known as 'rickets' which meant, when I eventually started walking, that my ankle bones were not strong enough to support even my meagre weight, and I had to wear surgical boots to keep me upright. I also developed an involuntary nervous tic in my face which was called rather frivolously 'St Vitus Dance'. Not a very promising start for a future actor.

I sometimes have this vision of myself walking down the street as a small boy with heavy-lidded staring eyes, a nervous tic, ears pinned back with plaster and wearing Frankenstein boots laced up to just below the knee. I must have frightened the shit out of the other kids.

I was named Maurice Joseph Micklewhite after my father, who was 36 at the time. He had returned from seven years' service in India with the Royal Horse Artillery to marry my mother and participate in my conception. A tough man with jet black hair and a strong hawk-like nose, he was only about five feet eight inches high but he was very thickset. Extremely intelligent and completely uneducated, like most of his class at the time he was conditioned to do only manual labour. For a couple of hundred years the Micklewhites had been porters in London's Billingsgate fish market, so even though he was one of the three million unemployed at the time of my birth, at least he knew what job he was out of. He eventually got back to work there when things picked up again, which meant getting up at four in the morning and carting about crates of cold fish smothered in ice for eight hours. The thing he most liked about the job was the fact that he could get home by midday in time to get round to the bookies. Gambling was his one consuming passion and although he earned good money at the market, he was broke all his life, which is why I started my acting career at the front door.

Although my father was a very funny man, he was never truly happy and I think that he eventually realised his job was a dead end. In spite of this, jobs at Billingsgate were very sought after because of the pay and lack of qualifications needed but you could only get in if you had a relation who already worked there. I remember him saying to me as I grew up that when I went to work he could get me into the market. He seemed very proud of this and I had to bite my tongue to stop myself from telling him that I had absolutely no intention of following in his footsteps.

When they eventually began to mechanise Billingsgate, my father gave me the following advice: Never do a job where you can be replaced by a machine. Based on that advice I thought how clever I was to become an actor, little realising I'd be facing competition from a tin shark, a green frog and the Terminator. The only other advice that he ever gave me was never to trust anyone who wore a beard, a bow tie, two-tone shoes, sandals or sun glasses. Having believed him for many years, you can imagine the panic I was in when I arrived in Hollywood. Never say never.

My mother was an absolutely traditional working-class 'Mum'. She was short, plump, rosy and cheerful, very funny – and as tough as nails. Her whole life was devoted to her home, her husband and her children and on top of this she worked all her life as a charlady. She was completely devoted to my brother and me, and I can't remember her buying anything for herself that was not second-hand. The first new coat I ever saw her wear was one I bought her when she was fifty-six years old.

Although we were very poor, I can never remember ever being hungry, cold, unloved or deprived of anything that was important to a growing child – thanks to my mother.

My arrival brought about a move from my parents' one room to a two-room flat in Urlwin Street in Camberwell. Number 14 was a tall Victorian terraced house, which had seen better days and was now converted into small flats. Our flat was at the top – three long flights of stairs up from the ground floor and five flights from the garden, where the only toilet for five families was situated. The location of this toilet was to take on major significance, as my weak legs meant that five flights of stairs were a tremendous obstacle for me, but as I grew and ran up and down these stairs my rickets eventually faded away and I developed very strong muscles plus a facility to control my bowels which has come in handy many times since, when filming in 'exotic' locations.

The flat consisted of two rooms: one was the bedroom with a big double bed for my parents and a little one for me, the other functioned as living room, dining room and kitchen combined. There was no bathroom. I was given a bath every Friday night in the tin tub which was used for the laundry. When my brother and I grew up, we always had a standing joke that we had a bath every Friday night whether we needed it or not.

The cooking was done on a gas stove, which my mother was always cleaning with lead. (I don't know what this might mean and I have been too scared to find out.) The lighting for the flat was also gas – very dim and very inefficient with a mantle so fragile that if you so much as touched it with the match, it would immediately crumble into dust. My father always liked a drink in the evening – or any other time for that matter – and he could put it away without visible results, except for a slightly trembly hand. He was the only one who lit the light as my mother was afraid to do it in case it 'went off', as she put it. (She said the same about the telephone I gave her many years later. I watched her speaking on it once and she was holding the phone a foot from her ear. When I asked her why, I got the same reply.) My father's trembly hand caused a high casualty rate in gas mantles and I was the one who always had to journey up and down the stairs to get another one.

One of the threads that winds its way through all my early memories is that of aching feet. Second-hand clothes were no great problem for me, but second-hand shoes certainly were. Trying to cram feet into someone else's shoes even if they are the same size makes life very miserable and it was actually a pleasure to wear the special boots for my rickets. Discomfort comes in many forms and perhaps the most humiliating ritual of my childhood was the dosing of syrup of figs my mother gave us after our bath on Friday nights. 'To keep you regular,' she would say, with a significance that I did not then understand. All I knew was that next morning I would suddenly have to tear down five flights to the toilet, before I had what my mother called on the one occasion when I did not make it, 'a nasty accident'. 'Where do they make this stuff?' I asked my mother one Friday, after I had choked down yet another teaspoon of the disgusting mixture. 'California,' she replied. One place I'll never go, I thought. Never say never again.

When I was about two and half years old I noticed one day that my mother's stomach was starting to swell up and I was scared she was going to die and leave me and my father alone. I remember watching her week after week as she grew larger and larger until she was almost bursting through her dress. I wanted to say something but I did not want her to tell me that she was going to die, so I kept quiet. My father, on the other hand, didn't seem to be worried at all – in fact he seemed happier than usual. Finally when I came into the room one day and found her being sick in the sink, I plucked up courage. 'What's the matter with you, Mummy?' I asked through my tears. 'I've got paint poisoning,' she said, 'from the fumes.' My father had just painted the bedroom and the place reeked. 'Is it the smell that's made your stomach swell?' I asked. 'Yes, that's it,' she replied quickly. 'Well I can smell it so why haven't I got it?' I demanded. She thought for a moment. 'Only women can get it,' she replied. I breathed a sigh of relief: 'Thank God I am a man,' I said.

The next day, when we got on the bus to go shopping there was a pregnant woman sitting opposite us. 'Have you been painting the bedroom?' I asked her, according to my mother who always went into hysterics when she told the story.

At around the time the smell of paint in the bedroom disappeared, my mother also disappeared and I was sent to stay with my Aunt Lil. When my mother came back, her swollen belly had gone and I had a new baby brother called Stanley Victor, who had been, I was told, found under a gooseberry bush. This sounded perfectly reasonable to me and I accepted it and my new brother immediately, although I was a bit put out when my bed was shoved into the corner of the bedroom and he was placed closer to my mother. My mother pointed out that he woke up a lot during the night, but then every time he woke up, so did I.

The impact of Stanley on my young life was nothing, however, compared with something that happened the following year. At around the age of four I was set on a journey of discovery that I haven't finished yet. I was taken to see my first movie.

When I was a teenager I used to read a lot of biographies of actors to see if I had anything in common with them, because by now I had dreams of becoming one as well. My avid reading as a teenager taught me that I had little in common with any actor – particularly the British stage greats. In fact they sounded as though they actually came from another planet. All their stories seemed to start from the same point: the first time that they ever saw an actor was when their nanny took them to the theatre, and as the curtain rose and the lights went up on the stage they just *knew* the theatre was going to be their life's work.

In stark contrast to this, the first actor that I ever saw was the Lone Ranger and it was at a Saturday morning matinée for kids, which in my area was a cross between an SAS training camp and the St Valentine's Day Massacre. The first obstacle in the assault course was the queue, which developed into a full-scale riot as some of the bigger kids who came late tried to push in front of others. Once inside, another riot started as everybody rushed for the front seats. And even when we were all seated comfortably and it seemed that our troubles were over missiles started hurtling around and an orange hit me on the back of the head. My friends had told me that after the lights went out and the picture started everything would be all right, but when I was plunged into darkness it turned out to be an overcoat which had been thrown down from the balcony above on top of me. It was finally dragged off me and thrown back up, accompanied by a lot of words that I did not understand but had heard before when my father stubbed his toe on the bed legs.

At last the lights went down, the film started, and on came the Lone Ranger. I sat there as entranced as those privileged actors before me with their nannies and I knew that this was what I wanted to be. A half eaten ice cream cone suddenly landed in my lap but even this could not break the spell; I just wiped it up, without taking my eyes off the screen.

After a while I got cramp, so I put my feet up on the back of the seat in front of me and stretched my legs. At this point the entire row of seats that we were sitting on tilted back on to the knees of the kids in the row behind. Yells of pain and indignation filled the air as the unfortunate patrons behind us tried to extricate themselves, but we were lying in our seats half over backwards with our feet flailing in the air. The lights went up, the picture stopped and the usherettes came rushing down to sort things out. I was pointed out as the culprit (there was no mention of the boys who had unscrewed the seats from the floor before we came in) and given a hefty whack round the ear. The lights went down, the picture started again and I sat there and watched through a veil of tears as my future profession unfolded before my eyes. I wonder what nanny would have made of that outing.

2

'Very flat, Norfolk'

At the age of about four I began school at The John Ruskin Infants' School in John Ruskin Street. I was a very pretty little boy with blond curly hair and big blue eyes and my teacher mistakenly christened me 'Bubbles' which had the obvious effect on the other boys. After two or three days as a walking punch bag I informed my mother that I would not be going to school again and she very quickly realised what was going on. One morning she paid an uninvited visit to the school during our play break and asked me to point out the boys who had hit me. This I did and, much to my surprise, she beat the shit out of all of them. I always knew that she was tough, but that surprised me.

My father, on the other hand, took the view that if anybody hit me I should hit back even if it meant getting pounded. 'There is no shame in losing a fight,' he told me. 'There is only shame in being a coward and refusing to fight.' When I told him that I did not know how to fight he said with a twinkle in his eye, 'I know, and I'm going to teach you how.' With that he got down on his knees in front of me, put his fists up and said, 'Hit me,' and after a bit of persuasion I did. Pretty soon I had no more trouble at school and was renamed by common consent 'Snake eyes' which was a source of great pride to me.

I once asked my father what I should do if someone picked on me who I couldn't beat in a fight. 'Easy,' he said. 'You bide your time, wait until he's not expecting anything, and then you get a bottle and smash him over the fucking head with it. It's very important,' he went on, 'that you never let anybody get away with an attack on you or you will become a target instead of a man.' And although I hate violence of any kind I have never forgotten this.

When I was nearing six years old the atmosphere in our flat began to change. My mother and father and friends and relations who came to visit us were somehow not as cheerful as usual and sometimes they were downright miserable, especially when they listened to the wireless. It was 1939.

My first inkling that things were going to change was when my mother sat my brother Stanley and me down for a very serious talk. We were going to be something called 'evacuated' and we were going to be sent away to the country because someone that neither of us had ever heard of called 'Adolf Hitler' was going to try to kill us by dropping bombs on us. Stanley and I discussed this at great length and decided that it was probably a mistake, because if we didn't know Adolf Hitler, he couldn't possibly know us and therefore couldn't know where we lived. We forgot about it until one day my mother asked me to go and get a tin of corned beef at the corner shop. I liked corned beef, so I asked her if it was going to be for dinner. 'No,' she said quietly, 'it's for your sandwiches when you go away to be evacuated.' So that was it. My brother and I were going away to do this word that we didn't understand. We both cried when my mother told us that she would not be coming with us, but we cheered up a bit when she said that all the school would be going.

Before we went, we all had to be fitted with a gas mask. When I asked what we wanted gas masks for, my mother told me that it was to protect us in case this man Hitler dropped bombs on us with poison gas in them. She said that the gas went everywhere on the wind and anybody who breathed it in without a mask would drop dead. At this point I started to take the whole thing seriously and became quite frightened. I pointed out to Stanley that if the gas travelled on the wind as my mother had said, this man Hitler didn't actually need our address to kill us and I took a different and much more alarming view of things. My first experience with my new gas mask at school the next day was not very reassuring either. We were all lined up in the playground and the teachers came along and gave each of us a rather nice looking mask that was

13

made to look like Mickey Mouse. We were told to put them on to see if they fitted, and were then told to run about the playground to make sure that we could breathe in them. Unbeknownst to me, the part in my mask through which I was supposed to breathe in was blocked and so there I was running around with the rest of the kids, only able to breathe out. Suddenly I keeled over like some miniature telephone pole and hit the deck. I was sent home early as some sort of weakling who had been the only one to let the school down. There it was again: injustice. The result of all this was that while all the other kids felt quite confident about surviving one of Hitler's gas attacks, I was determined to die rather than put that thing on again. A longer lasting legacy has been my lifelong hate of the smell of rubber.

On the day of 'Evacuation' my brother and I were up early, eager to start our first great adventure. Stanley was three and I was six. We were both dressed identically: sensible shoes, long grey woollen socks held up with elastic bands just below the knee, and short trousers, which I already hated. For this special day my mother had bought us new shirts which were made of a wool that felt like wire and were the most uncomfortable garment I had ever worn until I joined the British army. To this she added something completely new in our young lives: a tie. This instrument of torture was drawn tightly around the prickly collar that was already causing a rash around my neck. I hated this tie so much that I have never worn one since unless it was absolutely necessary. (Today I own five restaurants and in none of them are you required to wear a tie.) On top of all this we wore jackets – not school blazers because they were too expensive – which carried a label with our names and addresses tied into the button holes – in case we got lost, my mother said. We had a cardboard suitcase each which contained three of everything that we needed: 'One on, one clean and one in the wash,' as my mother explained. The working-class attitude to hygiene always strikes me as strange when I think about it now. My mother's other piece of advice in this area was: 'change your underwear in case you get run over'. Many years later as a soldier in Korea I realised how pointless this particular tip was.

Our only other burden consisted of a small cardboard box each with a shoulder strap made of string that contained the offending gas mask. The fault in mine had been discovered and I had a new one, but I was not inclined to test it and crammed my corned beef sandwich in there instead. If there had been a gas attack, I would probably have died from inhaling bread crumbs. So, equipped for our new role in life and having kissed our dad goodbye (it was the only day off from work that he had ever taken) we set off, each holding one of Mum's hands tightly.

The scene at the school was pandemonium with harassed teachers rushing about trying to get the children lined up into columns of three. I looked around for some coaches, but couldn't see any. Were we going to march somewhere, I wondered? My mother had told me that the country was a long way away. Things weren't looking too good so far. All along the line mothers were clutching their children and sobbing, some of them hysterically. My mother had done a real psyching job on Stanley and me and until this moment we had thought that this was going to be fun. Now it all fell apart, as it dawned on us that there must after all be something to cry about and we joined in the chorus which started my mother off as well. The teachers finally got a grip of the situation and off we started on what turned out to be a two-mile walk to Waterloo station. I held tightly onto Stanley's hand as we marched, only relinquishing my grip as we turned the corner for one last wave at the band of weeping mothers flapping limp soggy handkerchiefs. We kept waving until, suddenly, they were gone and Stanley and I were on our own for the first time.

Almost immediately, with my head held bravely high, I stepped into a great pile of dog shit and consternation set in amongst the ranks as my classmates tried to identify the source of the terrible smell. When I was eventually identified as the culprit there was great jostling as the other kids tried to get as far away from me as possible and I was banished in tears to the back of the line, to walk on my own. One of the teachers took my brother's hand and with a sneer walked on ahead leaving me in disgrace alone with tears streaming down my

15

face. After a while another teacher took pity on me and came back to walk beside me. Seemingly impervious to the smell, she gave me a hug and said, 'Stepping in that is good luck.' 'Is it?' I asked, with considerable disbelief. 'Yes,' she said knowingly. 'You'll see.' On the first day of shooting on the film *Alfie*, the opening shot was of me walking along the embankment of the River Thames by Westminster Bridge. Lewis Gilbert, the director, said: 'Action,' and I stepped into a pile of dog shit. 'Cut,' said Lewis. 'We'll go again.' As we prepared for the second take, having changed shoes very quickly (you always have two of everything on a movie set), Lewis said, with a hopeful smile, 'That's lucky.' 'I know,' I replied, 'my teacher told me.' He looked at me for a moment with a puzzled smile. 'Action,' he said, and I was off to make the picture that made me a star. You should always listen to your teacher.

When we got to Waterloo, my shoe was washed and I was allowed to join civilized society again. Although we were only going about forty miles out of London to Wargrave in Berkshire, the journey took hours, but we eventually arrived somewhere and were marched to a large village hall, where we were greeted with lemonade, sandwiches and large smiling country ladies with red rosy cheeks. Having stuffed ourselves sick with food we were made to stand in line and the local families came along and inspected us to choose the child they wanted to take care of for the duration of the war. Whatever type they were looking for it was not Stanley and me and after about an hour he and I were the only two left standing there, being circled warily by potential carers like farmers inspecting two mad bullocks. Suddenly there was a bustle at the other end of the hall, and it was obvious that someone of importance had appeared. Everybody seemed to straighten up a little as a wonderful-looking elderly lady with almost blue hair came charging towards us. She was out of breath and obviously late. 'Are these the last two?' she asked, not unkindly. 'Yes,' said the vicar in a hushed apologetic tone. He had appeared out of the blue to greet the new arrival who was obviously somebody important and rich because she spoke with a very posh voice. She looked down at the two of us. She had the most wonderful smile and a very kind face. I hope she takes us, I thought to myself and smiled my nicest smile back at her. '*Take us*,' I was saying under my breath. 'I'll take them!' she cried. Then she crouched down and gave us both a kiss.

The vicar ushered us outside and for the first time in our lives Stanley and I got into a car. This was bigger than any car that I had ever seen and very much like the pictures of the one the King drove in; it must have been a Rolls Royce. We were whisked away to a house so big it looked like a castle. There were servants all over the place, and our cases and our jackets were taken and we were each shown to lovely little bedrooms. Then we were told to wash our hands before being taken downstairs to a large dining room where we were offered a seemingly limitless supply of cakes and drinks until both of us were quite literally sick. I lay in the best bed and in the nicest room that I had ever slept in, relishing the luxury of a room of my own for the first time and thinking to myself that this was too good to be true. I was right. The next day an official came and said that according to regulations the house was too far from the school and we had to be moved closer. This was done with disastrous results all round. My brother and I were split up and were both placed with people where the milk of human kindness had run kind of thin, especially where children were concerned. I knew I was supposed to be protected from the Nazis, but being locked in a cupboard beneath the stairs for twenty-four hours seemed like overkill. My mother came and took us away back up to London, with the vow never to let us out of her sight again.

By 1940, the Germans began the Blitz in earnest and men came to build an air raid shelter in the garden of our flats. This consisted of a six foot deep hole dug in the ground and covered with sheets of thick corrugated iron which were in turn covered with a couple of feet of earth. They wouldn't save anyone from a direct hit but they were protection from shrapnel and incendiary bombs. Gradually the bombs began to drop closer to where we lived and Stanley and I started to

17

get very scared. Hitler was obviously no fool and he must have found out our address.

Despite the bombing we went to a sort of skeleton school made up from returned evacuees like us and children who had not been sent away from London. A strange phenomenon developed when Hitler started the daylight raids. The teachers told us that if the siren sounded as we were on our way to school and we were closer to school we should run there, but if we were closer to home we should run back. So at nine o'clock every school morning you would find groups of kids standing on the corner just out of sight of the school praying for the siren to go so that they could run back home for a day off.

As anyone who saw the Blitz first hand will know, there has been a lot of misunderstanding about it. It was not a continuous bombardment from the moment that war was declared and in fact it did not start for weeks afterwards. Once it started it kept stopping, too, as the Luftwaffe recovered from the severe maulings that they received from the RAF. There were also breaks after which they would come back with new and secret weapons that we had never seen before. When London was set on fire with blanket incendiary bombing on that infamous Saturday night during the Battle of Britain, my mother decided to take us to the country again, and this time to come with us. Even though we were to be gone for nearly five years we always came back during one of the lulls. A week after our first return the Luftwaffe hit us with the new Land Mine, a bomb on a parachute that exploded in mid air and spread the damage over as wide an area as possible. During the next lull we met the doodlebug or V-1, a pilotless aircraft loaded with explosives which wasn't particularly effective from the Germans' point of view. You could see it and hear its engine and it was an easy target, but it was very bad for the nerves, because the sound stopped just before it exploded and you knew that somebody was about to die. But the most terrifying bomb of all was the V-2 rocket which was launched in 1944. We had only been back a few days when in broad daylight, without the siren sounding, the street next to ours just disappeared. There had been no aeroplane, no anti-aircraft fire, no doodlebug, just a massive bang. An entire street and its people had gone for ever.

Eventually my father was called up to serve in the Royal Artillery and we left London with my mother to go to Norfolk on the east coast of England. Its main distinction is its flatness, made famous in Noël Coward's play *Private Lives* when the hero asks his ex-wife where her new husband comes from and she says, 'Norfolk.' Noël's reply is just: 'Very flat, Norfolk.' So there you have it from the master.

We were housed in a large disused farmhouse which had been refurbished to the standard to which country people expected we slumdwellers from London were accustomed. Which meant that it was very primitive indeed: oil lamps and wood stoves, and tin baths for Friday nights in front of the fire. There was one outside toilet for the ten families, who were divided between small two-room flatlets and a big main kitchen which was shared by all.

I had never been so happy in my life. This tower of Cockney Babel was attached to a wondrous place for a small London boy: a farm. I could not believe that I could get close enough to real animals actually to touch them and I worked unpaid at odd jobs on the farm whenever I could. It was an idyllic place for a scrawny little city boy. Although I had long ago lost my surgical boots, and the stairs in our London house and the trips to the toilet and the front door had strengthened my legs, I was still not strong. Here was a chance to run free in fresh air, away from the soot-laden fumes of London and get the sun on my face instead of the shade of dark buildings. For children like myself the war was lucky. We were taken out of our rotten environment and given a chance for a healthy life. There were no chemical fertilizers put on the food we ate, and so we were forced to eat organic food for five years. Rationing meant that butter, ice cream, cream and even milk were rationed so there was no chance of high cholesterol. Meat was rationed, too, so we ate a lot of chicken and fish but sweets, biscuits and anything made with sugar was almost unavailable. The government gave all the children free orange juice, cod liver oil, malt, and vitamins to supplement food shortages

19

and so they were actually giving us forms of nutrition that we would never have had in our diet if there had been no war. In our house we ate a lot of fried food and always red meat which my father insisted on every day. He thought that any man who ate chicken was a 'Nancy Boy' or ponce.

The farmhouse was loaded with kids and I immediately formed a gang from the most unscrupulous-looking ruffians that I could find. This move had become necessary because the village lads had decided to protect their territory from invasion by the Londoners. The parents of the country children were terrified that if their children mixed with us they would catch lice or fleas or, worse still, our Cockney accents. We didn't so much live in the village as infest it and our reign of terror began. The local Bobby immediately invested in a faster bicycle, but couldn't keep up with us as we raided orchards, stole milk off people's doorsteps, and nicked sausage rolls from the back of the baker's van while one of us engaged the baker in conversation on the front of the van (a particularly sophisticated plan of my own that I was very proud of). We also arranged fights with groups of the local boys provided we outnumbered them and they were not too big; we were tough, but we were not stupid. But on the one occasion the opportunity for real vice came our way and we found some cigarettes and a bottle of beer, we were sick as dogs and did not add them to the list of items to be provided for our entertainment.

Not all of our enterprises were dishonest. In order to get extra meat for the family, we used to catch rabbits which were regarded by the war-time Ministry of Agriculture as vermin, as they could decimate a very valuable grain crop in a week. Since none of us were old enough for a shot-gun licence we did the next best thing and trained ourselves to outrun them, which you might think an almost impossible feat, but believe it or not I and several members of our band could do it. The meat of the wild rabbit back then was delicious, and I always felt very proud to bring one home to my mother who was often in despair at the lack of food. Another way we helped our mother with the rations was by getting moorhens' eggs. These birds always built their nests out over the water on very thin branches to protect them from predators. As a relatively new predator surveying a nest one day I thought they had got me beaten until I devised a method of tying a dessert spoon onto the end of a long stick and just scooping the eggs out of the nest. Three years of our greedy harvesting resulted, however, in the moorhen being more or less extinct in that area.

After we had been in Norfolk for about six months my father came home on leave for a fortnight. We could not wait for him to tell us all the great adventures that he had had fighting the Germans, but we were very disappointed when he finally arrived. He didn't seem like the dad that we remembered and looked very tired and sometimes very sad. He slept, it seemed to me, for the first week but he eventually brightened up and took us into King's Lynn, the local town, to go to the pictures. When I asked him where he had just come from he said that it was a place in France called Dunkirk. I realise now of course what he had just been through, but at the time I thought that he probably didn't like the country.

Dad's arrival changed my life. He bought me an air gun, which steered my enterprises in a new direction: money. The Ministry of Agriculture had introduced a new scheme to get rid of more vermin which ran something like this: for every dead rat the inspector would give you sixpence, and for a dead starling, which is a very voracious bird which not only eats fruit but has the nasty habit of taking one bite out of every other piece of fruit on any tree, thus destroying the whole crop, he would give you threepence. I became a very good shot and, by my own standards, extremely rich. Rich enough to buy my own fish and chips when the travelling fish shop visited our village every Thursday.

When my father's leave was up he was sent to North Africa to join the Eighth Army. We didn't know it then, but we weren't to see him again for four years. When the time came for him to go he took my brother and me aside and told us that we had to be good and look after our mother and he gave us a long lecture on behaving ourselves. The next day my mother gave the two of us a little lecture herself, which I have never forgotten. Instead of moaning and whining about being left on her own with two small boys to bring up, she told us that we were going to have to be the men of the family now and replace our father in looking after her. This was absolutely untrue, of course – she was as tough as nails and needed no looking after by anybody – but it did give me a sense of protectiveness and responsibility towards women that has never left me. It has got me into trouble lately with the feminist movement who seem to regard good manners and respect for women as some form of sneaky male chauvinism.

After Dad had left life carried on as usual for a while until suddenly our peaceful Norfolk life was brought slap bang into the frontline of the war. Bombs were dropped around us, aerial dog fights spattered the skies and the peace of the countryside was shattered by planes taking off and landing and crashing all day every day. The Americans had entered the war and we found ourselves living right in the middle of a ring of seven massive US Air Force Bomber bases. Whichever direction we looked, we could see either the war actually being fought as German planes followed our bombers home and met our own fighters, or the results as pilot after pilot, mortally wounded, crashed in the fields around us in their attempts to make it home. It was like living in the eye of a hurricane. From our little vale of safety and peace we watched the killing going on every day and every night. It was an extraordinary experience for a small boy and sometimes, if we reached the downed planes before the police or Home Guard, a shocking one as we saw dead bodies for the first time in our lives. It was also the first time I realised that our side died as well – in all the films I saw, only the enemy died – and I certainly didn't connect it with my father fighting on the other side of the world.

Kids are hard-hearted, though. We eventually got an enterprise together to make Christmas and birthday presents for our mothers and little girlfriends which consisted of making rings and bracelets out of the cockpit glass of the crashed airplanes. The trick was to cut this stuff with a hot knife and paint in little jewels for our mums and the young ladies who were the object of our baser desires.

*

22

Every Saturday we went into King's Lynn to get the week's shopping with our mother. We always had fish and chips and we always went to the cinema in the afternoon. One Saturday when we arrived we found that the town had been invaded by men in strange uniforms with accents just like the Lone Ranger. They all seemed to be chewing something. 'Who are they and what are they all chewing?' I asked my mother. 'Americans,' and 'Gum,' she replied. 'Where do you get it?' I wanted to know. She pointed to a crowd of young kids following a group of airmen who were all shouting the same thing: 'Got any gum chum?' The airmen were passing out sticks to each of the kids. Stanley and I ran over to join the throng, and took up the cry, and we were eventually rewarded with a stick each which we put in our mouths and began to chew. It tasted great and I was hooked for life.

Over a period of time I got to know many of the guys from the air bases around the village and I was amazed at their generosity and their tolerance and good humour with all of us kids constantly begging from them. By this point I was besotted with the cinema and by the images of America that I had seen on the screen, but my life-long love affair with America and things American was clinched by the behaviour of these first real Americans that I had ever met. Their warmth, charm and generosity was so welcome and unusual in a country racked by shortages of everything and massive tension and fear. They would give us sweets which they called candy and biscuits which they called cookies and some of them were so generous that they even used to ask me if I had an older sister who would like some nylons. They always seemed very sad when I said that I had no sisters at all. Such generous people; we really missed them when they all went home.

The most exciting time of all in the farmhouse was Christmas. The kitchen was overcrowded with friends, all gathered round making decorations, preparing food, or chopping and fetching the stacks of logs in for the great fire that always burned in the winter. Our ration portion was doubled, including sweets which we rarely saw. Thick cream suddenly became available and, best of all, the government

23

made sure that every child had an orange and a banana each. These were rationed to one a year so there was great excitement when they finally appeared. Watching the last sliver of orange or the pointed end of a banana disappear for another year was the only sad part for me.

One of my favourite memories of my mother is of her sharing out our sweet ration one Christmas. There was one very hard-boiled sweet left over and not wanting either of her sons ever to feel more favoured than the other one, she got a carving knife and proceeded to cut it in half. Even when the knife slipped and she nearly cut off her thumb she went away to bandage it and then came back and finished sawing until the sweet broke in half equally. Even in the middle of a war she made Christmas wonderful and it was always the same, which is just what us kids liked. We always had roast turkey, sage and onion stuffing with sausage meat, roast potatoes, brussels sprouts, Christmas pudding with lashings of custard and home-made Christmas crackers, usually full of the rings we had made out of the crashed aircraft glass. And if anyone was still hungry after that lot, there were mince pies and Christmas cake smothered in cream or custard. I always remember it snowing at Christmas in those days, too, which it rarely does now.

The small elementary school that I went to during this time was run by a formidable-looking lady who eventually became a close friend. Miss Linton must have been about sixty years old and looked like a cross between Margaret Rutherford and Elsa Lanchester as the Bride of Frankenstein. She was quite scary to look at with a very strange haircut for a woman – just like my dad's, I thought – but behind it all there was indeed kindly old Margaret Rutherford. Looking back now it seems obvious to me that my first close female friend was a lesbian. Miss Linton spotted me quite early on after my arrival at the school and always took special care in teaching me. If I found something difficult she would invite me to her house, which was opposite ours and next to the village church, in the evenings – for a drink, she always said. She would drink whiskey and I would drink lemonade. Some of her lessons were very unorthodox. When I was having a problem with maths, she taught me how to play poker for real pennies and always arranged to lose so that I would go home a penny or two ahead.

I was always an avid reader but Miss Linton guided me into the sorts of books that I should read and, although I was only eight, allowed me to borrow books from the senior school library, normally meant for children over fourteen. Unknown to me she had an ulterior motive. At that time in English schools you had to take a scholarship exam to pass out of elementary school into the higher education of grammar school. No child from this little village school had ever passed this exam and she saw in me a possible candidate for glory before she retired or died. As she smoked at least a hundred cigarettes a day and one of my jobs was an almost continuous errand to buy her cigarettes, one pack at a time, the latter was more than likely.

After a couple of years of her personal tutoring I did indeed pass the scholarship exam and brought glory at last to my school. I never saw Miss Linton happier than the day she came rushing across the village green to our house to inform me that I had passed, her school gown flying in the breeze like big black wings, Margaret Rutherford as a fallen angel. Without her, my future life would have been such a dreary place. Not long afterwards, the cigarettes I had bought for her did their job and she died of lung cancer. I was so relieved that she had seen that I had not let her down before she went.

Just before I passed the exam, my mother got a job as a cook at The Grange, a big house on the outskirts of the village, and we were suddenly moved from the farmhouse into the servants' quarters there. This time I was going to get a close up of how the other half lived — in fact, up until then I didn't even know that there was another half. The luxury was unbelievable. My brother and I had our own bedroom with a bed each and my mother had her bedroom next door. Our flat was beautifully furnished and the sheets and pillows were the softest that we had ever known. There was a bathroom with a sink and a toilet in it beside a big bath and there was not only a tap for cold water but one for hot water as well — we'd never had that before. The first thing I noticed about the bath was that it had two sets of

25

taps, and when I turned the top one on I was drenched in a rush of water that seemed to be coming out of the ceiling. I switched the tap off quickly and standing there dripping I looked up to see a big brass funnel with holes in it.

The most remarkable thing of all was the electric light. I had never lived in a house with that before. It was very bright and clean, not like the smelly dim oil lamps and the smokey candles that I was used to. Most of the day we spent in the kitchen, which was enormous and had electric stoves and a big thing that buzzed all day but kept everything cold and even made ice which I thought was a great idea, remembering how in London we used to keep the milk outside in cold water in the summer. The kitchen was a fascinating place for me with its warmth and smells and the different types of food my mother prepared. I used to wait until the food came back from the front of the house – where we were never allowed to go – and anything that was left over that I didn't know I would try. There were black fish eggs called caviar which I hated (I have since changed my mind); there was pheasant and there was a paste made of a goose's liver which I did not like at all at the time – but I have come around to that one as well. Then there was wine and port, both of which I loved instantly but found that if I drank more than one sip I got dizzy, so I had to curb my enthusiasm there. I also tried cigars but they made me sick so I stuck to a couple of puffs on any cigarette ends that came out, only managing to reach faint nausea with these. The kitchen was a great success with me.

We moved into our new billet just before the holidays and before I had the result of my scholarship exam. During this time I got to know the master of the house, a very impressive-looking man called Mr English, who was about fifty-five years old. He was always asking me questions about myself and how I was doing at school and what I wanted to do when I grew up. My mother was very puzzled at the interest he was taking in my welfare for a while as in her experience people of his class did not normally waste their precious time in conversation with the son of the cook. The answer to his strange behaviour came one evening after dinner, when a message was sent through asking if my mother and I would join Mr and Mrs English in the drawing room. This was a big moment for me as I had never been allowed into that part of the house before. My mother and I crept nervously along the wide passage and knocked on the door which was immediately opened by Mr English himself. 'Come in and sit down,' he said with a broad smile. Mrs English, a tall aristocratic-looking woman with slightly grey hair was sitting on the sofa. We all sat down and he explained to my mother that the reason he had asked us in was to tell us that he knew that I had taken the scholarship exam, because he had asked Miss Linton all about me and he just wanted to tell me that if I did not pass the exam, he was going to pay for my education anyway, because – much to my embarrassment – he said I was much too bright a boy to let go to waste. We stumbled out of the room and the moment we were outside my mother gave me a big hug and told me that I was made for life if a man like Mr English had taken this much interest in me. As it turned out I passed the exam anyway, but it was nice to know that someone in this world gave a damn about what happened to the likes of us.

While listening to Mr English I had spent a great deal of the time looking around the room where we were sitting. It was enormous. I didn't know that you could get a room that big in a house. The furniture seemed so comfortable, with big, deep, soft armchairs and a great big piano shaped like a harp, not like the ones that I had seen in pubs around London. Sparkling chandeliers lit the room and great big beautiful paintings covered all the walls. Tall windows that you could walk through opened out onto a carpet-like lawn surrounded by a beautiful garden. What with the bathroom, the electric light, the cosy bedrooms, the wonderful kitchen and the great food and wines, the beautiful drawing room and magnificent gardens, one day, I thought to myself, I am going to live exactly like this.

Having won the scholarship place I now had to change schools. This was a change that turned out to be not only geographic and educational, but social as well: I was sent to a Jewish school called Hackney Down Grocers. As I had won a London scholarship, I had to go to the nearest London school

27

that had been evacuated to my area, and this turned out to be 'Grocers' as we called it. I had never knowingly met a Jewish person before and I had no idea what to think or expect, so I decided to do a bit of research and turned to my mother for answers. She informed me that my father's bookmaker was Jewish and so was the man who sold jellied eels at the stall Dad used to visit. (Let's straighten out the jellied eels question at this point. It is a cliché that all Cockneys love jellied eels and people always seem to presume that I love them. In fact I hate the bloody things.) My mother also told me that Jews were very clever because they ate a lot of fish, which was an obvious dig at me for refusing to eat the beautiful fish that my father had brought home from Billingsgate before the war. She also said that most Jews had plenty of money. This last remark had a ring of truth when I thought of the amounts of money that my father had lost to his bookmaker. The bookie and the jellied eel man – known as 'Tubby' Isaacs – were both fat. So I was now beginning to build up a picture of what to expect at my new school: the boys would all be fat, clever, fond of fish and with plenty of money. This did not bode well for me. I was very thin (I had shot up in the country and was five feet eleven at the age of eleven), I didn't like fish, I wasn't very clever and I had no money.

The first day at school was a bit of a disappointment. I had expected that Jewish boys would look different or strange in some way, but looking round the hall at assembly on the first day, I could see nothing to distinguish them from anybody else. Prayers were started and on came the vicar – but he didn't look like any vicar that I had ever seen and he started to sing a prayer in a strange language that I had never heard before. I asked the boy next to me what was going on and he told me that this was the rabbi and he was singing in a language called Hebrew. One thing that I noticed very quickly was that he sang much better than any vicar that I had ever heard.

I quickly settled in and made friends, and although I was one of only a dozen Christians in the school I was accepted at once. There were differences however, but the first one was very comforting. I came from a world where I was, invariably, the only boy called Maurice. At Grocers, it seemed to me, every boy was called Maurice, so I immediately felt quite at home, if a little confused. Sometimes when someone would shout 'Maurice', the response would be a bit like the Mormon Tabernacle choir. Not only were there a lot of boys with the first name Maurice, but a lot of them had Morris as a surname, and there was even one boy who was called Maurice Morris, although his first name was pronounced like the French, 'Maw Reece'. I learned not to use the term 'Christian' name, to say 'Happy Hannukah' instead of 'Merry Christmas' and to call Easter, 'Passover'. There were lots of other special holidays which was great for me because I used to get the Jewish holidays as well as my own Christian holidays which was my idea of a great school. I also found out that I was a 'goy', which was a good word, but that if anybody called me a 'yok' that was an insult. I was also told that I should never let anybody call me a schmuck. When I asked what this meant I was told that only a schmuck would ask a question like that.

The boys at Grocers were much better behaved than the boys at the other schools that I had been to and much more keen on their work. There were only a few dumb ones – and they rapidly became my friends; there was no way that I was ever going to be as diligent as the top students in the school. My particular friend was a boy called Morris (different spelling but there's that name again), and I spent a great deal of time at home with his family, who knew that I was on my own and made me an honorary family member. It was here that I could see where the difference of attitude towards education had come from in these boys. Morris's family absolutely doted on him and pressed home to him all the time the importance of education for his later life.

Morris's education was invariably the subject of conversation at every meal I had there. I found out very soon that my mother had been right about the fish, because we had fish at practically every meal. I never liked fish but I figured that if I wanted to be clever I had better eat it, so I used to choke it down in great portions to no effect. His parents were also much more religious than my own family and used to say a

29

prayer before eating, especially on a Friday night. This would never have happened at my house, I thought, and specially not on a Friday when my dad had got paid, and we would all go down to the eel and pie shop for a slap-up celebration.

The final polish on the education at Grocers was music. Everybody seemed to be taking violin lessons, and in order to be assimilated into this new society, I took the violin up too, with such disastrous results that the teacher refused to accept payment for my lessons at the end of term. 'Goyim' are not natural violinists, I was told, and I could not agree more. But at least I'm not a schmuck.

3

What I got for a chocolate bar

It was 1946 when I got back to London and what a shock that was. Whole streets around where we lived had disappeared, leaving great stretches of land piled high with rubble and dotted with the still standing remnants of ruined buildings. There was a continual smell of burning rubbish as the government sent teams of men in to clear the bomb sites, and this odour is one of my lingering memories from this period of my life. I could smell it inside and outside our home, and when I ate it was all I could taste. The smell got everywhere. When I first started to date girls, our heavy petting was always done in the darkness and privacy of these bomb sites. I am probably the only man in the world to whom the smell of burning rubbish is an aphrodisiac.

To add to the general misery of the time there was an added plague that came when coal went off the rationing list. The heating in most of the houses was by coal fires, and the smog that this produced was the most disgusting in the history of mankind. It was almost pure soot and impossible to see through at all. I once got lost for an hour, two hundred yards from my home. They worry about smog in Los Angeles, but they never had anything like this.

We had won the war but the shops were empty and even to get your legal ration of things you had to queue for hours. The one blinding light in the middle of all this gloom was the cinema, where I could escape for a couple of hours to somewhere better – usually America. I became an absolute fanatic about the cinema and besotted with what seemed to me the glamour of America. Most dreams are a let-down, but the cinema has been more fantastic for me than anything I

31

could have imagined in those dark, depressing days, and America itself greater than anything that I could have possibly imagined it to be. I really don't know what I would have done at that time without the cinema and the public library, the two places where I could escape the grim reality of everyday life. In short I had become what they always said in my school reports; a dreamer.

In the library again my influences were American. I became interested in books about the war. The British wrote about officers, with whom I could not identify, but then I found Norman Mailer's *Naked and the Dead* and James Jones' *From Here to Eternity*; great books, written by ordinary soldiers about ordinary soldiers. I unconsciously started to identify with my own class in the cinema as well. The British cinema also seemed to be about the lives of the middle class and the aristocracy, whereas people in American films seemed to me to be more like me.

It was in the library that I found a book on how to act in films, which claimed that actors should never blink before the camera. I walked around for months with a blank unblinking stare in order to prepare for my film career, scaring the shit out of any strangers with whom I happened to come into contact – but I managed eventually to go without blinking for first ten, then twenty minutes at a time, and was well on my way to Hollywood. I also managed to get an eye infection from the filthy air as the particles of soot built up in my eyes. One has to make sacrifices for one's art I am told, and that is an early example of one of mine. There were others to come, most of them involuntary.

On our return to London the local council gave us new accommodation, as not only was our flat now too small, but although it had missed any direct hits it had suffered a great deal of structural damage from bomb blast. My father had returned from the war unscathed, having gone right through from the battle of El Alamein to the liberation of Rome. I was now twelve years old, my brother was nine, and the council gave us a prefabricated house. These were sent over from Canada and America in ready-made asbestos sections constructed like a big do-it-yourself doll's house, and were intended to be temporary accommodation until the government could set about building proper homes for the victims of the war and slum clearance. In fact, quite a lot of slum clearance had already been done – by the Luftwaffe.

The maximum life of these homes, we were told, was ten years and before then we would be housed in a proper house. This we quite rightly took with a pinch of salt and my family lived in that house for eighteen years until I moved them with the first money I made in films. A house like this sounds terrible to most people today, but to us then it was the lap of luxury. Although it was small – only about three times the size of the motor home that I use as a dressing room when I am filming – we were for the first time in a home of our own, with electric light, a bathroom with a shower, constant hot water, central heating, a refrigerator and that other great luxury, an inside toilet that you could flush with water. Undreamed-of splendour and it was all ours. The house was on a former bomb site in a place called Marshall Gardens at the Elephant and Castle in the borough of Southwark. It was a five-minute walk from three cinemas, and one minute from the bus that would take me to school. Things were looking up – well, almost.

Wilson's Grammar School, the one that was to replace Hackney Downs Grocers because it was now the closest, came into my life. I will pass a veil over this area of my life; suffice it to say that I hated this school and the compliment was returned in spades. There was only one man there that I really liked, an English teacher called Eric Watson, who took the trouble to guide my rebellious mind into the world of literature. My only other interest was French, which I took to with great enthusiasm not so much because of a thirst to learn a foreign language but because the French teacher was the only female in the school. Mam'zelle used to teach sitting on the front of her desk. She had great legs and always wore short skirts, for that time anyway, which would ride up as she sat back. Once in position she would cross her legs every five minutes or so, at which moments there was an audible intake of communal breath and the briefest of pauses in the sound of scratching pen nibs. The first words that I ever looked up in my French dictionary were 'white knickers'. In case you're interested they are 'culotte blanche'.

Apart from French and English, I failed completely to get an education at this school and the only marks I have to show from there are on my arse as the result of the disciplinary ministrations of the then headmaster. My only other memory of this place is even more unpleasant. If you got into trouble in class, which I did on a daily basis, you were made to go and sit in the back row, which was the realm of a boy who used to masturbate more or less continuously all day. He was the most enthusiastic wanker that I had ever met before or since. It was very off-putting to sit there listening to him alternately tearing himself apart with great physical effort and then collapsing with a sigh followed by the relief of the shortest of silences before the underside of the desk started to thump again at an ever increasing fury. Needless to say he was the most exhausted little boy that you had ever seen and he seemed to get visibly smaller every week. I'm sure if we had stayed at school long enough he would have disappeared completely.

My main ambition while I was at this school was to spend as little time as possible there which I managed by playing truant whenever we had to play sport. The journey from school to the playing fields was long and unchecked, and as I was so bad at sports that nobody wanted me on their team, I was never missed. Sports featured on three afternoons a week which gave me plenty of time to indulge in my real love — surprise, surprise, the cinema. My mother would give me money for my lunch each day and on sports days I would spend half of it on a bar of chocolate to stop me actually dropping in the street from malnutrition and the other half would go on a ticket to the Tower cinema in Peckham. I knew then what I wanted to be, but of course I couldn't see how someone like me could make it in that world. It was my great escape and I loved it.

It was on one of my clandestine visits to the afternoon cinema that I had my first encounter with commercialized sex, which had a profound effect on me. I was about fourteen years old at the time and was, as usual, the first and only customer when the cinema opened. On this particular day, I approached the box office with my money in one hand and my chocolate bar in the other. Doreen, the girl selling the tickets was, to say the least, homely and a little on the dumpy side, but I had seen her many times before and she had grown strangely attractive to me. When you are a fourteen-year-old boy all girls, no matter what they look like, are inclined to grow strangely attractive. I gave her my money for the ticket and as I was about to walk away she said: 'Give me your chocolate bar and I'll show you me tits.' I stopped in my tracks, dumbfounded by this generous offer and sneaked a glance at the rather grubby sweater which veiled the offered exhibits. I had seen a couple of breasts before but these looked to be much larger than any I had previously encountered. What do I do? I thought. If I gave her the chocolate I would probably starve to death in the cinema and I was famished. But there was only a moment's hesitation as libido destroyed appetite and I passed the chocolate through the box office slot with a sweaty and trembling hand. Doreen looked furtively around, but there was nobody about; the picture was obviously not a hit. 'Here you are then, Romeo,' she said and very slowly drew up the left side of her sweater to reveal a slightly grubby brassière. Inserting her finger under the band of her bra, she pulled it upwards over the mound of her left bosom, until first a nipple emerged and then a complete white breast popped out with a slight bounce as it reached the bottom of its fall. I was entranced. It was not only the biggest breast that I had seen, but it was much bigger than it had looked underneath the sweater. Almost immediately she pulled the brassière down over the quivering mound and covered it all up with her sweater. As I turned and weaved my way rather unsteadily along the darkened corridor towards my lonely paradise a sense of injustice started to creep over me. I had been cheated. She had definitely said tits plural and I had seen only one. To add insult to injury I decided she had shown me the smallest one – the right one I was sure was much bigger. I sat there in the auditorium with my stomach rumbling audibly, seething with anger at myself for having been such a fool. I vowed never, ever again to pay for anything to do with sex for as long as I lived, and to this day I never have. Love at various times in my life has cost me a great deal, but I have never paid for sex.

Soon food started to get more plentiful in the shops and my father was earning good money at Billingsgate market, where he had returned after he was demobbed. My mother stuffed us full of food – mainly fry-ups, which consisted of sausages, bacon, eggs and tomatoes, accompanied by bread which had been fried after all the other stuff had been cooked. Although this may sound disgusting to a modern health freak, it was absolutely delicious to a growing boy brought up on wartime rationing.

I still had problems with fish. Dad would bring home loads of the very best stuff which had, he would always inform us, fallen off the back of a lorry. Lorries in those days were remarkably inefficient around our area; the amount and variety of stuff that fell off the back of them and found its way into our house was amazing. Sometimes Dad would bring home so much fish that it was impossible to get it all into our tiny fridge and it had to be placed in the coldest part of the house. My father was an old-fashioned man who believed that heat was bad for growing boys. Fresh air was the thing, especially in bedrooms, and Stanley and I had to sleep with the windows open. My parents' room had heat and closed windows because, my father explained, my mother slept in there and women were different, so consequently the coldest place for the overflow of fish was our bedroom. One day he put a great big plate of smoked haddock there. That night as I got out of bed to go for a pee I saw a shiny apparition hovering over the end of my bed, shifting and waving in the dark. I screamed blue murder, and my father came rushing in to see what was going on. I shouted, 'There's a ghost!' pointing at the apparition. Dad switched on the light and there was the plate of fish. 'You stupid sod,' he said, 'it's only the haddock.' 'But it was glowing in the dark,' I whispered. 'Of course it glows in the dark,' he replied scornfully. 'It's full of phosphorus.' I went to have my pee and came back still shaking. 'Can you leave the light on, Dad?' I pleaded, as he tucked me in. 'Grown men don't sleep with the lights on, son,' he said, and turned out the light. I put my head under the blankets so that I couldn't see the fish and lay there thinking, not many grown men have to sleep in a bedroom with smoked haddock, either!

The district we lived in was called the Elephant and Castle, but no one ever said the whole phrase. If you were asked where you came from, you only said 'the Elephant', and if you could keep a reasonably straight face, this was usually enough to strike terror into anyone from outside the area. I used to practise in front of a mirror at home. 'I'm from the Elephant,' I would say, with the hardest stare that you can muster as an extremely spotty, pale and skinny fifteen-year-old. I did not have a lot of confidence in what I saw in the mirror so I figured I had better try it out on people smaller than me – or girls –before I entered the big time. I tried it, but the only reaction I got was: 'So are we,' from a group of snotty-nosed kids. It didn't work, I realised, unless you went out of your own area, which of course you never did if you wanted to come back alive.

The Elephant was famous in those days for some very vicious gangs of criminals called, in the old London backslang for VIPs, spivs. As far as the people who lived in that area were concerned spivs were very important people indeed, and everybody was terrified of them. They were into gambling, black market and protection mainly and their favourite weapon of intimidation was an open razor which they wielded with relish, accompanied by the unlikely innocent phrase: 'Stitch that up,' as they opened up a ten-inch gash in the victim's cheeks. It always left a scar when it was healed and was meant to show forever that the victim had offended the mob in some way as a warning to others to stay in line.

This warning was not lost on me in particular: I saw myself in films as the handsome leading man who gets all the girls, and a scar on my face would mean playing villains all my life. In fact in real life it wasn't the guys with the broken noses or the razor scars who were scary; I was far more afraid of the men with no scars who had handed out the punishment. I used to walk in fear of these guys and run whenever I saw them coming. They always wore very wide trilby hats with razor blades sewn into the brims, and they used these hats as a weapon. I still duck if anybody starts to take off their hat.

Although I was afraid of the spivs, my father never seemed to be worried by them, and we would often stop and talk to them, which always panicked me. When I asked him why he wasn't afraid of them, his reply really surprised me and changed my attitude completely. 'Most of them are related to us in some way,' he said calmly. Maybe life wasn't so dangerous after all.

The next bunch to terrorise the neighbourhood were Teddy boys. The children of the spivs, they were every bit as vicious and of course, a lot more agile, so that if you saw them coming you had to run even faster. The Teddy boy was immediately recognisable by his hair which was worn long and then greased into a quiff about four or five inches high in the front. At the back the hair was combed round and formed into a very complicated shape which was known as a D.A. (duck's arse), which is exactly what it looked like from the rear. Teddy boys always wore single-breasted suits with narrow lapels, narrow peg-topped trousers and 'Brothel Creepers', big ugly shoes with soles made of crêpe rubber at least three inches thick. The overall effect was more of a demented stork than an intimidating gang member but they were, nevertheless, a really bad-tempered and dangerous lot.

I decided that camouflage was the best defence, and I went for a Teddy boy haircut and suit. The haircut was not a complete hit with my father, who pointed out rather unkindly that I looked like a skinny tart. When I turned round he also remarked that from the back it looked like a duck's arse, not realising that this was real proof of success. Dad also refused to give me money for a new suit, noting that I had a new one only two years ago, ignoring the fact that I had grown at least a foot in that time and could no longer wear it because the trousers were so short. At fifteen I was nearly six feet and as skinny as a rake, so tall and thin that my mother announced one day that she was afraid I would overgrow my strength. My father's only reply to this imminent problem had been to say: 'What fucking strength?'

To get the money for a suit, I took up a paper round and set off every morning for three months at the crack of dawn. Delivering was easy; the hard part was Sundays when I had to collect the money. I would see curtains part slightly and houses go quiet as I approached. Sometimes small children would answer the door and inform me that 'Mum is out,' and slam the door in my face, but not before I had peeped through the crack and seen Mum hiding behind the door, just as mine had many years ago. The psychiatrists were right, I think. I had indeed become – not for the last time in my life – what I was afraid of. Sometimes, if nobody answered the doorbell, I would peep through the letter-box to be assailed by the smell of stale boiled cabbage and cats' piss wafting through the small opening. On more than one occasion I can remember looking through the letter-box only to be met by another pair of eyes looking at me.

Eventually I amassed the twelve pounds it would cost to get my suit and I had enough left over to purchase a pair of three-inch-high brothel creepers. I picked my suit up one Saturday morning and rushed home and put it on. It looked great and fitted as perfectly as any twelve pound suit made at the Elephant was ever going to. Proudly I modelled it for my mother, whose only comment was to enquire if I was going to a fancy dress party. Nonplussed by her lack of understanding of modern fashion, I was off out to test my new outfit. It didn't take long because as I turned the corner of our street there was a whole gang of Teds coming towards me. Normally I would have run like all the other kids, but this time, with my heart thumping so loud I thought that people must be able to hear it, I walked straight on with as fierce a look as possible on my face. As we closed I kept on walking straight past all of them uneventfully until the last one, who was smaller than all the others, said, out of the corner of his mouth: 'Cunt.' My whole world collapsed. After months of the stinking paper round and twelve pounds straight down the drain, I had fooled nobody. I would never be a villain.

The Elephant was not exactly a classy district. The streets were as rough and dangerous as it was possible to get without anybody actually declaring war, and even my own personal paradise the cinema was not without its perils. There was always a queue if the film was at all popular, which invariably resulted in fights as people tried to push in front of others, and even inside no one was safe. Every cinema had its share of gropers prowling the dark looking for young women sitting on their own, and these encounters would erupt like mortar-bomb explosions all through the film. Suddenly there would be a screech and the sound of a face being slapped followed by a lady shouting: 'You dirty fucking bastard!' Ushers would arrive and the shame-faced dirty fucking bastard would be thrown out. All the while I sat being enthralled in the dark, ladies were being sullied around me – I felt really sorry for them.

One day I was sitting there engrossed in some film or other when I felt a gentle hand touch my knee and start progressing with light caressing movements towards my crotch. I sat there, just staring straight ahead not knowing what to do. I knew that men used to try and feel women up in the cinema and that women always made a fuss about it, but here was a woman doing it to me and I didn't feel like making any fuss at all. I finally plucked up courage enough to turn my head slightly sideways to see what my seducer looked like (not that it mattered very much, as the standard of beauty to get me aroused in my teen years was incredibly low) and as I turned to meet her eyes I found myself gazing into the stubbled face of a middle-aged bum who was smiling at me with toothless gums.

'You dirty fucking bastard!' I shouted, leaping to my feet and at the same time knocking him unconscious.

The ushers came and dragged him out and I sat there angry and mystified. I knew why men liked to touch women's legs – I spent most of my time trying to figure out how to do it myself – but a man wanting to touch another man's leg in the cinema was a complete mystery to me. When I got home I told my father what had happened. 'It was a Nancy Boy,' my father said gruffly. 'Stay away from them.'

Another mystery solved.

I've never forgotten the Elephant and I still like to go back and pay the area a visit. One time, I remember, I ran into Charlie Chaplin who had been born there doing the same thing. I introduced myself and although I was by this time famous, he had obviously never heard of me, but we talked for a while and he seemed to have a tremendous nostalgia for the place and shared my sadness at the way the developers had torn it apart. About three hundred yards from the prefab where I grew up there was the ruin of an old Music Hall called the 'South London' and Chaplin pointed it out to me and told me that before he went to America he had appeared there in a show called *Mumming Birds*. It was a cold day and it may have been that, but I could swear that he had tears in his eyes. He obviously did not want to be disturbed for too long by a rather pushy young actor, so he said a rather brusque goodbye and turned and walked away. He was a small sad figure, and although he was wearing an overcoat and a trilby hat, I could almost see the funny shoes and the walking stick as he walked away, passing unnoticed through the crowds of people who were the children of his past.

I was always very proud of the show business people who came from my area; I needed all the encouragement I could give myself when I started out and seized on any connection, no matter how nebulous. I never dreamed I would meet any of them. Alfred Hitchcock's family had a shop in the Tower Bridge Road where my maternal grandfather had a fruit stall, and Noël Coward had lived in Clapham, which was then a rapidly decaying genteel area. Noël told me his mother ran a boarding house in order to keep up appearances of prosperity. He said that he had to live in the top room because it was the smallest and most uncomfortable and therefore the smallest loss of revenue for her. As he became more and more successful he told me he kept renting a bigger and better room on a lower floor. 'As I went up in the world,' he told me with that wonderful false sneer of his, 'I came down in the house.' That was success, South London style.

When I was in Hollywood Hitchcock asked me to lunch at Universal Studios to discuss playing the killer in the movie *Frenzy* that he was hoping to make in London. I was very nervous, not only because I was going to meet the great man, but because I did not want to play the part in the film. I found the role as a particularly sadistic killer of young women really loathsome and I did not want to be associated with it, but I didn't tell him this because I wanted to meet him. The only

41

thing that I can remember about the lunch was plucking up enough courage to ask him if he had, as was reported, said that actors were cattle. 'No,' he said with a smile, 'I never said that at all. What I actually said was that they should be treated like cattle which, you must agree, Michael, is an entirely different thing.' He was right, of course, but it didn't sound much different to me. My agent turned the part down – I didn't have the guts to do it myself – and although I saw Hitchcock very often on the lot and in Chasen's restaurant where he used to have dinner every Friday night, he never spoke to me again. So much for Cockney solidarity.

4

Noses Off

There were two routes out of the ghetto: sport or show business. Sport was out for me, so show business was the only option, although I had very little practical experience.

When I was seven I appeared in the school pantomime with my fly open and got my first on-stage laugh which was very gratifying – until I found out why they were laughing. I learned two things from this début: always make the audience laugh *with* you and never at you; and always to check your flies before you go on. These days it's an automatic reaction with me. My second attempt at show business was at Wilson's Grammar School where I went to the first play rehearsal without reading through my part and found out that I had to kiss a small boy who was playing my wife – a necessity in an all-boys' school and one of the reasons why I am against them. I couldn't do this love scene; apart from the fact that Jenkins was not a girl he was also very ugly – even for a boy – and he had bad breath. I retired from the play.

After this I promised myself I would never do anything where I had to kiss a male. I only broke this vow once, when I did *Deathtrap* many years later. And I had three good excuses: I was kissing Superman (the other part was played by Christopher Reeve); his breath only smelt of the bottle of brandy we had drunk between us before we did the scene – and I got paid a million bucks to do it. My sense of values, as you can see, did not alter much over the years.

A lot of actors came into show business by the direct route. Charlie Chaplin was a Music Hall star, Cary Grant was a child acrobat and Roger Moore modelled so many pullovers no one could pull the wool over his eyes. For me it began at a youth club called Clubland, in the Walworth Road. There, I soon made friends and lost a bit of my 'loner' status. My best new mate was a boy called Jimmy Anderton who was the funniest and wittiest person that I had ever met. And then there was Billy Marle who wanted to be a jazz trumpeter and used to spend every waking hour playing his records. It was through him that I developed a love for jazz. Londoners have a habit of splitting up a big word and putting an expletive in the middle and Billy's father was an expert at this. One night we were at Billy's house playing cards while Billy was practising on his trumpet and he woke up his father, who was a bus driver on the early-morning shift. We all stopped playing as we listened to him plonking down the stairs in his bare feet. He flung open the door to the kitchen, his tousled head appeared and he looked at Billy and said: 'Why don't you learn to play the vio – fucking – lin.' An illustration of some of the speech patterns unique to our area and part of my cultural heritage, which everybody else seems to be so proud of these days. We were very impressed with this and practised our own versions, like the unmarried girl who came home and told her Cockney father that she was pregnant. 'Marvellous. Fucking. Marvellous,' he replied.

We young men were expected to tear into the gym, and start racing around after a ball or leap over wooden horses and climb ropes, to make us all too exhausted to start anything with the girls. Cold showers were slyly suggested, under the guise of being the tough and manly thing to do, but I cottoned on to this deception very quickly and dodged them to save my energy for the real task in hand: the seduction of some unsuspecting young lady. I was fifteen and I had never actually seduced a girl, but I had read about it in books and I was determined not to be exhausted by maniacal gymnastic practices should the opportunity to 'dip my wick', as it was rather unromantically known, come my way. To keep up appearances and being very tall I joined the basketball team, but as this was played in a rather genteel and lethargic way I never had to expend a great deal of energy on it. I was also of course only eating two lunches out of five each week because of my forays to the cinema in the afternoons so I was not in the best of physical shape in the first place.

Amy Hood was the object of my lust at the time and never having been in the society of girls before, I was very shy, so I had to work out a way to get close to her. One day I was making my way up the stairs to the gym for basketball practice when I passed a door with a little window in it, and there, framed in the window, was Amy, surrounded by all the prettiest girls in the club. I was leaning on the door staring at this bevy of potential romance when the door swung in and I found myself standing in the room, trapped. The girls all stared at me for a moment and then the teacher came towards me, smiling in welcome. 'Come in,' she said. 'We haven't got any boys,' she added mysteriously. 'You are the first one to join this year.' 'What class is this?' I mumbled. 'The drama class.' It came to me in a flash. I could kill two birds with one stone. I could learn to act and go to Hollywood and maybe get to kiss Amy in one of the plays. So I was on my way to becoming an actor for all the wrong reasons – typical of me. I did get to kiss Amy and all the other girls at one time or the other, but none of them ever succumbed to my blandishments to go further, but I didn't mind at all, because I fell in love with acting.

My first role was not overly ambitious (I thought it better to start slowly). I played a robot who speaks in a flat mechanical voice and only says one line in the whole play. This I thought was a modest enough début and was insurance against making a complete fool of myself. The play was a very intellectual piece called *R.U.R.* which stood for Rossums Universal Robots and was written by a Czech writer named Karel Capek. Not for the last time as it turned out was I doing a play in which I did not understand what the hell was going on or what anybody was talking about, including my own single line. There were many deep discussions of the meaning of the play, which only made it more confusing for me, so whenever, which was rare, my opinion was sought, I nodded sagely and would say that I thought the meaning would become clearer as we progressed through rehearsals. It never did.

The big night came and went very quickly. My only

45

memory of it was that I was far more nervous than I thought I was going to be and that everybody who was great in rehearsal was bad in performance and vice versa, a situation that, many years later, I found occurred in the professional theatre. As for my own performance, I got my first review in the Club magazine. I already knew and disliked the boy who was the critic, who struck me as being a sarcastic bastard, and for once my judgment of character was right on the button. 'Maurice Micklewhite,' he wrote, 'played the Robot who spoke in a dull mechanical monotonous voice to perfection.' Portents of things to come in later life.

Although my role was a modest one I felt a great sense of excitement in putting on the show and a feeling of tremendous achievement after it was all over that I had never felt before. For the rest of my time at the club until I was called up to serve in the British army, I was always in some show or the other. I was also beginning to make contact with show business people. I was standing outside the Trocadero Cinema at the Elephant one day to catch my first glimpse of a real film star. The film that was showing was David Lean's *Great Expectations* and Anthony Wager, the young boy who played Pip, was making a personal appearance. There was a huge crowd and we all pushed and shoved to catch a glimpse of the star as the big limousine drew up. The manager was waiting on a fairly red carpet and he greeted the young actor as he got out. He then turned to the crowd and shouted: 'Is there any boy here who has a birthday today?'

I couldn't believe my ears: it *was* my birthday. 'Yes,' I shouted.

The manager beckoned. I pushed my way through the crowd and he put his arm round my shoulder and asked me my name. 'Maurice here,' he shouted to the crowd, 'is going to have tea with Anthony.' So there I was in the manager's office having tea with a real actor. I was too shy actually to say anything; I just sat there staring at a real live movie actor for the first time. I was so nervous that I remember nothing about the tea, except that poor Anthony Wager seemed as shy and nervous as I was. But it was a start. I had actually spoken to someone who had been in a film; I was making progress.

At the club I met a man called Alec Reed, who was a tremendous film buff and used to run his magnificent collection of 16 millimetre silent films on a Sunday evening in the club theatre. This man knew more about film than anyone I have ever met, before or since. He spotted my interest very quickly and took it upon himself to educate me in the history of film and to a certain extent in the making of them. Every summer the whole club used to go on holiday to the island of Guernsey, off the south coast of England, and Alec used to make documentaries of our trips, letting me help with camera while he explained the lenses he was using and about shots and angles. He even gave me a director's credit on a film one year: my proudest moment to date when I saw my name on the screen for the first time. I knew from the giggles and sarcastic remarks around me as 'Maurice Micklewhite, Director' came up on the screen that if I ever got into professional acting I was going to have to change my name. A problem that was going to fill my every spare moment for the next five years.

I really enjoyed my holidays in Guernsey. I was always in love with some girl or the other and being away from home there was more chance of what we used to call 'snogging'. There was none of what the Americans called petting and especially not heavy petting. I find the lines between these rather confusing, but whatever they are I can assure you, there was none of it. Unfortunately there was almost no promiscuity amongst teenagers at that time and I am sure that nearly every girl in that club was a virgin until she got married. The moral code was very strict and if some unfortunate lad did 'Go Too Far' he would soon find himself the attention of the burlier members of the girl in question's family, demanding to know when the wedding was going to be. This enquiry would usually be accompanied by a black eye and various cuts and bruises in the ear, nose and throat area for having put everybody to this inconvenience in the first place. Morally speaking it was a bit like living in Sicily, but without the sun, wine or pasta. The sexual revolution of the 1960s was ten interminable years away, so snogging was all we did – but we did it with great enthusiasm.

The more I worked with Alec Reed on his films the more I

became interested in the technical side of movie making, but I wasn't very happy when Alec, after seeing me in several plays as an actor, subtly suggested that perhaps I should aim for a directing career instead. It wasn't surprising. Alec was a very kind man and I think he thought this young skinny unattractive boy with a thick Cockney accent, with absolutely no family history in show business and not even the remotest contact with anybody in it, was going to have the disappointment of his life one day, and he was trying to let me down gently as early as possible. I had a few doubts of my own. All the stars at that time had black hair and were very handsome – Robert Taylor, Tyrone Power and Cary Grant, to name but three stunning examples. Even the ugly ones like Paul Muni, Humphrey Bogart and Edward G. Robinson had black hair and were attractive in their own way. It was a great worry that being ugly and fair-haired meant that my future as an actor was not necessarily a foregone conclusion. And they were all Americans. After I had gone through the 'Nanny in the theatre' English biographies and moved onto the new type of American biography, I found everybody seemed to have been the child of show business parents. Most of these actors were very proud to have been born in a trunk as though they were the only people who really had a right to be in show business. My mother was no help. When I told her that most people in the theatre had been born in a trunk her only reply was 'Tell them you were born in a flat the size of one.'

I was also six foot tall and painfully thin and this brought about my next phobia: my nose was too big. The thinner you get the bigger it looks and there was no star with a really big nose except Jimmy Durante. Of course if you gain weight your mouth gets smaller, so there was no relief there either. These problems all sound insignificant to adults, but to teenagers they take on an almost suicidal importance. Teenage children spend a ridiculous amount of time looking in the mirror as their facial structure convulses, rises and sinks like a pot of boiling porridge. When all this is covered with a strategically placed veneer of pimples, you have the reason why most children never smile between the ages of thirteen and nineteen. It is a terrible period for most kids, but it is even worse for those like me with ambitions in the visual side of the arts. Help was at hand for me, though, in the shape of Spencer Tracy, who had blond hair, a kind of big nose and did not look like a Latin lover. When I first saw him my spirits soared, but the clincher came when I saw my first European movie. It was a French film, *Le Jour Se Lève*, which Alec Reed had taken me to see and it starred the man who finally convinced me I could make it. His name was Jean Gabin, and he featured everything that I thought could hold me back: fair hair, a big nose and a small mouth. He was the biggest star in France, so everything was now possible. The other thing that Spencer Tracy and Jean Gabin had in common was that they were both great actors – something that, with the best will in the world, could not be said of most of the movie stars at that time – or even now for that matter. Forget the looks, I told myself, you are going to have to become the best possible actor that you can be.

Today, of course, it's easier. In those days people like me would be cast as the best friends of the glamorous heroes — now these roles are top billing and filled by actors like de Niro, Pacino and Hoffman. I remember even Steve McQueen saying that if he'd been an actor in the 1930s he would have been the hero's best friend.

During my teenage years, I watched my father, whom I loved very much, for clues to success when I grew up. This was a very sad process for me because almost everything that I learned from him was negative. He was a gambler and always blew most of his wages on the horses, which caused a lot of unnecessary suffering for my mother. Although we still did not have enough money for luxuries, we hired a radio for two shillings and sixpence per week. I worked out many years later that with the money he paid in hire charges he could have bought at least twenty radios of his own. I never mentioned this to him, but the day after he was buried I rang the company and told them to take it back.

Dad used to take me to the fish market on Sundays to help with a process called 'icing up', which meant replacing the melting ice in the fish boxes so that the fish did not go off over the weekend. This was an unbelievably cold and bleak experience for me and I also realised that most physical labour could be replaced by a machine. I had decided by now that I would never follow my father into the market no matter what I did for a living. Dad's job is now done by forklift trucks.

I was sixteen now and sex with a real female was still tantalisingly elusive. Some of the older boys had done it, they said, and even if they were lying, it was certain from their graphic descriptions that activity had taken place. My sex life was more of a still life. I was introduced to a magazine called *Health and Efficiency* which was the house organ (no pun really intended), of the British Nudist Club. A holiday camp where everybody was naked seemed like a very embarrassing place to me. How, I wondered, could all those men walk around with all those beautiful nude women and not get an erection? I had never seen a naked woman and I was walking around with one practically all day long. I already knew what breasts looked like so the photos of the women had only one source of interest for me and that was below the waist. I had never seen a naked grown-up woman and the magazine was of no help because the censor at that time made them airbrush out the sex organs of both sexes. So while I knew what a male organ looked like, I had grown bored stiff with looking at my own – which seemed to be stiff even when I wasn't bored with it – I was quite unprepared for the female one when I eventually did see it, to find that it was covered with hair just like mine. I think I figured that since women didn't have to shave their faces, they wouldn't have any hair down there either. It was quite a shock I can tell you and started me on a path of hatred of all censorship – not for any ideological reasons, but because it can be very misleading in important areas.

I was very late in everything sexual but I eventually caught up with masturbation. The vicar and friends also issued dire warnings. Much to my relief I did not go blind, but I was diagnosed eventually as being short-sighted and in need of glasses so I guess I must have overdone it a little. Hairs did not grow in the palms of my hands as some of the older boys threatened, although there have been rather a lot in my nose lately, so maybe it's some kind of delayed punishment.

I was not the only culprit indulging in this unhealthy practice. One day in the shower at the club after one of the occasional basketball games I played to maintain some notion of masculinity with the other boys, I found four boys holding a competition to see who could come farthest up the wall. I had already heard that women were interested in size but I had never heard a word about their interest in distance.

The moral climate in England in the 1950s is summed up for me by two instances. The first was a newspaper article reporting the murder of a young woman. It said she had been stabbed twenty-seven times, but that she had not been interfered with. The inference seemed to me that murder was all right, but sex wasn't. I couldn't help thinking that she might have been better off if she had been interfered with. The second was something that a master told us at school. He was trying to teach us animals some social graces. He said if ever we were in the embarrassing position of walking into an unlocked bathroom and discovering a naked lady in the bath, to save her embarrassment we should say: 'Excuse me, sir,' and leave as quickly as possible. Can you imagine the effect that this would have on that poor woman? She would probably spend the rest of the day naked looking in the mirror at herself and the following ten years on a psychiatrist's couch.

If you look at British movies of that period, the villain is always the one that's making love to all the women. I found out all about this later when I made the film *Alfie*. Alfie's intention to make love to as many women as possible caused the most incredible amount of fuss. I was treated like Jack the Ripper. The only place where the picture was a failure was France. This puzzled me so I asked a male French friend of mine why. He replied that the story was so unbelievable it was a joke. 'What is so unbelievable about it?' I asked. 'An Englishman who makes love to eleven women? It is impossible for any French man to accept that as reality,' he said with scorn. These guys still think they are the only lovers in the world.

Some time during this period, politics entered my life in an unusual and exciting way. Coming out of the club one evening I was surprised to find myself surrounded by a bevy of very attractive (my definition of attractive was anyone with big tits and most of her front teeth) older women, about twenty or twenty-two years old. They were offering leaflets. I took one and one of the girls said mysteriously: 'Read it and let us know if you're interested. We'll be back tomorrow night.' What exciting proposition could this be, I thought as I walked home reading the leaflet.

From what I could make out I was being asked to join something called the Young Communists. I knew it was a political party, I also knew that they were very keen on it in Russia and that it had been invented by someone called Marx. I knew the Marx Brothers from the movies so at least, I thought, it might be amusing. The leaflet went on to something really interesting: there was going to be a re-distribution of wealth. I could not believe my luck! If they were going to do that, my family and I would have to come out ahead. The clincher for me, was that Communists believed in free love. I couldn't credit that I'd found a political party that offered wealth and love: my two absorbing passions.

I couldn't wait to get out of the club the next evening to meet the group of girls. I had a good look at them and picked the one that I wanted to have free love with the most. 'I want to join,' I said. 'Wonderful,' she replied and dragged me off to a small dingy office a couple of streets away. 'He wants to join,' she announced and then she disappeared. I was left standing in a room with four men, all doing smile impersonations. I was instantly suspicious. Remembering what my father had told me about spotting untrustworthy men, I had hit the jackpot here. Two of them had beards, one was wearing sandals and another one had a bow tie. The only thing missing were the two-toned shoes. The object of my free love had disappeared and here I was with a group of guys who obviously so far had not done very well in the redistribution of wealth by the look of them. One of them put a form on the desk in front of me and told me to sign it and pay over my subscription of five shillings. I saw at once what a mistake I had made: the distribution of wealth was to be mine to them, not the other way round. I fled – and a lingering suspicion of Communism has remained planted in my mind forever.

During my four years at the club, I did many plays but although I can remember every minute detail of anything sexual that happened to me, I cannot remember the name of a single play after the first one that I was in. This is probably the same of all teenage boys.

We decided to take one of the plays to some of the local youth organisations and it was on this tour that I met a guy named Paul Challen who was to become my life-long friend. We had gone to do the play at a home for orphaned boys – a depressing place, even by my lowly standards, and everybody there looked as unhealthy and as unhappy as they could be without actually killing themselves. After the show, I walked out of the creepy place as fast as I could, when out of the gloom on the dim lamplit street, a strange, gaunt figure appeared. He was about the same age as me and the same height, around six feet, but that is where the resemblance ended. I thought I was thin, but this guy really made me look quite portly. He had a gaunt sunken face with a pale white skin stretched tightly over cheekbones that looked as though they might break through at any moment. A pair of very blue eyes were sunk deep back in his head beneath a mop of straight black hair. He walked beside me with slightly hunched shoulders as though he didn't want anybody to notice him and the only sign of life about him was a mischievous glint in his eyes that I could occasionally see in the dark. 'My name's Paul,' he whispered as though it was a secret. He had a very gentle voice. 'I know your name from the programme.' I put out my hand. 'Pleased to meet you,' I said and that was the start of a friendship that has lasted for well over forty years and kept me from going insane at times.

'Do you want to be a real actor one day?' he asked. 'Yes, I do,' I replied. 'Do you know how to get started?' he asked. I had no idea and was taken aback when he suggested we tried to find out together.

Paul was the first person I had ever told that I wanted to be a professional; up until then it had only been a dream. Not only did he not laugh at me, which is what would have happened if I had told anybody else that I knew, but he wanted to be one too. When I did voice my ambition, people

53

did laugh – right up until the time I made a success of it. Then they said it wasn't right that I should have earned so much more money than they did. I've always reckoned that I was paid a reasonable sum for the acting and the rest is recompense for the years of pain, humiliation and rejection that you have to take when you are an unknown actor. I looked at Paul's frail frame under the lamp post and said: 'Come home with me. My mother will cook us something.' Just looking at him had made me feel hungry.

Paul never joined the club with me but he always met me outside each evening and we would walk the grim streets, sometimes until dawn, talking of what we were going to do and who we were going to be. I had had lots of mates and chums but Paul was my first real friend and he was to prove it over and over again as the years went on. My experiences as an evacuee were for the most part pleasant and most of the time actually beneficial, but I had always felt a bit sorry for myself for being so poor. By this time I had read hundreds of books and knew what life was like for people who had money. One day I asked Paul how he became an orphan. 'My mother,' he said, without any emotion, 'gave me some money to run round the butcher's and get some sausages for lunch.' He took the money, got the sausages, but when he was coming out of the shop, the air raid warning went, so he ran down to the nearest shelter. When the raid was over he ran back home quickly, but when he arrived his home was gone – and so was his entire family. 'That was it. All I had in the world were the clothes I was wearing, a pound of sausages in one hand and some change in the other,' he finished, still without emotion. We never mentioned it again, either of us, and I never felt sorry for myself again, either.

The Reverend Jimmy Butterworth who ran the club was also its creator. He was, as he always referred to himself, a little Lancashire Lad and he was only about five feet tall. In every other way he was a giant. He had created this youth club out of nothing in the middle of nowhere, through sheer guts, determination and the ability to prise open even the tightest purse. If you mention a youth club in a slum area to most people, they would imagine a bleak leaky shed. Clubland was a magnificent building with every modern facility, and it had been designed by the same architect who had designed Broadcasting House in London; Jimmy went for the best for us kids.

Jimmy had a unique ability to raise money and it was because of this that I met my first big star. When Bob Hope came to London and played the Prince of Wales theatre for two weeks, he gave his entire fee to our club. Bob, I know, is a generous man, but there were plenty of other charities to give to then as now, but Jimmy persuaded him to give it all to us. He also talked him into repeating it three times so I got to know Bob very well because he actually came to the club and talked to us. Bob was something else to me in particular: he was an Englishman who had become a star in America. As a kid I had already got the idea from films that anybody could make it in America, but the thought of making it in my own country coming from what we now call the underclass was beyond even contemplating for one moment.

Many years later I was in Acapulco for the film festival. I had been invited there because they were showing my latest film, *Alfie*. While I was there I did the Bob Hope Show for television and I wondered when he met me again if he would remember me from the days at the club. I did the show and he never mentioned anything so I presumed that he had forgotten it. After all, why should he remember a single scruffy kid from an incident which was already fifteen years ago? I left Mexico and went back to England and after about six weeks I got a call from my agent to ask if my fee for the Bob Hope Show had been sent straight to me instead of him which was the custom. I told them it hadn't and they said they would check it out. A week later I got a call from Bob Hope saying that he had sent my fee straight to Jimmy Butterworth at Clubland. 'You owe them,' he told me.

It was at Clubland that I met the guy who was eventually to become the basis of my portrayal of 'Alfie'. Jimmy Buckley had none of my problems with the opposite sex, in fact he had a surfeit of supply. He had some kind of magic with girls. The moment he joined the club he became my new best friend. Maybe he can teach me something, I thought, or perhaps by proximity some of his magic would rub off. I was even prepared to settle for the ones he didn't want, but still nothing happened. When I was playing Alfie later I used many of his little tricks to flesh out my portrayal. Over the years many people have confused Alfie with me, but nothing could be farther from the truth. Alfie and Jimmy would go with anybody; my only interest was in the unattainable, which was perhaps the reason why I found it so difficult to attain anybody at all. I have never had any respect for any woman who did not respect herself, except on those few occasions when I was drunk, it was late at night, and I was desperate.

My unbroken run of bad luck with the opposite sex was about to come to an abrupt and unexpected end. I had been invited to the birthday party of a boy who lived near me. As I didn't drink alcohol at this time I just sat around drinking lemonade and watching people gradually get pissed out of their minds until I was the only one who could walk without help. With one exception, that is. As I sat there wondering whether to leave or not as there was nobody left I could talk to and get a reply that I could understand, the back door opened and my friend's aunt beckoned me outside. She was drunk but not legless, but as I quickly noticed, she seemed to have lost her skirt somewhere. In no time at all, I had at last done the deed and a whole new field of endeavour was opened to me. I stumbled out into the night, unable to believe my luck and headed for home with a spring in my step and a whole new outlook on life. Here I was at the age of sixteen and already I had found, apart from acting, the other thing that I wanted to do for the rest of my life. I had never excelled or been really interested in anything until acting came along, and now here was this as well: something that I was equipped to do, had quickly got the knack of and, although I was very lazy in most things, was prepared to do any time and anywhere. In fact, like acting, I was prepared to devote the rest of my life to the pursuit of its perfection. I will not reveal Auntie's identity. She was about forty-five then, so she must be ninety by now, and if she is still alive, I don't want anyone tracking her down in case she's forgotten how good I was.

There was a rather strange sequel to my experience that

night, when a year later I was invited to the same boy's next birthday party. I accepted the invitation with great enthusiasm as repetitions of my experience with Auntie had been rather thin on the ground in the preceding year. I arrived late, and everybody was already very drunk, but there was no sign of Auntie. Suddenly, however, when nobody was looking, one of the boy's uncles dragged me into a bedroom and tried to repeat my experience with Auntie – only with me on the receiving end this time. I had no idea what was going on, but fortunately he was quite drunk and I managed to fight my way out of the place and wound up in the same street as a year before, not with a spring in my step but a black eye and a cut lip. My enthusiasm for birthday parties waned visibly after that.

When I told my father of my experience, his only reply was that it was probably a Nancy Boy. 'I'll bet that young boy will turn out to be a Nancy Boy, too, when he grows up, so stay away from him,' Dad said wisely.

I took offence at this. 'He's going to join the merchant navy,' I replied, to prove how masculine my friend was. 'Mark my words,' he said darkly. The boy did go away to the merchant navy and I didn't see him for many years until we met by accident in the street. 'Still in the merchant navy?' I asked. 'No,' he said in a strange voice I'd never heard him use before. 'I'm a ballet dancer.' My father was always right. It was annoying.

During my last eighteen months at Clubland I started work in a short series of dead end jobs, marking time until I started my two years of National Service. I had left school at the age of sixteen and a half with three or four passes in the final exams, much to everyone's surprise, including my own. I was never happier to leave anywhere than I was when I left school. The feeling, I was assured on my last day by the headmaster, was mutual.

I was free at last to get into show business. The nearest job to Hollywood I could manage was as an office boy with a little film company called Peak Films. This company made little 8-millimetre films of the sights of London to take home before the days of video cameras. I was just an office boy who did odd jobs, but I was allowed occasionally to carry the equipment when the cameramen went out shooting some new tourist spot. I got quite handy with the lights and the general electrics and on Sundays I used to help with the lighting at Jewish weddings. Mr Frieze, who owned the company, was Jewish so he had a lot of contacts and we did loads of weddings. I was the only boy that I know of who could sing *Hava Nagila* all the way through. We were filming a Jewish wedding dinner in a night club one Sunday evening and the cabaret featured a band called Eddie Calvert and his Golden Trumpet. When the time came for the cabaret, the lights dimmed, the stage opened up and a spotlit Mr Calvert started to ascend from out of sight below stage. Mr Jackson, the man who did all the actual filming, yelled at me that he wanted to get this shot and that I should plug in all the lights because it was so dark. Eddie Calvert's head was just appearing at stage level, his Trumpet was indeed gleaming Gold, and he was playing the ubiquitous *Hava Nagila*. Just as his chin was at about floor level, I plugged in my lights. The fuses all blew at once and the lift carrying Calvert and his band stopped immediately. People started to shout as bulbs and fuses started to pop all over the place. Mr Jackson fired me on the spot, in a very impolite manner and my last image as I fled the club was the head of Eddie Calvert blasting away on his Golden Trumpet like a demented but talented pumpkin.

During my time at Peak Films I had one experience that was to have a profound effect on me. Mr Frieze had been a colonel in the army and at the end of the war he had been the military censor who had made the then very difficult decision to release in the public newsreels the films of the concentration camps at Belsen, Auschwitz and Dachau. I had seen brief newsreel snippets of these many times in the cinema and found them very upsetting but I reasoned Hitler was dead, and it was all over and best forgotten. One day at the office we were discussing this matter and I remember saying how horrifying it all was and the guy who ran the projector said that what they had released was nothing compared with what they had decided to hold back. Mr Frieze had kept an uncensored copy and this he ran for us. I sat and watched in stunned disbelief as this record of obscenity unreeled, until I knew that I was going to be sick. Just before I ran out, my last thought was about the boys that I went to school with at Hackney Down Grocers. I wondered how many of the corpses on the piles flickering in front of me had been called Maurice.

My next job was with the biggest movie company in England at that time: the J. Arthur Rank Organisation. I was still just an odd-job boy, but now I was with a real film company. There would be directors and producers coming in to see Mr Rank, I thought. Maybe I would get discovered. It had happened to Lana Turner in a drug store called Schwabs in Hollywood. But for a movie company the atmosphere in the offices seemed very quiet and austere, rather like being in church. The reason for this was explained to me by my boss, a woman who did not turn out to be a barrel of laughs either. Mr Rank was very religious, she told me, and a very strict Methodist and there were certain things that he did not allow. She then began to list the things I was not allowed to do, which was just about everything, especially smoking. With my new-found wealth I had just taken this up but I soon found out that I could run down to the toilet and have a quick drag whenever the craving got too much. On the second day I was sitting there having a quiet puff when there was a loud knock on the door and a male voice yelled: 'Come out, whoever you are. You're fired!'

And I was.

Part Two

5

'If you can't move it, *paint it*'

After the war the British government started a scheme in which every eighteen-year-old boy learned to defend his country for two years. They called it National Service. We called it hell.

Eventually, my great day came and I went to join the Queen's Royal Regiment at a barracks near the town of Guildford in Surrey. The barracks consisted of dozens of wooden huts surrounding a large square and I was quick to notice that everywhere was spotlessly clean and brightly painted, and that everything made of brass let off a blinding gleam. Very neat and tidy, I thought, and was just wondering who kept the place so spotless when something my father had once told me about playing poker came into my mind. 'If after five hands you haven't worked out who the pigeon in the game is,' Dad said, 'it's probably you.' Dad was usually right.

I stood in a group outside one of the buildings along with about thirty other clones. We all had single-breasted gaberdine suits, brothel creeper shoes and a duck's arse hair cut. A sergeant came and stood before us and smiled for what was to be the last time for eight long weeks. Then he spoke to us in a voice that seemed to indicate that there was something wrong with his eyes; he obviously thought that we were standing a lot farther away than we actually were. 'You are now a platoon – or at least you will be by the time I've finished with you,' he yelled. 'I am your platoon sergeant. My job here is to replace your mothers and look after you.' (This last sentence sounded very unconvincing.) 'Get fell in in threes!' he screamed suddenly. 'For those of you who don't know, that is one behind the other twice.' Even with the added information it took us a little while to sort ourselves out to his satisfaction. He then gave us a couple of useful tips that would come in handy in our new lives. He'd obviously thought that we had moved farther away, because his voice went up a further couple of decibels: 'The basic rules are if you can move it, *pick it up*. If you can't move it, *paint it*. And if it moves by itself, *salute it*. Have you got that?' Even the most doubtful of us assured him that we had. He then lowered his voice, a device I soon learnt meant that he was going to say something funny. 'Now I am going to march you down to the cookhouse to save you walking.' So that was army humour. 'Left turn!' he screamed in such a frightening tone that the majority of us turned right. 'Troublemakers are we, then?' he roared. 'I knew you bloody lot would be trouble the moment I set eyes on you. Just for that we're going to double to the cookhouse. Left turn. Double!' And we picked up our suitcases and ran all the way. For the next eight weeks I don't remember walking anywhere. And the only time I saw a soldier on a bicycle free wheeling, a sergeant appeared from nowhere almost instantly and screamed: 'Pedal!'

Twenty-eight of us lived in one large room. I had never slept in a room with anyone other than Stanley and I was overwhelmed by the smell of this bunch of strangers. I had had athlete's foot at one time, but I'd cured it. As we all took our shoes off at the same time the first night I learnt that fifty per cent of my colleagues had obviously failed in this. The first waft of stale Brie cheese made me gag for a moment and I resolved only to go into the showers with sneakers on late at night when nobody could see me. Regular showers had not been a priority with some of the guys either, and I learnt to get used to the mixture of athlete's foot and unwashed armpits. Not unnaturally I developed a deep loathing of the male body, either clothed or naked and I vowed that once I was out of the army I would never bathe with anybody else or anywhere where strangers walked barefoot, sweated profusely or sat down with no clothes on.

Even sleeping I was never free from the smell of my comrades. Farts of varying volume and intensity would explode continuously throughout the night like a smelly artillery barrage in an undeclared war. At least there was no shrapnel, although the intensity of some of the efforts made you duck under the sheets in case there were. Apart from this there was snoring, sleep-walking and nightmares that would erupt with a sudden scream in the middle of our dreams and had us all out of bed instantly with our hair standing on end. Add to this the night-long sobbings of the more sensitive lad and the occasional suicide and you have a good idea of night life in the army.

If the nights were bad, the days were worse. We never stopped running from dawn till dusk and we were made to clean anything that we actually touched until it shone. We were given bits of equipment smothered with lumps of brass which had not been cleaned since the Second World War and were told to make them shine, to quote my sergeant 'Like a new tanner up a chimney sweep's arse.' We were given boots known as 'Ammunition boots' which were heavy, ugly and as rigid as iron. When we put them on we could not actually bend the sole as we walked, so we sounded like a conveyer belt of clumping Frankensteins. They would have been good weapons for kicking with if our legs had been strong enough to lift them off the floor.

The most incredible piece of bullshit that we ever had to do was on the occasion of a visit to the Regiment by Princess Margaret. I was personally detailed to both these tasks so I know that they are true. We had a pile of coal which was very ugly and was deemed likely to offend the view of Her Royal Highness and as it was too large to move in time we were told to whitewash it. This we did under the eagle eye of a sergeant who made sure that there was not a single piece of black coal showing. It was autumn so we had to sweep up all the leaves that had started to fall from the trees which was reasonable enough I thought, until on the morning of the actual parade, I was designated to climb all the trees and shake the branches so that no loose leaf would fall during Her Highness's presence. The army thinks of everything. I often wonder if Princess Margaret thinks that coal is white and the winter comes earlier in Surrey than it does in London.

Sartorially the army was a definite loser. It started with a haircut that was based on the principle that the hair under the beret was yours and the rest was the army's. So with berets on we all looked bald, while underneath was the shattered remnants of our civilian hair cuts. Every piece of clothing they gave us was thick and prickly to the skin. This we resolved by shaving it, inside for comfort and outside to make the battle dress look smarter. There were no sheets on the bed, so I even shaved my blankets. Our berets were black and also needed shaving, and were so badly made that we usually wound up with about a foot of spare cloth hanging down one side of our head, over our ear and dangling down almost to our chin. We got over this by shrinking them until we had a presentable hat that just covered one ear. All these fascinating little jobs kept us occupied and I soon settled down to hating the army and keeping a list of the number of days to go until I was demobbed. The first entry was 716 days.

Our basic training consisted of running miles in the pouring rain, assaulting assault courses that had assaulted us right back, and learning to shoot 303 Lee Enfield rifles which had been obsolete before the end of World War Two. We also learned to fire a machine gun called a Sten gun, which always either jammed after firing the first three of its twenty-eight rounds or kept going for the full blast even when the trigger was released. This last little idiosyncrasy had given us all our first taste of being under fire with live ammunition. We had been at the firing range when one of the lads' Stens had run away. He turned away from the targets with the gun still spraying to ask the sergeant how to stop it. The speed and urgency of our reactions as his bullets started to spray amongst us did not go unnoticed by our sergeant, who commented later that if we had moved that fast during training we would now be the top platoon instead of the bottom one.

My platoon was posted to Germany in a small town called Iserlöhn near Dortmund. This town had two main claims to fame. Chain mail had been invented here in the Middle Ages, and Field Marshal Rommel was buried there. This meant that reunions of ex-members of the Afrika Korps were held in the town. These meetings resulted in so many fist fights between us and them that we were banned from going into town when they came. I thought this was very strange behaviour for a conquering army – even though I had done none of the conquering personally. Why didn't they ban the meetings rather than us, I wanted to know.

The one thing that you must never do in the army is draw attention to yourself and I had always practised this scrupulously. I did not want promotion, and I certainly did not want a medal, which might mean taking risks with my life which I was not prepared to do for four shillings a day. I just did enough to blend in and not be noticed. I always stood in the back ranks on parade and I never ever made eye contact with anybody with a higher rank than me. I had been in the barracks in Germany for about two weeks, when one morning as we lined up in platoon formation for our daily inspection I made eye contact with our platoon sergeant. A little evil gleam came into his eyes. 'You,' he said, pointing at me. 'Me?' I replied innocently, having looked back over my shoulder to see if there was someone behind me. 'Yes, you. Come into the front row.' I moved forward to right in front of him. 'What's your name?' he enquired suspiciously. 'Private Micklewhite, sergeant,' I replied, my eyes wide open as a gesture of truth and innocence which did not fool him for one minute. 'How long have you been in this platoon?' he asked 'Two weeks,' I replied. 'Two weeks?' his voice was starting to choke him. 'You've been in this platoon for two fucking weeks and I haven't noticed you?' He was now yelling. 'What have you been doing back there?' he demanded as though some evil plot was afoot. 'Nothing, sergeant,' I said truthfully. He lowered his voice and put his face very close to mine and said, 'From now on I want you in the front row doing fucking nothing, is that understood?' 'Yes, sergeant,' I replied, my days of anonymity over and my troubles just beginning. From then on I learned to peel potatoes, scrub out dirty pots and pans, do guard duty while everyone else went into town and once, in a spectacularly imaginative form of punishment, I was given a box of old-fashioned razor blades and made to scrape the floorboards of the guard room clean. I was on guard on both Christmas days that I spent there and all in all I was a foul-up as a soldier.

Although my time in Germany was boring beyond belief, I had the good fortune to have entered the army with a bunch of guys who were just as much misfits as I was. We were all together in the same section of our platoon and Harry Wain, Lenny Ware, Frank Lawrence and Jack Taylor kept me sane for two years. We all came from South London and our attitude towards the army was the same: survive and get out. I imagine that in the upper echelons of our regiment there must have been meetings to find ways of palming us off onto another outfit and their opportunity came as a result of an army directive asking for suitable men to be sent to the Korean war to die. Our five names, I am sure, were the first on the list that the regiment put forward. We were given one chance to get out: we were all two-year national servicemen and we were told that if we would sign on for another year's service, we would not be sent to Korea. A quick meeting was held by the five of us and in no time at all we decided that we would rather die than spend another year in the army, so we refused to sign on and were hastily dispatched to London to join the Royal Fusiliers.

The Royal Fusiliers was the only regiment that was allowed to march through the City of London with banners unfurled and bayonets fixed. This we did with great pride and enthusiasm and were immediately moved to Warley Barracks in Essex, which had been condemned as unfit for human habitation in 1916. Here we were asked to make out another will. I had made one when I first joined the army and this had been done as a great joke, as I had nothing to leave and there wasn't much chance of dying in Surrey. This second will was a much more serious affair. I still had nothing to leave, but from what we had read in the papers, there was every chance of this will being put to good use.

The army in its great wisdom then took our regiment, which consisted of men who for the most part had been born and bred within the sight of the London docks, to Liverpool docks about two hundred miles away, to board our troopship. It was called *The Empire Halladale*, and, according to the crew, had been sunk twice in the war and salvaged both times. I had grown up in the slums, but I had never heard of a ship that had a slum area. The officers lived quite well, but deep down in the bowels of the ship was an area that outslummed the Elephant. Once we got into warmer seas I slept on deck the rest of the way.

Our first parade on the ship was a surprise even by army standards: we were paraded to sunbathe – to get our skins toughened to the sun in the Far East, we were told. I'd never had a parade in the army where you were ordered to lie down and do nothing but, as usual, there was a sting in the tail. If we got burned, we were informed, it would be taken as an offence and we would be put in the nick for malingering. So there we all were, rows of lily-white bodies laid out on the deck as the hot sun seared many of us to a crisp. I knew that my skin would not take a lot of sun so I started off with a very short period of exposure. I was the first one to leave the deck on the first day and the sergeant stopped me and asked why I had finished so soon. 'I burn very easily and I don't want to get burned and be charged with an offence,' I said. 'All right, son,' he said very kindly, 'but if you're not brown by the time we get to Korea, that's a fucking offence as well.' I knew that I could never win, but I did eventually manage to go a deep enough red to pass as brown.

Our first stop in the long, hot and stinking six-week journey was Colombo in Ceylon. We only had a day ashore, but it was great to be off the ship and, in my case, for the first time in my life to set foot on foreign soil. We started off very gently looking at the sights and visiting all the tourist places, but it was very hot and we all got thirsty and we found a place where we could get a beer. One thing led to another, we all got pissed and eventually we met some French soldiers. Very soon there was a fully-fledged punch-up going on with bodies and military police everywhere. Drunk as I was, I remained on the periphery of the fracas. These French soldiers did not fit the stereotypical Frenchmen I knew from the movies – Gérard Philippe reciting poetry to Anouk Aimée, or Fernadel being funny – none of these soldiers looked the least bit poetic or funny. In fact our lads suffered a humiliating defeat that day as it turned out the soldiers were from the French Foreign Legion and most of them looked as though they couldn't speak any known language at all, let alone French. They were on their way home from Dien Bien Phu in Vietnam, and they had suffered a terrible defeat and were not ready to be fucked about by anybody, particularly the Royal Fusiliers.

As our journey continued, so did our normal routine: clean up sick, shine brasses and sunbathe. I was now a fiery red and burning quite a bit, but I didn't want to get charged so I suffered in silence. I did manage to steal some lard from the kitchen but this only made me smell as though something even the army wouldn't serve was frying. After a couple of weeks we reached Hong Kong. We were ready for any battles that might take place this time, but our reputation had preceded us and the dock was lined with military police as we came ashore.

On we went out into the South China Sea on our last leg of the journey. After a couple of days we hit the tail end of a typhoon and most of the lads were sea sick this time. About twenty of us out of seven hundred were spared – until we were given the job of going round the ship and cleaning up the vomit. I tried hard to keep my mind off what I was doing as I shovelled the contents of my comrades' stomachs into a bucket, but I was surprised to see tomato skins floating freely all over the deck, despite the fact we hadn't had tomatoes for four weeks. Trying to keep the contents of my own stomach down, I eventually rushed to the side and threw up over the rail without thinking of the storm, and was nearly swept overboard by one of the giant waves that were battering our ship. I sat down on my bunk, soaking wet in a sea of stinking slime, when suddenly I remembered something, and I started to laugh. It was my birthday today; I was nineteen. Happy birthday, Fusilier Micklewhite, I said to myself and sat there wondering if I would ever see another one.

A few days later we arrived at Kure, a port in South Japan. Most of the people there wore traditional dress and it was like stepping back four hundred years. Even most of the prostitutes were in traditional clothing, although knickers seemed to be optional. Wherever we went, they would follow us saying 'I be your wy po.' I didn't understand this until an Australian soldier that I was drinking with explained to me that they were offering to be my wife. 'Do they want to get married to us?' I asked, rather innocently. 'No,' he laughed. 'This is how it works. Gonorrhoea is like a fucking plague here so if you want a girl you wait outside the pox clinic and when they come out they have a card that says that they are clean. You grab one while the fucking ink's still wet and you keep her for you alone for all the time you are here. That's the only way that you can be sure of not catching the pox here, unless you've got it already.' Apart from my already vowed contempt for commercial sex, I was petrified of catching anything since I'd seen the VD film they had shown us on the ship. I've seen some horror films in my time but that one scared the life out of me. There was a terrifying rumour going around, about a disease called Black Syphilis which, the story went, was incurable and you went insane and were locked away until you died and the army informed your parents that you had been killed in action. If I was going to die here it would be with a bullet, I decided. There was one joke that was repeated over and over. Whenever we saw someone limping, one of the guys would say: 'See that, it's syphilis.' Someone else would ask: 'Why is he limping because of syphilis?' and the answer was that his cock had dropped off and landed in his boot. The romance of the orient was not going to be for me.

After a couple of weeks we were deemed fit enough to die and we boarded another ship for the short journey to Korea. As we approached the shore we became aware of it long before we could see it. A faint but very unpleasant smell gradually started to permeate the air in our quarters down in the bowels of the ship. Suspicious glances were aimed at the more celebrated flatulents in our group, but as the smell became more penetrating and we scrambled up to deck gasping for fresh air, we found that it was even worse up there. 'You've smelt it, have you?' asked an amused sailor, as though anybody could have missed it. 'What is it?' I asked. 'Korea,' he replied. 'They use human shit for manure on the land.' Our port of disembarkation, Pusan, was immediately christened Phew san by the more humorous amongst us.

As bad as the smell was it did not prepare us for the actual

71

state of the place as our ship was dragged alongside the dock. The buildings mostly consisted of little huts made out of every available piece of scrap and waste material that the inhabitants could get their hands on. It gave the impression that someone had tried to build a city on a dung heap and failed miserably. The people here, just as they were in Japan, were dressed in traditional clothing and there were fires burning, everywhere. There was no wind and a pall of smoke hung over the whole place, giving it the appearance of some kind of medieval nightmare. I had to serve a year in this place and even without a war, it occurs to me that it was an accomplishment to survive that long: you could almost see disease in the air. I was beginning to become paranoid. All my life I had assured myself that although things were rough, at least they couldn't get worse. I had been wrong time and time again, but there was one consolation here at least, I was sure: I could not sink any lower than dying in this terrible place. It cheered me up in a strange way. From now on if I survived I definitely had nowhere to go but up.

With my usual run of fantastic luck, I was chosen to go ashore the first evening as one of the night guards on the train that was waiting on the dock to take us to the front line the next day. As our little guard squad marched towards the train along the brightly lit dock, I could see the piles of rubbish and filth everywhere and, sitting on top, these miserable little constructions that some poor bastard called home. I managed to get the first guard and the sergeant took me to a siding and told me to guard one of the two massive trains that were standing there. 'Micklewhite,' he said, very seriously, 'this train contains all the Regiment's equipment. Guard it with your life.' I'd never been told to do anything at risk of my life before. If anyone comes near this train they are going to get it, I decided, flicking the bolt of my 303 Lee Enfield and putting a round in the barrel ready for firing. I put the safety catch on but kept my thumb on it ready to flick it off at a moment's notice. So, ready to kill and scared shitless, I set off to explore my area of responsibility.

I crept alongside the train checking the doors with a torch to make sure they had not been tampered with. The moon kept coming out from behind the clouds, bathing the whole scene in white light for a moment and then plunging me back into darkness. I kept whipping round, certain that there was someone behind me, but there was nothing; all was quiet. I stood for a moment, listening for any sign of imminent danger, and suddenly heard a rustling sound and little squeaks coming from the end of the train. I crept towards the sound, my rifle ready to blow anybody off the face of the earth. When I got to the end of the train the noise became louder. I slowly peered round the last carriage, but all I could see, and smell, was another massive pile of rubbish. Just then, the moon suddenly appeared from behind a cloud and I saw that the whole pile of crap seemed to be moving. Rubbing my eyes, I approached quietly and turned on my torch and there, suddenly still as if frozen in the light, were thousands and thousands of rats, their eyes gleaming in the torch-light. The hair on the back of my neck stood up on end; I had never seen anything like it.

I started to creep away, very slowly, as I didn't want to upset them and switched off the torch. As I backed slowly round the train, never taking my eyes off the rats, I bumped into another human being. I yelled and spun around, safety catch off instantly, ready to blast the intruder into oblivion and found myself facing a very large American Marine. 'What the fuck you disturbing those rats for?' he demanded. 'I wasn't disturbing them,' I said. 'I was just looking to see what they were.' 'Well now you know they're fucking rats and don't go near them again,' he said rather unnecessarily. 'We put all the waste food on top of the heap or those motherfuckers will be running all over the yard.' 'Why don't you poison them?' I asked. 'How long you been in this country, son?' he laughed scornfully. 'When the Pied Piper of Fucking Hamelin got rid of the rats for those people he brought them here. This is the most fucked-up place I've ever been to,' he continued. 'There are more rats than there are flies and there are more mosquitoes than both of them put together. You'll see.' I smiled at this exaggeration, but later I was to find out how right he was. Those three creatures made our lives a misery for the next year. Them and a couple of million very pissed-off Chinese.

'You want a coke?' my new friend asked suddenly. 'A Coca Cola?' I asked in disbelief. I hadn't had a coke for weeks. 'You've got a coke?' 'Got a coke?' he said as we approached the American train that he was guarding. 'We're up to our arse in cokes,' he replied, sliding open the doors on his train to reveal crates of coke and nothing else. 'The whole fucking train is coke! You a Limey?' he went on. 'Yes,' I replied. 'Good,' he said. 'These cokes are warm.' He ripped the top off a can and offered it to me. 'You guys drink warm beer and live in cold houses, they tell me.' 'Yes,' I said. 'I suppose we do.'

We sat for a while and savoured our cokes. 'Is the weather bad here?' I asked tentatively. 'Bad?' the Marine snorted. 'It's the fucking worst anywhere. Hot as hell in the summer, below zero in the goddam winter and in the windy season you breathe human shit dust from the dried up manure on the fields. Even the rats would get out if they could swim that far.' I sat there, coke in hand, wondering whether it might be better to take my rifle and shoot my own toe off. I'd go to jail for a while and walk with a limp for the rest of my life, but at least I'd get out of this place now.

'Have you been with any of these whores around here?' my companion said, changing tack. 'No,' I replied truthfully. 'Good. There's a 100 per cent clap rate in this country right now.' He paused. 'Well, you infantry won't be seeing any broads in the front line where you're going, so you'll be safe.' I smiled at this novel view of a civilian life that was so dangerous that the front line could be described as safe and took some comfort from this small piece of optimism. 'The only broads you are likely to see up there are fucking nurses when you get your arse shot off,' he suddenly volunteered, and stood up to go. 'Good luck, kid,' he said. 'Remember what the fellow said: You are not here to die for your country, you are here to make the other poor bastard die for his.' I watched him walk away for a moment and as I turned to go he shouted: 'Welcome to Korea.'

6

'You never hear the one that gets you'

The next day we started the long journey north from Pusan to the front line which was now on a map reference known as the thirty-eighth parallel, which divided North and South Korea. The trip could not have been more than a hundred miles but the lines were so clogged with supplies moving to the front that it took two long uncomfortable days. We eventually disembarked at a place with the unlikely name of Yong Dungpo and from here under the cover of darkness we were taken into our position on the front line to take over from a battalion of US Marines. As this was our first time in the line, or so we were told, we had not been given a particularly dangerous spot. For this information we were all truly thankful.

Our position was on a hill about three hundred feet high, laced with communication trenches. Loaded down with our kit we started the long awkward haul up to the top, slipping and stumbling in the dark. There were muffled curses and whispers as we toiled upwards although we had been told to keep absolute silence, in case the Chinese heard us and sent over a mortar barrage. If this was supposed to be a safe place and the Chinese could hear us talking, I wondered how close did they have to be for it to be a dangerous one?

We eventually arrived at the top, sweating and cursing quietly, in order not to wake up the Chinese, and Harry Wain and I set about making ourselves comfortable. This was a relative term; the accommodation consisted of a hole dug in the side of a hill with a roof reinforced with wooden beams, two camp beds with one blanket on each and everything illuminated by a single candle. These bunkers were situated on the back of the hill and were connected by communication trenches to the weapons pits which were on the opposite side of the hill facing the enemy. The war at this stage was static and consisted of lines of reinforced trench positions like the First World War. The support artillery were a mile or so behind us and the enemy was in front.

We had hardly put our kit down before Harry and I were designated the first guards of the night from our section. Our sergeant guided us quietly along the trenches and around the hill to the front and pointed to a dugout from which two marines quickly scrambled, wished us a quiet good luck and disappeared, smiling into the darkness. Before he left, just to make sure that we settled in comfortably, our sergeant informed us that we must be very alert, because the Chinese were trying to find out which unit had taken over this position and had sent out snatch squads to grab someone last night. Harry and I looked at each other and then into the inky black night to see where we were. We stood there for a long while, absolutely motionless, our rifles cocked, safety catches off ready to blast away at anything that moved. As we stood there the enormity of our situation began to dawn on me for the first time. Harry and I were the first line in the defence of Western civilization from the dark bastions of advancing Communism.

After a time, some of the skills that we had thought so ridiculous in our training began to come back to me. I remembered that to get your eyes accustomed to the dark, the best thing to do was to shut them for a minute. I discussed this with Harry and we decided to take turns at this as we were too scared to stand there for a whole minute with both of us with our eyes closed. To my surprise the theory worked, and when I opened my eyes I could make out several shrubs on the hillside below. Harry shut his eyes and repeated the operation while I stared out into the night. Suddenly, my heart froze. One of the bushes was creeping towards us. We had been told that the Chinese were very patient people – something that I already knew from my experience with the Chinese waiters in Hong Kong – and that one of their tricks was to disguise themselves with bits of shrubbery and spend a whole night slowly crawling into a position of attack. I panicked, and nudged Harry. 'Can you see that bush?' I whispered. 'Is it moving towards us?' I demanded. 'Do what they told us,' Harry said. 'Don't stare, look at it sideways.' They had told us in training that if you stared at something long enough it would seem to start moving towards you and the trick was to look at it sideways. So, keeping our rifles at the ready, we stood sideways glancing at the bush, in a rather sardonic pose, not unlike Clark Gable delivering the 'Frankly, my dear, I don't give a damn' line in *Gone with the Wind*. The bush seemed to stop crawling towards us, but as we weren't too sure with the Chinese, we decided to do another bit of training and listen. This time the trick was to shut your eyes and expel your breath so as not to hear your own blood beating through your ears. Harry kept his eyes open and I held my breath, which I did for so long that I eventually collapsed in a dead faint from lack of oxygen. By the time I had recovered we had both decided that the bush was stationary.

Suddenly a series of dull thuds broke the silence. Was this it? We were both instantly frozen with fear. Should we run back and tell the sergeant that someone was firing mortars? Which one of us should go? Which one of us would stay on our own? We decided we would both stay and fight to the death, because we were too scared to do anything else. Standing there, scouring the hillside for movement over the top of our rifles, I learned an important lesson which was to come in handy later: to keep my finger in the trigger guard. I was so scared when the first shots went off and my hands were shaking so fiercely that it took me quite a while actually to get my trembling finger into the guard to squeeze the trigger. The first explosion in the air was followed by another and then another – and the entire surrounding area was lit almost like daylight as one flare after another burst open in the sky. For the first time, Harry and I could make out exactly where we were: right in front of us was a thick and high barbed wire fence and beyond that was a minefield, clearly marked, and between us and the barbed wire fence the ground was covered with masses of small dried twigs. Our confidence began to seep back: we were not exactly defenceless with that lot in front of us. It would be difficult to creep up on us without breaking one of the layers of twigs. This was an old trick that we had both seen in western films and we decided that the Marines had probably got some American Indians with them who had taught them this trick.

We could see the Chinese positions in the hills opposite, about a mile away across a valley covered in rice paddy fields. This sense of distance brought an even greater surge of confidence; maybe things weren't going to be so dangerous after all. Just then, a fire fight started over to our left and we could see hordes of Chinese charging up the hill to be mown down, seemingly oblivious to the danger. The first time a soldier sees the enemy in person is a chilling moment. The first thing that struck me was that there seemed to be a lot more of them than us. The second thing that struck me was that, unlike us in general and Harry and me in particular, they did not seem to be afraid of dying for their cause which was a sobering thought and a frightening prospect for the future. Finally, after what seemed like masses of casualties, they just gave up and retreated.

The fight finished as suddenly as it had begun, flares went out and we were left in complete darkness again. I let Harry have a sleep in the bottom of the trench and stood on guard alone. I'd seen our defences in front of me and I wasn't so scared now. If I had known how the Chinese dealt with this type of barricade I might not have been so relaxed, but ignorance is bliss so I was happy, relatively speaking. As I peered into the gloom another comforting thought occurred to me: the Chinese couldn't see as well as we did. I based this on the fact that every Oriental that I had ever seen in the movies wore very thick-lensed glasses. But standing alone with my thoughts, I began to wonder exactly what I was doing defending capitalism in a country I had never heard of against the red menace for four shillings per day. The people who had the real capital were not here and so far the system that I was defending for them had treated me like shit. I decided there and then that my father's advice about the poker game had been right: if after five hands of cards, you had not figured out who the mug was, it was probably you. I vowed at that moment that if I survived I would never be taken for a mug again – and, by and large, I haven't.

The bunker that I shared with Harry, apart from being cold – even in the summer – damp and dirty, was also infested with rats. These rats were absolutely fearless, but although we started off by killing as many as we could they just kept on coming. We would wake up in the middle of the night and feel them running across our bodies without a care in the world. After a while we got used to them and just used to lash out at them with a bayonet in the middle of the night then turn over and go back to sleep.

Our rats were very clever. We were issued with combat ration packs which included packets of dried milk, sugar and coffee – rather like the airlines do today, except these were easier to open. And we also had issue packets of cigarettes. After we had been in the bunker a little while, I noticed that some of these packets would keep going missing. I tackled Harry about this but far from nicking my rations he said that some of his packets were missing as well. It was only ever the milk, sugar and cigarettes that were missing; whoever was stealing it always left the coffee. We couldn't figure it out for ages, until one day when the rat population had become so numerous we decided that we had to tear the bunker apart and destroy the nests. We took all the roof beams off and started to kill the scurrying rats by the dozens. When we got to the nests which were loaded with young rats in all stages of development, we solved the mystery of the ration thieves. The rats had taken the milk and sugar to feed the young ones and had made their nests out of the tobacco from the cigarettes, but they hadn't stolen one packet of coffee. I guess they knew about caffeine before we did, but it didn't stop them staying awake all night.

Daytime guard duties were not so frightening, but the Chinese did have snipers so it was still hard to relax. Old soldiers' stories took on a new meaning as well. I remember once throwing myself to the ground when I heard the crack of a rifle from the other side, and my sergeant just laughed at me. 'There's no need to duck if you've heard the shot,' he said. 'You never hear the one that gets you.' It was a terrifying thought: you duck at every shot and bang but you die in silence. The first bloke to get wounded in our unit got hit by mortar shrapnel – not badly – and I went rushing up to him to ask if he'd heard it coming. 'No, I was just standing there,' he said in surprise. Something else to worry about: silence was more dangerous than noise. None of us would ever take the third light of a cigarette from the same match. This was another old soldiers' tale: the enemy sniper would notice the first light, aim as you lit the second cigarette and fire at the third cigarette. I always carried two boxes of matches.

Two of my major character faults showed up while I was in the line for the first time, apart from my inbuilt cowardice which must be obvious by now. The first is never knowing when I am well off. There was one bunker in our position that was the envy of all, especially me. It had no rats at all, not one, and I went to great lengths to get this abode. I offered the two guys in it money, cigarettes and the choice part of my combat rations. I was prepared to exchange all my frankfurters and tinned peaches for their mince meat, which was eaten on a dry biscuit and called 'Shit on Shingle' and all their tinned prunes. No deal. In the end I arranged with the sergeant that if anything happened to them – like going on leave, I added hastily, not to appear too cold-blooded – Harry and I could move in. One day as we were all sitting around earnestly cleaning rifle bolts, there was a terrible scream from my favourite bunker. We all rushed into the bunker to see what was going on – and immediately rushed out again. We knew now why there were no rats in there. The terrified occupant was lying on his bed with a snake at least six feet long dangling from the beam above him, its forked-tongued head hovering a couple of inches from his face. 'Shoot the fucker,' he yelled. Someone grabbed a rifle and we all stood and watched as he took aim at the swaying head. 'Don't fucking hit me!' the victim cried. We all smiled and waited, prolonging his agony (he had been quite a pain in the arse about the comfort of his bunker) and then the rifleman took aim and tried to follow the head movement. 'Shoot,' the victim shouted. 'But I might blow your brains out.' 'I don't give a fuck, shoot!' he screamed. The bang in the confines of the bunker was deafening, and as the dead snake fell on him he freaked out and came screaming out of the bunker. We were all laughing in hysterics and the rest of the platoon came running out fully armed ready to repel our first daylight attack. I went back to my bunker and greeted a couple of rats as they scurried away. If ever they disappear, I thought, I'm sleeping outside.

My other fault is that I never know when to keep my mouth shut, which is particularly dangerous in the army. Since my experiences in Germany I had managed to curb this failing, but one day I made the cardinal mistake and asked a leading question of my sergeant. 'Why,' I demanded to know, 'are we expected to fight a Chinese army which numbers in the millions with a bolt-loading, single-shot rifle. The Americans have at least a semi-automatic carbine for the same job.' Sarge thought for a moment and with a wicked gleam in his eye said: 'You've got a point there, Micklewhite. I'll see what I can do.' The next day I was made the platoon machine-gunner and given a great big .30-calibre US Browning machine gun and a quick lesson in how to load it, fire it, dismantle and assemble it – and worst of all, to clean it. This one was brand new and was covered in a thick layer of packing grease to keep it from going rusty.

I had quickly realised that if the army gave you a piece of equipment you would have to clean it to their maniacal standards or carry it for long distances if it did not carry you. When they asked me if I wanted to go into transport, I refused, trembling at the thought of cleaning an entire truck. The tanks corps was another option on offer, but that was even worse; tanks were enormous and got very dirty. I finally settled on being a rifleman because a rifle was the smallest piece of equipment that needed cleaning.

After several uneventful weeks in the line we were due for a rest. The camp that we went to was just outside the capital city of Seoul and we were allowed to go into town for a bit of R. and R. (rest and recreation). They should have called it B., B. and B.: Booze, Broads and Brawls. Seoul at that time looked as if they'd reconstructed an old western mining town in America out of bamboo wood: it consisted solely of bars, whore houses and military police, known as meat heads. It was like the height of the gold rush in America; very little law and plenty of everything else. Apart from the American army there was also a unit called the Commonwealth division consisting of troops from Australia, New Zealand, Canada, India, South Africa, Great Britain of course and a couple of regiments from Turkey and Greece. All these units had joined as allies to fight the common enemy, the Communists. From what I saw on my first night in Seoul, the bonds that tied these units together were very slender indeed. Each unit seemed to have picked its own particular enemy and the fights were literally murderous. Although I had thought that the front line was dangerous, an evening in Seoul was of far greater risk to life and limb: our division must have killed and injured more of its own people than the enemy ever did. For some unknown reason the New Zealand Maoris hated the French Canadian regiment, the Vingt-Deux. The Maoris were the biggest men I have seen and the French Canadians were mostly ex-lumberjacks, so once a fight got started between these two groups, nobody tried to break it up including the police. The Turks and the Greeks only had eyes for each other – black eyes, most of the time. The American Marines used to fight the ordinary American soldiers, whom they called dog faces and the Australians would fight anybody who was as drunk as they were. So an evening in Seoul was not without its perils for us Poms, as the Aussies called us. I once asked an Australian in a bar why they called us that and he said it was short for Pomeranian dogs, all yap and no size. We wouldn't have stood a chance in a fight with these guys, so we only went into town in groups of ten or more. If we went out in small groups we usually wore Red Cross armbands to make ourselves look like medical staff and as there were so many injured and sick scattered over the streets it looked quite convincing.

Apart from the brawls, Seoul was smothered in hookers. I remembered what the American soldier had said when I was on guard duty in Pusan: one hundred per cent gonorrhoea. One evening I was walking along with a group of the lads and we were stopped as usual by a group of whores, asking if we wanted a good time. One of the lads who was very drunk came up and grabbed her and she persuaded him to go with her against my dire warnings. Four days later I was proved right. I was having a pee in the latrine when the same soldier came rushing in after me. 'What does the clap look like?' he demanded in a terror-stricken voice, dragging out a very sad tearful penis for my inspection. 'Just like that,' I said, rather cruelly pointing at his listless organ. He burst into tears. 'How long does it take to cure it?' he demanded. 'About a week,' I replied. 'Thank God for that,' he babbled. 'I'm going home in a fortnight.' I knew why he was so relieved. Even if it was time for you to be demobilised from the army, they would not let you out while you still had VD. The phrase used for this amongst the more uncouth of us was 'Blobby Knob Stops Demob'. I could stand even chastity more than the prospect of another day in this place.

Something else that we did while we were out of the line was one of the saddest things I have ever done in my life. The Americans had a special train rigged up for children only. It was like a cross between a hospital and a children's nursery and was called The Mickey Mouse Express. It was covered on the outside with big cut-outs of cartoon characters. A very incongruous sight as it chugged through this stark, battle-scarred country, its job was to pick up orphaned Korean children and take care of them, and every unit when it came to their area would send out troops to find these kids. We did this and it was heartbreaking. You would find children as young as two wandering alone and unwanted, and babies still alive sometimes hidden under bushes. We would pick them up and deliver them into the loving care of the American nurses. Although it was very distressing it was also certainly the most worthwhile job that we did in that country.

My position in our platoon was that of sage and professor. I had left school at the age of sixteen and a half, but I was better educated than the rest of my comrades who had all left school at the age of fourteen. I used this position to end rows and answer all questions. I was known as Mick and my final pronouncement on any subject or argument usually settled it once and for all. I also wrote letters home for those who could not write and read the answers for those that could not read. This elevated state as the fount of all wisdom, plus my virginal status with the local ladies of the day and night, brought a new and embarrassing role for me as an expert on gonorrhoea. We had now been out of the line for a few weeks and the number of diseased Romeos was beginning to increase. Word of my correct diagnosis of my first case spread almost as quickly as the disease, and the latrine was turned into my surgery. Every time that I went to the toilet, some terror-stricken soldier would come in behind me and wave his penis at me begging for a diagnosis. If they were not weeping I would tell them that it was all right if it was at least six days since their last attempt at romance, but even this was not enough for some of them and they became so paranoid that they would think that the end of it was changing colour. I would tell them purple was supposed to be the colour of the end of it but they in their fearful imaginings could see other hues that no one else could spot. It eventually got so bad that I had to produce my own organ as a colour match for what a perfectly clear penis should look like. If a military policeman had ever interrupted my impromptu surgery, three guys standing there matching the colour of their penises it would have been quite difficult to explain.

The damage that this disease did was far more mental than physical. When I look back now at our innocence I wonder how we would have felt with AIDS as a lottery. Some of those guys committed suicide because they had the clap. I imagine that today if somebody goes to a doctor for a sexually transmitted disease and it is diagnosed as gonorrhoea, they would be so relieved that they would probably give a party to celebrate.

The biggest action that I saw in the war was on our next tour of duty, in a valley in which the enemy was only a quarter of a mile away from my section. Like everything else that is bad in life, it came out of the blue. I was on night sentry duty again with Harry in the weapon pit at the front of the hill. Everything was quiet. I was standing there in my usual trance-like state, dreaming of becoming an actor in the glamorous and heroic war films which bore so little resemblance to the real thing.

Suddenly a trumpet sounded, then another and another until the night was filled with an insane volley of tuneless blasts. 'What the fuck is that?' I yelled at Harry. 'Trumpets,' he shouted. 'I know they're trumpets, Harry,' I replied, 'but who's fucking blowing them?' At that moment, from behind our positions, hundreds of searchlights were switched on and aimed at the clouds that covered the valley below us. The whole scene was lit up like the brightest moonlight you have ever seen and there in front of us were thousands of Chinese troops led by hundreds of maniac trumpeters, advancing across the valley. The artillery opened up immediately and began to scatter holes in this wall of human flesh and then machine guns and rifles opened up from the trenches all along our section of the front. My platoon came tearing out of their bunkers, scrambling into their weapon pits, and then Harry and I joined in with the machine gun spraying the valley floor. There were so many Chinese down there we had to hit someone, but we couldn't actually see if we were getting results. It looked like a 'Son et Lumière' in hell.

We soon realised, with great relief, that the main thrust was not at our position, but at the Americans on our left. The Chinese seemed to have no regard for death whatsoever, and just kept charging through the most withering fire. Eventually, however, they retreated back across the valley as the artillery chased them right back to their positions. We both just stood there flushed with the combination of fear and accomplishment that all soldiers feel when they survive a battle, but what we could see through the binoculars did shake our confidence in the minefields and barbed wire that were our last line of defence. The first sequence of advancing troops had obviously been suicide squads, their task to blow up the mines by running through them. Anyone who made it without striking a mine had his next chance at glory by throwing his body onto the barbed wire. Eventually enough dead bodies would pile up to form a bridge over the wire to leave a free path for their young crack troops. The dead bodies had to stay on the wire until the next night because the

85

Chinese would open fire on anybody going to collect them in daylight, and by the end of the day there was quite a smell in the valley. When I saw the bodies that they picked off the wire I wondered again about the benefits of Communism: the suicide squads were all old men and boys, some as young as twelve years old.

The most frightening duty in Korea was the night-time observation patrol into No Man's Land. The thought of leaving our relatively safe trenches and going down the hill at night to see if the enemy were about, not only struck terror in my heart, it also struck me as unnecessary. The Chinese could wander about down there all night as far as I was concerned, as long as they didn't come up my hill. But some officer somewhere – who didn't have to do the patrol himself – had decided that we must control the valley at night. First of all we had to blacken all the bits of brass on the equipment that we had been cleaning until it glistened, so that they would not be seen in the dark. Then all these little bits of metal were tied down tightly with black bootlaces so that they wouldn't clink against each other. We then covered our faces with a mixture of mud and mosquito repellent.

Our patrol was made up of a wireless operator whom I didn't know, my own platoon commander Robert Mills (whom I later met in civilian life when we both became actors at the same time) and me as the escort.

We three guys from London were now ready to go down into a rice paddy and outwit the Chinese. Bloody ridiculous, I thought, as we crept as quietly as we could down the side of the hill, using a map to negotiate our way through our own minefield. We managed it, and then on we went into the paddy fields. It was here that the first mosquitoes picked up the delicious aroma of my repellent and immediately started to feed off my face and arms. They must have invited all their friends because our faces almost disappeared in a cloud of these ravenous creatures. We found what was laughingly called an ambush position and waited for what seemed like hours listening for the slightest sound. After a while, we advanced, which we did very slowly and quietly towards the Chinese lines. My heart sank lower and a lump of lead seemed to be forming in the pit of my stomach as we came right up to the base of the Chinese hills. I was sure that no British patrol had ever come this far before, and I didn't know why we were doing it.

Even though it was night, it was still boiling hot and humid and the insects were now really enjoying our bodies. After a while Bobbie Mills whispered, 'I know what we'll do.' 'Go back?' I answered, hopefully. 'No,' he said, with an unusually strong note in his voice. He was only about nineteen himself and very slender, but inside that frail frame I knew there beat a heart that was not only brave enough to risk his life for Queen and country – his father had been a general and had won the Victoria Cross for gallantry – but brave enough to risk ours too. I was right. He thought that he had judged my character perfectly: a coward, but mercenary. 'I'll give you both five pounds each if you'll come up the hill and snatch a Chinese prisoner with me.' I stared at him in disbelief and committed my only act of insubordination with an officer. 'Are you fucking mad?' I screamed in a whisper. He had judged me right but he had underestimated my cowardice and overestimated my interest in money. 'Does that mean you won't come?' he asked in his very upper-crust English voice. 'You're fucking right,' the wireless operator and I both said in unison. 'All right,' he said, rather petulantly, as though his nanny had said he couldn't go out to play. 'All right. We'll go back right now.' As though we were terrible spoilsports.

We started back immediately, not stopping for a rest until we were over halfway home. By this time we were almost exhausted and covered with insect bites. I could only just see through the slits in my eyes where my lids and surrounding face had swollen from the bites and almost completely closed off my field of vision. We sat breathing as quietly as we could as we tried to get our breath for the last stretch home. Just then, all three of us threw ourselves flat on the ground. Garlic was wafting on the air all around us and getting closer and stronger. We had been warned that the Chinese soldiers chewed garlic the way we chew gum and, funny as it may seem, this would probably be the first sign that we had walked into an ambush. They were probably doing their old trick, which was to follow one of our patrols back, see where the path through our minefield was and follow us through it.

We could hear them searching through the long grass, talking softly to each other. The lovely sound of Chinese which had seemed to me like raindrops when the girls had spoken it in Hong Kong, now sounded like razor blades swishing through the dank night air as they grew closer to us. I could see their shapes scuttling around us and cutting us off from our own lines. I was now trembling with fear and felt very sick, but I already had my hand inside the trigger guard. Then a strange thing happened: I gradually began to get angry, really angry. After all my struggles to get anywhere in my so far shitty life, and with all my dreams and ambitions, I was going to die here for no good reason. I decided then that as I was going to die, I would make them pay, and take as many Chinese with me as I possibly could. Suddenly we were a group of different men; we had a purpose and we were in control, which is not a bad way to die. Bobbie Mills decided that we would charge – not towards our own line but back towards the Chinese so that we would take them by surprise. The wireless operator said, 'I want a piss,' to which we all agreed and we knelt together having a communal piss. It was rather like settling our estate. After we finished, we smiled at each other and Bobbie said 'Go!' and we were up and running. There was nobody there. They had not surrounded us; the Chinese were all between us and our own lines. They started to fire in all directions but although they could hear us it was obvious that they had no idea where we were. We just kept running toward their lines and then, in a wide arc, back to our own. We seemed to run forever but the survival instinct drove us tirelessly through the night back to our own camp.

We felt we were heroes. We had met the enemy up close, and we had survived. For my own part, that night has always been important to me, because although I hadn't killed anyone or proved myself to be a hero, I had faced what seemed to me to be certain death and I had not been a coward. And I had learnt something about myself which I would value for the rest of my life: if anyone takes me, they're going to have to pay. In fact, I thought as I walked to my bunker, smiling to myself, not only will they have to pay, but the price will be fucking exorbitant!

My sense of heroism was shaken however when the sergeant saw me and yelled: 'Who are you?' 'Fusilier Micklewhite,' I answered, puzzled. He had known me for six months. I had forgotten about my face. 'Where the fucking hell have you been?' he roared, looking at his watch. 'You're two hours late.' I was about to explain my heroic exploits to him when I thought to hell with it and turned to walk away. 'Do something about that face,' he roared after me. 'It's enough to frighten the fucking life out of anybody.'

Harry nearly dropped dead with fright when he saw me in the half candlelight. 'It's me, Mick,' I said, before he had a heart attack. 'Christ,' he said. 'That repellent doesn't work, then.' 'Well, the mosquitoes like it,' I said, as I lay down on my bunk. I tried to smile but it was too painful.

My last trip into the front line coincided with the onset of winter and I nearly froze to death. There seemed to be no end to the ways that the army could think of to get me killed. It became so cold that if you touched anything made of metal you would burn the skin off your fingers. We learned new tricks: at night, when we were on sentry duty, we had to rub each other's faces every fifteen minutes in case frostbite had set in; in the daytime we would just look at each other now and again to see if the skin had changed colour. Some of the men had managed to get hold of the much prized American army parkas which were thought better than ours because they had fur round the hood but even this luxury came with an unexpected danger. With the fur drawn tightly around the face, some soldiers found that the moisture from their breath froze the fur to their cheeks and in some cases when the guys took the parkas off, they tore the skin off their faces and lips with it. The ugly British parka turned out to be the most practical. The best thing about it was the hood which had wire round its edge so you could shape it to cover your entire face, leaving just a tiny slit for your eyes.

Winter, however, meant presents from a grateful British public and government. My token of gratitude and affection from my country consisted of a pair of socks that had been darned twice, a comb with three teeth missing, a half pint bottle of beer and an old paperback book with some pages missing called *My Turn to Make the Tea* by Monica Dickens. I remember standing there for a long while looking at these articles in absolute disgust. Were we supposed to be grateful for this insult? I drank the beer and threw everything else in the direction of the enemy lines and made a vow never to risk my life or anything at all for anybody ever again.

Fusilier Micklewhite was going home a very different man.

Our demobilisation was very simple. We handed in our kit, put on our civilian clothes, now hopelessly out of date, and Harry, Lenny, Frank, Jack and myself walked out of the barracks together. Our regimental band were practising *Colonel Bogie*, the march made famous in the film *The Bridge Over The River Kwai*. We had our own words to it, as soldiers will, and as we crossed the barrack square we started to sing: 'Hitler has only got one ball, Rommel has two but very small, Himmler is very similar, but poor old Goebbels has no balls at all'. The refrain, which is repeated, goes: 'bollocks and the same to you,' which summed up our attitude to the military in general.

As we were singing this the band suddenly changed its tune and struck up our own regimental march which brought about an instant change in our attitude, because this was our march and we found that we did have some pride in what we'd been and what we had done. Without thinking, we all straightened up, formed a line and very smartly marched out of the army forever singing our own words again: 'Here we come, Here we come. Bullshitting bastards every one.' Once out of the gate we stopped, shook hands and each went in his own direction. As I sat on the bus going home to the Elephant, I thought, that's what I am – a bullshitting bastard. Show business is the right life for me.

7

'It's only malaria'

I had absolutely no idea how I was going to start to become an actor. I sat around the prefab, trying to work out my first step on a ladder that did not yet exist. After a while I started getting hints from my father about what I should do. 'Why don't you get up off your arse and go and get a job?' he demanded, until I went and got a job in a butter factory just to make some money. It was 1952, and butter was still on ration after the war. All I had to do was to lift crates of different grades of butter into a vat, where they were mixed into one standard type.

The butter factory was a long way from show business but it was here that fate started to be kind to me. Sometimes when I am asked if I believe in God, people are very surprised when I tell them that I do, but if you had lived my life and seen the luck I've had from extraordinary circumstances you would believe in Him as well.

The first example of this mysterious helping hand came to me right out of the blue. Working with me in the factory was a little old man who one day told me for no reason at all that he had a daughter in show business, a semi-professional singer who made quite a nice living out of it. I told him that I wanted to be an actor one day myself, but I didn't know how to go about starting. 'Why don't you get *The Stage*?' he asked. I didn't even know what *The Stage* was, and couldn't believe my ears when he explained. He told me that I could buy it on Fridays at a bookshop that still exists called Solosy's, on Charing Cross Road.

On Saturday morning I was at Solosy's when they opened and in I went, plucked up courage and asked for it. Making

91

my way to Leicester Square, I sat on a seat in the gardens there and started to read. The only suitable vacancy seemed to be for an assistant stage manager required to play small parts, and the address was a theatre in a small country town called Horsham in Sussex. Applicants were asked for a photo and stamped addressed envelope. There were few photographs of me in existence at all – another piece of fallout from my sort of background, but I soon fixed this by going to one of a group of chain photographers called Jemroe that were all over the country. The photos they produced always had a brown haze over them, as though there had been a light fog in the room. As well as the haze and my attempts to slick my unruly hair down, the photo made my lips look as if I had lipstick on and the rather sickly smile that I had mustered at the photographer's request, made the whole effect rather effeminate. I didn't have enough money for another go, so the only thing to do was send the picture off. Maurice Micklewhite seemed too long for autographs, so I changed my name to Michael Scott. Much easier.

A week later I got a reply asking me to put in an appearance at the theatre and on a Saturday morning when I was not working I set off to meet Mr Alwyn D. Fox, the owner of the company. When I arrived I was ushered into the theatre by a person of indeterminate sex and introduced to the boss. He was a small rather grisly man of about fifty and the minute he spoke I realised that he was a homosexual. Christ, I thought. I had been warned that actors were all 'poofs', and that I would never get on in the acting world unless I did what was called a 'turn'. I didn't know exactly what a 'turn' was, but I certainly had no intention of doing one. Mr Fox looked me over with a certain gleam in his eye, which was disconcerting to say the least because I suddenly realised that he was looking at me the same way that I looked at girls. I was twenty years old, six feet two, with long curly blond hair. I had done a lot of weight training over the years so I was very well built and I still had the residue of the sun tan I had got on the boat coming home. I also had a very butch, tough-looking face and was obviously not gay.

'You don't give the same impression in life that you do in

your photographs, do you?' said Mr Fox with a tinge of disappointment. 'I'm sorry,' I said, as though I had deliberately misled him. 'Nothing to be sorry about,' he said, with a smile. 'You might do. Edgar!' he shouted. From out of nowhere came a man even smaller than Mr Fox and very slender indeed. He reminded me of Léonide Massine, the ballet dancer. Another poof, I thought. I had no chance here. Mr Fox and Edgar both stood staring at me, each with one arm across his body, holding the elbow of the other arm and one hand up by their face with a finger on their pursed lips. I stood there trying to think of who they reminded me of and just as I realised it was my mother, Edgar said: 'Well, he'd be all right for those small butch parts like policemen that *we* have so much difficulty with.' 'Do you think you can do stage management?' Alwyn enquired. I had no idea what this was, but I answered with an immediate and confident 'Yes.' 'All right,' said Alwyn Fox, 'I'll try you out for a couple of weeks. Can you start on Monday?' I was on my way.

Stage management, I quickly learned, was doing everything that nobody else wanted to do. I made tea, shifted scenery, placed props, ran errands for everything from cigarettes for the leading man to Tampax for the leading lady, and on the weekends when the show changed, took back all the furniture that we had borrowed from various stores and begged them to lend us a new lot. These jobs may sound mundane but I was part of a theatre company and I was happy.

My sex life was picking up quite startlingly, too. Most of the actors in the company were gay so I had more than an even chance with the half dozen young ladies who seemed to be around most of the time. Some of them were working for nothing just to get experience, but I must say that from my point of view most of them seemed to have a lot more experience than I had – and that's without any acting at all. They were called trainees and in the case of one particular girl this term vastly underestimated her abilities. I was earning two pounds ten shillings per week, and as my room in a local theatrical boarding house cost exactly two pounds ten shillings per week, this did not leave a lot left over to entertain young ladies. I found that in the theatre women did not mind paying for themselves or even me sometimes, and as everybody in the company of course earned more than I did and even the trainees seemed to be heavily subsidised, I never seemed to be without. Part of the reason was that as the stage manager, I was responsible for the food that was eaten on stage and the cigarettes that were smoked. So at the end of each evening when the show was over I finished up what was left. All the cast used to gather in the pub after the show and I was always given drinks and my rent did include an evening meal so life was not too bad.

When the time came to play my first role as a professional actor, it was indeed as the butch policeman who takes away the villain at the end after he has been unmasked by the upper-crust amateur sleuth. I forget the name of the play, but I do remember my line which is amazing after forty years, because I had a great deal of trouble remembering it at the time. The words 'Come along with me, sir,' may sound simple but I was so nervous that I forgot to do my flies up – yet again! – and got a laugh the moment I walked on. As this was the end of a very intense drama it wasn't quite the effect that the company was aiming at. The unexpected laughter threw me completely and I forgot my line. When one of the actors whispered it to me, his voice was so soft I did not hear what he said and I replied, 'What?' in a normal voice. My first attempt at professional acting was over. I got a great bollocking from Alwyn and I did not appear for another three weeks.

I was cast in my next part out of sheer desperation on the part of the management: the role was that of a seducer of women and a cad. With the best will in the world, Alwyn must have realised that I was the only man in the whole company who looked as if he might do such a thing, which of course was not far from the truth. So, casting caution to the wind, he gave me the part. It was not a leading role but the scene did last about five minutes. I had to bring an innocent girl back to my flat and seduce her by plying her with alcohol.

On I came, looking as suave and as urbane as it was possible for someone to look who had no idea what these two words meant. The suit with which I had been issued when I was demobbed from the army didn't help: it had never fitted me very well at the best of times, but my diet at the theatre had lost me quite a bit of weight and it now sagged quite heavily on my shoulders. This, coupled with a feeling of abject terror at the thought of having at least two hundred lines to remember, meant that I did not cut the figure of the lounge lizard that I had fondly imagined. The actress who was going to have to convince an audience that she was about to be seduced by this terrified oaf was June Wyndham Davies and she was superb, not only on this occasion, but the many other times that she was forced to work with me. She was always patient, gentle and kind – virtues that are not, you may be surprised to know, abundant in the hearts of most leading actresses. She taught me so much in my time with her and I shall be eternally grateful to this long-suffering saint.

The conviction of June's performance was not helped by the fact that she had to get gradually drunk as I plied her with liquor from a bottle which in my nervous state I had forgotten to open. She eventually overcame this problem by grabbing the bottle out of my hand and removing the cork, and then inventing some mad plot twist where she suddenly drank the whole bottle down in one go just in time for her cue to collapse in a seductable state on the bed. When we came off at the finish of the scene she gave me a kiss and congratulated me at having made my real start as an actor. She told me later that all I said to her was: 'That was worse than anything I did in Korea.'

Much of the training continues with me. I still always check my flies before a take in memory of those first embarrassing entrances, and I always bring a pencil to rehearsals to write down the moves after having Alwyn scream at me, 'The first thing that you need to become an actor is a pencil!' He also screamed at me for a mistake during the performance of a play. There was a scene where nobody would speak to me and I had to sit in the corner downstage. One of the elderly ladies in the audience took pity on me because I was on my own and nobody in the cast was speaking to me and she got up out of her seat, reached over the footlights and offered me a sweet. Being always hungry, I took it. Directly the curtain came down, Alwyn was backstage yelling at me again. 'How dare you break the fourth wall?' he shouted. I had no idea what he was talking about. 'It's the invisible fourth wall between you and the audience. If you are in a room you have four walls; in the theatre we have an invisible fourth wall so that the audience can see us. You must never *ever* break it.' I apologized, wondering just how many more pitfalls there were for me to encounter.

By now I considered myself a professional actor and my money went up to three pounds per week. The people of Horsham had not the faintest idea what all this entailed and I remember being stopped in the streets on many occasions and asked what I did in the day-time.

Working in provincial repertory has many unforseen problems. The first time that it rained during one of my performances I found out that the theatre had a tin roof, which is where I got my first opportunity to practise my rather primitive miming skills. The real difficulty was with the audience – and there was little we could do about that. For this type of company in a small country town the patrons consisted mainly of elderly ladies, especially on matinée afternoons when the older ladies brought the really old ladies who could not come out in the evenings because they went to bed early. In fact some of them found it difficult to stay awake in the afternoons, judging by the occasional snore that could be heard ripping through our performances. Being of advanced years this audience had a higher coughing rate than the average and at that time they were beginning to watch television and had got used to the idea of talking through a show.

The most difficult people in the audience were the hard of hearing. There were always three or four of them and they made their presence known on the first line. Just before I'd speak the second one, a voice would pipe up: 'What did he say?' The companion, in an even louder voice because she knew her friend's problem, would repeat your line. The other one would then reply that she thought that was what he said, and by the time all this had gone on, several more lines would have been said on stage that neither of them would have heard. The next complaint you would hear was: 'I don't understand what is going on.' Not surprisingly.

The worst example of this sort of 'audience participation' always seemed to happen during a particularly tense scene in a thriller. Suddenly there would be a scuffle in one of the rows, accompanied by, 'Excuse me' and 'Sorry'. Then you would hear the following exchange: 'Why didn't you go before you came out?' 'I didn't want to go before I came out,' usually followed by a 'Where's my bag?' or a yelp and a stumble and a 'My foot's gone to sleep.' This whole process would take three or four minutes – and then the tension would build up as you waited for them to come back from the toilet. This procedure took longer than the original departure, because their eyes had been in the daylight and now they can't see in the dark theatre. 'Is this the row?' 'No, we were in H.' 'Excuse me.' A loud *Ouch*! is heard as somebody's foot is trodden on, the older one invariably sits on the lap of the person next to her for a moment and then they finally get to their seat and peace is restored. As ten minutes of the play have now passed, the final line you hear is: 'I don't like this play much; you can't follow the story.' Provincial repertory is a great training ground for actors – especially for their egos.

Apart from giving me my first professional job and continuing to employ me, Alwyn also gave me an entirely new perspective on homosexuals. He and Edgar were the first two gay men that I got to know well and they altered my attitude completely. I had heard horror stories about the theatre being full of queers, but at no time did Alwyn or anybody else suggest that I do anything with them, and once I had earned it I was treated with great respect by them. I felt at ease with homosexuals for the first time in my life – a great relief, because the theatre was as full of gays then as it is now. And of course there are the closet gays with the wife and two children so it does add up. (These are the ones who were described by a gay friend of mine as not being gay but willing to help out if the rest of us are busy.) After all this time I am now at a stage where three of my closest friends in the world are homosexuals.

When homosexuality was finally made legal between

97

consenting adults in the 1950s, I saw on the British television news a reporter asking British people returning home at London's Heathrow airport what they thought of this new law. They asked an old British colonel type what he thought of it and what he said sums up my attitude: 'I don't mind them making it legal as long as they don't make it compulsory.'

After about two months went by, I started doing bigger and better roles and doing them with ever-increasing skill, thanks to the encouragement and patience of Alwyn and the rest of the company. There was however one small blemish on my happiness. I had developed a bit of a chill, but despite taking the usual cold remedies, the shivering and shaking actually started to get worse. I hid this from the company, of course, because I was terrified of losing my job and I carried on until we came to *Wuthering Heights*. This, it turned out, was the all-time piece of miscasting. Edgar Grey, Alwyn's little friend, was cast as Heathcliff, the passionate and fiery gipsy, and I was cast as the weak, vacillating Hindley Earnshaw. We almost carried it off until the fight scene, when Heathcliff has to give me a thrashing. Edgar weighed about a hundred pounds wringing wet and was about five feet tall – I was six feet two and weighed a hundred and seventy-five pounds. The fight got a laugh from the start, and by the time he had beaten me to a pulp the audience was in hysterics.

By the end of the week of *Wuthering Heights* I was feeling so ill that when I went on at the Saturday matinée, I collapsed. I remember nothing more until I came round in a bed in the local hospital with a doctor bending over me. As I opened my eyes I heard someone say: 'It's infantile paralysis, I'm afraid.' I knew better for once. It was my old Nemesis, Korea, having one final go at destroying me.

I put my arm out and pulled feebly on the doctor's white coat. She turned and smiled down at me. 'Oh,' she said. 'Welcome back. How do you feel?' I felt as though I was going to pass out again soon. So I said as quickly and loudly as I could: 'Malaria. I've got malaria.' She thought for a moment and said, 'You can't catch malaria in Sussex.' Just before I passed out I managed to say, 'Korea.'

The next time I woke up my father was sitting with me. 'It's all right Maurice,' he said. 'It's only malaria. I've had it several times in India.' I felt reassured by this, tried a smile and passed out again. When I came round I was shaking and freezing cold and I was being lowered into a warm bath. The shaking was followed by sweating until I felt that my body was boiling and this was accompanied by a headache, which felt like somebody was driving red hot nails through my brain. At this moment the nurse came in and put me in a cold bath until my temperature came down again. This routine went on day after day as I went alternately from freezing cold to boiling hot over a period of four hours day and night.

I was starting to get worried. A lot of my family had been in the army overseas and had malaria but I had never seen them having anything like this. I was right to be suspicious. Although the attacks decreased in severity as the pills finally worked and I was ready to leave the hospital, they told me that my malaria was a very rare and severe type and it was incurable. And then came the clincher. The pills that they were giving me would have to be taken permanently and I would only be able to lead a normal life for about twenty years. I would be dead by the time I was forty or fifty. The army was giving me a disability pension of three pounds ten shillings per week (only half the normal pension, I was told, because although restricted by my now weak and permanent physical condition I would nevertheless be able to work at some jobs) and finally the hospital admitted that they had wrongly given me penicillin and I was now allergic to it and would have to carry a No Penicillin tag for ever more.

I thanked the staff for all their efforts on my behalf and went back to the Elephant for a few weeks in an attempt to get my strength back. My mother was a great ally in this. Out came the frying pan as she made an enormous effort to 'fatten me up', but my body seemed to be a very different mechanism now. I had lost over forty pounds in a very short time and I was very weak. I no longer had the strength to do manual labour, and one look in the mirror told me that my ambitions to become a leading man in the theatre were finished. I was so thin that you could see the outline of the bones in my skull, the little clothing I had now hung sadly on my almost skeletal frame and because of the pills my complexion had changed to a very sickly yellow colour. I had never been Robert Taylor or Tyrone Power in the first place, but now I looked more like a round-eyed Dr Fu Manchu with anorexia. Not exactly the stuff of stardom. Although I knew that I could never be a star now and in any case I did not have long to live, I decided to go back and make a living from the theatre for the rest of my life and be happy doing it. I knew for sure now that I could never be happy outside show business.

When I phoned him, Alwyn, God bless him, said: 'Where the hell have you been? We thought that you had forgotten us!' My heart came up in my throat and almost choked me. They wanted me back. I was so glad I was on the phone because tears started to roll down my cheeks. From the depths of my despair this little man had given me new hope and a new start in my life. 'You mean I can come back?' I said, trying desperately to hide the tears in my voice. 'I must warn you,' I said, to be fair, 'I look a lot different now.' 'I know what you look like,' he snapped. 'I saw you in the hospital. Don't worry, we'll do some horror plays.' He was always very sarcastic. 'You start rehearsal Monday morning,' he said and put the phone down.

Before I left the Elephant I managed to settle the one seed of doubt that lay in my father's mind. I was showing my mother some of the photographs that I had from the different productions at Horsham and my father, who was feigning disinterest, was picking up the occasional one to look at. He came across one of the photos that had been taken with my stage make-up. My father looked at this for a long time and then he said: 'Maurice, tell me the truth. Are you a Nancy Boy?' 'I'm not, Dad,' I replied, after a pause, where I caught his eyes and held them. He threw the photo on the table and stood up. 'Let's go round the pub and get a drink, then,' he said, taking his jacket off the back of his chair. I was nearly twenty-one years old and this was the first time he had ever asked me to do this. It was his macho way of showing me he had at last accepted that I was not gay.

I had only been back at Horsham for a few weeks when I

got a letter from the army saying that they wanted me to go back into hospital because they had found someone who thought that he had a cure for my particular type of malaria. I explained this to Alwyn who told me that there would always be a place for me in the company when I was ready, and reported to the military hospital at Roehampton, on the outskirts of south London, where to my astonishment I found my old friends Harry, Lenny, Frank and Jack all in the same terrible state as me. The disease had a very long incubation period, we were told, and I had to laugh at myself when I thought of all the anguish and frustration that I had gone through maintaining celibacy for a whole year for fear of catching gonorrhoea which can be cured in a week, only to wind up with malaria. There seemed to be some kind of poetic justice in the fact that it is carried by the anopheles mosquito and you can only catch it from the female; I felt as though all those Korean hookers that I had turned down had put a curse on me.

My little squad was gathered together by Colonel Solomons, the tropical diseases expert from the American army. I looked around at my mates and thought that with our bright yellow faces and emaciated bodies we really looked like a bunch of dying daffodils. Our saviour seemed like a very nice guy and, unlike the English officers, he did not talk down to us as if we were a bunch of morons. We were all suffering, he told us, from a type of malaria so rare that we were the only group of people at that time anywhere in the world who were suffering from it. We all immediately straightened up a little and began to feel kind of special; none of us had been rare before.

He was, he said, especially pleased because there was a group of us because he thought he had a cure and if it worked it would give him a chance to see how it affected different people. This on the surface sounded like good news, but his cautious phrases did not inspire a great deal of confidence. With my usual show of courage I ventured to ask if there were any risks attached to this treatment. 'This is a medical experiment,' he replied gravely. 'And there are always risks in that. Also,' he went on, 'even now you are finding the disease is very debilitating and eventually you will not be able to work at all. If you stay as you are, you will not live much past your forties. That's the down side,' he said quickly. At least he was right about that, I thought, waiting to hear the up side. 'The up side,' he continued, as though he had read my mind, 'is that I will be using two medicines that are both proven cures in other types of malaria but which have never before been used together. That is where the risk is, and although I think that it is minimal, you will be asked to sign a waiver of responsibility for your death if you want to go ahead with it. Think it over for a few minutes.' With that he left the room.

There didn't seem to be an option. None of us felt we had anything to lose. We signed the forms and the treatment began. It consisted of taking two tablets each day for ten days. I had a funny feeling there was going to be what Colonel Solomons called 'a down side' and I was right again. The tablets, he informed us, would make our blood so heavy that we would not be able to move at all. 'Even the slightest head movement,' he said, 'will knock you unconscious and give you two lovely black eyes.' With that, a team of nurses came in and strapped us securely to our beds. 'Remember,' he said as he was leaving the ward, 'I have left your heads free but don't move them.' I lay there for a while, wondering how I was going to take ten days of this and thought that I would test the head theory. I moved my head a little bit and nothing happened. Then I made a more jerky movement and still nothing happened. He was having us on, I thought, but of course the pills had not started to work yet. A little while later I lifted my head up off the pillow to see how the other lads were and knocked myself out cold. When I came round, Colonel Solomons was standing over me smiling. He held up a small mirror. I did indeed have two lovely black eyes. 'Told you,' he said and walked away. I didn't move my head again.

When the ten days were up we were unstrapped and informed by the smiling and triumphant Colonel that we were cured forever. If any of us could have walked we would have jumped out of bed and kissed him. I had never felt so good. He came and shook all of us by the hand and thanked us for letting him try his cure and we of course thanked him for giving us our lives back which sounded rather weak for such a tremendous gift but it was all we could think of. As he left he grinned and said: 'You know, you were cured in five days really, but I had to let the cure run its full course.'

After the hospital I went back again to the Elephant for my mother's cure, the fry-up. Not surprisingly I put on weight quite quickly and I was soon ready to go back to work, but when I phoned Alwyn at Horsham I was told that the company had gone bust and the theatre was closed. I never found out where Alwyn and Edgar had gone and I never saw them again. Many years later when I was living in luxury in a big house on the top of a Beverly Hill, I received a letter from a social security inspector in the London Borough of Hammersmith. He said that there was a very sick old man who was absolutely destitute in one of their hospitals, by the name of Alwyn D. Fox. The letter went on to say that Mr Fox had said that he was once a producer and he had discovered Michael Caine. Nobody believed his story but the inspector said that he was writing to me in case it was true and that if it was, could I please send a little money so that he could buy Mr Fox a few extra luxuries to make what he was sure were the last few weeks of his life a little more comfortable. I wrote a letter back immediately saying that it was indeed Alwyn Fox who had discovered me and given me my first chance as an actor and I included in the letter a cheque for five thousand dollars. Two weeks later I got another letter from the same inspector which contained my uncashed cheque and a note saying that Alwyn had been very happy to receive the letter and had showed it to all the staff to prove that what he had said was true. He then went to sleep and died that same night.

8

Nowhere to go but up

With the break-up of the Horsham company I had to start again, so the next Saturday morning I was back in the Charing Cross Road at Solosy's to get my copy of *The Stage* and there I made a wonderful discovery. In the 'Artists Wanted' column there was an ad for experienced juveniles and I suddenly realised that now I could apply in this category. I wrote off to several theatres listing the parts that I had played and, like all actors, I padded it a bit by adding parts in plays that I had never even seen. One of these caught me out. There was at the time a very popular repertory play called *George and Margaret* that was going to be the next production that I was to be in when I was taken ill at Horsham. So I wrote down as part of my experience that I had played George in *George and Margaret*. I was summoned to an audition at the repertory in Lowestoft, on the east coast of England, and when I walked into the theatre the first thing the producer said to me was: 'What have we here, then? Apart from a bloody liar!' He waved my letter. 'It says here that you played George in *George and Margaret*.' 'So I did,' I replied defiantly, hoping that he was not going to ask me if I remembered any of the dialogue. 'You are a bloody liar, all right,' roared the producer. 'It is obvious that not only were you never in the play, but you've never even seen the bloody thing or you would know that the plot of that play centres on the fact that the entire cast spends the whole duration of the play waiting for George and Margaret to turn up – and they never do.' After that I was questioned very closely about all the other roles that I had said I had played and fortunately I had not lied about them, so he gave me an audition and I got the job.

It was a lovely theatre and the standard of the company was a good step up from Horsham. The producer was a fabulous old man of about seventy who always seemed to have the right advice for any problem. I was playing a drunk scene in one of the plays that I did in Lowestoft and on the first rehearsal when I entered playing what I imagined to be a pretty good drunk, he stopped me and said, 'What do you call this?' 'I'm playing a drunk,' I replied. 'That's right. That is exactly what you're doing, but I'm not paying you to play a drunk, I am paying you to *be* one.' 'I don't understand,' I called back out into the gloom of the unlit auditorium. 'You are being an actor who is trying to walk crooked and speak with a slurred voice like a drunk. Don't you realise that a drunk is a man who is trying to walk straight and speak properly?' I got it in one invaluable lesson.

On another occasion I was on stage for a long period and had no dialogue. 'What are you doing?' he suddenly shouted at me during my long silence. 'Nothing,' I replied. 'I haven't got any lines for a long while yet.' 'Of course you have,' he shouted. 'No, I haven't,' I shouted back. 'You are listening to everything that is being said and you are thinking of wonderful lines to say, but you just decide not to say anything until your next line, that is what you are doing. Don't tell me again that you have nothing to do on stage. Remember always to listen – that is half of acting. And reacting to what you hear is the other half. It is as simple as that.' 'Thank you, sir,' I said sincerely. Those two pieces of advice had just described film acting, but I wasn't to find that out until later.

There is one other piece of advice that along with these two forms for me the basic trio of rules for acting in films. This rule was not told to me, but to Jack Lemmon, who told it to me when I first went to Hollywood many years later. In his first film he was being directed by George Cukor and in Jack's first scene in the picture, Cukor kept cutting the scene just after he had started it. 'Do less, Jack,' George said. They'd re-start the scene and George would cut it again. 'Do less, Jack,' George said again. They did the scene over and over with George saying, 'Do less, Jack,' and with Jack doing less each time as he was asked. Finally George cut the scene again and asked Jack to do less and Jack replied, 'If I do any less I'll be doing nothing,' and George said to him, 'Now you've got it, Jack.' That just about sums up movie acting. Easy, isn't it?

One of the things I learnt very early on provincial repertory was that there is an unspoken sexual hierarchy, which decrees that the leading lady only sleeps with the leading man, the juvenile male lead with his female counterpart . . . and so on down to the male and female stage managers. These rules, though unspoken, are fairly binding – but like all rules of course there is much more fun in breaking them than abiding by them.

I was the juvenile lead, but after a week or two I found myself being irresistibly drawn towards that forbidden figure, the leading lady. Patricia Haines was a very tall woman about five feet nine, an absolute beauty, two years older than myself and a wonderful actress. Much better than me, of course. In other words she was an impossible dream. This did not impair my growing fascination, however, despite the fact that my feelings were obviously not returned, for even after two weeks with the company, she had still not registered my presence as the new juvenile lead. I would place myself in her eye-line as often as I could, and after a little while she let me know that she had noted that I existed, but that was it.

She was always very polite but with never an inkling of anything more, until one Saturday night after the show, one of the actors gave a party in his digs to which the whole company was invited. This would be my chance, I thought, my first social occasion with her, but a polite hello was all I got. I wandered around the party dejected and lovelorn. My socially decreed sexual partner, the juvenile lead girl, had her fiancé down for the weekend and we were not suited to each other anyway, so there I was alone and dejected sitting in the corner trying to look romantic and to attract Pat's attention. Nothing. I knew she was not with the leading man because I can't remember his name now, and if he had been with her he would have registered with me, because everything about Pat had that effect on me.

As I sat there, it began to dawn on me that I was hopelessly and, as it turned out, disastrously in love with her. The party began to thin out as it got late and I slumped there getting drunk to drown my sorrow and taking no notice of anybody.

'Are you shy?' her voice said behind me. I turned, and Pat was standing there looking down at me, and I do mean down since I was sitting and she was standing in three-inch high heels.

'Shy?' I mumbled, lurching to my feet and spilling my drink down my trousers. 'Me, shy? Why do you say that?' I was trying to dry the front of my trousers and look sophisticated and romantic at the same time, and failing miserably to get even close to any of them.

'Because you have been fancying me ever since you came here and yet you've never made a pass.' She was a North Country girl and they have a reputation for being forthright, but even so I thought this was unfair. I had heard of people putting their cards on the table but she was putting mine. With her high-heeled shoes on she was the same height as me, and she stood there with her beautiful blue eyes staring straight into mine, challenging me.

I was about to collapse with excitement, not only at what she had said, but I had never stood this close to her before and I could smell her perfume now, and even feel the heat of her. She had known how I felt all the time . . . but how could she have noticed? I had never been anywhere near having a relationship with a woman as beautiful or as sophisticated as Pat. Although I was in love with her, I really thought that I was not good enough for her, and in this I'm afraid I was to prove myself tragically right.

At that moment, I decided the thing to do was put the rest of my cards on the table before she did, and see if she had any cards at all. I had to restore my pride, even at the risk of eventual humiliation. I looked her straight in the eyes and said, as calmly and coolly as I could, 'I am in love with you.'

There was a pause, and then she smiled. 'I know,' she said. 'Didn't you notice that I am in love with you?'

'No,' I replied truthfully, hardly able to believe my ears, through which the blood was pumping so fiercely that I could scarcely hear what she was saying, let alone take it in. What do

I do now I thought, and it came to me very quickly. I leaned forward and kissed her gently on the lips, a kiss that was firmly returned, and to which I responded until we were locked in each others' arms, not noticing that everybody had gone home and the host had retired to bed. I was the happiest man in the world. I was truly in love for the very first time.

We were married a few weeks later at the registry office in Lowestoft, with the whole company present. Pat's mother and father, Claire and Reg, had come down from Sheffield where they lived and where Pat was born. I liked my father-in-law immediately, but my mother-in-law was obviously a bit worried about her daughter marrying someone from my background. They were a typical middle-class family. Pat's mother was always very nice to me, but I think she knew that this liaison was doomed. However she kept quiet and made the best of things. At the party that evening, Reg introduced me to something called barley wine; it tasted quite innocent but had the same effect as drinking gasoline. I passed out and woke up with a terrible hangover lying next to my unconsummated bride. This was a rocky start for a marriage – and unfortunately, the course never altered.

We decided to try our luck in London and informed the producer of our intentions. With his good wishes we set off to make our fortune in the big city. Before we went, the producer called me into his office and gave me my first compliment as an actor. He told me that while I had been with him I had learned to listen. In fact, I was the best listener he had ever had in one of his companies. With this praise ringing in my ears, I knew I was ready for the big time.

Our first home was a small two-roomed flat in a run-down area of south London called Brixton. It was owned by my Aunt Ellen, then aged eighty, who was the first person in my family ever to own her own house. We only had to pay a nominal rent of a couple of pounds, which was just as well as things turned out.

From the start, neither of our careers prospered. Pat's was a little healthier than mine, but even then we only made just enough money to survive. I occasionally got small jobs on television – just walk-on parts, no dialogue – but eventually gave up looking for acting work because Pat was the more talented of the two of us, and had the most chance of success. We decided that I would get some ordinary jobs to keep the money coming in while she promoted her career and then, when she had made enough money, I could restart my own. So I began a long line of soul-destroying jobs. I worked in a laundry for a while, wheeling trollies of dirty clothes into the boilers. I washed up at a restaurant and also had a long stint as a plumber's mate. By now, I had met up again with my old friend from Clubland days, Paul Challen. He was now an actor himself, but finding the going as tough as we were, and having to do odd jobs as well.

During the preceding period, there had always been plenty of unpopular jobs that were traditionally available for actors to do while 'resting', but around this time the first great wave of immigration into the UK occurred, and the newcomers scooped up all the unwanted work which made things even more difficult for us. Paul was working at a food factory and he got me a job there on the night-shift, which was ideal because it left me time in the day to go for auditions. I worked for quite a long time with an entirely Jamaican crew, making fruit pies and doughnuts. As the only white man in our gang I was known as Sanders, after the white commissioner in the film *Sanders of the River*. I really got to know the new immigrants well and became great friends with them, for they seemed to share my sense of humour and general devil may care attitude to life. They also used to hold certain competitions with the ring doughnuts, in which I refused to join, knowing I would lose; however I did decide that I would never eat a doughnut again. Paul and I used to go up on the roof of the factory at Hammersmith and look out over the brightly lit city during our coffee break and talk about how we would conquer this place one day, neither of us ever thinking that we would.

In the meantime, things went from bad to worse at home, and then Pat became pregnant and had our daughter Dominique, who was named after my favourite heroine in a book, Dominique Françon in Ayn Rand's *The Fountainhead*. Although this was a happy event, in our financial circum-

109

stances it was the last thing that we needed, and our new baby was the wonderful straw that broke an already very weak camel's back. My luck grew ever worse and I just couldn't handle it any longer. I walked out on the marriage and Pat took Dominique back to her parents in Sheffield, who were marvellous and brought her up and turned her into a great young woman whom I love dearly, and am very proud of. The breakdown of the marriage was my fault entirely. I was too young and immature to take the triple burden of grinding poverty and personal and professional failure. If I had been as strong as Pat I think that we could have made it, but I wasn't and I collapsed like a house of cards.

The pain of having to live with the guilt of what I had done was so intense that I think if I had known in advance what the break-up and losing my baby was going to do to me, I would have stuck with the marriage at all costs, but I didn't know, and I was left with what I thought of myself, which was nothing. Out of work, penniless and in deep, almost suicidal despair, I was forced at the age of twenty-three to return to the prefab and rely on the generosity of my family again.

When I moved back in, things grew even worse, for my father was out of work, bedridden with rheumatism of the spine. I went out and got a job in a steelyard that even the most impoverished immigrant wouldn't take, just to bring some money into the house. At work, I had to cover thick heavy rods of steel with grease and pack them into large crates for shipping. Physically it was the hardest job I'd ever done, and the dirtiest, and as it was outside in the winter it was also the coldest I had been since leaving Korea.

Every evening I used to rub my father's aching back with liniment to try and get rid of the pain, until our doctor took me aside one day and explained that he had cancer of the liver, and had only a few weeks to live. I had thought that things couldn't get worse, but I learned never to think that again as I spent every evening of the following weeks massaging his back for a rheumatism that wasn't there, and watching him literally fade away. Very quickly he went from his normal fourteen stone to half that weight and still I massaged him, to

110

keep the fact of his true illness from him. Eventually an ambulance came and took him away to St Thomas's Hospital to die. I insisted on carrying him to the ambulance myself. It was so easy; he was this big man whom I had admired and loved all my life and here I was carrying him to his death as though he were the child and I the father. I went with him to the hospital, saw that he was comfortable and went back home, promising to return that evening.

Just as I was going in my gate, a voice shouted, 'How's your dad?' I looked around and it was the old man who lived opposite us who was leaning on his gate as usual. As long as we had lived there, this old man had leaned on his gate and he had always looked so frail and was always ill, and I thought it strange that here he was, still alive, and my father who had never been sick in his life was about to die. 'He's fine,' I said quickly, and went in to comfort my mother who by this time had realised that it was almost all over.

I visited my father for two days, during which time his condition deteriorated rapidly. He was in excruciating pain. I asked the doctor to increase my father's drugs and he told me that a larger dose would kill him. I looked at him for a moment and said, 'If this is living, can death be such a bad thing?' He thought for a moment, then asked me to go away and come back at eleven o'clock that night. I was back there at eleven on the dot. Dad seemed to be much more comfortable now and I sat there holding his hand for an hour or so. He didn't seem to know that I was there but occasionally he would squeeze my hand and I would squeeze back. The hospital is right opposite the Houses of Parliament, and I could see Big Ben across the river. Eventually it struck one o'clock, and as it did, my father's eyes opened slightly and he whispered, 'Good luck, son,' and died.

I told the doctor that he had gone and thanked him for all that he had done, and walked back down the corridor. As I was walking I could hear someone running after me. It was a nurse. She caught up with me, and holding out her hand she said, 'This was in your father's pyjama pocket,' and handed me three shillings and eightpence. This was everything that my father left to us. Nothing else after fifty-six years of working like a beast of burden. I thanked her and walked on slowly down the long dark corridor, my heart and mind hardening with every step until they set into an unbreakable determination that I would make a success of my life and my family would never be poor again.

We buried him a few days later with my mother in true hysterics and my brother and I having to drag her away from his grave as she tried to throw herself in with him. We half-carried her from the cemetery and into the car, got her calmed down eventually and then we just sat there quietly on the short journey home. My mother never went to church but she believed in God, so what she suddenly said surprised the pair of us. She looked up, and wiping the tears from her eyes she said, 'I will never forgive God for this,' and she didn't, but I did.

Soon I lost my job at the steelyard and now I really was at the bottom, I hoped, of any despair that I was ever going to feel. I was broke and out of work. I had lost my marriage, my child, and now my father as well. Everything came at once and for the first time in my life I felt that I could not cope mentally with any more disaster, but I didn't know what to do. I just sat there in that little house with my distraught mother, in a catatonic state. The only money that was coming in was from Stanley, who was working and had pulled himself together quicker than I could. What was I going to do?

My mother found the answer. She obviously saw the state I was in and fixed on a solution to my woes. Retrieving the insurance policies that she had taken out on my father all those years ago – the ones I used to lie about to the collector when she was short of money – she found the one she had taken out and paid in my name on which she had collected twenty-five pounds – the equivalent of an average working man's weekly salary . This she now gave to me, and told me to go away somewhere for a while and come back when I felt better. This was extraordinary; she had got some money from her other policies, but she needed all of it to pay off everything, so I refused.

'What about paying for the funeral?' I asked. 'Use it for that.' 'I had a separate one for that, so it is paid for already,' she smiled. 'Take it and go away for a while.' She pushed the money at me. I took it and I went to Paris.

It may sound strange to anybody reading this today, as you wouldn't get very far on twenty-five pounds these days, but my return fare on the night boat train to Paris was seven pounds ten shillings. Paris was my choice because it was close and therefore cheap, and also because I had been reading about it for years and actually felt as if I knew it. I had been particularly influenced by an American novel called *Springtime in Paris* by Elliot Paul, which centred on a particular street called Rue de la Huchette. From the book I knew that it was situated just behind the St Michel métro station on Place St Michel. The author had written about the life on this street and everybody in it during a period of one year that he had spent there, so at least I knew this street very well, and I also knew that there was a hotel in it and that it was cheap – so that is where I headed.

This trip was exciting for me, not only because I was going to Paris, but it was also the first time that I had ever been abroad as a civilian and on my own. The journey was entirely uneventful and I slept most of the way, but the great thing about the boat train was that I woke up in the morning in the Gare du Nord, right in the middle of the city. I got off the train and there I was, in Paris! The excitement hit me immediately, and even after all these years and the hundreds of times that I have been there, I feel the same thrill.

The first thing I noticed was that the air smelt different. I didn't recognize the smell but it was very distinctive. I found the métro and bought a 'carnet', which is a little notebook of tickets. I knew about all these things from the novel. I spotted St Michel on the map and made my way there, only getting lost twice. The smell on the métro was different, too, and even more pronounced, but this time I knew what it was – garlic and Gauloises, the very pungent cigarettes the French smoke. Finally I reached the right stop and rushed up the underground stairs and stood in amazement looking out at the Place Saint Michel for the very first time. It is a large square, right on the banks of the River Seine, with the Pont Saint Michel at one end, and a big statue with a fountain

113

gushing out of it at the other. On the corner right by the métro exit was a café where I went and sat for two hours just watching the world go by. St Michel is the centre of the student quarter in Paris and a sightseer's paradise. Everybody seemed to be young and full of enthusiasm about anything and everything. Among the passers-by was every nationality, colour, shape and style that you could think of, and the women were gorgeous, not just some of them but *all* of them. It has always struck me as strange that even the ugly women in Paris somehow make themselves attractive, the exact opposite of London, where the women are just as beautiful but never seem able to make the best of themselves like the Parisiennes.

In my schoolboy French I ordered a 'Citröen pressé'. The waiter asked me loudly in English why I wanted a squashed car. This was my first taste of how shitty the French can be with foreigners who try to speak their language. I had made a mistake in pronunciation, he pointed out like a schoolmaster. What I really wanted was a *citron* pressé – a squeezed lemon. I changed my mind immediately and ordered un café – at least I could handle that. (I did not order squeezed lemon again for many years.) With my coffee I asked for a sandwich with ham, butter and Emmenthal cheese in a 'restaurant'. Most people would order a baguette, the long thin French loaf which is my favourite bread in the world, but a restaurant, although nearly the same as a baguette, is twice as wide but only fractionally more expensive; on a budget like mine, the main object was to fill my stomach for as long as possible.

Although I sat there for a couple of hours, nobody asked me to leave when I had finished my food, which I made last for as long as possible. That was another nice thing about French cafés – you weren't obliged to move on once you'd finished. During my lunch I encountered another great smell which always makes me think of Paris and that was praline; a man was selling some nearby.

It was time now to find the Rue de la Huchette and off I started, down the Boulevard St Michel on the left-hand side. I knew it was very far down and just one block off the boulevard, so I turned left at the first street and as I began to walk along, suddenly everything looked strangely familiar. I was on it! I looked up at the corner and sure enough, there was the sign Rue de la Huchette.

But something was wrong. It took me a minute or two to work out what it was. The people – they were all Arabs. I looked at the shops and restaurants and they were all Arabic and so were the street signs. I eventually found the hotel, but this was obviously now an Arab place too, even though the name was still in French. The original inhabitants had gone and the whole quarter had been taken over by Algerian immigrants. The smells were foreign, not French; there were kebabs and all sorts of foods that I had never seen or smelt before being sold on every corner. Unfortunately, I had started to attract the attention of one or two of the more sinister-looking types hanging around – pimps, I quickly realised – while the young ladies loitering outside the hotel could only be prostitutes. That put paid to my lodgings, I decided. One of the pimps asked me in very poor English if I would like to fuck one of his relations, although I didn't quite catch which branch of the family he referred to. Suddenly I realised how conspicuous I was – a foreigner, fair-skinned, the only six foot two blond male on the street, obviously lost and carrying a battered suitcase. If ever there was a case for an early example of mugging, I was it. My initial dreams of Paris shattered, I fled back to the safety of the boulevard.

It was now starting to get dark and my first priority was to find somewhere to stay. Fortunately, this was the student quarter so everything was cheap. I spent an hour or so looking around at hotel prices and then I went into one and asked them for the cheapest room they had. For the equivalent of five shillings per night, I got a small dirty room with just a bed in it, and one window facing on to a wall that was so close I wondered why they had bothered to put a window there in the first place. On this wall was an outlet vent from the kitchen below, where they seemed to specialise in cooking garlic, which I still disliked because it reminded me of the Chinese soldiers in Korea. Often when I was asleep there over the next few weeks, the smell would wake me up in a panic, believing that I was walking into an ambush. The hotel was just off the boulevard down from the Rue de la Huchette, and I guess

115

that the Arabs had moved further along because the other feature of this room was the Arab music, which went on for twenty-four hours a day. I was beginning to think that at five shillings per night I was being overcharged.

The next day I set out to discover Paris and at the same time fell in love with the city forever. To save money, I walked everywhere – and Paris is the greatest city in the world for walking. Over a period of a couple of weeks I discovered every nook and cranny of it, and I loved everything I saw. I'll always feel grateful to the city because I am sure that my stay there saved me from a nervous breakdown. The place to me was like a therapy. I didn't speak to anybody, I didn't want to. I just kept walking day after day until my money ran out. Needless to say, I know the streets of Paris better than most Parisians. Soon I started to feel better and happier. I spent hours in cafés, just watching the very different worlds go by as I sat and drank my coffee very slowly and munched my way through restaurants in every quarter of the city.

The first big expense came as a surprise and bankrupted me: my shoes badly needed mending. This used up the last of my twenty-five pounds and one evening I suddenly found myself broke, without a job and what was more important, without a room. They did not give credit at my hotel. It was getting dark and late, and I was becoming desperate for somewhere to sleep, when I hit on an idea. In my exploration of Paris, I had come across the air terminal at the Gare St Lazare. I was carrying a suitcase, so I could pass as a passenger – and in an air terminal there must be lots of people who had to wait a long time and happened to fall asleep in the chairs. Off I went, and I was right, there were people everywhere dozing in armchairs with suitcases, so that's what I did too. There were a few obvious bums that the police threw out but I quickly took care of this problem. I sauntered over to one of the waste-paper baskets and took out an old Air France ticket stub that had been thrown away, and fell asleep in a very comfortable chair with my suitcase between my legs and the ticket stub clutched prominently in my hand. The police could not see that there was no ticket inside so it worked for two nights, anyway.

During the night when it was quiet, I grew very hungry. There was a young guy on a buffet bar at the end of the hall, and at about two o'clock in the morning, he started to pack up. I hit on another bright idea. I went over to him and asked if he had any stale sandwiches that he was going to throw away. I was speaking in my faltering French, but to my surprise he answered me in English, with an American accent. I got talking to him and told him my story, including the obvious fact that I was flat broke. 'You don't want to eat any stale sandwiches,' he said. 'I'll make you some fresh.' And he went out the back and returned with half a dozen beautiful fresh ones. I ate two of them and put the rest in my suitcase. He then gave me a hot chocolate and a couple of bottles of Coke to put in my case for later.

The next day I walked all over Paris searching for some odd job to do. I couldn't get a real one because I did not have a work permit. Unfortunately, I couldn't find a thing. The next night I returned to the air terminal, where my American friend filled me up with food again and supplied me with some for the next day, and then I bedded down again on the seat. I was eventually woken up just before dawn by a gendarme who wished to see my ticket stub. He threw me out with words that I did not actually understand, but I think I got the gist of them: something along the lines of if I came back he would shove his truncheon up my derrière.

I dashed out onto the pavement just ahead of a boot in the arse, and stood there looking around at the city as the sun started to come over the horizon. In spite of my grave circumstances, the city looked so beautiful that my spirit soared and I decided that I didn't feel so bad after all. I had my return ticket in my pocket, and if nothing turned up today I could always catch the boat train home tonight, but I knew that mentally I was not yet ready to go back and face my life in London. Where to go now was the next question. I thought for a moment and suddenly remembered a place called the Boulevard Clichy that I had come across in my explorations. This was a real low-life quarter, full of strip-clubs, pimps and prostitutes, but it had one advantage: it did stay open all night and there might at least be something going on there. So off I set and arrived just as all the night clubs were closing and the drunks and revellers were blearily facing their trip home to bed. As for me, I just sat on a bench on the wide pavement in the middle of the boulevard and indulged in my favourite free pastime, people watching.

I sat there for a long while as the sun came right up and slowly warmed my body and the day, and I started to feel more hopeful. The revellers were thinning out now as more sober citizens took their place, and ordinary little snack-bars began to open up. Opposite where I was sitting, one particular place was doing a roaring trade. It was just a hole in the wall joint that sold beer, coffee and hot dogs, and on the pavement outside was a machine that made French fries which were sold by the bag. There were about a dozen seats and a little bar. Only one man was running this place, and very soon he was getting overwhelmed. As I sat there I thought that maybe he could use an extra pair of hands to collect the dirty glasses and wash up, so I waited for a brief lull then went over and suggested it. He agreed to take me on for a minimal sum, all that he was prepared to offer, but there it was – at least I had a job. I put my case behind the counter and started work immediately. In the evening he gave me my money, which was just enough for another fleapit room in a fleabag hotel in which I seemed to be the only permanent tenant, for the rest of the rooms were let by the hour to extremely unromantic-looking couples. Although I only had very little cash left over after I had paid the hotel, my job at least supplied all the food that I needed. The work was hard, the hours long and the pay small. It was typical of me, I thought: here I was living in a brothel and only getting screwed at work, but I didn't mind – I could stay in Paris a little longer.

While I worked at the snack-bar I came to know some of the most unsavoury people in Paris: tarts, thieves, pimps and gangsters, and mugs who were soon parted from their money. I had always thought that I was pretty stupid, but some of the con-tricks that the mugs fell for made me look like Einstein. It was also a very dangerous area; killings and fights occurred every single night that I worked on the Boulevard Clichy. I must have been there for several weeks but since my mental

118

state at the time did not take in days or weeks, I just existed in this cesspit until I felt ready to go home.

When I eventually made it home, my mother greeted me with: 'Where the hell have you been? Your agents sent a telegram yesterday.' We had no phone.

'What did it say?' I demanded, praying that it would be work. She handed it to me and I read: *Call tomorrow. Have job for you. Urgent.* 'When did this arrive?' I asked my mother, practically gibbering.

'Yesterday,' she repeated.

'Have there been any other messages while I've been away?' I asked but Mum shook her head. My immediate thought was that there *was* a God, after all, and He had sent me home at just the right moment. Maybe He was going to change things for me this time. At least from where I was now, I had nowhere to go but up.

9

'It's only a small part . . .'

My agent, a lovely old Scotsman called Jimmy Fraser, was part of the big agency Fraser & Dunlop with smart offices in Regent Street near Piccadilly Circus. I can't remember now why they ever took me on, since I was far too small a fry for the big league type of work that they had to offer. I got a clue when I first started with him. I sat in his office and he looked across at me and said, 'You've got something, Michael. For the life of me I can't see what it is and therefore I don't know how to sell it, but I'll take you on for a while and see if it becomes a little clearer . . .'

Now he told me on the phone that he had got me a part in a film. A miracle – I couldn't believe it. Who would have me in a film? I hadn't even had a speaking part in television yet! 'What is it called?' I responded, trying to control the excitement in my voice.

'*A Hill in Korea*,' he replied. 'It's about the war that you told me you were in. It's only a small part, and they want you to be the technical adviser on the film because of your experience over there.'

How much was the pay and for how long – and where? were my next questions, asked all in a rush. A hundred pounds a week, for eight weeks, Jimmy told me, and we would be shooting the locations in Portugal and the studio at Shepperton, one of our major studios at that time. 'You start in six weeks,' he said, and put the phone down.

From that moment on, my life changed in a small but significant way, for ever. Until then, through good times and bad, deep down in my heart there was always a small grain of despair. All that disappeared now, never to return, no matter how tough things got. In its place was a seed of hope.

This was all very well, but the film was six weeks away, I was broke and Pat needed money to support herself and the baby, and I had to pay my way at the house. Stanley was working and my mother had her usual early-morning cleaning job but that only brought in a pittance. There was no chance of me getting a job for just six weeks so I was stuck – until my mother, as usual, came to the rescue. She drew all of her savings out of the post office and gave them to me – £400. 'Take it,' she commanded, 'and pay me back when you make the film.' Mum actually saved me from going to jail for non-payment of support, a brand new hurdle in my life with which Pat suddenly confronted me, as well as keeping me going until that all-important first speaking role in a movie. My mother was the greatest and toughest lady that I have ever met, and she really loved her boys.

Six weeks later I was up and away to Portugal with the cast and crew of *A Hill in Korea*. This was my first encounter with the star of a film. I had heard they could be very egotistical and snobbish – especially about talking to unknown actors doing their first film and with only eight lines to say. The star in this case was George Baker, who as I write is appearing on television as Inspector Wexford in the Ruth Rendell mysteries. George was, and is, one of the nicest actors in the business. He always treated me kindly. His treatment of me – a lowly actor with only a few lines – would become a valuable lesson in the proper behaviour to small-part actors when I eventually made it. As I said, I had eight lines, or one a week on our schedule and as each line came round I built myself up into a state of abject terror for fear of forgetting it, which of course I invariably did. On stage in repertory I could easily remember two hours of dialogue, but the tension and the technicality of film I found very disturbing, especially when all the noise of the technicians stopped and someone shouted, 'We are going for a take!' which to my ears then sounded like some monumental, impossible dream.

This is the routine of a take. The first assistant shouts 'Quiet!' and then there is indeed quiet, a silence in which you can hear your heart thumping. Then comes the instruction

'Turnover!' and the camera technicians turn on their respective machines. The sound man calls 'Speed,' the assistant yells 'Mark it!' and the clapper boy runs in with the clapper-board, places it right in front of your face and shouts, say, 'Scene thirty-three. Take one!' He then brings the loose piece of board known as the clapper down with a bang on top of the clapper-board, to mark the sound synchronisation spot on the sound track, which at that time is separate from the actual film. This done, he rushes out of the shot and stands still in order to maintain silence, at which point the director finally shouts '*Action!*'

By this time the inexperienced actor is paralysed with tension. His neck and shoulder muscles have tightened to almost breaking point, cutting off the flow of blood and oxygen to the brain and causing him to forget his one line. The director shouts '*Cut!*' and the assistant calls, 'We are going again, don't break it up' – meaning that everybody should stay quiet. The director in disgust says to the continuity girl at his side, who is holding the script open at the appropriate page, 'Give him the line,' and she tells him the one line which he knows rather well, since he has been learning it all week! The assistant shouts 'Going again!' and the whole process starts anew, with the actor even more nervous this time because he has now failed once. It doesn't help when he hears a technician in the darkness behind the camera mumble something like, 'One fucking line and he can't even remember that.'

The most famous story going round the British studios at the time was of the starving one-line actor who took twenty takes to get it right, but gave the excuse that he knew it on the bus. To which the director was alleged to have replied, with some justification, 'We're not paying you to say it on the fucking bus!'

The director of *A Hill in Korea* was a wonderful man called Julian Amyes, who gave me my first speaking role in a film, as well as in television. Some of the other unknown actors in the cast were Stanley Baker, Stephen Boyd and Robert Shaw. Stephen and I became friends and when we were shooting back in England, he used to give me a lift to the studios every day in an old banger of a car that he owned at the time. He was the first one of the cast to make it as a star, and shortly after the film opened he disappeared into the rarefied atmosphere of Hollywood. I never saw him again and he eventually died of a heart attack while still very young.

Robert Shaw and I also became friends and worked together several times before either of us were famous, but our friendship did not start well. As a matter of fact, it started with a fight, at dinner in our hotel in Portugal. The food there was not great, and everything was swimming in olive oil, which I didn't like at the time although it's practically the only oil that I use now. On top of this everything was loaded down with garlic, which I associated with fear and the smell of human manure on fields in Korea. I kept sending my meal back until there was not a trace of garlic anywhere, and this seemed to annoy Robert. Mind you, we had all drunk a few bottles of wine. He yelled at me, 'Eat it, you fucking Cockney Philistine! It's the best food you've ever had in your life, and you're sending it back.'

To say that this garbage was great food was a direct insult to my mother's cooking, so I took instant umbrage. I also had a feeling that some umbrage should be taken at being called a Philistine, but as I did not actually know what it meant at the time I concentrated all my rage on the first insult. Reaching across the table and grabbing his shirt-collar I asked the extremely irrelevant question, 'Who do you think you're fucking talking to?' to which he replied as he leapt across the table with slightly more relevance, 'I'll fucking well show you!' Pandemonium broke loose as wine, cutlery, crockery, Portuguese waiters and British actors went flying in every direction. I found out later that Robert was right about the olive oil and garlic. As our friendship grew, he told me that his father had died of a heart attack at the age of fifty-six and he was determined to beat him. Robert, being very competitive, achieved this. He died of a heart attack at the age of fifty-eight.

Stanley Baker was already on his way to becoming a British star, although he never made it in Hollywood. We were not firm friends but got along amicably enough. Many years later he told me that he actually remembered me from the film, which was a surprise. Stanley was the source of another major step forward in my career: he eventually produced a film called *Zulu*. A young actor called Harry Landis had the big Cockney soldier role in *A Hill in Korea* but things didn't work out for him and I never saw him again. There was a good-looking Welshman in the cast who I thought had the chance to become a star, but he died young as well – his name was Ronald Lewis. Michael Medwin starred; he had already played leads in British films, always it seemed as a Cockney – and I was amazed when I met him in the flesh to discover that he had a very upper-crust accent. Cockney is a hard accent to do and he did it brilliantly; he certainly fooled me. Michael is a great guy and we are still friends.

My function as a technical adviser was completely ignored during the making of the film. For example, I advised the crew to spread the troops wide as the latter advanced, which was militarily correct, but they replied that they didn't have a lens of sufficient width to take it all in! I also pointed out that the officer would have removed his signs of rank and worn a hat, the same as the other men, to disguise which one was in command, but George was allowed to go into battle with all badges and hat gleaming, every inch an officer. In a real fight, he would have lasted all of ten seconds. The most glaring mistake that I never brought to their notice was that Portugal did not in the least resemble Korea; if anything, Wales was more similar. I did not say anything because I wanted to stay in Portugal – I could go to Wales at any old time.

Life in the hotel in Lisbon was one long round of drinking and, this being an all-male cast, womanising, plus problems with the language. One day at breakfast one of the technicians came in, very angry about the fact that his laundry had still not been returned and he could not make the maid understand his problem. He was so angry and frustrated that he yelled out, 'Who *is* this Mañana who has got all the fucking washing?'

Finally the location part of the film was finished and we came back to England and started to shoot at Shepperton. I repaid my mother, sent maintenance to Pat and found myself a flat in Earls Court, then a very seedy area of cheap lodging-houses in west London. I teamed up again with my old friend Paul Challen who had been living there for quite a while, and he showed me the ropes. Bed-sitting rooms were all the rage in those days. They consisted of a room with a bed in it and a chair, and they were both very cheap and plentiful, judging by the number of ads in the windows of the local newsagents and tobacconists. Things were going to be all right, I thought – until I got close and started to read the small print. Beneath the descriptions of nice rooms at cheap prices was the warning: *No Blacks, Irish, dogs or actors*. This was my first contact with racial prejudice, and being an actor I also noticed the billing: not only were we last, but we were below the dogs.

Anyway, I found a room near Paul and we went about what we called our social lives, which in my case meant the search for nubile and willing maidens, of whom there seemed to be an increasing number. It was 1956, and the first stirrings of the sixties were in the air. I had money from the film – not a lot, but you didn't seem to need a lot in those days – and I was setting out to catch up sexually with my contemporaries. My history in this area was rather lax. I had had two enforced periods of celibacy while I was in the army and in Paris, and in any case I was a late starter. All my male friends seemed to have done it before I did, and even when I did finally do it they all did it again before I did – so I saw myself as the perpetual laggard in this area. I had been married to Pat for two and a half years and had never been unfaithful to her, so here was my first opportunity. I was unattached, with money and a room of my own. I was not looking for romance or marriage, simply trying to catch up. I was now twenty-three, but better late than never.

I finished the film and then had the time and the money to visit my daughter Dominique, who was now living permanently with Pat's mother and father in Sheffield. I went with a mixture of anticipation and dread. I wanted so much to see my daughter, but feared that I would not be received with exactly open arms by Reg and Claire Haines. As it turned out, I was wrong. Dominique was a beautiful little blonde girl, now one year old, and I fell in love with her immediately. It took me the whole weekend for her to get used to me, but I persevered and by the time I left I felt that I had at least started some sort of bond with her. My in-laws were so pleasant and made me so welcome that I actually stayed in their spare bedroom and a relationship began with them which lasted until they both died a few years later. Pat, they told me, had gone back to her career in London and they were going to bring the baby up themselves. I thought that this was a great idea. They had a comfortable middle-class home on the outskirts of the city, and were kind people who obviously loved Dominique very dearly. I went away happy with the situation, promising to support my daughter until she went to work and to visit her as often as I could – with their permission, which they gave with enthusiasm – so life was great. All my problems seemed to be receding.

But not for long. Jimmy Fraser saw the finished film and dropped me from his list of clients, stating that I would never get anywhere if I did not dye my eyelashes, and that he could no longer represent me. Not having seen the film myself, I jumped to the correct conclusion that my screen début had not been an unqualified success. The company held on to the film for ages before releasing it. After a year of waiting for the perfect moment, with true movie genius they premiered the film on the night that we invaded Suez. The picture went straight down the pan, and my movie career along with it. I bemoaned the fact that nobody had seen the film, until I actually saw it myself. I was terrible! My voice was awful, and I solved the mystery of Jimmy Fraser's last remark to me.

My eyelashes are blond and so are my eyebrows, which has the effect in close-up of something speaking that hasn't got a face, and it's not much better in medium shot. Screen presence is very difficult under these circumstances and far from lighting up the screen when I came on, in spite of my fair complexion the screen actually seemed to darken. My appearances were mercifully few, the editor having decided that the cutting-room floor was the ideal place for my first effort at international stardom.

10

Becoming Michael Caine

I found a new agent, a lovely middle-aged lady called Josephine Burton, and although her office was in classy Knightsbridge, she wasn't as high-powered as Fraser & Dunlop, and that suited me better. Work did not come pouring in but with a few odd jobs I managed to exist. Pat and I were separated but not divorced, and I was amazed to meet her in the street by accident one day. She was going to walk past without speaking to me, but I stopped her just to ask when our divorce would be through, at which she laughed and said, 'We've been divorced for weeks.' She then walked away and left me standing there wondering how I could be divorced and nobody had the courtesy to tell me. As she was moving away she turned and added, 'You're behind with the maintenance,' which was true, but something would turn up.

Jobs did not come thick and fast with Josephine, and I had to move out of my bedsitter and go back to living at the Elephant with my mother and Stanley. Christmas was approaching and I was getting desperate for any money at all when I was sent to the Theatre Workshop in the East End of London, where a brilliant woman called Joan Littlewood was putting on her own Christmas production of Charles Dickens' *The Chimes*. I knew the Workshop to be a renowned theatre for the working class; it was in a working-class district and was basically a Communist organisation. I did an audition and got a part in the show. I had not been too impressed by this system up to this time but I was prepared to give it a fourth chance. The people with whom I was working were real dyed-in-the-wool Party members, and even their dialogue was different from anything that I had known. It took me two days to pluck up enough courage to ask who the proletariat were – and I was very surprised to find out that it was me. With words like this, maybe I was more important than I thought I was! The wages, a measly two pound ten shillings per week, were back to the day I started at Horsham and here I was, twenty-four years old. Being a Communist organisation, however, they were aware of the workers' plight and we were issued with free vitamins every day.

Brilliant as Joan Littlewood was, she failed to notice my talent and I was in trouble as soon as I stepped on stage for the first rehearsal. As I appeared from behind the curtain, she yelled from the auditorium, 'We don't want any of that! Come on again.' I duly exited and re-entered not knowing what 'any of that' was. Again she stopped me. 'This is a group theatre, we don't want any of that.' So off I went, and on I came. She stopped me yet again. 'I'm not having it.' 'Not having what?' I asked, genuinely perplexed. 'Any of this star nonsense. You bury your individuality in the character for the good of the group and the play as a whole.'

I began to understand. This was a method group and we followed the principles of Konstantin Stanislavsky, the Russian naturalistic actor and theatre director. I tried to blend with the group and immerse my personality, but I never really did it to Joan's satisfaction and when the production finished, instead of taking me on in the main company she got rid of me with the most backhanded compliment that I have ever received. Her parting words to me were, 'Piss off to Shaftesbury Avenue. You will only ever be a star.' To Joan, 'star' was a dirty word. I did learn one important thing from her, though. She told me: 'Rehearsal is the work, the performance is the pleasure!' This has helped me no end, and for that I am grateful.

I only ever saw Joan Littlewood once after that. It was about thirty years later, in a very expensive restaurant, and all she said to me was, 'I've watched your career with interest and you have never given a performance since you left me.' With that remark she turned away and continued her conversation with her constant companion, that very well-known Communist Baron Philippe de Rothschild.

After Theatre Workshop, as bad as that was financially, things grew even bleaker. My new agent Josephine could just not get my career off the ground, so I went to the last resort of starving actors: a casting agency on St Martin's Lane near Trafalgar Square run by a man called Ronnie Curtis. Here you sat in the office literally all day, along with a large group of ever-changing hopefuls, and waited for the small studios to ring in and ask for someone to do something the next day for as little money as it was legally possible to pay. As the job did not go through your agent you saved ten per cent immediately, and as you were there in the first place Ronnie knew you were desperate and that he could screw you into the ground on the deal, which you had to make on the spot with him in person.

My first engagement from Ronnie happened like this. He was very cross-eyed and so when he came out and pointed at us and said, 'You,' three of us stood up. This did not seem to throw him at all – I suppose he was used to it. Then he asked: 'What size is your chest?' and, each still thinking he was addressing us alone, we answered in unison with our chest sizes. 'Who said forty?' he asked, and I put my hand up. Now I knew how Marilyn Monroe felt. The other two sat down now, sure that he was talking to me. 'What's your inside leg measurement?' he demanded. 'Thirty-two,' I replied. His eyes lit up. 'Perfect,' he said. 'Come in,' beckoning into his small office. When I got inside he explained to me that I would be playing a policeman in a small film the next day; I had been cast because I fitted the uniform that the company already had in their wardrobe.

I did quite a lot of these little jobs and they were always at the Merton Park Studios which specialised in second feature pictures. As rough and as badly paid as these jobs were, they saved the careers of many actors who later turned into stars. In some cases it would actually save someone's life. Over the next four years, the whole group of actors that I got to know had a very lean time and in the midst of it all every now and then one of them would give up, and rather than go back to 'Civilian life', would take their own. There were always five or six suicides a year of actors that I knew personally, so what the number was in all I hesitate to guess. Believe me, those days were very, very hard.

Apart from Ronnie Curtis's office, the other main meeting place for impoverished actors was the café under the Arts Theatre in Sackville Street. The attraction of this place was that it was warm and comfortable, the coffee was cheap and you could spend all day there on one cup and they would never throw you out. Also, you got a chance to mix with your own kind and see that as destitute as you were yourself, there was always someone worse off. News of any jobs going could sometimes be picked up, and so could budding young would-be actresses, which was a bonus to some of the guys but in my case was my main reason for going there. There are very few big British stars of my generation that I did not meet there. The café was a great place, warm, friendly, sensual and informative all for the price of a cup of coffee. It was a time of tremendous physical hardship, despair and worst of all rejection and humiliation. If you live an ordinary life just think of the trauma of being sacked and applying for another job, and of having to go through that process maybe seven or eight hundred times in your life. This on top of a dodgy lifestyle and basic insecurity, so you can see that starting out as an actor is not exactly a bed of roses. Of course we all chose that life, including myself, so it was our own responsibility, you might say, and I would be the first to agree with you. However ten years later when the papers reported my latest film deal, a response was published in the letter columns a few days later saying that the correspondent thought it was disgraceful that Michael Caine should be paid all this money when coal miners only earned two hundred pounds per week.

My view is that I was paid two hundred pounds per week to do the actual acting, just like the coal miner; the rest of the money was to pay me for the ten years that I spent trying to get to that position. As an unknown actor you are an outcast. You cannot get a hire purchase loan, rent a car, get insured or borrow from the bank. In most cases people are reluctant to rent you a room, and if you do get one, the telephone company will probably refuse to supply you with a telephone. The gas and electricity companies make you pay in advance for service. Ordinary people with regular steady jobs avoid you in the pub in case they buy you a drink and you cannot reciprocate. The world leaves us to our own devices – until one in a thousand of us survives this baptism of fire and then, it seems to me, they resent us when we are successful. Our job has no guarantees and that is why the survivors are paid so much.

The Arts café was the morning and afternoon meeting place, while lunch was either in the Salisbury pub in St Martin's Lane or the Legrain coffee shop in Dean Street. The pub was a wonderful warm place, a typical Victorian London drinking establishment, complete with red plush upholstered seats and brass fittings. If you had enough money to buy a round of drinks, this is where you went to meet other actors. It was a step up from the Arts because a lot of the actors there actually had regular work and therefore money, because they were in a successful show. So you could have a drink and a sandwich and possibly meet someone with enough to be able to lend you the necessary for a visit tomorrow. If you had a little money you went to the Legrain for the best coffee in London at that time, and the best lamb sandwich. It was cheap and clean and run by two charming old French ladies. When the licensing laws closed the pub at three o'clock, we would go back to the Arts for a coffee for a couple of hours and then go opposite to an illegal afternoon drinking club called Raj's, which was owned and run by an Indian who because of his religion didn't drink himself but was quite happy to help us to do so illegally night after night. At six o'clock we unknowns would rush to the phones in Leicester Square tube station, to contact our agents and see if there had been a job offer during the day. This was a soul-destroying task, to phone five nights a week, sometimes for months on end, to be told a flat 'nothing today'. One night when I was just about as near as I ever got to giving up the business, I phoned Josephine Burton and learned that she had finally got me a job on television, with a good speaking part. The play, she told me, was called The Lark by Jean Anouilh, and it was about the life of Joan of Arc. I was to play the small part of Boudousse the guard, who took Joan to Paris to meet the Dauphin. There was one problem, however. I had to become a fully fledged member of Equity, the British actors' trade union, but apparently there was already another actor on Equity's list named Michael Scott – my stage name at the time. Josephine said I must change my last name in the next half hour, because she wanted to send the contract off that evening! I promised to call her back and went and sat in Leicester Square, desperately racking my brains. All around were 'first-run' cinemas, and it was as I was looking at stars' names up in shining lights and trying to think of something that would look equally good up there some day, that I saw the name Humphrey Bogart, one of my all-time favourite actors. The film he was in at that time was The Caine Mutiny. I looked for a moment and decided that was the one, for several reasons. 'Caine' was short and sounded easy with Michael, and it was a word with which everybody was familiar, particularly those of us who had been through the British school system. The word 'mutiny' in the title also appealed to me, because at that time I was extremely rebellious and angry, but I couldn't call myself Michael Mutiny. There was another reason for my choice, a Biblical one. Cain was the brother of Abel who was cast out of Paradise, and I felt a great sympathy with him at the time.

Mission accomplished, I called Josephine back and told her to put me down as Michael Caine. I was puzzled about how I had landed a responsible little part in a prestigious production like this without even meeting the director or anybody else for that matter, and she told me that Julian Amyes, who had directed A Hill in Korea was directing this play and had asked for me. I owe him a debt of gratitude, for my first speaking part in both the cinema and television. Thank you, Julian, from the bottom of my heart – wherever you are today!

The fee for this job, Josephine informed me, was eighty guineas. This was a fortune for me at that time and it got me out of trouble for a while. So much of the way society was run

132

at that time aroused my fury, but one day in the Arts club I met an actor whom I knew vaguely who always seemed to be angrier about everything than even I was. I asked him why he was back from a season of rep in Wales so soon and he told me that he had been sacked. He was *really* angry now – and he told me that he was going to give up acting and become a playwright. He had already written a play that he was trying to get put on and it was called *Look Back in Anger* – the play that changed everything for the working-class actor in the British theatre. His name of course was John Osborne. His ideas led to the forming of a group known as the angry young men, and I was a minor one of them. In some ways I still qualify as a member.

The reason that the sixties started in the middle of the fifties was – adrenalin. It is as simple as that. When you are a performer in a show you get a rush of adrenalin and when the show is over, you feel very up and ready to do things and keep going. At ten-thirty in the evening in those days, when the show finished and the pubs were closing you did not feel like going home to bed and you certainly did not feel like dressing up and going to one of the snotty night clubs that were around at the time even if you had the money to waste, which most of us did not. So the actors opened their own late-night clubs. One was called Gerry's, and it was owned by an actor called Gerald Campion, who played Billy Bunter in the children's TV series. The club was in Soho and sold very good food and served drinks until two in the morning. The other was called the Buckstone and was in a little street behind the Haymarket Theatre. I don't know who started it, but it was for show people and writers – any of the so-called artistic professions. So here you had the basis of a night-life for all of the people. It was cheap and cheerful and fun – and there was no dress code to keep out the riffraff because we *were* the riffraff and the club was for us. Coupled with this was a subtle change in the way restaurants were run. Until then most restaurants were very stiff places that closed early, had a strict dress code, served bad food and were staffed by surly British waiters who spent most of the time after 9 p.m. looking at their watches and breathing very audible sighs of impatience as you tried to rush through your food so that they could go home quickly. The modern British waiter is of course different, I hasten to add! I own five restaurants and do not want to get lynched when this book comes out. Slowly the Italians began to arrive and restaurants changed to what they would be like in the sixties. The food was good and cheap, the waiters were pleased to see you and behaved as though they never wanted you to leave, no matter how late it was. The interiors of the restaurants were bright and warm and friendly, and most important of all, there was no dress code and they were open late at night. So there you have it: the sixties actually started in the late fifties, and my own date for when it ended was around 1972 when the Biba boutique in High Street Kensington closed.

Over the last years of the fifties, the least favourite decade of my life, I made as many trips as I could to Sheffield to see Dominique. I was allowed as much access to her as I liked, and whenever possible I would go up there for the weekend – but never on a week day when the agents were opened for fear of losing an audition. I tried to form a bond with her, no matter how slender, so that I would never appear to her as a stranger when she grew old enough to understand what had gone on. During this period of my life, I had the occasional piece of luck that always seemed to fizzle out. One day, for example, Josephine got me a screen test for a picture that starred the old American actor Charlie Coburn and a man called Nigel Patrick, who was not only a big British star at the time but was also the director. The screen test was between me and another actor and I got the part – much to my delight, only to find out Nigel was cutting my part out of the picture. He was very nice about it, and I was paid my full money, but I still had not had the chance to show what I could do in a film.

The actor that I had beaten for this role was called Sean Connery and he went off and did another screen test which he got, for James Bond. I had first met Sean at what was called a bottle party. This meant that if you turned up you had to contribute a bottle of booze. The trick with this kind of party was to buy a bottle of the cheapest drink going, put it on the bar and then get the biggest glass available and fill it to the brim from the best stuff that somebody else had brought. You had to do this very quickly because everyone else was doing the same thing. You did not want to wind up drinking the crap that you had brought yourself.

It was in the middle of one of these after-theatre Saturday night parties that Sean walked in. Most of us young actors were very weedy-looking specimens from our lack of food over the years, but Sean was enormous and very fit. I immediately wondered where he got the food from. He was older than me and had been an actor for a long time, I thought. He had no money – you could tell by his clothes and shoes, plus the fact that he was at this party. Yet here he was fit as a fiddle and very robust to say the least. I got talking to him and he told me that he was not an actor but a body-builder. He was from Edinburgh, and was in the chorus of *South Pacific* because the director, Josh Logan, had called an audition for chorus boys in which they had to be tough American sailors and sing *There is Nothing Like a Dame*. Chorus boys today are fit and tough-looking even if they are gay, but in those days British chorus boys had a tradition of not only being gay but being very up-front with their homosexuality. They tended to be very slender and feminine, they all seemed to walk with a very definite mince and talk with a lisp. People talk about gays 'Coming Out' today as though it was some big deal, but these guys were not only Out, they were flaunting it. As you can imagine, they were less than convincing dressed as American sailors singing *There is Nothing Like a Dame* so Josh Logan sent round all the gyms and auditioned all the body-builders and that, Sean told me all those years ago, about thirty-two or -three, was how he got into show business. But until James Bond it wasn't all roses for him either.

Somehow, as I got to know Sean better, I worried about him less and less. I've watched him for over thirty years grow from the very big man I knew then to the giant he is today. He oozes confidence and determination and has a directness that can sometimes be disconcerting. I always remember a dinner he and I had with Barbra Streisand when she asked him if he would allow her to direct him in a film.

'How many films have you been in?' he asked.

'Five or six,' she replied.

'I've been in thirty,' he said. 'Why should I let you direct me?'

At this point, not being a direct person myself, I took a tremendous interest in my soup and hoped the evening would end quickly. Streisand, I might add, was unfazed.

Sean was determined above all to be taken seriously as an actor. His big break was as James Bond, but few remember that these early movies, although tremendous Box Office, were often objects of great critical ridicule. Sean took all this without wincing and waited until he got the starring role in Sidney Lumet's picture *The Hill*, and for the first time we all saw the actor minus the gadgets. The critical reviews changed overnight. And the public learned that his name was Sean Connery, not James Bond.

11

Understudying O'Toole

Over the next few years, my situation remained much the same. I lived hand to mouth, being helped out by friends, with the occasional film bit or television part, but nothing that would shift my career an inch. For instance, I played an Irish gangster in a second-feature film until the director, who was a Scotsman, heard my Irish accent – and then I played a deaf and dumb gangster. I was in a very popular police TV series called *Dixon of Dock Green*, playing an Indian. This time, the director said I sounded Welsh, but I pointed out to him that the two accents were very close; he reluctantly accepted that. A few months later, I did another *Dixon* and I received a fan letter from Dennis Price – a very famous British movie star at the time. It just said: '*I saw you on* Dixon of Dock Green *and I always pride myself that I can spot star quality when I see it and you, Mr Caine, have it. I know that* Dixon *is not the greatest show but don't give up. You have what it takes. Good luck, Dennis Price.*' There was no return address so I could not write and thank him for what was a massive boost to my flagging resolve.

I got so desperate for money, I even tried civilian jobs again. For a time I was a night porter in a small hotel and café in Victoria in London, and worked from 8 p.m. to 6 a.m. This job was ideal for me because it left me free during the day for auditions – of which I did hundreds but with never any result. When I looked at the register everybody was called Mr and Mrs Smith.

I was back in a whorehouse but I didn't mind. It wasn't a bad life for a while – plenty of money, all the sandwiches I could eat and a lot of fun with the girls who used to come down and talk to me after their 'husbands' had fallen into

137

satiated slumber. Some of them were very pretty and amusing, and I enjoyed their company, but my close contact over a period of a few months did convince me of something I had always suspected: the golden-hearted prostitute of fiction was a myth. No matter how charming they were, these girls were as selfish and greedy as any group of people that I had ever met. My ingrained dislike of commercial sex prevented me from taking advantage of half-price offers that would sometimes come my way, and the images of the army VD film were still fresh in my mind after five or six years. Some films you never forget.

The end of this wonderful job came one night when six men entered together with six tarts. I put them all in their rooms and settled down for a quiet evening once the foul deed had been done. Several of them were very drunk and were asleep before the foul deed was even mentioned, and one by one the rooms went quiet until there was only one active room left; this was very active, and eventually got very frightening. It gradually dawned on me as I half-listened that what was going on in there was an actual sadistic act against the girl's wishes. He was beating the daylights out of her and she was screaming for help in agony. It sounded as though I was going to have to go in and rescue the girl. Unaccustomed to chivalry as I was, I kicked the door open with panache despite the fact that it was not locked, and noticed immediately and with some relief that the guy was the smallest one of the bunch. My confidence rose immediately and I dragged him off the girl and knocked him unconscious. When I turned to the girl, to help her on with some clothes, she was hysterical and covered with cuts and bruises. As I was comforting her, my career as a brothel-keeper came to an abrupt end. A bottle was smashed over my head and the friends, who I had forgotten were in the other room, kicked the shit out of me as soon as I hit the floor. I gave my notice instantly to the owner who was standing over me when I came round and went back into show business, never to leave it again.

As the end of the fifties approached, jobs became even fewer and of less calibre, if that was possible, and I was really despairing when my agent Josephine Burton went to New

138

York on business, got appendicitis, went in for an operation and died when they gave her the anaesthetic. She had a weak heart that neither she nor anybody else knew about, and it could not stand the strain. Apart from my personal sadness, since I was really fond of her, her loss was also a terrible professional blow; now I had no lifeline to work.

Paul, my oldest and dearest friend and constant companion, who was never really strong in the first place, succumbed to tuberculosis and went into a sanatorium for three years and left behind one of his lungs. With the loss of his companionship and great humour I felt more alone than ever. Two other young actors who were great fun and fairly good friends of mine called Johnny Charlesworth and Peter Myers, remained in good health but were mown down by the pressure – not only financial but the prospect, which we all shared, that maybe this business did not want us anyway. They took another way out and killed themselves.

I did get a new agent quite quickly called Pat Larthe, who was a very successful model agent, but her opportunities for actors were less than Josephine's so even that was a retrogressive step. The first interview she obtained for me sounded great, but turned out to be the worst possible thing that could happen to me at any time, let alone at that particular moment, when it almost put me in the grave alongside Johnny and Peter. It was my anger that saved me. One of the biggest movie companies in Britain at that time was Associated British Pictures, who ran their operation like an old Hollywood studio, with a rota of actors under contract. I was sent to see their chief casting director, a very powerful man called Robert Lennard. Here was a chance, I thought. If I could get under contract, at least I would have regular money. I was now getting behind with my maintenance payments and in danger of going to jail, and I owed small sums of money to people all over London, which made walking the streets in broad daylight dangerous for me. I was forever seeing one of my creditors coming and dashing across the other side of the road to avoid them. How I never got run over in that period I don't know.

Came the day and I was ushered into the magnificent office

of Mr Lennard, who turned out to be a very pleasant middle-aged man with a sympathetic smile. He obviously wanted to help me and so I sat there with bated breath listening to what he was going to do for me, and this is what he did. He said that this was a very tough business, which came as no surprise to me, and then he proceeded to say that he had a son who was a little older than I was but looked a lot like me. 'My son is an accountant,' he said, 'and he has more chance of success in this business than you do.' I sat there quite numb but smiling. He went on, 'This may sound unkind, but you will thank me in the long run. I know this business well and I can assure you that you have no future in it. Give it up, Michael.'

I stood up, still smiling, and said, 'Thank you for the advice, Mr Lennard,' and left. I have said that I was an angry young man, but now I was furious – and instead of driving me from the business it made me even more determined to succeed. Neither the studio nor he still exist as a going concern, but in gratitude for that piece of advice I would just like to point out Mr Lennard's own track record as a talent spotter. The actors that he had under contract as potential star material were called Vernon Gray, David Knight and Gary Raymond, to name but three people you've never heard of today. This was at a time when Peter O'Toole, Albert Finney, Sean Connery, Richard Harris, Terence Stamp and of course myself were all out of work and available. The moral of this little tale is good for everybody, not just show people, and it is this: if you want to do something with your life, never listen to anybody else, no matter how clever or expert they may appear. Keep your eyes open and your ears shut, and as the Americans say – 'Go for it.'

The other great sadness in my life at this time was the fact that as I grew ever more destitute, I did not have the fare to go and see Dominique. This was a double-edged sadness for me, not only because I missed seeing her so much but my mother and father-in-law began to think that I no longer cared. They could not understand that anyone could have so little money as to be unable to afford a train fare.

Every now and then I did get a job, which didn't improve

my standard of living but allowed me to pay off my debts to the more belligerent and larger of my creditors.

I did the television version of *The Caine Mutiny Court Martial*, and caught up with Sean Connery again in the television play of *Requiem for a Heavyweight*. Sean had the lead in this while I had only a small part. This started a new anxiety for me; my contemporaries were forging ahead and I was still making no real progress. This point was brought home to me again when I was given the part of a policeman in a film *The Day the Earth Caught Fire*. The star of this was my old friend Eddie Judd. Not only was I in deep despair, panic began to settle in. Was I being left behind? These guys had started out at the same time as me, and were beginning to accomplish so much. Perhaps I was really useless after all. I did not feel jealousy at their success, just fear at my own inadequacies. It was all fine while we were all in trouble together, but now I started to feel increasingly isolated. I completely screwed up my part in *The Day the Earth Caught Fire* and was told by the director that I would never work in this industry again. I didn't tell him how close I had come to that situation already, without his help.

Sex and booze are a great antedote to despair, and during this period I am afraid I overdosed on both from time to time. There was a limit to the amount of damage I could do to myself with booze, since for a lot of the time I just didn't have the money for it, but sex, like the best things in life, was free. I did fall madly in love during this period. I will not mention her name for reasons that I will give later, but I just wanted to let her know that she has not been forgotten, and that if she does not want to be in this book she isn't, so she has got it both ways. I am not sure that she will buy this book, but I know that she will read it. Only you know who you are, and your secret is safe with me.

Just one final piece of humiliation before we leave this terrible period. I was sent to audition for a film, and it turned out to be the shortest audition that I, or probably any actor, ever did. I waited outside the casting director's door for my turn on this particular day, along with a lot of other actors; we had to wait because he was late. The list was in alphabetical order so, being called Caine, I was asked in first. By the way, if you're going to be an actor, choose a surname starting with a letter as near to the front of the alphabet as possible. That way, if you are ever in an all-star cast, with billing in alphabetical order, your name will be at the top of the list. Anyway, when my name was called I got up, opened the office door, was just about to say a polite 'Good morning,' when the casting director shouted, 'Next!' and I was shoved out again by an assistant. I couldn't imagine what I had done wrong. I told the secretary what had happened and she explained it all to me. On the other side of the door as you went in was a mark. The star of the film was Alan Ladd, who was not very tall – and if you entered the room and were above the mark, you were automatically disqualified. So that was it. My luck was definitely out, as usual.

My career finally took off again with a play called *One More River*, which Sam Wanamaker's theatre company was going to do in a theatre up in Liverpool. Robert Shaw was in the cast, as were several other actors that I knew and liked very much – Dudley Foster, Dudley Sutton and Brian Pringle; like me they all enjoyed a drink and female company. The play wasn't a success but it got me out of London for a couple of months, gave me a bit of money, put me back on stage again after a long absence, and restored my own confidence in my ability – if nobody else's. I really liked the city and the Liverpudlians – they were poor, tough and cheerful, similar in a way to my own people.

Liverpool also gave us the first real clue to the fact that the sixties were coming, but we didn't spot it. One day we were rehearsing and when we broke for lunch, instead of having sandwiches in the bar we decided to go out and find a coffee bar and eat there. We walked around for a while looking for a good place and as we walked we started to hear music. We followed our ears and eventually arrived at a coffee bar where there was a small group playing. We thought of going in and eating there, but when we went inside the place was stuffed to the ceiling with teenage girls, so we decided to find somewhere quieter. The band was causing a riot and when we asked what they were called we were told 'The Beatles'.

Not bad, I thought, as the music faded and we travelled on in search of a sandwich.

Another small preview of the explosion of talent that was about to form part of the sixties phenomenon happened one afternoon when we had already opened the play. As there was no matinée, we all decided to go and see Charles Laughton in what I think was *The Birthday Party*. It was on tour prior to opening in the West End of London, and it marked Laughton's return to the British theatre after many years in Hollywood. He was of course, a favourite actor of all actors; some are like that – there are a lot of actors that other actors adore and the public don't know them at all. The supreme example of this was Wilfred Lawson. Never heard of him? That's OK. Every British actor has. Anyway, the entire cast of *One More River* turned up for the matinée and we all sat back to enjoy Charles Laughton, but it didn't happen that way. We enjoyed the show all right, but the reason was a young actor we had never heard of, who came on and acted Laughton right off the stage. Until that time, anybody would have told you this was impossible, but that young unknown did it. His name was Albert Finney, and he was the son of a north country bookie. Finney took the biggest gamble of his life by acting opposite Laughton. Like all bookies, he won.

Although my career did not go zooming into the stratosphere on our return to London, I did get quite a lot of television. I did another *Dixon of Dock Green*, and an episode of a series called *Mark Saber*. Another popular series called *No Hiding Place* gave me my next job, and then I appeared in a play called *The Frog* by Edgar Wallace. The parts were getting bigger and therefore better paid, so although it does not seem like a lot of work, it did manage to keep me going. In 1959 I was offered the job of understudy to a new actor I had never heard of in a play called *The Long and the Short and the Tall* by Willis Hall. This was a play about the British army fighting the Japanese in the jungle in the Second World War, and I was to understudy the role of Private Bamforth – one of the two leading roles. Not only was the play destined for the West End, but it offered regular money and the chance to stay in London, where the job prospects were. It was also going to be directed by someone I very much admired called Lindsay Anderson. The play had been written for Albert Finney, but he had an appendicitis attack during rehearsal so the part was taken over by an actor called Peter O'Toole. It was an all-male cast and two of my old friends were in it, Robert Shaw and Eddie Judd, and a new friend, Richard Harris.

The play opened and was an instant smash mainly due to the great cast, especially O'Toole. His performance was magnificent and nearly caused me to have a nervous break-down during the course of the run. As his understudy I knew the lines, but I also knew that I could never go on in that part and come even close to his performance, so I used to pray every day that nothing would happen to him. At that time we were all great drunks, but Peter was the worst of us all. He was never actually drunk on stage but he often used to turn up at the last possible minute, with me standing there dressed to go on and shaking in my boots. He never ever missed a performance, but I almost had a heart attack some evenings. Once, he even came in as the curtain was about to go up one evening and shouted at me, 'Don't go on!' as he ran along the corridor to his dressing room, taking his shirt and trousers off as he ran.

Considering that I never actually performed in that show, it's amazing that I wound up absolutely exhausted. My main function was to bring in the booze, and find the parties – at which I became an expert. Saturday nights after the show was always a dangerous time, and I quickly learned not to string along with Peter after my first Saturday night out with him. He asked me if I wanted to come to a party that he had found on his own and I foolishly said yes. My previous experience with Peter was to start his evening off, and then duck out. Anyway, after the show on that particular Saturday night, we were just about to set off when he suggested that we go into a fast food place in Leicester Square called the Golden Egg, and have something to eat. This for a start was a surprise because I had never seen Peter actually eat anything. I thought he was one of those people who could get protein from alcohol. I don't say this as a criticism of him, since I drank as often as he did but I used to pass out in my efforts to keep him company. So off we went to the Golden Egg, ordered a plate of eggs and bacon and toast, and that was the last I remembered until I woke up in broad daylight in a strange flat, lying next to Peter, fully-clothed including overcoats. Peter was already awake, staring with glazed eyes at something fascinating on the ceiling that I could not make out.

'What time is it?' I asked.

Peter was much more experienced at this sort of thing than I was, so he knew the relevant question. 'Never mind what time it is, what fucking *day* is it?'

We located our hostesses, who turned out to be two very dodgy-looking girls whose knowing looks stopped us from asking any leading questions like – what happened? Neither of us wanted to know. We were then informed that it was Monday afternoon and five o'clock. The curtain went up at eight. We asked where we were and they told us. Neither Peter nor I had ever heard of the place so we did not know how far we were from the theatre. We quickly ascertained that we were at least in London, and set off for work. When we arrived we were met by our stage director, who informed us that the manager of the Golden Egg had dropped by; henceforward we were banned from that establishment for life. I was just about to ask what we had done, when Peter whispered, 'Never ask what you did, it's better not to know.' So I kept quiet and I never went out alone with Peter again. As a matter of fact he never asked me – probably thought I was a bad influence.

145

12

Raw steaks through the letter-box

While Peter O'Toole became a big star and went off to make *Lawrence of Arabia*, I stayed behind and went out on tour in his role in *The Long and the Short and the Tall* for the next few months. This was great experience for me. Bamforth was a wonderful part and we had a terrific new director called Antony Page who had been Lindsay's assistant on the first production. We toured all over England, Scotland and Ireland and I learned so much, especially from a marvellous actor called Frank Finlay, who played the other male lead in the play. Frank never became a movie star so is not as widely known as he might be. However, when he played Iago to Laurence Olivier's Othello in the theatre, he almost stole the show from him – that is the calibre of actor he is. Also in the cast was a shy but very good-looking young actor called Terence Stamp, who came from the same background as me. We hit it off immediately and became firm friends for many years. In a way he reminded me of my younger self, and I think for him I was a sort of a father figure. In the first of his autobiographical volumes, *Coming Attractions** he described me as his first guru, and that is probably what I was. Right from the start I took him under my wing and trained him in the first two principles of touring at that time. One was that when you get to a new town, always grab your room in the boarding house first before the best ones go and two, check the local newspapers and see if a show called *The Dancing Years* is also in town. This was a very camp old-fashioned show by Ivor Novello that seemed to be permanently on tour.

* Bloomsbury, 1988.

In this story, which is set in Ruritania, there are at least a dozen village maidens, and a dozen village men. The attraction of the show lay in the title by which it was known on the touring circuit: *The Dancing Queers*. Most of the men in the show, for some reason, seemed to be gay – and this left a great many village maidens at a loose, sometimes very loose end. I imagine that gay actors had a similar interest in the whereabouts of the show.

Playing the lead role in a really good play alongside first-class actors gave me back my self-respect. And there is nothing like the nightly grind of a long tour to improve your handling of very different and unpredictable audiences. It was my happiest and most valuable experience to date, and I identify it as my first step towards becoming a star.

On my return to London after four months away, I had to find a new place to live. Terry Stamp said there was a room available in a flat he was sharing with ten other guys in Harley Street, a very expensive area but affordable because there were so many sharing. As I discovered when I moved in, there were twenty-three rooms in all, so nobody got in anybody's way.

After the tour I fell on my accustomed hard times again, but this didn't bother me over-much since I was used to it, after all. There was, however, a very traumatic experience in store for me that shook me out of my normal cavalier attitude towards poverty. I was lying asleep in my room in the Harley Street flat at about eight o'clock in the morning, which is the equivalent of dawn for an unemployed actor, when I was awoken by a very rough shaking. When I got my eyes open and the blinds of yesterday's alcohol slid apart, I could see two very burly middle-aged men in old-fashioned suits standing there. Alarm bells went off in my mind. One of them said, 'Mr Maurice Joseph Micklewhite?'

The alarm bell quickly changed to a toll of certain doom. Nobody in the business knew that name – it's not something that you boast about. 'Yes,' I answered sincerely. This might be the only truthful answer I was going to give to these two.

'We are police officers. You are under arrest for the non-payment of maintenance to Patricia and Dominique Micklewhite. Would you please get dressed and come with us.'

I did this and accompanied them to Marlborough Street Magistrates' Court, which is just behind the London Palladium but not as much fun. They did not have a car, they explained. It was such a nice day they thought it would do them good to walk. As we strolled along I asked them how they had got into my bedroom and who had told them which one of all of us in the flat was me. 'A Mr Stamp was very helpful,' was the cheery reply. That was a point I had forgotten to make in Terry's education: *never* tell a stranger where anybody you know is. The risks were immense. I would have to straighten him out as soon as possible. The policemen were very sympathetic. They knew I had no money and could see the conditions in which I was living.

'Would you like some breakfast, son?' the oldest one asked. I was starving, I hadn't eaten anything in the last twenty-four hours. I had drunk a lot, but it wasn't the same. I told him that I would, and they treated me to a real English breakfast, the best meal I had eaten for at least a month.

After this, I was taken into the bowels of the court and put into a cell and told that I would be brought up to face charges later. I found myself sharing with a man whom I would have told the police to avoid. He was taken up to the court after about fifteen minutes, and I was very glad to see him go. He had not spoken but I had a crick in my neck where my head had been in one position for the whole time he was with me, for fear of taking my eyes off him for even a second. I sat there for a while, listening to the noises from the other cells. There is an old saying in criminal circles: 'If you can't do your time, don't do the crime.' I would never be a criminal, I decided. I was starting to break up after three hours. The whole place stank of disinfectant and every sound was harsh. There was one guy, still drunk, who sang *Nellie Dean* over and over, accompanied by loud mumblings from someone who was obviously mentally disturbed, angry curses at the warders, the police and the world in general, with the occasional comic relief of an ear-shattering fart followed by hysterical cheers and laughter. I did not join in; they were going to have to do better than that to get a laugh out of me today. Eventually the slot in my cell door rattled and a little round metal protruberance in the middle of it opened and there was a hot cup of tea and a piece of very nice cake. I heard the warder say, 'Your morning coffee, sunshine.' Just what I needed – a cup of tea to cheer me up. It's true what they say about English people, a cup of tea does help us to face disaster. After a while the warder shouted out that there was one piece of cake left over and who wanted it? Immediately there were yells of, 'I'll have it!' from all the other cells. I sat there and thought, 'Stuff your extra bit of cake,' and refused to belittle myself by screaming for it.

Just then, the slit in my cell door opened again and the warder said, 'Are you an actor?' I told him that I was. 'Were you in *Dixon of Dock Green* the other night?' he asked. 'Yes,' I answered. I knew it was a big favourite with the police force because it showed them in a very good light. He slid a plate with the extra piece of cake on it through my slot and walked away without saying a word.

Late in the afternoon I was brought up before the magistrate and faced my accusations, and Pat and her lawyer. The case was made against me and the judge made the mistake of asking me if I could see any reason why he should not send me to prison. I had been very nervous until I was put in the box on my own and looked around and saw that the court was full of people. I had an audience, so I decided to give an impassioned plea and throw myself on his mercy. I had a vague recollection of a film that I had seen where this ploy had worked. I already had the sympathy of the court, I felt. Pat, as I have already said, was a great-looking woman and in high heels stood six feet tall. She had obviously been earning good money because her clothes looked expensive and like all actresses appearing in court she had dressed and made up to the hilt. In short she looked blooming and prosperous. I on the other hand was dressed in shabby clothes, not made any smarter by the fact that I had slept in them for a couple of hours while I was incarcerated below. I was very thin and looked pretty unhealthy, mainly due to a hangover which was killing me. Pat had made the biggest mistake of all in that she was wearing a brand new fur coat. I gave my plea, pointing out that if I went to prison I would not be able to pay anyway, so it was best to set me free. I had done two *Dixon of Dock Greens*, I mentioned, hoping that this would have the same effect as the cake incident, and sure enough all the representatives of the law visibly warmed towards me, so I invented a non-existent episode of this show that I would be getting shortly if I was free. I was halfway through my performance, which had lasted about twenty-five minutes, when the magistrate put a stop to it by yelling at the top of his voice, '*Shut up!*' I was told later that it was the third time he had done so.

'How much do you have in your pockets?' he asked. I turned them out. I had three pounds ten shillings. They took that away and then he said, 'You are ordered to pay three pounds ten shillings per week maintenance and if you come back here again for this offence I will send you to prison. Case dismissed.'

I was a free man. I smiled at Pat as I left and she rather surprisingly smiled back. She remarried, to an actor unknown to me who, I was once told by a friend of hers, 'Earns a bloody sight more money than you ever did' which was very nice for him, but not very difficult to do, I thought. Most prisoners sewing mail-bags in Dartmoor earned more money than I did. The outcome was a success for me but now I had more than burning ambition motivating me to become a success. If I did not, I would go to prison. I never saw Pat again. I am sorry to say she died of cancer in 1977.

The year was 1960 and after a rocky start things were beginning to move for me: financially, it was my best year so far. Right at the end of it I did a little job for a BBC book programme in which they dramatised a section of the book under discussion and I played a small part in it. Not exactly an earth-shattering job, but I did meet the director, a lovely guy called John McGrath who became a good friend. I had many much-needed quiet domestic evenings and good hearty dinners with him and his wife Liz McLennan at their flat in Earl's Court.

During this year I made contact with another figure whose star was about to rise. He was an actor whom I knew vaguely called David Baron, who had decided to give up acting and make playwriting his career. David Baron was only a stage name, he told me. As a playwright he was going to use his real name – Harold Pinter. The play in which I appeared was a one-act piece called *The Room* put on at the Royal Court Theatre in London along with another one-act play called *The Dumb Waiter*. My play was a very serious piece and rather obscure. As a matter of fact I did not understand a word of it, but just knew that it was good without having the faintest idea why. I took my problem to Harold one day and asked him what the play was about. His reply did not solve any of my artistic problems but it did put a damper on any further enquiries. His reply was, and I quote: 'How the fucking hell should I know?' I decided to accept this explanation at face value and just try to remember the lines and not trip over the furniture. I still think that Harold is a brilliant writer – and I still do not know why. If you ever get a chance to see *The Dumb Waiter*, don't miss it. It is one of the funniest plays I have ever seen. Don't ask me why – and, for that matter, don't ask Harold.

As my earnings were quite reasonable at that time and Terry was doing quite well too, we decided that by pooling our resources we could afford to move out of Harley Street, where many of the other rooms had been discovered by impoverished artists of all kinds. It had become much more like the YMCA without the swimming pool. The house that we chose was a small one in Ennismore Garden Mews, just behind Knightsbridge tube station near Harrods. Unfortunately, it only had one bedroom, which created a problem right at the start. What if by chance a young lady should fall victim to our charm and want to pursue that descent to the bedroom? We solved this problem by practising grabbing the mattress and bedclothes to see how fast we could move them on to the front room floor. By the end of the session we had got the time down to five seconds and managed to do it without unmaking the bed.

We soon settled in and life went on as normal, except that

as the rent of the flat was rather high, we suddenly found ourselves slightly more broke than usual. Food became a problem for a while, until I found a recipe for egg custard in a newspaper. The ingredients were cheap and nutritious, and it tasted great. So it was I found a new interest in and talent for cooking, which has by now developed into a passion. Terry's looks and charm paid dividends on the food front as well. He was having an affair with a beautiful and rich young neighbour, who somehow got wind of our financial plight, probably because he told her, and would put raw steaks through our letter-box in case Terry was too embarrassed to accept her generous charity. She had obviously misjudged him badly. So for weeks we lived mainly on egg custard and steak, a high-cholesterol diet that could have felled an elephant. We, however, didn't know about cholesterol so at least it did no psychological harm and in Terry's case, his love life was now taking off to such an extent that he probably ended up with a cholesterol deficiency anyway.

It was around this time that I scraped together enough money to go to Paris for the weekend with a young French model I had met in London. She had a flat there so all I had to pay was my fare. I was really excited at the prospect of returning to Paris while apprehensive that it might not live up to my original impressions. I need not have worried; it was better than I ever remembered, not surprising considering my change of circumstances from the first time.

My girlfriend of course knew Paris very well, but on the Saturday night, when she said we would be going to a nightclub, my heart sank. I did not have that kind of money. A nightclub for me was a place where you went to eat bad food, listen to a third-rate band and watch half a dozen very dodgy ladies who could almost dance, all this accompanied by bad service from snotty waiters in the company of people you would not want to meet in the daylight, and for these privileges you paid a fortune. I voiced my fears but she promised that it was a new kind of nightclub, and that I should wait and see. Off we went to the Boulevard Montparnasse, where we ate cheaply and well in an enormous café called La Coupole that I loved so much I tried to copy it at Langan's, my own restaurant in London many years later. It was bustling, loud, bright and fun. I had never seen so many beautiful and interesting-looking people in one place at any time and I could have stayed there all night, which was just as well because my companion assured me that there was no point in getting to the club before midnight. This of course sounded absurd to me, coming from London where some establishments had reached the heights of debauchery by closing at midnight. I obviously had a lot to learn and so did London, still does as a matter of fact compared with continental cities.

Eventually midnight came and off we set for this new adventure. The club was just a short walk along the boulevard and you could hear it before you could see it, with some really great music. There was a crowd milling around on the pavement trying to get in, a bad sign, I thought. If it was this popular the prices were going to be sky-high. When we got there it looked like any other old-fashioned nightclub I had seen behind its big neon sign that said *Jimmy's*. Yet the people, who were young, were dressed casually – not at all like the clientèle in London who were always middle-aged and strictly dressed as I was with a suit and a tie. I immediately felt out of place and took off my tie and put it in my pocket. I thought we might have trouble getting in with such a crowd, but my friend seemed to know everybody and we were ushered inside. The scene was madness, the music deafening but I could not see the band. When I asked where it was she laughed and pointed to a platform where a guy was playing records. I cheered up a bit – at least we did not have to pay for the band, and then I saw in the dim light the dancing. It was like nothing that I had seen before; the people weren't holding each other, were just gyrating in a frenzy opposite each other. The place was jam-packed and you had to shout to be heard above the music but I got an immediate buzz from the fantastic atmosphere and was hooked on this kind of club, whatever it was.

I was introduced to the owner, who was called Régine, and I asked her why the place was not called *Régine's*. She told me that she had bought the club off a man named Jimmy and she did not have enough money before she opened to change the sign. I told her that I was glad she had not got a band, because with them you only got a third-rate cover version of the popular songs of the moment, but with records you actually got the real song and artist. I complimented her on the idea. She laughed and told me that she had wanted a band, but did not have enough money for that either, so she had to settle for records. She said that she just wanted a nightclub, had taken what she could afford and this was it. She seemed as surprised by its success as the rest of the world would eventually be.

'It's a great nightclub,' I told her.

'It is not a nightclub, it is a discothèque,' she replied. Now I had heard of the cinémathèque, which was a museum of the cinema in Paris, but this certainly wasn't a museum of any kind, and I had heard of a bibliothèque and this was certainly not a library. I mentioned that and she said it was from those words and the French word for records – 'disques' – that she got the name. So there I was for the first time in a discothèque. There were none in London as yet, but I was sure that soon there would be.

Back in London, Christmas came and went and we were into 1961. Terry and I made a pact at the beginning of this year. Because our profession was so unpredictable and we never knew who was going to be making any money, we promised each other that whichever one of us was working, if the other one could not pay his share of the rent, the one with the money would cough up. We shook hands on the deal, a sign of the true bond and depth of our friendship, and that is how it remained until we eventually made enough money for flats of our own.

The year started with a bang. I was in a television play called *Ring of Truth* and then went straight into the two-week run of a play which was written by my new friend John McGrath. It was called *Why the Chicken?* Don't ask *me* why! I was not playing the lead but had taken the part because Terry was appearing in his first lead part at this time and I felt it might be a good idea to be around. The director of *Why the Chicken?* was Lionel Bart, a friend and the composer of the massive musical hit *Oliver*. I had auditioned for the part of Bill

154

Sykes in *Oliver* and failed to get it, which made me heart-broken at the time. It was a part I felt sure I could do well, one that was just right for me. Not getting it was one of the biggest disappointments of my career, especially as the show was destined to run for six years. I could have had a good living with no worries for all that time. Anyway, I was desolate. It was still on six years later, when I drove past the theatre in my own Rolls Royce, a brand new millionaire and a star not only in England but in America as well, where *Alfie* had just come out. I happened to look up as we slowed down in the traffic outside the theatre and could see on the billboard the name of the actor who had got the part instead of me. He was still in the show, and I shuddered at the thought that it could have been my name there, for then none of the great things that had happened to me in the intervening years would have come about.

As it turned out, Terry was fine and didn't need me but the play did have one very significant consequence that happened by accident, really. I got to know John McGrath even better and somehow I was in his office and he pointed to a script on his desk that he said was going to be his next television show. At this point he went out of the room for some reason and I picked up the play and started to read through it. It was not only good, a tense psycho-drama, but it was dead right for me. It was called *The Compartment* and was about two men in a railway carriage on a journey. One is a middle-class snob and the other a vulgar Cockney. No prizes for guessing my part. During the trip the Cockney tries to talk to the other man but because of the class difference the man will not respond. The Cockney eventually goes mad with frustration and anger, and tries to kill him. It was only a forty-five minute play, but it was a great part because it was basically a monologue with the other actor only speaking at the end when he pleads for his life. Here was something that would be the making of me as an actor on television, and I was so right for it. I was a Cockney, I had become an actor so I was more than likely insane myself and I hated the class system in this country – and here was my chance to have a swipe at it.

The writer Johnny Speight was to become famous as the

creator of the television series *Till Death Do Us Part*, a comedy and a tremendous hit, later adapted in America as *All in the Family*. *The Compartment* was his first attempt at drama. In the few minutes that I had to look at this short piece I knew that it was very powerful. John came back into the office and I confessed that I had been peeking at the script while he was gone and begged him for the part. I had never played a lead this big or as difficult on television before, but somehow he got his superiors at the BBC to agree. My old friend from the tour of *The Long and the Short and the Tall* Frank Finlay played the other part, so I had all the help I could want. The play was very well received; as far as I was concerned, it proved that I could carry a show and it brought me to the attention of all sorts of people and this was to be of great benefit later on. *The Compartment* also proved that I could remember forty-five minutes of solid dialogue – no mean feat when you consider that not only this play but all the others I had done on television went out live. We did have a lady with a script who followed the actors who were speaking at the time all over the set; if you forgot a line, she had a button in her hand which she would press to cut the sound on transmission and during the silence she would give you your line. I only used this method once, and it was the nearest I ever got to abject terror. It was rather like being a tight-rope walker and somebody telling you that your shoelaces are undone.

The most satisfying and beneficial sign that the play and I were a success came a little while after it was broadcast. Terry and I were walking along Piccadilly when we saw Roger Moore on the other side of the road. He was already famous in England for the series *Ivanhoe*, and just like anybody else we were thrilled to see someone famous in the flesh; we were standing there gawping at him when he spotted us and came across the road. We both wondered who he had seen and were looking around to see if there was somebody else behind us, but no, he was walking towards us and he was smiling straight at me. I smiled back nervously and he stopped right in front of me and said: 'Is your name Michael Caine?' I told him that it was. 'I saw you in the television play *The Compartment*,' he went on. 'I just want to tell you that you are going to be a big star.' He shook my hand and walked away, leaving me stunned and delighted. It was the biggest compliment that I'd had since Dennis Price wrote to me.

After thirty years of friendship, I can still count the differences between us on one hand, several of which were apparent that first time we met. He was famous, handsome, elegant and generous; I was obscure, ugly, scruffy and mean. I've caught up with him since on at least two counts. And two out of four's not bad.

That year, 1961, I did five major parts on television thanks to *The Compartment* and although it did not make me rich it did improve my standard of living. I was in a play by Troy Kennedy Martin, who later wrote the film *The Italian Job*, and I also did a play called *Somewhere for the Night* by Bill Naughton who, although it would not be for four more years, was to write the most important film in my life or any other actor's life – the one that makes him a star.

13

The first screen test

I have always disliked what is called the 'Kiss and Tell' type of
autobiography. Firstly because I have been the victim of
several, and have always felt in some way betrayed, and
secondly because if you are a man and the book is by a woman,
there is invariably an assessment of your sexual prowess.
While I am not afraid of this, I have a professional aversion to
being reviewed, no matter how favourably, for a performance
for which I was not paid. Especially when the critic was in the
show.

In writing this book I have been through a lot of old press
cuttings and have noticed that, invariably, the women who are
mentioned most were the least important in my past. Those
who mattered more are mentioned less often, while the
names of those 'special few' do not appear at all. The one
contradiction to all this is of course my wife Shakira. There at
last they got it right, for she is the most important woman in
my life ever, by a long long long way.

My last word on this subject is an absolutely true, but
cautionary tale, to all you ladies contemplating telling all. I
have a middle-aged friend who hates these revelations even
more than I do. Incredibly wealthy – he has twenty million or
more pounds in the bank – he has made a will in which he has
left a million pounds each to twenty ladies with whom he has
had satisfactory relationships in his long past. There is one
proviso: they never write or sell a kiss and tell article or book
mentioning his name. The catch is that he has not informed
any of them of this proviso. So far, two of his ex-ladies have
written about their affair with him and unknowingly forfeited
their million pounds. So 'Tell All' women beware! And any

158

lady who has known me in the Biblical sense can relax and read on – your secret is safe with me. I was once asked in an interview: 'How would you sum up your life in one line?' and I answered, 'All my dreams came true.' When I was young I used to dream a lot about female movie stars . . . and I shall offer no more clues.

The sixties had arrived in London. The Beatles were playing endlessly on the radio, the Rolling Stones were gathering fans and David Bailey was taking pictures of what he called 'dolly birds'. This particular breed was brand new and all of a sudden more numerous than the London sparrow. All at once it seemed that every pretty girl with no tits was modelling clothes and every pretty girl with big tits was modelling those. Mary Quant invented the mini skirt and every girl, pretty or not, was modelling legs. Brassières were discarded as breasts jiggled under blouses, but panties were retained as skirts rose higher to prove it. Eyes shone, teeth flashed and thighs gleamed. Cafés started opening up on the King's Road in Chelsea and we watched the weekend parade as we sat at our tables out on the pavement for the first time in London. The sixties were here at last – and the sun seemed to shine on London for the first time since the end of the war.

When Terry got the starring role in Peter Ustinov's film version of *Billy Budd*, we finally had enough money to move into a two-bedroomed flat in Ebury Street, and my mattress-moving skills became redundant forever. However I had to develop a new and much more difficult skill. *Billy Budd* not only brought Terry money, it brought him fame – and for the first time I saw what an irresistible aphrodisiac these two can be when combined. As I have said, Terry was a great-looking guy with no shortage of women but now the succession of individual dolly birds turned into a flock and I was the flight controller. Getting them in and out of the very busy airfield that our flat had become, without collision, meant keeping them on a very narrow and definite flight-path. I would give them coffee in the kitchen until I heard the front door slam as a signal that there was a runway free. Then tea in the lounge until I heard the bedroom window slam shut; it had been

159

opened to let the aroma of an alien perfume escape before a hangar was free. Incoming birds were not my only responsibility. Trouble-free take-offs had to be taken care of, careful guiding to runway two, the back door as incoming flights were delayed and imminent disaster threatened at the front door. Occasionally I had to take the role of hawk as birds unexpected and not 'dolly' threatened the smooth running of the whole operation. The job, though stressful, was not without its compensations as the odd damsel in distress was guided as an emergency on to my own private runway, bedroom two. Terry had bedroom one because, true to the deal we'd once struck, when I could not pay my now very substantial share of the rent he paid it for me and did so for a long time without any comment, before or since. A true if exhausting friend.

The sixties were characterised not only by certain clothes and a particular frame of mind, they were also very much a question of rendezvous.

The first restaurant to become the 'in' place to go in the sixties was the Pickwick in Great Newport Street, almost opposite the Arts Theatre and next door to Raj's drinking club. It was a club-cum-restaurant, and one of the people who started it was Leslie Bricusse, the composer of the musical *Pickwick* who later wrote the musical *Stop the World I Want to Get Off* with Anthony Newley. I met Leslie and liked him and his wife Evie right from the start, and they soon joined my very small circle of close and permanent friends. Another couple I met there were Bryan Forbes and Nanette Newman, two more friends from that same circle. Bryan had been an actor, but had given it up to direct and write. The Pickwick was comfortable and fun. It had no dress code, but did have a membership so that made it rather cliquey, which was no bad thing if you were part of the clique. It always seemed to be full of talented and beautiful people. Terry and I of course loved it. We now had a brand new place where we could dance, and one where we could eat.

When *Billy Budd* was released Terry was hailed as a new star, and all hell would have broken loose but for the fact that it already had, so the pandemonium stayed the same. He immediately got another film, *Term of Trial* and we were set for 1963, which was just as well because I did nothing of particular note that year except for one and very poorly paid job in the theatre, which was, however, to change my life dramatically.

Terry went off to Ireland, the airfield closed down except for the occasional flight of my own, and I settled down to a bit of peace and quiet. I now had a new agent called Dennis Selinger who had taken me on after seeing *The Compartment*. He was the biggest agent in England and I was a bit afraid that I was out of my class there, but he was very good with me and unlike most agents who are very greedy, he guided my career to the best work rather than the best paid. This was great for my reputation but not so good for my finances, although Terry was still paying my rent and slipping me the odd fifty pounds. Dennis and I hit it off right from the start and we are still friends to this day.

Despite our rapport, though, I still had not got a big job from Dennis and the next one he offered did little to inspire confidence either. He sent me a play from a producer called Michael Codron, a man of great taste and courage, and someone I already knew. I had done my small bit with Terry in *Why the Chicken?* for him. The play in question was *Next Time I'll Sing to You* by James Saunders. It was destined to be an artistic success, no doubt about it – so in other words there was no money in it. The deal was seven pounds a week for two weeks' rehearsal, and twenty pounds per week for the run, which I thought would be short. It opened at my old stamping ground the Arts Theatre. I won't tell you what it was about because I can't. This play made Harold Pinter's work look like *The Dancing Years* and it was ably directed by an American woman called Shirley Butler.

I argued with Dennis about doing this show, as I was afraid to miss a chance of getting a movie, but I need not have worried. The play opened and was a big hit with the critics although the audiences were on the sparse side. However we managed to stay open for long enough for word to get around, and we eventually became such a success that our wages were

161

doubled and we transferred to the Criterion Theatre in Piccadilly. There I was in the West End at last! I was thirty years old. The play was a great 'succès d'estime' and attracted a very select crowd. The first person to come back to my dressing room and congratulate me was Orson Welles. I later found out this was typical of Orson – he was very generous to other artists. Rita Hayworth, for instance, but for different reasons. Orson offered me a part in the film of the book *The Bible*. I think I was supposed to play Esau, who was 'an hairy man' which I was not, so I was still in the stages of worrying about how uncomfortable a chest wig would be when I was told that Orson was out and John Huston was going to direct, with Richard Harris playing my part, obviously being 'an hairier man' than I was.

While Terry was away his younger brother Chris moved in with me and I took him under my wing. He was a very gauche, shy boy of nineteen and needed showing the ropes as Terry had put it, so I took him out and started him off on what I thought would be a short-lived bit of fun before he went back to the East End and an ordinary job. However, Chris thrived in the heady atmosphere of the time and eventually found his own niche; his ambition, he had decided, was to be a rock and roll manager. I made encouraging sounds and sent him off fully qualified for a fruitless quest. A few weeks later I met him and asked how it was going, and he told me that he and his partner had found a rock and roll group playing in a pub and were going to manage them. The name of the group, he said, was The Who. That's how it was in those days. Everybody seemed to become famous. Sean was James Bond; O'Toole was Lawrence of Arabia; Richard Harris was starring in films; Tom Courtney had been successful in both films and theatre; Albert Finney was a stage star and even my own flatmate was a star, and to top it all, his little brother had hit the big time with The Who.

One night at the end of a performance of *Next Time I'll Sing to You* Stanley Baker, with whom I had worked all those years ago in *A Hill in Korea*, came backstage to visit me in my dressing room. By now he was one of the biggest stars in the British cinema and I was very flattered by this. He was very nice about my performance. In the show I played a Cockney comic character and Stanley explained that he was starring in and producing a film called *Zulu*, in which there was a Cockney character. If I was interested in trying for the part, I'd have to go and see Cy Endfield in the bar of the Prince of Wales' Theatre at ten o'clock the next morning. This I very quickly agreed to do and he left, wishing me luck.

At ten o'clock sharp the next morning I arrived at the theatre bar and found Cy Endfield sitting there alone. He was a tubby, slow-speaking, slow-moving, middle-aged American. As he stood up and shook hands, his first words were: 'I am sorry to have wasted your time, Michael, but we have already given the part to James Booth. We figured that he looked more Cockney than you do.' I knew Jimmy Booth, who was a very good actor and I had to agree, he did look more Cockney than me – very tough indeed. This was a terrible disappointment and the rejection would have floored me at one time but I had suffered so much of it, I just went into my current defence, which was numb mode. 'Sorry kid,' he said. 'That's OK,' I smiled. 'Maybe next time.' He smiled back. 'Yeah, maybe next time, kid.' I turned and walked out.

The bar was very long and I could not wait to reach the door and get out of there, away from yet another humiliation. I opened the swing door and was just about to disappear when Cy shouted, 'Michael, come back here!' I walked back across the room and stood in front of Cy, waiting for the man to speak. I certainly had nothing more to say. 'Can you use any other accent but Cockney?' he asked.

'When I was in rep, I was doing fifty plays a year,' I told him, 'using every accent from American gangsters to a Lord of the Manor. I can do any accent you want.'

'Can you do upper-crust English?' he probed.

'That's the easiest one of all,' I shrugged, hoping desperately that I could remember how to do it.

Cy stared at me for a while and then he said, 'You know, you don't look like a Cockney. You look like one of those snotty blue-blooded English guys.'

My thoughts raced. Was this a compliment or an insult? Was there something behind what he was saying? What the fuck was he talking about, anyhow? I looked in the mirror behind the bar; maybe he was right, I thought. I was six feet two inches tall, very slim with long blond hair and blue eyes. Yes, I was nobody's idea of a typical Cockney.

'In this movie,' Cy remarked, interrupting my thoughts, 'there is a character called Gonville Bromhead. He is a very snobbish and aristocratic lieutenant who thinks that he is superior to everybody, especially the character played by Stanley – who will be here in a minute,' he added. 'Would you mind waiting and reading the part with him?' I agreed to this instantly and afterwards stood there feigning disinterest while they huddled in a corner and discussed my suitability. Finally they turned to me and Cy said, 'Can you do a screen test with Stanley on Friday morning?' Of course I agreed. At last I had got what I always wanted, a screen test!

I walked out of the bar again but this time with an almighty spring in my step. As I went through the door I reflected on what would have happened if the bar had been shorter.

The screen test took place in the basement of a building in Fleet Street, at that time the headquarters of the British newspaper industry. Cy directed and Stanley came and did the scenes with me. I was suddenly petrified. Joan Littlewood's advice did not work that day; fear and panic were the rehearsal and abject terror the performance. Cy and Stanley could not have been more helpful and patient, and at last we got the take that Cy wanted and the ordeal was over. I stumbled up the stairs into the daylight still sweating with fear, knowing that it had not gone well.

I now had to wait the entire weekend before getting the result. Fortunately I was invited to a party on the Saturday night and I accepted with the idea of going there and getting absolutely bombed, missing out Sunday altogether and waking up on Monday morning ready for the result. I walked into the party and the first person I saw was Cy Endfield, with his wife. I tried to catch his eye but he ignored me. Obviously the film was not back from the laboratories yet and he hadn't seen it. Now I was faced with a quandary. I couldn't get bombed as I'd intended, or Cy would notice and think I was a drunk and unreliable. So I spent the evening politely sipping

164

beer and keeping tabs on Cy. He was one of the first to leave, and as he went by he caught my eye for the first time and came over. 'I've seen the test,' he said casually. My heart sank. That meant I had not got the part, or he would have told me earlier. 'It's the worst one I've ever seen,' he added. That was it. All over, I thought. 'But you've got the part,' he carried on. 'We go to South Africa to shoot in three weeks. Congratulations.' He shook my hand.

'Why did you give me the part if the test was so bad?' I asked rather stupidly, pushing my luck.

'I don't know, Michael, but I have a feeling that there is something there. Goodnight.' He walked away.

I also had a feeling there was something there. In the pit of my stomach. When I could no longer hear the sound of his shoes, I threw up all over mine.

Part Three

14

'When the magic happens . . .'

Zulu was being shot in the Drakensberg Mountains in northern South Africa so the first part of our trip was the flight to Johannesburg. In 1963 the planes were a lot slower than they are now; we flew out on one called a Constellation, and the trip took twenty-two hours. It was the first charter flight to Africa by Lufthansa, the German airline, and they pulled out all the stops. The food was great and the champagne flowed continuously; the hostesses were gorgeous and there were a lot of them. After a couple of glasses of champagne I sat there studying them to see which one would initiate me into the 'mile-high club'. After two or three more glasses I started to lose interest and after a meal and a brandy and a cigar, which I had never smoked before, I fell asleep. I must have slept for hours because the next thing I knew one of the beauties was shaking me gently and telling me to fasten my seat belt because we were landing to refuel in Lagos in Nigeria. Great, I thought, my first time on African soil. It would only be the airport but I was curious to look around anyway. When the plane came to a halt the pilot informed us that we would have to stay on board because it was too dangerous for us to disembark. It seemed that the Nigerians had just received their independence from Britain after two hundred years and as part of their celebrations they would not be averse to carving up a couple of representatives of their oppressors as part of the festivities. We stayed on board and let the Nigerians celebrate their independence on their own.

The next refuelling stop was Entebbe in Uganda, which had also just received its independence from the British. It seemed that they were even more disenchanted with us than the Nigerians. I know because I received this opinion firsthand. When the plane came to a stop and I stood up to stretch my legs, I was walking along the aisle when I was suddenly confronted by a Ugandan policeman who had boarded the plane. 'Sit down,' he ordered. 'I am not getting off the plane,' I started to say, but before I could finish he smashed me across the right arm with his truncheon. '*Sit down*,' he repeated, weapon raised to strike again. I quickly decided that I had stretched my legs enough and sat down, nursing my arm which soon became numb. I could understand his attitude, I suppose, but at the same time I felt a sense of injustice, which exists to this day. I may be a member of a country that was one of the greatest colonial powers in history, but me and mine – and the many thousands like us – got nothing out of all this. As far as I can see, we owe nothing to any race on earth, colonial or not, because we never took a thing from anybody.

We eventually landed in Johannesburg, jet-lagged and either hungover or still drunk. The doors were opened and a searing heat came racing through the plane. We staggered to our feet and on wobbly legs negotiated our way to the exit. There were no ramps in those days, and when a long steep flight of steps was wheeled up to the side of the plane, Cy and Stanley were the first off and I followed them. (I have noticed over the years on movie unit charters that people seem to naturally disembark in the same order of importance as on the credit titles of the eventual movie.)

Standing at the bottom of the steps was a reception committee of people who were either important or thought they were, all smiling and very pleased, it seemed, to see us. All eyes were on this group except mine, which, with their experience on the streets at the Elephant, immediately picked out two burly characters standing to one side, who, if they were pleased to see us, were managing to hide their feelings very well. They were each carrying large bundles of printed forms which I mistakenly took to be immigration papers. The men turned out to be the Chief of Police and his assistant. When we reached the bottom of the steps the Chief of Police stepped forward, shook Stanley's hand and said, 'Welcome to

South Africa.' At this point the person behind who was still drunk and only halfway down the steps succumbed to vertigo and fell headlong at his feet, unconscious. The rituals of civic reception were accomplished to the background of heavy snorings from the drunk who was still asleep on the ground, everyone trying to pretend that he was not there.

The two policemen then distributed the forms, which turned out to be copies of the South African inter-racial sex or Miscegenation laws. Heterosexual contact between black and white people was illegal here, and if you were caught the punishment was either a long prison sentence, twelve lashes with a whip, or both. We all stood around reading these laws and laughing, which went unappreciated by the Chief of Police, when Stanley suddenly piped up, 'If I get caught, can I have the twelve lashes while I'm still doing it?' We all roared, but this went down like a lead balloon with the locals. Quickly we were hustled into the terminal building and the welcome was over.

We were then driven for seven hours along what must be one of the dullest roads in the world. It is dead straight and goes for hundreds of miles through the veldt, which as far as I am concerned must be Afrikaan for 'boring'. There was nothing – not a house, a tree, a shrub, a river, a pond, a hill, a valley, and not a garage or service station, which meant that if nature called as it did on this long journey, there was nothing to pee behind to save embarrassment. Eventually we reached towns with names like Mafeking and Bloemfontein and Ladysmith, and it was just like driving through an old history lesson at school and about as interesting. Fifty-two miles after Ladysmith we eventually came to the Drakensbergs, a beautiful range of mountains, and settled in amongst them – a pretty little range of hills shaped like an amphitheatre. Snuggled down in the middle of all this were two hotels and nothing else. Except now of course our set, because here we were going to shoot *Zulu*.

The first couple of days were spent getting acclimatised, which in my case meant sitting on the loo for a couple of hours and passing the rest of the time putting stuff that did not work on bites from insects I'd never heard of. However I

171

was taken to meet a gorgeous cheetah who would share a scene with me and I fell in love with him instantly. In order to get him used to me, I had to take him around with me everywhere on a lead like a dog. He had a wonderful loud purr like a cat trying to impersonate a motor bike. We looked like becoming inseparable. Then there were a few ... incidents. Every day a car took us to the set. He would sit with me on the back seat, purring away happily, fascinated by everything in the car, including the shiny button on the back of the chauffeur's cap. One day the sun caught the button at a certain angle and the bright light started to flutter and sparkle. This caught his attention and he grabbed it, taking a considerable part of the chauffeur's scalp with it. After that we travelled to the set separately. I was still allowed to take him for walks, though, until the day he spotted the catering manager's German Shepherd dog sitting on the steps outside the unit canteen. He took off like the wind, and the heavy chain which was his lead was torn out of my hand, taking half the skin with it. The German Shepherd spotted him coming, and quicker than I have ever seen any dog move, he had bounded up the steps and into the canteen and – I swear this is true – *shut the door behind him*. The cheetah came to a skidding halt like Sylvester the cartoon cat, but he was going at such a pelt he went head over heels on the steps and knocked himself out. That was the end of that friendship.

The first scene that I did in the picture was a long shot on a horse coming back to camp on my own after a hunting expedition. I hadn't been near a horse since I was a boy on the farm. I didn't like them then and I found that things had not improved. The horse, being a dumb animal, smelled the fear on me and the two of us worked each other up into a state of hysteria until by the time we did the scene we were both gibbering wrecks. Cy shouted 'Action!' over the intercom and I set off. All I had to do was walk the horse slowly. What could go wrong, I asked myself. The reply came almost immediately. The horse, like me, did not want to go anywhere. Cy shouted for someone to hit the goddam thing, which the prop man did and up the horse went and started to do a short impromptu dance on its back legs. Meanwhile the cameras

172

were rolling and Cy's voice came over the air again. 'Tell him,' he yelled, 'he's supposed to be walking along quietly not auditioning for the fucking Spanish Riding School.' I heard this and the prop man and I pointed the horse along the correct path which was on the side of a hill, and along we went, the horse and I competing to see who had the nervous breakdown first. As it turned out it was the horse but through no fault of his own. He had been born and brought up on the flatlands of the Veldt and had never been on a hill before. As we rounded a rather sharp bend, he saw his own large shadow on the hillside for the first time in his life. One likes to think he could have coped with this minor shock, but he was now so strung out that he leapt off the path and carried the two of us up to a twenty-foot dead drop down the hill. The prop man came running down and grabbed the horse before it carried on and then asked me if I was all right. I wasn't. I had hurt my back and told him so. It was also obvious that I could not get back up on the horse for a couple of hours. He told Cy this over the intercom. Cy replied, 'Can you ride a horse?' The prop man said he could. 'The sun's going down and we've got to get this shot today. Take his hat and cape and do the shot yourself. It's so far away, no one will know.' And so my début in major motion pictures was not me at all but a prop man named Ginger.

The next day was no better. All I had to do was walk the horse very slowly across the top of a little waterfall only six or seven feet high. Again I thought that it would be simple, but no. The horse was calm and so was I, and we slowly picked our way across the shallow water while the camera panned with us, and as it moved the metal bit on it started to sparkle and gleam in the sunlight. Again the horse, being from the Veldt, had never had anything like this done right in his eyes, so he stood up on his hind legs and I went sprawling into the little pond.

'I thought you took riding lessons in London?' Cy bawled.

'I did!' I told him. What I didn't add was that the lessons were to take place on Wimbledon Common, but having been thrown in Wimbledon High Street and nearly run over by a bus on the first day, and actually run over by a bicycle when I had been thrown on the second day, I never even reached the Common and my first lesson, although I had learned in Wimbledon High Street on both days that I never wanted to see a horse again . . .

Each time I had an accident nobody enquired if I was hurt or seemed to care how badly. There was concern for the horse, for the sun, which was disappearing fast and for my uniform, lest it was ripped, but no one asked, 'Is Michael all right?' I brought this point up with Stanley who was not only the star but also the producer, and he said to me with a slight grin: 'You have only done two shots so far and you would not be expensive to replace. However, as the film progresses and you are in more and more shots you become very expensive to replace and your welfare will become progressively more precious to us all and the fuss, care and attention showered on you will be overwhelming until you have done your last shot – and then nobody will give a shit what happens to you any more. For that reason,' he continued, 'never do a dangerous stunt on the last day of a picture because they don't care if it goes wrong, you see?' I nodded my head. He looked at my forlorn face, winked at me and walked away. I knew he was kidding, but there was enough of a ring of truth in what he said to make me vow never to do anything dangerous in pictures again, especially on the last day – a rule that I have stuck to religiously.

Filming continued without further disaster and finally the day for which we had all been waiting for came. The Zulus arrived, two thousand of them dressed in their war costumes, not from our wardrobe but their own personal battle-clothes. It was a most impressive sight at dusk as they came over the hills from the north and down into our valley, long lines of magnificent-looking warriors with high head-dresses and loin-cloths of monkey skins and the tails of lions that they had killed themselves with just a spear and their bare hands. As they approached, their deep booming voices echoed across the mountains singing a slow mournful lament; this was dusk, the time they would be returning from a battle and the song was to mourn the dead. As this chant boomed off the side of the hills in slow time to the beat of two thousand spears hitting

174

two thousand shields, the hair stood up on the back of my neck and even the ordinary black African workers whom we had brought with us from Johannesburg, definitely looked on the nervous side. It was at this moment that I realised how brave the men we were making the film about must have been even to stand against such a formidable foe.

None of the Zulus had ever seen a movie so Cy set up a screen and a 16-millimetre projector and they all gathered to watch and see what they were supposed to be doing. The film was an old Roy Roger's western, and when it first came on there was a gasp from everybody at the wonder of it. As the film progressed they quickly settled down and almost immediately started jeering at anything that looked ridiculous and shouting lines in Zulu that I am sure were 'Look out! He's behind you!' when the villain crept up on Roy. Eventually they cheered every time Roy came on and made a strange sound when the villain appeared, which I assumed was a Zulu boo, but it sounded a little more serious than that. The biggest laugh came when Roy sang as he rode along. They obviously could not understand why a man would want to sing riding a horse alone on a prairie and were puzzled about where the music was coming from. But after ten minutes they figured it out and their reaction was the same as anyone else's would have been.

The man who played the chief of the Zulus in the film is the real-life chief today, Chief Buthelezi, the present-day leader of the Incatha movement. A woman whom I think was his sister – a princess of the tribe, anyway – was the tribal historian. The Zulus have no written history; everything is passed down verbally and this woman seemed to know every detail of the battle that we were filming. Cy said that she drew in the sand with a stick the movement of the Zulu armies and their battle formations in such detail that he used them in the film exactly as she said to great effect. They are some of the best battle scenes I have ever seen in a film. The Battle of Rorke's Drift was fought by a Welsh regiment, hence Stanley's fascination with the subject. To say that he was Welsh and proud of it would be one of the great understatements of all time. The Victoria Cross is the highest medal for

175

bravery that the British military bestow and the standard of courage needed to win it is so high that it is very rarely awarded and most often, posthumously. The extraordinary feature of this battle is that it was fought with such exemplary valour that eleven Victoria Crosses were awarded in one day, a situation unique in British military history.

Eventually the first rushes of my work arrived back at the set. 'Rushes' are the bits of film of just a day's work that are 'rushed' back to you to look at, to see if everything turned out all right on screen. Because we were in South Africa and the film had to be processed in the laboratories in England, there was a two-week delay before anybody saw my first work actually on a screen. Seeing the rushes is a big test for new actors. The stakes are high now; in my case particularly so since for all these years I had maintained that all I needed was a real chance on the big screen and then I would show everybody not only that I could act well but that I also had that indefinable something, 'star quality'. The closest definition of this was one I heard from David Lean many years later. He told me, 'When you are cutting a scene with an excellent actor you can cut as he finishes the line; but with a star you can hold the shot for at least another four frames, because that is when the magic happens.'

I sat there in a very cool room with the sweat of anxiety pouring down my back as the place filled up to standing room only. What if I was so bad they fired me, I thought as I sat there. The whole show business world would know and I would be finished. Suddenly the lights went out without warning, and the first thing I learned is that when this happens the technicians forget the actors are there and speak honestly about them, an experience I am sure nobody wants, but that is what I got. The screen lit up and a ghastly face appeared and started to speak in a terrible voice. I sat there for an instant and wondered who the hell this was – and to my horror it was me. My career was over. They were going to fire me but I didn't care. I was fed up with this place and I wanted to go home anyway. I could leave tomorrow. I did not have much to pack, I thought as I sat there and watched this apparition drone on. Behind me a voice said, 'Who let the silly bastard wear his hat pulled down like that? You can't see his fucking eyes.' This offended me deeply from an artistic point of view. In the film I wore an old-fashioned military pith helmet with a small peak on the front to protect the wearer's eyes from the sun. I had decided to use this as part of my characterisation. I would say some of the lines with my eyes in the shade and when I wanted to make a strong point I would tip my head back slightly and catch the full glare of the sun in my eyes. This had been worked out with great skill, I thought, and here was someone misunderstanding and calling me a silly bastard into the bargain. Ah sod it, I thought. What's it matter? I'm going home tomorrow. At this point I threw up all over my best costume trousers and boots, and fled from the room. I have never returned to rushes since.

I didn't have to work the next day so I spent a tense time waiting for the evening to come and the unit to return. I decided to make it easy for Stanley or Cy to fire me, so I stood at the corner of the bar where they would have to walk right by me as they came into the hotel. The evening arrived and I took up my position, had a couple of quick drinks to deaden the pain, and I waited. Eventually Cy and Stanley came in. Stanley caught my eye first and said, 'Not bad, kid, but you'll get better,' and they both walked on. Working on this picture was so important to me, I thought, that I was becoming paranoid.

Dissatisfaction with my performance was going to loom again, but this time it was neither paranoia nor nerves nor imagination. It came in black and white from the head office of Paramount Studios in London. When I first started to work on the character of Bromhead, the most important facet of the man seemed to be the fact that he came from a privileged background. Not having one myself I studied people who had, and I picked on Prince Philip and watched his mannerisms whenever I got the chance. The thing that I noticed about him was that he always walked with his hands behind his back. The psychology of this, I figured, was that he was a powerful man and well guarded so he did not have to be ready to defend himself as the unguarded lower orders do. He

177

never had to open doors or do other mundane things for himself; he didn't have to wave his hands about during conversation in order to attract attention. Here was a good piece of characterisation, I thought, and played the part with my hands behind my back at every opportunity. One day I was walking past the production office when one of the secretaries put her head out of the window, put her fingers to her lips and beckoned me in. My eyes lit up. She was a very pretty girl and I had fancied her for some time. Was this my chance? I walked into her office and she peered anxiously down the passage behind me as I entered to make sure there was no one about. I couldn't believe my luck. She turned and instead of throwing her arms round my neck as I had anticipated, she thrust a telegram in my hand. 'Read this,' she whispered, 'before anybody comes back.' It was addressed to Stanley and it was from a senior Paramount executive in London.

'*Actor playing Bromhead so bad doesn't even know what to do with hands*,' it said. '*Every shot seen here so far, hands behind back, suggest you replace him*.' Apart from the fact that I was shocked and desolate, I knew that this time it was *not* my imagination. Now I really would be fired. I learned a couple of valuable lessons, though. One, not all movie executives know what they are talking about; and two, very few people can understand rushes when seen in isolation from the rest of the work. One of the time-honoured epithets of the movie industry when a film opens and bombs is, 'Well, it looked good in the rushes.'

I spent two more days of agony waiting for Stanley to fire me. Everywhere he went he would suddenly find me standing in front of him to give him his opportunity to get rid of me. I could not tell him that I had seen a confidential telegram or I would get the secretary into trouble. Finally I invented a cock and bull story of how I had found the telegram on the floor and had picked it up to put it back on his desk and happened to read it in the process.

'I know that you have been told to replace me and I just wanted to thank you and let you know that I understand your position and it is OK. I don't mind going now,' I blurted out in one long breath. He stood and stared at me for a moment and I could see that he was quite angry.

'Who is the producer of this movie?' he finally asked. 'You are, Stan.' 'Have I said that you are fired?' 'No,' I mumbled. 'Well, just get on with your job,' he said and walked away. Then he turned and said, 'And stop reading my fucking mail or you *will* get fired.' At last the weeks of agony and doubt were over; I knew that for better or worse, I had the part – and that was that.

The weeks went by and although the work was fascinating, the evenings were long and miserable with absolutely nothing to do. There were very few women on the unit and masses of men, so for the majority of us there was no romance or even sex to take our minds off things. The few women that there were seemed to have all been snapped up before we even arrived. One evening I was sitting at the bar having a drink with Stan when I mentioned how boring the evenings were here and he gave me a typical Baker piece of advice. 'If you have got dialogue the next day, go to bed; if you haven't, get pissed.'

Although this was Africa, there was no actual danger of wild animals where we were, with the exception of baboons. Meeting a group of these suddenly when you are out for a walk on your own can be a nerve-racking experience. One day I walked around a bend and was confronted by a large pack of them, led by an enormous male. When they saw me they all stopped and stared at me. I was scared out of my wits. I kept my eye on the big male and very slowly I started to walk backwards, my eyes never leaving his. I knew that if I turned and ran they would see the fear and come after me. He had the most malevolent stare that I had seen in any eyes, and he never blinked. I could outstare anybody, but I'd never tried it with a baboon before, although I'd done it with quite a few gorillas in bars in London. Now, the first one to blink would lose and if it was me, I would probably die. I held his stare with bated breath as I slowly progressed backwards round the bend, and once I was out of his sight, I ran like hell.

I met the same baboon again a little while later. We had finished all the scenes in the Zulu village set that we had built and it had been left empty for a few weeks. However, we learned from the rushes a few weeks later that one of the scenes had to be reshot. When we returned to the village set, we found that this particular group of baboons had taken over the place and were living happily in the huts. We were to shoot outside the chief's hut, which of course was the biggest and best in the village, and I walked over to it with a couple of hunters to see if any of the baboons were in there. The hunters didn't shoot them, but just fired their guns in the air and the creatures ran away. As we reached the chief's hut I saw something move inside and we all stopped and waited and out walked my friend the lead baboon; he sat on the top of the steps and although there were three of us he only stared at me. It gave me an eerie feeling, as if he were saying, 'I remember you, mate, and I'll get you for this.'

One of the hunters fired his rifle, but my baboon didn't run like all the others. He just gave us all a look of disdain and strolled out of the village. I never saw him again, thank God. I am sure that he had it in for me.

I once read somewhere that 'modesty is a matter of geography', and there was one scene in *Zulu* that proved this theory beyond all doubt. It was a big celebration scene in which a couple of hundred girls do a traditional tribal dance. Some of the dancers were from the tribal lands and a few of them were Zulu girls who had left the tribe and lived and worked in Johannesburg. When it came to filming, Cy discovered that the correct costume for this dance was a tiny bead apron and nothing else. No underwear. Nothing. He asked the wardrobe department to run up a couple of hundred pairs of tiny black panties that would retain some modesty and prevent an apoplectic censor, but would still give the impression of the correct historical costume. This compromise was eventually accepted by even the most ardent traditionalists amongst the tribal dancers. Cy thought his troubles were over until he was informed that the Zulu girls from the city would not dance bare-breasted and wanted to wear brassières. This of course was completely out of the question for the tribal girls. They had already given way in the knicker department and they were not about to concede any further. There was an almighty row between the two sets of girls, with Cy in the middle trying to get the pants on one side and the brassières off the other lot. Peace was finally restored and we shot the sequence once, but had to shoot it again because as the camera tracked along the line of dancing girls, the camera operator suddenly shouted, 'Cut!' He pointed at one of the girls and said, 'That one's got no drawers on,' and indeed she hadn't. Her reply was translated back to Cy: 'I am sorry,' she had said. 'I'm not used to them and I just forgot.'

The Zulus were great jokers and I was the butt of their first bit of humour. One day I came on to the set and there were two or three hundred of them sitting around doing nothing but waiting. As I started to walk along a path between them they all stood up together as if by some hidden signal and, raising their spears into the air, spoke one word together as a sort of salute and sat down again. This went on for several days. No matter how many there were, when I came on the set they all stood up and gave this one-word salute and then sat down again. I was quite proud at first but started to get suspicious when nobody would tell me what the word meant. No one would translate, until one day the princess-historian told me they were saying 'lady's hair'. That was their name for me. I had long blond hair and the only time they had ever seen that colour was on a woman. She saw that I did not like it and it never happened again.

This was my first visit to South Africa and I had no preconceived notions about their politics or racial policy – nobody had. However as I worked and watched what was going on around me I was uncomfortable, then concerned and finally downright angry. Most of the workers on the set were black, but they were not tribal – simply ordinary carpenters and electricians from the city, just like anybody else. But all the foremen were white Afrikaans and they treated the black workers with an incredible rudeness the like of which I had never seen before. They literally talked to them as though they were dogs.

One day I saw a black worker make a mistake and I stopped

to watch him getting a real telling off, just as an English worker would in the same situation. To my astonishment, the foreman didn't reprimand him; he smashed a fist into his face instead. I was so shocked at this I couldn't move, and then suddenly I started to run towards the man, screaming at him, but Stanley got there first. I had never seen him so angry. He fired the man on the spot and then gathered all the white gang bosses together and laid down the law on how everyone was going to be treated on this film set from then on. He was in an absolute fury and so were the rest of the British contingent. It brought home for the first time what this word 'apartheid' really meant.

A source of great amusement for us was watching one of our English foremen 'go native'. He spoke to his workmates in their own tongue, ate their food and drank their beer with them, and no longer fraternised with his white colleagues. This was just an ordinary Cockney workman from London.

One day we were shooting a scene when right in the middle of it we heard the sound of an aeroplane. We had to cut the shot, of course – our story took place over a hundred years ago so we couldn't have even the faintest plane noise on the sound track. We waited for it to go away, but instead of getting softer and receding the noise got louder until we could make out not one plane but two helicopters, heading straight for us. As the helicopters got closer, though, we could see the sign POLICE written on the side of them. What the hell did they want? For the first time since we had arrived, Stanley looked really worried.

The helicopters landed and several policemen got out. The leader demanded to know who was in charge. Stanley stepped forward. Apparently our Cockney had gone a little more native than we all thought. He had moved out of the hotel into a mud hut, and had taken with him three Zulu wives. The policeman told Stanley that the man was under arrest. Later on we realised that one of our white Afrikaan foremen was in fact a police spy, placed with us for exactly this purpose. Worst of all, the policeman told Stanley that the production was closed down and we would have to leave the country. Stanley went to work on him immediately and after much

Left: The only picture that exists of me as a baby.

Below: Bombardier Micklewhite. My Dad in 1925.

Above: Mum and Dad obviously hate the hair-cut.

Right: My father at Billingsgate (extreme left). The footsteps I did not wish to follow.

Top: Clubland in Guernsey. I'm on the left, second row down.

Above left: Star material of 1953.

Above: My first job in films. In the mail room at Peak Films.

Left: We called it hell. National Service, 1952.

Far Left: *A Hill in Korea.* Is this *really* star material?

Left: A stiff upper lip in *Zulu.*

Above: My first rep company. Alwyn D. Fox is second from the left. I am standing next to him.

Right: Ma and her boys.

With Shelley
Winters in *Alfie*.

'And *you* can call
me Mike.'
Sleuth with
Laurence Olivier.

Protecting Sue
Lloyd in *The
Ipcress File*.

The men who
would be kings.
Sean Connery and I.

Shakira, in her first
and last acting role,
as the Princess
Roxanne in *The
Man Who Would
Be King*.

The Silver Bears.
Louis Jourdan, me
and Jay Leno.

Right: Maggie Smith got an Oscar for *California Suite*; I didn't.

Foot: In bed with Glenda Jackson in *The Romantic Englishwoman.*

Below: 'Don't ever kiss me again!' *Deathtrap* with Christopher Reeve.

Above: Working with Julie Walters on *Educating Rita*.
Below: Me with Hannah and no sisters.

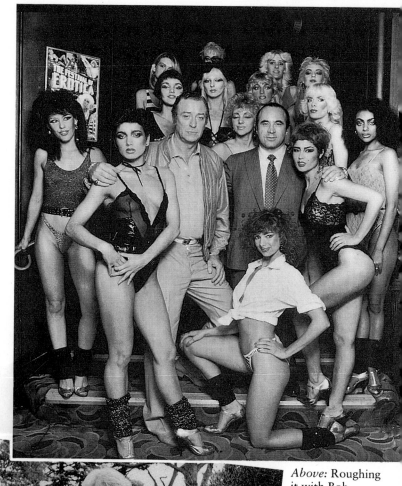

Above: Roughing
it with Bob
Hoskins on *Mona
Lisa.*

Scoundrels. Steve
Martin and me in
*Dirty Rotten
Scoundrels.*

argument they made a deal: the unit could stay, provided that Stanley guaranteed to get the criminal out of the country by midnight. Now I realised that apartheid was not a personal prejudice but a government-sponsored form of civil terrorism. I vowed there and then never to return to that country until they changed the system, and to this day, I haven't.

The film was coming to an end now after three exhausting months and we were shooting the final big scene where the Zulus come back after repeated attacks on the tiny British unit, this time in massive force. The script called for six thousand Zulus to line the top of the hills surrounding the British. I wondered how we were going to accomplish this with only two thousand warriors. As Cy shouted, 'Action!' the warriors started to appear as the camera panned, and there were our six thousand Zulus. The trick was simple. It was a very long shot and you could only just make out the lines of men. Cy had given each of the two thousand warriors a piece of wood with two shields with head-dresses glued on top of them. Cy had his six thousand warriors.

The film finished, we all got drunk as skunks and set off back to London. I was so homesick for my beloved city that I could taste it. As the plane took off from Johannesburg airport there was a loud cheer and I sat there, so happy that I almost cried. I was going home at last and I had made my first real film. Would my luck hold, I wondered, as I sat there guzzling free champagne – just in case it didn't . . .

15

$1500 a *week?*

Our hotel accommodation and meals had all been free in South Africa, and there was nowhere else to spend money, so I arrived back in London with most of my £4000 fee intact. I immediately went to see Dominique in Sheffield. By now she was a beautiful eight-year-old blonde, full of life. Her latest craze was horses. There was a stable near where she lived and she had practically moved in there permanently, her grandmother told me. I had arrived for the first time ever with my pockets full of money and more important, my heart empty of shame at not being able to give her all the things that a father should give a daughter. I knew what to do immediately. To make an early try at placating the guilt I had always felt about leaving when she was so young, I bought her a pony and set her on course for her future career; she became besotted with horses. I knew that I could not buy her affection, but I could buy her interest until I could afford time, for with children time is the currency that buys affection, and if you spend enough of it you might buy love. That was the principle I was working on, and I left Sheffield feeling pleased with the way things were going with Dominique.

My mother was my next concern. For a long time now I had been worried about her living in that prefab in such a rough area, and I finally hit on a solution to the problem. Apart from the dangers of elderly people living on their own, the worst enemy of old age can be loneliness, and since the death of my father I had worried about this affecting my mother. Stanley was still living at home but he was out most of the time, working all day and going out in the evening like any ordinary guy. I could certainly not afford the time to be with her,

184

unfortunately, and I definitely had no wish to come back to the Elephant. Things improved no end when I moved Mum into the flat at Brixton I had once shared with Pat. It was in a big old house divided into flats, and in each flat there were people who were actually related to her, and some of them were women of her own age. Perfect. So I moved her to Brixton, she felt safe and secure and she had company. As I made money and was able to improve not only my own life but to remove from grinding poverty my family and those around me whom I loved or cared for, I saw the happiness that my money could bring and it was a source of tremendous joy to me.

The third and last person I could help with my new wealth was Paul. He was out of the sanatorium now, in bad shape but on the mend, and I did what I could to make him more comfortable. I really owed this man. He had been so generous to me when I was down. Nothing was too good for Paul, I decided, and it was just as well that I did because his life ended up being one trial and tribulation after the other. However he never lost his sense of humour or his ability to make me laugh, which is not easy.

I was busy doing all this reorganisation of people's lives on my £4000, which to me was some kind of limitless fortune, but if I had taken the trouble to find out I would have learned that all my little unimportant debts added together came to more than I had. Dennis persuaded me to get an accountant and to open a bank account. Soon, I found myself surrounded by destitute family, friends and loved ones, up to my ears with responsibilities, with a bank account for the first time ever – which consisted of an overdraft of £1000 – and for the first time, an employee, my accountant, who was paying himself out of my overdraft. For eleven years I had worked and tried so hard, and this was all I had to show for it. Still, I was thirty-one years old, I was in London, it was the Swinging Sixties and we were all going to be stars.

Life at Ebury Street was still the same as when I had left, only more so. Terry was more famous, more rich and there were more girls. There was one change in Terry, however. He had now entered a more romantic phase which consisted of him falling in love with photographs of ravishing but unattainable girls in glossy magazines. The object of his long-distance passion when I returned was a stunning blonde girl. Terry showed me this photo with great pride, and it was at that moment that I achieved a god-like status in his eyes.

'I know her,' I said nonchalantly. He didn't believe me, so I told him the story. I had been rehearsing a play for the BBC one day and I went to lunch in the canteen which was laid out like an informal buffet. I collected my meal and was about to join some actors whom I knew vaguely, when I spotted this girl seated alone at a table in the corner. She was stunning. She was so stunning that she had actually frightened everybody off.

I had no scruples and went straight over and asked her, rather unnecessarily I thought, if the other nine empty seats at her table were taken. She informed me with a toe-curling smile that they were not, and invited me to sit down. I found out that she had just left drama school and was doing her first television show, a science fiction piece in which she was playing a mysterious heavenly body from outer space. The casting was perfection. She also informed me that she had no dialogue. I thought but did not say, that in her case dialogue was not necessary. After our first meeting I quickly realised that there was nothing here for me romantically but she was nice and I liked her. I saw her around many times after that and we knew each other as vague friends. Terry listened to this story enthralled and the moment I had finished he demanded to know her name. Julie Christie, I told him. He insisted that I arrange for them to meet. I did not know her well enough to ring her up and say come round and be ravished by my best friend, but there is a Machiavellian side to my character and I did bring about the meeting and subsequently a massive romance between the two of them.

Meanwhile, in the outside world, we were all dancing to the Beatles who had broken through in America where they had songs at numbers one, two, three, four and five. Nobody had done that before or since. The Rolling Stones were coming up fast behind them, in addition to a mass of other British groups.

The clubs had also changed when I got back.

The big disco now was the Ad Lib, situated in a penthouse just behind the Empire cinema, Leicester Square. This to my mind was the best disco ever. It was owned by two men who later become my friends, Johnny Gold, probably the greatest club host in the world and Oscar Lerman his silent partner, and I mean this literally, because Oscar rarely spoke and when he did I was always with him in the club and so I could not hear what he said above the music. What made the club so great, was the fact that you were dancing alongside the people who had made the music. The Beatles and the Stones would be grooving around next to you and in the dark corners you'd see Stamp romancing Julie Christie or David Bailey wooing Jean Shrimpton and in another corner would be Roman Polanski with Sharon Tate and everybody who was anybody was there and so was everybody who was nobody but going to be somebody tomorrow . . . There was the buzz every night of dreams coming true, and the charge of fresh dreams that would come true some time soon, and the shock as a record was played for the first time ever and you knew you were listening to a pop classic being born, and the new young genius who wrote it said, 'Sorry,' as he stepped on your toe as we all whirled like dervishes round the dance floor and into the history of our own chosen field of endeavour.

The sixties have been misunderstood: they should not be judged by standards of talent, skill, artistry or intelligence, or by the great works or artists that those years produced. The reason for their notoriety is far more simple than that. For the first time in British history, the young working-class stood up for themselves and said, 'We are here, this is our society and we are not going away. Join us, stay away, like us, hate us – do as you like. We don't care about your opinion anymore.' We created our own moral code, which may not have been ideal but was at least honest, especially in comparison with the hypocrisy of the rest of British society.

Back at home, Terry was in the middle of filming *The Collector* for the great William Wyler, director of *Ben Hur*, *The*

Best Years of Our Lives and *Wuthering Heights*. This, on the surface, would appear to be a tremendous advantage for a young actor, but in Terry's case it actually worked against him. After that experience, he never wanted to work with any director he didn't consider great which had, in my opinion, an adverse effect on his career. He waited for the great directors to come to him – which they did, but few and far between. Eventually, of course, it seems to me, if he doesn't speed up a bit he will have waited too long.

Terry was in love with a photograph again, this time of a model named Jean Shrimpton who was not only world famous, but the girlfriend of David Bailey the Cockney photographer, who had made her into a star. She certainly seemed the pinnacle of unattainment. I aroused his interest in other directions quite accidentally. We were sitting in the flat chatting one evening when I happened to mention in passing that several guys had been spreading the rumour that Terry and I were lovers. Well, we *had* lived together for a couple of years and *were* as close as two male friends could get, so some morons were bound to think the wrong thing. Terry asked me for names and when I finished, a determined look came over his face. I got very worried for a moment, since some of these men were very big and tough. 'You're not going to go and start a fight with any of them, I hope?' I queried nervously, thinking of Terry being massacred in his attempt to defend his macho reputation. 'No,' he said, and just smiled, but he did request the names of these gentlemen's wives, fiancées and girl-friends. I never found out what he did, but we never heard any more rumours . . .

The editing and final shooting of *Zulu* had now been finished for a couple of months, the music, a great score by my new friend John Barry, put on the soundtrack and the film was ready to be seen by the executives. This was a very important moment for me. When I won the role, I had met Joe Levine, the President of Embassy Pictures, the company that actually made *Zulu*. If you wanted to cast a caricature of a Hollywood movie producer, Joe would have been it. He was short, fat, loud and he always smoked a big cigar. In order to get the part

188

I had to sign a seven-year contract with his company. This was, he explained, to protect their investment in me. I thought this was fair and agreed with him, especially when I saw the numbers on the contract. The wages started at $1500 per week – a fortune – and doubled every year for seven years. This may sound very small in the modern world of mega-million dollar movie fees, but for me it was a dream. Like all dreams, however, there was a fly in the ointment, to mix a metaphor. The option was on their side only. They could get out of the contract at any time, but I could not. I was stuck with it no matter what happened. I didn't care and I couldn't wait for them to see the finished picture and decide to take up my option. I had not had any more work in movies and I knew I would not get any until the film came out.

One day I got the call that Joe was in London and wanted to see me. Stanley and Cy had been complimentary about my work in the picture so I went to his office full of confidence. Joe was a very charming man when he wanted to be and when I walked into his London office the charm was turned on full. 'Sit down,' he said, gesturing to a big armchair. 'You know I love you, don't you, Michael?' 'Yes, Joe,' I said warily. 'Remember what I said to you the first day you came into this office, about what was going to happen to you?' 'Yes, I remember, Joe.' He had told me that if I stuck with him I would be dripping with diamonds and I believed it. I had seen Mrs Levine. 'Well, you are going to make it, Michael. But not with us. We are not picking up the option on your contract.'

I sat there jammed back into my chair with the weight of this disastrous news. My well-used reflex mechanism clicked in. I smiled, 'That's OK Joe, but would you mind telling me why. Is it my performance?'

'No,' he said quickly. 'Nothing like that. Your performance in the picture is great.' There was an awkward pause and Joe took an unaccustomed nervous puff on his cigar. 'Now I don't want you to take what I am going to say personally and I know you're not.' He halted for a moment. 'Not what, Joe?' I asked, bewildered. 'Queer. I know you're not but you look like a queer on screen. Eventually, though, your face will mature and you will be OK.'

I got angry. 'I'm thirty-one now Joe, when do you think my face will change?'

'Don't worry,' he said. 'A lot of the big stars are queers but they look butch. Unfortunately you are butch, but you look queer. That's the wrong way round for movies.'

'Thanks, Joe,' I said and left.

I walked home wondering how I was going to tell Dennis that he should now look for gay parts for me. So I was too butch to play queer parts and looked too queer to play butch parts. What *was* I going to do? The answer was supplied for me by a wonderful television director named Phillip Saville, who cast me in my only classical role to date as Horatio opposite Christopher Plummer's Hamlet. This was the ideal part for a man with my quandary. Horatio is never completely identified as butch or gay, he fights for his friend and cries for him when he dies but he shows very little interest in Ophelia. The jury is still out on Horatio's sexuality and is liable to remain so. However, the part was tailormade for me at the time. We shot the play at the real castle of Elsinore in Denmark. Acting in Shakespeare was a very happy experience and also a very valuable one for me since I was after all an actor with no formal, let alone classical training, but I managed to make something of it. My old friend Robert Shaw played the King, and Donald Sutherland, a newcomer, played Fortinbras, a small part that nevertheless required star quality.

Location shooting, as always, was fraught with difficulties. The castle had just been redecorated, so although it was the genuine article it looked artificial, and they had to dirty it down. But the biggest problem was the fog, not because of the light but because of the fog-*horn*. The castle is on the shore of the straits that pass between Denmark and Sweden, and the fog-horn was on the castle roof; and sounded every fifteen minutes. Poor Christopher Plummer. We would all stand ready to shoot and wait for the fog-horn to go, Phillip would shout, 'Action!' and Christopher would try to get through a long soliloquy before the next blast. Not an ideal way to do Shakespeare but it added speed and energy and not a little suspense to some of our performances.

Back to what was now known as 'Swinging London' where the life, far from dying down, was unbelievably gathering momentum. Ossie Clark was designing clothes that girls could wear without a brassière; Mary Quant had not only invented the mini skirt, but had produced a new make-up range which was a big success, and a friend of mine, another Cockney boy who ran a small hairdressing shop and used to cut my hair as a favour, had introduced a startling new hair style. We all called him Vid but his full name was Vidal Sassoon. Our favourite painter was a shy young northerner from Bradford called David Hockney. Everywhere you went there was someone who was going to do something great – if not in show business then in something else, and if not now, soon. The energy was like a giant express train of talent that had no stops or stations. When you were where you wanted to be you took your life in your hands and jumped and that is how the people appeared, as if from nowhere. You met someone one day and the next they were all over the papers for some reason; they had jumped from the train and landed safely. I felt I was ready but I still hadn't jumped. I think I was hoping that there would be a station shortly. Time and time again you met someone who was no one and without warning they became someone. For instance, Terry took me to a talk show that he was doing and we were met by a young man in his first television job and all he had to do was look after us and show us the dressing room and take us to hospitality and supply us with drinks and sandwiches. Now this was really a nobody in a nothing job, but this guy really impressed the pair of us. He was great and he eventually became one of my current circle of close friends. His name, he told us, was David Frost.

At around this time, Terry took me to his tailor to see if I liked the tail-coat suit he was having made for a première. His tailor was a young guy called Douglas Hayward who became the official tailor of the sixties, and again a lifelong friend who has made all my suits ever since. When it eventually opened, *Zulu* was going to have a big première and I knew I would need an evening suit, something that I really could not afford just then. While Terry was having his tail-coat perfected I made a deal with Doug: I would get it for half-price provided that Doug himself, who was the same size as me, could borrow it on the rare occasions that he would need one. This worked out well enough, except for the fact that Doug and I became really close friends but nobody knew because we could never ever turn up at the same social occasions in the same suit. This state of affairs lasted until I made my next film and had enough money to pay for the other half of the suit. Even then Doug did not make himself one but still borrowed mine although, having paid for it, I had priority. Doug was not only physically similar to me, he was roughly the same age, came from the same background and had the same sense of humour. He was almost like a twin except for looks. The only other area where we differed was that he did not have my anger, bitterness or blinding ambition. In other words, he was exactly the same as me but much nicer and not such a pain in the arse. Doug became such a star in his own field that he now makes Ralph Lauren's suits.

Around this time I went to the theatre to see a play written by someone I already knew vaguely since I had been in one of his plays on television. I enjoyed my evening as it was a great play and very funny, but more important than that, it seemed like an ideal vehicle for me. The play was a big hit and the star was a wonderful actor called John Neville who was excellent in the role, but I had heard that he had a limited-run contract, and would be leaving shortly; the management were going to hold auditions for a replacement. My movie career was on hold and a short run in the theatre would do just right. I didn't really want to go back into the theatre as I had become completely besotted by the idea of movies and found that the subtlety of movie acting was far more fascinating than a lot of the overblown posturing that was taken for good theatre acting at the time, and which had started to look ridiculous to me. I think my divorce from the theatre, not to watch but as something that I wanted to do, came when I read a stage direction which said: *Act One: A Roman encampment 200 years B.C. Act Two: Twenty minutes later*. Anyway, the play I have mentioned was very realistic and natural, and so was John

Neville's playing of it. When he left auditions were held and I went along thinking that I was perfect for the part but to my surprise I didn't get it. They said I was not right for it. I smiled as usual and said, 'Thank you very much,' and concealing my disappointment once again I left. The play was called *Alfie*.

Zulu was about to be released and I was due to get my big chance before the critics and, more importantly, before an audience. There was a lot of publicity about the film, but there was none about me. I had a credit on my own with 'And introducing' before my name, and that was all the company did to recognise my presence in the film.

My first big publicity break came just a couple of days before the opening of the movie. Jack Hawkins gave an interview about the film and at the end of it he said, 'Watch out for an actor called Michael Caine.' Coming from Jack this was praise indeed. The very next day I got another break in the papers, this time from an entirely unexpected source and for a different reason. Edna O'Brien the Irish writer was doing a series for the whole week in the London *Evening Standard* on the five most attractive men in London – and I was Friday. It was such a relief for my sagging spirits. Thank you, Edna O'Brien!

I told Dougie Hayward that he could not come to the première because I would be wearing the evening suit, and I sat down to think which girl I could take. I had no special girlfriend at the time so it was rather a problem, but suddenly I had a brilliant idea. I would take my mother! I went rushing over to Brixton with the good news. She had never been remotely near anything like this before, it would be a great thrill for her and for me it would be just a small measure of thanks for what I owed her over the years. Like a lot of men I adored my mother but unlike a lot of mothers she had earned my adoration. Now, however, she turned me down flat. No matter what I said, or how I pleaded and begged, she would not come to the première with me and that was that. I even got angry with her, something I had never done before, but even that did not work so I went away defeated. As I left she made me promise to come the day after the première and tell her what it was like. She was trying to hide it but she was secretly proud of me, especially now that she had seen my name in the papers.

I am now going to get into trouble. I *did* take a girl to the première but can't for the life of me remember who it was. If you are reading this book, Sweetheart, I apologise. It was twenty-seven years ago, after all. The première came. I hired a Rolls Royce, I had a beautiful girl on my arm, the crowd cheered, the reviews had come out and mine were very good. Flash bulbs popped so fast that the light was almost continuous until all I could see was a green blur. I walked down the path made by policemen struggling to hold back the pushing crowds, and just before I entered the lobby of the cinema, through the green haze that was clearing from my eyes, I saw a face that filled me with astonishment and anger and, for some reason, shame. There, with her old hat pushed awkwardly over one eye and a policeman shoving her away, was my own mother in the crowd trying to get a glimpse of me. She had come over on the bus and must have stood outside all evening – for she was near the front – to be there at the moment of my first minor triumph. I was furious with her as I walked into the cinema. The next day I asked my mother why she had sneaked off to the cinema like that when she could have come properly with me. I was angry and about to give her hell. She said, 'I wanted to be there with you, but I didn't want to spoil it for you.' My anger subsided. What could I say? I was on my way at last.

16

The two minutes that changed my life

Let me tell you about the two minutes that changed my life and the guy who so generously gave me those two minutes of his time. His name was Harry Saltzman and he, together with 'Cubby' Broccoli, was responsible for the fabulously successful James Bond series.

I was in the Pickwick having dinner with Terry one evening, when a waiter came over and asked me if I would join a gentleman at an adjacent table. I looked up and saw it was Harry.

I went over and introduced myself and Harry invited me to join his party for a few moments. I sat. 'We have just come from seeing *Zulu*,' his wife said, and this was followed by many gratifying compliments, ending with the one crucial phrase that nobody had ever said to me before. Harry announced, 'We all agreed that you could be a big star. You really come over well on the screen.'

I blushed, my heart beat faster and my head started to spin. There it was at last, somebody had said it – and it was somebody who knew what he was talking about.

'Have you read a book by Len Deighton called *The Ipcress File*?' Harry remarked, changing the subject suddenly. As it happened, I was halfway through it at that time and I told him so. 'I am going to make a film of it. How would you like to play the lead?'

I sat there dumbfounded. I had only just met the man! 'Yes,' I said, trying to look as though people made offers like this to me every day. 'Yes,' I repeated, trying to control the wonder in my voice.

'And would you like a seven-year contract with my

company?' was his next question. I gave the same answer, with less control. 'Would you like to have lunch with me at Les Ambassadeurs tomorrow?' Harry, I found later, was not good at small talk.

'Yes,' I replied again, hoping that he was not getting bored with my replies.

'One o'clock tomorrow, then.' He shook my hand, I was dismissed.

I stumbled back to Terry and my by now cold dinner.

'What happened?' Terry asked eagerly.

'I've got a starring role in a movie and a seven-year contact,' I told him.

He looked at me with disbelief. 'You've only been gone two minutes,' he said.

'I know,' I replied, hardly able to believe it myself. 'That was Harry Saltzman the Bond producer and I'm having lunch with him tomorrow at Les Ambassadeurs. Er, where is it?'

Terry knew. He had been rich and famous for over a year now and had been to all these places that I had only heard of so far. 'It's opposite the Hilton in Park Lane.'

Mayfair, I thought – things *were* looking up. The waiter brought a bottle of champagne. 'With the compliments of Mr Saltzman,' he announced as he opened the bottle and poured us each a glass. I looked at Harry to thank him, and all three of them at his table had their champagne already. 'Congratulations!' they called and I called back, 'Thank you,' and as an afterthought, 'for the champagne as well.' Suddenly I felt rich and confident. This time I was going to treat Terry, he was always picking up the tab for me. I asked the waiter for the bill and he told me that Mr Saltzman had already paid it. As we were leaving I walked past Harry's table and thanked him for the meal and said good night. 'Wear a tie,' Harry replied with a smile but no small talk.

The next day was gorgeous, as warm and sunny as I felt. Harry and I ate in the glorious garden of Les Ambassadeurs, a very exclusive and therefore very expensive gambling club which was the meeting place for the rich middle-aged swingers of the sixties. The first thing that I nearly swallowed there was my own tongue when I saw the prices on the menu.

I had a quick look round at the other customers and very quickly realised that I was the only person there I had never heard of. It was choked with celebrities.

'Let's eat lunch,' said Harry. 'I've already ordered.' We started with caviar, vodka and blinis – the first time for me. 'First class all the way for you Michael, from now on.' I smiled, my mouth full of blinis and caviar. We ate in silence for a while and he could see that I was overawed by the place and the people and the occasion. Eventually he looked up at me for a moment and I knew that he was going to say something to put me at my ease, and he did. He asked: 'I wonder what all the rich people are doing today?'

We both started to laugh and I had a feeling that I had found a friend.

He told me that the picture was going to be directed by Sidney Furie, a new young Canadian director who had just had a hit with a small 'Biker' movie called *The Leather Boys*, and he talked about my seven-year contract in numbers that I could not comprehend. All I remember was that they were longer than telephone numbers and for the first time ever I heard the phrase 'hundred thousand pounds' and sat there bewildered and thinking what a wonderful language English was. Perhaps it was the vodka or the numbers that were flying around, or a combination of the two mixed with joy and adrenalin, I don't know, but as we walked out of there I never felt my feet touch the ground once. I was thiry-two years old: was life really going to change for me after all? I didn't dare believe that it would.

Terry was almost happier about my success than I was, and it wasn't because I would now be able to pay my share of expenses. He was genuinely upset that I had never made it, and told me so many times. I was eight years older than him and he really, rightly or wrongly, thought I was a good actor and could not understand how I had been overlooked; so my newfound good fortune had vindicated his faith in me and he was genuinely overjoyed. He was still moping around the place with the photo of 'Shrimp' as she was now popularly known, but being Terry he had not been carried away by this obsession and was 'walking out' as they say with a stunning girl who not only got us both into a little bit of trouble but was of great help to me as well. From time to time when Terry was not available, which was often, she would come round to the flat and have tea or a drink with me. On a few occasions she was accompanied by a handsome young Russian officer whom I found fascinating and used as research for *The Ipcress File* in which I played a spy against the Russians. He was very nice and charming and after a while I did not see him again and forgot about him.

One day I was in the flat alone when the doorbell went and I opened up to find two well-dressed but suspicious-looking young men standing outside. They flashed cards at me that said they were from MI5. This was very exciting, I thought – even more research! I had never even seen one of these people before let alone spoken to one of them. This was invaluable, but it was also worrying. What did they want with me? It was the Russian, they told me. They were checking all his contacts in London and I had been named as one of them. I started to get nervous at the word 'contact'. I had read enough thrillers to know that this word meant spies. They surely couldn't think that I was a Communist spy, I asked them. 'No,' they said, not very convincingly, they just wanted to eliminate me from their enquiries, which they eventually did after a pleasant afternoon of tea and on my part invaluable research. The Russian's name was Captain Eugen Ivanov and he was involved in the Profumo affair with Christine Keeler; he was a known agent, they informed me. As Profumo was the Minister of War at the time, his contact with Ivanov was, to say the least, suspect. For myself, I couldn't see how many military secrets could be leaked during a 'threesome' but I let that go and they let me go. A few weeks later I heard that Ivanov had been returned to Russia and had been shot. Never a dull moment in the sixties.

Terry got a film in America and I signed my contract with Harry, so there seemed no point in continuing to share a flat. I decided to set up in my own place. I found just the place I wanted, a little mews house in Albion Close just off the Bayswater Road near Marble Arch. Typical of my administrative abilities, I got rid of the Ebury Street flat before the new one was ready and was only rescued from sleeping in the street by my friend Vidal Sassoon, whom I had met years earlier around the London night scene. (Hairdressers don't eat lunch.) Vidal was a true child of the age. Deeply spiritual, he represented the very best of the flower children without the drugs. But life wasn't all about love and flowers and making ladies look good, so in spite of the fact that he was the most famous hairdresser in the world, this did not stop me from offering some advice to him in lieu of rent which he would not accept. I remember my talk with him with embarrassment now, considering that at the time he was ten times richer and infinitely more successful than I. I gave him a lecture on the way he was doing business, and the gist of it was something that I really believe you must do if you want to be mega-rich. It's simple. You must have something that is working for you while you are asleep. 'For instance, successful musicians have got it made,' I told him. 'Their records or music are being played all the time, every day, somewhere in the world. No matter what they are doing, they are still making money. You are a great hair-dresser,' I lectured him, 'but you can only charge so much for a hair-do and you can only stand on your feet for so long so there is a ceiling on the amount of money that you can make. So, you've got to make shampoos and other products that work for you while you are asleep.' He agreed with me and told me that that was what he was going to do. I think I paid for my stay.

There was still another delay with my house and I couldn't impose on Vidal any longer so I went and stayed with John Barry for a couple of weeks. By now, he was a top movie composer. He had done a great score for *Zulu* and was booked to write the music for *The Ipcress File*, which he did, magnificently. During my stay, he was writing the music for a James Bond film. I hadn't realised there was such a big drawback to staying with a composer: they compose all day and in John's case, all night. You wind up with no voice from shouting above the music. John could work for twenty-four hours at a stretch, and as he would not accept any rent either I took on the role of helpful gofer to his driven genius. I made the tea and sandwiches, did the tidying up and ran errands as he slaved away at the piano. One night I got no sleep at all, as over and over again for hours on end right until dawn he worked on the one same tune. I slept for short periods during the night and finally woke up with a start when the music stopped. I had grown so used to the noise that the silence had disturbed me. I decided to get up and make myself and John, if he was still awake, a cup of coffee. I went out into the living room and found him slumped exhausted over the piano. He had obviously finally finished the one tune that he had been slaving on all night. I made him some coffee and he played it for me as the sun came up and warmed the room. Not only was I the first person to hear this tune, I heard it and heard it all night long. 'What's it called?' I asked him when he finished playing. 'It's *Goldfinger*,' he replied – and fell fast asleep at the piano. Shortly after that my house in Albion Close was ready and I moved into my own home for the first time. A unique joy. That night I fell asleep in my strange new surroundings humming *Goldfinger* to make myself feel at home.

With Terry in America and me in a home of my own I knew that our friendship could never be quite the same again. His early success and my failure to become one had already created a divide in our lives but he had stuck with me loyally. Now, with *The Ipcress File*, I think he felt that I was on my feet at last and he no longer had to worry about me. Jean Shrimpton had left David Bailey, I heard on the London rumour line – which, by the way, then as now, was completely reliable and accurate – and the next I heard of her she had gone to America to work. I didn't have to wait long; I soon heard that she was now dating Terence Stamp of all people. Everybody said, 'Who would have thought it?' I didn't say anything. *I* would have thought it. Everybody felt sorry for Bailey, losing the most beautiful girl in the world, but we all reckoned without the sixties syndrome, which meant that no matter what went wrong it was going to be all right. While we were busy pitying Bailey, he turned up with Jean's replacement, a French actress called Catherine Deneuve. Sympathy for David cleared like mist and was replaced with the much more annoying envy. I'm telling you, the sixties were the only period in my life where nothing ever went wrong for anybody!

For those with little money, the world's first singles bar was on the King's Road and called the Kenya Coffee Bar. If you got lucky there and didn't have a lot of money for entertaining you could take your newfound friend to the Casserole, a very popular cheap restaurant just a little further along the King's Road.

Following their great success in *Beyond the Fringe*, Peter Cook and Dudley Moore opened a satirical nightclub in Greek Street in Soho called the Establishment. This quickly became the new 'in' place, especially when the American comedian Lenny Bruce arrived. It was here that he became the first man to say 'Fuck' on the British stage, causing an almighty uproar. It was also here that Peter Cook asked him not to say it on the night that Peter's mother and father were coming to see the show, and Lenny told him to 'Fuck off' – but not in front of his parents. The Establishment was great fun, but dangerous, too – not only onstage, where eventually Lenny had to stop saying the offending word because there were two police officers in every night waiting to close the place down if he said it again, but for the customers as well. I was walking out of the club one night when a petrol bomb was thrown from a passing car. It went over my head and exploded in the passage behind me. Although it wasn't a big bomb, and I wasn't hurt, my enthusiasm for the place was dampened even quicker than the ensuing fire. This I knew was the work of the local gangsters, who would come to a new business in the area and offer 'protection'.

Suddenly, 'satire' was everywhere – on television, in the theatre and in clubs like the Establishment, and the more ignorant amongst us all ran to our dictionaries to find out what the word really meant.

Dr Samuel Johnson once said that any man who was tired of London was tired of life, 'for there is in London all that life can afford'. As far as we were concerned, we never grew tired and knew that we would live forever. Like Johnson we had our own biographer as well. He was a journalist from the *Daily*

Express newspaper, his name was Peter Evans and he was the Boswell to all our Johnsons and the Pepys through all our windows. He and David Bailey produced the definitive sixties coffee-table book called *Goodbye Baby and Amen*.

This was a time when even our policemen were still wonderful, as the following story will illustrate. There is a working-class dessert called bread pudding which is made to use up stale bread. One Sunday, all of us London boys got our mothers to make one each and enter it in what we called 'The First International Bread Pudding Competition'. This prestigious event was held in the Playboy Club, which was on Park Lane at that time, and all the entries had to be in by one o'clock. Peter Evans was late with his and was caught speeding round Hyde Park Corner. When the policeman who stopped him asked where he was going, Peter explained that he was en route for The First International Bread Pudding Competition, and was running late with his entry. The policeman had obviously heard a few excuses in his time but he remained calm at this novel explanation and demanded to know what was on the back seat wrapped in tinfoil. Peter showed him his mother's entry, at which the officer commented that it looked like a winner. With that he got on his motor-bike and escorted Peter to the club, sirens blaring, just in time for him to avoid being disqualified – which was lucky, because Peter and his mum actually won. My mother and I came third. She had been a bit heavy-handed with the cinnamon, one of the main ingredients.

As well as our biographer, we had our own critic – Ken Tynan. He was not at all working class. In fact, he looked, walked and talked like a supreme example of an upper-class twit; his family and educational background were typical of that breed, but that was where the resemblance ended. Ken became the champion of the play *Look Back in Anger* in the late fifties, one of the few critics who actually understood what it was about and what was going on in the world generally. He knew what we were about, too, even though he didn't like some of it. What endeared him to us at the start was the legend that while he was at university he'd had a mistress who was a Polish bus conductress. That made him one of us. If we'd had a mistress while we were still at school it would probably have been a Polish bus conductress, too. However, what really made his reputation was the fact that he was the second person to say 'Fuck' in public, and his crime was even worse than Lenny Bruce's as he said it on television. Lenny had at least kept it in the context of a satirical nightclub, while Ken uttered the word where everyone could hear it! Pandemonium ensued. Middle-class, menopausal ladies aged ten years overnight, and immediately formed a censorship group which still exists in Britain today and which has done more than any other force or reason to reduce our once-great television network to the banal pap produced here today.

Like me, Ken hated all forms of censorship and he eventually put on the first all-nude show outside of stripclubs: it was called *Oh, Calcutta*! The logo was a picture of a beautiful young girl in a full-length evening gown. Seen from behind, she is looking back over her shoulder rather sexily, as well she might be, since a large round hole has been cut in her gown to reveal her very lovely and naked derrière. This, Ken explained, was a French painting, called in translation '*Oh, what a lovely arse you have*' – a title which, even with the new relaxation of theatre censorship, would have been unusable. In French the title was '*Oh, quel cul que tu as*'. If you say this quickly with an English accent, it comes out as '*Oh, Calcutta*'. He then went on about our film censor, who spent most of his time removing shots of ladies' naked breasts from films in case children should see them. This, Ken scoffed, was ridiculous – since children were the very people for whom ladies' breasts were invented. Somehow I could not argue with that. I got to know our film censor at the time quite well. His name was John Trevelyan, Secretary of the British Board of Film Censors from 1958, and one day he proved to me something I had always suspected of censors everywhere. He invited me to dinner and promised that afterwards he would show me a reel of shots that he had cut out of recent films. I didn't go, as it turned out, but my sneaking suspicion that the powers that be did not throw the 'dirty bits' away was

**vindicated. (My sneaking suspicion is that no one throws the
dirty bits away.)**

17

Butch cooking

I got to know my new boss Harry Saltzman very well. As a matter of fact I stuck to him like a drowning man to a straw, probably out of fear that if I did not see him at least once a day he would forget all about me and cast someone else in *The Ipcress File*. This fear was not without grounds, for I learned later that I was Harry's second choice for the role. Originally, he had cast Christopher Plummer, but Chris had been offered the lead opposite Julie Andrews in *The Sound of Music*, a much bigger film, and had turned this one down. Thank God.

I also came to know Harry's wife and children very well. Jacqueline Saltzman was a very attractive and vivacious woman aged about forty at the time, and as she was a Romanian from Paris and did not speak English very well, my French was put very much to the test. Harry had a large country mansion in Buckinghamshire and it was here that I started to spend every Sunday evening. The food was great and there was plenty of it, and the conversation was almost entirely in French because Harry would invite mostly French-speaking people for Jacquie's sake. Apart from their social aspect these occasions also served for business discussions – especially of course of *Ipcress*.

Our first problem was the fact that the book had been written in the first person, and the narrator had no name. One evening at the mansion we were sitting around discussing this when Harry said that this spy was to be the antithesis of James Bond: a very ordinary bloke, someone who could mingle unnoticed in a crowd and who should have an ordinary boring name. 'What's the dullest first name we can give him?' asked

Harry. Charlie Kasher, his partner on this film, myself and a couple of other people sat there meditating about this for a while and then, I suddenly, without thinking, blurted out: 'Harry is a pretty dull name.' There was a stunned silence as my *faux pas* registered, and all eyes turned to Harry who, for all his friendship and kindness, had a ferocious temper. He stared straight at me for a moment and then started to laugh. 'Let's call him Harry, then,' he said. 'My real name is Herschel.' Audible sighs of relief hissed round the room as the danger passed. Now we needed a surname. We all started to go through the dullest names we could think of – Smith, Brown, Jones, etc. None of them felt right. Finally, Harry said, 'The dullest person I ever met was called Palmer.' So that was it – the character was christened Harry Palmer.

It was during one of these Sunday evening sessions that our director hit on another idea for the character. I am short-sighted in real life and always wear glasses. During the meal Harry kept staring at me and finally remarked, 'I always hate it in films when actors who do not normally wear glasses are made to wear them and don't know how to handle them. You,' he said to me, 'know exactly what to do with them, so why don't we have Harry Palmer wear some in the film? It will also help to make the guy look more ordinary.' This, I thought, was a great idea – not only from the point of view of getting the character right but because of something else that had been niggling at me. If the first film was a success I would be doomed to play the same old character again and again, just like Sean Connery was doing in the Bond films and I had had several conversations with him lately in which he expressed his fear that the Bond character was now so popular that he was in danger of losing his own identity as an actor. Sean was afraid that this would make it difficult for him to get any other roles in the future. Here was my chance to put all of the identity of the Harry Palmer role into the glasses, a prop which, when removed, left me free for other roles.

Our efforts at making the man even more real went on to encompass him doing all the ordinary things that you could never imagine 007 doing. Remember, Harry was the co-producer of the Bond series at that time with Cubby Broccoli, and as *Ipcress* was his own production he wanted to get as far away as possible from the Bond image. We decided to have Harry Palmer shopping in a supermarket and pushing his own trolley full of groceries. Here was territory that Bond, brave though he was, would never have dared to tread. At this point, one or two of the fainter hearts started to demur – maybe we were making this Palmer guy just a bit too much of a wimp, but Harry told us not to worry. He would have Palmer fighting a duel with his boss, using the trolleys as weapons. I sat there listening to all this and worrying about the direction the project was taking in comparison with Bond. The latter had several million dollars' worth of special effects, a great name *and* a number – 007 – as well as a licence to kill. And here I was, winding up with glasses, a battle with supermarket trolleys and the dullest name that anyone could think of. Even my massive confidence started to wane from time to time.

Harry Palmer acquired yet another dimension after we had all gone to the home of Len Deighton, the author of *The Ipcress File*, for a meal one evening. Len is a great cook, and besides writing spy novels, at that time he also produced a cookery comic strip for the Sunday newspaper, *The Observer*. If you ever come across *Ipcress* on video or late-night television, keep an eye out for the walls of my kitchen in the film. They are plastered with Len's cookery strips. Anyway, that evening we decided to have Harry seduce the heroine *not* in the conventional way by taking her to a smart restaurant and plying her with booze, sweet music and romance, nor even by him going back to her place for a meal. No, he was going to take her back to *his* place and cook *her* a meal – an extreme reversal of the normal roles. Macho objectors started mumbling again. 'Everybody will think he's gay if he cooks the girl a meal,' someone objected.

'Don't worry,' soothed Harry. 'We'll do it all in a butch way.'

So Sid Furie the director and Harry went off to 'de-gay' my role in the script. The supermarket trolley problem had already been solved by having me use mine as a weapon. The glasses were satisfactorily 'butched up' in the seduction scene by having Sue Lloyd, who played the romantic lead, ask me if

I always wear glasses. I say, 'I only take them off in bed,' she looks at me for a moment, then reaches forward and takes them off . . . The cooking we made fast, expert and delicious. In that scene, I make her an omelette using the macho trick of breaking two eggs simultaneously and with one hand – very spectacular. I could not do this, however, as it is very tricky, so we had to use the hands of Len Deighton, who *could*. The only problem here was that being fair, my hands have blond hairs on them but Len's have jet black hair on them. No one seems to have ever noticed, though.

One of the great attractions of show business is its unpredictability, but this can be a two-edged sword, as our day number one of shooting on *Ipcress* was to prove. My first day of true movie stardom started out beautifully. I got up at six-thirty – the sun was shining already – and showered and shaved, only cutting myself slightly. It didn't matter, I was too happy to care. I dressed casually and studied my lines for the first scene for the thousandth time, ate a light breakfast and then was ready for the fray. Seven-thirty came and with it my chauffeur-driven car to take me to work. The driver held the door open for me and I stepped inside and settled back in the deep seats for my triumphant drive to Pinewood Studios. I sat there for a while savouring the moment and noticed an added bonus: the rush-hour traffic coming into town was jammed solid on the other side of the road but my side was empty, and would be again this evening. Life as a movie star was already easy, even on the roads . . .

My reverie was broken as the chauffeur's voice came zinging back at me like a sharp dart. 'What's this film *Ipcress* about then, salad?' I tensed up immediately; antagonism and insolence suddenly choked the atmosphere in the car.

'It's about spies,' I replied flatly, hoping in vain to end the conversation.

There was a short pause. 'Have you read it?' he asked, to my surprise.

'Of course I've read it,' I replied. 'I am the star of it.'

His next line surprised me as well. 'Well, I've read it and I think it's a load of crap.'

I sat there for a moment, stunned and absolutely furious at

this insult to my precious future. Finally I said, 'Don't speak to me for the rest of this journey.'

'If that's the way you want it,' he replied, and we sat there in deathly silence, my big day spoiled already and I hadn't even got to the studio yet.

When we eventually did arrive I leapt out of the car still in a fury, and for the first and only time in my professional life I fired someone. I also suggested that as he was such an authority on crap, perhaps he should get a job driving the 'Honey Wagon', which is our euphemism for the toilet truck.

I turned to walk away to my dressing room, only to find my way barred by a breathless assistant director who informed me that Sidney Furie wanted all the unit gathered on the sound stage at once. Still in a temper I joined him and the rest of the unit on the sound stage. When we were all assembled, Sid took his script, placed it on the floor and set fire to it. We all stood there aghast as the pages curled and squirmed in the heat as though the actual characters were dying in the flames. Finally my immediate future was a small pile of grey ash and the scene took on a funereal air as tears rolled down our faces from the thick cloud of smoke that hung over the set. We stood staring at Sid for a moment and then he said, 'That is what I think of that.' Then, after a pause, he said to me, 'Oh, what the hell. Give me your script. We've got to shoot this son of a bitch anyway.' I gave it to him and we finally went to work, my confidence shot to pieces. Sidney had just burnt the script of the best film that has been made so far: in show business you never know when you are well off.

In *Ipcress* we used the basis of Len's story but it fell to all of us, and me in particular, to create our own dialogue. Fortunately most of us were good at this and a lot of it turned out to be quite funny – but it was a nerve-wracking way to play one's first starring role. Sid also decided to shoot it as though the camera were someone else watching while hiding behind things. Thus there always seemed to be something between me and the camera, or else it would be very close and at an unusual angle, often shooting straight up my nose. Sid and Harry had a lot of rows, with Harry's temper living up to its reputation. I sometimes feared that he would have a heart attack, while the rest of the unit were *hoping* that he would – Sid, in particular. The climax to all these rows came one day when we were on location in Shepherd's Bush, a run-down area of west London. The first I knew of it was when Sid came running round a street corner and almost knocked me flying. To my astonishment, I saw that he was crying. He stared at me for a moment and then screamed through his tears, 'Fuck it, I'm off this picture,' and with one bound jumped on a number 12 bus that was just pulling away from its stop, and disappeared in the direction of Oxford Circus.

Shortly afterwards, Harry came charging round the same corner. 'Where's he gone?' he bawled at me. 'Down the Bayswater Road on a number 12 bus,' I replied, but Harry didn't believe me. 'Nobody leaves my set on a fucking bus,' he bellowed. I eventually persuaded him that I was telling the truth and his enormous Phantom Five Rolls Royce was brought up and we both piled in and the chase was on. We eventually caught up with the bus and stayed close behind it waiting for it to stop.

'Get closer!' Harry yelled at his chauffeur as he slid the window down. Meanwhile the bus conductor, who was standing on the platform at the back, was watching all this with great interest, not the least because the car we were in was exactly the same as the one used by Her Majesty the Queen on state occasions. He was peering intently into the car to see if Her Majesty was indeed there, when Harry leaned out of the window and yelled at him, 'Stop the fucking bus! You've got our director on board.' You could see it suddenly occur to the conductor that maybe Her Majesty was *not* in our car, but he quickly hid his disappointment and stopped the bus at the very next stop. Harry and I boarded it and after a fourpenny ride to Marble Arch, we managed to persuade Sid to come back and finish the film. Which he did without further mishap.

When *Ipcress* was finished there was a side-effect that I had forgotten about in my enthusiasm for my work. I was getting paid for all this – and very well, too. Suddenly and for the first time in my life I was able to indulge myself in all the material things that had been missing so far. However, the first effect of sudden riches came as a complete surprise to me. I had often thought about what I would do if I ever had a lot of money – I'm sure most people have. I considered luxury travel to distant places, great homes with staff and servants, cars, clothes, everything except what I did choose first. The most important luxury for me turned out to be hygiene. Poverty always seems to be synonymous with dirt, which is not surprising I suppose. If you haven't got enough money to eat, soap might well come quite a long way down your list of priorities. All my life I had spent making dirty shirts last another day, hiding holes in my socks, cleaning my teeth with salt because I could not afford toothpaste, going without shampoo for the same reason and sleeping in dirty bedclothes because I had no money for the laundry. With my newfound wealth I went completely mad, buying masses of shirts, sheets, towels, socks, tubes of toothpaste, bottles of shampoo and a complete collection of aftershave lotions until it was almost impossible to move in my bathroom. I showered in the morning and luxuriated in bubble baths for ages in the evening, until my skin started to softly wrinkle. I seemed to be trying to soak the grime and muck of my first thirty years out of my skin overnight.

I had now been earning ten thousand pounds per week for fifteen weeks – a situation which for me and I am sure anyone else with my background, was beyond belief. I was both stunned and delighted by the enormity of the sums. It was time to start re-equipping my new home in Albion Close and making it really comfortable. I had enormous fun going out and spending money on the place, acquiring luxurious items like an American fridge that apart from the normal functions also made ice and dispensed it crushed or in cubes as the mood took you, as well as delivering ice water from a tap. I bought the biggest colour televisions I could find and put one in every room including the bathroom. I also purchased the best and loudest hi-fi I could locate and taped that through every room. I filled the fridge and pantry with food, acquired all the latest records and, greatest luxury of all, I bought books – *hundreds* of them, and I read them all, though where I found the time I do not know. I selected a load of clothes for all occasions from my great friend Doug Hayward, and bought shirts to match from Turnbull & Asser. The measurements for the shirts, I was informed, could be taken at home in the evening if I was busy in the daytime. I was busy, I told them, and they said that 'Mr Michael' would be with me at seven o'clock that evening. The clock struck seven, the doorbell went and when I opened the door I was astonished to find a thirty-year-old boy scout, complete with short trousers and staff, smiling at me. 'I'm Mr Michael,' he announced, 'and I'm on my way to a scout meeting. I've just popped by to measure you for your shirts.' So there I was, able at last to afford shirts made by the most expensive shirtmaker in England, only to have my measurements taken by a boy scout. No matter what you expect, things never turn out quite like they should, do they?

This move was basically the end of my long and close relationship with Terry Stamp. Our lives, values and interests had already started to drift apart but the move, coupled with my sudden affluence, quickened the process. I still saw Terry from time to time and he was changing noticeably, as I was for him, no doubt. He had a goal: perfection and the top. I had a panic: survival and existence. Unnoticed by either of us, this was to be the first chink in the armour of our friendship. As I grew ever more materialistic, unbeknownst to me he was becoming more spiritual, so much so in fact that he along with many others of the sixties' generation finally wound up in a commune in India. It was run by a guru who taught that although you should be ashamed of your wealth, if you gave it all to him, he would then assume the burden of your share for you. Believe it or not, a great many normally intelligent people fell for this. I suppose its appeal was that so many of those who went to India did feel they had made their money too easily and did not deserve to keep it. By my own estimation I was not one of them.

In his autobiography Terry has written that our friendship ceased when I found us a new flat then grabbed the biggest bedroom for myself, leaving only a boxroom for him. This is not the way I saw it. I took the flat at Albion Close for myself alone; at no time was there any question of Terry sharing. Why would we share? I had plenty of money now and he had even more than I did. What actually happened was that Terry went away for a while to America, and came back with Jean Shrimpton. They had nowhere to stay and he asked me to put them up for a bit until he found a flat, which I did although I was very embarrassed about asking them to use the very tiny second bedroom in my flat. However, Terry said it was all right because it would only be for a few days. Actually it turned out to be a couple of weeks, after which he went off somewhere, leaving Jean with me at the flat and did not return to collect her for at least three weeks. Then they moved out. I was very upset when I read his account of this incident. He had been my closest friend for a couple of years, extra-ordinarily generous to me when I was down and there is *no way* that I would have repaid all this kindness with such shabby treatment.

What is ironic about Terry's version of my so-called 'selfish behaviour' is that during the time he was staying with me at Albion Close, he got a call from Lewis Gilbert, the director, offering him the part of Alfie in the film version of Bill Naughton's play. To my astonishment, Terry turned it down, and I actually spent three whole hours trying to talk him into accepting it. I still wake up screaming in the middle of the night as Terry takes my advice and accepts the role. The reason he didn't want to do it was because when he had taken the play to Broadway, it had flopped and he now wanted nothing more to do with it.

I never considered trying for the film role myself because I had been unable to get the part on stage. The film, as I later learned, was turned down by many British actors because it contained an abortion scene, and stars in those days did not want be associated with anything of that kind, in case it ruined their image. Behind the scenes my agent, Dennis, and Harry Saltzman were pushing for me to get the part but I knew it was impossible. However, something happened then to change everything: Lewis saw a rough-cut of *Ipcress* and offered me the part immediately. I read the screenplay and knew that it would work on film, especially those places where Alfie talks directly to the camera. I reached page two of the script, stopped reading and phoned Lewis and told him I'd do it. Then I read the rest of the script.

18

Alfie

Alfie had started out as a radio play called *Alfie Elkins and His Little Life*, so the dialogue was particularly good. The very first Alfie in this radio play was Bill Owen, who is now famous on British television in a series called *Last of the Summer Wine*. Another unusual thing about *Alfie* was the author himself. When you think of the subject and the hero, you would expect him to be a young swinger, but in actual fact Bill Naughton was even then pushing sixty. I had of course done another play of Bill's on television several years before – *Somewhere for the Night*. This was very good, but *Alfie* was much, much better.

I took an instant liking to Lewis Gilbert. He was a quiet, sincere man who loved actors and I felt a kindred spirit with him. I don't know why – perhaps it's that we do look a lot like each other. He too comes from a similar background of working-class London with a mother who worked, but in a different job from my mother's. Mrs Gilbert was a film extra. I worked with her many times subsequently, and on each occasion she informed me proudly that she was the mother of Lewis Gilbert who had directed me in *Alfie*.

When they were casting the rest of the roles in the movie, Lewis rang me one day and asked if I knew of a good actress to play the middle-aged married woman whom Alfie seduces, and for whom he has to procure an abortion. I knew immediately who I would cast for this – Vivien Merchant, who had been with me in the play *The Room* at the Royal Court Theatre. This, you remember, was Harold Pinter's first play and at that time Vivien was his wife. Lewis was happy to offer her the part, on condition that she did a screen test first.

215

Vivien had never made a movie before and so there was no film of her for a director to see. This is very important for directors, because no matter how well someone acts or how stunning they look, until you have seen them *on screen* you have no idea what you are going to get. However, Vivien refused to do a test and Lewis refused to employ her unless she did. Stale-mate. It was here that I did myself a favour. I stepped into the fray and talked Lewis into using her without a test. Vivien was brilliant in the film, a pleasure to work with and she was eventually nominated for an Oscar in America, so my judgment was vindicated – for a change.

Most of the film was shot on location, and the very first shot took place at night on the Embankment, just near the statue of Boudicca opposite Big Ben. If you remember from the beginning of this book, this is where I trod in some dog shit on my very first take, so it was a really lucky place for me. However, even I did not know just how lucky I was going to be . . .

Filming went smoothly for a little while and then we did the first scene where I had to talk straight into the lens. Lewis and I had studied two previous examples of this – Olivier in *Richard III* and Albert Finney in *Tom Jones*. Both were executed in a declamatory and theatrical style as though addressing a real audience. I decided to follow suit, but when we saw the rushes this technique did not work. It looked artificial in the modern realistic setting of *Alfie*. Lewis and I had a short conference – a very short one, as our entire budget only stretched to half a million dollars so we did not have the luxury of great lengthy artistic discussions. Lewis decided to bring the camera in very close and have me speak *not* to an audience, but to one close confidant. The intimacy of this worked so well with those who watched the rushes, that we decided to keep it this way. It allowed me to speak to the audience, even though I was on the screen with another actor – who, we presumed, could not hear what I was saying. I could also make asides to them, and in the scene with Eleanor Bron as the doctor who is examining me for tuberculosis, I actually do a whole scene directly to the audience, with asides to the character on screen. This turned out to be one of the funniest and best scenes in the picture.

As with all movies, I was to find that not everything went as smoothly as one would hope for, and that any problems usually came from 'straight out of left field', as the Americans say. Jane Asher, the young actress who was playing one of my many girlfriends, had a bedroom scene with me in which she appeared to be clad in one of my shirts and nothing else. As this shirt was not transparent and was about the same length as the mini skirts that were all the rage at the time, we thought that modesty was being upheld and that there was nothing prurient or salacious about the scene. However, Jane happened to be the girlfriend or maybe even the fiancée of Paul McCartney of the Beatles at the time, and we were discreetly informed that Mr McCartney did not approve of the length of my shirt, nor the amount of Miss Asher's leg that it exposed, so before we shot the scene our wardrobe department had to cut up one of my spare shirts of the same design and add about a foot to the length of the original one. With the shirt now reaching well below Jane's knees, Victorian standards of modesty were restored, except that with a shirt of that length, I should have been seven feet tall . . . but it was a comedy, so what the hell. Jane looked very fetching, did a very good job and Paul came on the set and approved and so life in the movies went on its eccentric way as usual.

I learned an important lesson on this movie – *never* smoke during a lengthy dialogue scene. There I was having done a long shot of a scene smoking a cigarette all the way through, and everything was fine until Lewis said, 'OK, we are coming for the close up.' I still hadn't spotted the difficulty until shooting was underway, when the continuity girl called for the shot to be cut because my hand movements with the cigarette did not match those in the long – which of course was absolutely essential if the editor was going to be able to cut between the two shots. We did the shot over and over as I took a puff on the wrong line and then blew the smoke out on another wrong line. It became a nightmare and eventually took fifteen takes to get the shot – a rarity on *Alfie*, where the majority of the shots in the film were take one, not because we were particularly brilliant but because we had very little money thus very little time. Needless to say, I never smoked in movies again. There was a time many years later when I asked the continuity girl on a movie I was making to give me the matching for a particular shot and she said in a very matter-of-fact, posh English voice: 'You get up from the chair on *Bastard* and you kick him in the balls on *Fuck you*.' This shot was a lot simpler to match than the one in *Alfie*.

Right from the very first shot there were good vibrations with this movie, and gradually everybody's attitude toward me changed from, 'Will he screw it up?' to 'Maybe we have got something here.' Lewis himself was marvellous – always there with a few words of encouragement when I got tired, for it was a marathon of a part. He could not get me to come to rushes, though, and he could never convince me that the film was going well, so one day he told me to listen outside the theatre door when they were showing the day's rushes. I did so, and was amazed at the amount of laughter. Suddenly, for the first time, I thought we might be on to a winner.

Things were moving along easily, too easily in fact, until I was at a stage where I was sailing through scenes with all the confidence of a Spencer Tracy when suddenly in came an actor called Denholm Elliott as the abortionist, who started to act me off the screen. Socks were pulled up and shoulders put to the wheel to combat this extremely charming new menace, but to no avail. I never ever managed to top him, only just managed to hold my own, in fact.

On top of this came a new experience for me, acting with a Hollywood 'Name' and the name was Shelley Winters. She came thundering down a corridor of the Dorchester Hotel in London where we were shooting a location scene. It was eight o'clock on a Monday morning, and I was just about to go into one of the hotel rooms that had been rented for make-up when I saw her. I decided to introduce myself there and then, which I did and she said, 'Let's do it before we go into make-up otherwise we will have to get made up again.'

'Do what?' I asked innocently.

'Screw,' she replied to my amazement. 'I always like to screw the leading man on the first day and get it out of the way because it can interfere with the performance sometimes.'

I stood there for a moment with my mouth agape, trying to reply but for once speechless and then I fled, her laughter echoing down the corridor behind me. She was not serious, of course. I think she was just playing the old pro trick of wrong-footing the other actor if you don't feel too confident yourself, which of course you never do on the first day.

Shelley and I became two disasters that were always about to happen but never quite did. When I was doing a love scene with her, rolling on the floor, one of the bones came out of the corset that I did not know she was wearing and went straight and painfully up my nose just as I was about to kiss her. Another time, in an extremely close close-up on a very hot day, I was just about to tell her that I loved her when her whole face rolled gently down her chin and settled on her neck. I stepped back and gazed in wonder at this, then watched as the make-up man reset the adhesive tape that had come unstuck behind her ears in the heat: an early and primitive form of face lift without surgery.

One morning, just before a shot in the studio, I watched as Shelley placed a small glass of water on a ledge out of sight behind the scenery. After a while I got thirsty, and when she was not looking I took a great swig of her water and nearly choked. The glass was full of vodka. 'What the hell do you call this?' I gasped, holding the glass out towards her.

'Acting,' she replied curtly, and that was the end of the conversation.

I had never thought of *Alfie* as being anything other than a parochial British movie with no market abroad, but I was soon to discover that not everybody agreed with me. The first sign came when I was post-synching the picture. This is a process whereby if the sound is not right on the original take, you go to a theatre and lipsynch your own voice on to the track in time with the picture on the screen. When I had finished the normal post-synching they asked me to do one hundred and twenty-five new loops in clearer English for a possible American release. I had never imagined that *Alfie* would be released in the US and had played the role in a very thick Cockney accent with lots of slang words that would have made it impossible for an American to understand. Shelley

Winters told me many years later that she had never understood a single word I said to her in *Alfie*, and had just waited for my lips to stop moving and taken that as her cue to speak.

One day, when the film was finished and awaiting its release date, I had lunch with Lewis and while we were eating and talking he very calmly dropped into the conversation a thought that had my head reeling: 'I think you will be nominated for an Academy Award for this one,' he said calmly, as if discussing the weather. This was Lewis's way of doing things. I did not believe it, of course, but the mere fact that someone like him thought enough of my performance to even mention it in the same breath was an unexpected compliment indeed. The film was finished and all I had to do was sit and wait for the verdict . . .

Meanwhile, it was out of the fantasy land of film and back to that true realm of make-believe, the sixties. It was 1966 – at least I *think* it was, but as someone once said, 'Anyone who can remember the sixties was not in London at the time.'

The Beatles released their song *Sergeant Pepper's Lonely Hearts' Club Band* with a record cover by the painter Peter Blake, who seemed to be the king of a new style called Pop Art. Frank Sinatra was a *Stranger in the Night* while his daughter Nancy was assuring us that *These Boots Are Made for Walking*. The Beach Boys had *Good Vibrations* and the Rolling Stones ominously sang *Paint it Black*. In the cinema, Julie Christie had a big hit in John Schlesinger's film *Darling*, Vanessa Redgrave was in Karel Reisz's *Morgan, A Suitable Case for Treatment* co-starring David Warner, and her sister Lynn had just made the lovely film *Georgy Girl* with James Mason. Sean had a massive hit with *Thunderball* and was following it up with *You Only Live Twice*. Peter Sellers was wildly funny as Inspector Clouseau in the Pink Panther films, and *A Shot in the Dark*. Richard Lester, an expatriate American director made the two Beatles films *Help!* and *A Hard Day's Night*. Another American expatriate, Stanley Kubrick, offered us *Dr Strangelove, or How I Learned to Stop Worrying and Love the Bomb* – a title that was strangely symptomatic of the sixties, as the threats of nuclear oblivion came and went with monotonous regularity. I think that part of the rationale of that period in London was along the lines of 'To hell with everything – we may not be here in four minutes' time.' That was how long it would take, or so we had been told, for a Russian nuclear missile to reach our capital city and annihilate us.

In the midst of this explosion of talent and excitement came the première of *The Ipcress File*, a title which was short for *Induction of Psychoneuroses by Conditioned Reflex under Stress*. It was not a true big movie première but opened on a Thursday night at the Leicester Square Theatre; the public was allowed in all parts of the auditorium except for the front two rows of the circle, which were reserved for those of us who had made the picture. Harry and I slipped out just before the end to stand in the lobby anonymously and eavesdrop on what the public said as they came out. The first man to emerge spotted me immediately, and came right over to us.

'Were you the bloke in that film?' he asked aggressively.

'Yes,' I replied, taken aback by his attitude.

'It was the biggest load of crap I have ever seen!' he yelled for everyone to hear, and stormed off. People stared at us as though we were criminals and we stared back as though we were guilty, which of course we were, if it was *that* bad.

I fled immediately in a state of depression to Dollies club and sat there with my friend Johnny Gold until dawn then went home very drunk and miserable. I dropped fully clothed on to my bed and fell fast asleep. I awoke not with a start but a tremor of fear, as I knew I would have to face the day of the critics. I showered slowly and dressed with the movements of a condemned man. I went round to the newsstand and bought every paper that was published at that time and took them home, resisting the temptation all the way to open one and have a peek at a review.

When I got back home I went into the living room and pushed open the big window there, took a few deep breaths of air and opened the first newspaper. This was my first true starring role in a movie, the one that really counted – and my name was above the title for the first time, too. That wasn't in my contract, but one day at the end of the filming, Harry had come to me and promised to do this. When I asked why, he replied, 'If I don't think you are a star, why should anybody else?' Good thinking. As if to confirm Armageddon, the first review that I read was a stinker. My future sank over the horizon. But, miraculously, the next one was good and my future started to dawn again almost immediately. The one after that was marvellous – and so on and on and on.

As I was reading the critics, a strange thing started to happen to me. I suddenly found myself sobbing uncontrollably, and screwing each review up into a ball after I'd read it and throwing them out of the window down into the street below as the years of stress, anger and pent-up frustration started to flow out of me in the form of tears, over my face and down to the floor where I stamped them into the carpet and oblivion, for ever.

How long I stood there doing this, I have no idea, but suddenly I became aware of someone watching me. I looked down into the mews and there was an old charlady from one of the houses standing looking up at me. 'You'd better come down here, my lad, and pick this lot up,' she said, gesturing at the rolled-up balls of newspaper strewn all around her. 'What are you crying for anyway,' she called gently, 'a man your age. It's time you grew up.' With that she turned and walked away, having unintentionally given me a great piece of advice. I went down and picked up the paper and from that day on I grew up as she had suggested. I'd made it at last and life was never going to be the same again. I was receiving real money and getting masses of publicity. Thank God. I was thirty-two years old.

I went straight up to Sheffield to see Dominique. She was nine years old now and I had spent a lot of time unable to see her. I wanted to keep up the close contact against the day when she grew old enough to choose independently to see me.

Back in London, I had to endure even more publicity, and the only problem with this was that they had cast me in the role of poor boy makes millions. Untrue of course, but it was very embarrassing for me because my mother was still working as a charlady and would not give it up, no matter how I pleaded.

I finally struck on a great idea. I had been going about things in the wrong way, by asking her to give up the job for her sake. Of course, this had no effect at all, so I put it another way: I said that now I was rich and famous, it would be very harmful for me if the press found out that my mother at the age of sixty-six was still getting up at 6 a.m. to scrub floors. If they knew that, I said, they would annihilate me!

'All right,' she said. 'If it's for you, I'll stop,' and she did. She never went back, once she realised that it would harm one of her boys. That's how she was.

19

Lemon and Micklewhite

The Wrong Box should have been a massive success if you went by its pedigree. Bryan Forbes had just directed *King Rat* and *Séance on a Wet Afternoon*; and the screenplay was written by Americans Larry Gelbart and Burt Shevelove, co-authors of *A Funny Thing Happened on the Way to the Forum*. It was also the film début of Peter Cook and Dudley Moore, and contained a wonderful cameo role by Peter Sellers as well as being stuffed full of great actors who were completely unknown outside Britain. Ralph Richardson and John Mills were famous, I suppose, but here were brilliant, internationally unknown stars like Tony Hancock, Cicely Courtneidge, Irene Handl and that most British actor of them all, Wilfred Lawson.

I was cast as a thirty-three-year-old virgin in *The Wrong Box*. This was only a small role, but it meant that I could work with Bryan and his wife Nanette Newman so I took it. It was on this film that Bryan and I cemented our friendship. *The Wrong Box* is a Victorian comedy that rapidly develops into farce, and is so British that it met with a gentle success in most places except Britain, where it was a terrible flop. I suppose this was because the film shows us exactly as the world sees us – as eccentric, charming and polite – but the British knew better that they were none of these things, and it embarrassed them.

Wilfred Lawson was an ageing alcoholic at the time, and Bryan had to stand for his insurance on the film because no company would do so. The picture was shot in the beautiful city of Bath and it was on the journey there before work even started that we discovered exactly why Wilfred Lawson found it so difficult to obtain insurance. He was bombed out of his mind twenty-four hours per day, but he was still one of the most brilliant actors with whom I ever worked.

Knowing his proclivity for the grog, Bryan had him put on a nonstop train to Bath by a responsible young assistant-director, to be met at the other end by another assistant, but Wilfred, they discovered, was not on the train. This was a mystery, and frantic phone calls flew between Bryan on the set where we were shooting, and Bath station. The train had not stopped anywhere en route, had been thoroughly searched, and yet our friend was nowhere to be found. Finally they gave up the search and moved the train out of the station, only to find Wilfred sound asleep on the opposite line, having got out of the carriage on the wrong side. He was dragged off the line just before the London-bound express came tearing through in the other direction.

In the movie, I have a romance with Nanette and we live a couple of doors away from each other in that beautiful Nash Crescent in Bath which has been used in hundreds of films now. The thing we liked about this arrangement was that Nanette lived in the actual house once occupied by Lady Hamilton, and I in the one where Nelson lived, at the time of their affair! Our film romance, however, was a very different matter and we both finished up unsullied.

I was staying at an hotel in Bristol, and one morning as I came out of my room to go to work, I saw a very familiar figure coming towards me. There were only the two of us in the passageway so as I reached him I stopped and said rather stupidly, 'You're Cary Grant.'

'I know,' he replied. 'What's your name?'

I told him, and he recognised it from something he had read in the paper about *The Ipcress File*. Mystified, I asked him what he was doing in this neck of the woods and he told me that his mother lived permanently in the suite next door to mine, and that he visited her every time he came to England. That short conversation was the beginning of a friendship that lasted until his death.

My *bête noire* returned in this film – as a matter of fact, there were two *bêtes* and they were *très très noires*. They were a pair of black horses pulling a funeral carriage which I, for some insane reason, had agreed to drive in the film. I'd had enough trouble with that one horse in *Zulu*, but now here I was driving two. My only consolation was that they were fixed to a carriage, and that the road ahead was blocked by the camera car which was filming a scene between Nanette and me as we drove slowly along. What could possibly go wrong?

I will tell you what went wrong. For the first time in its nine years of service, so the camera crew later informed me, the camera car backfired with a loud bang, right up the noses of my two horses. This kind of fright, I soon discovered, makes horses stand on their hind legs and flee sideways if the road in front is blocked. Being harnessed together but fleeing right and left separately, made the two horses part momentarily then smash together with a loud horsey grunt accompanied by loud farts in our faces as they strained to go in any direction. Driving coach-horses may look romantic, but even at the best of times, as any vegetarian will tell you, living things that eat roughage *fart* a lot – so when you see a dreamy carriage-ride in a film, just remember that the driver, if seated behind the horses, is suffering from near-asphyxiation and praying for the director to shout, 'Cut!'

Nanette and I were mere feathers behind these two frantic animals. I was heaving on the reins, but the horses noticed none of this. Nanette was threatening to jump but I yelled at her not to. And when she started to scream, she swears that I whispered to her, 'Don't scream! You will have to post-synch it!' – such is my dislike of the process.

The two horses did not appear to comprehend that they were shackled together. Each of them would race as hard as he could for a while, only to be surprised to find the other one had kept up with him. Eventually they gave up and called it a draw just before my arms abandoned hope completely and we all lived happily ever after.

Bachelors always have married couples as friends, somewhere to go for an occasional evening of domestic bliss far away from the trench warfare of the search for love, lust or romance. I already had Roger Moore and his wife Luisa as one haven and Bryan and Nanette Forbes and Leslie and Evie Bricusse as two other reliable ports in a storm. The only problem with all of the above was that they lived outside of central London.

One wonderful couple who lived right in the heart of London were Ken Adam and his wife Letitia. He was a German Jew who had escaped from Berlin and became a pilot with the RAF, participating in the Battle of Britain, while she was a truly fiery Italian from Ischia, who loved to cook and did so magnificently. I had met them when he designed the sets for *Ipcress*. Ken was better known as the designer of all the early Bond films. I became very fond of these two and spent a great deal of time at their home in Montpelier Square, which is opposite Harrods. You can't get more central than that.

Here I met a whole new group of people. One evening I was introduced to a mild-mannered little man who turned out to be Arthur C. Clarke, the great science-fiction writer. He told me of his experience with the press in the late forties, when he had given a conference to explain how the Olympics would very soon be broadcast simultaneously to every country in the world by satellite television beamed from outer space. Apparently, only three correspondents from the British press turned up, and one of those had walked out, laughing, halfway through his speech. It was reassuring to hear that someone really important had suffered the same derision as I had when I made my own predictions about the stars and me becoming one of them.

I also made friends with another fascinating man – the American director Stanley Kubrick. He had settled in England and I often used to go to his place just outside Elstree Studios to watch movies in his home cinema. He and his wife Christiana were another of my married couples, she a German girl who was a wonderful painter. When Stanley was making *2001: A Space Odyssey* I clearly remember him choosing the music for the film. He had a ticket for the local library, where you could not only borrow books but take out gramophone records, too – but only one at a time. This meant that Stanley would go to the library each day, come back with one record, listen to it then start the whole process all over again. One day, he announced that he had found the right theme for the film, and it was called *Also Sprach Zarathustra* by Wagner. I had no idea what this sounded like, but now it is familiar to us all as the theme from *2001*, courtesy of Elstree public library.

It was at the Adams' house that I met Albert Finney's wife, the French actress Anouk Aimée. She had been a pin-up of mine ever since I was a callow youth and had seen her in a French film called *Les Aimants de Vérone*. I became absolutely smitten at the time, and eventually the rest of the world caught up with me after her performance in the movie *A Man and a Woman*. I still grew a little tongue-tied whenever we met. For her part, Anouk always used to make a bee-line for me, as I was the only Englishman she knew who could speak French, and what is more, she really liked my accent, which apparently resembled that of a five-year-old boy and made her feel very motherly towards me, even though she was my junior. Typical! I had waited all these years to meet my idol only to find that she was married to a friend and had maternal leanings towards me.

One day I went to visit my mother and was surprised when she suddenly burst into tears as we were chatting. When I asked her what the matter was, she said that she had not seen or heard from my brother Stanley for at least six months. I promised her that I would find him, and went away not even knowing where to start. To begin with, I made a lot of enquiries amongst his friends but none of them had seen him for months, either. It was a mystery I could not solve. I had almost given up when one day I decided that I needed a much more luxurious sofa for my living room, so off I went to a very expensive furniture store called Heal's and started to inspect their handsome range of seats. None of them was nice enough so the salesman offered to have a new delivery brought out of the storeroom. I waited and eventually a lovely sofa was carried in by two scruffily dressed backroom labourers who were immediately dismissed from the show-room floor before any customer could see them. As they turned to go, I caught the eye of one of them – and it was my brother Stanley. I bought the sofa and told him to come with me there and then. I had never seen him so down and out. I was shocked and not a little guilty to have a brother in this condition while I was living in the lap of luxury. I took him back home with me and set about improving his life, which thank God I was able to do.

I was now coincidentally about to start to travel, so I asked Stanley to live at my flat while I was away and it all worked out just right. He had a home and I had someone I trusted to take care of it for me in my absence. Although I knew I would be travelling, I had no idea for how long, nor just how far I was going to go. This was my first foray into what I call 'career overdrive' – back-to-back film-making. Success had come late for me – *very* late, and I was not about to let anything stand in the way of my progress.

There was one more thing to do before I left London and that was to attend the première of *Alfie*. This time the première was a giant affair held at the Plaza Cinema in Piccadilly and everyone but *everyone* was there. All four Beatles came and all four Rolling Stones, plus Barbra Streisand and her current husband Elliott Gould. I sat next to Tippi Hedren, who fainted at the abortion sequence in the film and had to be carried out. There were many more British stars and celebrities, and so that she could see and meet them in the flesh, I had brought as my date for the show, my mother. This time I would not take no for an answer. The film went very well and we had a great party afterwards in a pub at Piccadilly called The Cockney Pride. My mother loved it and had to be poured out of the party at 2 a.m. I was pleased that she had finally experienced a little of the sort of life that I was leading. The reviews were great and the picture obviously going to be much bigger than any of us had ever anticipated, and it very definitely established me as a star – which means someone who can carry a movie, not just someone who has a kidney-shaped swimming pool in Beverly Hills (although I did have some ambitions in that direction one day for myself).

Now my long travels began. *The Ipcress File* was being shown out of competition at the Cannes Film Festival, and Harry Saltzman invited me to go over there with him and help publicise it for the foreign market. I was given a grand suite in the Carlton Hotel, which is *the* place to stay at Festival time in Cannes. If you are very rich – and here I am talking major money, you stay at the Hôtel du Cap at Cap D'Antibes. The price of a room here at Festival time would keep an Ethiopian family in Perrier water for a year.

At first I found the place very exciting, with its plethora of major stars from countries all over the world. Of course, many of these I did not recognise, but you could always tell which ones were stars by their entourage. Although I had a luxury suite, I could soon see that this was going to become a prison, once *Ipcress* was shown. Sure enough, I was unable to go out on the streets again as the whole town was a-jostle with press photographers and press agents – including my own, Theo Cowan, who was to become a lifelong friend. I introduce Theo here with particular sadness, because as I write I have just returned from his funeral: it is now December 1991. Theo was a master of the Cannes Festival, guiding me through the treacherous swamp which the movie press can be at times, and directing me to the right sort of journalists for my interviews. Theo always wore khaki shorts and a bush-shirt when he was in what he called 'the heat of Cannes' and he looked a bit like a stray from *The Four Feathers*, but he was a great press agent.

Sean Connery, who was already world-famous as Bond, came and was so engulfed by the press and autograph-hunters that he literally could not go to the hotel dining room for a meal and so left on the same day he had arrived, before his film was shown. The Beatles were there, too, and we all wound up one afternoon at a reception given by the British Consul in the ballroom at the Carlton. All the stars had to line up and shake hands with the people that the Consul had invited. I was positioned next to John Lennon. It very quickly became obvious to us that the guests were mainly old British expats who knew the Consul or somebody and had just come for the afternoon out. A lot of them knew nothing about films, the Festival and even less about England, where they had not lived for years, so John and I changed our names to see if anybody would react. He introduced himself as Joe Lemon and I used my real name of Maurice Micklewhite.

As each group approached us we would introduce ourselves (none of them having the faintest idea who we were) and when they asked us what we did for a living, John would point at me and say, 'I'm his assistant,' and I in turn would point at John and say, 'I'm in charge of him.' This was our little revenge for being made to waste our time with friends at court, so to speak, when we were supposed to be working and publicising our films.

That evening, I met up with John again at one of the big parties that were thrown every night of the Festival. This one took place in a great mansion overlooking the sea. Of all the Beatles, John seemed to me to be the most natural loner. An early example of this was his book *In His Own Write*. Even then, in the mid-sixties, it struck me as his first attempt at going alone. At that time he was very tough and abrasive – such a contrast to his later spirituality. At one point in the party I wanted to go to the lavatory and was trying each door-handle in turn, only to find them all occupied. I was getting desperate, when John came rushing up, also dying to go. I warned him that all the loos were engaged. 'Let's find one upstairs,' he said, and we both went charging around the bedroom of the hostess trying to locate the right door. We opened every cupboard on the landing before I finally found the bathroom door behind the hostess' bed. I rushed in, relieved myself and came quickly out to let John have his turn, only to find him peeing out of the bedroom window.

'I couldn't wait,' he explained, busy directing his stream through a narrow opening.

'You've done some on the curtains,' I hissed, looking round the door to see if anyone was coming upstairs. John finally finished and as we left the bedroom I said to him, 'You've ruined her bloody curtains.'

'They're rich,' he replied in his slow drawl. 'Fuck 'em.'

The lingering impression that I retain of those three days in Cannes are of flashbulbs exploding through an alcoholic haze, questions asked in deafened ears, wonderful food eaten I know not where, and a whiff of perfume I remember not whose. Suddenly I woke up one morning and was back at my

231

own flat in London. I had a hangover, but Harry assured me *Ipcress* was a great success, so maybe it had all been worthwhile.

While I had been busy with other things, *Alfie* had opened in America and had been such a big success that it was going to be put out on general release right through the country – an almost unheard-of event at that time for a small British picture. Not only had that happened, but *The Ipcress File*, which was already on show in the States in small 'art-house' type cinemas, where you would normally see foreign-language films, had been bought by Universal, and that was going on general release as well. I was being sent to New York to publicise the two of them.

At this point, my impossible dream came true.

Part Four

Part Four

20

'*If* you want to be a star in America . . .'

Suddenly there I was in New York – and it looked and sounded just like it did in the movies. As a Londoner I thought I would be well able to cope with the action, but the speed and energy of life there I found overwhelming, and after a long flight and a couple of hours of press agents telling me what I was supposed to be doing in America, I stumbled into bed and slept like a baby until six-thirty the next morning, when the phone rang to tell me that my press agent was in the hotel lobby and would like to come up and brief me about the first television show.

I stumbled out of bed and opened the curtains and there before me in all its morning glory was Central Park, shyly revealing itself as the slow dawn sun rose. I had arrived the night before in the dark, confused and bewildered by all the attention given me, and I suddenly realised that I did not even know what hotel I was in. I ran around the room looking for information and found it on the menu. I was in the Plaza Hotel, the great Plaza that I had seen in all the movies, and just like all those other stars I too had a room overlooking Central Park . . .

My reverie was interrupted by the doorbell and standing there was the man in charge of my publicity tour. He was slightly shorter than me and a little overweight, with long black hair. When he finally spoke he revealed a very pleasant Southern drawl, a sound to which I would grow very accustomed over the many years to come. What is more, he is now one of the foremost press agents in America, and his name is Bobby Zarem. How do you like that for an intro, Bobby?

All that was still in the future, though. My first reaction to him was one of annoyance. 'What the hell are you getting me up at six o'clock in the morning for, to do television?'

'You go on the *Today* show at seven-thirty,' he explained.

'I know,' I replied, 'but that is this evening, so why are you waking me at dawn?'

'You are on the *Today* show at seven-thirty *this morning*,' he explained patiently.

I could not grasp the idea that somehow they had television in the morning in America. In England we only had one channel, the BBC, which was very boring, and did not start transmitting until four o'clock in the afternoon.

'Nobody will be watching at this time of the morning,' was my next comment.

His reply surprised me. 'They have twenty-one million viewers,' he said, 'and you had better get ready and do the goddam thing, *if* you want to be a star in America.'

Off we rushed in the longest car I had ever seen, which had coffee and doughnuts and the morning papers in it, straight down Fifth Avenue to the NBC studio at the Rockerfeller Centre. When we got out of the car I rushed across the road and looked over the wall and there it was, just as I had known from the movies, an ice-skating rink. Bobby called me back and I was immediately surrounded by autograph-hunters. They all knew who I was and a lot of them had seen the movies that I was in. I was amazed that American people should know my identity. The police came and dragged me through the throng and into the studio. More coffee, more doughnuts, a quick puff of powder to take the shine off from the make-up girl and I was on television for the first time in America. Or so I thought – but I had forgotten something of which Bobby later reminded me.

A few months earlier I had been sitting alone at home in the flat at Albion Close, when the doorbell rang at about two in the afternoon. I went down and opened the door, and standing there was a very pleasant-looking young man who, when he spoke, turned out to be an American. 'Would you like to be on television in America?' he asked, much to my astonishment. Here it was at last, my chance to go to the United States, I thought.

'Yes,' I replied, a little too quickly.

He ran back down the mews to the corner and waved his hand at someone I could not see, then, before my baffled eyes, a Rolls Royce came slowly into sight followed by two vans full of television equipment. A small man with a very warm smile got out of the Rolls and shook my hand, suggesting that we go upstairs to my flat to see where we could do the interview. He explained that he was making a programme about the swinging sixties in London – yes, we were still swinging – and he would like to interview me because he had seen my performances in both *Alfie* and *The Ipcress File*. He thought the movies would do well in America and that I should do an interview with him as advance publicity for when they opened.

I stood there dumbfounded by all this as the technicians marched in, pronounced my living room too small and dark to film in, and asked if they could take two of my armchairs out into the mews and conduct the interview there, in the daylight. I agreed to all this, never having caught up with what was actually going on. The small man then explained to me that although I did not know who he was, everybody in America *did* – and he had a very popular talk-show there. Out of curiosity and just before we started the interview, I asked him his name. 'Merv Griffin,' he replied, with that same warm smile. Again, unknown to me, I had just met another dear friend. Merv was one of the reasons I was already a familiar face to some Americans.

On the *Today* show I was introduced by a young lady who had originally been a writer for the star hostess. The latter had just left the series and my announcer had only been fronting the show for the past two weeks. Her name, she told me later, was Barbara Walters. I was interviewed by the current 'doyenne' of film critics in New York, Judith Crist. Had I known this I would have been nervous but I was hardly awake. Everything went well and I was whisked off back to the hotel where I did an interview every hour all day long, until I was told that I would be on the *Tonight* show at eight o'clock that same evening. As far as the *Tonight* show was concerned, I was informed that I had a bit of bad luck. The star of the show

Jack Paar had just walked off the set last week and I would have to put up with being interviewed by a standby – one Johnny Carson. I did that show, and Johnny and I survived those testing times and are both still around today, although I have just heard that he is retiring this year after thirty years on the *Tonight* show.

After this 'ordeal', I was informed with great awe that I was going to be given the ultimate accolade – an interview by the *New York Times*. The next day in the Oak Room of the Plaza, I was indeed interviewed by a young and beautiful reporter called Gloria Steinem. She wrote an article headlined '*Maurice Joseph Micklewhite: What's he got?*' In it she decided that I did indeed have a certain 'je ne sais quoi' although it was never actually defined, but she did however manage to confuse Michael Caine with the character of Alfie, and when she later became a raging feminist I was always at the top of her list of international male chauvinist pigs, which I am not, of course. Is this fair, Gloria?

I don't know how I did it, but despite their brutal work schedule, I still found time and energy to wallow in the fantastic hospitality for which Americans are justly famous. I also managed to indulge myself to the full in what I can only describe as 'star' treatment. Here I was with two big hit movies, an unknown from England, suddenly hailed as a star. Parties were given for me, packed restaurants would suddenly find room for me, everywhere I went I knew I had the best table. At the 21 Club I found myself seated between Maureen O'Hara and Kirk Douglas! I found a new and lasting friend in Elaine, the owner of the legendary restaurant that bears her name. I knew I was at the correct table there because I knocked over Woody Allen's wine getting to it, and on my way to the lavatory later trod on someone's foot and apologised, only to find myself staring into the eyes of Ursula Andress. At the Russian Tea Room, where it always looks like Christmas because they liked the decorations so much one year that they left them up permanently, I was seated in one of the first three booths between Helen Hayes and Walter Matthau. I had definitely Arrived. Sometimes I felt that I was dreaming, but pinch as I might I never woke up from the dream that I was living, and probably still haven't, if the truth were known.

New York was also stacked to the rafters with some of the most beautiful women in the world, and to my surprise *they* wanted to go out with *me*. In the past, I had always had to chase the women I wanted, but now it seemed they were chasing me. Had I suddenly become handsome, or more charming? No, it was simply that now I was the possessor of the two most powerful aphrodisiacs: money and fame – and I didn't know how to spend either of them.

I was completely taken aback by all this, it was too much, but fortunately for my sanity my American experience soon came to an end. As a last gesture of thanks to all the people who had been so hospitable to me, I talked Paramount into paying for a little farewell cocktail party on top of the *Newsweek* building for about a hundred people. I had made friends with the married couple Jessica Tandy and Hume Cronyn during my time in New York, and when I invited them to my party they asked if they could bring Bette Davis with them. I of course said yes immediately – it would be great to meet her. When their party did arrive, Jessica and Hume came towards me and I greeted them, but Bette hung back by the door so I did not meet her immediately. I spoke to another couple of guests and eventually looked up to catch her staring at me, so I went over to greet her properly and to introduce myself.

'I hope you don't mind my staring at you like that,' she said, 'but when I saw you I thought of Leslie Howard. You remind me so much of him.' I was very slim in those days, with long blonde hair and other people had told me before that I resembled him. 'Did you know that Leslie screwed every woman on every movie he was ever in, with the exception of me?' she added, rather pointedly, I thought. I did know that he had that reputation, I admitted. 'I told him that I was not going to be plastered on the end of a list of his conquests,' she continued. I made what I considered to be a sort of approving moral grunt. 'The reason I was staring at you,' she continued, 'was that I was thinking what difference would it have made now if I had.' This last part had a sort of wistful tone about it.

239

'Would you have dinner with me tonight?' I blurted out.

'I wasn't making a pass at you,' she replied.

'I know,' I said. 'We could all have dinner together – Hume and Jessica, and you and me.'

'All right,' she said with a smile, 'so long as you put me in a taxi on my own afterwards.'

This I agreed to do and did, so my last night in New York was dinner with Bette Davis. I flew home to England, my dream complete.

Back in London I found I had become a Cinderella-type figure – the person from nowhere who becomes a star, rich and famous – a favourite story for any newspaper. It was in the papers that I also learned that I the actor had become indistinguishable from my character, Alfie. Here was this ignorant Cockney layabout, the story went, who had a bit of luck playing himself and unfairly became a star. Story after story appeared in the press of my consorting with all sorts of women, the majority of whom I had never even met. Like Sean with Bond, people confusing me with Alfie had always made me angry, and I tried to explain this one day to a reporter who had asked me: 'Is it difficult to play yourself in a movie?'

I paused for a moment to work out how long I would spend in prison if I strangled this guy right now, then choked back my fury and answered his question with another one. 'Have we met before?' I asked.

'No,' he replied.

'Well, if you don't know me at all, how can you assume that I played myself in *Alfie*?'

'It's obvious,' he replied. 'You're a Cockney, just like him.'

With this I had to agree. 'What else?' I asked. 'What about work? Would you say that Alfie was a man dedicated to a single and difficult profession?'

'No,' he said diffidently.

'Well, I am,' I said. 'I have been slogging my guts out for thirteen years to get to this position, and you dare to compare me with a layabout like Alfie. I have spent more time learning my profession than you have learning yours. In what other ways do you think I resemble Alfie?' I went on.

'There is one way that you do,' he said with a smile.

'What's that?' I asked, knowing what was coming.

'You screw every girl that's around just like him.'

This was another great myth. I was so far from being Alfie, I lectured my reporter, that if I met a girl and thought for one moment that she would have gone out with Alfie in real life, I would have dropped her like a barge-pole. I was always very fussy about my women – the very reverse of Alfie. I let the unfortunate man go eventually at the end of my boring lecture and when I read his article later, sure enough he stated that, just as he had thought, I was a real life Alfie in the flesh. You can't win with the press, but you can refuse to see them again, which is what I did with this guy.

London itself was changing gradually. Hippie clothes were coming in and with them came marijuana, which meant that people did not go out so much as smoking pot was illegal and you had to do it at home. Things were slowing down a little but there was always some big American movie shooting, it seemed, and all the American actors at that time whom I met seemed to be called George. I had been given a couple of brownies, a sort of American chocolate cake, which were usually served with hash or some other drug in them at parties and for a while I thought I must have been hallucinating, but I wasn't: all American actors were called George for a time. I met George Maharis, George Chakaris, George Peppard, George Segal, George Hamilton and George C. Scott, all in the space of a few days.

Dennis called me one day with the ultimate news for an actor like myself. Shirley Maclaine had seen me in *Ipcress*, and as her contract stated that she had a choice of leading men, unbelievably she had chosen me for her next film *Gambit*. I was sent the script, but I only read it as a formality: I would do *anything* just to make a picture in Hollywood. You see, at that time I had no sense of career moves or structure in my life; I was like a man just doing anything once that he had dreamed of before he died. And this was one of those dreams – to make a big Hollywood picture.

As it turned out, the script of *Gambit* revealed a very

charming little comedy thriller and I would have done it if I had been choosy anyway.

My first visit to the United States had been so fast and frantic that it was but a blur in my memory and I had no real impression of what America was like. A cocktail of hard work, no sleep, jet-lag and a sea of new faces, sights and sounds had just faded into the back of my mind and almost seemed not to have happened at all. This time it was going to be different. I decided to go via TWA – an American airline, so that I would be in an American environment from the start. This worked perfectly. The moment I walked on the plane, instead of saying, 'Good morning, sir,' as the British stewardess would have done, the American hostess said, 'Hi, honey.' This was more like it, I thought. The next part was a bit more puzzling. She asked me if I would like a beverage after take-off. I sat there wondering for a moment what sort of a drink a beverage was, until I suddenly realised that it was any drink. 'Vodka,' I said, then added for the first time in my life, rather sheepishly, 'on the rocks.' I had heard this phrase a million times in American movies, but did not know if people said it in real life. She just replied, 'Fine,' and walked away. So Americans really did say 'on the rocks'. I was learning already.

Eventually, exhausted, we arrived at Los Angeles where I was met by a minion from the studios with a Cadillac that had more leg room than the plane had. I was whisked off towards Beverly Hills. Los Angeles was hot, and the first thing I did in the car was take off my jacket and pullover, only to reveal a sweat-soaked shirt. I sat back boiling until the chauffeur turned on the air conditioner and then I froze as my sweat turned to a thin veil of ice under my shirt. As I surveyed my new abode out of the window, Los Angeles seemed a little disappointing at first, with endless used-car lots, parking lots, car dumps and car showrooms, interwoven with electricity pylons and telegraph poles, the whole thing dominated by massive freeways full to the brim with cars. I had never seen so many automobiles. Suddenly and incredibly the city's dominance by the car was made even more obvious to me as we started to go through a great expanse of oil-wells, nodding like iron donkeys, right in the middle of the city. The people here not only made, sold, parked and destroyed cars, but they pumped their own petrol, which I was soon to find out was called 'gas'.

Out of the blue I spotted something that was so familiar from those photographs in movie magazines: it was a great big water tower. I recognised its shape and knew what it would say on it when we were close enough to see – the letters MGM. Underneath it was indeed the fabled Studio. This was my first sight of a real Hollywood studio and now I knew I was really in the right place. Suddenly everything changed. The telegraph poles and electric pylons disappeared, the streets became cleaner and quieter, there were no used-car lots, just posh little shops with discreet car parks now and then, and tree-lined streets.

'We're in Beverly Hills now,' the driver called back to me. I rolled the window down. The people here even looked different – they were well-dressed, confident and laid back. They crossed the roads slowly in the wrong places and all the cars screeched to a halt to let them go. I told the driver that if people behaved like that in London they would be dead in five minutes. He replied that everybody in Beverly Hills was afraid to hit anyone with their car in case their victims were movie stars with high insurance, so the minute you saw a pedestrian you stopped and let him pass. As a person who could not yet drive a car and was a perennial pedestrian, this was beginning to sound like the right place for me. I asked him what had happened to all the telegraph poles and electric pylons and he said that the city had buried them out of sight of its illustrious and wealthy citizens. As I gazed out of the window I was struck by the number of old people around who looked as though they might soon be joining the pylons and poles. When I mentioned this to the driver, he told me that this was not only a movie community but also a great retirement place, as the geriatrics liked the weather and the leisurely lifestyle.

We drove up Beverly Drive which, when it crossed Santa Monica Boulevard, suddenly stopped its shopping parades and turned into very nice houses with lush gardens set well

243

back from the street. After several 'turnings' (or blocks) we came to another phenomenon: a street sign that said *Sunset Boulevard*. I sat in the back of the car feeling like a silly little boy who has just discovered that there is a Santa Claus, after all. We turned into Sunset Boulevard and there it was in front of us, pink and blushing in the hot sunlight and trying to hide behind a fan of palm trees: the Beverly Hills Hotel. I was here at last.

The car hissed up the hot black driveway and stopped under a shaded arch in front of the hotel. A doorman opened the car door for me immediately and porters came to grab my suitcases, which had looked so smart when I started out in London but now, in these plush surroundings and compared with the other luggage being handled, looked decidedly seedy. I dissociated myself from them instantly and walked in behind a porter pushing some very posh bags on a trolley, with only the occasional glance back to make sure that mine were following on. I was signed in and deposited in my room, and then I was alone. I was really jet-lagged for the very first time, but didn't know it. I just felt a strange dizziness and fatigue, but did not want to go to sleep. My eardrums seemed to have been left up in the sky, so every sound was diffused as though heard through water with a soft hiss, but the adrenalin was still flowing and I knew that I could not sleep. I was obviously not a star in this part of America yet, because my room was small, and my view one of a path that led to the exclusive cottages on one side of the hotel.

I showered, unpacked, put on a clean shirt and went to look round the hotel. First of all I visited the pool, which I left immediately as the pallor of my London face attracted incredulous stares from dark bronze shiny people, who looked at me in horror as though my pale skin might be catching. I smiled to myself in revenge as I anticipated the day when these same people would look like the suitcases I had just brought from London.

My next destination was the Polo Lounge. As I was on my own I was asked to sit at the bar, which I did, ordered a vodka on the rocks and studied the room. I knew that this was a haunt of the rich and famous so I looked to see if there was anyone I recognised. At this point I realised why the place was popular with the well-known: it was so dark in there that you couldn't spot your own friends unless you knew where to look. I had not been there long when a young lady with big tits asked me if I would like to buy her a drink. I mumbled something to the effect that I had an appointment, and fled upstairs to my room, surprised by the fact that commercial sex was available at the Beverly Hills Hotel. However, there were many more surprises to come, the first being that apart from getting a call from the production office to make sure I had arrived safely and was comfortable, and a call from wardrobe to set up an appointment for a fitting the following week, nothing happened. I just sat there in my room for two weeks watching television, which was nonstop day and night and had about twelve channels, which to me coming from two-channel England seemed like paradise, especially the all-night ones which carried me through my hours of lying awake at four in the morning as my body and mind began to adapt after the six thousand miles and eight-hour time change that it had gone through.

Occasionally I wandered past the pool for a little bout of mutual sneers and then back to the Polo Lounge where I was put out in the unfashionable seats in the back garden, and as I was always alone I ate at the small table by the kitchen door where all restaurants put lone diners. I had a little balcony off my room and discovered that the sun hit it for an hour or so each morning, so I decided to start a tan, which resulted very quickly in a peeled nose and a sort of semi-lobster hue. I paraded this past the pool one day, only to find my efforts rewarded with ridicule in place of the usual amazement, so I gave that up. I had now been there for a week with only the two business phone calls, and was beginning to despair of anything ever happening and to wonder if they had forgotten my existence. I didn't even see any film stars though I sat in the lobby for hours, for so long in fact that the desk clerk used to save all the old English papers for me to read.

One day, in desperation, I decided to venture across Sunset Boulevard and walk in the pretty little park opposite the Hotel, and this marked the real start of my life in

Hollywood: I saw my first movie star there up close. As I was walking round the fountain in the middle of the park, I noticed a little old man being taken for a walk supported by a very pretty nurse. I must admit that it was the nurse who first attracted my attention, but as I wandered slowly over towards them to get a closer look, I recognised the little old man as Groucho Marx. There he was, my first film star in Hollywood, so they did exist and I *was* in the right place after all. I was beginning to doubt it as my loneliness and the hot sun started to affect my sanity. As I passed I could not help staring at him and he said a very pleasant, 'Good morning,' to me. Apart from the hotel staff he was the first person ever to address me socially in Beverly Hills.

My next encounter was equally overwhelming. I was sitting in the lobby one day as usual, dismally reading a week-old British newspaper, when I felt a shadow cross my vision and stop in front of me. A female voice said, 'Is your name Michael Caine?' I looked up and my heart almost stopped. Smiling down at me was the unmistakeable face of Jane Russell. I stumbled to my feet and said that yes, I was, and to my astonishment she said, 'Would you like to have lunch with me?'

Again I mumbled that I would love to. You must bear in mind that I had not spoken to anybody let alone Jane Russell for days so I had got out of the habit of conversation or even understandable replies to quite mundane questions. I could not believe this. *I was being picked up in the lobby of the Beverly Hills Hotel by Jane Russell.* 'Where would you like to go to lunch?' I asked in a voice as calm as I could make it.

'It's all arranged,' she smiled, taking my arm and guiding me across the lobby to a large dining room, where a lunch was already in progress, with mostly middle-aged ladies at about thirty tables. Jane seated me at one of two empty spaces and introduced me to a lot of people whom I don't recall, and then explained what was going on. Her date had not turned up and she had gone to the Ladies and on the way back she had recognised me because she had seen something about me in the papers. She decided I looked lonely, which was very astute of her, I thought, and here we were. When I asked her

246

what the lunch was in aid of, she told me that it was a Christian Science lunch but it was OK if I wasn't one – they would still give me food anyway. Christian Science, I thought, with great disappointment. Not a lot of chance of getting laid here – and I was right. I had a nice lunch with no booze, a charming and albeit disappointingly innocent interlude with Miss Russell and then I was back in my room again watching television, but things were starting to look up.

The next incident that came my way was a real mind-blower. I was sitting in the lobby one evening at about six-thirty, when there was a tremendous threshing sound. It grew louder and louder until we all realised that there was a helicopter about to land in the park opposite. I got up and stood by the door to see who it was who was allowed to land a helicopter there – obviously someone of power and status, some amazing mortal like the President of the United States at least, or even the President of the Hotel, but nothing could have prepared me for the figure that strode across Sunset Boulevard and straight towards me in the lobby there. Smothered in dust and obviously fresh from location and dressed in full cowboy gear, came John Wayne. He marched up to the desk to get his key while I just stood there open-mouthed gawping at him. His eye suddenly caught mine and an extraordinary thing happened.

'What's your name, kid?' he said to me.

'Michael Caine,' I replied.

'That's right,' he said, as though there was some doubt in my mind. 'I saw you in that movie, what was it called?'

'*Alfie*?' I ventured.

'That's right,' he replied. He got his key and putting his arm round my shoulder guided me across the lobby. 'You're going to be a big star,' he said, to my delight. 'But let me give you a piece of advice. Talk low, talk slow and don't say too fucking much.'

I was about to thank him for this wisdom when he added mysteriously, 'And never wear suede shoes.'

'Why not?' I asked, truly puzzled.

'Because one day, what happened to me will happen to you. I was taking a piss in a public toilet and I was wearing a brand new pair of shoes. The guy next to me recognised me and turned in astonishment and said, "John Wayne!" and pissed over my suede shoes. So don't wear them when you're famous, kid,' and with that he walked away. This was the beginning of our acquaintance that lasted until John's death, but that is a much later story. A funny thing struck me as he walked away. I had been in Hollywood for nearly two weeks now and the only three people who had spoken to me in a social sense had all been movie stars. Maybe this place was not as tough as everybody in England had predicted.

The next day, I was finally rescued from my solitude by the wardrobe department, who called me to the studio for a fitting, thereby confirming the fact that I had not been forgotten. The first thing I learned on this trip was the geography of the place. Everybody calls it Hollywood, but there are now no studios there and none of the major movie people live there, either. In fact, Hollywood and Hollywood Boulevard itself is quite a sleazy kind of a place and you wouldn't want to be seen dead there. We passed quickly through it on our way to Universal Studios, where I would be working for the next three months. Universal is situated in the valley which lies beyond a range of hills inland from Beverly Hills, which is on the ocean side of the range. The Valley, as it is known, is in actual fact the San Fernando Valley, and is ten degrees hotter than Beverly Hills at any given time and twice as smoggy. It is now the wrong side of town. Although a lot of stars once lived there, very few do now, the main exception being Bob Hope, who not only lives in the Valley but seems to own most of it. So the Valley is a sort of downmarket Beverly Hills, and Hollywood a *very* downmarket Valley.

As we arrived at the gates of Universal, one of the guards surprised me by greeting me by name. 'Your parking space is down on the right outside your bungalow. You'll see your name on it. Good luck, Michael,' and he smiled and waved as I entered a Hollywood studio for the first time. I was dropped outside my bungalow and took the key that the guard had given me and entered my new world. As I looked around this bungalow – although it was just a dressing room – it was the most luxurious accommodation I had ever lived in. I met the make-up man, the camera man and the director, a marvellous old Englishman called Ronald Neame, who was not only a damn good director but had produced all of David Lean's early British films. For half a day it was a whirlwind of work and meetings, and then I was whisked off back to the Hotel to be left to rot again for another few days.

During this period of loneliness I discovered the actual town of Beverly Hills. It is only about a mile from the Beverly Hills Hotel. In Los Angeles at the time there was virtually no public transport and the idea of the taxi cab was in its infancy. One day, however, desperate with boredom, I committed the unpardonable sin of asking the doorman for a taxi. At the Beverly Hills Hotel, I realised one was supposed to rent a limousine not ask for a cab. After an hour the cab arrived and in five minutes I was deposited outside the Beverly Wilshire Hotel, right in the centre of the little town. Here at last I could walk, not very far but there were three streets with shops in them. The now world-famous Rodeo Drive was then a quiet little place with a few clothing shops and a lot of restaurants, and on the right was the place which later became my spiritual home – a discothèque called the Daisy. There were all sorts of little shops on Beverly Drive, which was the busiest street, and last and least was Canon Drive, which had a few shops but was not very interesting. For someone who had been stuck in an hotel for two weeks, however, all of it was fascinating.

When Shirley Maclaine arrived in town my life in Hollywood changed for ever. Although she had chosen me for the film role, we had still never met and to fix this she gave me a welcome party. I remember it was held in a big hotel ballroom somewhere. I arrived early, and when we were introduced, I was immediately enchanted by her; she made me feel instantly at home and welcome in this strange environment. There was no conceit or ego that I had been warned to expect of big Hollywood stars. She was and is a genuine woman full of warmth and friendship. Fortunately, we hit it off there and then, and have remained friends to this day. I was so overwhelmed by the size of the spread and the room that I asked her who else the party was for. She laughed

249

and said, 'Only you, Michael. Only you.' Perhaps she knew me in another life.

I grew nervous at this bit of information. 'Suppose nobody turns up?' I asked, worried that I would make a fool of her and myself at the same time.

'They'll turn up,' she said, with a confident smile. I did not of course realise at the time that her guests would be coming because she had asked them, and not primarily to meet me. My next problem was that I could not imagine who she could possibly have invited. Not real stars, of course, I thought. Wrong. The first guest to arrive was Gloria Swanson, who, much to my surprise, looked just like Gloria Swanson. She was followed by Liza Minnelli and Frank Sinatra who, because I was so petrified, also looked like Gloria Swanson. I was delighted, surprised and nearly fainted with nerves as I was introduced to these legends. Once over the first surprise, I took a couple of quick drinks and steeled myself to meet the rest of the guests, who turned out to be the entire Hollywood A Group.

Everybody seemed to have seen *Alfie* and *Ipcress* and they all assured me that I was going to be a big star. From not existing for two weeks I was suddenly a celebrity because Shirley had said so, and although I did not know it at the time, I was now socially launched in Hollywood for ever.

21

The Elephant to Beverly Hills

I was the new boy in town and all the hostesses wanted me at their homes. It was all very flattering and great fun, but they had an ulterior motive of which I was quite unaware at the time. Much more important than all my other accomplishments, I was a single man and *I was not gay* and I had not been tried out on any of the local single ladies. The matchmakers got hold of me. In my case, one in particular – a deceptively sweet little old lady called Minna Wallis. She became my new best friend and got me invited everywhere. The sister of the great Hollywood producer Hal Wallis, she had been a movie actors' agent in her own right for many years with her main and lasting claim to fame being that she had discovered Clark Gable. This was her public claim to fame. Her private claim to fame, which she confided in me one evening, was that on one momentous occasion Clark had actually made love to her. This seemed to give her more satisfaction than having discovered him.

Minna's raison d'être seemed to be to get me married off as soon as possible. Every time I went anywhere at her invitation, I would be targeted on to a single and desirable young maiden. The first one was Natalie Wood, with whom I became great pals but without those added ingredients of love, lust or romance. I was quickly reprogrammed and steered towards Barbra Streisand – with the same result. Minna's final attempt was with Frank Sinatra's daughter Nancy with whom I subsequently enjoyed a nice, platonic relationship. I was still completely innocent and I am sure that none of the aforementioned ladies knew any more about it than I did.

251

Deciding to move out of the Beverly Hills Hotel, which was very expensive on my meagre budget, I rented a furnished apartment in an old building called the Sunset Towers on 'the Strip' section of Sunset Boulevard. The Strip, I should explain, is approximately one mile long, just one section of the over thirty-mile-long Sunset Boulevard. It stretches from the boundary of Beverly Hills city towards the downtown area. Along this strip of Sunset then (and now) were situated all the cafés, rock clubs, discos, jazz clubs and comedy stores and restaurants. It is where all the kids gather on the weekends and in those days it was a meeting-point for all the fledgling junkies, pushers, whores and pimps before the police cleared the whole place up after the terrible trauma of the Manson case. In other words, it was just the sort of place that attracted me at the time. The Sunset Towers was an old thirties building, and in those days the tallest building around because of the old earthquake regulations. Now it has become a new hotel called the St James' Club. The apartments were big and well-furnished with their own kitchens, which meant that I could cook for myself, which was not only cheaper than room service but the food tasted better and was always hot.

I enjoyed living in the Towers very much. I was independent, free of ties and at the hub of the universe, or so it seemed to me. The Towers was also mysterious and glamorous, and strange things happened there. One morning I got into what I had always known as a lift but now knew to be an elevator, and there inside it was a tenant from the floors above. He smiled and wished me good morning. The bizarre feature of this man was that although he was very short and did not look even a little bit like a cowboy, he was wearing a great big stetson hat. A true eccentric, I thought sagely, and let him leave before I rushed to the porter and asked who he was. 'That,' he said proudly, 'is the great director George Stevens who made *Giant* with Elizabeth Taylor and James Dean.' Here I was living in the same building as George Stevens – great! I asked him if there was anybody else famous living there and he told me no – but that the penthouse was owned by Howard Hughes.

'Does he ever come here?' I pestered, thinking that I might just once see the elusive legend.

'Never seen him here, but he always keeps his latest mistress up there.' 'Have you ever seen her?' I asked, not having noticed any Howard Hughes-type mistress material floating around the place.

'Twice,' he said, licking his lips, 'and she's a beauty.' I of course spent the next few days haunting the lobby at times that I figured a mistress would be going in or out. Twelve-thirty for lunch, ten-thirty or three-thirty for hairdressing, or eight o'clock in the evening for an assignation with Howard. No luck. This lady proved elusive for a while until one day she walked almost literally into my arms as the elevator door opened and I stepped in as she stepped out. She was gorgeous, but she did not speak or catch my eye or even acknowledge my existence although we had bumped into each other. I saw her a couple more times before she disappeared from the building altogether, but she never made a sign at any time that there was another person present. I imagine that Mr Hughes had made her sign a contract which forbade her even having eye contact with other men. If he had, she certainly abided by the rules to the letter.

The Luau was a Tahitian restaurant halfway down Rodeo Drive in Beverly Hills. It was dark, and noisy with the sounds of laughter, loud music and even louder waterfalls. It also served the best Mai Tais in town and good Chinese-style food, but more important than all these things, it was where the 'in' crowd met. The 'in' crowd were the young, the beautiful, the handsome and the single – and as I was sure that I qualified on at least one of these counts, I went and got in with the 'in' crowd. The Luau was where we all met between seven and eight-thirty each evening to find out where the parties were, who was in town and to meet new people and old friends. In other words it was just the sort of place I was looking for in Hollywood.

It was at the Luau where I met my new best friend. His name was Steve Brandt and he said he was the editor of a movie-fan magazine. I never checked so I don't know which one. He was about twenty-eight years old and was the thinnest, palest person I had ever met. Steve also had long dark straight hair and large brown staring eyes. In other words, he looked weird and he was also gay. Steve and I were inseparable. Apart from the fact that we genuinely liked each other, he just happened to know every drop-dead beauty in town, and always appeared each evening with two or three in tow, and he had the endearing habit of disappearing God knows where at around one in the morning leaving me with the task of seeing these lovelies home – a great antidote to the machinations of Minna Wallis. He also knew everybody, everywhere, what they were doing and where they were going to eat, drink and be merry, so he was invaluable to me.

The social round would move on from the Luau to the best party available, and then on later to the Daisy, the best disco in Hollywood, and when we were thrown out of there, sharp at two o'clock in the morning (the Beverly Hills police were always strict about drinking-up time), we would all go to a café called MFK, which was actually inside the Beverly Wilshire Hotel, although there was a door from the pavement on Wilshire Boulevard. MFK seemed to be open twenty-four hours per day and served American diner fare. In fact, it looked like a forties' diner in an Edward Hopper painting. You could get lox and bagels, scrambled eggs, hamburgers, sodas, sundaes ... anything that was bad for you and you could get it all night. That was where the night ended, or if you got lucky late, began. There was a lot of late luck about in those days. This was the other side of Hollywood as opposed to the sedate and married parties of the Beverly Hills matrons. I could operate quite smoothly in both of these areas, but was happier at the Daisy than anywhere else.

Now and then there would be the big social and exclusive evening. My first experience of one of these came through Shirley and it also gives me my very first opportunity to name-drop. And boy am I going to drop some. Shirley did not have a date at the time and asked me to be her escort for this particular event. It promised to be a really hot evening for me, as we had been invited to have Chinese food cooked by

Danny Kaye himself in his own kitchen – a highly-prized invitation by anyone's standards.

We arrived at Danny's house, and although we had been told that we would be eating in the kitchen I was surprised to find that this was literally true. The kitchen was an enormous room with a table laid for eight on one side, and an enormous range of Chinese stoves blazing away on the other. It actually looked like the kitchen of a Chinese restaurant. Danny had on an apron and was slaving away with the help of a real Chinese cook. He took a little time off to say hello to me and make us welcome and then he introduced us to the other guests. These consisted of his wife, the brilliant writer Sylvia Fine, Danny's daughter Dina, a very suspicious-looking American with a completely bald head and very dark glasses, and two British naval officers – which I thought was strange until I saw the identity of the next guest. I seemed to spend a lot of time in Hollywood standing open-mouthed as I was introduced to someone astonishing, but this was really the last person I expected to meet here. Danny introduced me to his Royal Highness Prince Philip, the husband of the Queen of England. He stretched out his hand and smiling, said, 'You're old Ipcress, aren't you?' 'Yes I am, your Highness,' I replied and that was it – Prince Philip has called me Ipcress every time we've met since then. The last guest was Cary Grant. So there we were, and Danny started to serve the most delicious Chinese food. He never sat down himself, but would just lean over occasionally and take a little piece of something from one of our plates. At one point I asked him if he was going to sit with us, but he shook his head and whispered to me, 'I'll tell you a secret, Michael, I hate the fucking stuff.' Shirley sat quietly as the conversation flowed, staring at the mysterious bald-headed man. After a while she said to him, 'Is your name Smith?'

'Yes,' he said, very surprised that she should know this.

'What do you do?' she asked him.

He paused for a moment with a knowing glance at Prince Philip. 'I am the head of the secret service guarding His Royal Highness during this trip.'

Well, this all sounded very suspicious to me, more like the plot for a Marx Brothers' movie.

'Did you ever teach American history at a university at any time?' Shirley persisted.

'Yes, I did,' he replied, puzzled. 'When I came out of the army.'

'You taught me,' Shirley said. 'My name was Shirley Beatty then.' She was right – he *had* taught her and now here he was in the secret service with his past 'blown' as I would say in one of my spy films.

It had been a very 'Hollywood' evening, and another mind-blower for a newcomer like me. I escorted Shirley back home to the Valley at about three in the morning and as we approached her house I suddenly yelled, 'Your house is on fire!' and made a fool of myself again because of my lack of knowledge of the scene here. Above her house, very clear in the floodlights, a dense cloud of what looked like smoke was rising. Shirley chuckled and looked at me as though I was mad.

'It's all right,' she said, grinning. 'I've only left the pool heat on.' It was steam, rising from the swimming pool. I decided to keep my mouth shut in Hollywood in the future.

As you can probably tell, *Gambit* was proceeding so smoothly that it became secondary to the incredible social life I was leading. Ronald Neame the director was an expert at this sort of light frothy comedy, Shirley and I worked harmoniously together and Herbert Lom, who was the other star of the movie, was an expert *and* a sweetheart – so there was never a problem, apart from the fact that the movie was being shot in the Valley, which was notorious for its smog. Sometimes it was so thick you could not see a hundred yards in front of you, and it stung the eyes. Of course there was a snobbery about living in the Valley (the wrong side of town) or Beverly Hills. I once asked an actor, a resident of the Valley, what it was like there and he told me that it was fine – except 'at what age do you tell your children that they live there?' With Beverly Hills you got Rich Jokes like 'All the children in Beverly Hills learn to count by saying "a million and one, a million and two" ' and so on.

Even in a Shangri-la like Hollywood your past can catch up with you. One day I met a man called Jerry Pam who was and is one of the top press agents in the town and I wanted him to work for me as well. When we began talking, I discovered that not only was he an Englishman, but he had also attended the Hackney Down Grocers Grammar School in King's Lynn at the same time as myself. We hit it off immediately and he became my press agent there and still is to this day – an invaluable addition to the team that I hoped would make me a star in Hollywood.

Around this time I met and became firm friends with a wonderful old writer called Harry Kurnitz, who died in 1968. I think that he had done a rewrite on the *Gambit* script, but anyway we met and liked each other. Harry was about sixty-five years old then but still full of life. He liked to go out and eat and drink and stay up late – in fact, he shared most of my hobbies, so now we got to the stage where Steve, Harry and I were inseparable, a very motley and disparate crew, especially when gracing the dance floor at the Daisy at one in the morning. While the slim pale and gay Steve, the grizzled old Harry and the tall thin Englishman with the specs already made a sufficiently incongruous trio, we were about to become a staunch quartet that was even more improbable. One of Harry's friends was Frank Sinatra. Frank was out of town at the moment, but had phoned Harry and told him that he was getting married soon and as his fiancée was stuck in Los Angeles on her own, would Harry keep an eye on her and take her out if she wanted to go anywhere. Harry said of course he would take care of this for him, and informed us of his new responsibility, which by proxy and friendship became our task as well.

Harry rang the lady in question and asked if she wanted to go out and the answer was yes, very definitely, so out we took her, and that is how I got to know Mia Farrow, and how she became the fourth member of our night patrol. Mia at that time looked just as thin and waif-like as the fairy on top of the Christmas tree, but that was where the resemblance ended. She was tough and fun and as determined as we were to have a good time. We went to parties, dances, bars, disco, restaurants – everywhere together, always sticking to Harry's pledge to keep an eye on the future Mrs Sinatra. We kept all wolves, mashers and ne'er-do-wells away from her, so that there was never any chance of any scandal. This worked well until we all went to a première of a film. When we came out afterwards the press photographers took a picture of the four of us holding hands and smiling at the camera. The next day I was horrified to find the same photo in print, but minus Harry and Steve. There was just Mia and me, holding hands and smiling at the camera. '*Mia with new beau Michael Caine*' the caption read. I was on the phone immediately to Harry, instructing him to get on to Frank real quick and explain the photo. Frank, I knew, had very set standards for Mia *and* a short temper – and I did not want to be on the receiving end of any of it. Ever since then I have been very careful about who I hold hands with.

The Daisy was a kind of magical place. There were always some movie stars there, all doing the kind of things you expected of them, or so it seemed to me. The first time I ever went in there I watched a guy playing pool in the back room for five minutes before I realised that it was Paul Newman – it was that sort of place. I saw Sammy Davis Jnr dance and listened quietly as Bobby Darin sang along to his own record of *Mac the Knife*, which was popular at the time. It would have been glamorous for most people, but for someone like me who had always dreamed of going there, it was like paradise – but not every evening. As I waded my way through the champagne froth of the life I was leading, I was brought up suddenly with a short sharp shock.

Mia, Steve and I were in the Daisy at around midnight one evening when George came over and told Steve that there was a phone call for him. This was not unusual, as Steve got calls at all times of the day and night, no matter where we were, so we took no notice. He returned after about five minutes and asked us if we had ever met Rita Hayworth. Neither of us had, so when he enquired if we'd like to, we both jumped at the chance. 'When?' we asked, almost in unison. 'Right now,' was the stunning reply.

Steve ran us out of the club, we jumped in the 'limo' and in five minutes he was ringing on the door of a house just behind the Beverly Hills Hotel somewhere. I think we all expected a butler or maid to open the door, so what happened next was a shock. The door flew open and standing there drunk, with a half-empty bottle in her hand, was indeed Rita Hayworth. I think we all immediately regretted coming but it was too late to back out.

'Come in, Steve!' she yelled, and led us into the living room. I was upset by her appearance, as she was very overweight and dishevelled and was wearing a rather grubby terry-towel robe and house slippers, not at all what I expected. We sat and drank with her for a while and as I was pretty drunk already before we even got there I started to drift off after a while. The last image that I had of Rita Hayworth was of her inviting Mia to dance to the *Gilda* theme music with her, and as the two of them started to spin round the room, the waif-like figure of Mia, embarrassed but valiant, hugging the all too down to earth form of a fallen goddess as they twirled away to the theme for her greatest triumph.

Mia had put our hostess to bed when they woke me up, and we crept out of the house sadder and very much wiser than when we had gone in. That was just one of several warnings of how tough this town could be, even on the most successful.

22

Cannes

When Frank returned, we saw less of Mia, but I started dating his daughter Nancy, so we did meet up occasionally at family parties. Nancy was a very serious, straight kind of a girl but great fun to be with, and it seemed to suit us both to be together between more serious romances. I saw us as a breathing space for each other.

One day, Nancy phoned and said that we were all going to Las Vegas for the weekend, as her father was going to be singing at the Sands Hotel there with Count Basie. This was great news for me. I had never been to Las Vegas before, but it was better even than that; I was going as a guest of Frank Sinatra and he was the king of the place.

Friday evening came and I finished filming, but instead of going home I just drove up the road from the studio and got on his private plane at the Burbank airport. Frank was already in Vegas, rehearsing, as they were going to record this session, so it was more important than just an ordinary show. On the plane, which was a Lear jet, were just Nancy, Mia and myself. Forty-five minutes later we were there, rushing from the hot desert air outside into the cool, air- conditioned lobby of the Sands. To my surprise, Frank himself was there to greet us.

Nancy threw her arms round her father and gave him a kiss. 'Where am I staying, Dad?' she asked.

Frank pointed out of the window at a tall tower block which was situated a little way away across some gardens. 'You are at the top over there,' he said.

Some porters took her bag and whisked her off. Another porter collected Mia's luggage and led her off, leaving me standing alone with our host. 'Where am I, Frank?' I asked diffidently.

He gave me the look that only fathers give to their daughter's boyfriend and with a suspicious smile he said, 'You, Michael my boy, are down here right next door to me where I can keep an eye on you.'

With that I was indeed shown to the room next to his. I thought of telling him that my relationship with Nancy was innocent, but he did not look as though he was going to believe me.

The first thing I noticed about Las Vegas was that there were no clocks in the casinos nor were there any windows. This is a deliberate move to cut you off from normal time, and it works as a destabiliser. Several times while we were there I walked out into what I thought would be daylight and found myself in the dark and vice versa. The natives were also a suspicious lot, I noticed. Over each of the gaming tables were sinister-looking television monitors that were watching their own employees, though any among them trying to cheat the owners of these hotels must be either brave or stark raving mad.

Being a guest of Frank's opened all doors; we were treated like royalty with limousines there at all times to carry us off to the other hotels to watch shows, which seemed to go on all day, or gamble to our hearts' content. The whole place struck me as a twenty-four hour cacophany of music, gambling machines, and yells and groans as people won and lost at the crap tables.

That first evening we all assembled in the great cabaret room at the Sands. Our table consisted of about twenty of Frank's friends, among whom I recognised Yul Brynner and the old American actor Richard Conte. I was to see Frank perform many times in the future but I don't think I have ever seen him do better than on that particular night. It was a magnificent success, Frank was happy and we had a fantastic time.

In the early hours of the morning I saw Nancy home to her ivory tower and was taking a short cut across the gardens when something happened to convince me that Las Vegas was not like other towns, and that it was important here to stick to clearly-designated paths, both physically and figuratively speaking. As I stumbled half-drunk and tired through the shrubs I was suddenly stopped by two men with shotguns. They seemed to be interested in where I was going at this time of night. I immediately thought of the Mafia, this being Las Vegas, but somehow these two did not look the part. They were both young and fair-skinned with short haircuts and were both wearing navy blue suits and white shirts with very subdued ties. They looked more like young accountants than gangsters.

I explained my situation and who I was with, and the mention of Frank's name brought the change of attitude that I thought it would. They hid their guns and escorted me politely back to the main building. Intrigued by these two guys, I made enquiries the next day and found out that the guards were young Mormon men who were guarding their fellow Mormon Howard Hughes, who was at that time living in the tower. I stuck to the garden paths after that evening.

When I got to bed I was just about to turn out the light when I looked up at the ceiling, which consisted entirely of mirrors, I lay there gazing up at myself for a while worrying that there might be a television camera behind them and vowing that if romance did strike in this town, all activities would take place in the dark.

It is said that it always pays to be nice to everybody in this business, no matter how lowly their position, because you never know who they may become one day. Here's an example. While we were shooting *Gambit* at Universal Studios, someone had introduced the Universal Studio Tour. This of course is now world-famous, but at that time it consisted of a few open trams ferrying tourists around the studio for a couple of dollars a head. There were not many stars working on the lot at the time and the guys who were driving the trams were having a hard time making the little tour interesting for their customers. However, they were allowed to do something that only VIPs are permitted to do these days, which was to go on a real set for a little while and watch an actual film being shot, provided they remained quietly in the background, out of sight of the actors. Today there are masses of special features, purpose-built for the tour, like exhibits from *Jaws*, *King Kong* and *E.T.* and so on, but back in 1966 all you got was the tram-ride with an occasional glimpse of a star wandering about muttering the lines of their next scene to themselves. To pep things up a bit, the drivers would try to catch a star in the open and trap them for a close-up view before they could scuttle into hiding like lions in a safari park. Shirley and I used to watch and wait for a tram to go by then run from our dressing rooms to the set before the next one came along, otherwise, once caught, you had to be polite and sign autographs and pose for pictures with the tourists on the tram.

We both became very adept at dodging these trams, with the exception of one. The driver had worked out what we were up to and would wait for us to make a move then trap us. His tram always appeared out of the blue and it was very annoying to get nabbed two or three times per day, and always by the same man. As time went on I grew more and more annoyed, and after being cornered for the fourth time in one day I even thought of complaining to the bosses and having him replaced, but my better nature prevailed. After all, he was only some poor student or something trying to provide his customers with a good deal, so I suffered in silence and eventually grew to like him and admire his keenness for the job. This, although I did not know it at the time, was a very smart move on my part, since this young man twenty-five years later is the head of one of the most powerful agencies in the movie business. His name is Mike Ovitz and he is the Chairman of an agency called CAA (Creative Artists' Agency) of which I myself am a client. He was also responsible for brokering the deal to sell the same studio to the Japanese for several billion dollars. In short, Mike is one of the most powerful men in Hollywood today. So be careful whom you treat badly.

Although filming on *Gambit* was going like a dream, not all the movie-makers from England were having such an easy time of it. Sidney Furie, who had directed me in *Ipcress* was also working at Universal on a picture called *The Appaloosa*, which I found out is the name of a certain type of horse. It was a western starring Marlon Brando. Sidney came to my dressing room one day almost in tears with horror stories at how badly things were going over on his set. The main problem seemed to be that Brando would not take him seriously.

I had some free time so I went back with Sidney to the set

and met Brando, who was sitting on a horse at the time. We said hello and then Brando asked me what I thought of Sidney as a director. I told him that I thought he was excellent, and Brando said, in front of Sidney, 'I don't think he can direct traffic.'

Sid just stood there terribly hurt, and I found myself saying, 'It's a western – there *isn't* any traffic.' This got a slightly tense laugh after a moment while everybody waited to see if Marlon laughed, which he did and things lightened up a bit.

The scene required Brando to ride his horse up to the camera, stop in front of it, say something and walk on. They had rehearsed the scene several times and the horse, one of the beautifully-trained Hollywood western horses in contrast to the highly volatile nags I had worked with, stopped dead on the camera mark every time. This was fine, until they had to move the camera a couple of feet. The problem now was that the horse was so used to the original mark it would not go past it and so the whole shot had to be dismantled and started again.

I stood around for a while and watched as Sidney, the new director from England, tried to deal with the Hollywood old guard, and witnessed a superb example of the difference in approach. Anyone who has seen *The Ipcress File* will know that Sidney has a way of shooting that at that time was very unorthodox: he would film from angles taken above objects, through them and from the floor, shooting straight up to the ceiling, although in most movie sets then you never had a ceiling. Now I watched him set up a shot with the camera literally right flat on the floor. Standing beside him was the camera operator, a great big grizzled man obviously from the old school of picture-makers. Sid asked the guy to get down on the ground and look through the viewfinder at the shot that he wanted.

The old operator looked at him for a moment as though he was mad and said, 'I was the operator on *Gone with the Wind* and I never once had to get on the floor to shoot a shot, and I am *not* about to do it on this fucking movie!'

Sid looked at him for a second, realised he was beaten and changed the shot to a position where the operator could stand up. I glanced at him and shrugged. There was nothing to be done – they had decided to screw him and they had done it. I felt really sorry for Sid as I left him there, but I knew he would get over it and he did.

I returned to the wonderful atmosphere of our set and eventually finished the picture and thus ended my first incredible stay in Hollywood. I got on a plane and in what seemed no time at all was standing in the living room of Albion Close trying to convince myself that the past three months had really happened.

The Ipcress File had been a big success and the studio decided to film Len Deighton's third novel in the series, *Funeral in Berlin*.

I was back this time with my good friends Ken Adams, who had done the production design for *Ipcress* and Otto Heller, the wonderful old Austro-Hungarian cameraman who had shot both *Ipcress* and *Alfie*. Otto had been working in Germany in the twenties and thirties, and although he was Jewish, was one of the last anti-Nazis to leave Berlin. He had never really believed that the Nazis would do him any harm, although every one of his German friends had advised him many times to leave, including his own camera operator. He still took no notice, he told me, until one Monday morning early in 1939, when his own camera operator had come to work dressed in his SS uniform, looked at Otto and said, 'Now will you get out of Germany?' Otto said that he nipped off to the toilet, climbed out of the window and never stopped running until he got to England.

Otto was a brilliant lighting man, and always made a great fuss of waving a light meter about as though this were as important to him as it is to all other lighting men. Secretly we all suspected that he could light a movie without a meter if he wanted to. Otto was a man with whom I loved to work, and he was a great technician. I once asked him where he had become a cameraman and he told me that he had been an orderly in the officers' mess in the Austro-Hungarian army before World War One and when they

265

obtained this new thing called a film projector, they gave him the job of learning how to use it – and that was how he started in the movies.

Guy Hamilton, who had just directed the hugely successful Bond film *Goldfinger* was to be our director. He was from the old school of British directing, and having been in Intelligence during the war, was more at home with the shaken cocktails of the Bond films than the gritty realism that we were trying to achieve with Harry Palmer. Although at the time Berlin was one of the most fascinating and mysterious cities in Europe, I don't think we ever managed to capture its special atmosphere in the film. I personally loved the place, with the Wall and the guards on the other side watching us through binoculars at all times. One day when we were filming in the sunshine near the Wall, the East German border guards deliberately shone a mirror in our lenses until we had to move to another location. I had to go across Checkpoint Charlie in the film but as we could not use the real one, we had to build our own just a little way away.

A strange place, Berlin. One night we were shooting a scene in a gay bar that was full of transvestites, and I found myself shocked by the men who were dressed as women. I had seen feminine homosexuals dressed as reasonable examples of women before, but I had never seen big burly guys with beards and moustaches dressed like this. It seemed quite weird to me, especially the owner, who was a massive guy with a three-day growth of stubble on his chin and hairy forearms as thick as my thighs, who was standing at the door taking the money dressed as a very unconvincing schoolgirl. When he went on to do his act, which consisted of singing *On the Good Ship Lollipop* like Shirley Temple, I turned to the hat-check girl and told her just how strange I thought he was. She listened to me for a little while, then interrupted to say that he was her father!

As we were nearing the end of shooting in Berlin, I suddenly received a message that *Alfie* was being entered for the Cannes Film Festival. I obtained a few days off and flew direct from Berlin to Cannes. *Alfie*, unlike *The Ipcress File* when it had been shown there, was going to be shown in

266

competition. We were in trouble right from the start. The French thought it was a fantasy because it was about an Englishman who makes love to ten women and they, as we all know, think they are the only people who can do this. So the French hated the picture because it seemed to strike at their manhood, while Sophia Loren, the president of the jury which selected the films for the various prizes, hated it because of the very graphic abortion scene it contains. Well, in the end, they did give us a prize – and the French threw tomatoes at Lewis Gilbert our director when he came up on stage to collect the award. That was the end of my romance with the Cannes Film Festival.

One good thing did come out of the visit, however. *Alfie* was a Paramount picture and the company gave a big lunch at the Carlton Hotel, which is the headquarters of the Festival. Sitting next to me was a man I had never met before and we started talking. The first thing I noticed about him was his thick Austrian accent, although he spoke English very well. 'What do you do?' I asked him.

'I will not tell you what I *do*,' he said. 'I will tell you what I *did* – yesterday.' There was a little pause while he waited to see if I was interested. Some sixth sense made me look at him intently. 'Yesterday,' he pronounced in a loud voice, 'I bought Paramount Studios for one hundred and fifty-two million dollars.' A lot of people at the table of course already knew this, but those of us who didn't abruptly stopped talking and when we resumed our conversations, it was with a new topic and a new attitude to this little foreign man. His name, he informed us, was Charlie Bludhorn. 'Do you have any scripts that you want to make?' he asked. I did, and told him so – and that is how a couple of years later I made *The Italian Job*.

Back in London once again, I was faced with the prospect of another trip. A festival again, but this one seemed a much more exciting proposition than Cannes; it was held in Acapulco. I quickly got out an atlas to look up this place, and found it in southern Mexico. It was, I was informed, a beautiful, baking-hot holiday resort. It was starting to get cold in England so off I went to represent my country as *Alfie* once again. I was beginning to feel that I should be given an

Olympic-style T-shirt with *Screws for England* printed on it, above a pair of crossed ladies on a bed of Union Jacks as a logo . . .

23

Otto's Revenge

I had been in many hot places, but nothing could have prepared me for the heat in Acapulco. It was like walking into a blow-torch. The minute the plane doors opened, my shirt was drenched with sweat but I did not care as I scraped the pullover off my back and stepped into the sunshine, which dried my shirt in about two minutes. Acapulco was not as built-up then as it is now, and it was still a beautiful little town stretched out around a magnificent bay, with just a couple of high-rise hotels. I was deposited at one of these and was trying to make myself understood in the pandemonium which was the lobby, when I was rescued by the American movie actor John Gavin. In fluent Spanish he sorted out my problems and got me on my way to my room.

'I didn't know you could speak such beautiful Spanish,' I said in amazement.

'I am Mexican,' he told me. This was a surprise, I said, because he was so tall, taller than me in fact, and I had thought that all Mexicans were short. 'Anthony Quinn and I are both from Chihuahua – home of the biggest men and the smallest dogs in Mexico.'

Once installed, I found I was not there alone, and the purpose of my presence in Acapulco was explained – something of which I was ignorant at the time. At that point in my life, any free trip anywhere good was accepted by me and I asked questions later. Now I was introduced to my fellow British stars who made up our contingent, by an old ex-admiral with a beard and a great Greek wife. He, for some reason, was the Head of the British Film Association, I believe (although how an admiral got this job I can't imagine), and he was great fun, and we all loved him and his wife. My companions turned out to be Rita Tushingham and Lynn Redgrave. We were all there, apparently, because we had appeared in films that had already won awards at other festivals. This was the policy of the Acapulco Festival. I was there for *Alfie*, of course while Rita was there for *A Taste of Honey* and Lynn for *Georgy Girl*.

We had one day free before the activities of the Festival proper started, so I took this opportunity to go on the beach and get a second-degree sunburn and a nose that began to peel one layer at a time for the whole ten days we were there. The next day there was a press conference for the British stars, at which the entire South American press corps could scarcely conceal their disbelief that these three people represented some sort of cream of a nation's film colony. Their qualms about us were understandable. South American and Mexican film stars look like film stars and nothing else – that is what is wrong with their films. They are all stunningly handsome or beautiful and do not under any circumstances ever come close to looking like real people. What the pressmen saw was Rita, about five feet tall and weighing a hundred pounds wringing wet, with great big eyes in a tiny face and a little nose that pointed straight up to the sky; she looked cute, but like a little female elf. Lynn was pre-Weight Watchers, weighing in at around two hundred pounds and walking as though it was something she had seen done, but had never actually tried. Both of these ladies were pale to the point of transparency and made to look even more awkward when standing together, because Lynn was about five feet ten while Rita, when standing beside her, looked as though she might be her lunch. Add to this duet myself – a very tall and extremely skinny blonde man with glasses (a Mexican film star would go blind before he would wear specs) perched on a bright red face, out of which stuck a swollen nose flaking and throbbing like a red traffic light with a torn veil over it.

We were asked polite questions about our films, but sandwiched in between these was the query, were there any other British stars at the Festival, as though we had been brought on merely as an appetiser before the main course. The reporters were completely unable to conceal their disappointment when they were finally convinced that we were all they were going to get. The conference did not so much finish as melt away.

Neither Rita, Lynn or myself had ever been to a bullfight and we eagerly accepted an invitation to one the next day. It started, I was told by our Mexican minder, at three o'clock in the afternoon – 'tiempo Inglesi' – which he explained meant English time, or punctual. All Latin peoples are notoriously bad timekeepers and they had adopted this phrase to signify when a certain time would be on the dot. I have never been to a bullfight that started late, and I have never been to anything else in any Latin country that started on time. The seats, the Mexican told me proudly, were in the front and on the shady side of the ring – the best seats in the house. He took Rita, Lynn and myself to the ring, right up to our seats then left our strange little trio on our own.

Dead on three, a trumpet sounded, a gate opened and in came a parade of all the people taking part in the spectacle. It was a wonderful sight and we all sat back to enjoy the show. The bull was let in and he seemed terrifying and very large to our inexperienced eyes. Several guys teased him for a while and then came the picadors on horseback. This was where the trouble started. The shock that all three of us experienced as the horsemen started to grind their spear-like weapons into the top of the bull's shoulders, quickly translated into horror for poor Lynn. She passed out completely and slid down into the space between the seats and the front wall of the bullring. As this was very narrow and Lynn very wide at the time, she became wedged tight before she touched the ground. I reached down and hauled her back upright in her seat and held her there until she came round, which was quite quickly. She settled in her seat and lifted her eyes nervously back to the spectacle just as another spike jammed into the bull's shoulders right in front of us, with blood spurting every-where. This time I was ready and caught her before she fell again.

Lynn's bullfighting days were obviously over and I decided

to carry her out of the arena. This was no small task as at the time she weighed about what I weigh now, and I weighed then about what she weighs now, due in part to the recent help given by the ever-present Montezuma and his Revenge which I was experiencing. This last was still with me in a mild form and became quite a worry to me as I took the strain of Lynn's bulk and started to ascend the long flight of steps up the entire height of the bullring to the exit at the top. Small accidents started to occur almost immediately as I strained slowly up each step of the seemingly endless flight. My sphincter was as tight as flesh and blood could make it and held back any major flow, but small releases were unavoidable. These did not worry me, however, because I had taken the precaution of wearing very thick underpants and had on a newly-purchased pair of very dark brown trousers – a fashion statement which much to my surprise did not catch on in Acapulco that season.

By the time I was halfway up the steps the crowd had spotted what was going on and had turned their sadistic attention away from the bullfight to my plight. When I finally reached the top the entire bullring was shouting *Olé!* Rita was bringing up the rear, carrying our belongings, like Sancho Panza to my Don Quixote burdened with the lovely Dulcinea and we disappeared from the sight of the crowd and collapsed in a heap on the floor. This was the end of our outings together.

I slept most of the following days and spent the nights in a fantastic carousel. In Acapulco there was one of the most extraordinary discothèques I have ever been in. Somehow or other it always wound up at dawn like some miniature carnival in Rio. The queen of our nights there was Jayne Mansfield. As a matter of fact, that year in Acapulco she was Queen everywhere she went. One evening the British contingent gave a party and Jayne was dancing vigorously with the old admiral with the beard and Greek wife. She was wearing a dress that seemed to be held up solely by her very substantial breasts, and as the evening wore on and the dancing became ever more frantic, tension grew as the watchers on the sidelines, myself included, realised that even these admirable buttresses could not support the silken structure much longer. And so it was eventually with an almost audible sigh of relief that her bosom gave up the unequal task and relinquished its hold. The dress glided slowly to the floor, revealing that not only did Miss Mansfield have a beautiful, if slightly Rubenesque form, but that she also had a very bad memory, for it was immediately apparent that she had forgotten to put on any underwear. She stepped unperturbed out of the circle of silk on the floor, picked it up, threw it over her shoulder and retired to the Ladies, to reappear a little later with visible safety pins in strategic places. The Greek wife said something that I presumed went along the lines of 'Now that's what I call *chutzpah*' – but not speaking Greek I cannot be sure.

The night went roaring on until carnival at dawn was over, and suddenly I found myself out in the street with my friend and agent Dennis Selinger, who had recently arrived, and another man whose identity I never learned but I do remember a piece of startling information he passed on to us. The local whorehouse, he said, 'took American Express'. I had only just become the proud possessor of one of these, and so I felt a sense of real letdown that my new glittering prize could be used for such a purpose. What on earth would you put on the receipt as having been purchased? He had the answer: 'Breakfast,' and that, believe it or not, is what we did in the whorehouse for the rest of our stay. We had breakfast there at every dawn.

At last I left Acapulco and flew back to London, where I found that I had been offered a part in Otto Preminger's new film *Hurry Sundown*. Unbeknown to me, this was the start of a series of bad pictures made by people who had all the right credentials for success. Otto had created such wonderful movies as *Carmen Jones*, *Man with the Golden Arm* and *Anatomy of a Murder* so when I was invited to work with him I was so flattered and excited that I accepted almost without reading the part. As it happened it was a good one, but I had to have a Southern accent as the action took place in Louisiana. For this I obtained tapes and practised the accent all day long, and even had a bit of luck with an expert. One night I was having dinner in an old haunt, the Trattoria Terrazza, when

John Gielgud came over and introduced himself. He and his female companion had just seen *Alfie* and they were very nice to me about it. He eventually introduced the lady with him, who emerged from behind her dark glasses to be Vivien Leigh. Here was my chance!

'How did you practise the accent that you had in *Gone with the Wind*?' I asked, after we had been talking for a little while.

'I said "four door Ford" all day long for weeks,' she told me, except that when Vivien said it, it came out as 'Foah Doah Fohd'. So *that* was the secret.

For days after that I went around repeating this phrase over and over, but it did not help me with the good old class-conscious British critics. 'I could hear *Cockney* in his voice,' they shrieked, as though they had discovered leprosy amongst themselves. The strange thing was that in the Southern newspapers, I received the best reviews for my accent, and from the British critics, who knew the least about it, the worst ones. We were back at the *Zulu* thing again, when a critic who had never met me saw nothing wrong with my accent, and the only bad reviews I got for it were from those who knew my origins.

Everything started off very well on *Hurry Sundown*. I was given a very nice suite overlooking the swimming pool of a gigantic hotel situated on the road between Baton Rouge and New Orleans. The cast was great. Jane Fonda who was then married to Roger Vadim was playing my wife, and a new young star, Faye Dunaway, had another of the female leads. Diahann Carroll, the beautiful black actress, completed the trio of leading ladies. Apart from me there was John Philip Law and a talented young black actor called Robert Hooks. He and I became friends almost immediately. The older character parts were played by wonderful actors like Burgess Meredith, Bea Richards, George Kennedy and that great black actor Rex Ingram who had played 'De Lawd' in the movie *Green Pastures*. He was a particular favourite of mine because he loved to barbecue steaks. I was a big meat-eater at the time and he cooked the best steaks I'd ever tasted.

So there we all were, ready to go. The first evening we had a welcome party and a lot of us wound up in the swimming pool. Now this may seem quite innocuous to most people, as indeed it did to us, but we had reckoned without the racial situation down in that part of the world. We had committed an unpardonable sin and did not even know it until the middle of the next night. I was sleeping peacefully when I was awoken by a loud explosion just outside my bedroom. I looked out of the window, which had been almost broken by the blast, to see a strange sight. Someone had tried to blow up the swimming pool, a pretty difficult thing to do – blowing a hole in something which is already a hole, so the damage was minimal; it was obvious that the perpetrators were not exactly rocket scientists. The motive given for the attack on the pool was that it had had 'Niggers' swimming in it. Maybe Southern hospitality was not going to be all it was cracked up to be.

Otto, I knew by reputation, was a tyrant with a filthy temper who screamed at people a great deal, so I decided to take the bull by the horns and lay down some ground rules from Day One. When we were introduced, I informed him that I knew of his reputation and that he should know that I was a very shy little flower, and if anybody ever shouted at me I would burst into tears and go into my dressing room and not come out for the rest of the day.

He stared at me for a long moment and I waited to be bawled out immediately, as he was not used to being spoken to like this. Certainly, he did seem a little taken aback. Finally, however, he smiled and said, 'I would never shout at Alfie.' That was the key to the long friendship I subsequently enjoyed with this unpopular man. Like many other men I have met, he secretly saw himself as another Alfie, and as far as he was concerned, so did I. That was it – I never got a cross word from him during the whole picture and I even managed to take some of the pressure off poor Faye Dunaway, who became his 'whipping boy' right through the picture and seemed to end every day in tears. Through my friendship with him I was able to tell him from time to time to ease up on her, not something that most people on the picture would be keen to do, and it did always help for a couple of days – but then he would go right back to tormenting her.

Otto was an extraordinary-looking man, with a shaven

head, large watery eyes and a strange mouth that moved in a way that made you think his lips were made of soft rubber. As an actor he had scored a big success at playing Nazi officers in the Prussian mould of Erich von Stroheim. He seemed to relish his reputation as an ogre, to deliberately behave badly and upset people – not a nice guy to be around for long.

And yet he was, I discovered later, a man of tremendous taste and culture. He had started out as an assistant to the great director Max Reinhardt at his theatre in Vienna, and when I eventually went to his home in New York I found it loaded with paintings by great modern artists; he also had a small courtyard filled with a collection of statues by Henry Moore, Constantin Brancusi and Alberto Giacometti. The house, I was unsurprised to find, was furnished in a clean and uncluttered way with lots of cold stone and marble. In his projection room there was a coffee table with all the buttons to control the sound, lights, curtains etc, and at the end of the row I noticed a button that said *Destruct*. 'What's that for?' I asked.

'The workmen put it in as a token of their affection for me,' he smiled.

'It's nice to see that you have a consistent effect on everybody,' I said.

'I am completely predictable, Michael,' he replied without conviction. All right, I know, he did have some charm and good taste, but that is no excuse for the way he persecuted Faye.

Talking of Miss Dunaway, we eventually got some time off and had an evening in New Orleans where we were all introduced to the crowd in an enormous bar. None of them had heard of any of us except Faye Dunaway, and there was a big cheer when her name was announced. One woman who was sitting at the bar with her back to us and who was paralytically drunk, slowly swivelled on her barstool and stared at us for a second before slurring, 'Which one of you is Troy Donahue?' So much for fame.

We visited New Orleans several times, but the style of the place is not conducive to a good memory. One evening we started out at the bar of an old hotel where they had invented a very popular gin drink called a Sazarac. From there we moved on to a bar called Pat O'Brien's, where they gave you a drink called a Hurricane and you could take the glass out of their bar and get it refilled at any hostelry along Bourbon Street. I remember doing this at seven o'clock one evening then *nothing else* until I found myself having breakfast at Brennan's which at the time was one of the 'done' things.

For all the fun of New Orleans, though, most of which was supplied by black people – all the great jazz and rock musicians and the singers and dancers, there was still a strong racist bias to life there. One weekend, for instance, I saw an all-black revue that was great and told my friend Bobby Hooks about it. I asked him to come and see it with me the next weekend. Bobby being black was particularly wary of going to New Orleans but I convinced him that this place would surely be all right because everybody there, from the whole cast to the staff was black, so he finally gave in and came with me. We reached the door of the club and were just about to go in, when a guy came over and whispered to Bobby that black people were not welcome. I immediately started shouting and bawling, but Bobby grabbed me and dragged me out of there. It was a terrible thing for me. Bobby said it was always like that down there and he was used to it, but it was my first experience of prejudice in America close up – and it was honestly one of the few times in my life I have been ashamed of being white. All this, I am sure, does not apply now to the south in general and New Orleans in particular, but it did then.

The Ku Klux Klan had dubbed us 'the nigger picture' and tried to make life as awkward as possible for us, with little things like waiting until night then pumping our dressing caravans full of bullet-holes. Although the caravans were empty at the time it sure made you worry when you were in them during the day. There was one little town where they actually came in their white hooded gowns and told us to get out. Otto for once listened to what someone else said and we all obliged. A couple of weeks later I went back into the same little town with my friend David Lewin, who is Jewish and an English journalist, working then for the *Daily Mail*. He had been sent out to do a story on the film in general and me in particular as the only English actor in the cast. I told him about the various racial incidents and attitudes, and he clearly did not believe a word I was saying so I took him to the aforesaid town and was still trying to convince him, when suddenly there was a yell from the other end of the street. I turned and saw the sheriff coming towards us. As he approached he recognised me from the week before.

'You're with that nigger picture, ain't you?' he shouted.

'Yes,' I replied, 'but we're not working here, I was just showing my friend around.'

'I don't give a flying fuck what you're doing. I told you assholes to get out last week and I meant it so get the fuck out and take that kike with you.'

I took David by the arm and guided him out of town. He just walked by my side, his mouth wide open with disbelief. 'Now do you believe me?' I demanded. He grunted what sounded like an affirmative and we marched out of town at an ever-increasing pace.

Although Otto had let rip quite often so far during the filming, those who knew him assured me that I hadn't seen nothing yet. And indeed I had not – until we were shooting a particular scene in a real hospital on a boiling hot day. The temperature was further raised by our big hot lamps, and then the sound man committed the *coup de grâce*: he wanted the air-conditioning turned off because the sound of it was ruining his recording of the dialogue. When this was done, for a while it felt like a witches' cauldron in there. And then a major disaster struck. The heat was so intense that it set off the automatic sprinkler system in our section of the hospital and drenched not only us but thousands of dollars' worth of equipment. Otto exploded. I have never seen anyone so near apoplexy. His eyes bulged out of his head with fury and his vocal cords were torn in his throat as he spat curses on everyone in earshot. I had never witnessed anger like this. Eventually, having exhausted all of us and at last himself, he stalked out for the rest of the day.

The other time he blew his fuse I did not see him because he was up in a helicopter shooting the scene – a big one with hundreds of extras and masses of explosions. To get it all in the one take, because it could not be repeated without a great loss of time and money, Otto had aimed six cameras on it to take different angles of the action and he, as I said, was up in the helicopter with the main camera. It took all day to set up the shot and finally everything was ready. Otto shouted, 'Action,' and the explosions started and the extras began to run to their allotted marks when, driving through the midst of all this in his boss's 1966 Cadillac, came Otto's personal assistant. As the story of *Hurry Sundown* took place in 1945 the shot was completely ruined. I swear we could hear Otto's voice above the noise of the helicopter as it touched down. He came screaming out of it only to see his car do a quick U-turn as his luckless assistant fled in terror.

One of Otto's many minions was, in Otto's presence, one of the most obsequious and grovelling servants that I have ever seen. He lived in absolute terror, all day, every day. He was also responsible for a line which for my money is the all-time 'Yes Man' cop out. Otto was having dinner in his hotel room and having finished eating, ordered coffee, which was brought into the room by a waiter. The assistant, ever ready to ingratiate himself, took the coffee from the waiter and offered to serve it himself – which he did, but tripped over the carpet and poured the hot liquid straight into Otto's lap. The director screamed at the poor man, 'You are burning me, you idiot!'

'I can't be,' the man replied quickly. 'You never get hot coffee in room service.' What a get-out line – I love it!

By this time, word had got round the unit that I had told Otto never to shout at me – and this was taken as an act of extreme courage and folly. His assistant warned me that although Otto might have been nice to me at the time, he would never let me get away with it. Some time before the end of filming he would get his own back. Well, I watched and waited for several weeks and nothing happened, so I forgot all about it and dropped my guard – and that of course is when he got me. One day I had to do a scene in which I raped Jane Fonda, who was playing my estranged wife. I was looking forward to the scene with great trepidation, yet Jane seemed quite unconcerned about it. She was an extremely self-possessed young woman.

On the day of filming I asked Otto how I should go about it, but he just smiled and said, 'Jane will be in the room with the door locked. Just smash it down, get in there and rape her.'

I was still very nervous about the general lack of direction in this, so I asked another question. 'How far do we go with it?'

'Don't worry,' he smiled lecherously (and that was one smile he really could do), 'I will call Cut when we have enough.'

So I smashed the door down, came tearing in, grabbed Jane and proceeded to rape her as best as I could. I had no experience of such a procedure and this was an extreme example of 'on the job training'. Anyway, I got her on the bed and quite a bit of her clothing off, bearing in mind all the time the rigorous censorship laws in the United States, hence leaving her clad in brassière and panties. As I was kissing and trying to fondle less intimate parts of her body and occasionally failing, things began to get more and more 'advanced' until I felt that there was no way any of this could be used in the film. I stopped myself and said so, only to find director and crew all sitting there smiling with the cameras long since turned off, just enjoying the scene. There was a look of immense satisfaction on Otto's face and I knew, without a doubt, that he had got his revenge.

24

French hours

Cary Grant had once told me when we had dinner at Danny Kaye's house, that to be a star you had to make at least fifteen pictures before you became as familiar in people's lives as their favourite brand of tea or coffee. I was now, it seemed, taking his advice as I moved from one picture to another at great speed. I was off on my treadmill of almost nonstop pictures for the next few years. After *Hurry Sundown* I went from Louisiana, where the temperature rarely dropped below eighty degrees even at night, straight to Helsinki in Finland, where the temperature never went above zero even at noon.

My trip was in order to make the third and what proved to be the last in the Harry Palmer series of spy films, *Billion Dollar Brain*.

The cold in Finland was difficult to understand. If you did not wear a hat you got a splitting headache as your brain started to freeze, and the sea, which is after all a moving body of salt water, froze to depths of eight to ten feet. In the winter they run roads for ordinary traffic straight across the bay on which Helsinki stands, like a free bridge.

Towards the end of the picture I was doing a shot in which I run across the ice-floe as it breaks up, leaping from one floating block to another. As we were shooting this scene, one of the Finnish assistants ran into the middle of the action and yelled at me to get off the ice-floe immediately.

'What's wrong?' I queried.

'Where are your ice-knives?' the Finn demanded.

'What ice-knives?' I asked, not knowing what he was talking about.

'These,' he said, reaching back with both hands and

pulling two identical short knives from holsters on each hip.

'What are they for?' I asked.

'If you fall between the ice-blocks, how do you think you are going to get out with your bare hands? Without these you would be dead. We couldn't get you out.' I stood there shaking with more than the cold.

The morning continued with one disaster after another. The day before, the temperature had begun rising, comparatively speaking, and we could see the ice melting all around us, as cracks started to appear. I instantly recalled the saying from my boyhood days: 'Cracks it bears, bends it breaks'. I spent the entire morning searching the already cracked ice for signs of bending.

We continued shooting with one problem after another. The ice was now covered with about three inches of water and it became very difficult even to stand up. Then we lost the generator which powered all our lights. Being a very heavy truck it was the first thing to start sinking, so we had to send it off the ice and continue shooting with hand-held, battery-powered lights. By now we were frozen, wet and starving hungry and then the next disaster struck. The catering truck was too heavy to come out to us so we had to keep shooting until three without food.

By the time we finished the last shot, there was a definite feeling of mutiny in the air. I had not felt so uncomfortable and miserable since leaving the army. When the last shot was over, the director shouted 'Cut,' and the first assistant shouted, 'Check the gate!' This means the camera assistant takes the 'gate' the film has just run through out of the camera, and checks it for specks of dust or hair. This is necessary because even the tiniest speck or hair would be magnified so many times when the film is projected that it can look like a large spider running along the bottom of the screen. We all stood round waiting to see if the gate was clear and we could get back to our warm hotel and hot food, when suddenly a Cockney voice announced, 'If there's a sandwich in there, I'll fucking have it.'

At least one of us still had a sense of humour. Finally the assistant yelled 'Gate clear,' a cheer went up and we were off the ice forever and out of Finland the next day back to springtime in England. It was April and the daffodils would be out, I thought, as I slid across the ice to the shore and civilisation at last.

In London we worked day and night at Pinewood Studios on the interiors of *Billion Dollar Brain*. We had got behind schedule in Finland and needed to catch up. I could not wait to finish the picture; its plot had always been a bit obscure, but now at the end of shooting it would have befuddled Einstein. More importantly than that, though, when I had finished, I was due to go off to Paris immediately.

Shirley Maclaine was shooting a picture there called *Woman Times Seven* which was being directed by Vittorio de Sica. This part was my first 'guest shot' and was very small, with about three minutes' of screen-time and no dialogue. I played a private detective who just follows Shirley and Anita Ekberg, who plays her friend, all over Paris. I did this as a favour to Shirley, in return for the one she had done me by taking me to Hollywood for the first time. I also did it for other reasons, like the chance to do something, no matter how small, with de Sica, a man I admired so much. Lastly, I was looking forward to being in my beloved Paris again. This time I had a beautiful suite at the George V Hotel, for when producers are not paying your full fee they always give you great accommodation. What is more, we worked French hours. In England and America you always have to get up at the crack of dawn to go to work, not so in France. The hours were from ten in the morning until seven in the evening, with no break for lunch, just a running buffet. These hours, as you will see if you study them carefully, leave plenty of room for the important things in life, like partying all night and sleeping late in the mornings, with time to recover from a hangover and learn your dialogue. I was even more fortunate – I didn't *have* any dialogue, which gave me at least another hour of sleep in the morning. Add to all this the fact that it was springtime, and my cup ranneth over.

This movie got better and better. God seemed to be rewarding me for Finland. My first shot was on the Champs

Elysées and I could actually sit and have breakfast in Fouquet's, one of my favourite restaurants, and watch the crew set up the shot. The sun was shining, the coffee was great and the passing parade on the pavement was gorgeous. Work did not get any better than this.

My first shot summed up for me the attitude to life of the Parisian man. As the private detective in the movie, I had to follow Shirley and Anita Ekberg along the Champs Elysées, and as the pavement is so wide and Vittorio was shooting with a hidden camera in a van, he asked us to walk on the very outside edge of the pavement right next to the traffic. We started the shot with Shirley and Anita in front, me about twenty yards behind and the camera car following us, when an open sports car with two dashing young Frenchmen came along and spotted the two ladies. They slowed down the car by the side of them as they walked, so ruining the shot. I could hear Vittorio screaming in the van, but he was no match for Otto. The two Frenchmen, oblivious to what was going on, continued to try to pick up the two beauties until they suddenly realised who they were talking to and that they were going to get nowhere, so they backed up the car and stopped beside me. They did not know who I was – they just thought I was another guy like themselves following the girls with romantic intentions. They could see I was English and one of them said to me, 'My friend and I would like you to know that you have very good taste.' I love Paris.

Somewhere along the line I had picked up a two-picture deal with Twentieth Century-Fox, and the time had come to do the first one. This was called *Deadfall* and was about a sophisticated cat burglar who plies his nefarious trade in Spain. My old friend Bryan Forbes was the director and I was all set for a wonderful experience, but it didn't work out that way. Somehow between the writing of the script and the shooting of the film, something important got lost.

There was, however, one great compensation in making this movie. We were filming a big fancy-dress ball scene and a lot of the locals had come as extras, not for the money, just the fun. One day I was sitting at one of the trestle tables laid out in the sunshine and eating my lunch when one of these extras, an elderly man dressed as a sort of Arab Pasha, came over and sat next to me. His first question surprised me. 'Were you ever a Royal Fusilier?' he asked, mentioning the name of the regiment with which I had served in Korea.

'Yes,' I replied in astonishment.

'I thought you were, the moment I saw you. I was one as well once, in the First World War. My name is Robert Graves.'

My astonishment increased as I finally recognised the face beneath the funny hat and scrawny beard. Robert Graves was a writer whom I loved, and here he was actually talking to me! In actual fact, I thought that he had died long ago. He had written the classic account of the British soldier in the First World War, *Goodbye to All That* and the even more famous (now that it has been a television mini-series), *I Claudius*.

After that I spent a great deal of time with Robert Graves and went several times to eat in his home which was in a secluded and beautiful part of Majorca called Deia. It was not very fashionable at the time but now everybody has a home there, from King Juan Carlos of Spain to Michael Douglas. Robert told me a story which may not be true but it has a ring of truth to it. The Royal Fusiliers is a London regiment, and it recruits its men from south and east London, both districts very poor and working-class; into this area have traditionally come the waves of immigrants from Europe, as this is where the great London Docks used to thrive. Consequently there were always a great many Jewish immigrant families in the area and following on from that, in the Royal Fusiliers themselves. Robert told me that in the Great War he was a platoon commander and his sergeant was a Jewish immigrant who had anglicised his name and called himself Benny Green. The very next week, Robert confided, he was going to Israel to see his old sergeant as he had done every year for a long time now.

'What does he do over there?' I enquired.

'He's retired now,' Robert said with a smile, 'but he used to be the Prime Minister. He changed his name to a Hebrew one and called himself Ben Gurion.'

I was struck dumb. Ben Gurion – the giant of Israel – was

an ex-Royal Fusilier! It was unbelievable. Robert followed this startling information with a fact that I could readily believe. He told me that fourteen members of the first cabinet of Israel were ex-Fusiliers – now that really *is* feasible. When we finished the part of the film that had to shoot on the islands, we moved on to Madrid and I never saw Robert again: he died in 1985. It was a privilege to have known him.

25

Bardot tries it on

I have been in over seventy-three films in thirty years and by the time you read this it will probably be seventy-six. People often criticise me for not being discriminating enough and even for working so hard. Why bother? As far as discrimination is concerned I have a definite standard by which I choose films: I choose the best one available at the time I need one. Of course this has often led me down dubious artistic paths, but even they are not without their advantages. It is much more difficult to act well in a bad film with a bad director than in any other type of movie and it gives you great experience in taking care of yourself. It also means that when a good script does turn up you're ready for it. It's not unlike athletes in training who will practise running on sand so they find it easy to run on a solid track in competition. Plus of course there's the money. You get paid the same for a bad film as you do for a good one – because no one knows for sure if the bad film is going to be bad or the good film is going to be good until the première. You can wind up, as I do when a good role comes along, absolutely prepared, having worked right up to date, or you can sit there waiting for it for five years, scared and rusting. No one remembers unsuccessful pictures because no one went to see them. At the end of the day you are remembered for your hits – of which you must make a minimum of one in five or you're out. I came pretty close with four and a half flops on one occasion, but I'm still here.

I, of course, don't have the constraints of the great male Hollywood stars who will not play certain roles for fear of causing a lack of sympathy or letting down their fans. I cannot imagine a Robert Redford, Paul Newman or Clint Eastwood playing a transvestite killer as I did in *Dressed to Kill* or an overt homosexual as I did in *Deathtrap*. The main advantage that a foreign actor has in Hollywood is to play the flawed characters that the American stars don't want. The last three Best Actor Academy Awards have been won by British stars: Daniel Day Lewis as a horribly deformed man in *My Left Foot*, Jeremy Irons as a man on trial for the alleged attempted murder of his wife in *Reversal of Fortune*, and Anthony Hopkins, in 1992, who played Hannibal Lecter the homicidal cannibal in *The Silence of the Lambs*. Often nice guys finish last.

I had now settled into a period where I had no social life at all, but just went from one film to another, always with the best of intentions but mainly with that intense, overriding desire to make a lot of money before it all came to an end, which I expected it to do on an almost weekly basis.

The moment that I finished *Deadfall* in the studio in London, I was on a plane back to Spain to start another film, a Harry Saltzman production – a war film called *Play Dirty*. It was to be directed by the great French director René Clément. The script was reasonable and it had a good plot: a group of Israeli commandos are sent out in the desert war to blow up the German fuel dumps, but the British Army have got there first and they want the fuel for themselves. The Israelis are on radio silence so the British inform the Germans that they are coming in order to prevent them from destroying the fuel. On the surface it is a good action story, based on fact, with a moral to it and some controversy. So what could possibly go wrong? The short answer is – everything. *Play Dirty* is a prime example of how you can start out with a good story and the very best of intentions and yet get gradually worn down into mediocrity.

The moment that I signed to do the film, René Clément had a row with Harry and left the film. There was a much-vaunted re-write of the script, which in my opinion was not as good as the original, but we used it anyway. The powers that be always use the last script in film-making no matter how bad it is because they have to justify the additional expense to their financiers and dare not admit they have made a mistake. René

Clément was replaced by André de Toth with whom I had worked briefly when young in *A Foxhole in Cairo*. André came on to the picture so late that even he had no time to do his best work.

Once again I wound up in a film where the backstage action so to speak was rather more interesting than the film itself, but even that started off badly.

Play Dirty was due to be shot in a town called Almeria in southern Spain, and as there was no airport there I had to fly to Madrid and then take a train. This did not worry me unduly as I had visions of a very pleasant trip through the Spanish countryside in the comfort of a first-class carriage. The train, however, turned out to be a very ramshackle affair with no first-class compartments, only wooden seats – and no dining car. I was travelling with Johnny Morris, my stand-in and companion, and our first worry was food. We had been told that the journey took eight hours but no one had warned us that there would be no food available. The train itself was excruciatingly slow, and as a journey into the truly futile, we went the scenic route – at night!

Our trip finally terminated at Almeria and we hailed a cab to the hotel, only to receive the unkindest cut of all. A policeman stopped our vehicle and we sat and waited. After about five minutes I enquired what the hold-up was. Generalissimo Franco was coming, it appeared and all roads were to be closed. Franco was the Fascist Dictator of Spain at the time. We sat there for two hours in a temperature of ninety degrees with no air conditioning and sweated away what little liquid there was left in our dry frames after a nightlong bout with diarrhoea after buying dodgy snacks. Finally Franco came zooming past in a cloud of dust and we were allowed on our way. As we passed the policeman I asked him what Franco was doing down here. 'He is opening the new Almeria airport,' he said with pride.

Once in our rooms which, though a little spartan were very comfortable and clean with a nice view of the town, we unpacked, showered and descended to the lobby to find the action but there was none. Almeria at this time was the centre

289

of Italian 'Spaghetti Western' film-making since it had been discovered by Sergio Leone for his *The Good, the Bad and the Ugly* series. It had also been acquired by the desert-war film group, such as ourselves, when David Lean had shot the train-crash sequence in *Lawrence of Arabia* here. What nobody had told us was that there were only four sand-dunes – and if you did a high crane shot you had an almost immediate picture of the sea with the crowded beaches of the town of Almeria. We knew there were at least two Spaghetti Westerns being made there currently plus Sean Connery was also filming a western called *Shalako*.

Despite all this activity, it was now just after lunch and everybody was obviously still out working so the huge lobby of the hotel was empty. Johnny and I ordered a couple of ice-cold beers and took them into a shady corner and sat and had a chat. Or to put it another way, I sat and bemoaned the fact for half an hour that there were no women around and I was here for twelve long weeks. Johnny was happily married and not a great source of sympathy as is the way of married men faced with the enforced celibacy of bachelors. As I was droning on about my fate, three shadows fell across our table. We looked up and I thought I must be dreaming. Smiling down at us in her most seductive manner was Brigitte Bardot, and standing on either side of her were two other women, almost as attractive.

''Allo, Makell. We 'ave bin wetting fur yeww.' This last word pursed her already famous and naturally pouting lips into an even deeper *moué* and my eyes became hypnotically fixed on them as I rose to my feet, knocking over the coffee table on which our two beers stood in a vain attempt to muster an immediate air of worldly sophistication and *savoir faire*. Everyone laughed at this silly misfortune except myself as I felt my face burning with humiliation.

'Don't worry about zat,' said Brigitte airily. 'I 'ave a car outside and we will all go to my 'otel fur a drink.' Johnny and I followed this little group across the vast lobby, both of us struck dumb by what was happening as we weaved our way through a sea of empty chairs like rats following the Pied Piper.

I still had not spoken and was not yet prepared to try. I just could not believe that this was happening to us. Not only was my speech affected, but my walking started to go awry. I found myself suddenly swinging my left arm forward in time with my left leg and the same with the right. I hadn't even done this when I was learning to march in the army.

As we walked Brigitte introduced us to her two friends. The tall dark one was her Venezuelan secretary Gloria and the smaller fair-haired one was her French stand-in Monique. As a trio, she then informed us, they were known as Bri Bri, Mo Mo and Glo Glo. Outside the hotel we got into her white Rolls Royce which was driven by a black chauffeur. Obviously not a girl to do things by halves, I thought – correctly, as it turned out.

The first question that I managed to blurt out of a clogged throat as we glided quietly along the coast road to her beach-side hotel, was, 'How did you know that we were coming today?'

'Sean told me,' she replied. It was then I remembered that she was starring opposite Sean Connery in *Shakalo*.

On our arrival at the hotel we were taken straight up to her suite overlooking the sea and plied with drinks and room service. I sat there trying to keep up my end of the conversation as best as one can on the verge of a nervous breakdown. My mind was racing. What was going on? Could it be that Brigitte Bardot actually *fancied* me? Could I be that lucky? The answer was unfortunately no. It was her secretary Gloria who fancied me, and Bardot was setting it up for her. I was disappointed to say the least, for although Gloria was gorgeous, I had this intuition that here was the sort of girl who, having given herself, would be hard to persuade to take herself back. So I resisted all advances on this front and was also a little incensed by a feeling of snobbery, rare for me, that I had been sent for by Brigitte to screw her staff.

I hung around all during the shooting of the picture in the hope that Bardot would change her mind, but I soon found out that her taste ran to extremely beautiful dark Spanish boys, who all seemed to be in their late teens. I never heard any of them speak to anybody, including her, they just used to frolic behind her like energetic little puppies with their barks removed. Try as I might, and I did, I could not squeeze myself into this category. So I gave up all together and retired from her sphere of influence, which was quite wide down there.

The last time I ever saw Bardot was at the party for the end of *Shalako*. I was invited by Sean but sat deliberately out of the limelight with my friend the English comedian Eric Sykes, who was also in the picture. When Bardot came in Eric started to make me laugh. 'She is in love with me,' he whispered, 'and she can't stand it. Watch her as she goes by,' he hissed, as she approached our table. 'She'll pretend and just ignore me,' which is what she did. She walked straight past without even looking at us. 'I told you,' he said excitedly. 'She's trying to fight it – she's ignored me since the first day of shooting.'

By now I was in hysterics and Bardot noticed this and probably thought I was laughing at her. I went back to my conversation with Eric and we were just deciding to leave when a stale Spanish loaf hit me on the side of the head. I looked up and Bardot was grinning as she dusted bread-crumbs from her hands. I smiled through the pain in my head and left, flicking crumbs off my shoulder. That was the end of our relationship.

I didn't see much of Sean, as he was either shooting *Shalako* or golf balls, but we did meet for dinner a couple of times when the subject of my failed pursuit of Bardot was treated with great hilarity.

There was another side to the glamorous French actress that was very sensitive and surprised me very much. It is a sad little tale with a truly fairy-tale ending. We had on *Play Dirty* a transportation manager named Andrew Birkin, and one day his sister Jane turned up unexpectedly in Almeria from London, heartbroken and carrying her little baby. Her marriage to my friend John Barry the composer had broken up suddenly and she did not know what to do. She had just wanted to get away from London for a while and with her brother's help, sort out her life. Little did she know that she was not getting away from London for a while, but forever, and that the fairy godmother who was going to arrange all this for her was none other than Bardot herself. She met Jane Birkin and was immediately enchanted by her waif-like looks and her pretty little child. She took them more and more under her wing every day, and eventually brought Jane back to Paris with her and helped her find work as an actress, which she had been in England, until eventually Jane became and still is, a big movie star in France.

Shooting continued on *Play Dirty* with more than the usual share of setbacks. Some of the situations were truly farcical. As I said before, there were only about four big sand-dunes, which made for disaster when several units were shooting there simultaneously. One day we had a shot where the tanks of Rommel's Afrika Korps were advancing across the desert towards El Alamein, only to be greeted as they rounded a hill by a stagecoach being chased by American Indians coming in the other direction. At the sight of the tanks, of course, the horses panicked and threw their riders, and we had to wait while they were caught and the scene was cleared, and then in would go our local unemployed with brooms and shovels to wipe out the horses' hoofprints and pick up the horseshit, of which there was always plenty as the result of the sudden appearance of the tanks on the horses' digestive system.

The next little problem was that we would be delayed by the onset of rain, which was bad enough, but the following couple of days would be real murder as the desert there is full of seeds – and the moment that it rains the plants blossom very fast, transforming the dunes into a lawn. The labourers would then drop their shovels and buckets and spend a day on their knees picking plants out of the sand. Sometimes people ask me why films cost so much and I have often been tempted to tell them these stories. Unbelievable they may seem, but I swear they are all true.

Finally the picture came to an end and it was back to London for a short respite before returning to Majorca to make *The Magus* which, along with *Deadfall*, was the second of my disastrous two-picture deal with Twentieth Century-Fox.

Back in Majorca, it was, as Yogi Berra the American baseball player once said, 'déjà vu all over again', but even worse than that. The film *The Magus* was adapted from a novel by the great British writer John Fowles. I say 'great' not because I have finished any of his books – the closest I ever got to that was seeing *The French Lieutenant's Woman*, a film that I enjoyed very much because I almost understood it. I always think a writer must be great if I don't understand his or her work, and if the critics say s/he is great: intellectually, I am very modest. John fell into this category: I was told he was great, and did not understand him so he must be so. Of all his novels, for me *The Magus* was the most obscure but this is not surprising, as I was making this picture under a contract with Twentieth Century-Fox that I do not to this day recall discussing with anyone or, even more importantly, *signing* – so my chances of understanding *The Magus* were very slim indeed. I did not want to make the picture but I had to under the phantom contract.

When I was given the script, which I was told had been simplified, I read it and I still could not make head nor tail of the plot but when I confessed this to the producers John Cohn and Judd Kimberg, they said not to worry as they were going to rewrite the script themselves. This they did, turning the simply incomprehensible into the deeply unfathomable. They also worked on me an old movie trick, which was to say that they would 'fix it in the editing'. I eventually saw the finished film and the editing had made it even murkier.

I did learn one very valuable thing on the film, though – how to keep my eyes open in extremely bright light. It's a good tip for all people with blue eyes and fair hair. Billy was using a lot of light on the film to balance the brilliant sunshine you get in Majorca. I managed to cope with this until we got to a village set where the buildings had been newly painted a bright white. When we started to shoot, try as I might, I could not keep my eyes open without them watering. It became a terrible problem because we just could not shoot the scene. Suddenly from the back of the unit came an electrician with the same colouring as myself and he told me to stare at the sun with my eyes closed for a minute. This I did and a miracle occurred – I could keep my eyes open. That trick has saved me so many times. I put this bit in to illustrate that *The Magus* was not an entirely wasted experience.

There were a couple of other interesting experiences as well. My male co-star on the film was the Mexican actor Anthony Quinn. He did not appear in the film for a while, so a sort of tension built up as his arrival became imminent. Several of the technicians around me had worked with him before, and the general consensus was that not only was he difficult, but that he was going to eat me alive. So I awaited his arrival with some trepidation. Finally the big day arrived when Mr Quinn was due to start work. He was not expected on the set until eleven o'clock in the morning, but at about nine o'clock his stand-in brought out a chair similar to the ones we were all using – except this was a very expensive version made in leather – and plonked it down in the middle of us and left. A silence verging on gloom descended as we all stood and contemplated this omen of what was to come. In very big letters it had ANTHONY QUINN punched with great force into the thick leather. Silently during the morning one by one we circled it like natives in a film where they see an aeroplane on the ground for the first time. There was no question of anybody sitting in it or even touching it, so eventually we tried to ignore it.

At eleven o'clock, the great man walked out on to the set and without a word to anyone, sat in his chair, his character engraved on his face as deeply as his name was on the leather. Here was a man to be reckoned with, and nobody wanted to be the first so he was left alone for a few minutes. I was sitting a little way away from him in a cluster of chairs with the other actors, and after about a quarter of an hour I thought I had better break this pall that he was unwittingly casting over everybody. I dragged my chair over and sat right next to him and introduced myself. The first thing that he said to me was very indicative of the man himself and set the tone of our relationship.

'I read somewhere that you come from a very poor family.'

'That's right,' I replied. 'Why, do you?'

He smiled. 'Yes, I do – but the difference between a poor Mexican family and a poor British one is very big and I don't think you really understand true poverty.'

'I have spent most of my life trying to avoid finding out,' I said.

He found this very funny and burst out laughing, and there was an audible sigh of relief from around the set. He grabbed my hand and shook it. 'You and I are going to get on,' he said, and we did.

After the effect that the almost-ceremonious placing of his chair on the set had had on everybody, I could not help laughing to myself when he suddenly said, 'Ah, so this is where my chair was. I had been looking for it all morning.' It taught me never to listen to rumours of reputation because Anthony Quinn turned out to be one of the nicest and easiest actors with whom I ever worked. And Candice Bergen, still only twenty-two at the time, was the most intelligent beauty that I'd ever met. She ignored me from the start!

One day, about halfway through the picture, Dick Schaap who is now a famous American sports commentator, arrived on the set to do a piece on the film for *Life* magazine. He turned out to be a lovely guy and my dresser, Roy Ponting, a middle-aged gay man whom I loved dearly and who had worked with me since my start in films, helped him to do his story from a different angle. Dick wanted to write about what it felt like to be on a film as an extra, so Roy dressed him up as a Gestapo officer for one of the scenes. Came the day and Dick emerged from the extras' dressing tent in his full uniform and said, 'What do you think?' Roy gave one of his devastating one-word answers. He simply looked at Dick and said, 'Fraulein.' Dick never asked Roy another question.

I brought Roy into the story for a moment at this point because when writing a book like this you of necessity describe famous people – because those are your workmates and colleagues and let's face it – they are the people that readers are most curious to know about. With Roy and in a different way with Johnny Morris my stand-in, I had a close and long friendship and working relationship with them, and they became constants in my working life and so it was with Roy. He was an overweight effeminate man who worked with me on twenty-six pictures and eventually died of a heart attack. He was a source of great comfort to me during some very miserable locations and I still miss him. He was such an integral part of my early career and he always made me laugh so I will leave him with a line that he did on me on *The Magus*. There was a small-part actor around who was married with four kids, but he always seemed to me to be a homosexual, so I decided to ask Roy what he thought. I pointed the man out to him and awaited the verdict. Roy stared at him for a few moments and then said to me, 'No, I don't think he is gay, Michael,' and started to walk away. Suddenly he whipped round and added in a loud whisper, 'Mind you, I think he'd help out if they were busy.' I love that line. Thanks for everything, Roy, wherever you are.

26

'Oh yes – a Rolls Royce'

It had been three years and I was now finally home in London again. My first priority was to find a new flat. I was sharing this one with my brother Stanley which made it really crowded, I discovered, now that I was living there for a long period again. I didn't have to search for long. Like everything else in the sixties, real estate was cheap and available. I found a beautiful flat in Grosvenor Square, a hundred yards along from the American Embassy, which gave me the added bonus, although I did not realise it at the time, of a grandstand seat at all the anti-Vietnam riots which always wound up with a march on the Embassy and a fairly violent fracas with the police. It became my Sunday afternoon entertainment for the seven years that I lived there. I was also against the Vietnam war but I am not a political animal at the best of times and this was someone else's war and I did not know Vanessa Redgrave very well so I never joined the fray and sat, to my eternal shame, on the sidelines with an after-lunch cognac in my hand and watched out of the window as this battle nearer home was fought out.

The flat was stunning. There were three bedrooms, two large lounges, a big hall, an office and a vast kitchen in which you could dine, plus a dining room, which I immediately turned into a little cinema with a 16-millimetre projector. There were no videos in those days so they used to hire out actual films for projection. I also filled the place with state-of-the-art stereo and television equipment, bought all-new furniture and gave the old flat to Stanley with everything in it. Stanley was now working in the book department of Selfridge's where he was very happy.

He, like me, had always loved books, so he was in his element.

I caught up with my old friend Paul Challen again. He had been having a rough time but was now as robust as he was ever going to be, which was not very but at least he could keep up with me in my rounds of the discos and restaurants into which I plunged with my old enthusiasm intact. Not only was it great to have Paul back because he was my oldest friend, but there was another reason. The London scene had changed radically during my absence, and not for the better as far as I was concerned. Drugs had now taken hold quite firmly and I was very grateful to have Paul as a companion as he was, like me, a drinker. The big new drug was LSD which, like all new drugs, had been declared by experts to be not only harmless but actually beneficial in a lot of cases.

I was now comfortably ensconced in my new luxury abode and started to look at my life to see if there was anything else missing. After a great deal of consideration I came to the conclusion that now at the age of thirty-five, it was time for me to acquire my first car. I could not drive but decided I had enough money for a chauffeur, so it was now only necessary to choose the type of car that I wanted. A Rolls Royce it had to be, so I went to the Earls Court Motor Show and found the Rolls Royce stand with several samples on it. I chose a certain car but as it did not have the bodyline that I liked on a different version, I went up to the representative on the stand and told him that I wanted one car with the bodyline of the other. I could see that the guy thought I could not possibly afford one of his cars but that he was going to have to be polite and answer my non-profitable questions. The body I liked was a Mulliner Park Ward type which was not available on the car that I wanted, he informed me, delighted at the thought of choking me off so neatly.

'Listen,' I ordered him, rather snottily. 'You talk to your boss and tell him that that's what I want.'

He railed visibly at the thought of anyone assuming there could possibly be someone above him in the organisation, but then he smiled and gave me one of the best and biggest put-downs I have ever experienced. 'I think I can assure you myself, sir, that the Mulliner Park Ward chassis will never be available on the model you require because Mr Mulliner is dead and I am Mr Park Ward, so you are getting your information straight from the horse's mouth, as the saying goes, I think.' He stood there staring down at me although he was at least six inches shorter than I was. I hung around for a moment trying to figure out how he had managed this then fled. Here we were in the sixties and the British class system was alive and well – at least on the Rolls Royce stand.

Paul and I went out that night, which was a Friday, had a pretty rough time of it and didn't get home until three in the morning. We both woke up late with terrible hangovers but pulled ourselves together and slowly got ready to go out and do some urgent shopping before the shops shut. Saturday in those days was a half-day in London. In my bleary state I wrote a shopping list that read: cigarettes, toothpaste, Rolls Royce, sliced loaf and half a pound of butter. We set off in a rush, both of us without shaving and in our scruffiest clothes, did the small shopping first and then went round to the Rolls Royce showroom off Bond Street. We spent some time looking through the window at the models on show and the commissionaire who was inside the showroom began to keep a very wary eye on the two of us unkempt, unshaven individuals.

Finally I made up my mind which one I wanted and we entered the showroom. He blanched visibly as we dared to enter his hallowed domain. The salesman looked up, saw the two of us and made a sign with his hand that clearly denoted that the lackey should take care of the situation and get rid of us as soon as possible before anybody important saw us in there. 'What do you two want?' the commissionaire said gruffly. No 'Good morning, sir', or a polite, 'Can I help you?' I grew angry and faked a loss of memory, and took my shopping list out so that he could see what was written on it. Running my fingers down the list until I came to the right place I pretended to find what I wanted and said, 'Oh yes – a Rolls Royce.'

Steam was almost coming out of his ears by now but he kept his temper and hit back. 'How many do you want?' he enquired with great sarcasm. 'They're cheaper if you buy more than one.'

I put my mouth very close to his ear and whispered, 'Fuck you,' and we left to find another outlet that would appreciate my custom. This we found in another showroom nearby where, in spite of my accent and our appearance we were treated with kindness and courtesy. I later found out that the reason for this was that the salesman was a movie fan who had recognised me. I asked him to take us for a test drive, which he did with pleasure, then I requested a drive past the other Rolls Royce showroom. As we got closer I could see that the same commissionaire was now standing on the step outside and as we passed him, his mouth open in astonishment, I gave him the rude two-finger salute. Honour was satisfied.

The Italian Job – a comedy about a gang of English crooks who go to Italy to commit a robbery – eventually started shooting in London, directed by a young newcomer called Peter Collinson. Peter had grown up in an orphanage that had been financially supported by Noël Coward all his life and it was on the basis of this connection that Peter persuaded him to take the unlikely role of the boss of the British underworld in the movie. The boss masterminded everything from inside a prison cell. So I, as a small-time crook, had to break into it every time I needed to get my instructions from him. The picture of course was a comedy and also starred the British comedian Benny Hill, who tragically died in 1992. Also in the cast in a small part, was my brother Stanley, at the start of his shortlived career as an actor. The picture had a lot of car stunts in it, and a Frenchman called Rémy Julienne led the greatest car-stunt team that I have ever seen to this day.

   The Italian Job was a fun picture aimed at kids of all ages. It was very well made and become popular in Britain and Europe when it was released, but it flopped in America. This may have been partly because the game involved at the centre of the plot was soccer – virtually unknown in America at the time – but I think the advertising campaign they dreamed up over there was really to blame. When I arrived in Los Angeles to promote the picture I was stunned to open a newspaper and see an image of a naked woman sitting on the lap of a gangster who was holding a machine gun. The genius who thought that up was sending such a wrong signal about this U-certificate caper that I knew immediately that *The Italian Job* was doomed, so I got on the next plane and came home to England. After months of hard work, sweat and tears, it can sometimes only take one small mistake like that to screw the whole thing up.

The movie was shot on location in Turin and in the Italian Alps, where we spent days throwing little Mini cars off the top of Mont Blanc. Despite the fact that our Minis were in direct competition with his Fiats, Gianni Agnelli let us film a chase on the test track on top of his Fiat factory in Turin – a guy with a lot of class, as opposed to the bosses of our British motor company. We needed about sixteen Minis in all, what with crash cars, stunt cars, doubles and standby action cars, so we went to the car manufacturers and asked for help with this in return for what would be great publicity. Their attitude was that they did not need us to sell their cars and that they could only spare one. The picture was and continues to be the greatest publicity this car has ever had – but these moronic British businessmen were blind to that fact. No wonder we have lost our car industry. British bankers even now have not changed their attitude towards movies – they still think of them as something frivolous in contrast to the American banks, who know them to be a multi-million dollar worldwide business.

As a great admirer of the late Benny Hill, I was looking forward to working with him and getting to know him. The first part was a pleasure but the second part was impossible. Benny was very pleasant to all of us – unfailingly courteous, kind and professional, but it was not possible to make any real contact with him. He was a truly solitary soul and never mixed with the cast socially, even when we were all staying together in the same hotel. Like a lot of comedians I have known, Benny seemed a sad person.

Noël Coward was the complete antithesis – gregarious and *gay* in every sense of the word. Each Wednesday evening when we were shooting in England, I used to have dinner with him in the Savoy Grill. I always think of those occasions as one of the most quintessentially English things I have ever done. Noël had a free room for life at the Savoy, he told me, because during the war he had been playing cabaret there and had sung on right through a night of terrible bombing and kept the hotel's clients occupied and unafraid.

'I wasn't really being brave,' he told me. 'It was because once the air raid had started, people were not allowed to leave and so I had a captive audience for the first and only time in my life,' he gave that funny laugh of his, 'so I sang every bloody song that I knew before they could escape in the morning. Not only did I get the satisfaction of doing that,' he continued, 'but I was given a free room for life. Not a bad evening's work, really,' he ruminated with a smile.

Another evening, Noël brought as his companion Merle Oberon, who though no longer in the first flush of youth was still stunningly beautiful. She could stop a room dead and she did so that night as she glided into the Grill and over to our table. On yet another evening we got on to the subject of Vanessa Redgrave, who was constantly in the news at the time for leading demonstrations against the war in Vietnam. 'She should keep on demonstrating,' Noël sniffed disparagingly. 'She's a very tall girl and it will give her lots of opportunities to sit down.'

When we finally saw the finished product, *The Italian Job* was a good action film with a lot of the credit for its success going to Rémy and his stunt team. It was also a good start for Peter Collinson, who unfortunately, was to die of cancer at a very young age.

When my birthday came around again (I was now thirty-five) I waited for Harry Saltzman to give me my usual present. Most people who knew him would say that in business Harry was mean, tough and ruthless, but I saw a vastly different side to him. At the time of *Ipcress* he had signed me to a seven-year contract for money that was good at the time, but as I grew more successful, became outdated. I was hired out by his company for big sums of money, yet he was only obliged to pay me the small sums agreed in our contract. Harry had every right to do this, but he decided to be fair so every year on my birthday he used to sign a new contract with me at the

303

proper going rate. This year, however, when I opened the envelope it contained the contract itself, torn into small pieces and with a note that just said: '*You're on your own now. Happy Birthday.*' – and it was signed *Harry*.

But that was not quite the end of our relationship. Harry was doing a big blockbuster movie with an all-star cast – *The Battle of Britain* – and he wanted me to play one of the roles in it. The part was small, and no big challenge on the acting front either, but I took it and how glad I was, because it gave me an opportunity to talk to some remarkable survivors of the Battle of Britain. Over a period of a couple of weeks, I was privileged to meet two of the greatest British air aces of that battle: Ginger Lacey and Bob Stanford Tuck, who were on the film as technical advisers. They put me right on so many misconceptions, beginning with my own part in the film. When I suggested to Bob that at thirty-five I was surely far too young to be a Wing-Commander in charge of a whole airfield, he gave a surprised laugh. 'I knew men who were Wing-Commanders at the age of twenty-four,' he said. My first misconception shot down. My second one was about class. I always had the impression that the Battle was fought by brave upper-class young officers, but not so, as I found when I talked to Ginger Lacey. Ginger was from a working-class background and talked with a north-country accent and he told me that the majority of the men in the Battle of Britain were sergeant pilots, just like himself. Stanford Tuck, on the other hand, had upper middle-class origins and was made an officer straight away.

Our German technical adviser was none other than Adolf Galland, the Nazi air ace who had led the battle from the enemy side. The first time I met him I was absolutely dumbfounded. I was sure that either he had died, or had been executed at the Nuremberg Trials, but not so. Here he was, sitting opposite me at lunch in a tent in England. It was a bit like finding yourself eating with Hitler – in fact, he looked a bit like him, with straight dark hair and a little black moustache and of course his name was Adolf as well. Galland turned out to be a nice little man who only lost his temper when anybody mentioned the fact that the Luftwaffe lost the

304

Battle of Britain. My friend Harry was not known for tact and was forever bringing up the subject while Adolf was around. Galland would try to control his temper, reminding me irresistibly at these moments of Peter Sellers in *Dr Strangelove*, in which he played the Nazi who could not restrain his arm from making the Nazi salute. Finally, one lunchtime, Galland could control himself no longer and a blazing row broke out in which we witnessed the extraordinary spectacle of this elderly Jewish movie producer and the ex-leader of the Luftwaffe almost coming to blows over who had won the Battle.

The row finally ended when Galland told Harry that he knew nothing about air warfare and Harry replied that, on the contrary, he was now the boss of the eleventh biggest air force in the world. Which he was – since he had collected so many old planes for the film. This incident put World War Two into perspective for me. The long years of slaughter, agony and suffering were finally reduced to two elderly veterans arguing in a field on a summer's day in England forty-four years later. That, funnily enough, was the day the war ended for me psychologically – the last little battle between our side and theirs. Up until that time I had always taken a great interest in the war, reading histories and seeing films and television programmes about it, but my fascination died that day.

On my last day of filming, I had to do something dangerous – a situation I had always avoided like the plague, since as long as they get the desired shot, the team literally do not seem to care if you live or die once your part is finished. In his quest for realism, the director Guy Hamilton wanted to show the real actors in the open cockpits, going at speed along the runway as though we were actually taking off. For anyone like me, who can't fly a plane, this is a terrifying experience because if you get up enough speed, you could actually take off! The Spitfires we were using used to take off four at a time when they were scrambled in an emergency, and that is what we were doing on that day. Ginger Lacey was in charge of my plane; he showed me what to do to get it up to a reasonable speed, and more importantly for me, how to get it to stop. So there I was, sitting in the cockpit sweating with fear and waiting for the signal, 'Action!' when Ginger shouted to me, 'Look down by your left knee and you will see a red button.'

I looked down and indeed there was a very sinister red button. 'I see it,' I shouted back. 'What about it?'

'Don't touch it with your knee,' came the very ominous reply.

'Why not?' I bawled, already knowing that I was not going to like the answer.

'If you touch it,' he shouted, 'you'll take off.'

In a panic I zoomed my entire body over to the right of the cockpit, which is very small in the first place, then slowly and with much difficulty, crossed my left leg over my right to keep it absolutely clear of the offending button. In consequence I became the first pilot in the Battle of Britain to take off with his legs crossed – a very relaxed position which belied the terror in my heart.

27

My worst location

Friendship in show business is a matter of geography. Most films are shot on location which means that everyone you know and like is always somewhere else. The best location is, of course, near where you live, and failing that, a place where you would normally pay to go on holiday. I have a dream of opening a script and reading: *'As the yacht sailed in to St Tropez harbour . . .'* Usually locations do not come up to this standard.

The best location I ever had was for *Dirty Rotten Scoundrels* where the dream came true. It was shot in Cap Ferrat and Cap D'Antibes in the South of France. The worst location I have ever worked in was the Philippine jungle, where *Too Late the Hero*, a World War Two story of a battle between a small unit of British soldiers and one American against the Japanese, was filmed. Robert Aldrich, the director, kept us there for twenty-two weeks.

An enormous American naval base was our destination as we set off on the long journey through some of the poorest villages I had seen since Korea. All around us was dense jungle and great hill ranges. A lot of it was very beautiful – if you were short-sighted and didn't notice the human misery.

So shooting began, in some of the worst conditions I had ever encountered on a film. We were plagued by insects, thorns and 120° temperatures every day, accompanied by the highest humidity that it is possible to measure. The food, I was sure, must be alive with organisms unknown to modern science so my daytime diet consisted solely of sardines and Australian cheese which came out of tins opened in my presence and then consumed before anything else could touch them. The only thing that saved our sanity was our visits to the officers' mess in the navy base, where we could get a good shower, great food and cold drinks, and watch television. Life was perfect in the evenings, until we had to return to our mosquito-ridden cribs.

As conditions were so dire, Bob had us work for fourteen consecutive days and then gave us five days off, which was enough time to get out of the country.

The first place we went to was Taiwan, where I remember sitting in a hotel bar and then being whisked off by a very beautiful Chinese girl in front of an open-mouthed group of my friends. She was the daughter of a local bigwig who was a great fan of mine and wanted to give me the ultimate proof of her affection – no, not a signed photograph. Later, I was in bed fast asleep when the door burst open and three Chinese policemen with machine guns charged into the room.

'What do you want?' I asked, looking hastily round the bed for any sign of the girl. Fortunately she was gone.

'Papers,' ordered one of the policemen in English. I gave him my passport, he stared at it for a moment and then at me, his narrow eyes piercing into mine, when suddenly there was a look of recognition and he gave a big wide smile. 'I know you,' he said. 'You are Alfie.' I sat there amazed. 'I am the Chinese Alfie. I fuck many women all time,' he said proudly.

I thought for a moment that with over a billion Chinese around he wasn't the only one who thought he was Alfie but I just nodded and gave an approving smile as befitted the leader of the pack. He gave me back my passport and looked the bed over, hardly able to conceal his disappointment that I was on my own. I wanted to tell him that I hadn't been so that he would not think too badly of me, but he handed back my passport and said, 'Congratulations,' and shook my hand.

Cliff Robertson turned out to be the real-life star of the making of the movie *Too Late the Hero*. Part of the trip to Hong Kong was done in an old DC3, a veteran of World War Two. When we arrived to board it the crew were just putting the seats back in, having delivered a herd of cattle and then fumigated it – not very well, judging by the stench. The plane finally managed to get off the ground and everything was going fine until suddenly the door flew open and started to bang against the fuselage. Up sprang our hero, Cliff Robertson my co-star – a very nice man but given to the grand gesture, and shouted at me to follow him. As his co-star I was duty bound by the Hollywood star-billing code to follow him into danger. I could not afford for anybody below the title to take this opportunity to be brave. He said, 'Hang on to my belt!' – which I did, yelling for the others to hang on to me, and then he leaned out of the aircraft which was going at about two hundred miles an hour and was about fifteen thousand feet up, and grabbed the door and pulled it shut. 'Well done,' he said to me magnanimously as though I was the hero, and then he just sat quietly down again.

There was more to come, however. We changed planes and went to Hong Kong where the airport is difficult at the best of times, but as we were landing there was a very high wind and the pilot told us to hang on as it was going to be a bumpy landing. Cliff suddenly leapt to his feet and yelled, 'Put your cushion between your seatbelt and your stomach or the belt will cut you in half on impact.' There is sea on both sides at Hong Kong airport, so we were going to drown anyway which would take too long, I thought. I'd rather be cut in half so I left it. We finally hit the ground with a huge thump and screeched to a halt about three-quarters of an inch from the end of the runway. The moment we got to the hotel we showered and changed and met in the bar for a well-deserved drink after our ordeal, and that is the last I remember of our four days in Hong Kong. Various members of the hotel staff later remarked admiringly on our capacity to have a good time so I suppose we must have had one.

We decided to spend our next break 'at home' at the naval base. It was here that I met one of the toughest guys ever. He was a member of one of the American secret services, was six feet six inches tall and rejoiced in the name of Toy. He it was who took us on our first and only foray into the local town called Olongapo. This was a place with a population of about twenty thousand people, half of whom were prostitutes serving the naval base. We had heard tales about Olongapo but had been warned off it since it was dangerous for Europeans. We were all drinking in the officers' mess one night when Toy suggested that we should go and visit the place at least once. We told him about the danger and he said not to worry and pulled his jacket open to reveal a heavy .45 automatic in an underarm holster. A wave of courage swept over us and we decided to take a chance. Olongapo turned out to be just one long shanty-town main street, brightly lit with neon signs for wall-to-wall bars and discos, and with very dark alleys leading off the street at intervals.

'Don't move off the main street,' yelled Toy above the din of music from a thousand speakers. 'We'll never find the body if you do.' We all moved closer to Toy for safety, like ducklings on a pond and followed him into Sodom and Gomorrah.

The poverty and stench of the place were unbelievable. We finally found a bar that looked as though they changed the washing-up water at least once per day and went in. The moment we sat down we were smothered with ladies offering various specialities, some of which I must admit I had never heard of before. We all settled for whisky, which seemed to be the safest drink and ordered a round for the girls. I looked at them closely and thought that here I was, surrounded by young available scantily-clad girls, and instead of it being erotic or sexy or even interesting, it was just sad. I looked closely at their badly made-up, prematurely ravaged faces and saw the eyes go dead the moment no one was looking. These kids had been forced here by grinding poverty. Being an actor I not only listened to what they said, but to how they said it, and they all said exactly the same thing in the same way, as though they had all attended the same school, to be taught how to extract money from Europeans. Our drinks arrived and before I could pick mine up the girl next to me got out one of her breasts and dipped it into my drink. 'That will give it a good flavour,' she said. Not wishing to offend I 'accidentally' knocked over my glass and ordered an ice-cold beer instead, hoping that it would be too cold for anyone to be tempted to dip anything else in it.

We went the rounds of some of the other places but there

was such a depressing air of poverty hanging like a cloud over Olongapo that we fled back to the comparative gaiety of the naval base.

William Hall, a reporter on the now-defunct London *Evening News* was with us that evening, and he wrote a piece about our experiences that eventually won an award. As it happened his article was responsible for getting my films banned in perpetuity from Olongapo – not an earthshattering blow to my career, I admit, but one that still smarts. Bill had quoted me as saying that the women of Olongapo had flat chests – which they did, from what I saw and this made them take offence: a storm in a 'c' cup.

At long last, after what seemed like an eternity of heat, sweat, insects, and a particularly nasty sweatrash labelled appropriately by the Americans as 'the Crud', the location shooting was over and it was back to Hollywood for the studio work, with a few days off for partying en route in Manila. And boy, did we party. After a while, though, my social conscience began getting in the way. The gap between the rich and the poor here was the widest I had ever seen in a so-called civilised country. The poor were completely destitute while the rich, with whom we, of course, were mixing, lived in the kind of luxury unknown even in the super-rich countries of the west. I remember going into a party one evening, and seeing the local children rummaging through the rubbish bins from the house and eating the scraps that they found there, only to find inside that the cabaret for the evening was the cream of the Bolshoi Ballet flown in from Moscow especially for that one function. On my way home, I stopped the car at the garbage cans and watched the children for a while, thinking how fortunate I had been with my own childhood. Once upon a time I had thought it so poor but never again. The kids finally spotted me and came over to ask for money. I gave them all that I had on me and drove home with tears of anger in my eyes at a society that could treat its own people like this.

At another party the hostess came over and took me by the arm, saying, 'There is someone here that I would like you to meet.' She guided me to the end of the room to a dais that I had not noticed before, and seated upon it were two men deep in conversation. They stopped talking and stood up as we approached, and she introduced me to the leader of this system, President-for-life Marcos. Ferdinand Marcos had the sort of face that I associated with the children outside: the milk of human kindness had long since gone sour in it. My hostess then introduced me to the other man, a Mr Adnan Kashoggi, and I remember wondering who he was and what he was doing there, so close to the President.

It was at another one of these grand soirées that my hero Cliff Robertson again came to the rescue. The buffet table on this occasion was adorned with massive paper decorations and candles. Inevitably, halfway through the evening one of the candles burnt down and caught light to the paper, which started to burn quite rapidly. There were screams from the ladies and bewilderment from the men, myself included, but not from Cliff. 'Stand back!' he yelled manfully, with great flair (pun intended) and threw a decanter of cognac over it, setting fire to the curtains and eventually the whole side of the house. We all fled back to the hotel – another evening of fun in Manila over.

The last party that I went to there proved to be the most dangerous one. It was a very warm evening and we were partying outside. I suddenly felt very queasy and so rushed for the bathroom, which was always guaranteed to be empty. Recovering slightly, I was just standing at the sink throwing cold water over my face when I felt myself being grabbed from behind by my hostess. Without a word she shut and bolted the bathroom door then threw herself on me, her right arm going round my neck and her left hand down to grab a very delicate part of my anatomy.

'I have seen all your films, Michael,' she breathed, 'and I have always wanted you.'

While all this was very complimentary, it wasn't exactly a situation designed to arouse my ardour. Apart from her iron grip, I had been introduced to her husband earlier and he was not only fabulously wealthy but had two armed bodyguards who followed him everywhere. He also carried a gun himself and might come in here at any moment. I let out a small cry of terror at this thought, which Madame mistook for a passionate response and clamped her lips on mine again. Dragging her arm from my neck I fled the bathroom, the party and the house forever, and never stopped running until I reached the safety of my hotel room.

Finally it was time to go down to the bar and meet my friends – the Patrol – for the last drink of the evening, as we usually did, to have a post mortem on the latest party (which could have been only too apt for me on this occasion). They were all sitting there as usual. 'What happened to you?' asked Ronnie Fraser, always a stickler for good manners. 'The host thought you were very rude to leave without saying good night.'

'I didn't feel well,' I told them, deciding to keep my experiences to myself at least until I had left the country, which would be in the morning – Thank God!

As the plane took off for Los Angeles a few hours later, I breathed a huge sigh of relief. My worries were over. Then someone tapped me on the shoulder. I looked up, only to see Cliff Robertson. 'Did you have a nice time last night?' he asked innocently.

'Great', I replied, thinking – hell, I'm on another plane with Cliff: what's going to happen *this* time?

Fortunately, nothing did, and as we landed at LAX, as everyone in the know calls Los Angeles airport, I breathed a sigh of what turned out to be premature relief.

During his absence, Cliff had won an Oscar as Best Actor for a film called *Charlie*, and he had been very annoyed with Bob for not letting him come home to collect it in person with all the attendant publicity. However, Cliff being Cliff, he had thought of a way to garner some of the kudos, though it was a little late. He had a Filippino woodcarver make him an exact replica of the Oscar statuette so that when he got off the plane he would be carrying it and there would be no doubt who was this year's winner. We were on a charter flight so we did not disembark at the main airport but in one corner of the airfield, and we had to come down a long set of steps which were drawn up to the plane. As we looked out of the window, there indeed was the world's press waiting for him. It was their first chance to photograph him since he had won.

I let Cliff go first and followed right behind him. Cliff started to descend the stairs, the phony statuette clutched high in his hand for all the world to see, then suddenly we saw Gregory Peck, President of the Academy, coming and he was carrying the real Oscar, ready to make a surprise presentation to Cliff there and then. For a moment, Cliff did not know what to do with his phony Oscar but then, quick as a flash, he chucked it straight back over his shoulder and stretched out his hand to accept the real one. Standing right behind him, I received the full onslaught of the mahogany statuette in the forehead: it opened a small cut which nevertheless bled quite profusely. Apart from the nomination for *Alfie*, this was the nearest I had got so far to an Oscar. So with Cliff descending the steps beaming in triumph and me following clutching a bloody forehead I finished the worst location of my career – and when I eventually saw the picture, the most unnecessary one. The shots in the jungle were just a mass of trees that could have been taken anywhere. I was reminded of the old director King Vidor who, when asked why a certain film could not go on an expensive location, said, 'A tree is a tree – shoot it in Griffith Park.'

28

Elizabeth and me

Hollywood is a strange place. The unexpected is always happening and on this trip I did not know just how strange and unexpected things were going to turn out to be. Apart from being absolutely exhausted by our interlude in the Philippines, I was now on jet lag again and working as hard as we did, my memories of that time come in short recollections of strange things and pleasurable ones, completely disconnected – some of them quite stupid.

For this, my third visit to Hollywood, I decided to stay again at the Beverly Wilshire Hotel which was right on the corner of Wilshire Boulevard and Rodeo Drive. I still couldn't drive but enjoyed walking the admittedly small distances to my old haunts, the Daisy, the Luau and MFK. I looked up Steve Brandt and settled back into the swing of things. I made a new friend in Jay Sebring, a very famous hairdresser at the time, who used to cut my hair for nothing and bring his own case of Heineken beer over to my hotel room, and get through it during the day. One day, Jay took me to his house which he said had been built by Howard Hughes for Jean Harlow. This may or may not have been true, but there is usually a history behind any house in Hollywood.

One day I was being driven somewhere when I spotted a sign saying: *English fish and chips*. It was nearly lunchtime and I was hungry so I stopped the car and went in to get some. A big blond man was in there trying to mend a broken stove, and he informed me that unfortunately, there would be no food today. I started to leave when I had a funny feeling that I knew the man from somewhere. When I asked him if we had ever met, he said no, but that I might have seen him on the screen

315

when I was a kid. His name was Brian Kirkwood and he used to play the boxer Joe Palooka in the series with Leon Errol as his manager. Little things like this have always fascinated me about Hollywood and I talked to him for a while and found out that both he and Leon Errol were in fact Australians, and that Marilyn Monroe had made her screen début in that series.

Another memorable occasion was the night that Paul Newman and some of his friends opened a new discothèque called The Factory. This was the best opening night of a disco I ever experienced. The cabaret was Ike and Tina Turner. I didn't see much of Ike, but we certainly saw a lot of Tina and her trio of girls. I was seated on the floor about eight feet away from them. I don't know if you ever saw their act in those days, but it was the fastest and raunchiest act in rock and roll and could blow people's minds who were sitting hundreds of feet away. From eight feet away it was dynamite.

Other really 'Hollywood' things happened, like the one hundredth birthday party for Adolph Zukor the founder of Paramount Pictures. It was a massive do, with every Paramount star there including myself – a big honour. *Alfie* had been a Paramount Picture. Bob Hope was the host for the evening and when they wheeled the hundred-year-old Zukor out in a wheelchair looking very poorly indeed (he usually went to bed at seven and it was now eleven-thirty) Bob's opening quip was: 'If Adolph had known how long he was going to live he would have taken better care of himself.'

Zsa Zsa Gabor came on and Bob asked her what she would do if she lived to be a hundred. 'I vould say I vas ninety-nine, dahling,' was her honest reply. I asked Bob afterwards what would have happened if the old man had dropped dead during the festivities, which had looked very likely for a time. He told me with a straight face that they had a hundred magicians, one for each table in the room and if Mr Zukor had dropped dead they would all rip the white cloths off the tables to reveal black ones underneath.

But then I saw another side of Los Angeles that was eventually to become a sort of nightmare, and ended with the death of three of my friends.

One night I was invited to go out on night patrol with a detective called Rudy Diaz in an undercover car. He wanted me to see the other side of the city, he said, and curious, I agreed. We drove downtown to the main part of the city and to the central police station. After a sordid fracas involving two middle-aged bums and a raddled old hooker, who charged five dollars for the services as opposed to five hundred dollars in Beverly Hills, we started our patrol proper and drove around the very mean streets of downtown Los Angeles. Rudy pointed out things I might have missed. 'See that?' he said, pointing at an empty, blackened door. 'Last night there was a guy sleeping there and somebody came along with a can of gasoline and set fire to him.' We went round another corner and there was a bar with a lot of young guys standing around on the pavement outside it, drinking. 'You know what we call that?' he commented as we passed by the group. '"Crime looking for something to commit." I'll drive you through Watts,' he suddenly offered, speaking of the black ghetto where the 1992 riots centred. We drove through it at quite a pace, as sullen black faces looked menacingly at this car with a white guy in it. I started to get nervous and Rudy didn't help matters by remarking, 'If we break down here, we're dead.'

We drove through this nightmare to the accompaniment of the car radio which spewed out a continuous dirge of death, disaster and despair. As we left the black ghetto we drove into the hispanic one, where we immediately found two drunks fighting with knives outside a bar. Rudy stopped the car and opened a panel under the dashboard to reveal a pump-action shotgun. 'Keep the doors locked and if there is any trouble use that,' he said, pointing at the gun. He got out of the car and I locked the doors immediately. He walked towards the fight slowly, taking his leather jacket off as he went. When he reached the action he wrapped the jacket round his arm and suddenly leapt between the two fighters and laid them both out with karate kicks. He put the jacket back on casually and picking up the knives, strolled back to the car and got in.

'Aren't you going to arrest them?' I gasped.

'I'm not blowing my cover for assholes,' he said quietly as

we drove on through the night. As we went from one scene to another, I started to feel nauseated by the sight of the victims and guilty for being an uptown resident of the privileged Beverly Hills set coming down here as a sort of voyeur, staring secretly at the misery of these people. Dawn finally came and we mercifully drove back to the safety of Beverly Hills, but even there the inhabitants were about to get a rude awakening if they thought that this distant violence could not touch them. The trip with Rudy had at least prepared me for what was about to come.

I had become very good friends with Mama Cass, the lead singer with the Mamas and the Papas singing group, and one night she invited me to a party given for the birthday of some rock and roll singer. She introduced Johnny Morris and myself to a lot of musicians who were obviously famous, as one could tell by their entourages, who hung on their every word, or in most cases mumble. Steve Brandt came by for a while but had to leave, then Sharon Tate came in with a whole group of people including my friend and barber Jay Sebring. After a little while they left and I waved good night to them, not knowing I was never going to see them again. Johnny and I were beginning to enjoy ourselves when a scruffy little man came in with some girls who were not only scruffy but really dirty. They seemed quite out of place there and I couldn't think who could have invited them. Mama Cass introduced me to the guy who did not shake hands but just said, 'Hi,' and looked me up and down for a moment in a way that gave me the creeps. 'This is Charles Manson,' said Mama Cass. He smiled and walked away. Johnny is normally a fearless type of guy but he became immediately uneasy then, and when I asked him what the matter was he said, 'Let's get out of here. I don't like that little guy.' I laughed. 'No,' Johnny insisted. 'I mean it, Mike, let's go. We don't need to be with people like this.' How right he was. We left not only the party, but Hollywood as well a week later. After a couple of months as I settled back into life in London came the terrible news that Charles Manson and the girl with him that night had not only killed Sharon and Jay but the rest of the group that were with them there. Even that was not the end of it for me, however.

Several months later they found a death list belonging to the Manson Group and among the many people on it was my friend Steve Brandt, who became so terrified by this that he committed suicide. Johnny's gut instinct for villains had been right and I had lost three friends. Hollywood was by no means just fun, glitz and glamour, after all.

Soon I was free to set off for Innsbruck in Austria, my next destination, to film *The Last Valley*. I liked this film very much but it was not a success, due mainly I think to problems of timing. We were in the midst of the Vietnam War, and here was a story about the Hundred Year War in Germany, set in the Middle Ages. Even its exquisite musical score by my old friend John Barry couldn't rescue this film.

My troubles started almost immediately. I knew I would have to ride a horse in the film, and with my previous experiences always fresh in my mind, had made a point of stipulating that I must have a docile beast and that she had to be a mare. (Dominique, who was by now an expert young horsewoman, knew of my problem and had given me this advice.) Also, I said, I wanted a *small* horse. Came the day to meet my equine partner, I was taken to the stables from which emerged not just a big horse, but the biggest one I had ever seen. Was it a mare, I wondered and looked with horror at its rear, to find two immense testicles. When I asked his name the groom said it was a German one that translated into English meant 'Fury'. I immediately went into one but was eventually calmed down and assured that the horse was really a pussy cat, and that was why he had been chosen for me. I rode Fury for a bit and he did seem to be quiet – but that was without the costume I would wear in the film.

The first day of shooting, I mounted my steed and took him for a little trot which, without any effort on my part, grew faster and faster until we were up to a gallop. Soon I was hanging on to his mane for dear life as we charged off down a country road, going like the wind until we were finally overtaken by a jeep from the unit and stopped three miles away from the set. They took me back in the jeep, fuming with rage, and once there I really let rip. I have a filthy temper

319

sometimes, bordering on the psychotic, and on this occasion I ranted and raved for about ten minutes.

The director just sat there quietly with a faint smile on his face and let me run myself out. His name was James Clavell and he was first and foremost the author of such books as *Taipan*, *Shogun* and *King Rat*, which was a novel about life in a Japanese prisoner of war camp. This is where James himself had spent the war, and because of this he was about to teach me a very valuable lesson. He let my temper wind down and putting his arm round my shoulder, took me off into a deserted corner of the set where we sat and he talked very quietly to me. He said that after he had been captured by the Japanese, the only reason he had lived when so many others had not was that he had learned from his captors a few important lessons in the art of survival.

'You must never ever lose face,' he told me. 'With your display of temper just now you did exactly that – and it is only the first day of shooting. Not only have you lost face, but it will remain lost with these particular people in this situation and you will not regain it until the project ends. We all lose our tempers sometimes,' he continued, 'but you must never lose face in front of strangers. You belittle and demean yourself by showing such a great and personal emotion in front of people whom you do not know intimately, and the loss of control shows the other person that you are weak. Control, Michael,' he said. 'If you cannot control yourself, who can you control?' He smiled as he looked at me and he knew that I had got the message. I have never lost my temper in front of strangers again. (Well, almost never.)

As we walked back to the set he explained why my horse had kept increasing his speed. I was wearing a big sword, and as Fury started to trot, the scabbard had slapped his side as though I was urging him with a crop to go faster, and of course the faster he went, the stronger the sword slapped against him and so on.

The only other lesson I learned on that film was never to have the hotel room further down the corridor than the one belonging to my co-star, Omar Sharif. I don't know what went on, but the chambermaids rarely got past his room, so I'd come home in the evenings to find my room untouched.

I don't want to write any more about *The Last Valley* because it was such hard work and all to no avail. I knew the day we finished it that it was not going to work, and I arrived back in London quite depressed at the close of 1969 to witness the official end of the sixties.

This decade had been tremendous for me on every level and I was a little sad to see it go, thinking quite rightly that we would not see another one like it in London in my lifetime. Many of our former haunts had closed and old friends disappeared into the labyrinthine depths of drugs and alcoholism, some to be seen again and some not. Even those who had survived the era like myself had not come through entirely unscathed: I was up to two bottles of vodka a day and did not even notice it at that time. I didn't see the decade out in England. I got on a plane two days after Christmas with Dennis and Harry Saltzman and his family, and flew to Acapulco for a much-needed rest in the sun. Just before the plane went through the clouds after take-off, I looked down at my country for the last time in the sixties and watched it fade gently away. The Beatles were right, I thought. It had been a hard day's night, but now it was over and as we flew into the seventies I thought of the original phrase from which John Osborne had got his title *Look Back in Anger*. It was: 'Never look back in anger, always look forward in hope.' Goodbye baby – and Amen.

It was time to make some changes in my life. First, I wanted my mother to have her own house. My mother and her various relatives were still living together in the small block of flats at Brixton and although conditions there were not bad, I wanted her to have her own house. My experience as a child of dodging the rent-collector still haunted me and I wanted Mum to be in a situation where this would never happen again. Consequently I bought her a big house in a south London suburb called Streatham and split it up into flats so that everyone could move there with her.

The day my mother moved in, I went there and gave her the deeds to the house and told her that she now owned it and no one could ever take it away from her. She thought about this for a moment then said, 'What day does the rent man come?' I told her that there was no rent man – that *she* was the owner. This eventually sunk in and she then said with a smile, 'Can you afford this?' I assured her that I could.

'How much do you earn for a film?' she asked anxiously. At that time I was earning half a million pounds a picture and I told her so. She thought again. 'How much is that?' she said.

It was my turn to think for a moment. There was no way I was going to be able to explain to her that in ten weeks I earned more than my father did in his whole lifetime so I simply said, 'It means that you never have to work again, and you can go anywhere you want, and you can have anything you want for as long as you live.'

'I don't want anything and I don't want to go anywhere,' was her reply. I had no answer for that so I finished my cup of tea and left her sitting there, the mistress of all she surveyed for the first time in her life. As I was about to close the front door she shouted, 'I'd like a box of chocolates the next time you come.'

'I'll bring two!' I bawled back, and closed the door. As I got into my car I felt the happiest I had been in a long time. I had almost repaid Mum for all that she had done for me.

My next plan? To become a producer. This decision was based on the rather negative conclusion that as I had worked for several allegedly great film-makers and gone straight down the drain with them, I might as well go that route on my own for a change. For my first fling as a producer I went into partnership with a friend of mine named Michael Klinger. He was a producer by profession and had produced Roman Polanski's early films, the ones he had made in England. Michael had the rights to a book called *Jack's Return Home*, which we filmed under the title of *Get Carter*. This was a very tough story about a London gangster who goes to a north-country town in England to find out who murdered his brother and, of course, to avenge his death. For me it was a chance to show gangsters as they really are. The tradition in British films up until then, with the exception of Graham Greene's *Brighton Rock*, was that gangsters were either very funny or Robin Hood types, stealing from the rich and giving to the poor. Not a realistic portrait, as I think you will agree.

Another feature of movie violence that had always annoyed me where fights were concerned, was the scene we have all seen a thousand times in which the hero and villain slog it out for ten minutes; and then the following day, the hero turns up with a tiny piece of plaster on his forehead. In real life, every single punch in the face tears skin and cartilage and often breaks bones. We decided to make the movie more realistic in this respect. I was also always annoyed when people who were thrown off the tops of high buildings never hit anybody on the ground. I had a chance to remedy this in a scene where I threw a villain off a rooftop and his body landed on a car with a woman and two children in it. We had to show violence as it really was, Michael and I agreed.

We had a script and all we needed now was a director. I was watching a film made for television one evening and decided that whoever had directed this was our man. The moment that the film ended I picked up the phone to call Michael when the other line rang. I answered it and it was Michael. 'I know what you're going to say,' I said.

'Michael Hodges,' he announced, which is exactly what I was going to say. Now we had a director.

Michael Hodges wanted to give the film a tough look and so he chose as a setting a city in the north of England called Newcastle on Tyne. A shipbuilding town fallen on hard times, Newcastle has a grim Victorian beauty of its own and is eminently photogenic. It sits astride the River Tyne and has a bridge that immediately reminded me of the one in Sydney Harbour in Australia, which was not surprising because the one over there is a copy of this one and was even built by the same people.

By now I had seen poverty in different parts of the world that had made my own childhood look quite privileged, but I had never witnessed misery like this in my own country; it was Charles Dickens meets Emily Brontë, written by Edgar Wallace. Being in the far north of England, the weather was also dark and foreboding, the perfect atmosphere for our movie.

My hero John Osborne, the writer of *Look Back in Anger*, was cast as the chief villain and he was marvellous. He had not acted much since his success as a writer and he really seemed to enjoy his role of the ruthless gang boss, even though he was not typical casting for that sort of part. I don't remember who suggested him for the role but it was a great idea. I didn't get to know him at all as he was a very reserved sort of a man, so I left him to himself. He seemed to be someone who didn't like many other people so I kept out of his way, in case I was one of them. The only contact that I ever had with him was of his own volition. Every afternoon he would come into my dressing room and borrow my newspaper and in the evening, just before we finished work, he would drop by with his own glass for a shot of my vodka, which he had noticed in my room when he had first borrowed the paper. It was very cold up there and the vodka was necessary for medicinal purposes, we both agreed.

Sometimes in movies, little weird things occur unexpectedly and so it turned out on this film. There was a scene in a bar in which I enter in long shot, with a man standing in the foreground drinking a pint of beer. The next day, Mike Hodges asked me to come to rushes to watch this scene in case I noticed anything. I watched it through twice and still couldn't figure out what I was supposed to see, until Mike said, 'Look at the hand of the guy who is drinking the beer.' I looked and couldn't believe my eyes – he had five fingers *and* a thumb. I bet he never dropped his glass!

Mike Hodges did a great job on the picture, maybe too great since when it came out we were slammed by most of the critics for the violence. It was too realistic for these people who had become used to the choreographed nonsense you usually saw in those days. I happen to think that *Get Carter* is an excellent movie and I am very proud of it. It didn't make a great deal of money but it didn't lose any either, so nobody got hurt. Mike Hodges unfortunately did not live up to the promise that Klinger and I saw in him and *Carter* is still the best movie he ever made, but he is still a young man and he has time to prove us right.

The next film I made was the only one for which I was

never paid. It was called *Kidnapped*, and was based on the novel by Robert Louis Stevenson and was filmed on location in Scotland. I returned home to London in a terrible state. I had worked very hard for three months, but had not been paid and even worse, I knew that *Kidnapped* was going to be a dud. I was now drinking very heavily and smoking about eighty cigarettes a day and in consequence was not in the best of spirits. Even London itself had lost a lot of its former attraction. I was at a very low ebb. I felt as though I had been through a blitz and consequently decided to become an evacuee and take myself off to the countryside. I seriously set about looking for a country home, something I could now well afford. I was thirty-eight years old and since the end of my marriage fifteen years earlier, had lived a life that I could only ever have dreamed about. Now, however, it seemed suddenly urgent to return to the peace of the English countryside in which, even though I am a Londoner by birth, I had grown up. I badly needed a refuge, even if it was only for the weekend. I was in a state, mentally and physically, and needed rehabilitation, I decided.

The start of this came from a very unexpected source, Tony Curtis.

One evening I was at a party and smoking away as usual when suddenly I felt a hand go to my inside pocket where I kept my cigarettes; the pack was grabbed and thrown into the fire. I looked up from the fire where my cigarettes were burning aimlessly with nobody to inhale the smoke, and standing right in front of me was Tony.

'I've been watching you,' he said in a tone that reminded me of my mother. 'That is the third cigarette you have lit since you came into the room, and you've only been here twenty minutes.' He then proceeded to give me a long and biologically sound lecture on the dangers of cigarette smoking. This he did with such skill that I gave up there and then and haven't had a cigarette for the last twenty years. I do smoke cigars, which of course means inhaling some smoke, but at least I do not inhale it deliberately. As a matter of fact, when I sometimes have to smoke in a film (which I try to avoid) I find it impossible to inhale a cigarette now. I am still trying to give up cigars but I haven't seen Tony since so I have very little help.

My first hurdle crossed on the road to recovery, I set out to find my Shangri-la in the country. I had decided that I wanted to live on the banks of the River Thames and not very far from London, so I started to search in Berkshire which is more or less the nearest county to London that contains real country. I did not want to live in suburbia. My limited experience with the aristocracy had shown me that they always had an eye for the best of everything, including real estate, so I thought that I would look where they lived. The biggest aristocrat that I knew of was the Queen so I looked in Berkshire where she lived. After all, I thought, she has a castle there called Windsor, so that was where I started.

I could not have picked a better place, because I found what I wanted almost immediately. I am very thorough in most things that I do, especially where the spending of money is concerned and I had done some considerable research on how to buy a house. One thing I had read stuck in my mind. It said: 'When you look at a prospective home for the first time, take a couple of close friends with you and watch them carefully. If they sit down, buy the place and if they don't, don't.'

This place was a beautiful, two-hundred-year-old water mill in a little village just outside Windsor, called Clewer. It had a hundred yards of frontage to the Thames, a small stream running through the middle of it, and the actual house stood right on the main side-stream and millrace with the millwheel still in it. The house was too small and not in a good state, which suited me, as I did not want to pay for someone else's decoration and it would keep the price down. What is more, the garden was derelict, which is exactly what I wanted, because as part of my self-imposed therapy I had decided that I was going to create, for the first time in my life, a garden. This is something that I have done a couple of times since and like everything else that interests me, it now borders on obsession.

The first time that the agent took me to the Mill House, I remembered the advice I had read and took my mother and Paul with me, to see if they sat down. I fell in love with the

326

place immediately and was enchanted by the layout of the garden, although it looked like a rubbish dump.

'Of course,' the agent said rather snottily, 'the property is two hectares.'

I nodded wisely as though I knew what he was talking about. (I looked it up later – five acres is the answer.) 'Can we go back to the house?' I requested urgently. I wanted to see if my mother and Paul were sitting down. I could not have been happier, for when I got back to the house they were sitting outside in the garden having tea with the owner's wife. That was it – the final proof I needed that this was the place for me. I bought it for fifty thousand pounds. I knew that it needed a lot of money spent on it but that for me was the whole point: I was going to create my own paradise.

I remember once, many years later, when I was showing an American actor friend around the garden, he commented that I must have spent a lot of money on it if it was derelict when I found it.

'I did,' I admitted, 'but do you have a psychiatrist?' He did, he said, and it had cost him a lot of money over the years. 'My garden is my psychiatrist,' I told him, and I really believe that. Whenever I get in a state about anything, which is often in a business like mine, I just go and walk, or sit, or work in the garden and somehow it all seems to come out right in the end – just like a movie. Maybe those reporters were right about me being a moron.

A few days after I moved in I was working in the garden, smashing my way through the barrier at the end to try and find the real boundary and see what was there, and when I finally broke through, much to my amazement I found a small field, about three quarters of a hectare in size, with a horse in it! I phoned the former owner and asked him if he had a horse missing. He said not recently, but that he *had* lost one several months ago. He was most surprised when I told him where I had found it.

There was another feature of the house that had a particular significance for me. The garden on one side had a common boundary with Windsor Racetrack and there was a gate in the fence which, I was informed, gave me the right by ancient deed as the owner of the land to pass on to the racecourse without paying at any meeting. When I was told this, I thought to myself that this was God being ironic. My father, who had been poor all his life but loved gambling and the horses had now, too late, been given a son with a free pass to a racecourse, his own private gate and all the money that my father would ever have needed for his own modest gambling.

God had started to smile on me again. Not only had I found my own little portion of heaven, but Dennis telephoned and told me that he was sending a script for me to read, to star in a film with Elizabeth Taylor. I almost said, 'Don't bother to send it, I'll do it anyway.' Elizabeth at that time was the biggest female star in the world, but caution prevailed and I did read the script. It was called *Zee and Co*, and was written by my friend Edna O'Brien, who had given me my first little piece of publicity when I was doing *Zulu*. It was very much a woman's picture and a little ahead of its time, I thought, rightly as it turned out. We had just been through the Swinging Sixties, I knew, but I wondered if the world was ready for a story in which Elizabeth Taylor leaves her husband for another woman. It was, to say the least, not quite my style of thing, but I really wanted to work with Elizabeth so I took it and never regretted it for one moment.

The first great delight of the film was not Elizabeth, however, but the director, Brian Hutton. Without a doubt he was the funniest director I have ever met and possibly the funniest person, as well as being a man of enormous charm. I loved him. It was a great help for me to meet and like him so much before I encountered Elizabeth because I was unusually nervous at the prospect of meeting for the first time in my life 'a living legend' – because that is what she literally was, then. In addition, of course, I would also have to deal with Richard Burton who, I was informed, always accompanied his wife to the studio and stayed with her all day when he himself was not working. This at first I thought was great marital understanding on his part, but then someone suggested that he was coming to keep an eye on me because of my rather overblown reputation with the ladies. To me this seemed preposterous. I wouldn't know what to do with a dead legend – let alone a living one! So, apart from the normal nerves of the first day of shooting on any picture, I also had to deal with this living legend, with whom I had some very steamy love scenes. I had found heaven in Windsor, but had I found hell in Shepperton? Only time would tell.

So there I was, the first morning on the set and ready to go at eight-thirty in the morning and very nervous. It was at this point I discovered that Elizabeth was a true star: her contract stated that she did not have to arrive on set until ten o'clock. The consequence of this was that I did not do my first scenes with her, but with a lovely continuity girl called Penny Daniels who was an old friend anyway, so I was at least relaxed. That was how it was during the whole film: I would do scenes either with Penny or other actors for the first ninety minutes of each day. As I told Elizabeth later, I knew that she was a big star because she didn't have to turn up until ten, but I also knew that she was a professional because she was never late.

As we worked for the first ninety minutes that morning, the tension mounted as various messengers came scurrying in to report the imminent arrival of my co-star. 'She has left the hotel,' was the first one, followed at intervals by, 'She's in the studio . . . in make-up . . . out of make-up and into hair. She's out of hair and is getting dressed. She's dressed and on her way.'

As we all stood there in line waiting for her to enter, I was reminded of a royal film première and waiting to be presented to the Queen. Like the Queen, Elizabeth was preceded by various minions – in fact, quite a large entourage was finally lined up. The joke on the film quickly became that if the entourage alone went to see the film we would be in profit. Finally Elizabeth arrived and behind her as I had been warned was Richard. She was smiling, he wasn't. One out of two was not bad, I thought. I had never seen her in the flesh before and she was much smaller than I had expected. The next surprise was that she was holding a huge jug of Bloody Mary, and at some hidden signal a new minion came forth bearing two glasses and handed one of these to me and one to Elizabeth. She filled both of them, kissed me on the cheek, chinked her glass with mine and said, 'Hello, Michael. Good luck!' and we both downed a healthy swig. Brian the director shouted, 'Let's go to work,' and off we went.

My first actual scene went by in a sort of wobbly haze as the Bloody Mary hit my stomach, which was empty apart from a pint of adrenalin. As a matter of fact the whole picture went by in a relaxed sort of a haze, due mainly to the Bloody Mary jug becoming a permanent prop on the set.

Elizabeth turned out to be absolutely charming, no trouble at all and very professional – the only actor I ever worked with who never ever fluffed a line. We worked well together, quickly became friends and have remained so to this day. Our first shot together did produce one problem, however. The difference in our heights meant that in a medium two shot my head was sticking out of the top of the screen and hers was peeping in from the bottom of it. This was solved by having Elizabeth stand on a box so that our heads were at an equal height. After I had done this a couple of times, I told her that as everybody knew she was short, they would now assume that I was the same height. 'I am going to look like Mickey Rooney in this picture,' I commented. She laughed and that was it – to this day she still calls me Mickey and, I might add, she is the only person in the world allowed to do so.

Elizabeth has a wonderful sense of humour and could be relied on to take a joke against herself, although a couple of times I thought Brian went a little far with her. One day when there was a lull in shooting he told her of how, when he was preparing this picture at MGM in Hollywood (her old studio when she first started), all the older technicians who had worked with her then said that of all the young child stars at the studio at that time, like Mickey Rooney and Margaret O'Brien and others, she was the only one that was not a pain in the arse.

Elizabeth was very pleased with this and said, 'Why, thank you, Brian.'

There was a short pause and then Brian said, 'What I've been trying to figure out is when did you become a pain in the arse?' There was a brief intake of breath as we all waited for her reaction to this, but she just roared with laughter.

Another time we were shooting a scene and right in the

middle of it she stopped acting and shouted, 'Cut.' Now directors have a very proprietary attitude towards this word *cut*, and it is only they who are allowed to say it – unless there is an emergency.

Brian with mock anger said, 'What do you mean, *cut*? I am the only one around here who can say that.'

Elizabeth with great urgency replied, 'I'm sorry, Brian, but I have to go to the bathroom *right now* or there will be an accident.'

Brian looked hugely astonished. 'You mean to tell me that Elizabeth Taylor goes to the toilet just like the rest of us! I thought that in your case, fairies came and took it away in toothpaste tubes.' She didn't take offence this time either, just screamed with laughter and ran. Brian was always like this with her and far from being upset by his teasing she actually made her next picture with him.

There was, however, a tougher side to Elizabeth and one day out of the blue I witnessed it. We always had lunch in the back room of the Red Lion pub in the village of Shepperton and one day as we were returning to the studio and were entering the gates, she suddenly yelled for the car to stop.

'What's the matter?' I asked.

'Look up there,' she said, pointing to the top of the flagpole that stood at the studio entrance. I looked and there, on top of the pole, fluttered a flag with the sign of the Playboy Rabbit on it. 'What's that doing up there?' she asked angrily. I told her: Hugh Hefner's Playboy Pictures were shooting Roman Polanski's version of Shakespeare's play about the Scottish King whose name I won't mention. '*I* am working at this studio,' she suddenly yelled, 'and *I* don't work for Playboy. That fucking flag is coming down or we take this picture out of this studio.' She was really furious. Her instructions were given and we all sat in her dressing room for about half an hour until a breathless assistant came to inform us that the offending banner had been furled and back to work we went.

That wasn't the end of Elizabeth's problems with Mr Hefner. One day we were all sitting in her dressing room chatting as was our wont, when someone came in and said that he was outside and would like to meet her. Elizabeth told them to invite him in so we all stood up to go and leave them with some privacy, but she signalled for us to stay. Hugh came in and was introduced. I, of course, already knew him from my visit to his Chicago mansion. He had two other men with him and we all sat and chatted quite pleasantly for a few minutes. It soon became obvious that he had just wanted to meet her, as did the rest of the world at the time, or even now for that matter.

Everything was going fine and Hugh was very charming when suddenly I felt a sharp nudge on my arm. I turned and Ron, Elizabeth's make-up man, put his fingers to his lips to signify silence then handed me a piece of paper. 'Pass this to Elizabeth,' he whispered in my ear. I looked at what he had written and it said: *'The man with Hefner has a tape recording machine running behind his briefcase which is on the table.'* I looked across and could just see it hidden there.

I passed the note to Elizabeth and she read it and screwed it up and threw it on the floor. Suddenly she stood up and said, 'I have to go,' and walked out, leaving Hefner and his friends sitting there gaping in mid-sentence. The meeting was over and I think they knew why and just left.

Zee and Co went along as smoothly as could be and Richard turned out to be no problem. He would not have been much of a protector of Elizabeth, though, *had* my intentions towards his wife been dishonorable, as he was in the middle of his drinking problem and slept on the sofa in her spare room for most of the day. Susannah York was the other star of the picture but I never had many scenes with her as she was playing the other 'man' in our trio. Brian, as I said, was a delight and I had a wonderful time. The picture was good but a great deal ahead of its time so it never did as well as it should have done, but it still did OK and everything was great and I wouldn't have missed it for the world.

We finished a week before Christmas and had an end-of-picture party at the studio where we all got slightly drunk, which is on a par with being slightly pregnant. I kissed Elizabeth and Susannah goodbye and said a sad farewell to Brian, and just as I was going out of the door I ran into Richard. 'Happy Christmas,' I said to him cheerfully.

'Why don't you go and fuck yourself,' he snarled, with less than the usual festive spirit, I thought, and that was the end of that film. I eventually met Richard again and became quite friendly with him but I never asked him about the cause of his attitude towards me that day. Alas, it is too late now.

Part Five

29

Shakira

I was now drinking up to three bottles of vodka a day, and the trouble with doing something like that is that at the end of the day you can't count – so you don't know you are doing it.

In 1971 I flew off with Dennis and Johnny Morris for a couple of nights in New York to see the fight between those great boxers Muhammad Ali and Joe Frazier. The biggest and best fight of the evening was in Ali's corner after the main bout was over. I was sitting quite close to the scene, unfortunately, and got a chair over my head for my pains. So it was back to London bruised but unbowed, and beginning to flag. Paul and I went the rounds of all the usual places and found nothing but stupefying boredom there. Was this it, I wondered. The answer was no, but I of course did not know that. And then I made the decision that was about to change my life – but I didn't know that, either.

I decided that enough was enough and I was going to have a night at home. I put this proposition to a stunned Paul and invited him to my flat in Grosvenor Square where I would cook him a Cockney fry-up for dinner and then we would do the unthinkable and watch television for the whole evening. The truth was that I was just exhausted. Paul readily agreed to this treat of a fry-up because it was and still is very rare in London restaurants, although staple fare in more humble cafés. It consists of eggs, pork sausages, bacon and tomatoes all fried in animal fat and eaten with masses of sliced white bread smothered in butter and washed down with tea laced with full cream milk and white sugar. In other words, 'Cholesterol City' and then some. I always call it a heart attack on a plate. I still love it but rarely eat it, and when I do

I always have a feeling that my father is watching me with pride.

So I cooked up my treat and Paul and I ate in the kitchen and then we repaired to the lounge and settled down for an evening of television with the curtains drawn so that no one with binoculars could actually witness us indulging in this deviant act. There were only two stations in those days so there were no remote control devices, but even with two stations you had to change sometimes so I had a broom pole with which I could change them without getting up from my chair. With this device I think I can claim that I was the actual inventor of the first remote control.

We had been watching some show for a while and when the commercials came on I was just about to reach for my broom pole and switch over to the other channel when something caught my attention. The ad was for Maxwell House coffee and it had been shot in Brazil; it was banging on about the quality of the beans in the coffee and on the screen a Brazilian girl was dancing around holding up maracas filled with beans. (Apparently the beans not only tasted good but sounded good as well.) The girl with the maracas was dancing in a long shot, but there was something about her that made me hope that there would be a close-up of her before the commercial ended; then, as if the director had read my mind, there it was – a close-up of the most beautiful girl I had ever seen. The effect on me was extraordinary. My heart started to pound and I grew very agitated. The palms of my hands, I noticed, were beginning to sweat and I suddenly found myself down on my knees in front of the set trying to get a closer look at this vision, only to be confronted with a close-shot of a Maxwell House coffee jar. 'What's the matter with you?' said a very puzzled Paul.

'That girl,' I replied, hardly able to speak. 'She's beautiful.'

'I know,' said Paul. 'So what?'

'I want to meet her,' I told him.

'How can you meet her? She's in Brazil,' he said sensibly.

I got back into my chair and sat there stunned by what was happening to me. Even I did not understand it. I had never ever been turned on by just seeing a girl on a screen before.

We sat there all evening with me glued to the commercial station in case they ran the piece again, but they didn't.

Finally the station went off the air. In those days British television finished at about eleven-thirty so that the workers would go obediently off to bed and not be late for their jobs in the morning. Paul went into the kitchen to make some coffee and I just sat there trying to understand what was happening to me. I did know one thing: if I was ever going to have any peace again, no matter where she was, I was going to have to go and find her, and that was that. I knew I had no other choice; something strange and mystical seemed to be driving me.

Paul came back in with the coffees. 'Do you want to come to Brazil with me?' I asked him.

'To find that girl?'

'Yes,' I said.

'Are you mad?' he said. 'There are loads of beautiful girls in London.'

'Not like this one,' I replied maniacally.

Paul realised I was serious and agreed to come with me. 'When?' he said with immediate practicality.

'Tomorrow or whenever the first plane goes,' was my reply. We sat there in silence for a while drinking our coffees and I could feel Paul's eyes on me as though he was looking at a stranger.

Finally he said, 'I'm all for a trip to Brazil so I don't want to put you off, but I think you're fucking mad.'

I thought about this for a moment and eventually came to the conclusion that he was right. I *was* mad – madly in love with a girl whom I did not know and might never find, but I knew what I was going to do first thing in the morning. I was going to phone Maxwell House and find out who had made the commercial for them.

We had eaten and the television was finished but I was too restless to go to bed yet so I suggested to Paul that we set off for a walk. It was now about half-past midnight and Paul knew very well what a walk meant at that time of night. It signified a trip to Tramp, my favourite hangout, to see my friends Johnny Gold and Oscar Lerman who owned the place and were always good for a shoulder to cry on or an ear to listen to the troubles of the lovelorn. Johnny was there as always, but we now saw a lot less of Oscar because he had married Joan Collins' sister Jackie and she had decided to take up writing as a career so they came out less frequently.

Above the din of the disco music I sat with Johnny and screamed my story of having at last found true love with a girl I had only seen on the television. Johnny listened sympathetically to my protestations and ordered a brandy for Paul and myself like a doctor dispensing placebos, having heard it all many times before, though never from me.

'Look at that one,' he said, pointing towards the dance floor where a girl whose legs finished just below her armpits was wrestling with a possibly forbidden substance in time to the music. 'Gorgeous, isn't she?' he said, trying to take my mind off my impossible dream.

It was no good. I just sat there and suffered as the hours slowly ticked by to when the Maxwell House offices would open. Nine-thirty in the morning, I guessed, and looked at my watch. It was now a quarter past two. Only another seven hours and fifteen minutes to go and I could start my quest. I'd better get some sleep, I thought. I wanted to be fresh for the next day.

I was just about to leave when a guy I knew vaguely called Nigel Politzer came in and expressed surprise at seeing me sitting there with Paul and Johnny and no girl. 'I'm in love!' I told him.

'Oh yeah? Who with?' he asked, laughing at such a ridiculous statement.

'A girl I saw on television tonight,' I replied without embarrassment, having by now had three or four brandies.

'I've been watching television all evening,' Nigel replied. 'Which show was she in?'

'She wasn't in a show. She was in a commercial for Maxwell House coffee,' I said.

He roared with laughter and to my amazement said, 'The one with the maracas?'

'Yes!' I replied, in wonder. 'How on earth did you guess that?'

'I didn't guess,' he replied. 'I work for the company that made that commercial.'

I couldn't believe my luck! Here was someone who could actually help me locate her. 'Paul and I are going to Brazil tomorrow to find her. Do you know how we could contact her there?' I asked hopefully.

At this point Nigel went into hysterics and when he had finished and I was thoroughly pissed off at being laughed at, he said, 'She's not in Brazil and she's not Brazilian. She's Indian and her name is Shakira Baksh.'

'Shakira Baksh,' I thought. I had a name for her now. 'Do you know where she lives?' I asked Nigel rather diffidently.

'Somewhere in the Fulham Road,' he replied, which was about a mile from where we were sitting.

'Can you get her number?' I asked.

'Yes, the agency will have it.'

'Will you do me a favour and phone her, and ask her permission to give me her number?' I knew it would not look good if he just gave me it and I phoned out of the blue. Ladies, and that is what I rightly figured she was, don't like having their numbers passed round to strangers, and I didn't want to start off any relationship that might develop on the wrong foot. Nigel agreed and said that he would phone me the next day.

I strolled back to Grosvenor Square with Paul that night as happy as a kid just before Christmas, but still very nervous in case I did not get a present. It seemed like Fate to me, that I had gone to Tramp and met someone who already knew who she was, but things could still go wrong. Suppose she was married? I'd forgotten to ask Nigel that all-important question: she might be engaged or madly in love with someone! I started to panic as all these negative thoughts raced through my mind. It grew worse and worse.

Once back at the flat, I fell into bed and slept the sleep of the truly irrational, waking every half hour or so to check if it was time to get up and wait for Nigel to call. At one point I woke with a start and a new fear: suppose she was a lesbian! I flopped back on the pillow smothered in sweat and dozed off again with this prospect on my mind. Then I could hear a phone ringing faintly in the distance and suddenly my shoulder was being shaken and Paul was standing over me. 'Nigel is on the phone,' he said.

I grabbed the phone by my bed and in my haste, dropped it on the floor, picked it up and said, 'Hello.' Nothing. I'd forgotten to push the hold-off button. This I did and then heard Nigel's voice saying, 'She says it is OK to give you her number.' Still half-asleep I fumbled round for a pen and a piece of paper.

'What is it?' I gasped. He gave it to me and I thanked him profusely and put the phone down. I stared at the number for a moment and then started to get nervous again. Now it was all up to me. I had to phone this woman and get her to come out with me. I looked at the clock – it had just gone noon. It was not a good time to phone now, I told myself. She'd probably just be going out to lunch and would not have time to talk. With a sigh of relief I decided to call later. I spent the rest of the day nervously trying to imagine what her day was like and what would be the best possible moment to call her. Seven-twenty, I finally decided, would be the ideal moment to call. I don't know why, it just seemed right. When I telephoned, a girl told me that Shakira was in the shower and could I call back in half an hour. A girl had answered – that was a good sign, I thought. Maybe she shared a flat with another girl, which would mean that she wasn't married. And she couldn't be a lesbian or she would not have let Nigel give me her number.

Things were looking good. I'd already had two vodkas and a cigar to get up the courage to make the first call, so I had another vodka and another cigar to get me prepared for the second one, when I would surely be talking directly to her. I didn't want to sound nervous over the phone. I rang again and she answered this time. Her voice was cool and calm and very self-possessed. I started to tell her who I was but she stopped me and said that she already knew, she had seen me in several films. She didn't say that she liked them or me in them, she just said that she had seen them. Suddenly her voice hardened slightly. She said, 'I hope you don't think that I make a habit of giving my phone number to strange men, but I have seen you in films and feel as if I know you slightly.'

I quickly agreed that of course I understood this was not her normal behaviour, and as I had seen her in the commercial, it was as if we had already met, because we knew what the other one looked and sounded like; it wasn't like being complete strangers. This sounded half-witted, and I felt I was losing her interest. Help – what should I do? I asked her about herself. She told me that she was Indian, from a Kashmiri family, but that her parents had emigrated to Guyana where she had been born. She had come to England in 1967 as Miss Guyana to compete in the Miss World Competition. Wow, I thought. She must be beautiful if she qualified for that. Without thinking I blurted out, 'Where did you come?'

'Third,' she said.

I decided to take the bull by the horns. 'Would you have dinner with me some time?' I asked, in the least salacious tone I could muster, which actually came out sounding like a road company Dracula.

'I'm busy for the next week,' she said in a businesslike manner. 'Could you call me again in about ten days' time?'

'Wonderful,' I said, hiding my disappointment. 'I look forward to seeing you.' The phone went dead in my hand.

For the next ten days I walked around in a trance, unable to explain to myself, let alone others, what was happening to me. It was silly, I told myself. I had only seen this girl for a minute on television – what was going on? Nothing like this had ever happened to me before. Finally the time came to phone again. Another couple of vodkas and I was dialling confidently. She picked up the phone immediately and said yes, she would have dinner with me the next evening.

'Give me your address,' I said, 'and I'll pick you up at eight o'clock.'

'No, you give me your address and I'll pick you up in my car,' she said cautiously.

What did she think I was going to do – run out of petrol in the Fulham Road? 'Anything you say,' I replied obligingly, and gave her my address.

Another long twenty-four hours to wait. The suspense was killing me but I speeded up the passage of time with a couple of bottles of my usual poison. There I was the next evening, bathed, shaved and stone cold sober waiting for eight o'clock and my doorbell to ring. This was difficult – it was the most nerve-racking part of the whole thing. The first meeting – but I could not have a drink or smoke a cigar. I didn't want the smell of either around the place. The whole flat smelled of the green French perfumed candles that were so popular in England at the time and I was doused in whatever the latest after-shave was, and my mouth burned from having been swirled in mouthwash every half hour during the day and for the last minute I even had a small tube of Binaca, the little spray that you squirted straight into your mouth.

So there I sat in an armchair in front of a television that I would not put on in case I did not hear the bell. After a while I could feel sweat trickling down underneath my arms. Panic set in. I rushed to the bathroom and sprayed the whole shirt liberally with after-shave and went back to waiting. I looked at my watch: it was right on eight o'clock. She would not be dead on time, I thought, and had just relaxed back for another couple of minutes' respite when the doorbell sent a deafening scream through my ears.

I rose slowly to my feet and strolled to the door, determined to present what I laughingly called my 'man of the world' front, but somehow or other whatever holds up your knees had stopped functioning and my legs kept wobbling. I managed to get to the door and hang on to the handle where my knee-lock system quickly fell back into place and I looked through the peephole in my front door for my first sight in the flesh of this girl called Shakira. The distorting lens on a peephole is a pretty hard test but she passed it. She looked gorgeous.

I opened the door slowly, revealing her face, millimetre by millimetre from left to right as it went until it was wide open and there was no barrier between us. There, smiling up at me, was the most beautiful woman that I had ever seen in my life.

'Hello Michael,' she said, extending her hand, which I took but did not shake. To shake this woman's hand would have been like an act of violence. I just held it and suddenly thought of something that the French say about love: 'L'amour, c'est une question de peau.' Love is a question of skin . . . there are only two types of touch. One is when you touch someone for the first time, and can tell that it is possible to fall in love with them but not necessarily so, and the other is a touch that tells you that you could never fall in love with this person.

The vibrations from Shakira throbbed through my hands and I knew that I had at least passed the first French test. Love *was* possible here, and somewhere deep in my heart I knew at that moment that it was also inevitable, at least on my part.

I suddenly realised that I had not spoken yet and I said, 'Come in, Shakira,' but no actual sound came out. I cleared my throat as surreptitiously as possible, and had another go, and this time I produced a sound which was not quite the seductive baritone for which I was aiming, but it at least got the message across and she came into my flat and into my life forever. It was as simple as that. I had heard of love at first sight but never really believed in it, but here it was.

We sat and had a drink for a while and explored each other verbally like two people who had met on Venus and had no idea what to expect of the inhabitants or the terrain, each thinking the other was native there until we discovered that we were both visitors in this strange land of real love, and would have to explore together. My feelings for her were so intense that I quickly suggested we go out to dinner before I ruined it all by making some big pass at her. On the surface, Shakira seemed very shy and gentle but I rightly sensed that there was a thin but unbreakable core of steel hidden beneath that beguiling exterior.

After that evening we saw each other constantly, until she had to go off and do a modelling job somewhere and I had to go to Malta to make a movie called *Pulp*. This gave us a week or so apart and a chance to reevaluate our situation and see if we both wanted to continue what had now become an extremely intense affair. It was obviously not a brief fling, but something that could very well become as serious as it can get

– which in my case meant marriage. I was still having recurrent nightmares in which I woke up screaming in the middle of a wedding ceremony, so thoughts like this were strange and puzzling to me, along with long-forgotten words like 'permanent' and 'relationship' that flashed into my mind.

We talked as often as we could by phone from Mexico, where Shakira was working, to Malta where I was. Anybody who has ever moaned about any telephone system should have tried phoning Mexico from Malta in 1972. If anything was a test of true love this was it and we passed it. The moment she finished working in Mexico, Shakira came and joined me in Malta and we have remained together ever since. The commercial that I saw her in for the first time was, she told me later, directed by a man named Ridley Scott who is now a very successful director in Hollywood with hits like *Alien* and *Thelma and Louise* to his credit. Mr Scott has never given me a part in any of his movies but then he doesn't have to as far as I am concerned. He has already done me the biggest favour possible and I would just like to say thank you.

Coincidence is a funny thing. I have been writing these last few pages on 14 February 1992, St Valentine's Day and Shakira called me a little while ago to watch television for a few minutes, as they were playing that commercial and telling the story of how I met her.

Pulp was the second film that I produced with Michael Klinger after *Get Carter*, and Mike Hodges was again the director. It was a strange little piece and it had also been written by Mike as a sort of homage to John Huston. It was a real oddball of a movie that never really quite worked. Its heart was in the right place, but in a business where wallets are kept over the heart it did not count for much. *Pulp* never made any real money, but I again had a wonderful experience making it so I remember it with affection. It was winter in England when we arrived in Malta, where it was beautifully warm so we were ahead already. Shakira eventually joined me and the temperature got even hotter as we embarked on an idyll of really discovering each other in a hotel on the beach, which couldn't have been better had we planned it. Being absolutely besotted by this lady I don't remember much of the

346

actual film-making, even though I was supposed to be the associate producer, but Mike Klinger held it all together and gave us his blessing. He was a small rotund man with a perpetual smile on his face, and what with this look and his benevolent attitude towards Shakira and me, he always seemed like an elderly and slightly sinful Cupid.

One of the things that fascinates me about working in movies is the opportunity I occasionally get to work with stars familiar to me from my boyhood; in this film there were two – Lizbeth Scott and Mickey Rooney. Lizbeth was a strange will-o'-the-wisp sort of figure whom I never once met on any social occasion. She had always seemed to me to be a rather tough character on screen, but the first time we did a take together I got a surprise. We were sitting at a table having drinks in this particular scene, and as we rehearsed I noticed that every time she raised her glass to take a drink, her hand shook uncontrollably.

'What's the matter, Lizbeth?' I hissed when no one was looking.

'This is my first take for fifteen years,' she said sadly, her enormous brown eyes suddenly going soft and she sat there just like a little girl. We calmed her down and she got the take in one, just like the pro that she really is, but it proved one thing to me: no matter how experienced you are, you have to keep going or you lose it.

The other character, Mickey Rooney, was the complete opposite – noisy, outgoing and very funny, and full of snippets of good advice. The piece he gave me most often was simple and to the point: 'Save your money.' Mickey explained that despite all the large sums he had earned during his life, he was now completely broke. Until this movie he had been out of work and also out of favour for a while, but I noticed that after this film his luck seemed to change and he kept popping up everywhere. He was a contradictory sort of a character. He was very religious and belonged to some small sect or other and I remember how he used to tell me the filthiest jokes with every four-letter word imaginable, and then at the end of it he would clasp both my hands, a pious look would come over his face and he would say, 'God bless you, my son,' with complete sincerity and walk away. The film finished, it seemed to me, almost before it started, as I wallowed in the miasma of my newfound love and then we were all on our way home.

Back in England I invited Shakira to move into my flat in Grosvenor Square and we settled down to a sort of married life without the benefit of the ceremony. Very soon the lease on the flat was up and we decided to live in Windsor full-time without a London base. We quickly settled into a really idyllic life in the country and for the first time ever someone – Shakira, of course – actually pointed out to me that I was drinking two or more bottles of vodka a day. This came as a complete surprise to me and was such a shock that I gave up drinking altogether for a year. Since then I have only drunk wine, in moderation and only with food.

I felt great. I was sober, living with a woman whom I adored, and I had started my great therapy, creating a garden out of the mess that were the grounds at the Mill House. Life was suddenly completely different and absolutely perfect, and as if to top it all, I then received an invitation to star opposite Laurence Olivier in the film version of Anthony Shaffer's play *Sleuth*. My cup ranneth over, but with no alcohol in it this time.

I spent the spring planning and planting the garden with the help of an old Scottish gardener who had retired from Windsor Castle. His name, believe it or not, was Jock – and he had forgotten more about gardening than I would ever know. The two of us set about creating this city boy's dream and sort of 'return to childhood'. I once told someone what I did in the country and they surprised me by saying that I was practising 'Zen'. Not having the faintest idea what 'Zen' was, I was consequently surprised to be told that I was practising it. What I had said to this person that prompted their observation was that I loved to plant, pick, cook and eat my own garden produce. That, it turned out, was 'Zen' and what is more, a Chinese version of it! So there I was in love, physically fit (I did all of the manual work in the garden myself as Jock was over seventy), happy, I was going to star with Olivier and on top of it all I was practising 'Zen'. It doesn't get any better than that.

Shakira, it seemed, had saved me from myself – one of the most insidious of all enemies – and just as in the movies, in the very nick of time . . .

30

'Call me Larry'

I had now found my paradise. I loved the house and spent
entire days in the garden practising my newfound obsession
of creating environments of everything, from scented gardens
to cut flowers for the house, and organic vegetables to cool
wooded places in which to sit; most of all, to share this with
me I had Shakira. It is very hard to describe her without
making her sound like a paragon of all the virtues, which she
is not – nobody's perfect – but she almost made it. She is a
woman of great beauty but without the usual conceit and
arrogance of most of this species. She is gentle without being
weak, and when we first met and started to live together, she
was shy without being nervous. She is also a person of great
charm and humour, and if you add to all this the fact that she
is a very good cook, you will see how astonished I was at my
luck in those first few weeks at the Mill House as we got to
know each other. I was completely enchanted by her and
together with the house and the garden, life was perfect.

The months passed for me in an almost dream-like quality
as I gradually approached one of the biggest tests of my
career, playing opposite Lord Olivier in *Sleuth*. I was getting
exercise from working in the garden, I was teetotal and I had
given up smoking and nightclubs so I was now as fit as I had
been for years. I think now that I was unconsciously preparing
myself psychologically for the big fight against the world
champion – which Olivier was at that time.

Finally came the big day, time to start rehearsal, which would
take up the first two weeks of the schedule. The car arrived and
off I went to Pinewood Studios, where we were going to
rehearse in the actual sets, which had been beautifully designed

350

by my old friend Ken Adam who had done the sets for *Ipcress File* all those years ago. I sat in the car as we drove down the long country lane which is the final approach to the studio, and although I felt very nervous, I also decided that even if I could never hope to out-act Larry, I would never give in and never back off from him in any way. In other words, as they say where I come from: 'I would give him a run for his money.' And that is what I tried to do.

As the big limousine sped along that last country lane, I couldn't help but think back to the number of times when I had been playing minor roles in films at Pinewood and had to get off the bus at the end of the mile-long lane and walk that distance often in the freezing cold and many times in the dark, because the calls for the small-part actors are always hours earlier than the stars, in order to get them into make-up and out of the way before the leading players arrive. Today the sun was shining and it was just before ten o'clock in the morning, since we were only rehearsing, so I felt that life had improved greatly over the years as the car glided through the studio gate and up to my old friend Tom the doorman, who opened the car door for me and slung me up a salute – a sure sign that I had arrived.

Ever since I had been cast in *Sleuth* I had been bothered by a peculiarly English problem. Larry had a title and it would be rude to address him as anything but 'My Lord'. But since we were the only two actors in the movie, this was going to sound completely ridiculous. It was Larry, however, with typical forethought, who solved the problem. Two weeks before he had sent me a letter which began: 'It has occurred to me that you might be wondering how to address me when we finally meet. I think it would be a great idea if you called me Larry.' In spite of this I was still very nervous.

On the set, Joe came forward and shook my hand warmly and informed me that Larry would be here soon and then we could get started. He could see that I was a bit uneasy as I walked round just to see what Ken had done. I didn't want to get too familiar with the place because in the film I had to enter it as a stranger for the first time. That is a side of acting that people probably don't think about – the fact that you are either a

351

stranger in any set or, even more difficult, a set can be your own home. This situation needs a little bit of quiet rehearsal as you familiarise yourself with the way the doors and cupboards open and where, for instance, the light switches are – all things that you would know very well in your own home and not at all in a strange place. All these little touches help towards realism. It gives an immediately artificial effect if an actor walks into a supposedly strange place in the dark and then knows exactly where the light switch is. This sounds obvious, but I have seen it happen countless times in even the best movies.

Joe was watching me as I came back to him and he smiled and put his arm around my shoulder and said, 'Don't worry, Michael. I'll take care of you.' It was the best thing he could have said at that moment and I relaxed down to slight panic as the time came for the great man to arrive.

Dead on the dot of ten o'clock, in he walked – physically smaller than I thought he would be, and obviously a giant in every other way, especially in confidence. He didn't walk, he *advanced* like a conquering army across the set, ignoring Joe and Elaine, the continuity girl, and making straight for me, his right hand outstretched and a broad and genuine smile on his face.

'What a pleasure, Michael. We meet at last,' he said, shaking my hand.

And as I looked into his eyes for the first time and said, 'Hello, Larry,' I realised how much further I had to go on the journey through my own personal wonderland, the movies.

We all had a cup of coffee and a short chat to break the ice, which as far as I was concerned was thick enough to skate on, and then went to work, slowly reading through the script as we made our way around the strange set. I watched both Larry and Joe as we stumbled round the great room looking for positions to play out each scene. Larry, I got to thinking, was not only a great stage actor and director, he was also an Academy Award-winning movie actor and director, and when you add to that the fact that he had also been a great film star in the thirties and forties . . . I knew that what I had here was a very formidable opponent – or was it to be partner? I would find out during the next couple of weeks. In particular the Oscar for movie directing was not lost on Joe; even he seemed to be a bit apprehensive as he started to direct Larry, but behind his broad smile I could sense a steely resolve that would soon crush any attempt to usurp his authority, which in the case of film directors is always God-like, in Joe's case benignly so.

As the rehearsal progressed towards lunch-time, it became obvious that Larry was having a little trouble finding a line on his character. Even though it was only a rehearsal, his performance right from the start was as intense as if we were shooting it there and then, but he was very dissatisfied with what he was doing. I was amazed at the energy he was putting into what was, after all, only the first rehearsal. I spoke to him about this during lunch and he gave me a very good piece of advice. 'Always do the part out loud as though you are playing it, even the very first time that you read the script.' I took this advice and have followed it ever since: it works. For the rest of the afternoon Larry struggled with his role but could not get a handle on it to his liking and the day ended with all of us feeling just a little bit frustrated.

Larry left first and I stayed behind and was talking to Joe about something when suddenly Larry came rushing back in, a big smile on his face. 'Joe, I have a great idea for the part! I will show you in the morning,' he said with great secrecy and left. The next morning he came bursting on to the set full of enthusiasm. 'I've fixed it!' he cried, and with a great flourish he produced from behind his back a small moustache, which he held to his upper lip. 'What do you think, Joe?' he asked, modelling the small piece of hair as though it were a secret weapon.

'It'll be fine, Larry,' Joe replied. 'If you think that it is necessary.'

'I do, Joe. I do,' Larry stated, almost in desperation. 'I suddenly realised what was wrong as I was leaving here last night.'

And 'What was that?' Joe was eventually forced to ask, as Larry left a pregnant pause that almost had a miscarriage.

'I can't act with my own face!' Larry yelled. 'I always need some sort of disguise.'

353

'Well, use it,' Joe said immediately, and so Larry did and that was that. He was right into the part from the moment he put the moustache on. It was quite amazing to watch the change as he wore it through all the rehearsals, which went along smoothly for the rest of the time.

Finally we came to the moment to start shooting. Right from the first shot on the Monday morning it was obvious that Larry was in trouble again; he seemed to be preoccupied with something more important than the movie, and most amazing of all -- he could not remember his lines even in the shortest scenes as Joe started to cut down the length of the shots to help him. None of us could understand it. Here was a man who had just done a play by Eugene O'Neill that was three and a half hours long, and yet now he was struggling to remember a couple of simple lines.

We stumbled through for a couple of days, our hearts going out to him and our spirits sinking lower. On the third morning we discovered the reason for his condition but not from Larry – we read it in the newspaper. For years Larry had been building a National Theatre Company in London; he had worked so hard to get the funds for the company and to build a theatre complex and then, just at the time for the official opening, he found that he had been thrown out. This was, of course, a most terrible blow to him and a poor reward for the years of hard work.

Although this affair was partly responsible for his current problems on the set, we eventually learned the true cause of Larry's extraordinary loss of memory. He had been taking some pills to calm him down, and one of their side-effects was memory loss. Once he stopped taking them, he was just fine, back to normal and very powerful once again, so much so that I suggested he go back on the tranquillisers for my sake. He laughed at this, but he certainly was a handful to deal with once he was fit again.

Laurence Olivier, you must remember, had been the foremost star and director in the theatre for many, many years. He had worked in an atmosphere of autonomy and extraordinary power, where the job of everyone around him had always been – other actors included – to get the great

354

man's performance on the stage. I found myself suddenly in a similar, and very tricky, situation. He would place himself in the best possible location for a scene and then leave me somehow to act *around* him in a very theatrical way, rather than playing a scene realistically, as you must in a movie. If I had a line that interfered with one of his moves, he would just tell Joe to cut it. Eventually I went to Joe and told him of my problems, as if he hadn't noticed, and he said, 'I told you that I would look after you. Every time Larry has suggested that I cut one of your lines I have promised I will cut it in the editing.'

This was true, I remembered, but then I said, 'Did you see the two shot this morning, which was supposed to be a fifty-fifty? He went upstage and pulled me round until you could only see the side of my face.'

'I saw that,' Joe said sympathetically. 'The next time he does it, turn right around until your back is to the camera and I will come in over his shoulder from the other side for a close-up on you. He'll soon stop it.' He smiled. 'Don't worry, Michael. This isn't the theatre – we do have editing and close-ups.' I returned to the fray with my confidence boosted and a very valuable new trick that I have used to great advantage ever since.

A couple more days' shooting passed and we gradually came to work more as a team until finally I had my most difficult scene in the picture, in which Olivier's character holds a gun to my head and tells me that he is going to shoot me, and I have to break down in hysterics and cry for mercy. We did this scene and it went very well for me, and as we were walking back to our dressing rooms, Larry put his arm round my shoulder and gave me the greatest compliment I had ever received. He whispered softly in my ear, 'When we started on this film, I thought of you as a very skilled assistant.' He gave one of his little dramatic pauses and then added, 'I now see that I have a partner.' We reached my dressing-room door first and he just kissed me on the cheek and continued on to his. From that day our friendship was sealed and truly did create a partnership that was very good for the film, and also made my life so much easier.

As he was still quite shattered over the National Theatre dismissal, I made an arrangement with Larry that I would never disturb him in his dressing room, but that if he wanted to discuss anything with me, my door was always open and he could come in at any time. He liked this because he was always thinking up new little bits of business to do. One day he came in and stopped at the doorway, rooted to the spot.

'What *are* you doing?' he asked in absolute amazement.

'I'm watching the tennis,' I replied, which I was. Wimbledon was on the television.

He came slowly into the room, his eyes wide with astonishment. 'You have a *television* in your dressing room?' he said, as though I had performed some kind of miracle.

'Yes. Why – don't you?' I queried in a deliberately matter-of-fact tone.

'No,' he said. 'What a wonderful idea! I would never have thought of that.' He seemed completely bowled over by the fact that I had got one.

'Would you like to watch the tennis with me?' I asked diffidently. 'It starts at two and is on all afternoon, so come in at any time.'

'Thank you, Michael,' he said, like a kid being given a special treat. He sat down beside me to watch and never missed a moment until the last day when Evonne Goolagong won the Ladies Championship. I don't remember the men because we were working when they played.

Once Larry lightened up, the film became real fun to work on. Joe and he were always telling old Hollywood stories and I remember two of them in particular because they were both trying to outdo each other with Sam Goldwyn stories. Sam was a big producer for whom both of them had worked at various times. He was famous for his rudimentary grasp of the English language. Larry told us how he had been working for Sam on the day that the American Air Force dropped the first atom bomb on Hiroshima. Sam called him into the office and showed him the banner headlines in the paper and pictures of the terrible destruction. They discussed the awesome power of this new weapon for a while and as Larry was leaving to get back to work, Sam called to him and said, 'Larry, that atom bomb is dynamite!'

Joe then countered with *his* Goldwyn story; when he was working as a writer for Sam, Joe had given him back a script that he had rewritten for him. When Sam had read it he called Joe and told him that he liked his rewrite very much: the new script now had warmth and charmth.

I had never met Goldwyn, but I told them the one that I knew – when he said that a verbal agreement wasn't worth the paper it was written on.

One day we were talking about how unpredictable show business is and Larry told Joe and me about the time in 1939 when he had the hit movie *Wuthering Heights* playing on Broadway and Vivien Leigh, his then wife was starring at another theatre in *Gone with the Wind*. They were the two biggest hit movies of the year and he and Vivien had opened in a live theatre production of *Romeo and Juliet* just down the street, convinced that this would be a big hit – and then the show had bombed. Larry shook his head in disbelief and said, 'I still don't understand it.' But of course we all did – it was show business.

One day Joe showed up a typical side of the movie business. Ossie Morris our cameraman had won an Oscar for his photography in *Fiddler on the Roof*. He couldn't go and collect it, of course, because he was working with us, but the director Norman Jewison had collected it for him and he came to our set, secretly, with Ossie's Oscar one afternoon just in time for the tea break. Champagne was laid on instead of tea and Norman jumped out from behind the scenery and presented a surprised Ossie with his award. The celebration was quickly over and we went back to work on a new set-up and I stood there and watched the following.

Ossie was on one side of the set with his Oscar in his hand and a viewfinder in the other, looking to see where to place the camera for the next shot; on the other side of the set Joe was looking through his viewfinder to see where *he* wanted to put the camera. There was obviously an unspoken difference of opinion as to where the camera should go. Finally, Joe called from his side of the set to Ossie on the other side, 'Ossie, I've got four of those,' pointing to the Oscar in Ossie's hand, 'and the camera goes over *here*.' Authority restored, we set to work again.

After fourteen exhausting weeks, during which time I had spent two weeks getting to the studio at four in the morning to have a very difficult prosthetic make-up applied, the film finally came to an end and it was back to my little paradise at Windsor. In the years since I made *Sleuth* many people have asked me if I learned anything from Larry and the answer to that is – no, nothing specific, just how to take care of myself. However, one day I was privileged to witness something straight down the barrel of a gun: Larry in full flight at the peak of his power in a very emotional scene. For a moment it was like being in the eye of a hurricane. He was one of the people with whom it was a privilege to work, and an honour. There are so few in this business. Maybe that is what I learned . . .

I didn't want to work again for a while and so I stayed at the Mill House with my garden and my love, and tended them both with care. The summer passed so quickly and soon we were in the autumn and the nights started to draw in and fires were lit for the first time and the leaves turned to gold and brown and fell, making beautiful carpets on the lawn.

One day I was going past our bedroom when I heard Shakira crying, a sound that I had never heard before. I was stunned. What had happened? I could think of nothing for her to cry about. I strolled quietly into the room and there she was sitting on the bed with tears rolling down her cheeks.

'What's the matter?' I demanded, alarmed and upset.

She looked up at me for a moment and said, 'I'm pregnant.'

My heart skipped a couple of beats, I'm sure, and jumped for joy. We were going to have a baby. 'That's great,' I said, sitting down beside her and taking her in my arms. 'So why are you crying?'

'I didn't think that you would want one,' she replied with a little laugh through her tears.

'Of course I want a baby,' I said, forgetting that I had never mentioned it and then suddenly I remembered something else that I had forgotten as well. 'Will you marry me?' I asked.

'Yes,' she said, and stopped crying. 'You're not doing it just because I'm pregnant?' she asked suspiciously.

'No,' I said truthfully. It had never occurred to me that we would ever part again. Shakira was an integral part of my life, so mentally I was already married.

So now for the ceremony. We discussed it and eventually decided that we wanted no fuss and that we would do it quietly with just a couple of close friends the next time we went to Las Vegas. The only time proviso, we both agreed, was that it had to take place before the baby was born. I had no movie coming up in America so it meant a special trip to Los Angeles which we always enjoyed anyway. Life was perfect again, for the time being at least. Neither of us had any idea of the ordeal to come. Like the fella said, 'Life is what happens while you are making your plans.'

Shakira and I settled into the Mill House for the winter and like two squirrels, began to store up for a really big Christmas that I wanted to give my family. I suppose it went back to my wartime experiences and the lack of things to buy, but I overloaded the house with every conceivable luxury and laid on everything. I particularly wanted to repay my mother for all the grim Christmases that she had lived through.

On a logistic and practical level it was a great success; the emotional side, however, was not so hot. There were rows and people ate or drank too much and got sick and the whole thing quickly fell apart. I had tried my best and my mother had a wonderful time and that was all that mattered, and I never gave an extended family Christmas party again. I was waiting for any comments that might surface on a race-prejudice level because I had recently announced that I was going to marry Shakira who, as I have said before, is Indian. There were very few and none of them serious. I waited with bated breath for my mother to come up with something but she didn't for a while, and then one day she made her only racial comment on the subject of Shakira.

I went into the lounge one Saturday morning and found her sitting watching television. I had invited her for the weekend. 'What time is it?' she asked. It was eleven o'clock in the morning and I told her so. 'Where's Sharika?' she demanded, getting her name wrong again; she never quite got it right.

'She's still asleep,' I told her. It was then that she said it. 'Indians sleep a lot, don't they?' she remarked, and that was it – her only racial comment ever.

When Shakira's mother Swabera came to visit us, she quickly became known as Saab to all of us except my mother, who was a real Mrs Malaprop and insisted on calling her Bass. We never corrected her, there was no point. I now had not only a great future wife, but the best mother-in-law a man could have. Saab was a wonderful woman who had a special Indian outlook towards the elder members of the family and made such a fuss and took such great care of my mother when she was with us that Ma became absolutely devoted to her.

I received only one comment of a racial nature from the press and that was very mild. When we were finally married, a reporter asked me why I had married an Indian woman and I told him that I hadn't – I had married a woman who turned out to be an Indian. The other question I was asked a couple of times was on the subject of us living together or 'living in sin' as one reporter put it. I pointed out to him that sin was not a fact but an *opinion* – and you can't live in an opinion. That ended that conversation. Apart from those few minor incidents, nobody has ever said anything adverse to me directly. If you could see my face when anyone brings up the question of race, you would understand why.

I now had a great piece of luck. *Sleuth* was ready for release and the studio wanted me to go to America to publicise it so we went to Los Angeles immediately after Christmas, which gave us a chance to go to Las Vegas and get married. We stayed in the Beverly Wilshire Hotel and I worked all week doing publicity and on the Friday night Shakira, my press agent in Hollywood Jerry Pam, Dennis Selinger, who had come with us to America specifically to give the bride away and pay for the wedding, and myself boarded a plane and headed for Las Vegas. Nobody knew what we were doing and we got there with our secret safe, or so we thought. When you get married in Las Vegas you have to first go to the Clark County Court and get a licence, which takes about twenty minutes, and then you can go and get married in any of a dozen little chapels dotted about the town.

As we came out of the courthouse my heart dropped. Standing there with a smile on his face was a man covered with cameras: we had been found out. He introduced himself as a local photographer and said that if we let him take the pictures of our wedding, he would give us a free set and not tell anybody else, the inference being that if we did not agree we would be smothered in local press in five minutes. None of us had brought a camera and here was a chance to get some pictures of the occasion and as we *did* want a quiet wedding, I agreed. Off we went back to town to find a place to get married. As we left I asked the photographer how he knew that we were coming to get married when not another living soul apart from those present knew what we were doing. He explained to me that his girlfriend was a hostess on our plane and she had phoned him the moment we had landed with the information that we were coming to get married. Were we that obvious, I asked. We had deliberately not talked about it on the journey in case one of the hostesses or the other passengers overheard us.

'No, she just knows by looking at people that they're coming to get married,' he explained. 'She does it all the time for me.' I suddenly realised that this was a business and she was a kind of partner. Good old Las Vegas.

We finally chose the romantically named 'Little Chapel on the Green', which owed that name to the fact that it was surrounded by a ribbon of astroturf. We showed the man in charge our licence, he put in the date, 8 January 1973, and asked us to be seated. Then he telephoned the Justice of the Peace who, he informed us, would be there in twenty minutes. During the wait the clerk addressed himself mainly to Dennis once he learned he was footing the bill. The ceremony would cost seventy-five dollars but there were extras, should we choose to have them. Would we like Polaroid pictures of the ceremony? Yes, we would. Dennis paid up. A sound tape recording of the ceremony? That, too. Dennis paid again. Would we like some orchids and a spray of flowers for the bride? Yes, please. Dennis forked out a bit more cash. The orchids came in little tiny sealed plastic vases filled with water, the significance of which became

361

clear after the ceremony. These were pinned to the gentlemen's buttonholes while Shakira was given a small spray of orchids also in a small sealed vase of water. There were no more extras so we all just sat and waited for the Justice of the Peace to arrive and listened to a tape of church-like waiting music.

Suddenly I noticed some Polaroids of former satisfied customers pinned up on the walls. Among them I recognised Tony Curtis and a couple of other Hollywood characters who had plighted their troth in this establishment, but the display did *not* inspire quite the confidence that the management had intended. I recalled that all these people were now divorced from the smiling partners in the photographs.

Finally the Justice of the Peace arrived, sweating and harassed, to inform us that Friday night was the busiest night of the week and with that, the ceremony took place. It was very short – possibly it took longer on less busy nights. The music was turned up louder as he finished, everybody kissed the bride, Polaroids were taken and then real photographs by our friend from the courthouse, and it was all over. We were given the Polaroids, and the tape of the ceremony. At this point the reason for the orchids being in water became obvious. It was suggested to Dennis that he might like to sell the flowers back to the management for half-price. This he did, but not Shakira's: she wanted to keep hers. The clerk then quietly suggested that perhaps a little tip for the Justice of the Peace would be in order and somehow by inference Dennis got the message that one for himself would not come amiss either. Dennis then gave back his refund on the orchids and added a bit for good luck. The photographer suggested a couple of pictures outside so off we went into the boiling heat and blazing lights of night-time Las Vegas. We all posed on the astroturf, he took our addresses and, promising to send us all a set of pictures, he disappeared – probably back to the courthouse to await his next victim, and leaving us all doubting that we would ever see any of his photos except in the papers. However, we were wrong. We each received a lovely set of pictures a week later.

It was all over. I was forty years old and married again, and much to my surprise, deliriously happy. As we all turned to go out of the little gate in the picket fence that opened so incongruously on to the main strip of the town, I looked up and saw something that made me roar with laughter. I had always said that I wanted a quiet wedding, that I did not want it to be turned into a circus: I had used that same phrase over and over for weeks – and now all I could see was an enormous neon sign which was flashing into the sky the words *Circus Circus, Circus Circus* – advertising the name of the casino right opposite the Chapel.

Now for the wedding party. We strolled along the strip for a half an hour looking for a good place to eat. It was too early for the big shows and in any case we wanted to catch a plane back to Los Angeles that evening so we finally settled on having our wedding meal in a big fish restaurant which had the added attraction of Louis Prima and Keely Smith as a cabaret. Dennis footed the bill for dinner, jokingly grumbling that this wedding had already cost him at least five hundred dollars, and then off we went to the airport and back to the Beverly Wilshire Hotel.

Here, unknown to us, word had got back to the management about our wedding. When we arrived, we found that we had been moved to one of the bridal suites, and I suppose because of Shakira's nationality they had put us into the Indian one, which was a very nice thought on their part, but it did create some difficulties for me. The bed was not on legs like a normal one, but suspended from the ceiling on four chains so that when you got on it, it swung with your movement. Added to this, according to the hotel's version of Indian tradition, there were four bells dangling on the bed so that the people outside the room could listen and make sure that the marriage was being consummated. This last piece of equipment seemed to have absolutely no purpose in the case of either India or ourselves. Shakira was already pregnant and in India with their population problems I should imagine that the last thing they wanted to hear was the ringing of those bells. The result of all this was that I spent the first two hours of my honeymoon night trying to get the bells off the bed before we got continuous room service running in all night.

363

Room service did, however, come in handy when I couldn't get the bells off, or stop them ringing. I ordered four hamburgers and stuffed the buns in the bells. So the newlyweds eventually drifted off into silent slumber as the bed swayed gently from the ceiling.

31

Natasha

The weekend we spent quietly in the hotel, and that was our honeymoon because immediately after that I had to go off and fly round the States on a twenty-two-city publicity tour for *Sleuth* – something that I had never done before and have never done since. On the Monday morning, Shakira and I flew to New York, me to start my tour and she to see her mother, who had now emigrated to America and lived in Queens. The main purpose of Shakira's visit, apart from telling Swabera that she had just got married, was to confess that she was pregnant – something about which she felt rather apprehensive. She rang me the next day and told me that she had taken her mother out to lunch and had finally plucked up enough courage to tell her that she was already three months' pregnant, at which her mother had just smiled and said, 'I know. I read it in *Suzy's Column* in the *New York Post* a month ago.' So much for secrecy in show business.

It was winter, and the cold once I got outside of Los Angeles was brutal but not as brutal as the mindblowing repetition of interview upon interview on the same subject, with the same answers to the same questions for days on end in different cities on a different airplane every single day until you don't know where you are, who you're talking to – and what the hell you're talking about. Add to this the fact that I was missing my new bride and was terribly homesick as I sat alone each evening in a different hotel room that was somehow exactly the same as the one that I had left the day before . . .

The tour reached its nadir in Atlanta, where I arrived on a Sunday to find out it was dry. There was only one thing to do

– go and see a movie. I got the Atlanta paper and found that *Young Winston*, the story of Churchill, was playing so I went to see that. Choked with emotion I sat and watched this very English story unfold and then suddenly I remembered that last summer the crew had filmed a scene at the Windsor Racetrack next door to me. I waited with anticipation as the scene at the races finally came around and there – behind Bob Shaw's shoulder (he was playing Churchill's father) I could actually see some of my own garden and the roof of my house! I stayed and saw the film around twice more and finally sat out what was probably the most boring day of my life.

Things could only get better, and at last my nightmare ended and I flew back to London and joined Shakira who had flown home earlier. Now that I had a real home and a family to come back to I was happier than I had ever been about returning to England and so we settled down to welcome the baby and the spring but not in that order. The baby wasn't due until July, which was an awkward date from my point of view because that was just when I was scheduled to start a new movie called *The Black Windmill* – a movie that I remember almost nothing about, because of what lay in store for us.

Spring came and went as I prepared the garden for summer and Shakira prepared the house for our new arrival, and eventually the time came and she went into labour and into a nursing home in St John's Wood in north London. Dr Bourne, a good name for an obstetrician, liked the father to be present at the birth, so I decided I would be in the room all the time. I only hoped that I wouldn't faint or do something equally stupid, a thought that returned very forcefully on the big day when they gave me my costume for the delivery room and it included a pair of white wellington boots that came halfway up my legs. How much blood was there going to be, I wondered frantically, nearly fainting at my own question, let alone the reality, but I could not back out now. I had my instructions: 'Hold Shakira's hand and push when she does.' I could not leave her in the lurch, I told myself sternly.

The labour time was seventeen hours, a lot of which I spent in the waiting room with Luisa Moore, Roger's wife. Even though she was seven months' pregnant herself, she the eternal Italian mother figure, was there to make sure everything was going well and only left when she was sure it was. I waited another few hours until around six-thirty in the evening when I was told to get dressed and come in as the birth was imminent. I put on my white smock and hat and with trembling hands the offending rubber boots and was led, Zombie-like, into the room by a nurse who obviously regarded me as a source of possible trouble.

Shakira was already in the first throes of the birth and looked as if she could manage without me if I passed out. I was led to the head of the bed and given my wife's hand and told to do my job, which was to push with her. This I did for another hour and a half with such enthusiasm that I knew I was setting myself up for a hernia or piles in later life. I had a quick look around to see which was the best direction to fall if I did keel over, and saw with some satisfaction that there was enough space quite close by on the floor that could safely contain my inert body without disturbing the proceedings if the worst came to the worst.

After a while I grew used to the atmosphere and felt that I was going to be all right. Everything was going fine. We were in time with our pushes, she would smile up at me occasionally between bouts and it was at those times that I felt so glad that I had decided to be with her. Suddenly, with a cry of enthusiasm, Gordon Bourne grabbed a pair of scissors and started to snip at something at the other end. I could not see what he was doing and it was here that my imagination ran riot and I nearly collapsed.

I was just about to stagger out when he held up one hand and in it was a lock of hair. 'It's got a lot of hair and it's black,' he announced triumphantly. Followed by, 'We're nearly there now. Just a few more pushes from the two of you,' he said, urging us on. Together we gave our final heaves and out it came, bawling its head off immediately. 'It's a girl.' I didn't care what sex it was. I was waiting for the next report. 'And she's perfect.'

I looked at my child as the doctor held her up and she was truly perfect. I almost cried with relief and happiness, as something being wrong with the baby had always been my big worry. I knelt by the side of the bed and cradled Shakira in my arms and kissed her until the nurse came and put the baby between our two faces and there she was, perfect, or so we thought. Eventually it was time for my wife and baby to rest, and so I was ordered out and went home for the night.

I left the nursing home walking on air. It was all over and Shakira and the baby were fine. I badly needed a drink. Dennis' home was nearby and I had arranged to go round and see him after it was all over, so off I went and told him all about it over a glass of wine. And then another glass of wine and then another . . . I had not realised just how stressed out I was until after a little too much to drink I started to really relax and feel great.

It was about ten o'clock that evening when the phone rang and Dennis picked it up and then gave it to me. 'It's for you.' Alarm bells went off in my head immediately. Shakira was the only person who knew that I was with Dennis. I took the phone, my hand starting to shake already, and I was right to be afraid.

It was Dr Bourne. 'There is a problem with your baby, Michael,' he said, as the bottom dropped out of my world. 'Don't panic. She is going to be all right.' I panicked instantly but kept quiet. 'We have had to move her to the intensive care unit at King's College Hospital,' he continued. 'I am there now and I want you to come over here.'

I put the phone down and ran out of the house searching for a taxi. When I arrived at the hospital I was taken into the intensive care unit, which was a big room with twenty or thirty incubators in it, each with its own tiny premature baby. This was the first thing that I did not understand. Our baby was not premature or underweight. She had been six pounds twelve ounces at birth which, although it is not large, is quite normal. I was only six pounds two ounces at birth myself. I asked the doctor about this and he told me what had happened. The night-duty nurse had been doing her rounds after everybody including himself had left, when she noticed that our baby was having difficulty in breathing. She had called him and they found that the little one's lungs had collapsed: only the nurse's quick response had saved her life.

There had been absolutely no sign of any problem before, and as Dr Bourne pointed out, I myself had heard her bawling her head off from the moment that she was born – a sure sign that her lungs were all right.

It was a problem that could be solved, he assured me, and she had a seventy per cent chance of survival. This cheered me up slightly for about ten seconds before I started to worry about the other thirty per cent. A nurse came and took me over to the incubator where our daughter lay breathing pure oxygen, surrounded by an alarming array of tubes, gauges and other instruments. The most disconcerting thing for me, however, was a monitor above the incubator which gave an audible bleep in time with each beat of my daughter's tiny heart and a visible blip of light on a screen. For me this particular instrument took on a sinister and threatening presence. This was not something that was proving that my daughter was alive, it was a mechanical signal that could stop at any moment and take her with it.

A nurse came and gave me some special antiseptic soap with which to wash my hands, and then she gave me a chair and sat me down beside our daughter. She pointed to a hole in the side of the perspex bubble that covered the incubator. 'Put your hand through there,' she said quietly, 'and you can touch her.'

I have very big hands and could not squeeze one right inside the incubator, so I put one finger through and found I could just touch the tiny hand that was nearest to me. My baby's eyes opened as we made contact and looked straight into mine. I tickled her hand for a moment and then slowly it curled round my finger and gripped it very tightly and just stayed like that. This had an extraordinary effect on me. I immediately felt less impotent. Here was something physical that I could do, that might possibly help her. It was not much, but anything was worthwhile if it made even the slightest difference. At that moment I felt a tremendous bond with her that has never left me, plus the fact that it seemed to me that she had taken some comfort and strength from our contact. Her eyes closed and she fell asleep, her tiny hand still gripping my finger.

The moment this happened, my eyes flashed to the heart monitor, but there was nothing to worry about. It was still beeping and blipping softly. I never took my eyes off that monitor for the rest of the evening, because with my darling's eyes shut it was the only way I could tell that she was still alive. I don't know how long I sat there for, but eventually a nurse came and told me that I had to go home. I slowly withdrew my finger from my daughter's hand and left quietly, with several backward looks to make sure that the monitor was still functioning and my daughter with it.

The next day things got even worse. Early in the morning I received a message that Shakira had developed some kind of complication. Although it was not serious she was really quite sick and as she did not know about the baby's condition, I decided not to tell her until it was absolutely necessary. I moved in with Dennis who lived near the nursing home where Shakira was, and spent the next two weeks dashing from one side of London to the other as Shakira and the baby both started to get better. I eventually had to tell my wife what had happened because as her health improved she demanded to see the baby. The little one was fortunately out of danger by the time I had to explain what had happened. It had been an absolute nightmare for me and the real tower of strength was my friend Dennis, who stood by me as I came and went to and from his home at all hours of the day and night in all sorts of emotional and irrational states. Never once did he complain or leave me alone when I needed someone to talk to. He was there for me all the time – a true friend. I know this is what friends are supposed to do but I think you'll agree that many people you thought of as friends tend to disappear just when you need them most. Dennis was there for me the whole time.

As I sat there for the two weeks holding hands with my daughter I became so impressed with the courage and professionalism of the nurses in this particular ward. The care that they lavished on these tiny tots was quite extra-ordinary. It must be one of the most difficult types of nursing because your patients are so small and helpless and you know that you are going to lose a percentage of them no matter how hard you strive. I was talking to one of the nurses one day, when I had got up to go for a walk round the ward to stretch my legs, and I asked her how they dealt with the losses. She told me that they gave all the babies silly names deliberately (none of them had names yet anyway) and the favourite names were those of the Seven Dwarfs. While I was there I had often heard nurses talking about 'Grumpy' or 'Sleepy' or 'Dopey' – and had never understood why. Apparently, with silly names like that it hurt the nurses less when they lost one; it was their way of dealing with the pain.

I often think of those girls and the job that they do, when I see the spoiled and pampered members of my own profession going into temper tantrums because a newspaper has published an unflattering picture of them, or some other equally ludicrous crisis to do with their massive egos and sense of self-importance. For me, the greatest actor in the world comes way below the most junior nurse in that ward or any ward like it anywhere. So to all my peers and colleagues I would just like to remind them that we are no big deal really, but we *are fun* – which is not unimportant, so we do have a right to be here.

Shakira recovered first and was released from the nursing home, and a little while later the baby, who was now called Natasha, joined us in the haven of the Mill House. During this period I had started to film *The Black Windmill*, but as I said before, it all passed in rather a blur. My close shave with both of my ladies had bonded us into a tight family unit. Being with Shakira at the birth had brought us even closer. I had thought this impossible, but I was learning all the time that there are no limits to love. The emotional link that had been forged with Natasha during those long days in the hospital was quite extraordinary. Both of these bondings were deeper than I could ever have imagined and, as I now know, were permanent.

I had chosen the name Natasha as a Christian name and Shakira, who is a Moslem, chose her other name of Halima, which means wisdom. This way, we figured, with a Christian name and a Moslem one, when she grew up she could choose which religion she wanted, if any, and would have a name for either of them.

After a few weeks at home with us Natasha progressed very quickly and was soon back to normal. I had been worried that there might be some after-effects of her experience, but our doctor assured me that there would not be, and he was right. It is now nineteen years later and everything has worked fine for her.

Winter finally came and was a bitter one, so for the first time in my life I chose to do a film for convenience rather than quality. I was offered a part in *The Marseilles Contract* (known in the US as *The Destructors*) and took it because it was being shot in the comparative warmth of the south of France and I wanted to get the family, especially Natasha, out of England for the worst couple of months. The picture, incidentally, turned out to be a flop, but I didn't care. We had a wonderful time and it was good for our baby. I always try to get my priorities right.

32

Gucci shoes

I am not a political animal, but I am a human being and although I had not known much about apartheid when I started *Zulu* in South Africa, I knew a lot about it when I finished. My abhorrence of this system lay dormant for many years – as it did for most of the world – until a chance came for me to do something concrete about it. The film was called *The Wilby Conspiracy*. While it was set in South Africa, we were not allowed to shoot in that country because the theme of that film was anti-apartheid.

My co-star was Sidney Poitier, whose hatred of apartheid was predictable – and very real. This film was my first foray into that very risky realm of 'message' pictures, and as such proved to be a bit ahead of its time, but I am still proud that I made it anyway.

The first thing I noticed when we reached Kenya was that Sidney was not only a wonderful actor, a movie star and, as it turned out, a great friend, but in Kenya he was also a god. Everywhere he went he was treated with awed respect. Something else I noticed was that nobody there had the faintest idea who *I* was. My first inkling of this was at the airport in Nairobi when we landed. I stood in the hall with Shakira and Natasha and all our bags looking around for the person who had been sent to meet us when finally I noticed a white man who seemed to be looking for someone. I went up and stood right in front of him, but before I could open my mouth he walked straight by me and went up to a little old fat man with a bald head and asked him if he was Michael Caine.

My fame had obviously not spread to Africa, but I remembered the advice from my old repertory producer:

'Use the difficulty.' Great, I thought. Here was my first chance in years to walk down any street without being asked for autographs or bothered by people wanting to talk to me or have their picture taken with me. It would be wonderful to be anonymous for a while. Or so I thought, but after the last few years and the sort of fame I had enjoyed, I soon started to get paranoid, imagining that I had sunk into obscurity. The public indifference also reminded me of my early years as an actor, a period that I wanted to forget forever. My paranoia was particularly prevalent when I was anywhere near Sidney, for he was always surrounded by fans and/or journalists, and when we were both in restaurants at the same time, Sidney would be at the best table while I would find myself at the one by the kitchen door.

This was again a very happy picture to work on. We were living in the Kenya Safari Club, which is a luxurious private club situated in a breathtaking site at the foot of Mount Kenya. We had a beautiful bungalow in a huge communal garden, with Sidney and his wife Joanna as our next-door neighbours, and Nicol Williamson and his then wife Jill with their small baby. It was paradise again. I used to sit there every evening looking out at the great mountain and wait for something to go wrong, but it never did. The work went well and we continued to feel that for once we were doing something worthwhile. A great friendship developed between Shakira and myself and Sidney and his wife – two of the nicest people that I ever met in show business.

Sidney was also given the final accolade in Kenya at that time: he was invited to an audience with the president, Jomo Kenyatta. It was a great and rare honour, he was informed, and he was rightly proud of it. The big day came and Sidney was whisked off by air to Nairobi and the famous meeting. All day long we waited impatiently for his return to get the low-down on the big occasion. In the evening his plane returned and we waited for him in the small airfield. Sidney got out of the plane and walked towards us with a slight look of disappointment on his face. When we asked him eagerly what had happened, 'He asked me what I did for a living,' Sidney said and strode on by as miffed as Sidney ever gets, which isn't very. I at least felt a little better after that about being unknown here.

We in the so-called civilised world do not realise just how far we have retreated from what should be our natural state. This is a subject to which I must confess *I* had not given much thought either, until something happened in Kenya which brought it home to me. Shakira and I had gone to a party one evening in a car driven by a Kikuyu driver. The Kikuyu are the main native population of Kenya. On this particular evening we were a long time at the party and when we came out at about two o'clock in the morning, we found our driver, who had waited for us all evening, fast asleep in the car. I shook him to wake him up, but he did not move. I shook him again and nothing happened. Everybody had a go at waking him up and still we could not rouse him. It gradually dawned on us that he was dead.

A doctor was called, an Englishman who had been born in Kenya. He eventually arrived, obviously annoyed at being woken up at this time in the morning. We waited for him to pronounce the man dead and possibly give us the cause of his mysterious demise. Shakira and I had been in close contact with him in the confined space of the car for quite some time that evening. We had all heard horror stories in Africa of diseases unknown to science striking people down for no particular reason. My first thought of course was, was it infectious? Or had his local witch doctor put a spell on him for some indiscretion? We had heard those stories as well . . .

The doctor finished examining the body and turned to me and yelled, 'What the bloody hell do you think you are doing, getting me out of bed at this time of night to attend to a man who is fast asleep?' I stood there shocked for a moment. I, and others, had felt for the man's pulse and heartbeat and found none, a fact I immediately communicated to the irate doctor. 'Feel again,' he said, taking my hand and placing it on the driver's chest. For a moment I could feel nothing, and then eventually I felt a low thump and then after a few seconds another one and then another on in a regular pattern, but it was beating slower than I thought could have been possible with the owner still alive.

'There you are, you see!' the doctor snarled at me again. 'He's just bloody well asleep.'

'Why isn't he dead with a heartbeat that slow?' I enquired.

'His heartbeat isn't slow. It's how all our heartbeats are supposed to be when we are asleep, except that we all live a "civilised" life in stinking cities with noise, stress and our water and air filled with chemicals and we take pills to make us sleep.' The lecture went on for a bit and then the doc left, with the parting shot that nothing would wake the man until he was good and ready so we had better get another driver.

So that was the secret, I mused as I watched the medic drive away into the night. I looked at my driver and thought, 'If only I could sleep like that . . .' but of course I never would. *I* was civilised.

On this trip I fell in love with Africa and Kenya in particular. The vastness and the savage beauty of it all was so different from my native England, a small and gentle land. The values of the people were different as well, to say the least. The Masai for instance believe that flies are the spirit of their dead ancestors and therefore never kill them. They just let them walk all over themselves and more dangerously, their babies. Being just about the only nation in the world that does not kill flies, the news had obviously got around the fly world because the place was smothered with them, with millions more recipients of the good news arriving every day, or so it seemed. It occurred to me one day while visiting a Masai village that this notion about flies and ancestors could have been dreamed up thousands of years ago; possibly some bright elder had watched his villagers fight a losing battle against this neverending plague and decided to invent the story so that they no longer had to spend so much time killing flies and could get on with more important stuff like standing on one leg all day – which a lot of the young men seemed to do. At first I thought this posture was quite useless, until I found out what the Masai initiation ceremony was for young warriors: they prove their manhood by killing a lion on their own, armed with just a spear. I subsequently felt that some of the participants in this rite might well need to know how to stand on one leg for extremely long periods. Nothing in Africa is without its purpose, if you look deep enough.

There was something else that I noticed about the Masai warriors. As a matter of fact it was very difficult *not* to notice. Their clothing consisted mainly of a sheet of animal skin, draped over their shoulder and hung down their front in a vain effort to conceal their private parts. It was not so much that the sheets were small that made concealment impossible, but that what they were trying to conceal was so large. Never slow to miss an opportunity for self-improvement, I enquired about the diet of these people and I have bad news for all male vegetarians: their meals consist almost entirely of oxblood and cows' milk. I must add quickly here that I am *not* a vegetarian – but I was toying with the idea until I met the Masai men.

Filming for the most part is great fun and, as on this occasion, sometimes a delight, but even at the best of times you can never afford to relax. There is always danger somewhere and it comes as it did with Sidney and myself on this particular day, right out of the blue. We had to do a travelling shot in a jeep, just him and me, going very fast along a rough track and as there was no room for the crew and no dialogue, they strapped a camera on the front of the jeep and had us turn it on ourselves and just drive for a while. Sidney was at the wheel and I was sitting next to him, and as it was supposed to be a chase he got us up to a very high speed and we were jolting about when suddenly the camera, which must have weighed at least fifty pounds, broke loose from its straps and tore through the small space between our heads, miraculously without touching either of us. It went like a massive bullet, and if it had hit either one of us, our heads would have been crushed to pulp. Sidney and I took several days to get over the shock of our near-deaths, and this incident brought us both down to earth with rather more than a bump.

Although we shared many lighter moments, I always sensed in Sidney that he was forging a bond with Africa. One afternoon, during a break in filming, I was leaning against an old hangar on the grass airstrip, smoking a cigar and watching the impressive figure of Sidney at the end of the short runway silhouetted against Mount Kenya. Over the top of the mountain a large black cloud was advancing bringing with it rain. Sidney looked up, saw it and snapped out of his reverie. He started walking back towards me and as he passed I said, 'Feeling your roots, Sidney?'

He smiled for a moment. 'They don't go through Gucci shoes, Michael.'

As he walked away, looking at the man, I knew that he was wrong. They had.

The animals of Africa are a particular delight. To me, camels are ugly and nasty, all of them, but in Kenya I saw a Somali camel that was actually nice and beautiful. It had straight silken blonde hair and big brown sad eyes with long eyelashes, and was actually very sexy. I remember thinking at the time that if Marilyn Monroe had been a camel she would have been a Somali.

There is a beautiful little deer in Kenya called the Dik Dik, which we always loved to see jumping around the plains. However, when we booked into the sumptuous Norfolk Hotel in Nairobi and all rushed down at Sunday lunchtime to sample their world-famous buffet of fifty different kinds of curry – all labelled – and the first label read '*Curried Dik Dik*', it was hamburgers and french fries all round. There was an enormous tame eagle owl in another restaurant on an island somewhere who had only one eye, but he looked as if he was wearing a pair of big brown-rimmed spectacles. Coincidentally, at the same time I was wearing big brown-rimmed spectacles, and every time I went to eat at this place he would come and sit opposite me and stare at me all through the meal. It was very disconcerting at first, this dangerous-looking bird the size of an eagle just sitting there fixing me with his one eye, but I learned to like him and looked forward to seeing him there. I tried to guess what he was thinking when he looked at me, and I decided he had concluded that I was another owl of a different species.

One day, I asked the owner how the bird had lost his eye and he said, 'I will not tell you how, I will *show* you how,' and took me out to a garden at the back of the restaurant where he had a small menagerie full of little animals. On one side there was a glass case with a large wicked-looking snake in it. 'This is the spitting cobra,' he informed me. 'Put your face up against the glass.' I did as he asked and waited. The snake uncoiled, drew its head back and struck with lightning speed. I jerked my head back involuntarily and there, on the glass right where my left eye had been, a glob of poisonous venom was now slowly rolling down. '*That* is how my owl lost his eye,' said the owner proudly.

'Are there many of these snakes about?' I asked faintly.

'Quite a few,' he replied casually.

On another occasion I stayed at a hotel on an island where the owner had a similar sense of fun. To get to this place they put me and my cases in a flimsy canoe which seemed to clear the water by about an inch and as we were starting to leave the small dock, the owner inexplicably shouted, 'Lulu!' I looked up at him standing there, thinking that he had gone raving mad when suddenly the water by my elbow parted with a great rush and the head of a hippopotamus with its great jaws wide open broke the surface. It was a terrifying experience and I thought that my end had come until I saw the owner laughing down at me. 'It's all right,' he roared. 'She's only a pet. She wants her tongue tickled,' and he was right. This great hippo was just lolling there with her tongue out, so I tickled it, which she obviously enjoyed because she seemed to laugh right into my face and as I reeled from the rush of foetid breath that hit my face, she sank slowly back into the depths ready to terrify the next unsuspecting customer.

The island was a delight and full of formerly wild but now tame animals. We all stayed in little native huts with communal toilets, which were to be my undoing. In the middle of my last night on the island, I got up to go for a pee and in the dark I fell over a sleeping buffalo. The only way I can describe what happened next is to ask you to imagine that you are in an earthquake that has horns and a temper to match. As I tripped I draped myself over its back. It leapt to its feet in a terror only marginally less severe than my own, and with horns tossing at an invisible foe it tore off through the garden, dumping me in true slapstick form into a very thorny plant, of which Africa I might add is also full. The next day it was time to go home and the thought of my quiet Mill House at Windsor had never been so attractive . . .

Back in London we completed the film at Pinewood Studios without any noteworthy incident, but something that was to prove of enormous significance in my future did occur, as these things sometimes do, without anyone noticing it or attaching any importance to it at the time.

During the course of filming in London, Sidney and Joanna and Shakira and myself would go out to dinner a couple of times a week. When I was the host it was always to a different restaurant, but when Sidney was in charge, for some reason that I never fathomed, he would only take us to eat at one particular restaurant called Odins, situated in Devonshire Street just off the Marylebone High Street. Odins was a very beautiful restaurant and the food was wonderful, so although it was the same place every time, we did not really mind.

One evening after we had eaten there a couple of times, a short tubby man came in on his own, clearly very much the worse for alcohol. He spotted Sidney immediately and came reeling over to our table. He slobbered 'Hello,' over Sidney and Joanna, whom he obviously knew very well, and then stood there, his head rocking as he tried to focus on whether he knew Shakira and me, which he didn't.

'This is the owner of this restaurant, Peter Langan,' Sidney said with a smile at the look of astonishment on my face as this last bit of information sunk in, 'and this is Shakira and Michael Caine.'

Langan stood there for a moment as this information finally took hold and then stumbled over to me, holding the back of my chair for support. 'Michael Caine,' he repeated, and then found what he was looking for.

'Sidney told me that you wanted to open a restaurant.'

'He's right,' I said. I did want to open a restaurant in London that would be a big noisy brasserie like La Coupole in Paris, but I didn't volunteer this last piece of information, in case he stole my idea.

'Well, when you do,' he said, bending over me and breathing into my face a mixture of what I rightly diagnosed as banana Daiquiri, expensive champagne and Chinese take-away food, 'get in touch with me, kid' – he always called me kid, even though I was at least ten years older than he – 'and I'll be your partner.' With that he heaved himself off the back of my chair and weaved his way to the back of the restaurant and out of sight, much to our collective relief.

'Is he really the owner of this place?' I asked Sidney.

'Yes,' he said, 'and he is also a very good cook.'

'Is he always that drunk?' I asked.

'I don't know,' said Sidney kindly. 'But I have never seen him when he wasn't.'

I sat there and thought for a moment and finally came up with one of my usual great statements. 'I'll tell you one thing,' I said. 'If I ever do open a restaurant, he would be the last person I would take as a partner.' This pronouncement either comes under the heading of 'famous last words' or 'never say never', because I did eventually go into partnership with this man and I made more money through my investment with him than with any other, but more of that later.

I always get slightly annoyed when I read things about myself in the press that have been written by lazy journalists who have no knowledge of me, have never bothered to interview me yet who make assumptions about me.

At around this time, mild annoyance turned to fury when my press agent sent me a cutting of an American article by the feminist journalist Gloria Steinem. I remembered her writing an article on me for the *New York Times* many years before after a brief lunch together. This new article made me see red because it not only attacked me, it attacked my wife Shakira. What Steinem actually wrote was, and I quote: *'Michael Caine is only attracted to subservient women and now he has found one.'* This statement is not only completely uninformed but I found it the most offensive, patronising and condescending thing ever written about me and what is more important, an ignorant and hurtful criticism of my wife.

In her book *The Golden Thread* the Indian lady writer

Zerbanoo Gifford wrote the following about Miss Steinem's statement: *'Feminist journalist Gloria Steinem wrote in one of her articles, "Michael Caine is only attracted to subservient women and now he has found one", meaning his wife Shakira. Shakira has her own flourishing business and a happy marriage, despite living amid the lurid life of show business, accomplishments of which any person could be proud. To infer that she is a nameless doormat is hurtful as well as untrue, yet Shakira's reaction was simply to think how sad it was to think like that. So often it appears that women who claim to fight to liberate others become substitute authorities, judging by their own criteria the "true role" of women. Shakira's choice to value her husband and daughter ahead of her own ambition was not a means by which to deny herself personal satisfaction, but one through which to gain it. The blind spots of certain Western feminists might make them unable to perceive that fulfilment can be gained through the giving of self as well as the promotion of self.'*

Long before Miss Steinem made her snide comment about Shakira and myself, I had started to get uncomfortable with the direction in which the women's liberation movement was going. Suddenly we started reading statements like: 'Why should women have to stay in the home and face the drudgery of housework and bringing up small children?' Those chores, I readily agree, are no bed of roses, but this attitude is, I think, a product of an educated middle-class woman's point of view; her life certainly might seem dire in contrast to her husband's, who may be out all day meeting interesting people, having wonderful business lunches and possibly intercourse, too, with gorgeous secretaries on the side. If you are the wife of an ordinary worker, say in a steel mill, a coalmine or car factory, or working in agriculture in all weathers, the prospect of staying at home and looking after the baby sounds rather more attractive. And please reflect on this: for every lone woman going out into the masculine world and making it (which should be the right of every woman without prejudice from men), there is usually some other woman – from an ethnic minority or a lower class – doing their housework for them.

What I have against the Ms Steinems of this world is that

they seem to be preaching that this 'emancipation' is the *only* acceptable course for women.

So many times I have heard feminists ask why it is necessary for the woman and not the man to stay at home with the children, and the answer to that one seems obvious to me: a mother's breasts produce the milk on which babies used to feed before infant formulas and vanity took its place. My last, equally heartfelt disagreement with some members of the radical feminist movement concerns their claims that all men are potential rapists. I certainly resent this, as I am sure would most other men. What women like this do not understand, is that most *men* are seeking affection and understanding just as desperately as their female counterparts, and would never *ever* contemplate attacking a woman for sex. As with most normal people of either sex, there has to be mutual attraction.

Please, Ms Steinem, don't attack my wife or me again because I shall never write another autobiography and so will not have the platform to reply.

Apart from the upsetting article by Steinem, our lives returned to the bliss of living in the paradise at the Mill House. Natasha was well and growing fast and Shakira and I, who had thought that we were deeply in love when we got married, were surprised and delighted to find that as we came to know each other more and more, our love for each other deepened, a process I might add that has continued with a few minor blips right up to this day. I immediately got a movie in England, which was great because we had travelled a lot since our marriage and it gave us a chance to settle down for a while.

It was called *The Romantic Englishwoman* and was my first (and hopefully last) foray into the realms of 'artistic films'. If for nothing else, this film should go down in film history as one of the monumental examples of *triple* miscasting! Glenda Jackson was to play my lovelorn and romantic wife, Helmut Berger the insatiable seducer of women and I a wimpish husband who stood by and did nothing while his wife was being unfaithful right before his eyes.

The film was not only very convoluted it was also

downright grim, but I decided to do it because of the director, Joe Losey, who had a tremendous reputation for being 'artistic', but better than that, had made a couple of pictures that had actually produced a profit without being discarded by the critics. One of them was a favourite of mine – *The Servant*. Joe seemed to be a very nice man on our first meeting, but he also had a rather grim face and outlook on life. On the first day of shooting I bet one of the crew ten pounds that I could make Joe laugh before the end of the film – and I lost my money.

To add to the festivities, Helmut and Glenda seemed to hate each other at first sight. Nobody knew why and they never said, but I had a theory that he secretly wanted to play her part. My off-stage role immediately became that of roving ambassador between the realms of Jackson and Berger, because they both seemed to like me and I liked them. So there I stayed, stuck between them like the Channel between England and France. Although I was not present at the shooting of their love scenes together, when I saw them later it was apparent that Glenda and Helmut had been very professional; however, I did detect a small lack of sparkle and chemistry between them. My own short love scene with Glenda did not fare a great deal better, not because of any emotional thing, as we got on well and to say the least she is a brilliant actress. But she did one disconcerting thing just before the take where I was to make love to her.

We were in bed and we had just got everything right and were ready to turn the camera over when she said, 'Stop! I've forgotten something,' and reached under her pillow, pulled out a little piece of toilet paper rolled up in a ball and proceeded to unravel it under the rapt and mystified gaze of myself and the entire camera crew. Slowly, a small sliver of false tooth was revealed. Glenda slipped it into her mouth, filling a gap between her teeth that I had never noticed before. 'Ready,' she said, with a wider smile than any of us had hitherto witnessed. *'Action'* – was shouted and we went into our passionate clinch with the same lack of fire and chemistry that had dogged her scenes with Helmut – but for different reasons.

Glenda is now the Member of Parliament for Hampstead in north London, and it has just dawned on me that I have made love to an MP and a Socialist one at that. There's no business like show business.

While we're on the subject of love scenes, I dislike doing them intensely. Especially directly after lunch when the leading lady has just had garlic salad.

Love scenes that require any nudity at all for the actress are always tense. No matter how uninhibited they think they are, when it comes to it they're not. Take Julie Walters for instance, who when she had to do a nude scene, conned the whole shooting unit into taking their clothes off as well, by telling them it was a new Equity ruling. On my own picture, *Blue Ice*, Sean Young had to do a short nude scene and made all the crew strip down to their underpants.

My dislike of nude scenes is personal. The first asset I or any other actor has in movies is his eyes. If you're naked, no one will be looking at them. The second asset is his voice, but no one will be listening either because they'll all be discussing what's on display – which in the case of a man can be much smaller than normal on account of nerves and therefore can give a false impression.

Simulated love scenes are not as sexy as you think, because both the man and woman wear a form of padded cod-piece to avoid genital contact. The sum total of all this is that for the artists and the crew the filming of this type of sequence develops into nerve-wracking chaos while the audience loses all track of the story. So the next time you see me making love on screen to a beautiful naked woman, I hope I'll have your sympathy.

The only actress I ever met who was not shy at all during her nude scene was Glenda in *The Romantic Englishwoman*. She reacted throughout as if she had been fully clothed. As a matter of fact, I was more embarrassed than she was, which I suppose says more about my uptight attitude than it does about her. But with or without clothes she was an extraordinary actress to work with and I'm glad that I did the film, if only for that reason.

The Romantic Englishwoman not only flopped financially,

but the critics didn't like it much either, which was very ungrateful of them since we only seemed to have made it for them in the first place. While we are on the subject of critics, I would like to make a couple of observations. Early in my career, I once wondered who became a critic in the first place. In my days in repertory, after receiving a particularly brutal savaging from the local paper, using it seemed, direct quotes from the Marquis de Sade, I set out for the pub where the journalists hung out and located the drama critic. He turned out to be a spotty youth all of nineteen years old who explained to me that he had been forced to review our show because he had been late into work that week more times than any other reporter. This, he further enlightened me, was the normal criterion applied in choosing the critics to review our shows. I know of course that many critics are consummate professionals but whenever I get a bad review I remember that lad and feel more cheerful.

An idyllic summer then passed in the Mill House as I gardened myself literally into the ground and became a lifelong fanatic of this peculiarly English obsession. Comes the first sound of the cuckoo, which coincidentally I heard about an hour ago as I was writing here, and the urge to go out and buy new plants gradually overtakes me. It is doing that, now, but I daren't go. I have a deadline with this book and I now know why it is called a deadline – it's killing me.

We were so confident about the Mill House now that we had started to entertain. One week for instance we had a group of people down for Sunday lunch, which is my favourite time for entertaining in the country. Peter Sellers came with his girlfriend Liza Minnelli, and her father the director Vincent Minnelli came with his companion Kay Thompson, the Broadway musical comedy star. Jack Jones the singer was there with his then fiancée Susan George, and my agent Dennis made up the group. It was a wonderful Sunday. Peter and Liza were obviously very much in love as were Jack and Susan, and not least of all so were Shakira and myself. Natasha, who was then two, decided to show Liza how to dance, and Liza returned the compliment so well that Natasha, now aged nineteen, is a great dancer even though she does it to music that I do not like or understand, but as she has said so often – that's *my* problem! Peter was always the one among us to have the very latest electronic invention. This week's gadget was the Polaroid camera. We all took pictures of each other and although the technique was familiar to me from my wedding, they gasped in astonishment as the snaps developed before their eyes. I remember one particular photograph that I took of just Liza and Peter together, which I gave to Peter. It was Liza's birthday on the following Tuesday and the party was going to be at Rex Harrison's apartment in Wilton Crescent in London, because Rex also had a birthday around that time. We all split up on the Sunday and looked forward to meeting again at the party.

Tuesday evening came and off we went to Wilton Crescent to enjoy the evening, but when we got there a big surprise was waiting for us. In the past twenty-four hours, Peter and Liza had split up and Liza was almost in tears for most of the evening, obviously very upset but managing to control herself for the sake of the rest of us. At one stage she got me in a corner and showed me the photograph of them that I had taken.

'Turn it over and look at the back,' she said. I did, and there on the back was written: *'Thanks for the memory, Peter.'*

Later in the evening I helped myself to food from the buffet and as I went towards one of the dining tables with my food I noticed a familiar face, but not someone whom I knew personally. It was a woman who was past middle age but had obviously once been very beautiful. The table was discreetly lit by candles – at her request, I later discovered. She was or had been a big star, I knew that, but with the combination of the candlelight and the champagne I couldn't think who it was. She looked up and smiled at me and gestured for me to come and sit in the empty seat next to her. As I slid into the chair at her side I nearly dropped my plate. It was Marlene Dietrich.

'Is your name Michael Caine?' she asked, rather sharply. What have I done, I thought, and said aloud, 'Yes.'

'Are you a good friend of Peter Sellers?'

'Yes, I am,' I replied.

'Will you be seeing him soon?'

387

'Next week,' I mumbled.

She suddenly sat up straight in the chair and fixed her incredible eyes on me as I sat there like a rabbit trapped in headlights. 'Well, tell him from me when you see him that I think he is a rotten bastard for the way he has treated my beautiful Liza.' I mumbled a promise that I would do this and started to eat my food. 'Why do you have friends like this?' she asked suddenly.

'He has always been very nice to me,' I protested through a mouthful of food. Although I knew that she was a virulent anti-Nazi during the war, the combination of the German accent and the cold blue eyes lit only by spluttering candles gave me the feeling that I was being interrogated by the Gestapo.

I half-expected her to say, 'Ve haff vays off making you talk,' but instead she said, 'She is my god-daughter, you know.'

I was now wolfing down my food so that I could escape to the next course at another table, and as I finished and was leaving her, she gave me one parting shot. 'You should dress better when you come to a party,' she yelled. 'You look like a bum.'

So that was the end of my brief relationship with the divine Marlene – and the end of a very long weekend.

33

The Man Who Would Be King

Shakira and I have spent mini-honeymoons in Paris, usually over a long weekend every three or four months. It is always the same – very simple and completely sybaritic. We eat in all the best restaurants, stay in a luxury hotel, dance all night and sleep all day and spend all our time just with each other and that's it.

At this particular time we were staying in the Hotel George Cinq. As I sat up in bed having my first coffee of the day, the phone went and a voice that I immediately recognised but could not place, asked, 'Is that Michael Caine?'

'Yes,' I replied.

'This is John Huston.' I nearly dropped the phone! Here I was, speaking to the one director whom I actually idolised. I couldn't say anything for a moment. 'Michael,' he said after a few seconds.

'Yes, Mr Huston,' I choked.

'Call me John,' he drawled. 'I am in the Hotel Prince de Galles next door to you. Could you come over and see me for a few minutes this morning?'

'Yes, I'll be there in ten minutes,' I said, a little too quickly.

'That will be just fine. I'll be in the bar,' he said, and rang off.

I sat there, stunned. Could this be a job he wanted to talk about? It must be, for what other reason would he want to see me? We didn't know each other. Of all the directors in the world, he was the one with whom I would most like to work. All these thoughts rushed through my head as I scrambled out of bed, washed, shaved and dressed and got myself to the lobby of the Prince de Galle in eight minutes flat. It was about eleven o'clock in the morning and the place was empty, and as I entered the bar a voice called, 'Over here, Michael,' and there he was sitting at the counter, a cigar in one hand and a glass of vodka in the other.

He had white hair and a white beard separated by smiling blue eyes that looked as though they had seen it all and decided that it was OK anyway. He looked like God after a bad night out, and after I heard his voice in real life for the first time I always thought that if we ever heard God speak, that was exactly how He would sound.

'Hello,' he said, stretching out his hand.

'A great pleasure, John,' I whispered.

'What'll you have?' he asked, pointing to his own drink.

It was too early really but I thought – what the hell? I'm never going to meet John Huston for the first time again. 'A large vodka,' I said nonchalantly. A broad smile with a hint of relief spread across his face. I had passed the first test. I was obviously a man after his own heart. And so began a friendship that was to last until his death a few years ago.

My vodka came, we touched glasses without a word and both downed a slug. He watched me to see if I could take it, but I was experienced at this stuff and didn't flinch. I felt as though I had passed another test when his face broke into a satisfied smile.

'Now let me tell you what this is all about,' he said, settling himself comfortably on the bar. 'For twenty years now I have been trying to make a film of a short story by Rudyard Kipling called *The Man Who Would Be King*. I had it all set up at one time a couple of years ago. As a matter of fact I was sitting in this very bar when I brought together the two stars I was going to use.' He paused for dramatic effect and took a swig of vodka.

I couldn't resist. 'Who were they?'

'Clark Gable and Humphrey Bogart,' he replied with a smile. 'We had it all set up and then they both went and died on me, and what's more, it would have been the first time that they had worked together,' he added wistfully. I waited for a while to see where I was going to figure in this. I was intimidated by these two names and could not imagine myself

Above: Shakira and me with Paul Challen (left) and my brother Stanley (right) in Las Vegas, 1971.

Our wedding in Las Vegas, 8 January, 1973.

The remains of the Olongapo patrol, *Too Late the Hero*.

Hollywood veterans: From left to right, Fred MacMurray, Shakira and me, June Haver, Irwin and Sheila Allen.

Sean Connery, Joe Louis, me and John Huston in Los Angeles, 1980.

John Huston and me on *The Man Who Would Be King*.

The four-legged chicken hits home. From left to right, me, our host, Holmes Tuttle, Her Majesty the Queen, Tony Richardson and Nancy Reagan.

Above: The two James Bonds and me. Circa 1983.

Above: Shakira and Natasha, my favourite picture.

With Jackie Collins and Shakira, my two Hollywood wives. Circa 1985.

Above: We lost the game, but I won an Oscar anyway. Los Angeles 1987.
Below: Irving and Mary Lazar at their 1989 hot Oscar party at Spago.

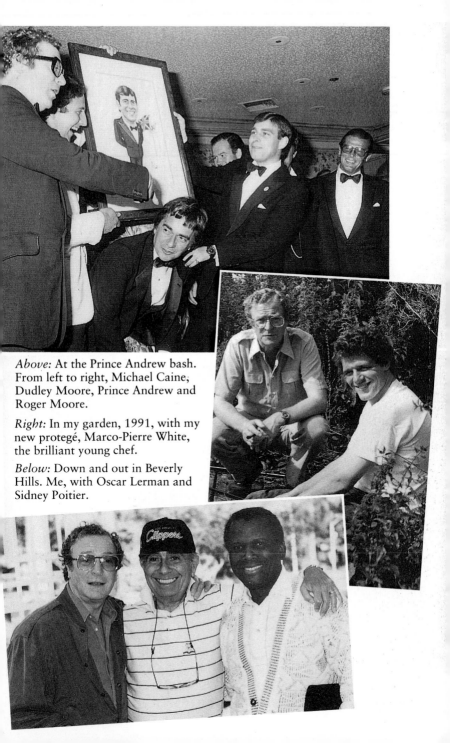

Above: At the Prince Andrew bash. From left to right, Michael Caine; Dudley Moore, Prince Andrew and Roger Moore.

Right: In my garden, 1991, with my new protegé, Marco-Pierre White, the brilliant young chef.

Below: Down and out in Beverly Hills. Me, with Oscar Lerman and Sidney Poitier.

Dominique's wedding with all the trimmings.

Below: My two girls – Niki and Natasha.

being associated with any project that was to have involved such legends as Bogart and Gable. Finally he said, 'We have now got the backing for the movie and I want you to play a character called Peachy Carnehan.'

Instead of saying, 'Thank you,' or 'I'll read the script,' I found myself blurting out, 'What part was Bogart going to play?'

'Peachy Carnehan,' John replied, knowing he'd got me.

'I'll do it,' I said suddenly.

'Don't you want to read the script?' he asked, surprised.

'John,' I said. 'With you directing, a story by Rudyard Kipling and a part that Bogart was going to play, what have I got to lose?'

'I hope you're right,' he replied laconically. 'Do you know the story?'

'No,' I said.

'Well, read it. It's very short. As a matter of fact it is so short that we have had to add from other writings of Kipling to make a full-length movie out of it, but every word is from Kipling. The other leading character – they are best friends in the movie,' he went on, 'is called Daniel Dravot, the part that Gable was going to play.'

'Who do you want to play that?' I asked with bated breath, hoping that it would be an actor I liked.

'Sean Connery,' he replied.

This was great. I told John that I would shortly be going back to London and he said he would send me the script there and we would have a read-through in a couple of weeks' time.

I said goodbye and then rushed back to the George Cinq and told Shakira the great news. She was as delighted as I was and little did she know at the time that there would be something in it for her as well. She then had to go and meet some ladies for lunch and as I was not invited I walked the streets of Paris alone once again as I had done so many times before, but this time with joy in my heart and a spring in my step. I loved this city, I thought. It had always been lucky for me even in times of great despair. I rambled along the great boulevards for a couple of hours no longer dreaming the impossible dream but *living it*. I remembered how, as a boy,

391

my impossible dream had been to become an actor. In a Huston film I had seen called *The Treasure of the Sierra Madre*, a bunch of misfits were looking for gold, which was their impossible dream, and in it I had identified with the Bogart character, the 'nobody' trying to become a 'somebody' – that was me. Now here I was playing a part that was meant for Bogart and even in this story, Peachy and Danny were two British Army sergeants in India, who set out on their own quest to become the kings of an ancient realm of fabulous wealth called Kafiristan. I was *doing* the impossible dream – making a film with Huston – *about* an impossible dream, and it was all coming true. Paris was really lucky for me.

The Man Who Would Be King was shot in Morocco, and our base was a beautiful old French colonial hotel called the Mamounia in the city of Marrakesh. This was a favourite hotel of Winston Churchill and I was put into the suite that he had always used. Much to my surprise it was a very modest suite but very comfortable and with a great view over the hotel gardens, which were magnificent, towards the Atlas Mountains. To cap it all there was a painting on the wall by Churchill of the view out of the window, and from what I could see, it had not changed a bit since he had painted it.

I soon learned that the way of life in this north African society was very different from our own and that we'd all have to adapt – or go nuts. It started with my bath that evening. As I was sitting there I noticed that two tiles had come unstuck from the bathroom wall and had been neatly placed, unbroken, beneath the soapdish. I reported this to the management, who promised to have it fixed within the hour. Of course it was not fixed within the hour nor within the day, the week or the month, in spite of my regular reminders. As a matter of fact I went back to the same hotel three years later and at my request was given the same suite. The moment that I walked in, without unpacking or doing anything else, I rushed into the bathroom and there they were – the two unbroken tiles still placed neatly under the soapdish. I hasten to add that this was all a very long time ago and the Mamounia is now under new management and is one of the most efficient luxury hotels in the world.

Another example of the time-frame difference between the Eastern and Western mind occurred one day when Sean was driving me back from location in his van. My car had lost its windscreen on the road and he had picked me up to take me back to Marrakesh. On the way we saw a very old man with a large load moving slowly along the road so we stopped to give him a lift. It was obvious that he was making for the market in Marrakesh. We drew up in the van and I asked him in French to join us and he told me no, because that meant he would get there two days earlier than he had done for the last forty years, and he would not know what to do with the extra time in the city. Also, he added, the people that he knew along the route would miss him and as he was very old they would think that he was dead and that would cause unnecessary sorrow so, all in all he went on, it would be better if he did not accept a ride and left life just as it always was. The logic, though not typical for a Westerner, was after a little thought unmistakeably correct and a lesson for us all. Time is not something that is passing but something to be spent – wisely, of course.

So we all settled into the Mamounia and began to prepare to start shooting. Christopher Plummer arrived. I had played Horatio to his Hamlet on television a few years before and he was an old friend of mine. He was to play Kipling himself who featured in the story, probably truthfully, as a newspaper correspondent. Oswald Morris and his camera crew were next. This pleased me particularly, as they were the crew who had shot *Sleuth* and I knew them very well and got on with them. The camera crew and sound boom operator are very important for a movie actor. They are always the nearest people to you when you are acting, so it is necessary to have good vibrations around you. Also on the unit and a complete surprise to me was our first assistant director whose name was Bert Batt. I knew him well as he had been the first assistant on *Zulu*. It's a small world, is show business. Shakira also met someone who impressed her very much. She has a great interest in fashion and design and she became very close friends with our designer, the great Hollywood mistress of this profession, Edith Head. John Foreman the producer was there, of course – a wonderful guy, something you can't say of a lot of producers, so we were in luck because along with Huston you could not ask for better people at the top, and as the saying goes, 'A fish goes rotten from the head down.'

John Foreman was also something that you need on all movies – a hypochondriac. He had the most wondrous bag of medicines with him at all times and saved at least my sanity if not my life on a couple of occasions.

John Huston's wife Cee Cee would join him later, we were informed, and he arrived with a Mexican maid whom Cee Cee had sent along to look after him. John had come from Mexico, where he now lived permanently. Also with John was a small plump middle-aged lady with glasses whose name was Gladys Hill. I thought at first that she was his secretary, but I could not have been more wrong. Gladys was his almost-silent partner in his writing and as I watched them together I realised that she was an indispensable part of John's career as a writer-director, a very important partner in his life and not at all the self-effacing little assistant that she would have us believe. So there we all were, ready to go . . .

The night before we started shooting we were all having dinner in the hotel dining room when John Huston dropped the bombshell that the girl who was to play the part of the beautiful Indian princess was no longer available: we had to re-cast immediately. The question was, where could we find someone at such short notice to play the part?

My wife Shakira was sitting there innocently eating her dinner when she must have felt the atmosphere change, because she suddenly looked up to find us all staring at her. She cottoned on immediately and said very firmly, 'I am not going to play the part.'

John put on his most charming smile, winked at me and said, 'We'll talk about it in the morning, honey,' and we all continued eating.

The next day, Shakira came out to the location to watch the start of shooting. During the course of the morning John had a moment free and he took her aside for a while and they both came back all smiles. John announced that Shakira had agreed to be our Princess Roxanne. I was very surprised at this because I had spent the night before trying to talk her into playing it but with no success. The old charmer, however, had done it again.

For me, the first three days of shooting were murder. I do not like make-up at the best of times, but in the opening scenes of this picture I had to have a face that had been terribly scarred. It took two hours to put all this on, which meant that I had to get up very early which I also hate. Getting up late is the only good thing about being unemployed. The make-up was really uncomfortable to wear, and what with the heat it kept melting and had to be redone. Unfortunately, when those first three miserable days were over and the rushes were sent back to London, we received a message that it was not satisfactory and I had to go through the nightmare process all over again.

Whatever else happened on the film though, one thing was certain – John was a joy to work with. He did what very few directors ever do with actors. He left you alone to get on with it until he saw a basic flaw, and then he had the rare ability to put you back on the right track with the minimum of words and fuss. For instance, I was doing a long speech on the second day when suddenly he stopped the take. I hadn't made a mistake and could not understand why he had stopped the shot. 'What's wrong, John?' I asked, and he replied: 'You can speak faster, Peachy. He's an honest man.' With that one sentence he had explained my character in a nutshell. You will also notice that he called me Peachy and not Michael. Once we started to play the parts, John only ever addressed Sean and myself as Daniel and Peachy. This lasted all through the film and for months after it.

The only other time he stopped me on a take was in a scene with Christopher Plummer. I had to tell him of our plans and his reply was that it was very dangerous. In response to this I had the line: 'We are not little men,' which I said with the accent on the word 'not'. John cut the shot and asked me to say the line with the accent on the word 'little'. I did it his way and when we cut the shot I looked over at him. He was smiling, the inference being obvious, that we were all big men around here, and it was true – we all seemed to increase in stature as we worked with him.

Eventually we moved to our biggest set, which was the temple of a secret religious sect on whom we had stumbled during the course of our adventures. John had wanted to cast a local Moroccan actor in the part of the High Priest but he still hadn't found one and it was nearly time to start shooting. The problem with all the actors so far was that they looked too modern and sophisticated. What he wanted, he told me, was the natural look of someone who had spent a hard life in the mountains and showed it. The scenes we were shooting took place in the Atlas Mountains which are very beautiful but would be very rough to live in. His casting as usual was perfect and a complete surprise.

One morning we were all on the set very early for a 'dawn shot', and as we all sat there waiting in the cold half-light for the sun to peek over the horizon, a little old local man came strolling by, carrying a little bag and a long sort of shepherd's crook. He looked to be about a hundred years old, with a face that his years and the sun had dried to almost parchment.

'Who is that old man?' John yelled to one of the assistants.

'He's the nightwatchman and he is just going home,' came the reply.

'Stop him! I want to talk to him!' John shouted back. He went for a walk with the little old man and the interpreter, and came back a few minutes later to announce that we had found the High Priest, and he was right on the button. If you have ever seen the film you'll know that the old man was perfect because he possessed two qualities that many of us lose early in the so-called civilised Western world – innocence and dignity.

His innocence almost became his undoing as well. After four days of shooting it became obvious that the old man was really exhausted. When asked what was wrong, he told the interpreter that he was not getting any sleep because as well as working on the film all day, he was being the nightwatchman all night. No one had thought to tell him that he did not have to do both things any more, and out of a sense of loyalty to his post he had carried on with it: a reversal of the old theatrical saying, 'Don't give up your day job.'

John's other great task with someone who had not acted before was of course with Shakira. She was a little nervous when the time came for her to start work, but I on the other hand was so concerned for her that I was almost a basket-case and in actual fact was so nervous that John barred me from the set on the days that she worked in scenes in which I did not appear with her. I need not have worried. Shakira was surprisingly good naturally, and of course working with John she came out of the whole thing looking absolutely marvellous and what is more important, very real. There was one difficult scene that she had to do that I knew John had improvised. The day before we had shot a scene with some Berber women dancing and one of them had suddenly gone into a cross between a fit and a trance. He obviously picked up on this and had Shakira's character do the same thing. It was a difficult scene even for a professional actress, but with John's help it turned out fine. I was very proud of her. When she had finished her part I asked Shakira if she would like to become a professional actress. The answer was a very firm 'No.' There was from this, however, a very important benefit to our marriage. My wife had now done my job and knew what pressures and stress were part and parcel of it, so now when I do come home from the set a bit exhausted, she does know why and what I am talking about. I know that it is impossible, but I have always thought what a great boon to all marriages it would be if that could happen.

Working with Sean was a real pleasure. I had rarely worked with any actor who was so unselfish and generous, so much so that you could experiment and take chances and not expect to find a knife in your back if it went wrong. We did all sorts of improvisations which are less easy in films than in the theatre because of the technology involved, but it was all done in a completely relaxed atmosphere, because John trusted us and we trusted each other. It is rare to do a long dialogue scene in a film where your fellow actor will turn you full face to the camera for your important line, and you return the compliment, but this is what Sean and I did with complete ease all through the film, and I like to think that our personal relationship and trust came through on screen and helped the picture. Sean is also the consummate professional – which is the highest compliment that I can pay him. The scene in the picture where we march in and are given a sharp rebuke for our behaviour by the Governor of the Province was completely unscripted and improvised on the set by Sean and myself. A little scene of which we are both very proud.

Life back at the hotel went on as usual, with its little ups and downs. Sean for some obscure reason moved to another hotel round the corner and tried to talk me into going with him. I went round to his suite for a drink and to inspect the new hotel, but I didn't like it. I think that my mind was made up when he ordered a drink for the pair of us and when the waiter came with them and knocked on the door, everyone along the corridor shouted, 'Come in.' I had lived in too many fleapit hotels with thin walls to want to stay awake again all night listening to the sexual successes or failures of my fellow human beings, so I stayed on at the Mamounia. This was not without its pitfalls, either, however.

There was a middle-aged American couple who drank quite a lot and when they were in their cups the wife would always get the idea that I was Peter Finch and pester me for my autograph. I always insisted that I was not him and refuse to sign, at which the woman would go back to her seat and have a few more drinks and the husband would get pissed off at me as he too imbibed, until it was time for them to go to dinner. As he passed me on the way out he would always say, 'I think it's Mickey fucking Rooney,' or on another night it would be, 'Donald fucking Duck,' and so on night after night with different names each time, which was OK so long as my guests were sitting there to witness the whole performance. It was sometimes very disconcerting for those who arrived late to suddenly see a drunk American looking at me and yelling, 'I think it's Bela fucking Lugosi.' Never complain and never explain became my motto.

For a few weeks now we had all been looking forward to meeting John's wife Cee Cee. Her arrival date kept being put off, however, until she became built up in all our minds as some mythical figment of John's imagination. Eventually, one evening as we were all sitting in the lobby having a drink after work, he came down from his room to announce that Cee Cee had finally arrived. A great air of expectancy and curiosity descended on the group, but she had apparently gone to the Souk or local bazaar, and would be here shortly, we were informed. We all sat patiently sipping our drinks with half an eye on the front door of the lobby, waiting for this legendary figure to appear, which she finally did when the front door burst inwards with such force that it almost came off its hinges and a woman roared through the lobby.

'Over here, sweetheart,' yelled John.

She stopped for a moment and surveyed our group, and then yelled at us, 'The Souk sucks!' There was silence for a moment as the legend, now with slightly clay feet, proceeded upstairs and disappeared. We all turned and looked at John, who smiled back and said, 'That's my wife Cee Cee.' We never saw a lot of her, as she didn't visit the set at all but she did join us for another three nights to inform us consecutively that 'The Mamounia sucks', then that 'Marrakesh sucks', and finally 'Morocco sucks' and the following day she flew back to California and out of our lives forever. Although we did not know it at the time, it was out of John's as well. I later learned that he had divorced her and married the Mexican maid who was actually looking after him.

Marriage was also in the air for Sean. He was and is a fanatical golfer, but even for him the preoccupation with the game seemed obsessive until we found out why. He had met a lovely Frenchwoman on the golf course and she had become the obsession. Her name was Micheline and she became and still remains Mrs Connery.

The work continued apace with me suffering from my usual dysentery, thanks to the buffet at the Mamounia, held on Sundays by the pool with the food laid out for the flies to sample before we got to it. Again I hasten to add that this does not happen nowadays. With the new management, the food is covered in refrigerated displays. The direct result of my condition was that most of my physical scenes in the picture were done through gritted teeth, with one eye on the shortest route to the 'honey wagon' – the special toilet truck that travels with you on all locations. My first act of every day's shooting was to ascertain the exact location of this vehicle, which in some situations took on an aura of paradise. The guy who looked after it had a very novel idea of hygiene. One day I went rushing over to it in a grave state of emergency, only to find that the entire truck was covered with the thickest cloud of flies I had ever seen and the stench was incredible. The attendant was sitting reading the paper. 'Why haven't you used any disinfectant today?' I yelled at him.

'I forgot it,' he replied calmly. 'I left it in Marrakesh and it is too far to go back for it.'

I was furious and desperate. 'It's impossible for anybody to go in there,' I screamed at him. Suddenly I saw a brilliant idea glide across his face.

'Why don't you come back at lunchtime?' he suggested. 'All the flies will be in the kitchen then.' The logic was inescapable and I held on till lunchtime and he was quite right.

We finished the scenes on the big temple set and around Marrakesh, and then it was time for us to cross the Atlas Mountains and go down to a town called Ouarzazate on the edge of the Sahara Desert. Up until now the film had been physically very hard, but nothing could have prepared us for Ouarzazate. It was basically a camel stop with a couple of fleapit hotels and bars and amazingly, a discothèque. It was boiling hot in the daytime and freezing cold at night. The place had dirt roads and dirt air, as the wind blew off the desert and whipped up a mixture of dust, sand and dried camel-shit. This last item or ingredient may sound amusing or improbable, but it was no laughing matter. It made the smog in Los Angeles seem like the air in a Swiss sanatorium, and it was actually very dangerous, as I was to find out. The diseases you could catch from breathing in this filth were diverse, and in my short time there I got around to most of them, ranging from the severest sinus headache it is possible to imagine, to infected eyes and throat, right through to a mild attack of typhoid. I say mild because I had been injected against it before I came, but it got me anyway. Now a mild typhoid attack is very insidious. You don't know you've got it until you wake up one morning, get out of bed and then go flying round the room with your entire sense of balance gone, and when I say gone I mean it. It is so severe that of course your first instinct is to sit on the floor, but you are so unbalanced that you cannot even fall over. I went reeling round the room for what seemed like for ever until I was accidentally bounced back on my bed where I hung on as the bed turned on its side and eventually upside down with me yelling for help which eventually came in the form of the hotel doctor and a very worried John Foreman. They shot around me for a couple of days and I was soon fit enough to go back to work, but I was still suffering from the sinus and an eye infection. These problems were taken care of by Foreman with the aid of his little bag of Beverly Hills medicines the British National Health Service probably did not even know existed, let alone possessed. I remember him coming into my room after work one particularly bad day with some large multi-coloured capsules wrapped in a Kleenex.

'Take one of these every four hours,' he said, as though he had just created the dosage.

'What are they?' I asked.

'Never mind, but just make sure that there is at least four hours between doses.'

Alarmed, I said, 'Why, are they dangerous?'

'Trust me,' he said soothingly, which instantly alarmed me even more because it is well-known in Hollywood that if anyone says those words, you should immediately reach behind you and take the knife out of your back.

'All right,' I said, 'what colour do I take first?'

'It doesn't matter,' he said quickly, and my confidence waned.

'If it doesn't matter,' I asked suspiciously, 'why do they make them all different colours in the first place?'

He thought rapidly. 'It's a marketing device,' he said airily, and made for the door where he turned and added 'good luck,' with his peculiar humourless chuckle, which always sounded as if he was rubbing his hands together even when he wasn't.

I lay there thinking to myself that I was going to die anyway so I might as well take the pills. I took the first one and passed instantly into a state of complete euphoria for the three days that the pills lasted. I woke up in the middle of the night with a smile on my face and listened to the jackals going through the garbage cans outside my window and snuggled back to sleep in a state of bliss. I went to work treading on air. Shakira came and pronounced me the nicest that she had ever known me since we got married, and spoke of finding a permanent source of the tablets. Natasha, who was only a toddler, had been left at the Mamounia with the nanny for the two days that she would be in Ouarzazate, a good idea considering what had been happening to me. Wherever I went Foreman would keep checking on me, but strangely he never asked me how I was feeling. I only realised after it was all over that all he was worried about was whether I was still alive! My recovery was complete and I never got sick again while I was in Morocco. I never asked Foreman either what those pills actually were . . .

A few days later, Sean came to my room in the evening and suggested that we check out the local discothèque. Shakira had done her little stint at that location and had fled back to Marrakesh so I was free and off we went, having no idea what a disco in this terrible place would be like. I was amazed that one even existed. It turned out to be a seedy café with a jukebox and a bar that did not serve alcohol. Devout Moslems do not drink it and all the customers were men. Devout Moslems do not allow their women to go out to discos or many other places, come to think of it. We stayed for a while and listened to the music and downed Coke after Coke as we watched the men dance with each other. The effect of this was not at all like a gay club. There was no romance or touching, it looked just like a load of butch guys dancing with each other because there were no girls. There was one suspect couple in a dark corner but we will ignore them.

After the fourth or fifth Coke, the atmosphere and the rhythm of a rock and roll record that was at least ten years old, started to get to Sean and I could see that he wanted to dance. Our two Moroccan drivers were with us in the disco and they were both getting into the mood of the evening, but I could see that Sean was eyeing my driver as a potential partner and the reason was because his own driver was not very attractive. Not to put too fine a point on it, he was downright ugly. He had a broken nose, and no front teeth and breath that would make a camel flinch. My driver was sitting there obviously dreading the thought that Sean was going to ask him to dance, when suddenly it all got too much for Sean.

'Do you mind if I dance with your driver?' he asked politely.

'Not at all,' I replied and off they went. Sean's driver was about to ask me to take the floor but I pre-empted this by limping out to the toilet. So another riotous evening of fun in Ouarzazate came to an end.

One day we had to go out into the desert from Ouarzazate to a new location. Sean and I went on ahead of the main column in a car which, right in the middle of nowhere, broke down. We were stuck on the road for an hour or so until the main unit caught up and rescued us. We sat there for a while talking to pass the time when our driver asked us if we had ever been in the desert before. Neither of us had so we told him so. He then asked us to get out of the car because he wanted to show us something. We both got out and stood there, with nothing to see but desert in every direction, right to the horizon. We seemed to be marooned on a small island of tarmac in the middle of an ocean of sand.

'Stand still and don't make a noise,' said our driver mysteriously, 'and listen.'

We stood there, Sean and I, for a few moments, puzzled at what we were supposed to hear.

'I always do this with Westerners when they come to the desert for the first time,' he told us. 'Stand still and keep quiet, and you will for the first time in your lives hear the sound of complete silence.' We both stood there for a while and all we could hear was the sound of our own blood pumping through our ears and then gradually, even this sound faded and there it was – complete and utter silence. We stood there for a long time and let it wash over us; it gave us a strange, relaxed feeling, almost like taking a drug.

Eventually Sean broke the silence, and in a very simple way he summed up the different attitudes between the Easterner and the Westerner towards time and distance: 'I can see now why no Arab has ever won a hundred yard sprint in any international competition.'

'Why is that, Sean?' I asked, accustomed to the very shrewd pronouncements on the human condition that he occasionally passed on to the rest of us.

'Because if you said to an Arab, can you run from here to there,' pointing to a spot a hundred yards away, 'he would say to you – why should I, because it is exactly the same over there as it is here, and I have got all day to get there anyway.'

Sean is a very logical man, and there was no escaping the logic in this statement. I think he summed it all up beautifully.

Although *The Man Who Would Be King* was a hard film to make physically, it was a very happy experience, due mainly to the friendship that developed between Huston, Foreman, Chris Plummer, Sean and myself. At the end of the shoot we knew that, even if we had been so before, we were no longer 'little men'. There was, however, one sad postscript: the dancers and musicians whom we used in this picture were from a special tribe called the Blue Berbers, and they lived high up in the Atlas Mountains, out of contact with the rest of the community. We had to send trucks to bring them down to the relative civilisation of Ouarzazate. Even the local Moroccans were curious to see these people. They had only ever heard about them and many people believed that they did not exist at all, so for them it was a bit like seeing a legend. In the eight weeks that they worked for us the Blue Berbers grew used to the so-called joys of civilisation. They listened to the radio, saw television, ate what was for them good food, and slept in real beds in warm rooms for the first time in their lives. This was all too much for them and at the end of the film they refused to go back to the harsh conditions of life in the mountains. The last we heard of them was that the Moroccan army had had to be brought out to force them to return to their native territory.

This saddened us all tremendously and made me wonder whether the sudden surge of work and money that movie units have for years been bringing to the poorest of people in Third World countries has always been the great benefit that I fondly imagined it to be. I hope and believe that in most cases it was. Incidentally, in poor countries when a movie unit is packing up, a little ritual takes place in which the continuity girl suddenly becomes the focus of attention for all the local workers. The reason for this is because she has the only Polaroid camera on the unit. This is essential for the locals to get a reference to work on the next unit to arrive. My driver came to me one day, dragging the continuity girl with him and posed beside me for a Polaroid photograph to be taken by her. This was not done for vanity but as proof that he had truly worked for me. On the back I wrote a glowing reference for him to show to the next production manager to come his way. That is how the poorest of the world's peoples get their jobs.

The last scene that we shot in *The Man Who Would Be King* was the one in which the religious sect who have captured us, execute Sean by making him stand in the middle of a rope bridge over a deep ravine, and cutting the ropes to send him plunging to his death hundreds of feet below. The bridge was a very unstable affair, handmade by the locals, and I had come there the day before with Sean to have a look at it. I had only managed to get a little way out on the swaying bridge before vertigo overtook me and I retreated to the safety of the top of the ravine. Sean had gone out further than me, but then of course he was the one who was going to have to do the scene. However, even he did not manage to get right to the middle as the bridge swayed dangerously in the wind. So, finally, there we were ready to shoot the scene and Sean had to go right out to the middle of the bridge this time. We were all quite tense, particularly Sean of course, and even John was a little worried I could see – not a customary emotion for him, being a man of immense personal courage.

There was a long silence as we all surveyed the swaying and suddenly flimsy-looking structure. This silence was suddenly broken by Sean. 'I was here yesterday and the bridge looked OK,' he said with some trepidation, 'but today it seems to be leaning over to the right.'

John looked at Sean for a moment, a twinkle in his eye. 'The bridge is exactly as it was yesterday, Sean,' he said. 'The difference today is that you have to walk out on it, so you're looking at it from a different point of view.' Sean glanced at

John for a moment, accepted the challenge in his eyes and without a moment's hesitation walked straight out to the middle of the bridge. In this scene, Sean has to sing as the priest cuts the ropes and this he did as the first phony ropes were cut and then he came off the bridge, visibly relieved. His place was taken by a wonderful, really experienced British stuntman called Joe Powell, who was going to do the actual drop when the ropes were cut.

I looked over the edge of the ravine and a couple of hundred feet below I could see the mound of boxes and mattresses that were to break his fall: it looked about the size of a postage stamp. With the wind blowing and the bridge swaying as the axes cut the real ropes holding it, we all stood there watching, frozen with nerves as it dawned on us that to leap off this moving platform and hit the target so far below was an almost impossible task. My heart was thumping as I watched and I wanted to shout out and stop the stunt, but the final rope split, the bridge collapsed and down Joe went, hurtling towards the jagged rocks below, manoeuvring himself all the time as he plummeted and as the wind tried to drag him on to the rocks. At the very last minute, he straightened himself out and hit the centre of the mattresses. An audible sigh of relief went up, immediately followed by a great cheer as we saw Joe get up uninjured and make his way towards his assistants at the side of the mattresses. John was not an impressionable man, nor one given to easy compliments, but at that moment he turned to me and said, 'That is the darnedest stunt that I ever saw.'

The film was finished and I instantly felt a tremendous pride that I had been in it. And I was right – I think that *The Man Who Would Be King* is one of the finest films in which I have ever appeared, and one that I think will last long, long after I am gone.

34

Biting the customers

The most glorious summer I ever spent in all the years that I owned the Mill House was in 1976. On the opening day of Wimbledon the temperature was 110 degrees on the centre court, and I had got a movie in England on location in a place called Mapledurham, an even more beautiful spot on the River Thames than my own, and just fifteen minutes upriver.

The film was called *The Eagle Has Landed* – the story of a band of German Commandos who were sent to England during the war to assassinate Winston Churchill. The cast was marvellous: my old friend Donald Sutherland, the brilliant American actor, Robert Duvall, Donald Pleasence, Anthony Quayle, Jean Marsh from *Upstairs Downstairs* and an American actor who was eventually to become world famous as JR in *Dallas* – Larry Hagman. Considering that he now gets very angry if anyone smokes in his presence and carries a small electric fan in restaurants to point at people who are smoking, you may be surprised to know that on this picture he was chainsmoking cigars. The producers Jack Wiener and David Niven Junior were old friends of mine, so with long hot sunny days on the bank of the Thames, life was perfect. Treat Williams made his movie debut in the picture and lovely Jenny Agutter was the romantic interest.

The summer was great, as were the actors, and location . . . everything was fine, or almost. The picture was being directed by the Hollywood old-timer John Sturges, who has just died, and we were all very pleased that this illustrious veteran had agreed to direct our film. That is, until one day when I was talking to him between set-ups and he informed me that now he was older, he only ever worked to get the money to go fishing, which was his passion. Deep-sea fishing off Baja, California, he added, which was very expensive. The moment the picture finished he took the money and went. Jack Wiener later told me that he never came back for the editing nor for any of the other post-production sessions that are where a director does some of his most important work. The picture wasn't bad, but I still get angry when I think of what it could have been with the right director. We had committed the old European sin of being impressed by someone just because he came from Hollywood.

Robert Duvall is a brilliant actor and eventually won an Academy Award but although he was a nice man and easy to work with, I always sensed that he had a very short fuse, and I was right. One day we were at a different location for a short time in Cornwall, which is famous for lobsters, and as lunchtime approached we were informed that they had just brought in six fresh ones and so we all reserved one each. Came lunchtime, we all got our lobster except Robert, who was informed that his had been given mistakenly to someone else. 'That's OK,' he replied calmly, then walked over to the pub door and punched out the glass panel with his bare fist.

A small blot was beginning to form on my horizon around this time. It was destined to grow bigger and bigger until it engulfed my life in England, but I was not taking too much notice yet. Ever since the first day of shooting on *The Ipcress File*, when Harold Wilson became the Socialist Prime Minister of Britain and during the ensuing years when I started to make good money, the Socialists had been in government for most of the time and had brought in really punitive tax rates for those of us who were in the Super-Tax bracket. Not being a political animal myself, nor for that matter being someone who was used to having large amounts of money, I had not taken a great deal of notice of what was actually happening to me. I was happy, I seemed to be rich – what could go wrong? The answer was a lot. My accountants had for a long time been trying to persuade me to do the unthinkable and leave my country – a prospect I did not even consider. If only I had listened to them then! Some of the actors I knew who were shrewder than me and less sentimental about living in England had long since departed, including Sean Connery, Richard Harris, Richard Burton, Rex Harrison, James Mason, Julie Andrews and now even Roger Moore. I was beginning to feel that if I left I would have to turn out the lights, but still I stayed on, purely out of an emotional attachment to my country. Meanwhile, the government took eighty-two per cent of my earnings and reviled me and my kind for being a success. Anyway, I forgot about all this for a while and went on with my life.

I plunged into all sorts of projects. I had finally been granted planning permission for an extension to the Mill House, a process that had taken a couple of years. The delay was due mainly to a concerted attack by the middle-class local council against me, a vulgar, nouveau-riche upstart movie star with no taste, who was sure to ruin this gem of historic British architecture! The fact that the garden was a dump when I bought the place and the house had needed repairs costing thousands of pounds just to keep it standing (which I had happily spent) seemed to be ignored in this class-conscious community.

Once the permission was through I started to build and ignored the locals completely for the rest of my time there; of course then I was attacked in the local press for being snobbish and standoffish. There was, however, tremendous support for me among the poorer people in the area. I remember one Christmas a knock came at the door and there stood two of my neighbours, delivering an enormous Christmas card with five hundred signatures on it stating that they were on my side in my battle with the council. They had put a sixpenny stamp on the bottom and asked a lawyer to sign over it which meant, in England, that it could be used as a legal document if it came to a battle with the planning authority. I was deeply moved.

A little bit of racism also reared its ugly head when we first moved in. One evening the doorbell rang and my wife Shakira answered it. 'I must see Mr Caine urgently,' the male visitor said, handing her his coat and hat, obviously under the impression that she was the maid. She pointed through to the living room where I could be seen advancing toward the front door. 'Mr Caine,' he said, his hand outstretched. 'What a pleasure,' and then he introduced himself. 'Can I have a word in private?' He indicated the presence of Shakira.

'Certainly,' I said, and took him into my office.

Once inside with the door shut, he said conspiratorially, 'I didn't want to speak in front of *her*.'

'What's the problem?' I asked warily, certain now that there was one.

'There is a house for sale in this street,' he began, 'and I know that it is about to be bought by an Indian.' He paused for a moment to let the full horror of this sink in, and when I didn't respond he continued, 'and you know what will happen if one of *them* gets in, don't you?'

'No – what?' I replied.

'The whole street will go. Once you get them in you never get them out again!'

I opened the office door and guided him out. 'If you think it will be difficult getting them out of the street once they are in, imagine my problem,' I said, walking with him into the living room where Shakira was now sat watching television, much to his surprise. 'This is my wife,' I told him. 'Once you get them in the house, you can never get them out.' He fled, grabbing his coat on the way out and I never saw him again.

Another project that I plunged into was buying the right of way that went along the back of my garden and through which horses passed on race days to the adjacent Windsor Race-track. I have a passion for privacy and this invasion every race day really made me mad, even though I had known about it before buying the place. I had imagined that it would just be for horses and jockeys, but members of the public used to sneak through, too, some for the short cut and others because it was my garden and they were curious. On race days I used to be out there in a rage even before anything happened, turning back people who had no right to use the path. It was a trivial matter, I know, but it really used to upset me. One day, I nearly had apoplexy when I saw someone actually driving a Range Rover across my land. I went storming over to it and was just about to give the driver an obscene volley of vituperation when I caught the eye of the passenger, a lady in

410

a headscarf who was sitting there smiling. I bit back the words just in time and with a flourish and a bow, allowed Her Majesty Queen Elizabeth II to pass though my humble garden and there and then made the decision to buy back the right of way before I wound up in the Tower of London!

Up in town one day I ran into Peter Langan again and almost didn't recognise him, as he was sober. We had a cup of coffee together and he asked me if I was still serious about opening a restaurant. I was about to shrug it off when something told me not to. The difference now that he was sober was surprising. Here was an extremely serious, well-educated, charming Irishman, with a great deal of successful experience in the restaurant business.

'Yes, I am,' I said, knowing that I was letting myself in for a harrowing experience, once he was back on the booze. He was not drinking at the moment, he told me, because he had a bet with someone that he could give it up for a month.

It seemed to be a good risk to go into business with him at the time, and so it turned out. Years later, whenever I used to criticise his drinking he would always reply by asking me to name anyone else with whom I had made so much money for such a small investment. I couldn't.

'I'll be in touch when I have found some premises,' he said as we finished our coffee. 'Is it a deal?'

'A deal,' I said, and shook his hand. What had I let myself in for, I wondered as I watched him walk away. 'When do you finish your month of no drinking?' I shouted after him.'

'Tomorrow,' he yelled back.

When I met up with Peter Langan once again, he not only wanted to open the restaurant, but had found the ideal premises. How he had accomplished this was something of a mystery, since he was blind drunk and judging by his suit, which was always white, or a sort of dull cream on this occasion, he had obviously been sleeping in it for several days. After a while I became expert at identifying where he had slept the night before, as he could never remember himself. On this occasion everything pointed to the rubbish tip outside the Ritz, as it was being refurbished at this time using a particular shade of blue paint that also featured rather

411

noticeably on Peter's suit in a series of footprints across his back!

We sat in the lobby of the Ritz to have our business meeting. The only reason he had been allowed in was the fact that he was wearing a tie: I never ever saw him without one. He always wore red braces to keep up his decidedly dodgy trousers and two-tone shoes, brown and white. Just the sort of man my father had warned me about all those years ago, and here I was going into business with him. Through an alcoholic haze, he outlined his plan. He had taken on the lease of a very well-known 'society' restaurant called the Coq D'Or, one of those very old restaurants which had enjoyed a great reputation before the war with the upper crust, but now the crust was on its uppers and its time had run out.

My share, it turned out, would be a third of the action and the price was twenty-five thousand pounds. I sat there for a moment staring across the table at this sad, inebriated Irishman, the last person on earth with whom you would choose to do business, and for some unknown reason I said, 'OK Peter, I am in.' There was no reply – he was asleep. I woke him up and repeated my promise and off we went, very unsteadily, to view the premises. Fortunately they were just across the road from the Ritz, in Stratton Street, Mayfair.

At first sight, the restaurant was very unpromising. It consisted of a long narrow, L-shaped room, absolutely enormous, and decorated with a deep-red flock wallpaper. To counteract its great size, the room had been divided into five sections with phony walls, in order to make it seem like five cosy little restaurants – a disaster. I also noticed a couple of trolleys that had been used for flambé-ing food – always a dead giveaway in a restaurant as far as I was concerned. If the chef was so good, why were the waiters doing the cooking? I strolled through the premises, my heart sinking at just how many changes there would need to be, and I turned to Peter to give voice to my misgivings, only to find him fast asleep on the floor behind me. Yet I still had faith in him, and was proved right.

We went ahead. Peter designed the place himself. He tore down the partitions and opened it all up so that there were no corners, and everybody could see everybody else at all times. This was one of my provisos, based on my expertise as a customer. A restaurant, especially a big one, should be a spectacle where you are the show when you come in and the audience when you sit down, so you must be able to see everything. One feature of the Coq D'Or that I liked was its windows. I had a theory that you would never get anyone in for lunch if you could not see daylight.

Peter tore up all the dirty old carpet and just left the wooden floor, and he painted the walls an attractively warm, dull-orange colour that looked as if it had been there for years. He then covered the wall space with paintings of all different types in a completely random fashion, giving the impression that they had been collected over a long period of time. All of this made our spanking new restaurant look comfortably old and well-established. When he brought in some lovely old lights from Paris, none of them matching, he listened to my one piece of advice that at no time should anybody be able to see a light-bulb. We lit the tables from the ceiling with spotlights containing silver-coloured bulbs, so you did not look into a light even if you happened to glance up, yet the tables were still well-illuminated. By the time we opened, our restaurant looked as if it had been there for ever, and it had that most elusive and essential of all ingredients – *ambience*.

Langan's Brasserie opened very quietly on a Monday night with just a few friends and passers-by who happened to come in, and everything went very smoothly.

We had taken on a very good chef who came from Alsace. The only problem with his dishes, which originated from that area, were that they are designed for farm labourers, people who have toiled in the fields all day, and there we were serving this stuff to secretaries and typists. Hence, although the food was good the waste was incredible, but word soon got round that the most enormous meals were available with us at a reasonable price. On the second night we were full and on the third night, diners were standing in line in the street and we actually did the unthinkable – we ran out of food!

So there we were, off and running, and our restaurant

immediately became *the* place to be seen, not only for the food, but for reasons not unconnected with Peter's behaviour – which very quickly became celebrated in all the gossip columns. His favourite ploy, I discovered, was to go up to the most nubile of female customers and say, 'Show us your tits!' – not very original, but if you are drunk you can get away with anything. Mind you, one of the girls did one day – and he ran away. Another of Peter's foibles was to get under the table and bite the lady's leg. Of course, we lost a lot of customers that way but the publicity made up for it. At one time people used to come merely to be insulted by him. This kind of thing is fine when you're opening a restaurant but it is no way to build a long-term business.

After we had been open for a couple of years, Richard Shepherd, the chef we had wanted originally but who was under contract elsewhere, became free and we made him a partner. He was responsible for turning Langan's into the prosperous business that it still is today. Richard is a great chef and a brilliant administrator, and it is to him that the restaurant owes its success, not the antics of Peter as the British press wrongly believed.

35

The Swarm attacks

My next acting role required a short trip of five days to Holland, where I was to play a guest shot in Richard Attenborough's film about the courageous but futile attack by British paratroopers on the bridge at Arnhem in World War Two. It was good money for very little work, but I did wonder at the time where the market for such an expensive film would be. Although the battle was fought bravely and with honour, it was after all a defeat.

My acting role, meanwhile, was proving somewhat embarrassing. For the very first time in my career I was playing a real person who was actually present on the set as a technical adviser during the whole time that I was working. Lieutenant Colonel Joe Vandeleur was the Commander of the tank column that had tried to rescue the paratroopers trapped at the bridge at Arnhem. He soon put me at my ease, however, when at the end of the first day I asked him how he felt about the way I was playing him. 'You are taller than I am and funnier,' was his reply, so I guess he was satisfied.

The only other thing I remember about my short involvement with this film is my very first shot, when Dickie Attenborough played a rotten trick on me. In the real battle, Colonel Vandeleur had been leading his tank column when he was ambushed by the Germans. In order to recreate this same element of surprise, Dickie had placed me in my scout car at the head of a column of tanks, and asked everyone to keep quiet about what was going to happen. There was a camera on me, of course, as we rolled film, and I stood in the conning tower of my car, waiting in blissful ignorance for Dickie to shout, 'Action!' This he duly did. My convoy started forward very peacefully and then, at some invisible signal, the whole countryside erupted and the tanks behind me started to explode. I had never seen so many special-effect explosions in my life. Everything around me was blown to smithereens over a course of about five minutes as I stood in the scout car stunned and not knowing what the hell to do, especially when the tank right behind me blew up. Finally Dickie shouted, 'Cut!' and I stood there in a cloud of thick stinking smoke, my nerves shot to pieces, surveying the scene of devastation.

Dickie came over to me, smiling. 'Great, Michael,' he said approvingly.

'Why the bloody hell didn't you tell me what was going to happen?' I replied, still shaken by the experience and almost deaf.

'I wanted the element of surprise that Joe Vandeleur must have experienced in real life to show on your face,' was his reply. I couldn't argue with that. I saw the film and I was very realistic – in that bit, at least.

That summer at the Mill House was so special. I remember in particular one wonderful hot afternoon in our garden, with a sky so clear there seemed nothing between heaven and us. Our dearest friends – I now realised our friends for life – were gathered there for Sunday lunch; the Moores, Bryan and Nanette Forbes, of course Dennis Selinger and others. I could not imagine a moment as perfect as this. It was, that Sunday afternoon, as if no cloud could ever pass over us.

In the cold clear light of Monday morning everything looked different, especially when my accountant wanted to see me on an urgent matter. The sum total of our lunch together was that I must cut my standard of living drastically, die penniless or sell up everything and leave England. I thought about dying penniless for a while but rejected it as a possible option. Lowering my standard of living I had to reject too because I couldn't think of any way of telling Shakira. I was left with the last sad resort. I decided to leave England, adding 'some time in the future' as a proviso. Our Labour government of the time, it seemed, was not bothered with Super-Tax as an economic tool, as the majority of the people who were required to pay it had already left the country, so

416

they were actually collecting less tax from the rich than the Conservatives had with much lower taxes – so what was their motive if it was fiscally unsound? The answer came when I saw a Socialist minister on television making a speech in which he said that the rich were going to be taxed 'until they screamed'. I concluded that we were not talking about economics here but emotion, and that particular emotion – envy, is not a good basis for government.

These punitive taxes proved a tragedy for Britain because of all the talented, and ambitious people who left – the trained, the skilled, the best and the brightest . . . They all flooded out of this country in a torrent that left us high and dry, forever one step behind all other advanced industrial countries of the world. It may well take us another fifty years to recover from this terrible blunder engendered solely by envy. I come from the poorer class of my country and I have an understanding and, God knows, a sympathy with their problems; I should ideally be a Socialist. I agree that we high-earners should all pay taxes to help the less fortunate and build a just and equal society. I also agree that the 'super rich' should be taxed more heavily than ordinary earners, but not to the extent of bankrupting or exiling those people most likely to pay these taxes. Hence I rejected Socialism, but I still did not vote Conservative because, coming from my class, I did not trust them either. I was forty-four and had never voted for anybody.

Shakira and I quickly made the decision to move to Los Angeles, a place we both knew well and liked very much and where we already had friends. However, property out there was very expensive and my accountant informed me that I was now more or less penniless – with the exception of the money I could get for selling the Mill House. Panicking, I accepted the first offer of work that came along, to make a picture called *The Silver Bears*. This was completely unremarkable except for two things. One that I worked with an actor called Jay Leno, whom I thought very funny and who in fact became a famous comedian and chat-show host in America. And two, Louis Jourdan and his wife Quique joined our set of Hollywood friends.

During filming, a tragic incident occurred that brought me up sharp. It stopped me feeling sorry for myself in my current parlous state. One of the last scenes in the film took place in the vault of a bank that was filled with silver and the director had real silver bars brought on to the set, accompanied by several security guards. It was about two days before Christmas and the last day of the film so we were all in a very cheerful mood, even the security guards – all except one whom I noticed sitting quietly in a corner all on his own. During a break in the filming I went over to have a chat with him and much to my surprise, he turned out to be a boy with whom I had gone to Wilson's Grammar School. I remembered him very clearly and we were getting along fine when I had to leave to go and do the last shot on the movie. As I moved away I wished him a Happy Christmas and he returned the compliment almost in tears. 'What's the matter?' I asked quickly, with the assistant director yelling for me to get on the set. He leaned forward and whispered to me, 'This is my last Christmas. I have incurable cancer. Goodbye, Michael.' He took my hand and shook it and I was dragged away by the assistant. When I had finished the shot I looked for him but the silver and the security guards were gone, and I never saw my old schoolfellow again. I was shocked by what he had told me. I was exactly the same age as him and it brought home to me how close we always are to death. Having to emigrate to America for financial reasons never held quite the same importance for me after that incident. I regarded it as a warning shot from God to get on and make the best of it. Like the fellow said: 'This is not a dress rehearsal – this is the real thing.'

My daughter Dominique was safely ensconced at the home of Marion Mould, where she was continuing her chosen career as a show-jumping horsewoman and my mother was in her new home at Streatham with all her relations for company so she would be OK if I left. I could, of course, come back and see them any time I wanted, so long as I didn't stay for more than ninety days in any one year. The worst part was going to be the first year, because then you can't come back at all. That turned out to be a real problem, but here was something even worse: my friend Paul had developed multiple sclerosis. I managed to get his treatment sorted out, however, before I left so I was now basically free to go, but I still hadn't made up my mind exactly when.

A big push in the direction of Los Angeles was then given to me by my old friend Irwin Allen. He was a producer whom I had known for quite some time through my many visits to Los Angeles, but I had never worked for him. Saying it was best for my career if I came to live in Hollywood, he offered me a picture called *The Swarm* to help me earn the extra money I would need to buy a house in Beverly Hills, where prices were like telephone numbers with noughts added. This picture was one of the worst I ever made, but it got me to America and opened up all sorts of opportunities for me. As a matter of fact I quite enjoyed making it. I knew the script was a bit ropey, but I also knew that Irwin was the master of the 'disaster' movie: he had just made the extremely successful *Towering Inferno* with Steve McQueen and Paul Newman, and the equally popular *Poseidon Adventure* so his pedigree in this genre was impeccable.

I had not been involved in this kind of movie before so I left it all in the hands of the special-effects people, who were after all the stars of the picture. However, I made the fatal mistake of not taking into account the *quality* of the element of danger in the film. While *Towering Inferno* had a skyscraper on fire and *Poseidon Adventure* was about a giant liner turned upside down in the middle of the ocean, *The Swarm* merely offered a thrill-hungry public bees, which do not give the same kind of 'buzz' no matter how hard the special-effects guys worked. The movie was doomed but we didn't notice, especially not me as I was trying to buy a house that I had seen for 350,000 dollars a year before and which was now back on the market for 1,200,000 dollars. Poor Irwin went straight from being the master of 'disaster' movies to making movies that were a disaster.

The Swarm almost had the double function of starting and finishing my career in Hollywood at one and the same time, but Irwin's heart was in the right place. He was the only one who offered to help me and I loved him dearly before he offered me a movie anyway. The actual making of *The Swarm* was somewhat weird because you were forever standing in front of a blue screen acting to something that wasn't there and would be put in after the actors had finished. Some of the filming was quite dangerous because a lot of the action was done inside big glass cages with real bees, millions of them. They were all supposed to have been destung but the destingers had missed quite a few and these ones that had got away with their stings intact were known as 'hot ones'. Every now and then, even during a take, you would hear a yell of pain, and the plaintive cry of, 'Hot one!' would go up round the set. You can learn all sorts of odd facts on a movie like this. For instance, we had a scene for which a million bees were locked in boxes ready for the take inside our enclosed area: at the allotted time they were released and the scene proceeded with the bees, all destung, whirring around us. What the bee experts hadn't confided in us was that bees never 'go' inside their habitation so there we were, Henry Fonda, Fred MacMurray and I all scientists in white smocks and when the take started and the bees were released, they must have been busting for a crap, because we noticed our dazzling white smocks gradually turning a shade of pale brown as the stingless bees took their final revenge. Unfortunately when the picture eventually came out, the critics did exactly the same thing.

The wonderful part of *The Swarm* for me was the opportunity to work with great old-time stars like Henry Fonda, Olivia De Havilland and Fred MacMurray – and even that worked against me one day. I was doing a long lecture scene to a gathering of scientists and during the take I happened to look down in the audience and when I saw these three great stars sitting there listening to me I became a sort of film fan again, and grew completely overwhelmed and lost control of the entire scene. I had to have them removed before I could regain the confidence to go on with the scene.

Hank Fonda taught me a good technical trick. I was doing lines off for him during a closeup, which meant that I was standing by the camera out of shot doing the scene while they just photographed a close shot of him. The normal way of doing this is to look straight into the other actor's eyes as you do when you act the scene together, but Hank didn't want this. He had me stand to one side and a baby spotlight put by the camera where I should have been, and he did the scene staring into the light instead of my eyes. This gave a very startling effect, which I have used myself on a few occasions since. It was great to work with someone as experienced as him. We also hit it off on another level, for like myself he was a very keen gardener and when I eventually moved to Los Angeles, he was very helpful with tips on gardening out there about which I, of course, knew nothing. He used to grow the most beautiful melons called Ambrosia and he kept bees – very handy on this film, and was always giving me small pots which just said on them, *Hank's Honey* written in biro. Whenever he gave me some it always felt like I was receiving an award.

Fred MacMurray was very charming as well and we became very friendly with him and his wife June Haver when we finally moved out there. Olivia De Havilland was, as I expected, the quietest and the shyest of them all.

I love Hollywood, I thought, but I still flew back to London at the end of the film with another quarter of a million dollars after tax towards my new home out there. In spite of all the dire warnings I had been given, and the decision I had made to leave, I was still hesitating about when exactly to go but like most important decisions I have made in my life, it came about for very mundane reasons. Something went wrong electrically in the house and I sent for an electrician to mend it. He arrived, I showed him what was wrong and then left him to get on with it. I was about to go out. My driver had taken my Rolls Royce out of the garage and I was standing there as he parked the car at the front door and went inside to do something. About three minutes later the electrician suddenly brushed past me on his way out. 'Have you fixed it already?' I asked in amazement, never having had this kind of speed and efficiency before.

'No I haven't and I am not going to,' he replied truculently. 'Why not?' I asked, puzzled.

'I am a Communist,' he announced proudly, 'and it is my

belief that no one should live in such luxury. I refuse to work here.' I was surprised at his idea of luxury. He must live in a pigsty, I thought, as although my house was extremely comfortable it was not even bordering on the luxurious. 'People like you shouldn't be allowed to exist,' he continued, as he kicked the tyres of my Rolls. Getting into a small German car he yelled back at me, 'It's people like you who are ruining this country,' and with that he drove off, leaving me standing there in a fury. What kind of people had my countrymen turned into? They were not only envious but stupid too, I thought. It was the last straw.

I walked back into the house and called upstairs to Shakira, 'Pack your bags – we're going to Los Angeles!'

'How long for?' she asked.

'For good,' I shouted back.

There was a long silence and then she came tearing down the stairs and threw her arms around me.

Part Six

36

Welcome to Beverly Hills

I just hope my timing as an actor is better than the way I time my personal decisions. It was 3 January 1979 and we were flying to New York on our way to Los Angeles. With my normal shrewd intelligence and impeccable timing, I had just lived through the last sixteen most lucrative years of my life under one of the most brutal taxation systems in the world and was now jetting off just as a Conservative government was about to be elected and remain in power for the next eighteen years at least.

We stopped in New York so that Shakira could see her mother and three brothers who now lived there. They had all been forced out of their own country Guyana – coincidentally by left-wing extremists – so Shakira was experienced at this type of migration and was well able to cope with it. It was a new experience for me, however, and I wasn't so sure that I could cope – a doubt that was to come back and haunt me.

I had sold the Mill House to Jimmy Page of the rock group Led Zeppelin for three-quarters of a million pounds, and also had a hundred thousand pounds left in the bank after making a down payment on my new home in Los Angeles, which had a mortgage of a million dollars. I was, in actual fact, broke as far as cash was concerned, a refugee from my own beloved country and living in a strange land. Now if I had been lazy or unsuccessful, this might have been understandable, but I had worked hard and enjoyed enormous success for sixteen years.

The moment I got off the plane in New York I felt a tremendous sense of relief, not from politics or tax but from class. Suddenly nobody listened to my accent and judged my intelligence on it; they listened instead to what I said – and

425

then made their judgment. Nobody looked at my clothes and tried to assess my wealth, because they did not care! There was no one with an inherited, unearned title and even those with inherited money did not feel superior to those of us who had worked for it. Among the rich and powerful there was no nouveau, there was only riche – and those with power had earned it, albeit unjustly in some cases. On a personal level, no longer in the papers would I see written that most insulting of all epithets –'Cockney actor Michael Caine'. Here I was just treated as an experienced and skilled professional – what a relief and a delight! And when I eventually drove my Rolls Royce, other people did not glare at me and wonder how they could destroy me and my car – they just wondered how I had obtained it and vowed to do the same one day. America I know is far from perfect, but I had not then, nor to this day been in a country where there was so much opportunity and equality. On that first day as an immigrant I felt strangely free in a way that I do not feel even to this day now that I am back living in my own country; however, there are other compensations for that which I will come to later.

Two cars were waiting for us at the airport, filled to capacity with all our portable worldly goods; our furniture was coming on a ship – the slow boat to China as it turned out. We drove through Beverly Hills up Rodeo Drive, which was still as I had first seen it, not yet the up-market shopping street that it is today. Across the lights at Sunset Boulevard we went and up Benedict Canyon about half a mile and then left on Angelo Drive and then up and up to a thousand feet above the city, a right turn on Davies Drive and then a left at the only gate on this side of this very short street and into number 1309, our new home. It was a very pretty single-storey ranch-style house, set in three acres of garden, with a patio and swimming pool with 'R.4.TC.' – which is Beverly Hills real-estate shorthand for 'room for a tennis court'. This house had cost me one and a quarter million dollars, very cheap for a Beverly Hills house, but then it was not actually *in* Beverly Hills, it was in BHPO; this stands for 'Beverly Hills Post Office' which, as the title suggests, means that you can use 'Beverly Hills' in your address, which is very handy for those of us who are a bit short of money but who wish to create the right impression. The most important thing about BHPO was that it meant we were under the jurisdiction of the Beverly Hills police and ambulance service, guaranteed to arrive in ten minutes as opposed to the Los Angeles ones who could only guarantee twenty minutes. As far as the police were concerned we hedged our bets even further and hired a private security force called Armed Response, which could guarantee to arrive in three minutes. For our further comfort, I noticed after we had lived there for a while that the Armed Response cars used the small parking space outside our gate to have their coffee breaks at night, so for most of the time, rather than being three minutes away, in case of emergency they were usually there before any potential criminals. This was very reassuring for us as my paranoia increased when I found out that we were living six hundred yards from the house in which the Manson Family had killed Sharon Tate and her friends.

Here I was in the midst of making all these apparently wrong decisions when in fact they turned out, as in this case, to be life-saving, preventing a great tragedy. I had left England at the wrong time, had bought a house in BHPO which I could not really afford but God must have been watching over me as He encouraged me in this sublime stupidity, because everything was working for the best in the long run as we progressed innocently towards potential disaster in our little family.

The house was charming: it had great vibrations and we knew we would be very happy there. Architecturally it would have won no prizes. The view over the city to the south was blocked by an eighteen-foot-wide fireplace, the swimming pool was at the back of the house and facing north, and the master bedroom was right by the garages at the front of the house. One of the best views was from over the kitchen sink! For a professional architect to have made so many howlers was a mystery which I solved by finding out the history of the place from the real estate agent who had sold it to me. It was in fact his own home, but being a sentimental soul he had sold it to me the moment I had reached a price he could not refuse.

The house had been built by the Woolworth heiress Barbara Hutton as a birthday present for her son Lance Reventlow, with the stipulation that it should be built in the shape of an L: hence the aesthetic mess.

We loved it instantly. Friends had already put in temporary beds for us all, which included my English secretary Joan. A dining table and some chairs had been hired (you can rent anything in Los Angeles), there were saucepans and cutlery, and they had filled up the fridge with essentials, for Los Angeles, that is – Perrier Water, Arugala – a kind of lettuce I had not come across before – skimmed milk, mint tea and tofu ice cream, non-alcoholic beer, diet Coke and bran muffins. Everything that the stomach craved, in fact. We were off and running in our new life of glamour and luxury in the fabled Beverly Hills, but with one important item missing – a telephone. It was Friday afternoon before I noticed this omission. I rang the telephone company to switch us on, as there was already a receiver in the lounge and the bedroom; but the guy said it was too late that day and they were too busy on the Saturday morning. He promised to come on the Monday. Now I did not need a phone really urgently, but for some unknown reason I insisted that he come on Saturday morning. I said there would be a little something extra for him if he turned up, and he said OK, he'd come. Little did I know that my insistence would prevent the near-tragedy that was just twenty-four hours away.

The next day, the Saturday, was very busy as we were getting in food and odds and ends. The telephone man arrived and fixed it up, and that evening, our old friends Leslie and Evie Bricusse gave a sort of welcome party for us at their home on San Ysidro Drive, where I had stayed so many times when visiting and working in Beverly Hills. We knew lots of people there and the party was fun even though we were tired and quite stressed; it served to calm us down and reassure us of being amongst so many good friends. Halfway through the evening a silly thing happened. Shakira was wearing a leather belt that snapped suddenly, and everyone joked about gaining weight and being pregnant, and then we thought no more of it. It was a danger sign – but none of us noticed it. The party eventually broke up and we went home and collapsed exhausted into bed. I fell asleep the moment my head touched the pillow.

A clenched fist smashed me on the bridge of the nose and I woke up in the dark with a yell of pain and bewilderment. For a moment I thought I had been hit by an intruder, but as my eyes grew accustomed to the dark, I could see that Shakira had thrown her arm over in my direction and hit me accidentally. I yelled at her to be careful and turned over and went back to sleep, but just as I was dropping off again, Shakira's fist hit me, this time in the side of the ear. I grabbed her hand and put it back over by her side and told her in no uncertain terms to be more careful. I laid down again, furious when the fist hit me in the mouth once more. That was it! I sat up and turned on the light and was just about to tell her off when I froze. Her eyes were half-open and I could only see the whites. Her face was a deathly grey and she was obviously almost unconscious and was banging out her fist to try and get my attention before she passed out, which she did as I was looking down at her. I grabbed the phone and dialled 911 and got the paramedics on their way. I yelled for Joan my secretary who was sleeping with Natasha in the next-door bedroom, and they came running in.

'Get dressed!' I shouted. 'We're going to the hospital. Shakira is ill.' I quickly got dressed myself, went back to the bed and started to feel for my wife's pulse. There wasn't one. I listened for a heartbeat. There wasn't one. For a moment I panicked. I thought – was she dead? I felt her face – she was very cold, but I couldn't tell. Her eyes flickered for a moment, so she was still alive, but only just. I gathered her in my arms in an effort to try to warm her and sat there rocking her back and forth, trying I suppose to make her move or the blood to run through her veins. It was stupid, but it was all that I could think to do. I held her like that while Joan got some things together for her to take to the hospital. I just sat there holding and rocking her until the paramedics came, which was fairly soon. They were both quite young; one was black and one was white and they both looked as though they knew what they were doing. They searched for a pulse or a heartbeat and couldn't find either and one of them said to me, 'Has she got any pants on?'

'No,' I replied, puzzled at the question. 'We were both in bed asleep.'

'Well,' he said, 'for modesty's sake will you find a pair and put them on her.'

With that they both rushed out of the room. I couldn't find hers – there were unpacked cases all over the room so I borrowed a pair of my secretary's and put them on her.

'What are you going to do?' I asked them as they rushed back into the room with a pair of what looked like great big rubber bloomers. 'We are going to put this on her and pump it up and force all the blood into the upper half of her body and try to get a heartbeat or pulse showing.' This they did until she looked rather like the bottom of the Michelin tyre man.

After what seemed an age, as they explored her upper body with a stethoscope they found some faint signs of blood beating through her veins and immediately went to work on her with all kinds of injections and drips. All this time they were on the phone to a doctor at the UCLA hospital who was giving them instructions and listening to their description of symptoms, trying to diagnose the illness. I could see now why her belt had broken. Her stomach was so swollen and tight it looked as though the skin would burst at any moment. 'Feel it,' one of the medics said. I touched it and then pressed. It was like trying to dent steel. The doctor diagnosed the illness as peritonitis, which is a burst appendix; her stomach was awash with poison. The paramedics actually saved her life at the house, as they had rigged up a whole life-support system.

We all got into the ambulance and headed very slowly to the hospital. There was no hurry now, they told me – she would last at least a couple of hours and the hospital was only twenty minutes away. We arrived at the emergency entrance at about seven o'clock on the Sunday morning and it looked as though there had been a war on Saturday night. The operating rooms were overflowing with victims of gunshot wounds, knife attacks, heart attacks and every other kind of assault that you could think of. Shakira was quickly wheeled into a theatre and I was left with the comforting phrase, 'Go and see the cashier.'

I went and saw him and waited while he checked on what was happening and then he said to me, 'That will be five thousand dollars, please.' I stood there dumbfounded. I had grown up in a country where we had a National Health Service and no one paid for any operations.

'I'll send you a cheque,' I said – and then he stunned me again.

'We have to have the money before we do the operation.'

I screamed at him: 'My wife is dying in there and you are telling me that you are going to do nothing until I give you the money. It is seven-thirty on a Sunday morning, I have on a pair of jeans and an overcoat, where the fucking hell do you think I am going to find five thousand dollars?' I was almost apoplectic with rage and fear that they would hold up the operation.

His next question almost paralysed me with fury. 'Aren't you an actor?' he asked, completely unaffected by my attitude. I thought he was going to ask me for my autograph.

'Yes,' I said through clenched teeth.

'Are you a member of SAG?' he continued. SAG is the American movie actors' trade union, the Screen Actors Guild.

'Yes, I am,' I replied.

'Why didn't you say?' he continued with a smile. 'You and your whole family are covered for all medical bills.'

I signed a form and staggered back to my waiting position in the passage outside the operating theatre. There were all sorts of people lying on stretchers all along the corridor. One man in particular caught my eye as I paced up and down. He had obviously had a heart attack and looked very ill indeed; he was holding an oxygen mask over his face as he struggled for the breath of life. I leaned on the wall beside his stretcher, absolutely exhausted and trying to collect my thoughts when I happened to glance down at him and saw a look of recognition come into his glazed eyes. Then he did a strange thing. He took several deep gulps of oxygen and then, taking the mask off, he gasped, 'I loved you in *The Man Who Would Be King*,' and collapsed. I quickly grabbed the hand with the oxygen mask and placed it back over his mouth. I did not want to lose such an ardent fan.

After what seemed like forever, a doctor emerged and told me that Shakira was out of danger. I could not see her until later, so I might as well go home and come back and visit her in the evening. I got a cab and as I sat there driving back to my new home, several startling thoughts came to me. First of all my decision to insist on the phone being put in on the Saturday. If I had waited until the Monday, Shakira would certainly have been dead. The paramedics told me that she had about five minutes of life left when they got to her. As for my decision to live in the Beverly Hills Jurisdiction, the Los Angeles paramedics would have taken at least twenty minutes longer than the Beverly Hills ones and might not have been paramedics at all, just ordinary ambulancemen. In that case Shakira would have definitely died, too, but the most incredible decision of all that I made was to leave England at that particular moment. Where we lived at Windsor, on that particular weekend, the ambulancemen were on strike and were not answering any calls.

I got to pondering the subject of death as the taxi slowly ground its way up the hill to our new home, and it occurred to me that with Shakira's close brush with it, all three of us had now been through this experience. Natasha when she was born had almost died and I had faced an early death from malaria, had the doctors not used me as a guinea pig for a cure. God, it seemed to me, had contemplated taking us all at one time or another but had changed His mind at the last moment. Since that time I have always felt that He is watching over our little family to see what we will do with the extra time that He has given us. I've tried not to let Him down. I wouldn't want Him to change His mind.

Back at the house I reassured a tearful Natasha that her mother was not going to die, and to prove it I took her to the hospital that evening to see Shakira, who was still very ill, but would recover quite fast now, the doctors assured us. Back and forth we went over the next couple of weeks as she grew stronger until about a week before she came out, I was visiting her on my own one afternoon and was just leaving when I heard a familiar voice hailing me from the room two doors down. I went in and said hello to John Wayne, whom I had not

432

seen in years. He was in there suffering from what would prove to be his final bout with cancer. He seemed genuinely pleased to see me, and we talked for a while until a nurse threw me out. From that day on, every time I went to see Shakira, I would pop in to see 'Duke', as he liked to be called. It was a very strange experience because as the days passed I grew happier as Shakira recovered and sadder as 'Duke' grew worse. I always remember the day when I asked him how long he was going to be in hospital. I had no idea that his condition was terminal. He seemed to have been beating the 'Big C' as he called it, for years. 'It's got me this time, Mike,' he said with a smile, as though it was a fair fight but he'd lost. 'I won't be getting out of here.' I sat there, feeling both embarrassed and deeply saddened by the answer. I suddenly realized that tears were welling up in my eyes. He spotted them immediately and said, 'Get the hell out of here and go and enjoy yourself.' I fled, grateful for the excuse.

It was only a few more days before Shakira was fit enough to leave and always after my visit with her I would join Duke in his daily walks which were taken up and down the long hospital passage. On the final day when Shakira was leaving, I saw him walking down the passage on his own, this giant of a man, now slightly diminished, wearing pyjamas, a dressing gown and a baseball cap. I was going to say goodbye, but couldn't. We got to the corner of the passage and I looked back just at the moment when he got to the end too and turned and saw me. He waved and so did I and that was the last time I saw him. He died a few weeks later.

Shakira was now fit and well and we plunged into our new lives with enthusiasm. We furnished the house and fixed it up in no time at all – another contrast with life in England, where it was impossible to get anything done immediately and difficult to get anything done at all. The efficiency and standard of service in Los Angeles was beyond belief for someone who had lived all their lives in my country. For instance, when I wanted some additional telephones, which in England would have meant at least a three-month wait, here it was done in half a day. At the supermarket someone actually packed your purchases at the check-out counter, thus speeding up the number of customers they could serve and ladies, who do most of the shopping, were helped with heavy bags. The assistants would actually take them out to your car for which, by the way, there was plenty of room to park.

Of course we all know there are usually one or two serpents in Paradise, and Los Angeles was no exception. Gardening was my first fall from Grace. I just couldn't get the hang of the fact that there really are no seasons out there. I remember being in a garden centre and asking the assistant when a particular shrub should be planted, meaning what time of year, which is so important in England, and his reply was a disdainful, 'When you get it home.' My efforts with daffodils met with even less success. I was told that if I wanted to plant daffodil bulbs in that climate I had to put them in the refrigerator to simulate the frosty conditions that they normally grow in, so I did this and our new maid, who was from Guatemala, found them and made 'onion' soup with them and nearly wiped out the lot of us. Also in the gardens there I found pests that you don't find in England. During our first year I planted masses of roses and the deer promptly came and ate them all, so I had to put an enormous fence all round the property. I dug a pool and stocked it with goldfish, and the racoons came and helped themselves. Every night coyotes rooted in the garbage cans and this was not all they ate. Natasha was only six when she arrived and was mad about pets so we were always buying her kittens, until even she noticed the fast turnover in felines; the coyotes were eating them.

Insects were not rife up there but when they came they really made their mark. I was sitting watching television one evening when a scorpion came out of the fireplace, walked straight across the room and disappeared down a hole in the wooden skirting that I had not noticed before. The same thing happened with an enormous tarantula spider, except that he or she went out under the front door. I never saw either of them again, but they certainly got my attention, even though I was assured the California Tarantula did not sting. As far as I was concerned, it didn't have to: it could frighten you to death just looking at it.

We had bought an Alsatian dog for extra security and he saved me one evening. I was again sitting in the living room watching television in my favourite place – a big swivel armchair when the dog came in and froze and then started to bark at something under my chair. I bent over to see what it was and found myself staring into the eyes of an enormous snake which was coiled round the swivel mechanism of the chair. I leapt three feet into the air and rushed out and got a walking stick and beat it to death, only to find out the next day that I had done the wrong thing. I called the pest control man to see if there were any more about, like a wife and children. This thing had scared me so much that I naturally assumed it was male. When he arrived I showed him the body and he looked at me sadly. 'You shouldn't have killed that sonofabitch,' he informed me sadly. 'I know people who would pay money to have one of these suckers around.' He obviously wasn't talking about anybody that I knew.

'Why, what is it?' I asked.

'That,' he said with great authority, 'is a King snake. It is non-poisonous and it kills every other motherfucking snake that you can think of.' I had obviously boobed and he wasn't going to let me off the hook. As he left he said, 'I hope that you've got another one around the place, but if you haven't you might get some nasty ones up here now. If you see any, give us a call,' he finished rather unnecessarily.

One of the biggest drawbacks for me living in Los Angeles was the fact that I could not drive a car. There are two reasons to drive a car there. One is obvious – there is no public transport to speak of, but the other is that whenever you purchase anything there with a credit card they always ask you for your driver's licence as proof of identity. I quickly learned that if you did not have a licence, people became very suspicious. I encountered shop assistants who had never met anybody who could not drive a car, and I used to spend ages explaining why I did not do this essential thing. I was pointed out to other assistants as I went round stores as an object of curiosity, some kind of freak. It was all very embarrassing so I decided to learn to drive. I had a brand new Rolls Royce by this time and it seemed a pity not to be able to drive it. By the way, a Rolls may sound like a big deal anywhere else in the world, or even in America, but in Beverly Hills the women go shopping in them. It took me just six lessons to learn to drive and on the second one my instructor forgot his briefcase and he had me drive for twenty miles on the freeway. I was terrified but didn't show it and it conquered the whole fear thing for me. I'm sure that he never really forgot his briefcase – I think he was just testing me. I passed the test first time and now at last I was prepared for life in the fast lane in Los Angeles. The first time that I went out driving in the rain, however, I had a very funny but quite frightening experience. It was the first rainfall for at least eight months and it began to pour. Suddenly all the cars on the freeway started sliding all over the place as though they were slightly out of control. It wasn't even slippery yet, so I couldn't figure out what was wrong, until I eventually realised that it had not rained for so long that everybody had forgotten where the windscreen-wiper button was and were fumbling around desperately looking for something to push . . .

37

Dressed to Kill . . .

Before I even set foot in Hollywood I had been told that the people there were false, artificial and ruthless. How can it be, then, that in all the time I spent there, I have only encountered charm, sincerity and warmth? There are unpleasant people there, as there are everywhere else, but you just don't go to dinner with them – if you do, you pretend that they are not and they are usually so surprised that they manage to be nice for the evening. Try it, it works.

In this scheme of things in Beverly Hills Sue Mengers, my wonderful agent and hilarious friend, was definitely the senior duchess at the time. The senior dukes were Irving 'Swifty' Lazar the literary agent, whom I never ever call Swifty since he doesn't like it (and by the way, Elizabeth Taylor hates to be called Liz – in case you ever meet her). Irving was destined to become one of my closest and dearest friends; he also became my literary agent and was in fact responsible for talking me into writing this book. He and his wife Mary were two of the most genuine and charming people we met there. They gave the best, most discreet and high-powered parties of anyone in Hollywood. Irving, as a matter of fact, opened up the whole of Hollywood society for us. He is now a crown prince, having thrown the hottest ticket party in town for several years – the alternative Oscar party at Spago's restaurant. If you can get in there, you are made socially in Hollywood.

Kirk Douglas and his wife Anne were another duke and duchess who also gave wonderful dinner parties, and an invitation to their home was also a hot ticket. They were always very kind to Shakira and myself, the two strangers in town. I was amazed at how readily and quickly we were accepted into this rarefied atmosphere, but I shouldn't have been, since Americans have always been the warmest and most hospitable of people to strangers, possibly because they are a nation of immigrants and know what it feels like. Billy Wilder, another duke and his wife Audrey, the nicest of duchesses give very small intimate dinner parties. They live in a flat, which is unusual for this circle, and it is filled with paintings, as Billy is an avid collector. Whenever I've been there paintings are stacked everywhere with no room left to hang them on the walls, although I noticed recently that he auctioned off thirteen million pounds' worth. I haven't been to the apartment since the sale, but imagine you can probably get to the bathroom now without tripping over them. Billy and Audrey only invite guests who are clever and amusing. He has a tremendous sense of humour, all of it caustic, and likes people who can keep up with him. Fortunately we could and thus were always invited back, and so became firm friends. The quietest of all the dukes, a man who became a really close friend of mine, is a producer called Leonard Goldberg. He and his wife Wendy, who is *not* quiet, are really lovely genuine people and Shakira became very close friends with Wendy, which drew us all together even more. I always thought of Beverly Hills as a place that consisted of nothing but glamour but was surprised to find ordinary amenities, too. There used to be a hardware store right on Beverly Drive where you could buy mundane things like nails and string, but where you could see the most extraordinary people buying them. I once saw Fred Astaire buying sandpaper and Danny Kaye buying one light bulb. The most frightening sight I ever saw in my whole stay in America was in that hardware store. I hid behind a shelf of tools and watched Klaus Kinski buying an axe. It cleared the store.

For a while I thought our ready entrée into this society was down to my own intoxicating charm and wit, but it was not so. The real reason was simple – Shakira. Here was a woman of incredible beauty whose equally lovely nature did not go unnoticed, especially by the wives of Hollywood; and she was accepted even more readily than I was. I first noticed this when she started being invited to women-only lunches by the wives of men who did not even deign to speak to me! So, rather than being an appendage of the male star, which is often the lot of Hollywood wives, she quickly became such an entity in her own right that I remember once warning her that if we ever divorced, I would sue her for loss of status. I have always thought that anybody who becomes somebody, has, at some time in their lives, to invent themselves and it was here in Beverly Hills that Shakira invented herself. It was here that she blossomed and really became her own woman because she knew at last exactly who she wanted to be, and it was here that she truly belonged for the first time in her life, and that is the way she still feels about it. Her grandparents had been born in Kashmir in India, had emigrated to Guyana and then had been driven out of there, with Shakira winding up in London, which she loved, and now she had been forced to move on again and this time she had hit the jackpot. She absolutely loved Beverly Hills and I must say the feelings were reciprocated. I had never seen her so happy and of course I was delighted for her. For myself, I liked it very much and I only had the occasional twinge of homesickness.

My work situation, however, was not quite so rosy. Before I left England I had done a short stint on a brilliant movie called *California Suite* written by Neil Simon, who is also partially responsible for this book as he often told me that he thought I could be a writer. The picture was for the worst part fun, as I was working with that brilliant actress Maggie Smith and under a great director, Herb Ross. For the first time in my life I was playing a homosexual and thinking that maybe I could use what Joe Levine had once said about me looking like one. As it turned out I must have been quite good at it because when the film was shown I received a letter from the president of a homosexual organisation congratulating me on a convincing and for once dignified portrayal of a gay man. I was very flattered by this. Not all homosexuals were that generous, however. I met one gay fellow who asked me who I thought I was, that I could play something I was not. I pointed out that I had portrayed murderers with no experience, and with much less knowledge of the actual people than I had of gays.

439

California Suite got good reviews and so did I, which helped after the tanning we received for *The Swarm*. The only problem with the part from a financial point of view was that it was only one of four separate segments in the film and so I only got paid a quarter of my fee. I quickly looked round, desperate for something to help me get to America, and I found it – a picture called *Ashanti*. 'I've never heard of that one,' I hear you cry – at least that is what I hope I hear, because *Ashanti* was the worst, most wretched film I ever made. I knew it, but I was desperate and I did it. What is more, after a week of shooting in Kenya, I was sent back to England for two weeks while 'changes' were being made. These changes turned out to be the removal of the director, the leading lady, the art director and anybody else who was standing around at the time, or so it seemed. The picture was never properly released, although I was paid. Once I was living in Hollywood, I was rescued by my old friend Irwin Allen again, who invited me to star in *Beyond the Poseidon Adventure* – a sequel to his successful *The Poseidon Adventure*. I had no qualms about this one, but I should have done. My first qualm should have been the fact that Irwin had decided to direct – his second attempt, *The Swarm* being his first! While I loved Irwin, and he was a great producer, a director he certainly wasn't, so although the picture was not as dire as *Ashanti* it was not *Gone with the Wind* either. I did, however, learn to scuba dive on this picture, and I solved a little personal Hollywood mystery, too.

Working on *The Swarm* I had noticed that Hank Fonda, Dick Widmark and Ben Johnson were all slightly deaf, and on this picture I was acting alongside the old cowboy actor Slim Pickens, and he was partially deaf as well. I asked him one day why so many of his generation of Hollywood actors had this problem and he said, 'Can you speak up a bit?' I raised the volume and he told me that it was because they had all done Westerns in the old days, and had their eardrums injured by the explosion that you always see when the cowboy looks out from behind a rock and a bullet pings right by his ear and he ducks back.

Beyond the Poseidon Adventure was not a complete flop, and as a matter of fact, financially, Irwin saved my bacon again. The story was about an ocean liner that has capsized at sea. A lot of the action took place underwater, and one of the critics kindly suggested that it should have taken place underground. He needn't have bothered because the rest of his colleagues buried it anyway.

Back in Hollywood our life continued apace. We had now been granted our green cards, which gave us residential status and allowed us to work. We had to report downtown to collect them and to swear allegiance to the United States – a big moment for all of us and especially me because every time that I went to work I had to get a special work visa called an H.1 which all foreigners need and which is only issued per job, or in my case, per movie. We were greeted in a small office by a very sour-faced black lady of about sixty, who did not seem to want us to stay in America, but she soldiered on with the ceremony. Finally it was all done and this very serious lady's face broke into a big smile. She picked up Natasha and gave her a smacking kiss then shook both our hands and said, 'Welcome to the United States.' We were now almost Americans, and in true style and in deference to Natasha who was now seven, we celebrated with a slap-up nosh at Macdonalds. I'd never eaten there before: it was delicious and I felt very American.

Socially, things were settling down fast. In Hollywood, society is divided into three: the 'A group' which consists of powerful people who can give jobs, the 'B', which is a powerful group of stars who *have* jobs, and the 'Fun' group which, as the title suggests, consists of people who are fun and who, more importantly, are not looking for jobs or power. The A group and the B group very rarely mix because in the first place a lot of the B group are single stars and either turn up with or are beautiful young women, which among the higher strata of Hollywood wives goes down like a lead balloon. The A group who are mainly executives are also socially well behaved, while some of the stars are barely house-trained. The 'Fun' group on the other hand can mingle with either the A or B groups. This is the category into which Shakira and I fell. We couldn't be in the A group because I didn't have any power, or the B group, because I was not a big American star and because I was too well behaved. So we were in the Fun group and invited everywhere.

Professionally my luck was still running cold, although the next film that I was offered, *The Island*, had all the right credentials for success. Written by Peter Benchley, the author of *Jaws*, its producers were Richard Zanuck and David Brown (producers of *Jaws*) and we had a very good director called Michael Ritchie. The location was the Caribbean; it was a thriller-cum-horror story and we also had a nice big budget – so what could go wrong? It's elementary: a thriller-cum-horror story needs a villain or villains that are *really frightening*. Here we had a bunch of people on an island that time had passed by, who had grown into savages, preying on passing boats and slaughtering everybody in sight – in other words, terrifying monsters. These people should have been portrayed by actors with the right kind of frightening presence, and yet those who were chosen (some of whom were very talented) stood no chance. Their roles and the way they were made to play them just gave a ludicrous impression, the exact opposite of what it should have been. The only thing I found at all scary about the movie was that every time I had to dive into the sea, sharks turned up. It was no consolation Dick Zanuck assuring me that during the making of *Jaws* they had never seen a single real shark.

Although the sharks didn't get us the critics did, and there I was sitting in Hollywood with four clunkers in a row. I needed a miracle.

This came in the shape of a film entitled *Dressed to Kill* and a director called Brian de Palma. My role was somewhat bizarre, and a very big departure for me. I was a transvestite, psychiatrist-murderer – not a lot of laughs but just the sort of good role that a British actor could get his teeth into. As I've said, none of the big Hollywood stars would accept it through fear of damaging their images.

My first, most pressing problem was the wardrobe fitting. I had to wear an entire female wardrobe, including underwear

442

and tights. I had worn tights in *Hamlet* but they weren't like this. I had never worn female clothing before, I swear, and my first worry was – supposing I became a transvestite! I was truly so anxious about this that I refused to wear the panties (because nobody was ever going to see them) and kept my own underpants on as a sort of safety shield against a lapse of masculinity. I needn't have bothered. I hated wearing the costume and, as my agent Sue Mengers said later when she saw the film, 'I don't want to upset you, Michael, but you look like shit as a woman.'

The second hurdle was having my legs shaved. This chore had to be repeated often because the hairs there seemed to grow faster than those on my face. I loathed wearing the wig and I never really mastered high-heeled shoes so all in all I was rather a mess as a woman. Lipstick I hated as well. It kept getting on my cigars.

My double was a real woman. The same height as me, she was slimmer than I was so they padded her out, gave her a false nose that looked like mine, and with sunglasses on, which my female character always wore, it was very difficult to tell us apart. She did a lot of the film instead of me, which was handy but also got me into considerable trouble. In the story, my character slashes a woman (played by Angie Dickinson) to death with a razor. At this really horrific death scene I was not present, as it was acted out by my double. When the movie was released there was an outcry at the sadistic way that Brian had the victim killed, and because it looked as though I had done the scene I also came in for a lot of censure. I must admit I was very shocked when I did finally see it myself: Brian had a well-deserved reputation for being preoccupied with blood and gore and he had really gone to town in this scene. When I asked him why, he said that as there was only one death in the film, he wanted to make it last in people's memory, and also so that fear would pervade the film. This he certainly accomplished. I was in England when it opened, in the North Country town of Bradford where the Yorkshire Ripper was terrorising women at the time and the film had to be withdrawn there after protest from many social groups. While I could understand the hysteria I could not agree with some of the statements made to the effect that the film had encouraged him. The Ripper had already killed nine women before *Dressed to Kill* was released.

De Palma, I thought, was one of the greatest directors, technically, that I had ever worked with, but personally he was a very quiet almost shy man with what seemed to me to be a slightly chilly nature, so while I liked him and was happy to be working with someone so talented, no great friendship blossomed on this picture. A small incident happened one day that illustrated to me just how unemotional even people who knew him well thought he was. When my character is finally unmasked by the police I had to break down and cry in hysterics and collapse on the floor. Not an easy thing to do, even for me. Who can cry at the drop of a hat? Anyway, we did the scene and I wound up exhausted on the floor. Brian shouted 'Cut,' and then came over to me and, stretching out his hand, helped me up from the floor. In his other hand he had the remains of the cigar that I had been smoking before the scene. He handed it to me, lit a match and gave me a light. He had never been so attentive to me before and I was touched by this gesture, even more so when one of the crew who had often worked with him came over to me and said, 'He must really like you. I've never seen him be that emotional with anyone before.' The picture was a big box-office success, which was just what I desperately needed at the time, and now I could walk round Hollywood with my head held high once more. Brian had not only helped me up off the floor personally, he had done the same for my career.

We had made the film in New York and when I arrived back home I had with me an extra suitcase full of the clothes that I had worn in the movie. If the clothes that you wear in a picture are good, you may keep them at the end and thus obtain a free wardrobe – although some of the meaner companies do charge you half-price for them. That's why actors like to play well-dressed rich people – you get good clothes to take home. This time along with my clothes I took home the dresses I had worn in the picture as a joke present for Shakira. She is very clothes conscious and has been on the 'Ten Best-Dressed Women in the World' list so many times

444

that they have recently put her in the Hall of Fame. My joke backfired however, because when she unpacked the case, which I deliberately asked her to do, she later told me that for a moment she thought that I had been unfaithful and she had caught me with my lover's clothes in my case. When she looked at the clothes, though, she knew I would never be seen with a woman built like that, and with such bad taste!

My next film I did for two reasons: one it was a horror film and I had never done one before, and two the director was a young man making his first feature film who impressed me so much that I wanted to join his team. The film was called *The Hand*, and although it was well made, I suppose it was just too weird to gain acceptance and thus it was not a success even as a cult movie. I was surprised to find that I did not actually enjoy the physical act of making a horror movie, it depressed me and I vowed never to do another one again. The young director, however, I found fascinating. It turned out that we were both ex-infantrymen and that he had been in Vietnam and had become wounded and was decorated for bravery. Gradually our whole conversations were based on our experiences in this field of endeavour. Every day he used to talk about how a proper film of Vietnam had never been made and how, one day, he was going to do just that – and show what it was really like. Our other main topic of conversation was also based on our infantry backgrounds and that had to do with the assassination of President Kennedy. His theory, with which I agreed, based as it was on his experience as a soldier, was that Oswald could not possibly have shot Jack Kennedy with the rifle and ammunition that he carried, at his distance from the car at the time.

The director was an extraordinary personality, very volatile and with a tremendous intelligence. Even though *The Hand* flopped I was absolutely certain that I would hear of him again, and I did. His name was Oliver Stone.

There was someone else on that film who became a runaway success – a very unlikely character. In the story I lose my hand in a car accident; no one can find it and it takes on a life of its own and runs around in the night killing people. Just think of it – here is a director who is destined to make *Platoon* and *JFK* and this is the story I am doing with him. I sometimes smile when people tell me that I have been very lucky in this business. Anyway, the special-effects man – a wonderful guy called Carlo Rambaldi – had to make a model of my hand. While I was over at his workshop and sitting there as they put plaster all over my hand I had this weird feeling that there was someone else in the room staring at me. I kept looking around but there was no one there except Carlo and his assistant. Finally, in a corner amongst a whole group of arms and legs and masks I saw this strange little creature with big blue eyes peering straight at me. It was obviously a doll but so realistic that it gave me the creeps. I asked Carlo what it was and he told me it was called E.T. – he had made it for a new film by Steven Spielberg . . .

38

Ma in Beverly Hills

We had now been in our new home for three years and were settled in sufficiently to have my mother out for a holiday. It was the middle of a very severe winter in England, and yet was really beautiful weather in Los Angeles. I still think that winter is the best time there – lots of cool breezes, sunshine, no smog, and no tourists. My mother was now eighty-one, and although she was very fit and healthy, the time could not be far away when she would be unable to make the punishing trip.

I picked her up at the airport and on the way back to the house she stared out of the window, fascinated by everything. She had hardly travelled overseas before. I had taken her to Cannes one summer, but that had been a very short trip and so disastrous that I had not tried it again until now. The heat had been too much for her, and although I pleaded, I could not get her to take off her very old-fashioned corset. She hated the tea and the food, and she thought that the swimwear on the beaches, what there was of it, was disgusting so we cut short that trip. This time it looked more promising. It was cooler and the food would be more to her liking. We had the correct tea and the white wine was good in California. My mother never drank alcohol until she was fifty-six, and then she drank more or less a bottle of white wine a day for the rest of her life. I guess she thought she had some catching up to do.

As we progressed through the mundane suburbs of LA then swung into the more lush vegetation of the Beverly Hills gardens, my mother was amazed at the amount of flowers and plants, and the fact that there were leaves on the trees. It was

447

winter in England, of course, and all the plants were bare. 'What do you think of it, Ma?' I asked.

At this point my mother, who was a sort of Mrs Malaprop, always mispronouncing words, gave the best description of Beverly Hills that I have ever heard. 'The gardens are so lovely,' she said, pointing out of the car window. 'Look at all that hysteria growing up the walls.' Innocently and with a misused word she had hit the nail right on the head and she hadn't even got there yet.

My mother had always misused words with telling effect. On politics her best statement had been: 'The trouble with the unemployed is that we are subsiding them.' Her favourite singer was Mick Jaguar and her favourite record at the time was by a trumpeter called Halb Erpert. When the war in Europe was over she proudly announced that the happiest day in her life had been VD Day.

My mother settled into the sybaritic life of Beverly Hills as to the manner born and loved it, but she still worried about money and my ability to pay for all this. She told me that if her trip had cost me too much, I could change her airline ticket from first-class to tourist as she had short legs and didn't need all that room. I assured her that I could manage the fare and she gave in reluctantly.

Another example of how a British working-class mother perceived Beverly Hills came when the painter David Hockney, who was a neighbour at that time, brought his elderly mother, who was also visiting him there, over for tea at my place with my mother. During the afternoon I said to David's mother, 'How do you like Beverly Hills, Mrs Hockney?' and she replied, 'I think it's lovely, Michael, but there is one thing I've noticed that I don't understand.'

'What's that?' I asked.

'Well,' she said, 'there is all this beautiful sunshine and nobody has any washing hanging out.'

In England, of course, where sunshine was at a premium and before washing machines were invented, the moment that the sun came out, all the women would tear into their little gardens and peg out their washing. I thought for a moment about what would happen if you did hang washing out in Beverly Hills: you'd probably wind up on Death Row.

Dominique flew over, too, which made me very happy to see all the family together for once. It had been so long. The moment she arrived, she put on a swimsuit and some sun-tan lotion and we never saw her again except for meals. Eventually I took her and my mother on a trip to Las Vegas, which they both adored, Dominique because she got to see a load of shows, and went backstage to meet the stars. The Osmonds were the big thing there at the time and she actually saw the show business début of Marie Osmond – a moment in history. She was great, actually.

My mother, I suppose, liked it because of her hard early life. In her old age she never wanted to go to bed while there was still something going on, so Las Vegas was paradise for her as there was something going on for twenty-four hours a day. She revelled in it and we never once got her back to the hotel before three o'clock in the morning. We were staying at the newly-built Caesar's Palace, which has an enormous lobby filled with all kinds of gambling machines and music and noise. I remember we got home one morning at our usual three o'clock, all of us exhausted except Ma, who finally admitted to being a little tired and ready for bed and as we went through the door of the lobby and into all the din and mayhem that was going on she turned to me and very innocently said, 'It's nice to be home, isn't it?' I managed with some difficulty to keep a straight face.

Of course being Ma she did not like everything about Las Vegas. The décor in her bedroom, for instance. 'It's not a bit like home,' she grumbled, not understanding that that was the idea – you wouldn't lose money at home and not worry about it. The thing she disliked most, however, was the mirror above her bed. 'What was the idea of that?' she asked. Here was a woman who turned the light out before she undressed when she was on her own, so there was no way that I could explain the true reason for its presence. I thought quickly and told her that it was there for women to put on their make-up in the mornings without getting out of bed. She paused for a moment but finally bought my story and her only reply was, 'Lazy cows.' Got out of that one.

Back we went to LA where Ma suddenly decided that she wanted to go home to England as she had missed three episodes of some soap opera she had been following and didn't want to lose the thread of the story. We all have our priorities and this was hers so off she went back to Streatham.

Natasha's school holidays came around and we all followed Ma to England for a short holiday until it was time for me to go to Hungary and start a new film called *Escape to Victory*. This was a special pleasure for me because it meant that I would be working again with John Huston, who was going to direct, and with Freddie Fields, who was going to produce.

My co-star in the film was Sylvester Stallone, popularly known as Sly, who was flushed with success from *Rocky One* and *Two* – so the film had a chance of making it in America, despite its subject-matter, which was football. Not American football, but European soccer, which I thought would be death in America and fine in Europe – and this was exactly how it turned out, so it wasn't a complete loss. John was not at the height of his powers then, to say the least. A lifetime of fun was beginning to catch up with him, but Freddie was so supportive of him and instead of playing the big producer as a lot of them do, he was one of the best 'hands-on' producers I have ever worked with; he was there on the set every day and leading from the front. Sly was fine to work with, but very exhausting. He never stopped exercising or running during the entire shooting of the film. Every time we finished a scene we all slumped in our chairs and watched Sly run con- tinuously round the nearest open space, or if there was no open space, he would do push-ups and sit-ups. (I lost three pounds just watching him, which was the nearest I ever got to exercise in those days. Now I exercise every day; having installed a full-length mirror in the bathroom several years ago, I quickly spotted the need for it. Middle age creeps up very stealthily.)

Sly was very easy to get along with but had developed one or two 'Hollywood Star' idiosyncrasies, the main one being that he did not like to be called to the set if he was not going to be used instantly. He was busy writing *Rocky Three* or *Four* in his hotel room at the time, so would get a trifle moody if he was summoned and everything wasn't ready. It all came to a head one morning when he was called very early and then made to wait three hours because the weather changed and we had to shoot something else. At the end of the day he announced that whenever his call was for the next day, he would be three hours late to make up for this débâcle and so he was. We all sat for three hours the next morning, waiting for him because we had nothing to shoot without him. All eyes were now turned on me, since I was also a star in the movie and everybody was curious to see my reaction to being kept waiting so rudely for three hours. I think they secretly hoped I would have a row with Sly, but I had other plans. When he finally arrived I asked very pointedly if I could have a word with him in private for a moment, and the tension increased on the set as everybody thought, here it comes – the big bust-up – but I took him aside and told him that I had been to a party the night before and had not had time to learn my lines. He had saved me, I said gratefully, by giving me time to learn them with the delay. I added that I was going to another party that night and had a lot of dialogue tomorrow. Could he possibly be a couple of hours late again, because I would need the extra time and did not want to take the blame for the delay? He was never late again.

Another thing that bothered Sly was John's 'economy' of direction. He kept asking me if John had given me any direction at the end of the day, and when I told him that he hadn't, he informed me that John hadn't given him any either. Sly had directed *Rocky Two* and he told me that he was always giving specific instructions to his actors on how to play the scene.

'Let's go and talk to John about it,' I suggested, and off we went.

Sly put his problem about the lack of specific direction to actors and John replied, 'If you've cast your actors correctly, Sly, there is not much you *have* to say to them. Only directors who don't know how to cast actors have to talk to them all the time.'

A suitably chastened Sly backed off and left it at that, but as he departed he whispered to me, 'I still think a director should say something to the fucking actors!' and the subject never came up again.

There was another thing John did in filming that I complained about, and I got caught out this time. To move the camera in a tracking shot you have, of course, to put down tracks for the camera to move on and this is usually done alongside the route that actors are taking in the scene. With John there always came a point where the tracks crossed our paths and the camera changed to the other side of us during the take. This was very awkward, because there you are, doing the dialogue and looking at the other actor, and eventually you have to step over the tracks without looking as if you are doing it, and without, of course, looking down. I tackled him about why he did this so often when it was so uncomfortable for the actors and he said, 'If you step over the tracks, Michael, that means that they are not there, which in turn means that the camera is not there either, which is the first principle of directing a movie; *you make the camera disappear.*' I thanked him for the lesson and retired suitably chastened.

Sometimes movies are like a kid's dream come true. In this film I was the captain of our football team, which included such great names as Pele the Brazilian football genius, Bobby Moore, who was the Captain of England the last time that we won the World Cup, Ossie Ardiles the great Argentinian player and the Polish World Cup Captain Kazimierz Deyna. Add to this the fact that I had Rocky and Rambo in goal and then among others the great British footballer Mike Summerbee, who retired immediately after the film and now makes my shirts, it truly was like a schoolboy's fantasy come true. These guys were also great company, to say the least. It was a very happy film to work on, while we were on the set, but the evenings could get very depressing. Hungary being a Communist country was not exactly a barrel of laughs. I say this quite literally, for whenever we went to restaurants in Budapest I picked up a strange atmosphere and one day realised what it was: in my whole three months there, I never saw one group of people laughing in a public place. I was told that just before we arrived, Hungary's greatest poet had killed

452

himself live on television. A further proof of how depressed everybody was there was evident in their birthrate, the lowest in Europe. If you can't even make babies, you *must* be depressed. Budapest looked beautiful at least, and seemed somehow familiar to me. I discovered that the reason for this was that it had been designed by Hausmann, the same architect who had designed parts of Paris, but that was the only point of resemblance. It was certainly not a city of romance, gaiety and light like Paris.

However, there were a couple of good restaurants, one in particular that was always full of people who sometimes smiled, if not exactly chuckled, and most of the patrons, I very quickly noticed, were middle-aged men with very attractive young female companions. I was puzzled by this because other restaurants in town were filled with very harassed-looking people studying the menu for prices, not dishes. I took a Hungarian friend there one day and he solved the mystery for me. He told me that before the Revolution, this had been where all the rich capitalists brought their mistresses to eat, and it was now very expensive, he added. 'Well, who are all these guys here now?' I asked.

'They are Communist Party Commissars with their mistresses,' he explained sadly. Nothing had changed at the top; it had only got worse for people like him who had never joined the Party, he went on.

'Are there many Communist Party members here?' I asked.

'Oh yes,' he replied, 'but none of them are Communists. They only joined for the privileges.' He then leaned over and whispered in my ear, 'Somewhere in Hungary there is a Communist but we can't find him. If we could, we would kill him and then we would all be free.'

I found this counter-revolutionary humour all over the place. I was standing at the door of my hotel one day waiting for my car when a cab full of Russians drew up. The doorman came forward and opened the cab door for them and ushered them inside the hotel without a word. I was surprised, as he was normally very chatty. 'Don't you speak any Russian?' I asked when they had gone.

'Yes, I do,' he replied. 'I can say Thank You but I have

453

never found an opportunity to use it,' and he gave a subversive grin.

I remember saying to Shakira on her brief visit to Budapest (she fled after four days) that I thought that in the next ten years Hungary would be free of Communism. I also remember adding that the end of the Communist empire had commenced with the Russian invasion of Afghanistan; that country had proved the beginning of the end for the British Empire and I was sure that the same fate awaited the Russians. I was right on both counts, I am very proud to say, but I would never have believed that the entire system would collapse so quickly. In that summer of 1981, however, there were signs in the air that the end was beginning. My first inkling of even the slightest chink in the iron curtain had come, of all places, at a Sunday lunch with Roger Moore and his family in a very luxurious restaurant on the banks of the River Thames in England called The Waterside Inn.

Roger was playing James Bond at the time and it seemed very strange to us when the waiter informed us that the party at the next table was the Russian Ambassador and his family. At the end of the meal as we were drinking coffee, the waiter came over to our table carrying a plateful of candies wrapped in coloured paper and accompanied by a note. Roger read it out loud. It said: *From Russia with Love.* We all looked over at the Ambassador, who raised his glass of wine in a toast. We all did the same and said something in Russian that I can pronounce but can't spell, then we ate the sweets and waited to see if we were poisoned. We weren't and I began to think there was hope for the world yet.

Now my efforts to get out of Budapest as often as possible became more frantic and a sort of joke at the airport every weekend. As soon as we finished work on the Friday I would go tearing off to the airport and try to catch the plane to London, where Natasha and Shakira were staying while I was filming.

I could now legally spend ninety days per year in my own country, so I tried to use them up every year. We no longer had a home, of course, but we always went back for the summer and rented furnished flats. I was enjoying my life in

Los Angeles but I knew deep down that my heart was still in England.

At the airport, if there was no plane to London I would wave my American Express card and buy a ticket on the next plane anywhere west, usually with minutes to spare, so they soon got used to my Friday visits and even the four banks of security police started to treat me lightheartedly and wave me through unchecked as I almost missed my planes, weekend after weekend. The picture went well, although John was now becoming quite weak from the emphysema which was eventually to kill him. Afterwards we flew to London for a brief but glorious holiday during which I checked up on everything and everybody.

Langan's was now a big hit. Out front Peter Langan himself was creating havoc with the customers as he sunk ever deeper into alcoholism. He was a great source of amusement and/or disgust and dismay with our customers and his antics were in the gossip columns every day. Although this created a lot of free publicity, it brought in all the wrong type of customers for all the wrong reasons. I just felt deeply sorry for his sad wasted life, which had so much potential, and even got a friend of mine who was a member of Alcoholics Anonymous to go after him. He told me that he had never had a failure. Peter was his first and almost drove *him* back to drink. There was nothing to be done, I knew, but I kept trying. He had now taken to sleeping all night at the restaurant under a table in the bar and on many days would still be there when we opened for lunch. None of the staff would wake him up because if they did, he would fire them. Sometimes no one even noticed him until the first customer sat down and had their ankle bitten. The number of free meals that we gave away to nerve-shattered people was phenomenal.

Of my family, Dominique was thriving at her riding school, Ma thank God was happily settled in her new house, but the other person who worried me besides Peter was my old friend Paul. His multiple sclerosis was increasing in severity now very quickly. I remember buying him a walking stick one day after a lunch at Langan's, because every time we got up to leave, after a meal, he would stagger a bit and people would think that he was drunk, so I talked him into buying his first walking stick for the sake of appearances. I don't remember the exact chronology of it, but every time I went back to England things seemed to have deteriorated. He went from one stick to two and then sadly into a wheelchair, and then into a flat designed for the disabled. I found an article in the paper one day that said some of the symptoms of MS could be relieved by placing sufferers in a diving bell. I tried to obtain this treatment for Paul, but was informed that he was unsuitable because he only had one lung. 'Some days,' as the Americans say, 'you can't make a dollar' and that is how life was most of the time for Paul. I made him as comfortable as possible and disappeared just ahead of the British income tax authorities. My ninety days were running out, so it was back to the sybaritic lifestyle of Beverly Hills.

Sean Connery and his wife Micheline had temporarily moved into a flat in Century City. The real estate that Twentieth Century-Fox had lost in the Cleopatra Disaster was now a big thriving city centre. David Niven Junior, an old friend from England who had produced *The Eagle Has Landed* with Jack Wiener, turned up and settled down and even Jack himself would look in occasionally. Bryan and Nanette Forbes came, and so did Roger and Luisa increasingly often as the British film industry went into almost terminal decline. The result of all this invasion of the Brits was that I would often cook a traditional British roast beef Sunday lunch, which we all ate in temperatures of sometimes a hundred degrees, purely out of nostalgia or homesickness, a twinge of which I was beginning to get from time to time, but I took no notice. I knew that it would go away with time. Wrong.

Strange things happen in Hollywood. Apart from the films that you do there are the films that you might have done that worry you, and this one haunts me still. One day I had a call from Orson Welles. We had been casual friends for many years and we had always agreed that one day we would like to work together. Over the years we had suggested various subjects to each other that had never got a unanimous decision until one day he called me with an idea for one that broke my heart because I already knew we couldn't do it. He

456

wanted us to do the film of the stage play *The Dresser*. It would have been a brilliant vehicle for the two of us. A wonderful atmospheric British play about the relationship between an old ham stage actor and his gay dresser, it was perfect, but I knew that it was already going to be filmed with Tom Courtney and Albert Finney. So much for my chances of winning an Oscar.

My old friend Robert Bolt suddenly showed up in LA on his way back to England from Bora Bora, which he described as boring, boring. He had been there for months as part of his ongoing partnership with David Lean. This time he was writing the screenplay for what should have been their version of *The Mutiny on the Bounty* but which unfortunately was destined not to be made – not by them, anyway. He was obviously tired and seemed to be on the verge of a breakdown of some kind. Just how tragic a collapse, we were soon to find out. I invited him to stay with us and rest up a bit before he continued his journey back to England. Romantically speaking, he was on his own, either divorced or separated from his then wife Sarah Miles. By chance, Mia Farrow had turned up, and she was now on her own having long since divorced Frank Sinatra, so Shakira and I being the matchmakers that we are tried to put these two obviously lonely and, we thought, compatible people together. I was now doing what had been done to me when I had first come to Hollywood on my own – I was matchmaking. The relationship was a complete success until disaster struck and Robert had a massive stroke. He was rushed to hospital where they just managed to save his life but he was left terribly damaged by it.

Robert is one of the greatest writers in the English language. His play *A Man for All Seasons* I think ranks as one of the best this century, or any other century, and I remembered him at our Mill House enthralling people with his thoughts and language. However as a result of the stroke, after he had been in hospital for quite some time, I recall standing there on one of my daily visits watching him trying to speak, which he had to learn to do all over again, and on another occasion learning the alphabet. It was a terrible tragedy for a giant intellect like his.

Mia stayed on for a while and looked after Robert, but it was obvious that any potential romance was over. He would be disabled for quite some time and she had to go to New York to do a play. So that was the end of that strange, tragi-romantic episode. He seems to be much better now, thank God, and more or less back to normal, but only after a tremendous struggle of guts, determination and willpower. Bob's illness also had a tremendous effect on the way that I behaved. From that moment on I began to take notice of my health and the way that I was treating, or ill-treating my body.

In the New Year I went to New York and Shakira and Natasha followed me later when Natasha's school holidays started. I went to make *Deathtrap* for director Sidney Lumet – a really smashing person. If only all directors were as nice and understanding of actors as Sidney is. I just loved him. I was delighted to be co-starring in this one with Christopher Reeve, whom I already knew from London, when he was making the film in which he was to find fame and fortune, *Superman*.

Deathtrap was an adaptation of a play that was in the same kind of English country-house thriller mould as *Sleuth*, and it had almost as many plot twists and turns as that convoluted piece. This, however, was by the American writer Ira Levin, who had also written *Rosemary's Baby*. Christopher and I played closet gays who 'came out' in no uncertain terms, by murdering my wife. I had now played an outright gay, a transvestite and here I was playing a bisexual. Joe Levine, who had told me I would never make it in movies because I looked too gay, must have been laughing on the other side of his face. A movie set in New York about two gay men was particularly topical, because in a very similar way to the heterosexual revolution in England in the 1960s, in the 1980s there was a massive homosexual revolution going on in America, and apart from San Francisco it was mainly based in New York. The gays had a tremendous effect on the nightlife of New York, and the daylife too, come to think of it, and they weren't selfish about it, either. Anyone, including straights, could join in the fun. The main headquarters for all this 'gaiety' was a disco called Studio 54. It was here that the gays, straights, and

Don't Knows mingled until dawn every night of the week. The first time I went there I made the mistake of wearing a very tight leather motor-cycle jacket. I think it must have meant something in gay code, because when I went to the cloakroom, it took me fifteen fairly nerve-racking minutes to get back to my table. It was also kind of complimentary. I was forty-seven years old at the time – maybe old 'rough trade' was in that year, I know that everything else was.

When I first arrived in New York, I did what I always do there and went to see my great friend Elaine at her restaurant of the same name. This was my staging post for the start of all my visits to the city, because if I didn't find my friends there, which was rare, Elaine would know where they were and if they were in town. My main friends in New York were Bobbie Zarem the press agent, his brother Danny who was in the menswear business and a producer called Martin Bregman and his wife Cornelia. I had met Marty many times there over the years and we have now got our own company together and have just produced our first movie, *Blue Ice*. I followed my usual route of lunch at the Russian Tearoom, dinner at Le Cirque, plus of course finishing the day always at Studio 54. At the same time I was also making *Deathtrap*, which was very satisfying apart from the fact that the studio was in what resembled an old warehouse a long way uptown. I think it was about 110th Street. Now in New York, the further uptown you go, the less likely it is that you'll ever be returning downtown again. This is where the drug culture starts and a lot of life ends. It is only a short distance from the ritzy part of town where I was staying – in the Pierre Hotel on 61st Street – fifty-nine blocks actually, but the difference is sudden and terrifying. At seven every morning I would leave the hotel and drive through the quiet and green beauty of Central Park, entering the gate by the Plaza Hotel, which is almost opposite and proceed with great serenity uptown with the driver pointing out the same landmark every day – a heavily disguised Jacqueline Kennedy, jogging round the huge reservoir which is in the centre of the park, and then when we had come almost to the end of the park we would turn out of it on to the normal streets. On my first day it was a shock to draw up at the traffic lights and see groups of men talking to drivers ahead and realize that they were selling dope of various kinds, quite openly in the daylight. I had never seen this before and grew quite nervous when the driver told me that we still had to go several blocks further north to the studio. This turned out to be a ramshackle building in an extremely undesirable neighbourhood, and I felt like calling in the SAS to make the trip from the car to the door, but I was never harmed so I suppose it was all right, but uptown is not the place for me.

The filming went very well for a while in spite of the fact that Sidney, I very soon discovered, specialised in long takes. He is one of the few directors who can make a film interesting doing this. Woody Allen – as I was to find out – was another. There was one scene, however, that I was really dreading. There usually is in any film; my main experiences of this so far had been when I had to ride a horse or a camel (I hate both of the bloody things and the feeling is mutual). What I had to do in this film was going to be a first for both Christopher and me. Neither of us was looking forward to it, but as those actresses say who do nude scenes, 'It was an integral part of the story.' Christopher and I had to indulge in a very passionate lovers' kiss.

Now I had never kissed a man on the lips before, not even my father, and I experienced the same anxiety as with wearing a dress for the first time: supposing I liked it! I had been kissed on the lips by two men before, one of them by coincidence Sidney Lumet and the other Burt Lancaster, who always seemed to meet me on the days when he hadn't shaved, but this was just a mild form of greeting. Came the big day and we rehearsed it a few times, our lips always miming the kiss and as the tension mounted and the moment for our take crept closer, we were now quite drunk. We had been sipping brandy all afternoon to get up some Dutch courage. By the time it actually came to the take, the bottle was empty and Christopher and I were feeling quite jolly. I was still feeling a little upset, though, because Chris is a lot taller than I am and I didn't want to look like the feminine part of the couple. I was still trying to hold on to some masculine dignity, but even that was denied me. Finally we did the take and the last thing I remember saying to Chris was, 'Whatever you do, don't open your mouth,' and there followed the tightest-mouthed screen kiss in the history of the cinema. The shot was fine and for the one and only time in the movie, Sidney printed the first take and didn't ask for another. It was over and neither of us had enjoyed it. The rest of the film was easy. When *Deathtrap* came out it was quite a success critically and did some moderate business.

Weeks later, I ran into Mia again, who was by now doing her play on Broadway and we arranged to go and see it and have dinner at Elaine's afterwards. When we picked her up after the show she asked me if I knew Woody Allen and I told her that I did, vaguely, and she said she knew that he ate at Elaine's, which he did most evenings. I said he would probably be there that evening and she asked me to introduce her if he was. I had a feeling that I would be doing my match-making again. Sure enough, he was there and we all sat at the table next to him. When we were joined by Bobby Zarem and some other friends, I told Bobby who was sitting closest to Woody that Mia wanted to meet him. He introduced her, and that was how their romance started. I have gone into detail about this introduction in order to assuage the annoyance of my friend Bobby, for I once told a journalist that I had introduced the couple. I thought I had, but the moment he read it in the paper Bobby was on the phone to me saying that I had taken credit for something that he had done, so this last bit is a sort of apology to him.

After the film and the riotous living we all arrived exhausted back to the peace and quiet of Beverly Hills. Here the social life was much more sedate than in New York with everybody packing up the evening at around ten o'clock so that they could leave by ten-thirty. The centre of social life was still dinner parties at people's homes but there were several very 'in' restaurants. The smart one was the Bistro, where you had to wear a tie and they served the best chocolate soufflé in town to drip down it. For lunch we would go to Ma Maison, a very successful restaurant that was so exclusive its telephone number was ex-directory – a typical Hollywood syndrome.

461

The restaurant had started life as a small building with a parking lot in front of it; it was run and owned by a very shrewd and engaging Frenchman called Patrick Terrail. The chef was an as-yet unknown Austrian called Wolfgang Puck who has found success and fame as the owner of Spago, now Hollywood's most popular restaurant for the last few years.

Ma Maison was such a big hit that it soon overwhelmed the small building and Patrick had to put tables under umbrellas in the parking lot. These tables became so popular that nobody would sit inside, so the parking lot became the restaurant and Patrick bought the building next door and pulled it down to make another parking lot, and so the original little building remained empty – except for Orson Welles, who would eat inside out of sight of the rest of the Hollywood Glitterati. I've heard of favoured seating in restaurants, but this must be the first time in the history of catering that the restaurant became 'Siberia' and the prime tables were in the parking lot.

39

The Queen and I

It was about this time that Peter Langan arrived to carry out his long-threatened opening of a restaurant in Los Angeles. In London, we have a tolerance and sympathy for drunks and some people even find them amusing, but not so in Beverly Hills where people have nervous breakdowns and heart attacks in their efforts to keep fit and lovely. Drunks are regarded with absolute horror by a group of people who, you must remember, drink Perrier in moderation. Anyway, Peter arrived and did absolutely nothing to disabuse them of their opinion.

My job, he informed me imperiously, was to find the million dollars he needed to open this establishment. Feeling, rightly, that I owed him in part for some of the success of Langan's in London, I went ahead and did so. I arranged a meeting of several of our town's more substantial citizens at my home to give them and Peter a chance to talk. Came the day, we all gathered to discuss this business arrangement and waited half an hour for Peter to arrive, which he eventually did and collapsed in a drunken stupor on the floor. There was a long pause while our potential partners assessed the situation from a purely business point of view. One of them finally spoke. 'If we invest in this restaurant,' he said guardedly, 'who will be spending our money?'

With as much dignity as I could muster, I pointed to the crumpled, and now snoring, heap on the floor. 'He will,' I said as they all stood up and left without so much as a goodbye – and that was the end of my business relationship in Los Angeles with Peter.

Socially my patience came to an end with him after I

foolishly invited him to lunch at Ma Maison. I knew from his behaviour at Langan's that he made a speciality of insulting celebrities, but the California sun must have gone to my head. The lunch was surprisingly quiet as Peter sat there, for once dumbfounded at the array of stars eating all around him. He had never seen the likes of this, even at Langan's, so he was suitably subdued. After about an hour of his usual lunch of champagne and banana daiquiris, he not unexpectedly wished to visit the cloakroom, which was inside the restaurant (we were eating outside). He was a bit drunk so I decided to accompany him to make sure he found the right place. Once inside the building, he immediately spotted Orson Welles and before I could stop him was over at the table and speaking to him. 'Orson Welles?' he asked innocently. Orson said, 'Yes.' Peter weaved his way up to near his full height and announced with great dignity, 'I think that you are an arrogant fat arsehole.'

Pandemonium broke out instantly. The owner Patrick Terrail came and barred him from the restaurant forever, and I got a telling off for bringing him. We were both ordered off the premises. I stayed behind to apologise to Orson while Patrick and Peter left immediately, with some anatomically unfeasible advice to Patrick as to what to do with his restaurant. As I went out to follow Peter to the car, I heard another scream and dashed out already guessing the cause – and there was Peter relieving himself in the line of flowerpots that decorated the entrance. Peter left LA shortly afterwards and I didn't go back to Ma Maison for weeks. I have made a lot of profit out of Langan's Brasserie but over the years that I spent with Peter, I feel that I earned it.

I had quite a break between films at this time and I settled down in Los Angeles to what was now my normal routine when not working – shortwave radio, British newspapers and Sunday nights with the Public Television station. During these periods of resting – a harmless-sounding phrase that we use in show business to describe enforced periods of unemployed terror and frequent bouts of deep paranoid imaginings that one will never work again – I became a sort of

British Social Ambassador whenever royalty or the aristocracy came to visit us. I gave a dinner for Princess Michael of Kent at Morton's, a new restaurant and fashionable rendezvous opened by Peter Morton, an American whom I had known in London. He had opened the first Hard Rock Café there at around the same time that we had opened Langan's. Morton's very quickly became *the* place to be seen, so I took the Princess and her group there and we were seen and we saw. Whenever you get a visitor to Los Angeles you always feel that you have to take them somewhere where they will see movie stars and nine times out of ten on the night that you go, no stars turn up. This night, however, we got the ultimate accolade: Warren Beatty himself came in and stopped at our table and said hello.

Princess Margaret came to visit us, and my American agent Sue Mengers somehow got herself chosen to host the party for the Princess at her home. This was a great source of pride for Sue, who adores the British royal family and a great source of fear when it came to the night of the event. Sue was one of the toughest agents in Hollywood, but when the time came to meet the Princess at the door of her home, she almost collapsed with fright but was ushered through the niceties of the meeting by her charming and very calm French husband Jean-Claude. He was as impressed as her but like all the French, he would die rather than show it. I already knew Princess Margaret so I was considered socially safe enough to be seated at her right hand at the dinner table. On the other side was Governor Jerry Brown of California, who started his conversation with her with the biggest gaffe that you can make with British royalty. The protocol with them is that nobody leaves the occasion, no matter what it is, before they do, and this is very strictly adhered to. Governor Brown's first words were very proper – he had obviously been advised of the correct form of address. 'Good evening, Your Highness, I just dropped by to say hello. I have another appointment so I'm only staying for the first course.' The Princess did not stop smiling, but she just turned her back on him without a word and engaged me in conversation until he left.

There was worse to come. The Governor's companion that

465

evening was a singer called Linda Ronstadt, and she had been seated at another table. As the Princess was at our table we were served first and Miss Ronstadt came over to the Governor and stood behind him saying, 'What are we having to start?' She then leaned over his shoulder and took a piece of food off his plate and tasted it. Apart from these rather casual table manners, in so doing she committed a ghastly gaffe. In your dealings with the British royal family, you never *ever* touch them. Miss Ronstadt not only put one hand on Brown's shoulder when she leaned over rather rudely to look at his food, but she put the other hand on Princess Margaret's shoulder. I have seen people shrug many times, but the Princess's shoulder shrugged that night like a punch from a boxer and with almost the same effect on Miss Ronstadt. She almost overbalanced and fell on the floor. The Princess never again during the evening acknowledged Jerry Brown's presence nor his departure when he finally left.

The rest of the evening was a big success. Your status when visiting Hollywood is judged by how many glittering stars accept invitations to your welcome party. Princess Margaret hit the jackpot, not only because of the stars who turned up but because she had Sue as a hostess. If any one could get the glitter out it was Sue. At our table were Barbra Streisand, Jack Nicholson and Clint Eastwood, plus Barry Manilow (who was, I understand, a special request). Some of the stars are so reclusive that you often find on an occasion like this that they are actually meeting each other for the first time. The rest of the half dozen tables in the room were also filled with glitterati so the whole evening was judged a success, especially by the Princess who enjoyed herself immensely but did not like that dreadful man at all, as she told me when she left. Unlike the Governor, I knew the protocol and stayed until she had gone and comforted Sue as she almost collapsed with relief that it was all over and had gone so well. A great evening.

The next royal occasion I attended was a much bigger affair: the visit by Her Majesty the Queen. The fact that she herself was coming was enough to make the best hostesses in Los Angeles quake with terror at the thought of being asked to entertain her. Not only that, it was the first ever visit of a

British monarch to Los Angeles. The number of people who wanted invitations to this affair was so great that the party was held in an enormous sound stage at Twentieth Century-Fox Studios. The British Hollywood contingent were seated at a raised dais on either side of the Queen and the rest of Hollywood society was seated below at tables laid out all over the studio floor. Also seated on the dais were one or two Americans. Nancy Reagan was there, as was the multi-millionaire Cadillac dealer who had financed the evening. Because of his generosity he got to sit next to the Queen and I sat on the dais next to him. On the other side of the Queen sat the late Tony Richardson the British director, whose credits included the film *Tom Jones* and being the ex-husband of Vanessa Redgrave. It was a very formal affair but went quite well anyway.

Once on the dais, though, the whole evening stiffened up a bit. The car-dealer sitting between the Queen and myself seemed either paralysed with nerves or just plain tired, because he hardly moved or spoke during the entire evening. The Queen seemed OK when she was talking to Tony on her other side but she was obviously finding it uphill work when the time came to talk to the other guy until there was complete silence, I noticed as Tony chatted to Nancy on his other side. There seems to be a protocol at all dinner parties that you talk to the person on one side of you for about five minutes, and then turn to the other one. I've always made the terrible faux pas of finding the most interesting person on one of those sides and talking to him or her for the rest of the evening. Once, when I was seated next to the most boring dinner companion whom I have ever encountered, without thinking I said, rather arrogantly in retrospect, 'I have a reputation for being amusing so hostesses always sit me next to the dullest people.' She didn't find that amusing at all. I was sitting there pondering on all this, miles away, when suddenly I heard a familiar voice. 'Mr Caine.' I looked around behind me – nobody was there. 'Mr Caine.' The voice came again. Suddenly I saw the Queen's head appear round the car-dealer – she was addressing me. I didn't know the Queen at all, I had just met her for the first time that evening in the line-up at the entrance. I peered round my side of the car-dealer.

'Yes, Your Majesty?' I blurted out, hoping that it was the correct form of address and wondering what I had done to be noticed at all.

'Do you know any jokes?' she said with a smile.

'Yes, ma'am,' I replied quickly, 'but very few that I could tell you.'

'Have a go,' she said, 'and then I will tell you one.'

And that is what we did for the rest of the evening, swap jokes. I had always seen the Queen as a very serious figure and it was a revelation to me that she had this funny side to her. For the first time I saw her laugh out loud. I was always very pleased to get a laugh, but to get one from the Queen was a true accolade. I actually have a photograph in this book of Her Majesty laughing at one of my jokes. This is what she found so funny:

There was a guy driving along a country road when suddenly, to his surprise, his car was overtaken by a chicken with four legs. He couldn't believe what he'd just seen, so he speeded up and overtook the chicken which was now doing eighty miles an hour and really *did* have four legs. The chicken then speeded up to one hundred miles an hour, overtook the car again and turned off the road into a farmyard. The driver followed it and stopped by the farmer who was standing at the gate. 'Did you just see a chicken with four legs go through here at one hundred miles an hour?' the driver asked. 'Yes,' the farmer said. 'It's one of mine. I breed them.' 'Why do you breed chickens with four legs?' asked the driver. 'For the local restaurant who sell a lot of drumsticks,' the farmer replied. 'What do they taste like?' the driver persisted. 'I don't know,' the farmer said. 'We never caught one.'

Well, the Queen liked it anyway.

When the end of the evening came we all stood up as the Queen left and she moved along the dais shaking hands with all of us and wishing us goodnight, and that was the end of that, we thought, until she reached the end of the dais and realised or was informed that she had only said goodnight to the people on her righthand side, and in any case the exit was at the other end. So back she came along the line of us having just said goodnight and said goodnight all over again. This obviously struck her as extremely funny and she started to laugh as she made her way back and we all got a fit of the giggles at the ridiculous situation that we all suddenly found ourselves in. When she reached me again without thinking I blurted out, 'We've got to stop meeting like this!' and immediately thought, Oh my God I shouldn't have said that, I've gone too far – a place where I usually wind up, but she just laughed even louder and continued on her way.

Sally Field had just won an Oscar for *Norma Rae*, and I was offered a picture with her, but I turned it down in favour of *Educating Rita* playing opposite Julie Walters who would now be making her cinema début. Not an ideal situation on the surface, but there was more to it than that. First of all the picture was going to be directed by Lewis Gilbert, who had directed me in the all-important *Alfie* and secondly, Willy Russell, the original novelist and playwright had also written the screenplay, and had opened the play out from what it had been in the theatre, turning all the moments in their lives that the two main actors had only been able to talk about on stage, into actual action on film. This was one stage play that just cried out to be opened up. Added to this there was a technical aspect about the difference between theatre and film acting that was also to my advantage in making any impression in a play that was so obviously a vehicle for the female lead. In the play, Rita does all the moving about on the stage, while the man, for most of the time, just sits at his desk and listens and reacts. Now the theatre is about 'acting'; the cinema is about 'reacting'. When Rita said something, the camera had to cut to me for my reaction. You can't do that on stage, and that is what helped to balance the weight of the two parts in the film and made it acceptable to me.

The basic story is about a working-class girl who tries to better herself with education, and her relationship with the professor who becomes her mentor. Both the film and the play were compared in tone at least to Shaw's *Pygmalion* or as

469

we now call it *My Fair Lady*, with Rita as the Eliza Doolittle figure and me as a sort of Professor Higgins. While there are elements of *Pygmalion* in it, and I could very easily have taken that route, that is not what I based my role on at all. Higgins and Eliza are both attractive people who wind up falling in love with each other, but I didn't see *Educating Rita* in this way at all. I saw it with an under-theme of an ugly professor (he is an alcoholic in the story) who has an unrequited love for an attractive student, and I therefore based my performance not on Professor Higgins but on Emil Jannings' role as the professor who loves Marlene Dietrich in *The Blue Angel*. So I started by trying to look like him. I grew a beard and gained thirty pounds so that there was no chance that Rita could possibly fancy me. Changing myself physically in this way was a great help, as for the first time in my life I was playing a character with whom I had nothing in common, a man for whose ideas, outlook on life and in particular his relationships with women, I had absolutely no sympathy. Any woman who did not requite my love the moment it was declared, was very quickly forgotten. I did, however, have a firm basis for my characterisation – Emil Jannings – and for the alcoholic side of the man I used my long relationship with Peter Langan to guide me in the blunderings of the drink-sodden mind. For the professorial aspect, I called on my friendship with Robert Bolt, who had once been a teacher himself, to flesh out this side of the man.

We made the film at Trinity College in Dublin during the summer when all the students were on holiday. It was ideal for us and Dublin is a favourite city of mine. I had been there many years before with the play *The Long and the Short and the Tall* but had never found the time to go back. I like the people there and the general atmosphere of the city, especially the attitude towards three of my own main interests – food, drink and the arts. It was a wonderful summer of work. Lewis was still the warm, charming, shy man I remembered from *Alfie* and Julie Walters was smashing company.

Lewis and I were a little concerned at first, this being her first film and her with a theatrical background. Both of us had worked on films before with basically theatre actors and it is always hard to pull their performance down from *acting*, which is the theatre, to *behaviour*, which is film acting. On stage you have actors so you expect them to act, but in films you have real people and they don't act, they simply behave and react. Our concern turned out to be groundless, because Julie understood all this instinctively and mastered it so quickly and so well that she was eventually nominated for an Academy Award for her role in the film. Lewis, like John Huston, left the actors to get on with it, until he spotted some potentially fatal flaw and like John, he could put you back on the right track with very few words.

In the film I played a professor of English and on the first day of shooting, as we waited to do the very first shot, in fact, in the courtyard of the college, I spotted a familiar figure coming towards me. As he got closer I realised that I did not know him, but the reason he looked so familar was because he mirrored the way that I looked now. He was overweight and had a straggly beard, and his face was still flushed from last night's drinking; to top it all off, he was carrying a case of red wine. He said hello as he drew level with me and I said to him, 'You wouldn't be a professor of English, by any chance?'

He stopped and stared at me in amazement. 'As a matter of fact, I am. However did you know that?'

I smiled. 'Just a lucky guess,' I said. He laughed and walked on. Maybe I was on the right track with this character after all, I thought, even though he was such a stranger to me.

A couple of weeks into shooting Lewis sidled up to me one morning, just as he had on *Alfie*, and whispered, 'I think you will get an Academy nomination for this. Julie as well.' As usual he was right on both counts, but more of that later.

40

How to lose an Oscar

I went off on my own to Mexico to shoot my next film, which had come to me via a lovely lady producer friend of ours from London called Norma Heyman. I hated leaving without my family but Natasha was happy at Marymount School in Westwood and Shakira was deliriously content with her life in Hollywood. She now had so many good friends that I did not lose a lot of sleep over being missed and off I went to Veracruz to make a film version of Graham Greene's novel *The Honorary Consul* in which I was to play the Consul himself. The film was directed by a very tough little Scotsman called John Mackenzie who had directed the excellent gangster film *The Long Good Friday* starring the sensational newcomer Bob Hoskins. Bob was also appearing in this film with me, with Richard Gere making up the third main player. Hoskins is very much a 'what you see is what you get' man. On screen he looks as though he might be a wonderful guy if you ever met him, and that is exactly what he is, besides being a brilliant actor. Not a bad combination if you are going to work with someone in a tough place for a long while – and Mexico is a tough place to work.

Richard Gere on the other hand is the complete opposite of Bob, in as much as what you can see of him is very little, and not necessarily what you are going to get. He is a very shy, inward-looking man until he gets to know and trust you and then, as I very quickly found, he is as charming as Bob and almost as funny. He was also, unlike Bob and myself, a very spiritual sort of a man and a devout Buddhist. As an actor he was also the opposite of us, for we are very similar in style – relaxed but forceful. He was very intense, both as an actor and a person, but very gentle with it. The one thing my co-actors had in common was their high level of professionalism, so again the actual work was a pleasure, which is more than I can say for the conditions.

Everybody went down with dysentery almost immediately except for me. I had found not a cure but a preventative. It worked this way. I started every meal with a straight vodka on an empty stomach, drank wine all through the meal and finished it off with a straight brandy. As far as the dysentery germs were concerned, I figured that if they could survive that onslaught, they deserved to be able to make me sick. The only problem with all this, of course, was that although it worked and I didn't get the disease, the treatment almost killed me. The weather was boiling hot and the wind blew dust in your face constantly and every location we went to seemed to be filthier than the last one. Richard was very unwell at one time and when I asked his girlfriend, Sylvia, a beautiful Brazilian painter, where they had eaten the night before, she took me on to the beach outside our hotel (a rubbish-strewn stretch of sand lapped by waves from a toxic nightmare) and indicated a small café there. At dusk a couple of nights before I had gone for a walk on the beach and as I was walking back to the hotel, I passed that same café, which had been closed at the time. As I approached I saw a sight I had never thought to see again after I left Korea, but there they were – thousands of rats who, when they saw me, ran under the café where Sylvia and Richard had eaten that night.

I did become ill myself, eventually, but in a rather bizarre way. The Consul whom I played in the film was a drunk who also had the ability to chew aspirins all day without ill-effects – the complete opposite of myself, who had never eaten an aspirin in my life or any other pill for that matter. So in order to be seen eating these aspirins by the handful, they had to make up dummy pills for me out of chalk. My first shot on the film featured this habit; the prop man handed me the dummy pills but there had been some mistake. I was given real aspirins instead, and as I chewed them all through the scene I quickly began to feel a bit strange, then became very wobbly on my feet and of course everybody thought I was drunk. That was very unpleasant for someone like me, who prides himself on being professional. I don't drink in the daytime when I am not working so I certainly wouldn't do it during a film. Anyway I eventually collapsed and was carted off back to the hotel to recuperate and remained in good health for the rest of the film.

Richard and I did, however, find ourselves in another near-deadly situation down there. We had a long weekend free so we hired a little plane between us and went to Mexico City for a break from Veracruz. His girlfriend had gone on ahead and Shakira was flying in from Los Angeles to join me there. I had told her not to come to the location, as it was too boring. We had a less than great time in the city. The moment that Shakira got off the plane, her lips swelled up as the result of an allergy to a shrimp cocktail that she had eaten on it – a great start to a romantic weekend. Aeroplanes by the way are another place where I practise my dysentery-preventing scheme, and if you drink enough it also cures fear of flying. We met Terence Young the director there, and over the course of the weekend he talked me into doing a duff film for which I nearly never got paid. So far my weekend in Paradise was not going too well. Terence is a very sophisticated fellow and always knows anybody who is anybody and at his invitation, although we knew no one in the city, we were soon invited to dinner with the cream of Mexican society. Like all good things the weekend came quickly to an end. Shakira flew back to Los Angeles vowing to fast on the plane and on the Monday Richard and I took the same little plane back to Veracruz. However, by this time the location was changed so we had to land at a grass runway airport at a small place with an unpronounceable name.

As we were coming in to land I was looking out of the window on to a road that ran alongside the airport and there was a small convoy of Mexican soldiers tearing along it at terrific speed. I pointed them out to Richard and said, 'I wonder where they are going in such a hurry?'

The question was of course rhetorical, or so we thought, but we were about to find out that it wasn't. The plane landed and we gathered up our things and descended the little steps on to the grass. We both stood there for a moment looking around and then, very slowly, we put our bags on the ground and raised our hands above our heads. Now we knew what the soldiers were doing there. They were standing in a half-circle with their rifles pointed at us.

An officer came forward and told us in broken English that this was a notorious drug-smuggling airfield. He pointed to the other little planes lined up along the field, and they were all full of bullet-holes. Our Mexican pilot intervened and explained who we were, but not nearly quickly enough for me. I was looking over the barrel of the rifle nearest me into a pair of eyes that just wanted to kill a gringo. I hoarsely whispered to the officer if he could ask his soldiers to lower their rifles. 'Yes,' he said, to my great relief. He barked an order and the rifles were lowered, the last one being that closest to me, with the soldier almost in tears from disappointment.

That was the last of anything remotely interesting on this film and after an eternity we all flew quickly back to our loved ones. The picture was not well received anywhere, but when it was finally released in America they hammered the last nail in its coffin by changing the title to *Beyond the Limit* which not only effectively got rid of anybody who had read the book or was a Graham Greene fan, but also made it sound like a science fiction film. A couple of years later I was eating dinner in the dining room of the Connaught Hotel, when Graham Greene walked in. I flinched visibly. He was notorious for hating the films of his books and I ducked down in my seat. I had never met him but he might just recognise me. He did, and came straight over. He was smiling, which was something at least. He introduced himself and told me that while he had hated the film, he liked my performance, then he walked away. I never saw him again. I continued my dinner, rather pleased with myself.

I had been in Hollywood now for five years and had made some tremendous friends and enjoyed a happy, comfortable life, but I had left my country to start a new life at the age of forty-five, which was of course too late, even in a country and with people that I loved so much. I had been very unhappy for some time now and Shakira being the incredible wife that she is, had seen what this was doing to me and although she adored living there, for my sake she made a deal with me. The deal was this: we both agreed that my performance in *Educating Rita* was the best I had ever given, possibly the best I ever would give, so if I didn't get the Oscar for that, there was no professional reason to continue living in the town and being unhappy doing it.

Just as Lewis Gilbert had predicted, both Julie Walters and I were nominated for an Oscar for our performances in *Educating Rita*, and we duly turned up for the ceremony. I honestly did think that my performance in that film was my personal best, and I did believe I stood a chance of winning that year – until I saw the other leading actor nominees. I realised immediately that I had no chance, and I even knew who was going to win. The nominees were Albert Finney and Tom Courtney for *The Dresser*, Tom Conti for *Reuben, Reuben* and myself for *Educating Rita*. All four of us were British actors and then there was one American actor, Robert Duvall, who was nominated for a film I have never seen called *Tender Mercies*. Robert's performance in his film was brilliant, I was told, but even if it hadn't been we all thought he was going to win.

The ceremony was in the Dorothy Chandler Pavilion which is situated 'downtown' – a phrase which strikes terror in the hearts of all true residents of Beverly Hills because you know that it is going to take forever to get there. It all starts very early, around five o'clock, so that it catches prime-time television on the east coast, which is three hours ahead of Los Angeles. With the traffic holdups this means that you have to start out around three-thirty to get there on time, and as the ceremony is formal you find yourself struggling into evening dresses and bowties immediately after a large lunch. The lunch is large because you know that you are not going to eat again until at least eleven o'clock that night. You also cut down on taking a lot of liquid because you probably won't be able to have a pee until the same time as well. The interminable drive ends and you get out to cheering crowds and batteries of cameras as television interviewers from all over the world try to grab you as you progress slowly along a wide, red carpet like deposed European royalty going to the wedding of a relative who still has a country. The security is heavy and so is the insecurity.

This hurdle overcome, you get inside and are shown to your seat. Now, if you are nominated this moment is of the greatest importance because while the Oscars are scrupulously honest and no one but the Price Waterhouse accountants know the actual results, the television producers of the spectacle, for the sake of speeding up the programme, have to make an educated guess and try to seat potential winners near to the steps up to the stage where they will collect their awards, or at least on the aisle seats for quick access. I knew in my heart that I wasn't going to win and as I was shown my seat, it verified this instinct. I was seated four seats inside a row a long way from the stage, and when I looked to see where Robert was seated, there he was in the front row with nothing between him and the steps up to the stage. For the next three hours I practised my gallant loser's smile in readiness for the moment that he was announced as the winner and the cameras cut one by one to a sadistic close-up of the reaction of the losers. I was good at this, having done it twice before for *Alfie* and *Sleuth*. Being experienced I also knew to put my programme on the floor so that I could be seen clapping enthusiastically when the result was announced. I had been caught out with that on my other two losing occasions, and they weren't going to get me this time.

Robert won, I smiled and clapped, and the smile was really genuine, but for another reason entirely. *I was going home.* My last four films had been made in Hungary, New York, Ireland and Mexico, my next two were in Brazil and the Caribbean, and none of the numerous British directors who had come to America and made massively successful careers had ever offered me a part in their films, so there seemed to be no point in staying on and being miserable. So I sat there applauding Robert with a genuine smile on my face.

Winning the Oscar can be one of the most important moments in a movie actor's life, but *not* winning the Oscar is one of the least significant moments you can think of. When the result is announced and you haven't won, there is no sadness and no misery. It is just as if nothing has happened, which is, of course, the case: a complete negative.

As tricky as it was to get to the ceremony, retrieving your car afterwards used to be a nightmare, because after the awards are given, the governors of the Academy give a party, and in those days it was always somewhere else. This meant that everybody tried to get their car at the same time, which led to a wait of, in our case that night, an hour standing on the pavement. One of the best things about winning was that you got your car quickly! It doesn't happen now. The dinner and the ceremony are held in the same place so the requests for cars are staggered. If you lose, the Governor's Ball can be a bore because everybody comes up to you and commiserates as though you are about to commit suicide.

Having been to the Governor's Ball and suffered these commiserations twice before, I didn't fancy doing it again and tonight my luck was in. I was going home! I didn't know when, but I was some day soon, and tonight Irving Lazar was giving the first of his now legendary Oscar parties. This one was not in Spago as they are now, but in the private room upstairs at the Bistro restaurant, our favourite formal place in town. At Irving's party the guests are all those who have not been nominated that year, nor asked to present an award. The first arrivals after the ceremony are the losers and later the winners come. You get to see everybody. When I arrived I was completely taken aback at the reception I received – after all, I *had* lost, but I stood there dumbfounded by a standing ovation from what was really the élite of motion pictures. It was like an honour in itself. I suddenly found that tears were streaming down my face as Cary Grant came forward and gave me a hug and whispered in my ear, 'You were a winner here, Michael.' I stood there for a long while and it gradually dawned on me just how many genuine friends I had in this town, and even though we had just made the decision to leave it, both Shakira and I knew we would be back some way or the other. Irving's party was a tremendous success and another Hollywood tradition was born. Even though I had lost, it was one of the happiest evenings of my life. I did win the Golden Globe for the performance, however, and the British Academy Award so *Educating Rita* was not ignored completely.

Blame It On Rio was my next project – an adaptation of a French film. It was a very risqué comedy about a man who is seduced by his best friend's young daughter. Just *how* risqué it was we didn't discover until it was released. I saw the French film and liked it very much. It was light-hearted with a kind of innocence with which only the French seem to be able to treat sex. The film was directed by Stanley Donen, who had made many successful films including *Singing in the Rain*, *Funny Face* and one of my all-time favourites, *Charade*. So I was delighted to be working with him. The script by Larry Gelbart was very funny, and although the story was a bit dangerous we all believed we could get away with it. Stanley cast a beautiful unknown young girl who had never made a movie as the daughter of my friend. Her name was Michelle Johnson. Besides being beautiful, this girl had a stunning figure and this is where we started to go wrong, because Stanley shot a lot of scenes of her topless, against my wishes. But Stanley shot on regardless and what had seemed so innocuous on the topless beaches of St Tropez where the French film had been made now suddenly seemed vulgar and gratuitous in our film, and did us a lot of harm. Unbeknownst to us, there was worse to come.

My daughter in the film was played by a beautiful, young and very skilled actress who impressed me so much that I can remember telling her that I thought she would be a star one day, and how right I was. Her name was Demi Moore. My best friend was played by a wonderful funny man called Joe Bologna, who was a particular delight because, like me, he enjoyed doing comedy schtick and we used to practise this all day together until we got to a point where we figured, quite wrongly I am sure, that we had an act we could take to Las Vegas! Michelle worked very hard and did a very creditable and surprisingly good job for a newcomer, first time out. So the film itself was a very happy experience in spite of my nagging worry about the nudity.

The great joy for me of course was, not only was I in Rio – a town I had always wanted to visit, but added to this Natasha was on school holidays so she and Shakira came as well. We stayed at the luxurious Rio Palace Hotel in the presidential suite right on the end of Copacabana Beach where Ipanema Beach starts so the location and the accommodation couldn't be bettered. It was boiling hot when we arrived in the middle of March, so hot in fact that we went to the Brazilian Grand Prix motor race and it was held up for a while because the track was melting. The first Sunday there I remember very well because it was my fiftieth birthday. We had a small dinner party to celebrate, and this is where I got my first experience of the way that things work in Brazil. I ordered a bottle of red Bordeaux wine and was amazed to see the waiter go to a very smart refrigerator at the back of the restaurant, take the wine out of there and bring me it, all frosty. I told him in no uncertain terms that I didn't want the wine from the fridge as red Bordeaux should never be served cold but always at room temperature. 'I know,' he said with an expert's smile. 'That is why I put it in the fridge. I was trying to get the temperature down to the same as a room in France.' There was no arguing with this logic but I finally settled for a bottle out of the back room where it was a hundred degrees. I'd rather have red Bordeaux boiling than frozen.

The next day was a Monday and we started shooting at night on the beach, where disaster struck almost immediately. I had to chase Michelle in the dark and I fell over a rock and broke my little toe. This may sound funny and inconsequential, but it left me in agony for the rest of the film. I tried to keep my special shoe on whenever Stanley shot a scene in which you couldn't see my feet, but he had made his mark shooting tap-dancing films and so my feet always seemed to be visible; then I had to wear the now unbearably tight costume shoes. There were few other setbacks, apart from sudden torrential storms which lasted fifteen minutes and left everybody drowned out for the rest of the day, and a peculiar moral question that sprang up out of the blue.

Like everybody else, I had heard that Brazil in general and Rio in particular were very liberal places sexually speaking. I'd only been there a couple of days when the English electricians had taken me on a boys' night out to have a few beers and see the local striptease. The latter reinforced my view of Rio, as the opening act consisted of three couples in sexual congress. The girls on the beaches wore the tiniest of thongs to just cover their fronts and completely reveal their rather gorgeous behinds, but the one thing none of us had anticipated until we came to do the scene where I see Michelle on the beach topless, was that topless bathing and sunbathing for women in Rio is illegal and the law is strictly enforced. What's more, when we found a remote beach where it was possible to shoot it, it was very difficult to find any Brazilian women who would appear in the film topless, which is particularly strange when their bottom halves concealed nothing, and when every Brazilian film that we had ever seen contained sustained scenes of total nudity. However, the assistant directors refused to give up looking, diligent lads that they were, and eventually found some extras in the end, but the whole thing was a big surprise for everybody. I had a theory that this regulation had been introduced by the women, since I couldn't help noticing that while almost every one of them had a great derrière, they were not so hot in the breast department. Vanity, I thought, was the mother of morality there.

Many things are not quite what they seem to be in Rio, we discovered as our sojourn there progressed. Brazil has a reputation for beautiful women and many of them are in actual fact stunning, but all the women on our film were quick to point out that the men on the whole were even more attractive than the women. I am not an expert on this, but I took their word for it. Of course, not only are the men attractive but some of the most beautiful women there are transexuals – an operation which seemed to be very popular there; thus one had this strange anomaly where the men were not only the most attractive men, they were often the most attractive women as well. Confusing.

Rio de Janeiro was at that time the centre of plastic surgery – a position now, of course, usurped by my then home-town of Beverly Hills so it is not surprising that the best friend we

481

made in Rio was the celebrated plastic surgeon, Ivo Pitinguey. He was a most charming and hospitable man and, like everybody else we met in Rio, fabulously wealthy. We only met rich people in Rio because Brazil is one of those countries like the Philippines where there are only the very rich and the very poor – and the very poor don't want to meet you, they want you to give them something. Cracks were beginning to appear in the façade of this country which even I in my insulated world could not help noticing and being angered by. Ivo, however, took care of us socially and we had a marvellous time with him, especially on weekends when he would fly us all to his own private island that was really the nearest I ever came to Paradise. He had stocked the place with every tropical animal and plant that it was possible to buy, and for Natasha who loved animals so much, it was heaven. The place was extraordinarily beautiful in a primitive jungle sort of way, but the accommodation and amenities were luxurious and completely modern.

The food was great and the drink flowed constantly, along with a flow of interesting people, but it was Ivo himself who was the most fascinating of all. He told strange stories of his patients, never of course giving away identities. He recounted the day that a woman came to see him with an enormous nose, and as they were doing the preliminary interview he was looking at it and wondering how to set about improving it when to his surprise she told him that she wanted her breasts, which were actually quite firm, lifted, and never once did she mention her proboscis. He had taken me to his office to see how things were done before we left for the island, and I had noticed that he always had a nurse present in the room with him. I asked if that was a sort of insurance against being accused of some misdemeanour when examining a woman patient. No, he told me. The woman was a top psychiatrist disguised as a nurse, who was there to evaluate the mental state of the patient. Sometimes people's appearance problems indicated psychiatric problems as well. No wonder he was so successful: he seemed to have thought of everything! A Russian ballerina whose breasts he had just done arrived one weekend and treated us all constantly to an exhibition of Ivo's work, at the drop of a brassière, even at meal-times if someone new arrived.

One day I tackled him about the gap between the rich and the poor in his country and the way he treated the very rich for cosmetic reasons when there were so many wretches who really needed him and his skills, and he very quickly informed me that he spent one day a week at a free hospital for the children of the poor, treating burn victims. Ivo had some weird and wonderful ideas. One day we were having dinner when he suddenly said to me: 'What was the greatest physical development in the evolution of the human being?' I suggested speech, making tools or making fire but he said, no – the greatest development was the human thumb. 'Until the thumb, nothing could really be accomplished by the human being.' I laughed at first, but he told me to try to get through the day of a modern man without the use of the thumbs. He was right, of course. It is impossible.

Another man I met up with in Rio was an old friend from Los Angeles, the Brazilian musician Sergio Mendes. He had come back home for a holiday. I talked to him one day about the abject poverty of the masses in his country which was beginning to act on my feelings of guilt at the life I was leading. I came from a poor family in England, I told him.

'You think you come from a poor family?' he scoffed. 'Let me take you to where I come from,' and he took me to a place on the shore exactly opposite Copacabana Beach, but so far away that it was almost out of sight. He drove me round there and showed me the beach and his little home town – the kind of place that tourists never see. It was terrible: the beach was strewn with so much filth that instead of seagulls scavenging, there were vultures, hundreds of them.

I never visited the Favelas, the poor shanty towns, as it was too dangerous. The people, I could see even from a distance, lived in conditions disgusting beyond belief. The most upsetting part of it all was the orphan children of the streets. They slept outside the door of the hotel where we were living and begged from us every day, and I had got to know some of them quite well. I am certainly not a rabid Socialist, but I do think that some form of taxation of the rich to provide welfare for the needy, the children and the sick and old is absolutely necessary before any country can call itself civilised. The mentality of these children had been conditioned by the streets, and to survive they would steal anything. One day I was sitting just outside the hotel at an open air café with some of our English electricians and they were talking to some of these kids and accusing them of being a load of little thieves, when their leader took offence at this slur and protested that they were all as honest as anybody else. One of the men produced some coins and said that he would prove they were thieves. He gave the kid the cash and told him to go and buy him a cheap disposable lighter. As the gang ran off he shouted, 'I bet you don't come back with the lighter!' The leader called as they disappeared round the corner, 'We'll be back and you will see how honest we are.' We sat for a while, about half an hour, with all the other electricians teasing the one who had given the boy the money and telling him that he had seen the last of the lads. Suddenly, after about an hour, when we had given up all hope of ever seeing them again, the gang reappeared with the leader in front. He went to the man who had given them the money and said, 'There you are,' and gave him two lighters *and* his money back. 'Don't ever say we are dishonest again,' and they all walked away, proud at having proved their point once and for all.

Just before we left, I discovered that Natasha had a talent I had long since suspected. We decided to go to the top of Sugar Loaf Mountain on the cable car, a very beautiful but slightly hairy trip. There is a restaurant up there with a great view of the whole of Rio and a sort of mini-carnival for tourists every night. I love the music of Brazil and brought back about two hundred cassettes, but we had missed the real carnival by a week. We had been told that it was no good starting the film until the carnival was over because none of our Brazilian workers would turn up. So here was a chance to get at least the flavour of it, and it was really good. At the end the whole cast of dancers and musicians came on stage and invited members of the audience to come and dance with them. Natasha, who was only eight years old at the time, went up and started to dance absolutely on the beat and in no time

484

was copying the professionals around her and making a great job of it. I sat there open-mouthed. My little girl was a great dancer even if the significance of some of the movements she was copying escaped her.

We had all had a marvellous time, but all too soon Natasha had to go back to school. The night before my wife and daughter left, we had been invited to dine with the richest host and hostess in all Rio – an honour indeed. And a disaster.

The hostess, it turned out, fancied me and sat me next to her at dinner, while Shakira was planted miles away in the corner with a group of people who did not even speak English. I did not know this at the time, I was enjoying myself but a bit worried by the hostess' intimate attention and anxious in case Shakira could see what was going on. Shakira, I might add at this late juncture, is a very jealous woman. She never had many problems because most women give up any evil intentions they may have towards me the moment that they see her, but not this particular one. She carried on blithely unaware of what was coming. I knew that Shakira had a temper, but it was slow to rise, and I had no idea there was any real fury in her. I also knew that she used the occasional swearword, which I'm sorry to say she had learned from me, but nothing could have prepared either me or my hostess for what happened next. The party had been held in their enormous penthouse on top of an office building, and when it was over the host and hostess accompanied us all downstairs to say goodnight in the street as we picked up our cars. When it came to the point where the hostess said goodnight to me, Shakira was slightly in her way and she brushed her aside and kissed me on the lips. That was it. Shakira, who had been boiling now for four hours, exploded. Never before or since have I seen her in such a fury. She called this women every single filthy name you could think of, in a voice range that I never knew she possessed. The entire assembly stood on the pavement in stunned silence as Shakira ripped this woman apart. Finally, her energy sapped and her voice almost gone, she collapsed into the car, satisfied. I jumped in beside her quickly and told the driver to go as fast as possible. Shakira and Natasha left for Los Angeles the next day and I stayed on for another few days to finish the film, with plenty of time to ponder a whole new side to my wife's personality.

Socially, the phone never rang again for me in Rio, which didn't bother me. I had seen and done the rounds and for the most part enjoyed it, but I was now thoroughly sickened at the disregard of these greedy, over-privileged people for the disgusting poverty of their fellow countrymen. I had always wanted to go there, but I couldn't wait to get out, and as I left I realised that I never wanted to go back again unless the whole fabric of their society changed to a more just and caring one.

When *Blame It On Rio* came out it ran into a tremendous hammering and even I was stunned by the vehemence of the critics. After all, it was only topless. There was no full frontal nudity at all and in a picture that ran for two hours there was less than four minutes of it. The fuss reminded me of *Dressed to Kill*, when people asked me why I had made a movie with so many murders in it. When I told them that there was only one, some people called me a liar. I think that you see what you want to see, especially if you are a hypocrite. The most hysterical reviews came, I noticed, from female writers. I made a particular study of the reviews of this picture, as I was so taken aback by the over-reaction to what I saw as a rather amusing little light comedy. I eventually came to the conclusion that we would have fared better with the lady critics if Michelle Johnson's breasts had been uglier and smaller.

There was, however, a more serious reason why we were slated when the film came out in America. A big anti-incest campaign was in progress, and for some obscure reason the film became involved in this, the critics missing the point that I was having an affair with my friend's daughter. The cant and hypocrisy that was wheeled out by the American critics when the film appeared was beyond belief. *Blame It On Rio* never got the same phony moral reception in any other country in the world. Two reviews in particular incensed me, by critics whom I knew personally. They complained hotly about the disparity in age between our two characters. Michelle Johnson was eighteen years old and I was forty-five. A romance between two people of those ages was quite possible, I believed. After all, one of the critics was fifty-six and living with a girl of nineteen. I can't help noting how the same female writers who screamed about *Blame It On Rio* now write with glee about fifty-year-old women having satisfying relationships with 'toy boys'. I am glad to say that the film went on to make a lot of money all over the world, despite all this fuss.

41

Paradise Found

In 1984 Prince Andrew, whom I had already met in London, paid a visit to Los Angeles and we gave a big party at our house for him. For one evening of my life I decided to play Minna Wallis with the new bachelor in town. There were of course guests with conventional pedigrees – Henry Kissinger, the British Ambassador and Lew Wasserman, the head of Universal Pictures, with his wife Edie. Sprinkled among the heavyweights, however, were the beauties we had invited, much like Minna had done for me so many years ago; Jamie Lee Curtis, Ursula Andress and Linda Evans among them. They all wanted to meet the world's most eligible man, but they couldn't get past the security that surrounded him eating our hors d'hoeuvres and chatting up the women themselves. Prince Andrew went home alone, with four security men. But for us, it was definitely an A crowd evening – such a tremendous success that even Shakira admitted that we couldn't top that socially, so it was as good a time as ever to start looking for a home back in England and we never really gave another big party in that house again.

The summer of 1984 was beautiful in England, and there was only one small fly in the ointment. With my usual perfect timing I had chosen to relocate just as the bottom started to fall out of the Beverly Hills real estate market and British property prices were going through the roof.

Shakira and I were staying at Arlington House again and our luck, which was to hold all summer, started early here. Dorrit Zarach, a great friend of ours, knew the owner of the block, a very wealthy Arab called Mahdi Altijir and she brought him to tea one day at our flat, which had been booked at the last minute and was not the best one in the block by a long shot. When Mr Altijir saw it he decided it was not good enough and gave us his penthouse flat in the same block, explaining that he had several homes in England and would not be using that one this summer. We were delighted to accept and immediately moved into this beautiful and sumptuously decorated apartment. It was so sumptuous in fact that I nearly got a hernia the first time I tried to move one of the dining-room chairs – they were made of solid silver and weighed a ton. So instead of paying a fortune for a mediocre flat we were now living in the best apartment in the block for nothing – a good start to the visit.

Unlike many prospective house-buyers I knew exactly what I wanted and where it should be, so we set out on our search with the confidence of the truly innocent or stupid. I wanted another house like the Mill House, on the banks of the Thames, but further away from London. Windsor, where we had lived before, had now become like a suburb rather than countryside. My next proviso was that the house had to be on a stretch of the river with the longest distance between two locks. The Thames rises after it leaves the tidal stretch in London and there are masses of locks to raise the boats as you go upriver to its source. The locks finish at the town of Tedding, which is where the tidal part ends. Hence the name Teddington, which actually started out being called 'Tide end Town'. I wanted to have a small river boat and I didn't want to have to go through a lock, which were always crowded at weekends and holidays, every time I went out on a little trip. I found the longest distance between locks lay between Benson Lock and Cleeve Lock in Oxfordshire. The stretch between these two was six miles, the longest on the Thames, enough for a good Sunday-afternoon cruise without having to go through either of the locks.

I also wanted direct frontage to the river, and as a lot of the river bank is open as public footpath, this narrowed it down further. I went to see one house which had a towpath or public footpath on the banks of the river and no direct frontage, because the estate agent told me that it was interesting, and he

489

was right. It was a big gloomy Victorian house and I knew immediately that I did not want it but with typical English good manners we went round the house mumbling grunts of interest and looking at our watches whenever the agent's back was turned. We had wasted hours with this form of polite behaviour when we were looking at houses in America. You always know instantly when you don't want a particular house. On the other hand I had reminded Shakira of the old business adage that enthusiasm is the enemy of the bargain, so we did not repeat the experience we had at one beautiful house in Beverly Hills where the moment she walked in, she said very loudly, 'It's lovely! We've *got* to have it!' The price of course shot up half a million dollars instantly and we couldn't afford it. On this trip she had learned her lesson so well that she was sometimes downright insulting, especially if the owners were present, so we had to calm that down as well and try to achieve a middle-of-the-road lack of enthusiasm.

Anyway, the agent showed us through this house, which was not only gloomy on the outside but grim on the inside too. The previous owner had obviously been gone a long time because the whole place was covered in a veneer of dust and it had that peculiar empty-house smell you get when nobody has opened a window or door for months. The other strange feature was that the former owners had not taken anything with them. The house looked as though it had been vacated quickly, with everything left in place – there was even a table laid for a breakfast that had never been eaten. It soon dawned on me that the last owner had died here and had moved up instead of on. This belief was reinforced when we came to the bedroom where, from being grim and gloomy, the house now became downright macabre. The bedclothes were turned back as though a body had been taken out and there was a half-finished bottle of medicine on the bedside table and at the foot of the bed was a fading doctor's chart. By now the place was giving us the willies but we were hooked and wanted to get to the bottom of the obvious mystery about it. We were next shown the office where the former owner had obviously worked, and this was very strange as well. It was about sixty feet long but only about ten feet wide with a desk inside the door and the rest of the room lined with bookcases filled with books on medicine and poisons and anatomy. It was all very strange and I could contain myself no longer. I asked the estate agent to whom the house had belonged. He seemed surprised that we hadn't been told before because, he informed us, the house would have to be maintained as a museum and we would have to build a new house in the grounds.

'Who lived here?' I interrupted, both of us now dying to find out.

'Agatha Christie,' he replied. 'This is where she died.'

We informed him that the place was not quite what we were looking for and carried on our search along that section of the Thames. Eventually we saw every house that was up for sale but had no luck. There were another couple of provisos which were making it even more difficult. I wanted the house to be in a village that was a cul de sac, so that there was no passing traffic and one that had no pub or shop, in other words no communal meeting place where the villagers could discuss the new owner of whatever house I bought. I had been a celebrity and lived in the English countryside long enough to know that down that road lay gossip and curiosity and trouble. Having looked at all the houses that we could find for sale and been unsuccessful I decided to find a village that suited my requirements and wait for a house to come up for sale. After a long search we discovered a small village on the non-footpath banks of the Thames which was a dead-end and had no pub or shop. There was nothing for sale the first time I went there but the second time a week later there was one house. We looked at it and although it wasn't absolutely right it did meet all my main requirements, and we were tired and desperate by now so I went ahead and made a deal. Now property prices as I have said were booming in England and the market was very volatile. Sellers often indulged in a practice called 'gazumping', which meant that after you had made a deal, they would suddenly say they had received a better offer and ask for more money. This is what happened to me. I told the guy to take the new offer and refused to pay more and the deal fell through.

As we left the house with the estate agent, to my surprise he said, 'You do know that there is another house for sale in this village, don't you?'

'No, there isn't,' I replied instantly. 'I know every house in this village and there is nothing for sale.'

'Yes, there is,' he insisted. 'The sale of a house that went through before you came here has just fallen through and the property is back on the market today.'

'Where is it?' Shakira and I said together. Both of us, we agreed later, immediately felt that our luck was being changed for us by this little bolt from the blue.

We got back in the car and drove to the other end of the little village and turned into the lane that led to the church. We first came to a lovely little cottage garden and then a row of three, pretty little Tudor cottages on the right, while on the left were a couple of farmworkers' cottages and then some barns and the wall of the farmyard which led down to the gates of the churchyard at the end. This was perfect. It was not only a dead-end village, but this lane was a dead-end as well, literally in this case, for at the end of it was the church and graveyard. Back on the right was a gate set in a wall and a faded sign that said *Rectory Farmhouse*. The gate was open and we drove in past a lodge on the left which was a staff house, we were informed, and down a drive that bent slowly to the left and gradually revealed the house. Shakira has an instinct that other people don't have. I'm not saying she's a witch exactly, but she does have a very uncanny side. We had not even reached the bend in the drive and could not even see the house when she leaned across to me and whispered in my ear, 'We must have it.'

'We haven't even seen the bloody house from the outside yet. Wait a minute,' I whispered furiously back in case the agent had overheard her quiet enthusiasm.

As we came round the bend, a serenity swept over me as we saw the house for the first time. It was about two hundred years old and a mass of steep gables in the roof, with old-fashioned diamond-shaped leaded windows, and although it was painted an incongruous white, most of it was hidden by ivy, wisteria and climbing roses. On the right was a kitchen garden hidden behind a hedge and on the left a very old stable

492

block and a huge barn. So far it was Paradise and perfect, and no matter what the rest was like I had decided that Shakira was right. We had to have it. We also had another proviso, that the front door should be correctly placed. This was very important. In Los Angeles Shakira had a friend who was a brilliant cook, an old Chinese lady called Madame Wong and when Shakira had told her that we were going to look for a new house in England she had passed on an old Chinese proverb about houses. 'If your front door opens directly on to the street your money will quickly flow out of the house.' This front door was far from the street, so we were all right, or so I thought until I bought the place and got the builders in. There must have been an ancient road that had gone right past the front door at one time!

We went inside and met the owner, an old lady who had recently been widowed, hence the sale of the house. It was beautiful inside, with old oak beams and pillars and enormous open fireplaces. Some of it was three hundred years old and some two hundred, she proudly informed us, ignoring the dreadful extension, circa 1957. That had to go, I decided immediately, and a lot of money needed to be spent on the place. It was very shabby and neglected, however when we went out of the other side of the house, there was masses of room for the extension that I was already planning. The garden was a mess but right outside the house I could see the remains of a huge croquet lawn crouching beneath the weeds ready to spring into life at the slightest bit of attention.

The house was two storeys high and the bedrooms were just as quaint as the rest of the house, with beams and odd quirky corners. It was all delightful and just what I had always envisaged in my dream home. There were eight British bedrooms i.e. a tiny room with a bed in it and no bath en suite; these could be turned into three good bedroom suites. On the ground floor was a formal lounge and library, which is now my office and where I am writing at this moment. The small lounge where the former owners spent most of their time was in the 1957 bit that had to go, but it was right for my new living room because it faced west and the setting sun – another one of my stipulations. It was all there, we had found it at last. We looked right round the outside of the house. The kitchen garden was huge and there was a small orchard. The stables were derelict but would make a wonderful guesthouse, I quickly decided, and there was a tennis court that nobody had ever played wearing shorts, by the look of it. The whole place reeked of neglect and decay, but that suited me. I wanted to start afresh and make my own home. At least I wasn't going to have to pay for decoration that I hated and would have to replace.

The estate agent informed us that there was two hundred yards of direct frontage to the river, but it was not possible even to see the river from the house, as the land in front of it was so overgrown. It was obvious that there were about five acres there that had never ever been cultivated. The old lady told us that this was designated 'Flood Plain' as it flooded to a depth of two or three feet every winter so it was impossible to cultivate it. We borrowed a chopper and after half an hour had hacked a path through the dense undergrowth and reached the river bank, and there it was – the Thames, only about forty yards wide this far inland and we were situated on the start of a wide bend, a stunning sight.

By now we had fallen completely in love with the place and knew that we must have it. On our way back to the house from the river we spotted a small lake with an island on it teeming with water birds, and we saw the quick blue flash of that good-luck sign of the superstitious countryside, the very rare and exquisitely beautiful Kingfisher. We also spotted another good-luck sign – a mulberry tree. This plant is so difficult to grow that if it flourishes in your garden, it is a sign of good luck. Seeing the lake solved the problem of five acres of wasted and unplantable flood plain: the solution was obviously to build another lake and with the extra soil, make a garden that was a foot higher than the floodwater. This I eventually did and now have two beautiful lakes and two wonderful raised gardens.

The old real-estate adage that you should take a friend with you when you look at a new house and see if he or she sits down and if they do, buy it, took on a new meaning here. We sat and had tea with the owner and bought the house on the spot for £380,000. As we were very reluctantly leaving a couple of hours later, she started to leave with us. She told us that she did not live at that house any longer, but at another one that she owned nearby. 'Rent us the house for the summer,' I blurted out suddenly. She thought for a moment and then asked for a sum of money that she thought was exorbitant. We were really the victims here of enthusiasm being the enemy of the bargain but we no longer cared and the sum she asked was negligible for us, so the next day, we actually moved in and started one of the happiest summers of my life.

Saab, my lovely mother-in-law, brought Natasha over from Los Angeles at the end of term and we all settled down to an idyllic summer even though the standard of living by comparison with our Beverly Hills home was a trifle primitive; we exchanged the standard of living for a quality of life. I have always described the difference between these two states as follows: a standard of living is two cars, two television sets, two refrigerators, one psychiatrist and some pills. A quality of life is one car, one television set, one refrigerator and no psychiatrist or pills. As a contradiction to this theory, we found that there was only one black and white television set in the house so we went out and bought a coloured one. We hired a car and bought three bicycles, cutlery, plates, pots and pans and some tennis rackets and some balls. The cooking was a bit on the Third-World side as we only had an Aga stove which ran on coal and we all took turns at being stoker for a day. We filled the place with groceries and booze, including a sizeable order of Pimms and lemonade, and we were ready for a blissful summer holiday, English country-style. With Natasha we had a tremendous piece of luck. There was a wonderful farming family living up the road and they had a young daughter called Catherine who was the same age as our daughter, eleven, and they became firm friends so there was a very important problem solved as any of you with children will know. Whenever you go to a strange place it is absolutely crucial to find your kid a friend and we found a great one. The sun shone constantly and we had our new home and life could not be better. Shakira spent her time getting the old house in shape, while I spent mine designing the new house and garden and Natasha was always over at Catherine's farm, where with her great love of animals, she was in her element.

Some of the things we did that summer were so peculiarly English. We were invited to lunch by the authoress Barbara Cartland, which was a bit of a surprise because we didn't know her but were curious so we went anyway. The other guests were Douglas Fairbanks Junior, Buzzer Haddingham, the President of the Wimbledon Tennis Club at the time, and General Sir Robert Ford, who was the Commanding Officer of the Chelsea Barracks, that home for the old soldiers known as the Chelsea Pensioners. It was a delightful lunch at Ms Cartland's home in Hertfordshire, but still a bit of a mystery was the reason for the occasion and what we guests, who did not really know each other, had in common. The answer, I eventually discovered from Douglas, was that Barbara had always nursed a secret passion for Lord Louis Mountbatten, and the common bond that we all shared was that we knew him! Another very English thing we did was to go to the Derby for the first time, and to Wimbledon for the first time. We dined by the Thames at The Compleat Angler in Marlow and at the Waterside Inn at Bray. I was doing many things now out of nostalgia for the way of life in my own country that I had never done when I lived there, and having a great time doing it. This was also the year that we gave our first 4 July party at Langan's. Because it was the summer and the time of the Wimbledon tennis tournament, a lot of our American friends were in England, and as 4 July coincides with the last days of Wimbledon, it is a weekend when our English friends are in town. Most of the people whom we know never spend summer weekends in London, so it worked out very conveniently for everybody. This was the first of several annual parties that we gave at Langan's, and they were always star-studded: Bjorn Borg, Jack Nicholson, Mick Jagger and Jerry Hall, Nureyev, Johnny Carson, Joan Collins, Tom Selleck. The guest list was so staggering that we sent waiters out on to the street with champagne and sandwiches for the crowds of paparazzi who had waited so long. It would be their last chance to photograph a group of celebrities en masse as the

496

British entertainment industry disappeared over the horizon in all directions.

Meanwhile, as I was finishing the film *Water* I received an invitation to go straight from that film into another. *The Holcroft Covenant* was going to be directed by John Frankenheimer, who had directed one of my favourite films *The Manchurian Candidate*. The book was by a great thriller writer, Robert Ludlum, so it sounded like a winner. Wrong again. The only certain thing was that my summer idyll was over, because as the part had originally been given to James Caan and he had dropped out at the last moment, I had to finish *Water* on the Friday night, and whizz off to Berlin to start filming on the Monday morning. It all happened so quickly that I didn't even have time for a wardrobe fitting and wore my own clothes in the movie. Even more to the point, I didn't have time to read the script properly, and only too late did I realize that I couldn't understand the plot, so God help the poor audience who would eventually see it. However, my fee came in handy for my plans for the new house, which were now becoming megalomaniacal.

After ten really fun weeks in Germany making *The Holcroft Covenant* (it's amazing how much fun you can have making a bad movie – part of the charm of this business) it was back to Los Angeles to join my family who had gone on ahead of me, as Natasha was due back at school. Autumn is the real party season there and this year was no different, except for the first three that I went to when I got back. Irwin Allen had always known that I was a big comedy fan and loved American comedians, so one night he gave me a surprise party in a private room in the Beverly Wilshire Hotel, where the guests were comedians only and their wives. The list of guests was impressive: George Burns, Milton Berle, Danny Thomas, Bob Newhart, Steve Allen, Dick Shawn, Red Buttons, Sid Caesar and my friend the comedy writer, Larry Gelbart. I was very touched by the trouble that Irwin had gone to and the fact that they all turned up. I knew all their acts very well, but the material that night was new to me. I think they used the occasion to try out new jokes. A lot of the time I was the only one laughing because comedians do not laugh at jokes, they sit there committing them to memory. George Burns said the funniest line for me that evening. He said, 'Acting is simple. All you have to do is be sincere and then learn to fake it.'

Milton Berle hit me with a funny line the moment I came in the door. There was an old band-leader in America at the time with a very old-fashioned orchestra and his name was Lawrence Welk. As I walked into the room that evening Milton was smoking one of his cheap cigars and I asked what brand it was. 'A Lawrence Welk,' he informed me. 'What's that?' I asked, walking straight into the trap. 'A load of shit with a band round it,' he replied. Milton is notorious for overstaying his time on stage. When he does his act, once he starts getting laughs he goes on and on. That evening, the first line he said was, 'Tonight my act will be very short, and if you believe that, you'll believe that there is going to be a Liberace Junior.' He also told us Ed Wynn's – the old comedian and father of the actor Keenan Wynn – description of the difference between a comic and a comedian. A comic, he said, is a man who says funny things. A comedian is a man who says things funny. To end his spot Milton raised his glass to me and said: '*L'chayim.*' It was a Hebrew word for 'life', Milton explained. 'As a matter of fact,' he continued, 'I have an uncle who is doing *L'chayim.*'

As we left that evening he was standing by a big blown-up photo of Charlie Chaplin which was part of the décor for the party. In the picture, which was a scene from a film, Charlie was with a woman who was holding a baby. Milton then said a strange thing about the picture which I didn't believe for a moment, but then Steve Allen came along and convinced me that it was true. The woman in the picture with Chaplin was Milton Berle's mother, and the baby in her arms was Steve Allen. It is moments like that which fascinate me about Hollywood. The evening was for me one of the best I ever had in Beverly Hills. It was also a privilege.

Not all dinner parties in Beverly Hills turned out so well. Zev Brown, a producer friend of mine, was making a picture that Muhammad Ali was involved in and he knew that I was a great fan of Ali's and had never met him, so when he had a dinner for him he invited me along. Everything went well for a while. I had heard rumours that all was not well with Ali, but when I finally met him he seemed fine and we were overwhelmed by his ebullient personality, which close up was even more overwhelming than on television. He was a great joker and at one point said to me, 'Do you want to see my right hook?' A bit apprehensive, I said yes, hoping that he would miss my chin in the demonstration. He stood absolutely still for a second or two and then said, 'Do you want to see it again?' He was full of fun and life as we sat down to eat, but I always remember talking to him about the time he lost his title to Joe Frazier. I was present at that fight, I told him, and I could not understand why, towards the end, he seemed just to stand there and take the punches without putting up any defence. Ali's answer has stayed with me to this day. He told me that Frazier had hit his arms so often and so hard that he had in fact paralysed them. At the end of the fight Ali could not even lift them to defend himself.

Our conversation at the dinner party continued, when suddenly in mid-sentence and speaking quite normally his voice went into a terrible, incomprehensible slur for just a few sentences and then returned to normal. It all happened so quickly that I thought I had been mistaken, and no one else reacted to this so I just carried on talking with him and after a few minutes it happened again. A string of completely unintelligible sentences came out and then it was back to normal conversation again.

I looked around the room but again no one had taken any notice. Then I caught Zev's eye and he made a sort of face that said, 'It's OK, take no notice.' At this point I realised that it was only Shakira and myself who did not know Ali; everybody else in the room knew him well and were used to this so it was ignored, but for me it was a terribly sad moment to see this great man in this condition which I figured was some sort of brain damage from boxing, and something that could only get worse. If indeed it was the result of punishment in the ring, it seems a terrible price to pay for such a short glare of fame.

Part Seven

42

Working with Woody

I have always been a great admirer of Woody Allen's – even now, as events in his personal life have become more traumatic than any he has ever filmed. In November 1984, I went to New York to film *Hannah and Her Sisters*. The producer obviously agreed with me as he offered me half my usual money, which I accepted. I had heard so many conflicting stories about working with Woody that I wanted to find out for myself. So off I went to New York and this time I stayed in the Helmsley Palace Hotel. This establishment was run by the now infamous Leona Helmsley, wife of the owner. Dudley Moore, who had just made *Arthur* in New York, told me that they had enormous suites there for long-stay guests. The ones I had stayed in before had all been a little cramped for living in for weeks on end, but these were large, and even better, they didn't start until the fiftieth floor of the hotel. They even had a special lift, well away from the lobby, and this lift did not stop for the first fifty floors. This was paradise, for when you are a well-known face in a hotel, if you don't get caught by autograph-hunters in the lobby, you get in-carcerated with a talkative fan for an eighty-floor ride in an elevator who extols your virtues to the trapped audience for the trip, and very often after the fan has left you are faced with irate passengers, usually drunk and wearing funny hats, who want to know, 'Who the hell are you, then?'

The other obstacle in getting to and from your room can be the elevator operator, who becomes a critic and as every day goes by, catalogues your career with progressively less flattering comments. So a hidden elevator that skipped the first fifty floors and didn't have an operator was heaven on earth and I moved in, although every time I told New Yorkers where I was staying, they clucked with sympathy and secretly thought my career was on the skids. My suite was enormous, and Leona Helmsley could not have been nicer, although she later took my views on taxes to the extreme. She arranged for a larger television, a stereo set and a bar to be installed and did everything she could to make me comfortable. First of all I went and had dinner at Elaine's as usual, where I met up with all my special New York friends, like Danny and Bobby Zarem and Martin Bregman and everybody else, it seemed. New York was still vibrant and joyful but some of the edge had been taken off the fun as AIDS began to decimate the ranks of the gay community who were responsible for a great deal of the city's energy. Shakira came with me for some of the time and so did Natasha, when she was on holiday from school. Our special trip was to the ice-rink at the Rockefeller Centre where we would sit in the hamburger bar by the rink and spend my free afternoons, which weren't many, watching the skaters and stoking up on hamburgers and French fries. It was walking back from one of these jaunts one afternoon that I lost a lot of money on a deal that Natasha suggested. We were passing a building site on Fifth Avenue when we saw an office which was selling apartments in the block that would eventually be erected there. 'That would be a great place to have an apartment in New York,' she said, with an eye on the proximity of the ice-rink, so I went in and got the details of the place. The price of the apartments seemed very reasonable, so I started to make a deal but was eventually talked out of it by friends who knew more about New York than I did, so I never bought a flat for Natasha in 'the Trump Tower' which eventually turned into one of the most exclusive condominiums in New York.

One Sunday I went to lunch with Boaty Boatwright, a lady agent who had been a great friend of ours when she lived in England. Now she had moved back to New York and gave the most interesting Sunday lunches in her flat in 'The Dakota', the famous apartment-building on the upper west side. You could never tell who you were going to meet there, but whoever it was they would be fascinating. On this particular

Sunday lunch had been somewhat alcoholic and I wound up in the kitchen, feeling slightly the worse for wear and talking to three other men whom I thought I recognised but could not put a name to. They all seemed to know who I was – well, it's easy with actors – so eventually I stopped the conversation and told them of my plight, at which they all introduced themselves. They were Kurt Vonnegut, Joseph Heller and Tom Wolfe – three of America's greatest writers. I had read all of their books and the reason I thought I knew them was that I vaguely remembered their faces from the dust-jackets on their books. Very embarrassing.

Apart from all this fun and frolic, I was of course in New York to make a movie with Woody Allen, a man of many myths, which were soon to be dispelled. The first one was about the script. People always said that you never saw a script on his movies until you were ready to shoot – and then you only received the part that you were in. Wrong. I had a script of the whole movie weeks before we started. All he said about it was that he would appreciate it if I never showed it to anyone, or told anyone the plot, because it took the edge off the movie when people saw it. A reasonable enough request, I thought. Another thing I had been told about Woody was that he didn't like going into the countryside. This was OK I thought, until I went to his apartment on Fifth Avenue and saw it had a great view overlooking Central Park and not only that, it was a penthouse and on the roof was a small country walk complete with shrubs and quite big trees. I immediately realised that it wasn't a case of Woody disliking the country, he just preferred the country to come to him.

Being an actor himself, Woody was wonderful to work with. He understood the problems and was very tolerant of them and he was a specialist in detail. One time I did a rehearsal and then a take and he cut it and said, 'Why didn't you do that movement with your hand like you did in the rehearsal?' I had no idea what I had done with my hand and he showed me and we shot it again with the movement in. He never missed a thing. He also did very long takes with no cuts or room for close-ups, so it was impossible to speed up a scene or cut into it if it was too slow. We all had a clause in our contracts to say that we would come back and reshoot any scenes where he had a problem with this. I agreed to this, knowing that it would never happen, but it did. I couldn't believe it – nor did I want to. I found myself back in New York several months later, reshooting a scene and playing it faster.

When people hear that I have worked with Woody they often think it must be a very amusing experience, but in fact the exact opposite was true. He was a very quiet and sensitive man who liked to work in a very quiet atmosphere, so even the crew on his pictures – who for the most part have worked with him many times, were the quietest crew with whom I have ever worked. The atmosphere on Woody's set was a bit like working in church. People also think that he will say funny things all the time. Not so. Like all comedy writers he doesn't say funny things, but listens to hear if you say something funny that he can use. His style of using a camera is very different from most directors, as well. I was doing a scene where I had a lot of dialogue and I had to go from one room to another as I spoke. When we rehearsed I noticed that the camera didn't follow me when I was speaking, and when I asked him why not, he told me that the camera was like his eye, and if he was looking at me as I was talking and I went into the other room still talking he would not get up and follow me there if he knew that I was coming back, so the camera did the same thing. In Woody's films you will see all the time characters walk in and out of shot while they are talking. Even in a scene where I was on the phone all by myself, he had me walking in and out of shot. This gives his films a strange kind of reality, as though the camera is a voyeuristic intruder that can't manage to see all the action. His camera is similar to a voyeur who is secretly watching a lady undress and every time she gets near to be being naked she disappears behind a curtain and comes back with a dressing gown on, but his camera is different in that it only catches the interesting bits and leaves the dull bits out. Woody's films consequently have such an air of reality that people often ask if you ad lib most of the dialogue. Of course the opposite is true: the dialogue, which is written by Woody, is carved in stone unless you can come up with something on the spur of the moment that is better than the material he has spent months perfecting. Highly unlikely.

In *Hannah and Her Sisters* I play a man who is married to Mia Farrow, yet seduces her sister, played by that gifted actress and lovely woman Barbara Hershey. When I first read the script I was surprised to find that Barbara and I had a rather explicit love-making scene to do. I had never seen this before in one of Woody's films and thought that by the time we came to shoot it, it would either be toned down or cut entirely, but it wasn't. There was no nudity in the scene. It was a sort of stand-up screw with all our clothes on – something we used to call a 'knee-trembler' when I was young. I never actually participated in one as I had weak ankles, remember, so I had no chance at all in that area. Anyway we shot it, to the great embarrassment of both Barbara and myself, because although you couldn't actually see anything, the movements had to be realistic and we were both relieved when it was finally over. I was still worried that it did not really belong in the movie, and in fact Woody cut the whole sequence from the final film.

The picture was a joy for me to work on. I was reunited with Max von Sydow, with whom I had worked on *Victory*, and I was also working with Carrie Fisher whom I've always considered to be wildly funny. There was also an old American character actor in the cast whom I had seen in films since I was four years old – Lloyd Nolan. For me it was a thrill just to meet this charming and legendary man, let alone work with him. Mia, of course, was fun. While we had known each other now for about twenty years, we had never worked together, so the filming was a joy. *Hannah and Her Sisters* was, I think, the warmest film that Woody has ever done, and sometimes during shooting it felt so intimate that it took on the atmosphere of a home movie. Mia's mother in the film was played by her real mother, Maureen O'Sullivan, the first and most gorgeous Jane that I ever saw in a Tarzan movie. In the film, Mia and I have children and these were played by her real children, and the flat that we lived in in the film was Mia's real apartment. It got so domestic that when we were shooting the sequence there, I would often see Mia serving up food to her numerous offspring. I think she had about seven at the time – she's up to nine now. The assistant director would come into the kitchen and say, 'You are wanted on set, Miss Farrow,' Mia would stop ladling out food, take off her apron and go into the other room and start acting and at the end of the scene she would rush back into the kitchen.

When we got to the bedroom scenes, which were shot in Mia's real bedroom (although for propriety's sake I think we had a different bed), things became even more cosy until one day I wound up doing a love scene in bed with Mia in her own bedroom, and being directed by her lover! This was nerve-racking enough but got even worse when I looked up during the rehearsal to find her ex-husband, André Previn watching us from the other side of the bedroom. He had come to visit the children and found us all there. It took all my concentration to get through that scene!

To complete the intimacy, there was a little old man who came on the set from time to time selling watches. This surprised me, as Woody kept a very closed set. That was Woody's father, I was told. There was still one further, subtle example of domesticity that was so subversive that I didn't notice it for a while until we came to a scene in which I have a row with Mia and have to say the line: 'I hate the country and I don't particularly like kids.' The first time I said this line in rehearsals Mia made a funny face and it occurred to me that I was saying as the character a lot of the lines that Woody might have wanted to say to Mia personally. (Perhaps he's now said them.)

Dianne Wiest was another actress in the film of whom I had never heard, but I soon saw how good she was and was hence very surprised when Woody started to give her a tough time, making her do scenes over and over again. I think I figured out what he was doing. She was playing a neurotic in the movie, but was so happy at having got the part she was having difficulty in being miserable, so Woody fixed it. She wound up with the Oscar for Best Supporting Actress. She wasn't the only Oscar winner on the film: I won as the Best Supporting Actor when the film came out later that year. So all in all, *Hannah and Her Sisters* proved to be that most unique of all films – one that was enjoyable to make and an artistic and commercial success.

Now, of course, it is hard not to view the making of *Hannah and Her Sisters* through the distorting lens of hindsight. But the fact that Mia and Woody – two vastly different people – ever came together was a source of great astonishment to me; the manner of their parting an even greater one. As someone who likes them both very much, the news of their split came as a deep shock. Whatever the outcome of the whole sad business I can only hope that they will find again the happiness that they first found in each other.

In LA once again, Shakira and I started to have long, deep discussions about our pending new future. We decided that life was a lease, not a freehold, and as the years dwindled down it became less valuable but more precious. We were going to cut out all the dross, we agreed. We were only going to go where we really wanted to go, and be with the people whom we really liked and loved. After the age of fifty you become aware that your stay here is not permanent. I was fifty-two, so I already had two years of pondering this insoluble problem, plus there was another sign of age creeping up that men get – hairs in the nose – very unattractive and difficult to cut. The only advantage about snorting cocaine was that you burn all the hairs out of your nose, but a couple of thousand bucks a week seemed rather a high price to me so I stuck to nose scissors with the little blunt bits on the end.

Our friendship with Barbara and Marvin Davis – the legendary Texan oil billionaire turned Hollywood mogul – was now blossoming and we went to a party at their house for the first time. Sometimes, seriously rich people can be surprisingly mean and inhospitable. Not so the Davises: their hospitality and generosity are legendary in Los Angeles and they are very down to earth. The proof of that can be seen in their children who are un-neurotic, pleasant and happy individuals. Marvin's character can best be summed up by an incident that occurred when I visited their house, and was admiring the paintings in it.

509

'Would you like to see the most expensive picture of all?' he enquired. I had seen most of them and wondered what could possibly be more valuable than a Renoir or a Matisse. Marvin took me into the enormous living room that looks out over Los Angeles and pointed to a small photograph in a silver frame on a side table. He was now in the film business, remember. 'There it is,' he said ruefully, pointing at the photograph of Sly Stallone and Dolly Parton when they were making the ill-fated film *Rhinestone Cowboy* for Marvin's company. 'That picture,' he grinned, 'cost me twelve and a half million dollars.'

While on the subject of luxury, I have two supreme examples: one was an Indian Maharajah who, when you stayed as his guest, gave you a personal servant to be at your beck and call for twenty-four hours a day. This fellow even slept on a mat outside your bedroom door in case you wanted something during the night. A friend of mine, who told me this story, said he was very upset by the way the man was being treated and when, after a week, he discreetly complained that the servant was being grossly overworked, the Maharajah assured him that everything was all right because all of his servants were identical twins so as not to disturb his guests by having to get used to a new face! The other incident happened to me personally in the South of France. One summer I met a Mexican man who invited Shakira and me on his yacht for lunch one day. This ship was one of the most luxurious private boats I had ever seen. Instead of being ready for lunch when we got there we were informed that we would be having apéritifs on this boat and lunch on his brother's yacht which was anchored off the beach at Cannes. We sailed round there and found his brother's boat which was the exact replica of his – and people think that movie stars are rich! My idea of decadent luxury when I finally made a lot of money was to get myself some prescription sunglasses.

During a charity show with Bob Hope in London on, I think, his eighty-second birthday, I came on and told the story of how I had met him when I was a young boy in Clubland. In reply to this he said that if he had known how rich I was going to become, he would have adopted me!

The next day I had to go to a wine festival in Antibes in the South of France, to be made a Chevalier in a wine-tasting society. I was given the freedom of Antibes which is, by the way, the only thing you will get for nothing there. I visited all the stalls put out by the local vineyards and tasted their wares, but forgot to spit out most of them like everybody else, so by the time it came to the ceremony where I received my award I was rather far gone, but I still managed to remember enough French to give a thank-you speech, which got a lot of laughs, some of them unintentional, I'm sure. I cringe when I remember telling them that as my real name was Maurice, I was now Maurice the Chevalier. That got a really big laugh. We were staying at the Hôtel Du Cap which, although one of my favourite hotels in the world, is horrendously expensive. The price of having a shirt laundered there is about the same as buying a new one anywhere else. The restaurant there, the Eden Roc, is another of my favourite places. It is beautifully situated on a ledge of rock at the water's edge, half in the open air and the other half inside; to my mind it is one of the most beautiful places to eat in France.

After a wonderful riotous weekend in Monaco with the Bricusses and Régine, Shakira and I were both longing for some peace and quiet so it was back to London, where we stayed at the St James' Club. It was pleasant enough, but I wanted to get to the country and see what was happening to our house, where they had started building work. It was chaos, and terrifying to see the scope and eventual expense of what I had planned, but at least the men had started. I was so enthusiastic that I got a camp bed and slept in the barn for several nights just to be on site. Shakira, of course, went back to the luxury of the St James' Club. I eventually became fed up and went back to London where something happened that I'm sure happens to everyone in all walks of life. One evening I met Peter Weir, the great Australian director of *Gallipoli*, in the bar at the Club and he told me of an idea he had for a film that I might like to make with him. It was a comedy about the trials and tribulations of someone like myself who emigrates to America. I thought this was a great idea and potentially very funny, and we parted vowing to keep in touch and eventually make the film. Nothing happened, of course, until 1991 when I saw the new Peter Weir film advertised: it was the same story about a foreigner in America and was called *Green Card*, starring the French actor Gérard Depardieu.

I stayed on in England as long as I could until my ninety days were running out, spending most of my time in the country overseeing the daily disasters as our new house, Rectory Farmhouse, started to take on a skeleton shape, but finally I had to leave, and back to California we all went.

In June we visited a place in America that I had always longed to see and never had. My friend Marty Bregman invited me to play a small but smashing part in his new film *Sweet Liberty*. My role was of a conceited, arrogant movie star – a part I found strangely accessible and for which I had already done masses of research! This cameo role would give me lots of time to spend with Natasha and Shakira, something I had been short of lately. I remembered something that President Reagan's speech-writer, Peggy Noonan, had written once. She said: 'There are only two things you can give your children, and they are roots and wings.' Natasha wasn't ready for wings yet, she was only thirteen years old, but here was a God-given oportunity to dig some more roots for her.

The film was going to be shot in the Hamptons at the end of Long Island outside of New York, the affluent New Yorkers' seaside playground. It is called the Hamptons because it is made up of East, South and Westhampton. What happened to North Hampton I have no idea; it may be there for all I know but nobody goes there, I can assure you. There are four very fashionable towns in all and the other two are called Montauk (which is at the very end of Long Island, and the journey along it takes about three and a half tedious hours) and Sag Harbor, which is where we stayed. A beautiful little town, it is still basically the same small whaling town that it was at the turn of the century. The great American steam-roller called Development and Progress has fortunately been kept out. All four towns have a very different atmosphere from each other, however. Southampton is the grandest, the centre of the old-money families. Easthampton is nouveau riche and show business, but Sag Harbor is gentler and quieter than the other two and caters for writers and painters. All three towns are quite close together and then there is Montauk, which is about another hour's drive away and seems to be for the eccentric and the reclusive, and the extremely famous in search of privacy.

We were staying on a private estate just outside Sag Harbor, with quite large houses, each in about an acre or two of its own garden. Ours was not only right on the seashore, but it also had a swimming pool in the lounge, which made it a bit dangerous if you came in drunk at night, but was great for the kids.

I had gone on earlier, because I had to work right at the beginning of the film, which suited me fine as it got some of it out of the way before my paid holiday started. When I first arrived I thought someone had been playing a joke on me, because as we turned off the public road and into the estate I saw the name of the road: it was called 'Actors Highway'. The reason for this was explained to me later. The whole place used to be the eastern estate of Mary Pickford and her husband Douglas Fairbanks, and they had built houses all over the huge estate for their friends to come on holiday, but the original estate had been destroyed by a hurricane many years before and was now just an ordinary residential area. The house was two storeys with four bedrooms and was probably fifty years old but like most American houses it was completely up to date technologically speaking. There weren't too many plants in the garden because we had regular visits from a beautiful herd of deer, which were now so tame that you could feed them by hand. Natasha eventually arrived at night and I was trying to show her what it was like and extolling the virtues of the place. We were looking out of the lounge window across the lawn that was lit by bright moonlight and I was telling her that she would see deer there sometimes, but she didn't believe this last bit. Being the daughter of an actor, she was used to my over-imaginative descriptions of things, and just as I was trying to convince her, a beautiful deer strolled slowly across the moonlit lawn. I felt so proud as she looked up at me in amazement. Dad was not only telling the truth, he was capable of magic! (I was greatly relieved because at that time I had not seen any deer myself. I'd just heard about them from our next-door neighbour.)

The star of *Sweet Liberty* was Alan Alda, who also wrote and directed it. He had proven himself to be very talented in all these disciplines, and was also a devoted family man who worked for lots of good causes. He was such a decent, gifted and very nice man that I always felt slightly inadequate and wicked when I was around him. I hadn't done anything wrong for years and I agreed with all his many causes, it was just that he was so good and nice, he was almost saint-like, and I had very little experience of being around people like that. He was also very physical, and whenever he wasn't working, which was rare, he was throwing himself into some game or competition or swimming pool. Alan was on a diet at that time and of course he stuck to it rigidly, which made me feel a trifle uneasy. I had gained all that weight to play my role in *Educating Rita* and had had terrible difficulty in getting rid of it so I even felt guilty when I ate with him, which was as seldom as possible. Alan was not an ideal companion for my secret, sybaritic holiday but he had so many responsibilities on the film that we saw very little of each other. On the other hand, my great friend Martin Bregman, who was the producer of the film, and his wife Cornelia, who loved a fun time and to entertain lavishly, had rented a beautiful house in Southampton, next door to Bob Hoskins and his wife. Bob was also in the film, so I had a small nucleus of funloving friends, which increased rapidly as the summer went on. The days were spent on the beach or in boat trips and the nights at parties; the weekends consisted of two parties a day, one at lunch. Shakira and I are very social animals; we base our life in part on a quotation from St Augustine, who said: 'Life is a book and he who stays at home only reads one page.' That's our excuse.

The summer was a kaleidoscope of parties. We went to the home of Bill Paley, the tycoon who owned CBS at one time and was recognised as the father of modern television. He had a wonderful house which had once been the Southampton theatre – the auditorium was the living room, the stage was his office and the dressing rooms were the bedrooms, very impressive. Bill was over eighty then; he'd had a reputation as a ladies' man all his life and age had not dimmed his appreciation, as I found out when I walked into his party with Shakira and two of the female stars of *Sweet Liberty* – Michelle Pfeiffer and Lois Chiles. His eyes lit up when he spotted my companions and he was over introducing himself in a flash. I instantly became his new best friend and Bill never gave a party all that summer without inviting me. Michelle was not yet the enormous star she is today and I remember being surprised that someone who was such a stunning beauty and could act so well, had not already made it. She used to sometimes talk sadly about having possibly missed her chance, but I was sure she would get there and told her so many times and happily, I was right. She was wonderful to work with and I also had my longest screen kiss with her – four and a half minutes. If you're going to have a long screen kiss, I can recommend Michelle, but mind you, we were laughing most of the time. You cannot keep up a passionate kiss for four and a half minutes, but of course in real life nobody does that. After a minute or two you get on to other things.

Love scenes are also difficult from a married actor's point of view. When your wife sees a film – and you can be playing anything from a serial killer to an SS officer – she will compliment you on a wonderful performance. If you put the same realism into a love scene, she will say: 'You're not *that* good an actor, you must have fancied her!' In my own defence I've learned to be slightly bad at love scenes.

Although we were party animals, the people we met here were quite different from those in Los Angeles. President Kennedy's sister Pat who had been married to the actor Peter Lawford gave a housewarming bash and we went to that, and met the entire younger Kennedy clan. I don't remember any of them individually, as there must have been about fifty of them and their similarity of clothing, accent and family resemblance made it a bit confusing. They all seemed very well-mannered and considerate of others.

Among many other interesting and stimulating social

occasions, Shakira and I also had a wonderful lunch at Alan's beautiful home in Bridgehampton. His guests included Peter Jennings, anchorman of the ABC nightly news, and Don Hewitt, producer of my favourite American television show *Sixty Minutes*. All these people were so far removed from the Hollywood scene. I am a great news and current affairs buff so meeting Peter and Don was fascinating for me.

Bridgehampton, by the way, is a mixture of old money and people who know how to use new money properly. You don't flaunt it, seems to be the basic rule. There are certain conventions in the Hamptons about dress and I was caught out by them. I was having lunch one day at someone's very proper Southampton home when the man to whom I was talking looked down and said, 'I see that you are wearing socks.' This was indeed true. There was an implied criticism in the way he said it so I looked round the room at the feet of all the other men and – lo and behold, to my eternal shame, I was the only man there wearing socks. I had been found out, I was an outsider.

I later discovered that you could rate the different towns according to socks and jackets. (I had quickly noticed while assessing the lack of socks that all the men wore jackets, except for me.) Southampton, I concluded, was no socks but with jacket. Easthampton was socks and no jacket, Bridgehampton jacket and socks and Sag Harbor was no socks *or* jacket! I do so hope I have straightened that out for the socially unaware.

Irving Lazar arrived and stayed with us for a while. Despite his age, for he was nearing eighty even at around this time, his enthusiasm for life and all that it has to offer continues to be a lesson for us all, and his facility for enjoying himself is endless. We call him 'the Life Enhancer'.

The talent that Irving possesses that most of us lack is that he gets his priorities right. He lives his life; he has never spent it. One of the reasons he has lived so long is that he's always got some in the bank. He is physically not a big man, but that's the only small thing about him. The rest is gigantic: his love of life, his friends, and today and tomorrow. Professionally he is one of the greatest agents in Hollywood. He has represented clients from Ernest Hemingway to Humphrey Bogart, who gave him the nickname 'Swifty' because of the speed with which he does deals. He was also the first man to get a million dollars for the film rights to a Broadway show – *My Fair Lady*.

I love this man dearly, but he is not only my friend, he is my literary agent and responsible for the book you are reading now. But I am one of his lesser lights when you consider the names of some of his other clients: Betty Bao Lord, Elia Kazan, David Brinkley, Joan Collins, Larry McMurtry, Lauren Bacall, Kirk Douglas, Quincy Jones, Carole Matthau, Helen Gurley Brown. To each of us he dispenses wisdom, hospitality and experience and to me, once, a lesson in his beloved priorities. He asked me to dinner one evening and I had to tell him I was dining with someone else. He asked me who it was and I told him. 'You can't have dinner with him,' he said, 'he's a lunch.'

43

Moving back

Keeping one eye on our house in Oxfordshire, I fixed the other eye on Langan's, which was still going very well although Peter was becoming increasingly eccentric. While I was there he had a row with our partner Richard Shepherd, who was also the chef, set up a table outside the restaurant in the evening and stopped anybody from going in. Richard got round this by standing in the street before the customers reached the entrance and Peter, and taking them in through the kitchen. It was very amusing to everybody except Richard and myself, who were after all trying to run a business. Peter was also getting violent these days, Richard informed me. Now, instead of just sleeping in the restaurant all night he had started to smash up the chairs and tables in a drunken fury. Before, he had always been a harmless and to some people, Richard and I excluded, an amusing drunk. This violence was something new, and unknown to us at the time, the first signs of the tragedy that was to come.

While I was in London I checked up on everyone. My mother was nicely settled at Streatham, and we took her out several times. She was getting a little frail now she was eighty-five, but she was still good for the occasional malapropism. Somehow or other our conversation turned to the Middle Ages one day and I asked her if she would like to have lived then and she said that she wouldn't, because everybody died of the Dubonnet plague in those days. Her mind was getting old but she still loved to go out, especially to Langan's, where she would sit at dinner until one o'clock in the morning watching the crowds of people coming and going who now packed the place every mealtime. Her other favourite treat was Sunday lunch at the Connaught Hotel.

Dominique was happily married. The wedding had taken place in November 1981 and she had married a fellow-equestrian, Roland Fernyhough, who was perfect for her – and so he was perfect for me. She wanted a wedding with all the trimmings and it was my pleasure to supply it. Paul seemed reasonably well; although the multiple sclerosis hadn't got any better, it hadn't deteriorated – and remission is a sort of blessing with a disease like that. Shakira and I kept up our usual crazy social life. We would spend days and weeks without going out or seeing anybody, and then we would go into a frenzy of social activity. David Frost, another old friend from the 1960s and his marvellous wife Carina invited us to dinner, where I met up again with Prince Andrew. A wonderful evening. Dinner at the Frosts is always very warm. A bigger party at the White Elephant, another favourite restaurant of ours, followed, this time to celebrate Roger Moore's birthday on 14 October. As the years have gone by, my affection for and friendship with Roger has deepened. I find now that I have some friends to whom I could go for help if I'm in trouble, but Roger is one of the very few who would offer it before I asked.

Eventually my ninety days in the country were nearly up and everybody was settled so it was off back to Los Angeles to start thinking about packing. The actual move was still two years away but things were progressing on our house. I could tell this by the way my bank balance was rapidly dwindling. With Natasha back at school in Marymount, as we watched her develop it gradually dawned on us what a great school this was for her. She was a bright and kindly child with none of the qualities of the loathsome Beverly Hills spoilt brat. The actual quality of caring for others that the school instilled in the pupils was illustrated when our daughter told me that whenever they heard an ambulance go past the school, they were all made to stop work and say a short prayer for the recovery of the sick person. Natasha is still a very caring young nineteen-year-old woman today.

One of the extraordinary things about Hollywood is that

you keep bumping into people whom you expected to be dead. An instance of this came at an American Film Institute dinner where the Lillian Gish scholarship was to be awarded. At this point a white spotlight hit the table next to me and Lillian Gish, in a white dress, pale make-up and with grey hair, stood up. For several moments many of us there thought the award was for special-effects and she was a hologram. Even George Burns agreed with me, because when he met her afterwards, he said: 'I thought we were dead.'

In February 1986 I went back to England to film Freddie Forsyth's novel *The Fourth Protocol*. This was directed by John Mackenzie, who had made *The Honorary Consul* with me and the much more successful *Long Good Friday* with Bob Hoskins. The book was very wordy and a little short on action, and although I tried to get Freddie who was writing the screenplay to try to turn the ratio around a bit, it is very difficult for a writer to cut his own lines. We wound up with a wordy action movie which, although it was quite a good picture and did fair business, never had the speed and pace of the best American action movies. I remember an American once saying to me that the Americans made moving pictures and the British made talking pictures and I agree with him. Part of the failure of the British film industry to make any impact on the world market has been due to this failing. A lot of British films are not even talking pictures, they are photographed radio. Also, if you are going to have a talking picture, the talk had better be brilliant à la Woody Allen, for that's the only way you'll get away with it. We do produce moving picture directors, but they flee to Hollywood where they can join up with moving picture writers. Ridley Scott and his brother Tony, Adrian Lyne and Alan Parker spring to mind. It's difficult to do in England and I am living proof of it. In Hollywood there is an old saying about the movement of the camera and it is: 'Spray it like a fire hose and keep it on the money.' In other words, aim at one point, the star, and keep it there, unless you are on the villain but once you are with these two, you stay there. Old-time stars were so aware of this that they even had in their contracts the minimum number of close-ups that they should have. There is the story of Ray

Milland who was so impressed with a young actor that he said to the director, 'Give him one of my close-ups.'

In *The Fourth Protocol* we had scene after scene where we cut away from me not to the villain, who was played by Pierce Brosnan – but to other characters in Russia who appeared to be in another movie altogether and Freddie, a stickler for reality, had them speaking as Russians speak together. It seems that every time they address each other they start the sentence with other fellow's full, long and unpronounceable patronymic, so for long sequences in the film we not only had a talking picture, but a lot of talk, and even worse, most of it unintelligible. I went there as the star and associate producer and one might have thought this would give me sufficient authority to put my own strongly held opinions into practice, but no chance. Even I in my exalted position wound up making a talking picture when it should have been a moving one.

I had gone to England on my own this time and spent a great deal of time on my camp bed in the barn, overseeing the renovation of the Rectory. As I watched the outline of the extension I noticed for the first time that it was twice as big as the original house. When I wasn't working I went there as often as my nerves would stand, but I soon gave up these visits as an impending breakdown loomed and I fled back to the comparative sanity of Los Angeles the moment the film was finished.

Shakira, Natasha and I packed our bags for what was to be our last summer trip to London before we moved back permanently. This trip in July of 1986 was, however, unique: it was to attend the wedding of Prince Andrew to Sarah Ferguson at Westminster Abbey. The Prince was the only member of the royal family whom we knew well, and still is, so we were not used to moving in such exalted circles. It was a very exciting opportunity for us to see a state occasion, which I think the British do better than anyone else in the world. Another invitation, without the grandeur, but just as exciting because of the intimacy of it, was to attend the royal family party for the occasion a couple of days before the wedding. This was a dinner party held in a tent on Smith's Lawn, the famous polo ground near Windsor. It was a full dress affair, of course, for about two hundred people. I know that I said it was intimate, but for the likes of us to be with the entire royal family plus a couple of hundred people counted as intimate.

It was an absolutely beautiful evening with the royal family relaxed and comfortable amongst the people they knew and loved the most, showing a side of themselves that we as members of the public had never seen before. The last thing I remember about it was dancing with Shakira and as we moved round the floor exchanging smiles and comments with people as you would at any normal party, except that these people were the Queen and Prince Philip and Princess Diana and Prince Charles. There was no hint that evening of the family turmoil that was unfortunately to come.

The night before the wedding, Charles Price the American Ambassador and his wife Carol, who had been friends of ours since they first came to England, gave a party at their residence Winfield House in Regent's Park. We had been there many times before and they were great hosts. Charles was also one of the best American ambassadors we ever had. The party was great, as usual, but there was one incident that I remember very well. It was the first time I met Mrs Thatcher. We had a short conversation. I was introduced and she said, 'I am so glad that you are coming back to this country, Mr Caine,' and that was it. At least someone was glad I was coming back! I was not very popular with the British press when I left England and in some areas I was just as unpopular for coming back. Not that this mattered to me, of course. I have always run my life for the good of my family and myself and could not care less about anybody's opinions of my actions – then, now or ever. I had thought of asking Mrs Thatcher if there was any chance of the income tax being cut any further. It was now down to sixty per cent, from the eighty-two per cent when I had left, but by now I was so homesick I had abandoned my principles.

The next day was the wedding – a massive and impressive occasion. Shakira and I had very good seats, I noticed. Having owned restaurants for a long time I was very aware on formal occasions if I had been seated in Siberia. We were right on the aisle, quite a long way up the Abbey. I had no experience of these occasions, of course, but I quickly noticed that all those further up the Abbey were closer friends of the royal family than ourselves, or had titles. We seemed to be in the first row of the hoi poloi so honour was satisfied.

For all the breathtaking pomp and circumstance of the occasion, the very first inkling that the ceremony had commenced was for me the most stunning. There had been organ music to while away the time as the guests assembled but suddenly it stopped and there was complete silence in that great church as everybody waited to see what was going to happen next. But it wasn't a sight that came, it was a sound that echoed round the silent Abbey, a steady and rhythmic bump as wood hit stone followed by the high sound of many pieces of metal coming together like steel tambourines and then the sound repeating itself in a slow and steady thud: clang, thud, clang, thud, clang. We eventually realised it was coming from one of the side aisles and tried to see what was happening over the top of the crowd, but all we could see was the heads of about twenty ageing men topped with ceremonial hats adorned by white plumes. They were obviously a guard of honour, and if we could see their heads over the crowd they must all be at least six feet four inches tall, but the strange thing was their age: the faces were all well over fifty. Their slow march continued until we could see the source of the sound. The bump was as the long lances that each man carried, hit the stone floor in absolute unison and the clang of metal came as each man's high leather riding boot hit the ground and the gleaming silver parts of their spurs struck together. This was obviously no ordinary guard of honour but the cream of the British aristocracy, the Knights of the Garter.

As they passed us in complete silence except for the uniform sound of their boots and lances, their already formidable height was enhanced by the high heels on their boots and the foothigh plumes on their hats. Their scarlet tunics were ablaze with military medals and honours and their ageing backs ramrod straight, their wrinkled aristocratic faces set in stone but enlivened with a light of fierce pride gleaming in their eyes. A strange thing happened to me as I watched this: the hairs on the back of my neck actually stood up. Never had I seen up close such a naked example of the establishment of my country and my reaction was ambivalent. I suddenly felt a fierce pride at being an Englishman and part of the history and power that these men represented, but on the other hand, I hoped that they thought I was a part of it as well. I still had my doubts, for with my background I was as always still suspicious, but at least I had got this close, so I let it go for the rest of the day and got on with enjoying the wedding.

During the long wait I had been chatting to the man next to me, who turned out to be the Captain of the ship on which Prince Andrew had served during the Falklands War. He said a funny thing to me which showed just how many mistakes you can make when you judge by appearance alone. After the dramatic procession of knights had passed, along came the family and VIPs and they walked past us up the aisle to the celestial positions at the end of the Abbey nearest the altar. As they walked by, because we had been at a party with them the night before they recognised and acknowledged us. The Queen smiled at us, Prince Philip gave us a friendly nod, Princess Diana also smiled our way and Prince Charles said, 'Good morning,' as did Mrs Thatcher. I could feel the officer observing all this recognition in disbelief and when everybody had moved on he turned to me and said, 'You know everybody, don't you, Michael?' The truth, of course, was that I really knew nobody except the bride and groom.

The service went off without a hitch and it was all very English and mind-blowing and then off they went to lead what has turned out to be only a few years of marital bliss.

After working on a small-budget movie called *The Whistle Blower* in the South of France, we fled back to Los Angeles to do more packing. All through that autumn there was not a job in sight. Instead of working, I was reading the bills for the house that flowed in on an almost daily basis now. The costs were horrendous and like all building expenses, over twice what I had imagined. On top of all that Christmas was coming, with all the expense that entailed. I was almost on the verge of a nervous breakdown when I was offered a small part in the fourth of the *Jaws* series of films at a tremendous fee and I took it. I have never seen the film but by all accounts it was terrible. However I *have* seen the house that it built, and it is terrific. What is more, the film has now gone but the house is still with me and continues to be one of the greatest sources of pleasure and happiness in my life. So if you ever see the film and don't like it, which is almost certain, and you wonder to yourself, 'Why did he make this?' now you know.

The most important thing that happened while I was shooting the picture in Nassau in the Caribbean (another good reason for doing it – the family had a great holiday) was that much to my surprise I won the Academy Award as Best Supporting Actor for the film *Hannah and Her Sisters*. The award was picked up for me by Sigourney Weaver, which meant that I never got to make my speech, which I had prepared for my first three nominations when I was there in the flesh. In case I never get nominated again my speech would have gone as follows: 'I would like to thank all the little people who helped me win this award. The director, who was five feet two and the producer who was only just five feet tall, the writer who I never saw standing up and the leading lady who stood on a box all the way through our scenes together.' I always want to make that speech whenever I hear actors talking about 'the little people'. One of the things I appreciated most about my award was that the Academy members remembered my performance in a film that had actually been released before the last year's Oscar ceremony had taken place. Anyway *Jaws – The Revenge* will go down in my memory as the time when I won an Oscar, paid for a house and had a great holiday. Not bad for a flop movie, right?

Life is contrary. All the time I had lived in Los Angeles I had only made one film there, and now here I was leaving and I had been offered a film that was actually being made in the City of the Angels. It was a comedy that didn't work, alas, and when a comedy fails it cannot be redeemed or rescued in the way you can handle a slightly ropey drama. I was surprised that it flopped since I had a marvellous co-star, Sally Field, and a director who is still one of the funniest men I have ever met – Jerry Belson. The script too seemed pretty hilarious, but as Harry Saltzman once said to me: 'It's amazing how often the public is wrong, isn't it?' And to repeat Sam Goldwyn on the subject: 'If the public don't want to go and see a movie you can't stop them.' That's what happened to *Surrender*, the last movie I was to make as a resident of my youthful dreamworld, Hollywood.

And Surrender is what we did. After eight and a half fascinating years we got on a plane and went back home, leaving behind a host of great friends and a wonderful life, knowing even as we left that somehow, some day and in some way we would be back.

Despite having cost the earth, the house was perfect and in summer 1987 we set about the pleasant but daunting task of starting a new life all over again in a new home. The house was everything I wanted it to be. I was now into health in a big way, so there was an indoor pool. I'd had an outdoor one at the Mill House and had swum in it four times – and caught a cold on two of those occasions. There was a jacuzzi steam shower and a sauna, plus all sorts of gymnastic paraphernalia, some of which I have still not conquered to this day. The layout of the living area was very Californian i.e. open plan. I always hated the way a lot of big houses are divided into a warren of rooms, the majority of which are never used, like a dining room, a formal drawing room, what the Americans call a family room – that's the one with the television in it – a bar-room and a breakfast room. All these are in one enormous room in my house, including a kitchen for the family because Shakira, Dominique, Natasha and myself are all enthusiastic cooks. I had found in other houses that when I cooked for guests I was always stuck away in the kitchen and cut off so I put our kitchen in the living room and built a bar in it so everything is in the same place while the staff have their own kitchen out at the back. There are big open fires everywhere, backed up by very efficient central heating. I loathed going to big old English country houses and freezing my arse off. All the bedrooms have clothes closets and bathrooms, as another thing that niggled me about old English country houses was wandering blindly down a dark, draughty passage for a pee in the middle of the night. There are enormous windows in the living room looking west and leading on to a large patio where you can dine outside overlooking the garden that leads to the River Thames and, of course, see the sunset in the evening. There is also double glazing on every window, which not only keeps out draughts but the noise of any violent storms at night. It is not a luxurious house by any means. There are no gold taps, no onyx or marble, but it is extremely comfortable and efficient. It is not a showpiece but exactly what it was meant to be, a home, and I love it.

As far as the garden was concerned, I fenced off about two acres and left the area around the lakes as a nature reserve – my small contribution to the ecology. I also planted six hundred yards of hedgerow as a minute contribution to replace the miles of hedge that are being rooted out in the British countryside so that we can grow food that nobody wants and will be stored in sheds all over Europe. My days were and still are until I started writing this book, spent in the garden, a place that fascinates me, and the long winter evenings so dreaded by country-dwellers are spent either planning my garden or swanning around Europe on my satellite, finding out what is happening in the rest of the world. For me, this is perfection.

We gave a party for Natasha's fourteenth birthday although we still had no curtains in the living room. My mother, now eighty-seven, was invited. She still liked to go out and see people, although mentally she was not grasping situations quite as well as she always had done. Proudly I asked her what she thought of the place and she said, 'Bloody awful. No curtains up or pictures on the walls. You'd think that with all the business they're doing they'd do something about it.' Surprised, I asked, 'What business?'

'Well, look at all the customers,' she replied, pointing at my guests. 'The worst pub I've ever been in.' I realised that she didn't know this was my home and thought it was a pub. 'Are you short of money?' was her next surprising question.

'No, Ma,' I said. 'What makes you think that?'

She pointed to Shakira who was busy giving people drinks

527

and collecting empty glasses. 'Why have you got Shakira working, then?' she asked accusingly.

I decided to leave her with her own ideas of what was going on and just said, 'It's only part-time work,' and left it at that.

Not all our time was spent in the country; as I started to rediscover London myself I found a startling difference. The depressed place I had left was now a city full of energy and life with a tremendous sense of purpose. Buildings were going up all over the place and the old ones were being cleaned, restaurants and theatres were full and so were the shops. Everything seemed happy, bustling and prosperous and I was happy to be back and part of it, especially as if to welcome me home Mrs Thatcher put maximum income tax down from sixty per cent to fifty. That livened up the economy still further, and I have never seen so many smiling faces – including my own, of course. Langan's Brasserie was doing incredible business; the archaic and paternalistic licensing laws of my country had changed and now we could keep on serving right to the end of the meal.

The one cause for concern amidst all this euphoria was poor Peter Langan. He was now sinking fast into the depths of alcoholism and had gone from a semi-coherent and sometimes funny man to a dirty mumbling wreck. This time, instead of trying to get him to join Alcoholics Anonymous again (it was too late for that), I tried to get him to see a doctor, but again I failed and he wandered off God knows where to drown himself in alcoholic oblivion.

Eventually, of course, I failed completely. Peter, in some drunken nightmare, managed to set fire to himself, surviving in agony for five weeks in Intensive Care until relief came from the pain of the day and the demons that had been trying to destroy him for so long.

I still miss him.

44

Scoundrels

It was about this time that I changed agents in America, which is just a matter of changing initials. I went from ICM to CAA (pdq). These, along with William Morris, are the three most powerful agents in Hollywood, their ranking shifting as powerful clients ebb and flow on whims of iron. Hollywood used to be run by powerful studio heads with agents dependent on them for work for their clients. Modern agencies now package their own deals, with the studio heads dependent on *their* largesse, so it is very important for an actor to be with an agency which he believes is occupying the number one spot. In case you don't know, for all this power and Machiavellian machination, they only charge 10 per cent!

I've always been lucky. At ICM I had Sue Mengers until she retired. I had left them once before to go to William Morris where I was with the legendary and much-loved agent Stan Kamen, whose clients also included Al Pacino, Barbra Streisand, Steve McQueen, Robert Redford and Goldie Hawn. The one unforgettable evening that I spent with Stan was dinner at Mortons. He seemed not to be feeling well and half way through the meal excused himself and went to the men's room. After he had been gone for a while I got worried and went looking for him. I found Stan leaning on a wash basin in obvious pain. When I asked him what the matter was, he raised his shirt and showed me his back where there were several blueish marks like bruises on his flesh. He said he didn't know what it was, but he had some ointment for it. I didn't know it then but I was looking at the lesions from *Kaposi's sarcoma*. It was 1983. Three years later, Stan died of AIDS.

Our world was changing and we didn't even know it.

On Boxing Day of 1987 we were invited to lunch by Mrs Thatcher at Chequers, the traditional home of British prime ministers. We had only met her once, at the American Ambassador's party and that was only briefly, so the invitation was a bit of a surprise: it was surely to welcome us back to England, I thought. She'd mentioned it at the party, and we of course had never been to Chequers before so this was going to be more exciting than the day after Christmas usually is, normally spent nursing a hangover and trying to force down cold turkey. It's easy to see why stopping drugs or smoking suddenly is called cold turkey.

It was an icy cold day and the roads were quite dangerous so we were not looking forward to the long drive when my friend Lord Hanson, whom I had known since he was James Hanson, came to the rescue and dropped in at our house, with his wife Geraldine, in a helicopter and whisked us off to Chequers in ten minutes instead of what would have been an hour's drive. As we came down over the wide lawn in front of the house, policemen with sub-machine guns appeared from all over the place and surrounded us. I was seated nearest the door and had to get out first and was immediately confronted by a policeman who recognised me and looking at the helicopter (we were the only ones, the other guests had all arrived by car) he said with a slightly disapproving air, 'I might have known it was you.'

I felt like saying, 'It's not mine, it's his,' and blaming James for the extravagance, but I didn't and we all plodded up to the front door and rang the bell. I expected the door to be opened by a flunkey in full costume but instead Mrs Thatcher herself opened it, all typical smiles and energy.

'Come along, ladies,' she said in the manner of a teacher showing some new girls round the school. 'I'll show you the cloakroom,' and in they went leaving James and me standing there like lemons. Mrs Thatcher looked back over her shoulder as they disappeared and shouted, 'You men can look after yourselves.'

This we did and went inside to the first reception room

which was crowded with people from all walks of life, many of whom I recognised and the ones that I didn't I instinctively knew had accomplished something. I was right. The first person I spoke to was a very pleasant, robust-looking lady who turned out to be the captain of the English ladies cricket team; she was rather aptly named Rachel Heyhoe-Flint. The place was loaded with faces I had seen in the *Financial Times* and a great many members of the government, but very few show business types. What impressed me most was the actual house itself. It seemed to be mostly Tudor or Elizabethan, with high timbered ceilings, and it had been beautifully kept, absolutely immaculate. My recollection of whom I met that day is very dim. I had a hangover and the place was jammed with people. I do remember being seated at Mr Thatcher's table at lunch. Shakira was with Mrs Thatcher and I sat next to two marvellous people whom I did not recognise. They were a married couple, middle-aged or older and very funny, and after a while I asked the man what he did for a living and he told me that he was the ex-Chief Rabbi of Britain. It was that sort of lunch and at our table there was a lot of laughter. We were surprisingly the fun table. People kept looking over and wondering why we were having a better time than they were.

The first course was a buffet and it was at this point that I spoke to Mrs Thatcher for the only time at the lunch; actually she spoke to me. As I was leaving the table with my plate full she was standing there sort of overseeing the operation and as I went by she said, 'Mr Caine, you haven't got any caviar. You must have some – it's wonderful. Mr Gorbachev gave it to me.' I went back to the table and helped myself to a great spoonful of it and held it up to her as I passed on my way back again. She smiled approvingly and said, 'So glad you came back,' and that was it, I was officially welcomed home. The food was great, the wine flowed and before I knew it I was back home and waking out of a deep slumber on Boxing Day evening, to be offered turkey soup and that was the end of Christmas 1987.

The first thing that the New Year brought was a demand from

the British Inland Revenue, our tax authority, for over a million pounds in back taxes, and there I was thinking they'd forgotten all about me. On top of this, the dollar had gone into a decline and was now zooming down to a third less in value against the British pound. All my money was in dollars, so there I was in financial trouble again. On top of all this, the house had cost me twice as much as I thought it would and I had found a flat that I loved in a new estate they were in the process of building at the end of King's Road, called Chelsea Harbour, and although I loved the whole project it still cost me £200,000 more than I intended to spend on a flat in London. The property market in the capital was still spiralling upwards at an alarming rate, and as if that wasn't enough, I finally sold my house in Los Angeles as the property market there started to nose dive; it had been on the market for a year. Happy New Year.

With my new financial predicament I had to work so as there were no films being made in Britain and I didn't want to leave my family and go abroad I went back to television for the first time in twenty-five years. A writer-director called David Wickes sent me a marvellous script based on a new and intriguing theory of the true identity of Jack the Ripper; I was to play the real-life detective who investigated the Ripper case. It was a mini-series with an American television company attached to the deal so I received the same fee as I would have for making a film. Television had come a long way from when I used to work for the BBC and get paid in guineas, and very few at that, and when the money was called for some unknown reason 'increments'.

The show was shot in London and was great fun to make, even if the schedule was a little brisk for someone used to working at the leisurely pace of feature films, but I never liked hanging about at work anyway so it suited me. The show was a massive success when it was shown on television both here and all over the world. In Britain it got the highest viewing figures on television except for the wedding of Prince Charles and Lady Diana. It also knocked one of our soap operas out of the number one spot in the ratings for the first time in over twenty years.

As if all this was not good enough my luck got even better. I was offered an absolutely marvellous part in a comedy movie that despite some of my disastrous experiences in this genre looked absolutely foolproof. The movie was called *Dirty Rotten Scoundrels* and I was to co-star in it with someone whom I knew, admired and liked – Steve Martin. The film was to be directed by Miss Piggy from the Muppets or, as he likes to be called, Frank Oz. I had only met him once before, in Central Park in New York when I had been walking with a very young Natasha and we had accidentally come across the Muppets shooting there. I loved the script and Steve and Frank came down to the country for lunch one Sunday. Steve, of course, I knew. I had made a picture with his wife Victoria Tennant and he and I had got along really well. He is not at all like the zany characters he plays in movies. As a matter of fact he is the complete opposite, come to think of it. He is a very shy, quiet man, uneasy with strangers. He does not seem to have any of the madness of his characters, but has a very analytical mind, and is quite a computer expert and he doesn't make friends easily.

The lunch on that Sunday had already been arranged for a large group of my friends and I had asked Steve and Frank to join us because it was the only time that they could make it for a meeting with me. A moment came when we were alone at one end of my enormous sitting room and were looking at the other thirty guests milling around, when Steve said suddenly: 'You know, I'd love a house like this.'

'Why don't you get one? You've got enough money,' I replied.

'I wouldn't have enough friends to fill a room this size,' he said wistfully, and I believed him. He is so shy I don't know how he became friends with a noisy individual like me. I liked him very much and I was looking forward to working with him.

As far as Frank was concerned it only took the one lunch to find out that he was one of the real sweetheart people in this business. I love him dearly, plus, as the picture shows he's a wonderful director.

So there I was sitting at Sunday lunch with a great part and a great script, a co-star I liked and a director I trusted from the moment that I met him. My luck was in, but there had to be a catch and I thought I knew what it was. The story in the script was set in the South of France in the summer – a very expensive time to make a film there. I had seen this done before: you usually wind up in some crumby seaside town in Yugoslavia with some hastily erected signs in French over the shopfronts and a guy with a beret, moustache and a string of onions on a bike riding by in every other shot just to give it a bona fide atmosphere. I waited until nearly the end of lunch to ask my last and most important question: 'I know the film is set in the South of France, Frank,' I said confidently as though I didn't care if we shot it in Yugoslavia, 'but where are we actually going to shoot it?'

Frank smiled at me as though I was slightly simple. 'In the South of France, of course,' was the wondrous reply. 'We are based in the studios at Nice.'

The miracle was complete. We were going to work all summer while Natasha and her friends were on holiday from school in one of the places that we most loved in the whole world.

Shakira was on the phone the moment that they left talking to Luisa Moore at her home near St Paul. We wanted a house for the summer near theirs – could she help, Shakira asked. Thanks to the Moores, we got a great house with all the trimmings in three days about three hundred yards from theirs. We started very quickly on the film so we all moved out to France almost immediately. There was one slight flaw in our new paradise, evident in a note from the owner that lay on the bedside table when we moved in. It said: *In case of intruders there is a rifle under the bed. Be careful, it is loaded.* I looked under the bed and there it was. I picked it up and opened the breech and yes, it was loaded. Fortunately we never had to use it, but no matter how good things get reality is never far away.

Although the title *Dirty Rotten Scoundrels* was new to me, the story did seem familiar and I suddenly remembered why. It had been offered to me under the title of *The King of the Mountain* and the idea was that I should do it with one of the then new crop of young American actors known as the Brat

Pack, but we couldn't get the money to set it up. The young American actor with whom they had wanted me to do it was called Tom Cruise. As I write he is getting fourteen million dollars for his next movie. The story, I eventually found out, was even more familiar to me. I had already seen the film many years ago. It was a very unfunny comedy starring Marlon Brando and David Niven called *Bedtime Story*. Steve was playing the Brando part this time and I was playing the Niven part. When I found this out I asked Steve and Frank why we were remaking a comedy that had flopped the first time round. They said that there was no point in remaking a successful film because you can't improve on success but you can, however, improve on failure – a whole new approach to Hollywood thinking.

I had arrived early and was living in the house on my own for a week or so, which was handy in a way because it gave me time to prepare the house making sure that everything worked and having extra bolts put on doors and windows, since the lesson of the rifle under the bed had not been lost on me. It also gave me a chance to start work with no interruptions. Comedy is difficult enough but the main problem I had here was how to play opposite some of the zanier characters that the plot called for from Steve. In the film we played conmen who lived off well-heeled, middle-aged ladies, and the way we used to get rid of them was for Steve's character to play some really outlandish characters who appeared as relatives of mine, just when my relationship with any lady got too serious. I knew that Steve could get away with the madness because people were used to that from him in other films, and of course they knew that he was acting this way for the plot. My problem was how to react to this madness and I chose the route that I have always taken with comedy in films – play it for reality as though you were in a drama and let the laughs take care of themselves. I never for one moment joined in the joke and played everything absolutely straight, and according to the critics and the audiences, when the film came out, I was right. *Dirty Rotten Scoundrels* is a very funny film and any attempt on my part to be funny would have ruined it.

They had cast an actress called Glenne Headly whom I had

never heard of as the female lead, and our luck still held, as she turned out to be fabulous both as a comedy performer and a person. The fourth member of our quartet of con artists was the local police chief who was played by a British actor called Anton Rodgers – another nice guy whom I had known for years. He played the Frenchman so well that I suggested we do parts of some scenes in French and he told me that he didn't speak it but not to worry, he would make up his own French. Much to my amazement, this he did, and it was very funny. So there were the main players and not a lemon in the group, another little miracle.

Frank Oz had turned out to be a master comedy director and as he had been an actor himself, very sympathetic towards all of us. Actors love directors who have been actors; they excuse your limitations because they remember their own. So the work went well right from the start – a situation that never changed. The actual locations for the picture looked as though I had chosen them. My character's house in the picture was an incredible villa with acres of land overlooking the sea at Cap d'Antibes, right next to the Hôtel Du Cap, which meant that for us the studio canteen was the Eden Roc restaurant there – my idea of heaven. A lot of the picture takes place in a luxury hotel and for this we used another hotel, the similarly named Hôtel Du Cap at Cap Ferrat. Often in life we find that we didn't know when the good times were until they have gone, but in this case we definitely knew it and made the most of it. Somewhere deep in my soul I just knew that I was loving this picture so much that one day I was going to have to pay for it. I didn't know just how soon that day would come.

Now my world was made complete by the arrival of Shakira and Natasha, and my daughter's friends Missy and Stacey, so everybody was happy, especially me. I hate going anywhere without my family. The arrival of the girls was timed perfectly. We were filming a scene in a discothèque on the beach at Juan les Pins and I had my driver pick them all up at the airport and bring them straight to the beach. They arrived pale and tired from the journey and the weeks they had spent indoors studying for the end of term exams that they had all just taken. They got into their swimsuits, immediately rushed into the sea and then stretched themselves out on the sand in the blazing sun while I rushed back and forth plying them with ice cream and soft drinks. I topped all this luxury treatment off with extra parts in the discothèque, where they danced behind me in a scene with Glenne so they had now all been in a movie for the first time and what is more they got paid for their work, and kids love to earn their own money, especially Natasha. So in the course of a short afternoon they were all restored to their normal selves and we did not see them again for the rest of the holiday except at mealtimes and bedtime, and on one occasion when they worked again.

This was on the sea front of the main street in Villefranche. We had received an urgent request from Hollywood for a 'teaser trailer' for a conference of movie exhibitors that was taking place shortly. We didn't know what to do so Steve disappeared into his motor home and came out twenty minutes later with a scene in which he and I walk along the front as a voice over extols our virtues as human beings, while he on screen pushes a little old lady into the water and I jam a little boy's candy floss in his face. This was so popular with everybody back in Hollywood that it was eventually used as the trailer for the film, but it backfired on us because a lot of people who saw the picture were disappointed when the scene that they had enjoyed as a trailer wasn't included. If you ever see it, watch out as the camera tracks along the street. It passes three young girls talking – they are Natasha, Missy and Stacey earning their second day's pay.

We did a night sequence at the beautiful casino at Beaulieu and at the end of it I walked out of the building and stood for a moment looking out over the bay and watching a huge sun come steaming out of the sea. As I stood there feeling really tired, having worked straight through the night, I experienced a sense of déjà vu and suddenly realised its source. Across the bay I could see a beautiful house on the water's edge that I knew very well. It had belonged to a friend of mine who was now dead, and I had spent many wonderful days there in the company of this witty and charming man; my feeling of sadness was intensified by the fact that I was now playing his

537

part in a remake of his film. I was looking straight at David Niven's house.

David was a man of immense charm, great taste and miniscule ego. An example of his modesty is that I went to lunch with him the day his publishers had told him that the following Sunday his autobiography, *The Moon's a Balloon*, would be Number One on every bestseller list in the world. He knew it; I did not. He never mentioned it once.

45

In my own write

The super-rich own yachts; the smart super-rich rent them. Our first invitation onto one that summer came via Roger and Luisa Moore, who took us for lunch on a yacht rented by a very rich man called Kirk Kerkorian. We arrived by tender from the pier at the Hôtel Du Cap (a very fashionable way to board a yacht down there) and were greeted by our host and his ladyfriend Barbara Grant, the widow of Cary Grant. Also on board were Frank and Barbara Sinatra. Frank talked to me as he always does about his love for London. It was the place where his, at one time, waning career had turned round. He had seen a showing of *From Here to Eternity* in Soho, for which he eventually won an Oscar and he said to me: 'I knew then that I was on my way back up again. And I walked for miles through the streets of London in the rain.' I had always felt that part of my friendship with Frank was based on the fact that I came from the city he loved so much. We had a great time on the yacht. Of course, a couple of years later it became infamous as the vessel from which its owner was to fall overboard and drown, in mysterious circumstances. Kirk had rented it from him for one week that summer. The yacht was called the *Lady Ghislaine* and belonged to Robert Maxwell.

While we were having lunch, I began to think what a marvellous way this would be to have a holiday, so I asked Kirk very discreetly what it cost to rent. Now I had always thought of myself as rich until I asked this question, but his answer soon dispelled any delusions I might have on this score. He told me that it cost 25,000 dollars a day. 'And then there are the extras,' he added. 'You have to pay for the fuel and your food and drink – and of course you have to supply the crew's provisions as well.'

'How many crew are there?' I asked.

'Thirteen,' he said – and that was the end of my summer holiday aboard the *Lady Ghislaine*.

A week later I went on David Bowie's new yacht, and the lunch he gave that day was in fact his 'maiden' one, again around the Bay of Cannes. We were late arriving and as we were driving along the seashore I could see the boat out at sea and watched carefully to see if they had given up on us and were upping anchor and setting sail, but there was no movement in that direction as yet. I asked my wonderful French driver to give me the car phone so that I could tell them we were nearly there and he said to me, 'If you make a call from here, the message will go thirty thousand miles into the sky to a satellite, bounce off it to a station outside New York and then be bounced to the ship and back again to the car when you answer.' He pulled a handkerchief from his pocket and stopped the car. 'Why don't you get out and wave this at them?' he suggested. This I did; they saw me and waved back, and the situation was saved. I just wanted to point out how practical the French are and what a sensible attitude they have to modern technology – the correct one, I believe.

David had only had the boat for two days and was still in that first euphoric stage of ownership. There are a mass of sayings about buying a yacht, and one of them is that there are two great days in owning a yacht – the day you buy it and the day you sell it. David was still in the first phase. David has a tremendously exotic aura and a sort of mystery as an artist. But he comes from exactly the same place as I do – South London – and started out as a small-part actor a few years after I did. So when I talk to him the conversation is on a less ethereal plane. His yacht like himself was sleek and unfussy with no luxurious trimmings like the *Lady Ghislaine*.

By the end of the year I was absolutely exhausted with the pressure of work, a lot of which was accomplished in tandem with our hectic social life. Some of our time was spent in London, where we started to go to the theatre. Having been

540

away so long, there were many productions we wanted to see. One night, during a visit to the Olivier Theatre at the National Theatre complex, I ran into Larry Olivier, who was in the bar with two of his children. I was very shocked by his appearance. I had not seen him for a couple of years and the physical change in him was startling. He had suddenly become a frail little old man. For a moment I didn't recognise him as the powerful giant who had almost overwhelmed me in *Sleuth*. I had heard that he had been ill, but it was more than that: age seemed to have caught up with him suddenly.

During the interval, we were having a drink when a thought suddenly struck me. This was the Olivier Theatre and here he was, seeing a play in it. I asked him the obvious question: 'Do you have to pay to come in here?'

He stood for a moment pondering this new thought. 'Yes, I bloody well do,' he told me, 'and I am going to do something about it!' At that point the bell went and we all made our way back to our seats. He died the following year.

At around this time we moved out of our furnished flat in Cadogan Square and into the apartment I had bought in a brand new development at the end of the King's Road in Chelsea. It was on the site of an old power station by the Thames, so I was on the river bank now in both my homes. This place was absolutely ideal: a modern, fairly small yet completely private apartment, sufficiently high to have an unobstructed view over London, but not so high that you needed a tranquilliser to venture out onto the balcony. It not only looked over the Thames on the south side, but on the north side it gave onto the harbour – an extraordinary sight in the middle of London. Chelsea Harbour is a private estate so it is kept spotlessly clean, all cars are parked underground so there is no noise and an independent security force makes it as safe as anywhere is going to be. It is a delightful and serene place in which to live.

I didn't work for a while in 1989 which gave us a chance to go back to Los Angeles for the first time since our grand departure. Irving and Mary Lazar gave a dinner for us the

541

night after we arrived at which I think Irving for the first time mentioned to me the idea of writing my autobiography. On that occasion I said no, simply because I didn't think I would be able to remember anything. His reply was that this might not be the case now, but that if I left it very much longer, it certainly would be. I promised him that I would think about it.

Well, I did think about it for a while, but it was Jackie Collins who – in the nicest possible way – bullied me into actually doing it. She always told me that she thought I would be able to write and I asked her why. 'Because,' she said, 'as a talker you can tell a story. Just write the way you speak.' By this time Jackie was a multi-million-dollar bestselling novelist, so I took this advice seriously – especially since I hadn't taken her seriously when she told me she was going to be a writer over twenty years before.

It may surprise you to know that the author of *Chances*, *Lucky*, and *Lady Boss* lived the ordinary life of a happily married woman: getting up in the morning, making breakfast for the kids and taking them to school. Only after she had finished the household chores did she sit down to write. In other words, the author of *Hollywood Wives* was a Hollywood Housewife. I thought to myself, if she could do it, then maybe I could too.

The final push for me came when Irving – who had been so aptly named 'Swifty' – came up with a deal with the Random House Publishing Group. Here was a god-sent opportunity to take a rest from filming and spend a great deal of time on my own at home, working when I felt like it. It was a chance to go back and reflect on my life. To try to find out for myself what it had really been all about.

But, typically of me, first I had to do a small-budget thriller called *Shock to the System*, with a first-time director named Jan Eglson. This was shot in New York, and as it coincided with Natasha's school holidays, we rented a penthouse at 63rd and Second Avenue and lived like native New Yorkers for a few weeks.

Domestic life in New York turned out to be great fun. The variety of food and shops was amazing, and it seemed to us cheaper than London. Within a five-minute walk, there were

542

at least twenty cinemas, all with the latest summer releases. Our greatest find, however, was a local Italian restaurant called Primola. We all loved this place, which became our second home. The picture was a nice little movie and everyone was very agreeable. Natasha and her friend Missy had a big heartthrob moment one evening when they came to visit the set. Matt Dillon, whom I knew from the 'Night of a Hundred Stars' show, turned up to see a girl who was working on the movie. We were shooting down in Soho, a very vibrant 'fun' district situated south of a street called Houston – hence 'South of Houston', which became 'Soho'. It is an area of restaurants, cafés, delicatessens, art galleries, dance studios, little theatres and night-clubs, and the place never seems to close. I always found it very exciting down there and the girls thought it was fascinating, too, especially since, when I introduced them to Matt and he learned that they had never been there before, he and his friend took them off for a tour and dinner. When he eventually brought them back to the set at about midnight they were in a daze. He said goodnight and off home he went. I tried to talk to the girls but it was no use; they were both fifteen and in love with the same guy – but they were being friendly about it. I don't remember either of them ever speaking again the entire time we were in New York!

A strange thing happened once when we were shooting at this same location in the daytime. My motor home was parked in a very dodgy spot right outside the Methadone centre, which is where the heroin addicts come to get their drug substitute that is supposed to wean them off the hard stuff, hence there were some fairly weird and hairy passers-by when I looked out of the window. Two guys in particular looked really scary. I took them for pushers, since they never stopped looking around to see if anyone was coming, although they didn't try to sell anything to anybody and hung around all morning unaware that I was watching them. Eventually I was called on the set, did the shot, and was standing there talking to the sound man while we waited for the next set-up when suddenly the two villains appeared at my side. They both got out wallets and flashed police badges and told us that they were working under cover.

'Are you the sound man on this movie?' one of them asked my friend.

'Yes I am,' he replied.

'Do you have a directional microphone?' This is a microphone that can pick up conversations at long distance.

'Yes I do,' our sound man replied.

'You see those two guys over there?' said the second officer, pointing to the other side of the street, where two men were standing and watching the filming and talking to each other.

'Yes,' the sound man replied.

'Get your directional mike. We want to hear their conversation,' the first policeman ordered.

'Who are they?' my friend asked.

'That's John Gotti and his second-in-command,' the policeman replied calmly.

The sound man went a dull grey colour and as the nerves in his throat constricted he just managed to croak, 'Me, put a directional mike on John Gotti? Are you out of your fucking minds!' With this he stumbled away mumbling to himself.

'Asshole!' the policeman shouted after him.

Not all the New York police are quite like that – especially the New York Movie Police, a special squad set up by the Mayor just to take care of movie units that want to shoot in the city. These officers have become very knowledgeable about the art of film-making over the years. I was standing with one of them one night watching a scene, and when the director shouted 'Cut' and designated the next shot, there was a hiss of disapproval from my police friend. 'What's the matter?' I asked.

'Woody would have gone in for a two-shot there,' he said – and he was probably right.

On my return to England I plunged straight into my second mini-series for television again working with David Wickes, the producer-director responsible for our successful *Jack the Ripper*.

I was once asked the difference for me between theatre, film and television. They were like three women, I said. The

544

theatre was a woman I loved, but who didn't love me back and treated me like shit. The cinema was a woman I loved, who loved me back so deeply she didn't care when I treated *her* like shit. And television was a one-night stand.

The Strange Case of Dr Jekyll and Mr Hyde – yet more villainy in a Victorian setting – took five weeks, but it also taught me a lesson. The make-up for Mr Hyde took four hours to put on and another hour to take off. It was hellishly uncomfortable all day, plus of course nobody wanted to have lunch with me looking like that, so I vowed there and then that never again would I do a picture where I had to wear that kind of make-up. It also gives people a chance to be funny at your expense. The first day I wore it I walked out of the make-up room looking absolutely hideous and rather looking forward to some horrified reaction from the first stranger who saw it. This turned out to be one of the technicians, who just looked at me casually and said, 'Hi, Mike,' which was very upsetting after four hours of agony!

At least the agony was layered on by my own make-up lady, part of the team that has accompanied me throughout my career. A lot of stars have an entourage; I have a team. A team is a group of people so indispensable that the movie company pays for them. I would like to take this opportunity to name and thank them for all the wonderful work they have done with me over the years, and many more years to come, please God. They are Lois Birwell my make-up lady, a very small and loving person and a joy to be with, even if I do have to crouch down every time she does touch-ups on the set. She also makes-up Mel Gibson when he doesn't work in America and I have been meaning to ask her how she manages to make him look so much more handsome than me . . . Betty Glasow does my hair. She started with me on *Alfie*, coming straight to that picture from the Beatles film *Help!* and created the 'Beatles haircut' that started that fashion. Jim Smith has been my dresser since *Zulu*, and Roy used to take his place when he wasn't available. Jim is a small quiet man of super-efficiency and an unflappable nature. He can keep his head when all about are losing theirs and blaming it on anybody they can – a daily occurrence on most movies. In these situations he always has the same cry, 'Don't panic!' Brian Weske is my driver, a companion who takes care of all those things that go wrong. Apart from being a wonderful driver he can turn his hand to anything. I have never mentioned a job that he hasn't done or can't do. Reg Turner, my stand-in, is a real East End Cockney who always has a smile on his face and always knows where the food truck is parked. He has perfected my walk and mannerisms so exactly that I get lots of days free when he does the long-shots. Last but not least is Dave Jones, who looks after and drives my motor home – which is not only home to me but all of the above. Dave is mentioned last because it took me a long time to persuade the movie companies to spring the money for the luxury American Winnebago that he drives, runs and hosts. Always ready with a cup of tea or a glass of brandy (for medicinal purposes only on cold nights, of course) Dave is ever willing to fiddle with the television aerial when we get in a dicey spot.

These, then, are the people with whom I was so happy to be working again that summer, and the people who have done so much for me in not only their own particular jobs, but by keeping me going when things got rough and never once letting me down.

In July 1989 Larry Olivier had died, and in October I attended the memorial service where his ashes were interred in Westminster Abbey: he is only the second actor ever to be accorded this honour, the other being Edmund Kean. Buried with him were certain articles of significance from his career and actors who had had special relationships with him were invited to carry one of these items. Peter O'Toole was one, I remember, and Paul Scofield was another. The memento that I was asked to carry in the procession was his script for the film *Henry V*. It was a sad and solemn, but beautiful occasion and a great privilege for those of us who participated. For me, like so many, his death marked the end of an era.

46

A sting in the tail

On 12 December 1989, my brother Stanley's birthday, our mother died. She had for many years now been living in a nursing home that was just like a private house, where she got tremendous and thoughtful help. Typical of this was when Ma was unwell and needed to see a doctor. She was then about eighty-seven years old and had never ever seen a doctor for anything, nor been into hospital – with the exception of the time when she had her babies. She informed her nurse, Gemma, that she was not about to start seeing one now. She was of the firm opinion that if you ever saw a doctor he was going to find something wrong with you, and that would start you on a slippery road to a quick death. As she was really ill, Gemma solved this problem by finding an Indian doctor and telling my mother that it was Shakira's brother – a ruse that worked, once she thought he was a member of the family.

My mother's last days remind me of a story about George Burns. When he reached the age of ninety, a friend asked him if he still smoked cigars and he said, 'Yes.' Did he still drink wine at his age? 'Yes.' And did he still chase after women? 'Oh, yes!' The friend then enquired what his doctor had to say about all this. George Burns replied: 'Oh, him – he's dead.'

My mother had, for the last twenty years of her life, smoked her way through eighty cigarettes a day, drunk a bottle of white wine per day, and eaten traditional British meals like the fry-up. All this was washed down of course, with endless cups of tea containing white sugar and full cream milk. On 11 December I had gone to see her because Gemma had phoned to say Ma had a bad cold and always now that she was eighty-nine I went immediately, knowing that even the slightest illness could kill her as she was very frail by now. However, when I got there that day she was as bright as ever and on the mend so I went away relieved and happy. The next morning I received a frantic phone call from a hysterical Gemma who kept saying, 'Ma's not alive. Ma's not alive.'

'You mean she's dead?' I asked. It is strange how human nature reacts in times of extreme stress. No matter how many times I asked Gemma if she meant that Ma was dead, she could not say it. She just kept repeating, 'Ma's not alive.'

I went straight over and found everybody in tears. Gemma told me that Ma had done her usual thing after I left – she'd eaten a hearty meal, smoked her cigarettes, finished a bottle of white wine and gone to bed happy and had died in her sleep. A great end, I thought, to a tough life and she deserved to die without pain; there had been enough along the way.

Gemma and I went into her bedroom where she was lying peacefully as though asleep, almost a smile on her face. I bent down and kissed her lips for the last time and managed to stand up straight again without bursting into tears, but then I caught Gemma's eye and she went first and that was too much for me. I let go and Gemma and I just stood there holding each other and sobbing for what must have been a few minutes. Eventually I pulled myself together and tried to put on a macho front before I left the bedroom and had to face the staff. They gave me that universal British panacea, a cup of tea, and I recovered somewhat and left. The funeral was a few days later on a cold and miserably rainy day. My brother Stanley was unable to come as he was in bed with pneumonia so Shakira and I were the only family mourners. It was the end of that period of my life – or so I thought, but Ma had left a little surprise for Stanley and me which I am coming to quite soon.

Ma was gone, taking some part of me with her, and the year ended badly for everyone, it seemed. The stock market had crashed in October and a hurricane had scythed through the country, taking twenty-five of our favourite trees with it. It seemed as if nothing would ever go right again.

During the summer of 1990 I received my second invitation to dinner from Prime Minister Thatcher. The dinner wasn't actually for me, it was for Prime Minister Mulroney of Canada, but Shakira and I were included and were very intrigued to actually go inside 10 Downing Street. My first impression was how different it was inside from what you would expect, looking at the building from the outside. I had always thought of it as a very modest terraced house – not really good enough for our prime minister. However, when you enter through the little front door, you suddenly find yourself in a great mansion with a magnificent staircase leading to a group of enormous reception rooms and a beautiful dining room that can seat at least forty people. To this day whenever I see 10 Downing Street on television I still cannot understand how all those great rooms can be fitted in behind that tiny façade. I hope that the house is symbolic of the government – more than meets the eye.

Mrs Thatcher was very pleasant, as she had been the first time we met at Chequers, but it was a big busy evening and I never got to know her any better than the image I had of her from the press and television. The evening was very memorable, offering both good food and the company of interesting people whom I recognised from television although I did not always know their names or what exactly they did in the government. When we sat down to dinner, I noticed a man who was seated one lady away from me wearing a yarmulke, the little hat that Jewish men wear in the synagogue or that orthodox Jewish men wear all the time in public. Now this man was not only wearing a yarmulke, but he also had a paper bag with him containing his own kosher food. I suddenly thought back to the dinner at Chequers where I had sat almost next to the ex-chief Rabbi of England and I figured out that this time I was seated almost next to the current Chief Rabbi of England. When I asked him if indeed this was the case he said no, he was Paul Reichman, a Canadian real-estate developer, and he was building a new project in London called Canary Wharf, which included the tallest building in Europe. The tempo of that evening was all so positive – so powerful and unassailable – and as we left,

Mrs Thatcher, too, looked secure and confident as she bade us good night. Everything was going to be all right, I thought. Wrong again, as usual. Now, of course, even Canary Wharf is in trouble, and my mind goes back to that dinner at 10 Downing Street, when the future seemed so bright such a short time ago.

Six months later, Shakira and I were invited to have another meal with Mrs Thatcher, but this time it was in very different circumstances indeed – nowhere near as grand but much more comfortable. The occasion was Saturday lunch in the country-house kitchen of our friends, David and Carina Frost. Mrs Thatcher was the 'guest of honour'; the other guests were Lord Hanson, Lord and Lady Snowdon, Sir Mark and Lady Weinberg and two sets of token commoners, Mr and Mrs Thatcher and, of course, Mr and Mrs Caine. Mrs Thatcher had just been ousted as prime minister two weeks before and we were all fascinated to see how she had taken this terrible blow. At first sight she seemed to be the same tough, uncompromising Maggie but as the lunch progressed it became apparent that it had been a terrible trauma for her and she wore the haunted look of bitterness and frustration of someone who believed that they had been betrayed. Don't get me wrong – she was still just as formidable as ever, and although I would never have presumed, on such a short acquaintance, to call her Margaret, I was always so nervous of her that I even foolishly called her Prime Minister – and take my word for it, I don't scare easy. All the others, who knew her much better than I did, still called her Mrs Thatcher, for although she is very friendly and charming, it is always at arms' length.

I tried to cheer her up in my own way by talking to her about the book deal she could make on her life story, as being halfway through my own I now considered myself an expert on the subject. The gist of my thrust, if I may put it so boldly, was that she should make the deal on the book as soon as possible, before it went 'off the boil'. She accepted my advice graciously with a slight frown at my suggestion that anything she would do could possibly go off the boil and that was that, the end of a lovely lunch with charming friends, all of whom I had known before they got their titles. I was not hobnobbing with the aristocracy for social advancement, but I was definitely cultivating the Frosts because I knew that their steak and kidney pie was great – I'd had it before.

After lunch we repaired to the sitting room for cigars, liqueurs and coffee, all but Lord Hanson (my friend James, actually) and Mrs Thatcher, who sneaked off into an adjacent bedroom for an innocent private talk. Half an hour later, we were all still there, chatting and drinking, when the door opened and the pair emerged from the bedroom and stood in the sitting room entrance way like two teenagers at a party who have been up to something naughty. As if by a common signal we all stopped talking and stared at them for a moment, while they hovered looking almost guilty until James broke the silence by saying: 'It's all right – we're engaged.' That was the biggest laugh of a day that could have been rather awkward.

1991 started out with the Gulf War. Interest rates were high and the bottom had dropped out of the property market. To cheer ourselves up, at least once a week Shakira and I would go up to London and go out to the theatre.

I was especially pleased when the show *Me and My Girl* was revived, because the opening number of its second act was a big song-and-dance rendition of *The Sun Has Got His Hat On*, a song I had sung to Natasha ever since she was a baby. She had no idea that it was coming up and she was surprised and delighted – two emotions not easily come by in teenagers, as any parent will tell you. It was a cold and filthy night and we had to walk for a while before we found a cab. As we made our way along the Strand, I became terribly aware that something, apart from the recession that we were now in, had gone dreadfully wrong. Every doorway along this once fashionable street was filled with cardboard boxes containing homeless children, some even younger than my daughter, sleeping rough. When I had left this country twelve years before, it had been in a state of chaos, populated by a tired directionless people and I had great admiration for Mrs Thatcher, who had come along and proceeded to galvanise everyone with

551

aspirations and a sense of purpose, but I began to comprehend that she had made a big mistake – one which had eventually caught up with her. She had got the people of my country up off their arses and onto their feet, but she had forgotten about those who only made it to their knees.

Winter turned to spring; the daffodils appeared, those glorious golden harbingers of the Oscars, but even though I was free I didn't feel it was right to be enjoying myself while some of my countrymen's lives were at risk in a war, so I stayed glued to the television and my keyboard for the next few weeks. Relief from my depression came in the form of an offer that I could not refuse. Peter Bogdanovich, who had made such films as *Paper Moon*, *What's Up, Doc?* and *The Last Picture Show*, phoned to ask if I would play the stage director in the movie version of *Noises Off*. It was a wonderful role and not only that, Shakira was ecstatic because it was due to be made at Universal Studios in Los Angeles, her 'home town'. Even I was ready to get out of this country for a while, not that the gloom was any less in America but at least it was a change of depression, which is almost as good as a rest.

We rented our favourite temporary home in Beverly Hills that had so many fond memories for us, the Bricusses' house on San Ysidro Drive. Natasha had spent her first birthday in this house and that summer she celebrated her eighteenth birthday there. It was while we were staying here that we had bought our house on Davies Drive, our home for the nine years of our residence in Beverly Hills – would we do that again?

We had almost decided to buy another house here and were going to use the free time on *Noises Off* to investigate. Our welcome back and the joy of seeing our old friends again was considerable, so within three days we had decided to at least start looking.

Noises Off takes place in one set in a theatre, so that all of it was shot on one stage at Universal Studios. This meant we could all lead a normal home life with regular hours – the very thing I had gone into show business to avoid, but which was now so important to me.

Farce is a difficult medium, even in the theatre; in film it is almost impossible – and so it proved for us, at least from the American reception of the film. As I write it has not yet opened in England, so there is still hope. We worked so hard to get it right but in spite of a magnificent cast and everybody going full blast, it seems that we never made it. Such a disappointment. It was nobody's fault, just one of those things. The play was brilliant and we kept very close to it, and the actors could not have been better. Denholm Elliott was in it, along with my old 'boyfriend' from *Deathtrap*, Christopher Reeve. I had never seen him do comedy before but in this film he was marvellous.

So there you have it – all the ingredients for a wonderful film. The people who saw it loved it, but we could not get the general public into the cinemas. It seems that they don't really care about what happens to actors – or stories about them, unless they are scandalous or tragic. They think we are spoiled, overpaid and lucky, which is true and I will settle for that and live with it as the reason for the honourable failure of *Noises Off*.

Our search for a small Beverly Hills home was successful: we found one almost immediately, with one of the most spectacular views of Los Angeles. Everything seemed perfect. Natasha received the wonderful news that she had got into university – the first person in my family ever to achieve this, so after the doom and gloom of the beginning of the year, the sun had finally got his hat on once again.

There was, however, a sting in the tail – there usually is.

One Friday evening during the shooting of the film, I reached home from work just as the phone was ringing. I rushed in and picked it up and discovered the legacy my mother had left me. . .

47

David

He had been born with epilepsy which in 1924 was not medically as easily treated as today. From a social point of view it was very easily treated – as a form of insanity. When he grew to adulthood, he was automatically put into a fully fledged lunatic asylum where he spent the next fifty years. Add to these circumstances the fact that he was the illegitimate child of a destitute mother and that he was born in a Salvation Army hospital, and you have a life that was over even before it started.

And this man was my half-brother.

I was shocked when the reporter from the English tabloid *The People* gave me the news that I had an illegitimate half-brother. His name was David.

Noises Off was running over schedule, so it was a long time before I managed to get back to England to see him, but in the meantime I did the only thing possible at such a distance and used money to improve his circumstances. A few weeks later I finished the film and rushed back to London to see him. I was very nervous about this, and told Shakira that she didn't have to come, but she spotted my nerves and insisted on being with me for moral support.

David was living in a nursing home, in a very pleasant quiet country lane just south of London. I didn't know what to expect, and I became more and more worried as we walked along the short corridor to his room. I had seen a black-and-white newspaper photograph of him, but what I found as I opened the door and saw him for the first time stunned me. I had no idea of the severity of his condition. The nurses had gently tried to prepare me for this first meeting, but it was still a shock. He was a very small man, with very dark, slightly greying hair, but in spite of his terrible life he did not look all of his sixty-seven years. This was the only pleasant surprise. He was confined to a wheelchair – he had been all his life – but most upsetting of all was the fact that when I held out my hand to shake his and said, 'Hello, David,' I realised he could not speak. I wondered why the nurses had not told me this and it was not until I had spent some time with them and David that I realised that they could interpret the noises he made. They did not see him as someone who could not speak, they saw *me* as someone who could not understand.

David had been transferred from the lunatic asylum in which he'd spent most of his adult life to a nursing home for the last few years after the authorities had closed many of those terrible institutions. The most extraordinary information I was given, however, was the fact that for sixty-two years of his life, with the exception of the Second World War and her time with us in Beverly Hills, my mother had visited him every Monday, without my late father, my brother Stanley or me ever knowing anything about it.

The love of my mother for this secret son was quite astonishing to me, when I thought of all the secrecy and lonely subterfuge she must have had to endure for so many years. Her passion for secrecy was so great that after I became famous, Ma would make any new nurses swear on a Bible that they would never reveal to anyone, particularly the press, that David was my brother. She was convinced that news of his existence would hurt my budding career, and she would have gone to any lengths to protect me. The nurses kept her secret for all those years.

The name of the asylum where David was kept was Cain Hill. I will always wonder what my mother must have thought on the day I told her that I was going to call myself Michael Caine. She was an incredible woman, but she is still surprising me, even from the grave.

David of course was completely institutionalised and there was nothing that I could do for him physically. I could not even communicate with him on my own so I did the only thing I could which was to make sure that the rest of his life would be as pleasant as possible. Our visit had, the nurses told me later, reassured him that he had family in the world, because my mother had told him that I was his brother and he had seen me many times in old movies on television. My brother Stanley had been able to visit him before I did, so now he knew that our mother had not lied to him about us. As I left David that day, I couldn't help thinking to myself: and I thought that *I* had a tough life.

You never know when you're well off, do you?

My discovery of David forced me to reassess myself. It's funny about things like this, there are secrets so close to you that they can alter the very foundations on which you have built your life.

So, 1992 has begun and this is where I stop. This is not the end of my story, however, but I suppose that at the end of an autobiography I should be winding up my life for you. I can't do that.

I have new things to do and new places to go and I intend to keep dealing with the unknown and the unpredictable, two dangerous elements that have been the norm in my show business life. In this year alone, for instance, I have produced *Blue Ice*, my first film with Marty Bregman, which is now in the cutting stage, and the first word from the front is good, so we will get to make another one in the series. My partnership with Marco Pierre White for our new restaurant 'The Canteen' in Chelsea Harbour has gone through, and we are in full-time construction and planning to open this autumn. And I am currently in the middle of making the Muppets' movie version of Charles Dickens's *A Christmas Carol* in which I play Scrooge – the only adult human actor in the film – which is due for release this Christmas. And then there is this book. I have really enjoyed the process of writing. It is marvellous not to have to deal with seventy-five strangers on a daily basis in order to make a living. So I am up and running and filled with excitement and not a little fear.

There are things that I have done in my life that I should regret. I don't – because I started with the firm conviction that when I came to the end, I wanted to be regretting the things that I *had* done, not the things that I hadn't. When I was young I took only half of the saying: 'Don't get mad get even' on board, and I just got mad. Now, at last, I am even. The first twenty-nine years of my life were rough and the last twenty-nine have been great, so now, at the age of fifty-nine, I am not only even, but ahead for the first time in my life.

My half-brother David died a couple of months ago and his ashes are buried with our mother's in my garden. I can see the spot from here as I write. My great friend Oscar Lerman finally succumbed to cancer earlier this year, and Beverly Hills will seem strange to me without him. My brother Stanley is living far away in Cornwall, Dominique is happily married and living on her own farm in Gloucestershire and Natasha is away at university, so Shakira and I are now alone again, in a sense, but as happy as we have ever been. I have been and still am blessed.

So what *was* it all about? In my case it was about ambition and anger and despair and determination, the everyday driving force of the poor who wish to find a ladder out of the well of hopelessness. It was also about my companions on my journey through show business. We are not, of course, without our faults. For the most part we are spoiled if we are successful, and bitter if we are not. We can be conceited and arrogant, and we are all, without exception, insecure. Finally, we are all slightly mad, or we would not be in this business in the first place, and only cling on to some sanity by a thin thread of incurable optimism. Most of all, my fellow travellers have been fun to be with and, most of the time, a joy to work with. To all of you I want to say thank you. It has been an honour and a privilege to share my life with such a bunch of rascals.

And to all of you who have come this far with me, a special thanks for allowing my story into yours for a little while. God bless and good luck. Just for the record, that's what it was all about.

Acknowledgements

First, last and always to my wife Shakira, without whose support and strength I would have given up long ago, not only on this book but many other things.

To Irving Lazar, without whom I would not even have thought of starting, let alone finishing, a book, and to Mary Lazar, a friend indeed in times of all our needs.

To Dennis Selinger, my guide and friend, without whom there wouldn't have been any good stuff to write about. And to Sue Mengers and Fred Spector, my two other agents along the way, who have also been responsible for a lot of the good stuff.

To Tony Lloyd, my American make-up man and companion on so many lonely locations.

Last, and definitely not least, to my two editors, Joni Evans in New York, and Kate Parkin in London. I had no idea what book editors did before I started; now I know that without you, there would not have been a book at all. Your work and your skill has amazed me and taught me so much. Thank you.

Thank you to everyone who helped.

Picture Credits

All photographs are from the author's collection.

My father at Billingsgate:
©Hulton-Deutsch Collection

Clubland:
S. Hills

Ma and her boys:
©Rex Features: Richard Young

A Hill in Korea:
©Movie Acquisition Corporation Limited

Zulu:
Embassy Films

Alfie:
Paramount Pictures

The Ipcress File:
Copyright © 1965, Universal. All rights reserved

Sleuth:
Twentieth Century-Fox

The Man Who Would Be King:
©Copyright 1975 Allied Artists Pictures Corporation. All rights reserved

The Silver Bears:
Raleigh

The Romantic Englishwoman:
Independent

California Suite:
Columbia Pictures

Deathtrap:
Copyright © 1982 by Warner Brothers Inc.

Educating Rita:
Columbia Pictures

Hannah and Her Sisters:
©1985 Orion Pictures Corporation. All rights reserved. Photo by Brian Hamill

Dirty Rotten Scoundrels:
Orion Pictures Corporation

Mona Lisa:
Island Pictures

561

Hollywood veterans:
Nate Cutler Photo

Connery, Louis, me and
Huston:
Mike Joseph Photography

John Huston and me:
Allied Artists Pictures Corp.

The four-legged chicken:
© 1983 *Los Angeles Times*

The two James Bonds:
Jackie Collins

We lost the game:
Natasha Caine

Irving and Mary Lazar:
Jackie Collins

In my garden:
Shakira Caine

With Jackie Collins and
Shakira:
Oscar Lerman

At the Prince Andrew bash:
Alan Berliner/Gamma-
Liaison

Shakira and Natasha:
Mirella Ricciardi

My two girls:
Shakira Caine

Extract from *The Golden
Thread* by Zerbanoo Gifford
is reproduced by kind
permission of Grafton
Books, A Division of
HarperCollins Publishers

Index

Academy Awards, *see* Oscars
Acapulco, 55, 267, 268–73
Ad Lib, 187
Adam, Ken, 227, 228, 350
Adam, Letitia, 227
Afghanistan, 454
Agnelli, Gianni, 302
Agutter, Jenny 407
AIDS, 84, 504, 529
Aimants de Vérone, Les, 228
Aimée, Anouk, 69, 228
Albion Close, 198, 200, 211, 236, 265
alcohol, 325, 337, 348
Alda, Alan, 514–17
Aldrich, Robert, 307–14
Alfie: MC auditions for play, 193; film, 16, 51, 55, 155, 213, 215–23, 229, 232, 237, 240, 266–8, 270, 308, 314, 316, 469, 470, 477, 545
Alien, 346
All in the Family, 156
Allen, Irwin, 419, 440–1
Allen, Steve, 497–8
Allen, Woody, 238, 460, 461, 503–9, 520
Almeria, 289–90
Ambassadeurs, Les, 196–7
Amyes, Julian, 122, 132
Anatomy of a Murder, 273
Anderson, Lindsay, 144
Anderton, Jimmy, 44
Andress, Ursula, 238, 488
Andrew, Prince, 488, 519, 521–4
Andrews, Julie, 205, 409

Angelo Drive, 426
Anouilh, Jean, 132
apartheid, 170–1, 181–3, 373
Appaloosa, The, 263
Ardiles, Ossie, 452
Arlington House, 488–9
Army, *see* National Service
Arnhem, 415–16
Arthur, 503
Arts Theatre, 130–1, 133, 160
Ashanti, 440
Asher, Jane, 217
Associated British Pictures, 139
Astaire, Fred, 438
Atlanta, 365
Attenborough, Richard, 415–16
audition, shortest, 142
Augustine, 514

baboons, 179–80
Bacall, Lauren, 517
Bailey, David, 159, 187, 188, 200, 202
Baker, George, 121
Baker, Stanley, 122, 123–4, 162–5, 170–83, 189–90
Baksh, Shakira, *second wife see* Caine, Shakira
Baksh, Swabera, *mother-in-law*, 360, 365, 495
Bardot, Brigitte, 290–2
Barry, John, 188, 199–200, 319
Bart, Lionel, 154–5
Basie, Count, 260
Bath, 224–6
Batt, Bert, 393

Battle of Britain, 18, 227, 304–6
Battle of Britain, The, 304–6
Beach Boys, The 220
Beatles, The, 142–3, 159, 186, 217, 220, 229, 230, 321. *See also* Lennon, John *and* McCartney, Paul
Beatty, Warren, 465
Beaulieu, 538
Bedtime Story, 535
bees, 419
Belson, Jerry, 526
Ben Gurion, David, 285–6
Ben Hur, 187
Benchley, Peter, 442
Benedict Canyon, 426
Bergen, Candice, 296
Berger, Helmut, 383–6
Berle, Milton, 497–8
Berlin, 266–7
Berra, Yogi, 293
Best Years of Our Lives, The, 188
Beverly Hills, 242–50, 251–9, 425–36, 461
Beverly Wilshire Hotel, 249, 254, 315, 497–8
Beyond the Fringe, 201
Beyond the Limit, *see Honorary Consul, The*
Beyond the Poseidon Adventure, 440–1
Biba, 134
Bible, The, 162
Billion Dollar Brain, 281–3
Billy Budd, 159, 160–1
Birkin, Andrew, 292
Birkin, Jane, 292–3
Birthday Party, The (Pinter), 143
Birwell, Lois, 545
Bistro, 461, 478
Black Windmill, The, 366, 371
Blake, Peter, 220
Blame It on Rio, 479–87
Blitz, 17–18, 32
Bludhorn, Charlie, 267
Blue Angel, The, 470
Blue Berbers, 404–5
Blue Ice, 385, 459, 556

Boatwright, Boaty, 504–5
Bogart, Humphrey, 48, 132, 390–1, 517
Bogdanovich, Peter, 552–3
Bologna, Joe, 479
Bolt, Robert, 457–8
Booth, James, 163
Borg, Bjorn, 496
Bourne, Gordon, 366–8
Bowie, David, 540
Boyd, Stephen, 122
Brando, Marlon, 263–4, 535
Brandt, Steve, 253–4, 257, 315, 318–19
Brazil, 480–7
bread pudding, 202
Bregman, Cornelia, 459, 514
Bregman, Martin, 459, 504, 512, 514, 556
Bricusse, Leslie and Evie, 160, 226–7, 428, 511, 552
Bridge over the River Kwai, The, 90
Bridge Too Far, A, 315–16
Brighton Rock, 322
Brinkley, David, 517
British Academy Awards, 479
Brixton, 108, 185
Broadway, 357
Broccoli, Cubby, 195, 206–7
Brosnan, Pierce, 521
Brown, David, 442
Brown, Helen Gurley, 517
Brown, Jerry, 464–5
Brown, Zev, 498–9
Bruce, Lenny, 201, 203
Brynner, Yul, 261
Buckley, Jimmy, 55–6
Buckstone club, 133
Budapest, 452–4
Burns, George, 497–8, 520, 547
Burton, Josephine, 127, 129, 131, 132–3, 134, 138–9
Burton, Richard, 409
Buthelezi, Chief, 175
Butterworth, Rev. Jimmy, 55–6
Buttons, Red, 497–8

CAA, 263, 529

Cadogan Square, 541
Caesar, Sid, 497–8
Caesar's Palace, 450
Cain Hill, 555
Caine, Natasha, *daughter*: birth,
    366–8; health problems, 368–72;
    dancing, 386–7, 484–5; love of
    animals, 434, 482, 496; New
    York, 458–61, 504, 542–3; Rio,
    479–87 Marymount, 519; Sag
    Harbor, 512–17; Nice, 534–8;
    Matt Dillon, 542; university, 557
Caine, Shakira, *second wife*: MC first
    sees, 338–42; early years, 346,
    361, 372; MC first meets, 344–5;
    living together, 346, 348;
    character, 350, 411; pregnant,
    358–9; marriage, 360–4; birth of
    Natasha, 366–8; problems with
    baby, 368–72; Nairobi, 373;
    Gloria Steinem and, 381–2;
    Paris, 389–92; Marrakesh, 393–
    403; acts, 394–5, 397; gravely ill,
    428–33; and Hollywood wives,
    438–9; Budapest, 454; New
    York, 458–61, 504; Rio, 479–87;
    Nice, 534–8
Caine Mutiny, The, 132
Caine Mutiny Court Martial, The,
    141
California Suite, 439–40
Calvert, Eddie, 58
Campion, Gerald, 133
Canary Wharf, 550–1
Cannes, 229–32, 266–8
Canteen, The, 556
Cap d'Antibes, 307, 536
Cap Ferrat, 307, 536
Capek, Karel, 45
Carlton Hotel, Cannes, 230, 267
Carmen Jones, 273
Carroll, Diahann, 274
Carson, Johnny, 238, 496
Cartland, Barbara, 496
Casserole, 201
censorship, 203
Chakaris, George, 241

Challen, Paul, 299, 327, 337;
    friendship with MC, 53–4, 109,
    125, 139; and Rolls, 299–301;
    and Shakira 338–42; multiple
    sclerosis, 419, 455–6
Chances (Collins), 542
Chaplin, Charlie, 40–1, 43, 499
Charade, 479
Charles, Prince, 522, 524, 532
Charlesworth, Johnny, 139
Charlie, 313
Chasen's, 42
Chelsea Harbour, 532, 541, 556
Chequers, 530–1, 549
Chiles, Lois, 515
Chimes, The (Dickens), 127–9
choice of material, 287
Christie, Agatha, 491
Christie, Julie, 186–7, 220
Christmas Carol, A (Dickens), 556
Churchill, Winston, 392, 407
Clark, Ossie, 191
Clarke, Arthur C., 227
Clavell, James, 320
Clément, René, 288–9
Cleopatra, 456
Clewer, 326
close-ups, 521
Clubland, 44–59, 109, 510
Coburn, Charles, 134
Codron, Michael, 161
Cohn, John, 294
Collector, The, 187
Collins, Jackie, 340, 542
Collins, Joan, 340, 496, 517
Collinson, Peter, 301–3
Colombo, 69
Coming Attractions (Stamp), 146
Compartment, The (Speight), 155,
    156, 157, 161
concentration camps, 59
Connery, Micheline, 399, 456
Connery, Sean, 134–6, 140, 141,
    162, 206, 220, 230, 240, 290,
    291, 292, 391–406, 409, 456
Conte, Richard, 261
Cook, Peter, 201, 224–6
cooking, 338, 526

Coupole, La, 152–3
Courtneidge, Cicely, 224
Courtney, Tom, 162, 457, 476
Cowan, Theo, 230
Coward, Noël, 19, 41, 301–3
Crist, Judith, 237
Criterion Theatre, 162
Cronyn, Hume, 239
Cruise, Tom, 535
Cukor, George, 105–6
Curtis, Jamie-Lee, 488
Curtis, Ronnie, 129–30
Curtis, Tony, 325–6, 362

Daily Express, 201–2
Daily Mail, 277–8
Daisy, 249, 254, 257, 258, 315
Dallas, 407
Dancing Years, The (Novello) 146–7,
    161
Daniels, Penny, 329
Darin, Bobby, 258
Darling, 220
David, brother, 554–7
Davies, June Wyndham, 95
Davis, Barbara and Marvin, 509–10
Davis, Bette, 239–40
Davis, Sammy, Jnr, 258
Day the Earth Caught Fire, The, 141
De Havilland, Olivia, 420–1
de Niro, Robert, 49
de Palma, Brian, 442–4
Deadfall, 284–5, 288, 293
deafness, 440
Dean, James, 252
Deathtrap, 43, 288, 458–61, 553
Deighton, Len, 195, 207, 208, 265
Deneuve, Catherine, 200–1
Denmark, 190
Depardieu, Gérard, 512
Derby Stakes, 496
Destructors, The, see Marseilles
    Contract, The
Deyna, Kazimierz, 452
Diana, Princess, 522, 524, 532
Diaz, Rudy, 317–18
Dickens, Charles, 556
Dickens, Monica, 90

Dickinson, Angie, 443
Dien Bien Phu, 70
Dietrich, Marlene, 387–8, 470
Dillon, Matt, 543
Dirty Rotten Scoundrels, 307, 533–8
discos, 153–4, 536–7
Dixon of Dock Green, 137, 143,
    149–50
Dollies, 221
Donen, Stanley, 479
Doreen, 35–6
Douglas, Anne, 437–8
Douglas, Kirk, 238, 437–8, 517
Douglas, Michael, 285
Dr Strangelove, 220, 305
Dressed to Kill, 288, 442–4, 486
Dresser, The, 457, 476
driving lessons, 435–6
drugs, 299
Dumb Waiter, The (Pinter), 151
Dunaway, Faye, 274, 275, 276
Durante, Jimmy, 48
Duvall, Robert, 407, 408, 476–8

Eagle Has Landed, The, 407, 456
ears, 5
Eastwood, Clint, 287, 466
Ebury Street, 159, 185, 199
Eden Roc, 511, 536
Educating Rita, 469–71, 476, 479,
    514
Eglson, Jan, 542
Ekberg, Anita, 284
Elaine's, 458, 461, 504
Elephant and Castle, 33, 37, 39–40,
    127
Elizabeth II, 329–30, 410–11,
    466–9, 522, 524
Elliott, Denholm, 218, 553
Elstree, 227
Embassy Pictures, 188–9
Empire Halladale, The, 68–9
Endfield, Cy, 163–5, 170–83, 189
English, Mr and Mrs, 26–7
Ennismore Garden Mews, 151
Entebbe, 170–1
envy, 421–2, 425–6
Equity, 132

Errol, Leon, 316
Escape to Victory, 450–4
Establishment, 201
ET, 262, 446
evacuation, 13–17
Evans, Linda, 488
Evans, Peter, 202
Evening News, 311
Evening Standard, 193

Factory, The, 316
Fairbanks, Douglas, 513
Fairbanks, Douglas, Jnr, 496
Falklands War, 524
Farrow, Mia, 257–9, 260, 457–8, 461, 507–9
feminism, 381–3
Ferguson, Sarah, 521
Fernyhough, Dominique, *daughter*, 121, 418, 449, 557; born, 109–10; MC visits, 125–6, 134, 140–1, 185, 222; love of horses, 184, 319, 455; marriage, 519
Fernyhough, Roland, 519
Fiat, 302
Fiddler on the Roof, 357
Field, Sally, 469, 525–6
Fields, Freddie, 450–4
Financial Times, 531
Fine, Sylvia, 255
Finland, 281–3
Finlay, Frank, 146, 156
Finney, Albert, 140, 143, 144, 162, 216, 228, 457, 476
Fisher, Carrie, 507
Fonda, Henry, 420–1, 440
Fonda, Jane, 274, 279–80
Forbes, Bryan, 160, 224–6, 284, 416, 456
Ford, Gen. Sir Robert, 496
Foreman, John, 394–403
Forsyth, Frederick, 520
Foster, Dudley, 142
Fountainhead, The (Rand), 109
Four Feathers, The, 230
Fourth Protocol, The, 520–1
Fowles, John, 294
Fox, Alwyn D., 92–103

Foxhole in Cairo, A, 289
Franco, Gen., 289
Frankenheimer, John, 497
Fraser, Jimmy, 120, 126
Fraser, Ronnie, 313
Frazier, Joe, 337, 499
French Lieutenant's Woman, The, 294
Frenzy, 42
Frieze, Mr, 58
Frog, The (Wallace), 143
From Here to Eternity: novel, 32; film, 539
Frost, Carina, 519, 550
Frost, David, 519, 550
Fu Manchu, 100
Funeral in Berlin, 265–6
Funny Face, 479
Funny Thing Happened on the Way to the Forum, A, 224
Furie, Sidney, 197, 207, 209, 210–11, 263–5

Gabin, Jean, 49
Gable, Clark, 77, 251, 390–1
Gabor, Zsa Zsa, 316
Galland, Adolf, 304–5
Gallipoli, 511
Gambit, 241–2, 256, 262, 263
Gavin, John, 269
Gelbart, Larry, 224–6, 479, 497–8
George, Susan, 386
George and Margaret, 104
Georgy Girl, 220, 270
Gere, Richard, 472–5
Germany, 66–8
Gerry's club, 133
Get Carter, 322–4, 346
Giant, 252
Gibson, Mel, 545
Gielgud, John, 274
Gifford, Zerbanoo, 382
Gilbert, Lewis, 16, 213, 214, 215–23, 267, 469, 470, 471, 476
Gilda, 259
Gish, Lillian, 520
Glasow, Betty, 545
Gold, Johnny, 187, 221, 339–40

Goldberg, Leonard and Wendy, 438
Golden Egg, 144–5
Golden Globe Awards, 479
Golden Thread, The (Gifford), 381
Goldfinger, 200, 266
Goldwyn, Sam, 356–7, 526
Gone with the Wind, 77, 264, 274, 357, 440
Good, the Bad and the Ugly, The, 290
Goodbye Baby and Amen (Evans/Bailey), 202
Goodbye to All That (Graves), 285
Goolagong, Evonne, 356
Gorbachev, Mikhail, 531
Gotti, John, 544
Gould, Elliott, 229
Grant, Barbara, 539
Grant, Cary, 43, 48, 225, 281, 478, 539
Graves, Robert, 285–6
Gray, Vernon, 140
Great Expectations, 46
green card, 441
Green Card, 512
Green Pastures, 274
Greene, Graham, 322, 472–4, 475
Grey, Edgar, 92–103
Griffin, Merv, 237
Grosvenor Square, 298, 326, 348
Guernsey, 47–8
Gulf War, 551

Hackney Down Grocers Grammar School, 27–30, 33, 59, 257
Haddingham, Buzzer, 496
Hagman, Larry, 407
Haines, Patricia, *first wife*, 127; brief marriage, 106–10; parents, 108, 110, 125–6; baby, 109–10, 121, 125–6; and maintenance, 121, 125–6, 148–50; death, 150. *See also* Fernyhough, Dominique
Hall, Jerry, 496
Hall, William, 311
Hamilton, George, 241
Hamilton, Guy, 266, 305
Hamlet, 190, 393, 443

Hancock, Tony, 224
Hand, The, 445–6
Handl, Irene, 224
Hannah and Her Sisters, 503–9, 525
Hanson, James and Geraldine, 530, 550–1
Hard Day's Night, A, 220
Hard Rock Café, 465
Harley Street, 147, 151
Harlow, Jean, 315
Harris, Richard, 140, 162, 409
Harrison, Rex, 387, 409
Haver, June, 421
Hawkins, Jack, 193
Hawn, Goldie, 529
Hayes, Helen, 238
Hayward, Douglas, 191–2, 193, 212
Hayworth, Rita, 162, 258–9
Head, Edith, 394
Headly, Glenne, 535–6
health, 5
Health and Efficiency, 50
Hedren, Tippi, 229
Hefner, Hugh, 331–2
Heller, Joseph 505
Heller, Otto, 265–6
Helmsley, Leona, 503–4
Help!, 220, 545
Hemingway, Ernest, 517
Henry V, 546
Hershey, Barbara, 507–9
Hewitt, Don, 516
Heyhoe-Flint, Rachel, 531
Heyman, Norma, 472
Hill, Benny, 301–2
Hill, Gladys, 394
Hill, The, 136
Hill in Korea, A, 120–6, 162
Hitchcock, Alfred, 41–2
Hockney, David, 191, 448
Hodges, Mike, 323–4, 346
Hoffman, Dustin, 49
Holcroft Covenant, The, 497
Holland, 415–16
Hollywood, 242–50, 251–9, 262–5, 315–19
Hollywood Wives, (Collins), 542
Homme et une femme, Un, 227

568

homosexuality, 458–9; in theatre, 97–8, 100; suspicions of MC and Terence Stamp, 188; MC's looks, 189–90, 439
Hong Kong, 70, 76
Honorary Consul, The, 472–4, 520
Hood, Amy, 45
Hooks, Robert, 274
Hope, Bob, 55, 248, 316, 510
Hopkins, Anthony, 288
horses, MC and, 172–4, 225–6, 319–20
Horsham, 92–103
Hoskins, Bob, 4, 472, 514, 520
Hôtel du Cap: Antibes, 230, 511, 536, 539; Cap Ferrat, 536
Hôtel George V, 284, 389–91
Hôtel Prince des Galles, 389–92
Howard, Leslie, 239–40
Hughes, Howard, 252–3, 262, 315
Hungary, 450–4
Hurry Sundown, 273–80, 281
Huston, Cee Cee, 394, 398–9
Huston, John, 162, 346, 389–93, 450–4, 455, 471
Hutton, Barbara, 428
Hutton, Brian, 328, 330, 331

I. Claudius (Graves), 285
ICM, 529
In His Own Write (Lennon), 231
Ingram, Rex, 274
Innsbruck, 319–21
Ipcress File, The, 195–6, 198, 199, 200, 205–12, 221, 225, 227, 229, 230, 232, 237, 241, 264, 265, 303, 351, 408
Irons, Jeremy, 288
Iserlöhn, 66–8
Island, The, 442
Italian Job, The, 157, 267, 301–3
Ivanhoe, 156
Ivanov, Eugen, 198

Jack the Ripper, 532, 544
Jackson, Glenda, 383–6
Jackson, Mr, 58
Jagger, Mick, 496

Jannings, Emil, 470
Japan, 70
Jaws, 262, 442
Jaws – the Revenge, 524–6
Jemroe, 92
Jennings, Peter, 516
Jewison, Norman, 357
JFK, 445, 446
John Ruskin Infants' School, 12
Johnson, Ben, 440
Johnson, Michelle, 479, 480, 486
Johnson, Samuel, 201
Jones, Dave, 546
Jones, Jack, 386
Jones, James, 32
Jones Quincy, 517
Jour Se Lève, Le, 49
Jourdan, Louis and Quique, 417
Juan Carlos, 255
Juan Les Pins, 536
Judd, Edward, 141
Julienne, Rémy, 301, 303

Kamen, Stan, 529
Kasher, Charlie, 206
Kashoggi, Adnan, 312
Kaye, Danny, 255, 281, 438
Kaye, Dina, 255
Kazan, Elia, 517
Kean, Edmund, 546
Keeler, Christine, 198
Kennedy, George, 274
Kennedy, Jacqueline, 459
Kennedy, John F., 445, 515
Kenya, 373–80
Kenya Coffee Bar, 201
Kenya Safari Club, 374
Kenyatta, Jomo, 374
Kerkorian, Kirk, 539
Kidnapped, 325
Kimberg, Judd, 294
King Kong, 262
King Rat, 224, 320
Kinski, Klaus, 438
Kipling, Rudyard, 390, 391
Kirkwood, Brian, 316
Kissinger, Henry, 488
Klinger, Michael, 322–4, 346–7

Knight, David, 140
Korean War, 68, 69, 71–4, 75–90
Ku Klux Klan, 277
Kubrick, Christiana, 227
Kubrick, Stanley, 220, 227–8
Kurnitz, Harry, 257–9

Lacey, Ginger, 304–6
Ladd, Alan, 142
Lady Boss (Collins), 542
Lady Ghislaine, 539–40
Lancaster, Burt, 457
Langan, Peter, 380–1, 411–14, 455, 463–4, 470, 518, 528
Landis, Harry, 124
Lark, The (Anouilh), 132
Larthe, Pat, 139
Las Vegas, 260–2, 359, 360–4, 449–50
Last Picture Show, 552
Last of the Summer Wine, 215
Last Valley, The, 319–21
Laughton, Charles, 143
Lauren, Ralph, 192
Law, John Philip, 274
Lawford, Pat and Peter, 515
Lawrence, Frank, 68, 90–1, 101
Lawrence of Arabia, 146, 290
Lawson, Wilfred, 143, 189–90, 224–6
Lazar, Irving, 437, 478, 516–17, 542–3
Lazar, Mary, 437, 542–3
Lean, David, 46, 176, 249, 290, 457
Leather Boys, The, 197
Led Zeppelin, 425
Legrain Coffee Shop, 131
Leigh, Vivien, 274, 357
Lemmon, Jack, 105–6
Lennard, Robert, 139–40
Lennon John, 230–1
Leno, Jay, 417
Leone, Sergio, 290
Lerman, Oscar, 187, 339–40, 557
Lester, Richard, 220
Levin, Ira, 459
Levine, Joseph, 188–9, 439, 458

Lewin, David, 277–8
Lewis, Daniel Day, 288
Lewis, Ronald, 124
Life, 296
Linton, Mrs, 24–7
Littlewood, Joan, 127–9, 164
Lloyd, Sue, 207–8
Logan, Josh, 135
Lom, Herbert, 256
London 'Swinging', 124, 133, 142–3, 159–60, 186–7, 191, 220–1, 241, 299, 328
Lone Ranger, 10, 23
Long and the Short and the Tall, The (Hall), 143–5, 146, 156, 470
Long Good Friday, The, 472, 520
Look Back in Anger (Osborne), 133, 202, 321, 324
Lord, Betty Bao, 517
Loren, Sophia, 267
Los Angeles, 242–50, 317, 360, 417–18, 419, 433–5. *See also*Beverly Hills *and* Hollywood
Losey, Joseph, 384–6
love scenes, 385, 515
Luau, 253, 315
Lucky (Collins), 542
Ludlum, Robert, 497
Lumet, Sidney, 136, 458–61
Lyne, Adrian, 520

Ma Maison, 461–2, 464
Macbeth, 331
McCartney, Paul, 217
McGrath, John, 150, 154, 155
McMurtry, Larry, 517
Mackenzie, John, 472–4, 520
Maclaine, Shirley, 241, 249–50, 254–6, 262–3, 283, 284
MacMurray, Fred, 420–1
McQueen, Steve, 49, 419, 529
Magus, The, 293–7
Maharis, George, 241
Mahdi Altijir, 488–9
Mailer, Norman, 32
Majorca, 285, 293–7
make-up, 545

malaria, 98–103, 247

Malta, 346–7

Mamas and the Papas, The, 318

Mamounia Hotel, 393–406

Man and a Woman, A, 228

Man for All Seasons, A (Bolt), 457

Man Who Would Be King, The, 390–406, 431

Man with the Golden Arm, The, 273

Manchurian Candidate, The, 497

Manilow, Barry, 466

Mankiewicz, Joseph L., 350–7

Mansfield, Jayne, 272–3

Manson, Charles, 318–19, 427

Mapledurham, 407

Marcos, Ferdinand, 312

Margaret, Princess, 65, 465–6

Mark Saber, 143

Marlborough Street Magistrates' Court, 147–8

Marle, Billy, 44

Marseilles Contract, The, 372

Marsh, Jean, 407

Martin, Steve, 533–8

Marx, Groucho, 246

Marymount School, 519

Masai, 376–7

Mason, James, 220, 409

masturbation: prodigious, 33; and poor eyesight, 50; distance trials, 50

matchmaking, 251, 457, 461

Matthau, Carole, 517

Matthau, Walter, 238

Maxwell, Robert, 539

Maxwell House, 338–41

Me and My Girl, 551

Medwin, Michael, 124

Mendes, Sergio, 483

Mengers, Jean-Claude, 465

Mengers, Susan, 437, 443, 465–6, 529

Merchant, Vivien, 215–6

Meredith, Burgess, 274

Merton Park Studios, 129

Mexico, 472–5

MFK, 254, 315

MI5, 198

Michael of Kent, Princess, 465

Mickey Mouse Express, 83

Micklewhite, Ellen, *mother*: poverty, 3; character, 7; Norfolk, 19–27; cooking 24, 36; charlady, 121, 193; Brixton, 184–5, 222–3; *Zulu* première, 193–4; bread pudding, 202; *Alfie* première, 229; Streatham, 321–2, 418, 518; Mill House, 327; and Shakira, 360; in Cannes, 447; in Beverly Hills, 447–50; Malapropisms, 447–8, 518; in Las Vegas, 449; Rectory Cottage, 527–8; David, 554, 555, 556; death, 547

Micklewhite, Maurice, *father*: character, 6–7, gambling, 6, 49, 328; and homosexuals, 20, 40, 57, 100; final illness, 110–12, 184

Micklewhite, Stanley, *brother*, 112, 121, 184, 557; birth 9, evacuation, 13–17; Norfolk, 19–27; father's death, 112; hard times, 228–9; MC's flat, 298; actor, 301; and David, 556

Miles, Sarah, 457

Mill House, 326–7, 348–9, 350, 358, 359, 383, 386, 407, 409, 416–7, 425

Milland, Ray, 520–1

Mills, John, 224

Mills, Robert, 86–8

Minnelli, Liza, 250, 386–7, 388

Minelli, Vincent, 386

Mona Lisa, 4

Monaco, 511

Monroe, Marilyn, 129, 316, 378

Moon's a Balloon, The (Niven), 538

Moore, Bobby, 452

Moore, Demi, 479

Moore Dudley, 201, 224–6, 503

Moore, Luisa, 226–7, 366–7, 416, 454, 456, 519, 539

Moore, Roger, 43–4, 156–7, 226–7, 409, 416, 454, 456, 519, 539

Morgan, 220

Morocco, 392–403

Morris, Johnny, 289, 290–1, 296, 318, 337
Morris, Oswald, 357, 393
Morris, William, 529
Morton's, 465
Mould, Marion, 419
Mountbatten, Lord, 496
Muhammad Ali, 337, 498–9
Mulroney, Brian, 549
Mumming Birds, 41
Muni, Paul, 48
Muppets, The, 533, 556
Mutiny on the Bounty, The, 457
My Fair Lady, 469–70, 517
My Left Foot, 288
My Turn to Make the Tea (Dickens), 90
Myers, Peter, 139

Nairobi, 373
Naked and the Dead, The (Mailer), 32
name changes, 5, 132; for a joke, 230–1
National Service, 57, 63–74, 75–90
National Theatre, 354–5, 356, 541
Naughton, Bill, 157, 213, 215
Neame, Ronald, 249, 256
Neville, John, 192–3
New Orleans, 274, 276–7
New York, 235–9, 425, 503–8
New York Post, The, 365
New York Times, The, 381
Newcastle upon Tyne, 323–4
Newhart, Bob, 497–8
Newley, Anthony, 160
Newman, Nanette, 160, 224, 225, 226, 227, 416, 456
Newman, Paul, 258, 287, 316, 419
Newsweek, 239
Next Time I'll Sing to You (Saunders), 161, 162–3
Nice, 534–8
Nicholson, Jack, 466, 496
Nigeria, 169–70
Niven, David, 535, 538
Niven, David, Jnr, 407, 456
No Hiding Place, 143

Noises Off, 552–3, 554
Nolan, Lloyd, 507
Noonan, Peggy, 512
Norfolk, 12–27
Norma Rae, 397
nose, 48, 509
nude scenes, 385, 507
Nureyev, Rudolf, 496

Oberon, Merle, 303
O'Brien, Edna, 193, 328
O'Brien, Margaret, 330
Observer, The, 207
Odins, 380–1
Oh Calcutta!, 203
O'Hara, Maureen, 238
Oliver, 154–5
Olivier, Laurence, 146, 216, 348, 356–8, 541, 546
Olongapo, 309–11
One More River, 142
O'Neill, Eugene, 354
Osborne, John, 133, 321, 324
Oscars, 216, 220, 288, 313–4, 357–8, 408, 437, 457, 471, 476–9, 508, 525, 552
Osmonds, The, 449
O'Sullivan, Maureen, 507
Oswald, Lee Harvey, 445
Othello, 146
O'Toole, Peter, 140, 144–5, 146, 162, 546
Ouarzazate, 400–3
Ovitz, Michael, 263
Owen, Bill, 215
Oz, Frank, 533–8

Paar, Jack, 238
Pacino, Al, 49, 529
Page, Anthony, 146
Page, Jimmy, 425
Paley, Bill, 514–5
Pam, Jerry, 360
Paper Moon, 552
Paramount Pictures, 177–8, 239, 267, 316
Paris, 113–19, 152–4, 283–4, 389–92, 453

Parker, Alan, 520
Parton, Dolly, 510
Pat O'Brien's, 277
Patrick, Nigel, 134
Paul, Elliott, 113
Peak Films, 57–9
Peck, Gregory, 314
Pele, 452
People, The, 554
Peppard, George, 241
Pfeiffer, Michelle, 515
Philip, Prince, 177, 255–6, 522, 524
Philippe, Gérard, 69
Philippines, 307–14, 408
Pickens, Slim, 440
Pickford, Mary, 513
Pickwick, 160, 195
Pickwick restaurant, 160
Pinewood Studios, 208, 283, 350–2, 380
Pinter, Harold, 151, 161, 215
Pitinguey, Ivo, 483–7
Platoon, 446
Play Dirty, 288–93
Playboy Club, London, 202
Pleasance, Donald, 407
Plummer, Christopher, 190, 205, 393, 395–6, 404
Poitier, Joanna, 374, 380
Poitier, Sidney, 344–81
Polanski, Roman, 187, 322, 331
Politzer, Nigel, 340–2
Polo Lounge, 244–5
Ponting, Roy, 296–7
Portugal, 120–6
Poseidon Adventure, The, 419, 440
Power, Tyrone, 48, 100
Preminger, Otto, 273–80
Previn, André, 508
Price, Charles and Carol, 522
Price, Dennis, 137, 157
Price Waterhouse, 477
Prima, Louis, 363
Pringle, Brian, 142
Private Lives (Coward), 19
Profumo, John, 198
Puck, Wolfgang, 462

Pulp, 345–7
Pusan, 71–2, 82
Pygmalion, 469–70

Quant, Mary, 159, 191
Quayle, Anthony, 407
Quinn, Anthony, 269, 295–6

racism, 359–60, 409–10
Raj's club, 131, 160
Rambaldi, Carlo, 446
Rand, Ayn, 109
Rank Organisation, 59
rats, 79–80
Raymond, Gary, 140
reading, 31–2
Reagan, Nancy, 467
Reagan, Ronald, 512
Rectory Farmhouse, 492–6, 512, 521, 524–5, 526–8
Redford, Robert, 287, 529
Redgrave, Lynn, 220, 270–2
Redgrave, Vanessa, 220, 298, 303, 467
Reed, Alec, 47–8, 49
Reeve, Christopher, 43, 458–61, 553
Régine, 153–4, 511
Reichman, Paul, 549
Reinhardt, Max, 276
Reisz, Karel, 220
Requiem for a Heavyweight, 141
Reuben, Reuben, 476
Reventlow, Lance, 428
Reversal of Fortune, 288
Rhinestone Cowboy, 510
Richard III, 216
Richards, Bea, 274
Richardson, Ralph, 224
Richardson, Tony, 467
rickets, 5
rifle under bed, 534
Ring of Truth, 154
Rio de Janeiro, 479–87
Ritchie, Michael, 442
Robertson, Cliff, 308–14
Robinson, Edward G., 48
Rockefeller Center, 504

Rocky, 450, 451
Rodeo Drive, 249, 315, 426
Rodgers, Anton, 536
Rogers, Roy, 175
Rolling Stones, The, 159, 186–7, 220, 229
Rolls Royce, 17, 155, 299–301, 426, 435–6
Romantic Englishwoman, The, 383–6
Romeo and Juliet, 357
Ronstadt, Linda, 466
Room, The (Pinter), 151, 215–6
Rooney, Mickey, 330, 347–8
Rosemary's Baby, 458
Ross, Herb, 439
Rothschild, Baron Philippe de, 129
Royal Court Theatre, 151, 215–6
RUR (Capek), 45
rushes, 176–7
Russell, Jane, 246–7
Russell, Willy, 469
Russian Tea Room, 238, 459

Sag Harbor, 512–17
St James's Club: Beverly Hills, 252; London, 511
St Olave's Hospital, 4–5
St Paul, 534
St Vitus' Dance, 5
Salisbury, The, 131
Saltzman, Harry, 195–7, 205–12, 213, 221, 222, 229–30, 232, 288, 303–6, 321, 526
Saltzman, Jacqueline, 205
Sanders of the River, 109
Sassoon, Vidal, 191, 199
Saturday-morning cinema, 10
Saunders, James, 161
Saville, Phillip, 190
Savoy Grill, 302–3
Schaap, Dick, 296–7
Schlesinger, John, 220
Scofield, Paul, 546
Scott, George C., 241
Scott, Lizbeth, 347
Scott, Michael, 132
Scott, Ridley, 346, 520
Scott, Tony, 520

Screen Actors Guild, 431
screen test, first, 164–5
Séance on a Wet Afternoon, 224
Sebring, Jay, 315, 318–9
Segal, George, 241
Selinger, Dennis, 161–2, 185, 190, 213, 273, 321, 328, 337, 360–4, 368, 370–2, 386, 416
Selleck, Tom, 496
Sellers, Peter, 220, 224, 305, 386–7
Seoul, 81–2
Servant, The, 384
sex, 141; and chocolate, 35–6; in cinema, 40; snogging, 47; 'Auntie', 56–7; leading ladies, 93–4; theatre hierarchy, 106; commercial, 137–8, 245. *See also* AIDS; homosexuality; masturbation; venereal disease
Shaffer, Anthony, 348
Shakespeare, William, 146, 190, 331 393, 443
Shalako, 290, 291, 292
Sharif, Omar, 320
Shaw, George Bernard, 469
Shaw, Robert, 122–3, 142, 190, 366
Shawn, Dick, 497–8
Shepherd, Richard, 414, 518
Shepperton, 120, 124–5, 329
Shevelove, Burt, 224
Shock to the System, 542–3
Shogun (Clavell), 320
Shot in the Dark, A, 220
Shrimpton, Jean, 187, 188, 197–8, 200, 213
Sica, Vittorio de, 283, 284
Silence of the Lambs, The, 288
Silver Bears, The, 417–8
Simon, Neil, 439
Sinatra, Barbara, 539
Sinatra, Frank, 220, 250, 257–8, 258, 260, 457, 539
Sinatra, Nancy, 220, 251, 260–1
Singing in the Rain, 479
Sixty Minutes, 516
Sleuth, 348, 350–8, 360, 365, 458, 477, 541

Smith, Jim, 545
Smith, Keely, 363
Smith, Maggie, 439
smoking: and filming, 217–8; MC
  cuts down, 325–6
snakes, 79–80, 378–9, 435
Snowdon, Lord and Lady, 550
Soho: London, 112; New York,
  133, 543
Solomons, Col., 101–3
Solosy's, 91, 104
Somewhere for the Night (Naughton),
  157
Sound of Music, The, 205
South Africa, 169–83, 373
South Pacific, 135
Spago's, 439, 478
Speight, Johnny, 155–6
Spielberg, Steven, 446
spivs, 37
Springtime in Paris (Paul), 113
Stage, The, 91, 104
Stallone, Sylvester, 450–4, 510
Stamp, Chris, 162
Stamp, Terence, 140; friendship
  with MC, 146, 147, 148, 151,
  154–5; *Why the Chicken?*, 154–5,
  159; girls, 159–60, 185–6; *Billy
  Budd*, 159, 160–1; *Term of Trial*,
  161; and Julie Christie, 185–7,
  220; gossip concerning MC, 188;
  Collector, 187–8; success,
  196–8; and MC's success, 197–
  8; in America, 198, 200; and Jean
  Shrimpton, 188, 197, 200, 213;
  end of friendship with MC, 212–3;
  offered *Alfie*, 213
Stanislavsky, Konstantin, 128
Steinem, Gloria, 238, 381–3
Stevens, George, 252
Stevenson, Robert Louis, 325
Stone, Oliver, 445–6
Stop the World I Want to Get Off, 160
*Strange Case of Dr Jekyll and Mr
  Hyde, The*, 545
Streatham, 321–2, 418, 518
Streisand, Barbra, 136, 229, 251,
  466, 529

Stroheim, Erich von, 276
Studio 54, 458–9
Sturges, John, 407
Summerbee, Mike, 452
Superman, 43, 458
Surrender, 526
Sutherland, Donald, 190, 407
Sutton, Dudley, 142
Swanson, Gloria, 250
Swarm, The, 419–21, 440
Sweet Liberty, 512–17
Swinging Sixties, 124, 133, 142–3,
  159–60, 186–7, 191, 220–1, 241,
  277, 299, 328
Sydow, Max von, 507
Sykes, Eric, 292

Taipan (Clavell), 320
Tandy, Jessica, 239
Taste of Honey, 270
Tate, Sharon, 187, 318–19, 427
tax, 408–9, 416–7, 426, 528, 532
Taylor, Elizabeth, 252, 328–33,
  437
Taylor, Jack, 68, 90–1, 101
Taylor, Robert, 48, 100
Teddy boys, 38–9
Tender Mercies, 476
Tennant, Victoria, 533
Term of Trial, 161
Terrail, Patrick, 462, 464
Thatcher, Denis, 531, 550
Thatcher, Margaret, 522–3, 524,
  528, 530–1, 549–51
Theatre Workshop, 127–9
Thelma and Louise, 346
Thomas, Danny, 497–8
Thompson, Kay, 386
Thunderball, 220
ties, dislike of, 14
Till Death Us Do Part, 156
Today, 236, 237
Tom Jones, 216, 467
Tonight, 237
Too Late the Hero, 307–14
Towering Inferno, 419
Toy, 309–10
Tracy, Spencer, 49, 218

Tramp, 339–41
Treasure of Sierra Madre, The, 392
Trevelyan, John, 203–4
Trinity College, Dublin, 470–1
Trump Tower, 504
Tuck, Bob Stanford, 304–6
Turin, 302
Turner, Lana, 59
Turner, Reg, 546
Turner, Tina, 316
Tushingham, Rita, 270–2
Twentieth Century-Fox, 284, 293, 294, 456, 467
21 Club, 238
2001, 227
Tynan, Kenneth, 202–3

Uganda, 170–1
Universal Studios, 262, 488, 552–3
Upstairs Downstairs, 407
Ustinov, Peter, 159

Vadim, Roger, 274
Vandeleur, Joe, 415–6
venereal disease, 71, 82, 83–4, 101
Victory, 507
Vidor, King, 314
Vietnam, 298, 303, 319, 445
Vonnegut, Kurt, 505

Wager, Anthony, 46
Wain, Harry, 68, 75–81, 84, 86, 89, 101
Wallis, Hal, 251
Wallis, Minna, 251, 254, 488
Walters, Barbara, 237
Walters, Julie, 385, 469–71, 476
Wanamaker, Sam, 142
Ware, Lenny, 68, 101
Warner, David, 220
Wasserman, Lew and Edie, 488
Water, 497
Watson, Eric, 33
Wayne, John, 247–8, 432–3
Weaver, Sigourney, 525
Weinberg, Sir Mark and Lady, 550
Weir, Peter, 511
Welk, Lawrence, 497

Welles, Orson, 162, 456–7, 462, 464
Weške, Brian, 546
What's Up, Doc?, 552
Whistle Blower, The, 524
White, Marco Pierre, 556
White Elephant, 519
Who, The, 162
Why the Chicken? (McGrath), 154, 161
Wickes, David, 532, 544
Widmark, Richard, 440
Wiener, Jack, 407, 408, 456
Wiest, Dianne, 508
Wilby Conspiracy, The, 373–80
Wilder, Billy and Audrey, 438
Williams, Treat, 407
Williamson, Nicol and Jill, 374
Wilson, Harold, 408
Wilson's Grammar School, 33–4, 43, 418
Windsor, 326; Castle, 348; racecourse, 327–8, 366, 410–11; Smith's Lawn, 522
Winters, Shelley, 218–9
Wolfe, Tom, 505
Woman Times Seven, 283–4
Wong, Madame, 493
Wood, Natalie, 251
Wrong Box, The, 224–6
Wuthering Heights: film, 188, 357; play, 98
Wyler, William, 187–8
Wynn, Ed, 498
Wynn, Keenan, 546

York, Susannah, 332
Yorkshire Ripper, 443–4
You Only Live Twice, 220
Young, Sean, 385
Young, Terence, 474
Young Communists, 52–4
Young Winston, 366

Zanuck, Richard, 442
Zarach, Dorrit, 488
Zarem, Bobby, 235–6, 459, 461, 504

Zarem, Danny, 459, 504
Zee and Co., 328–33
Zen, 348
Zukor, Adolph, 316

Zulu, 124, 163–5, 169–83, 188–9, 193, 195, 199, 226, 323, 373, 393, 545
Zulus, 174–5, 180–1, 183

Who Does She Think She Is?

Martine McCutcheon

The autobiography of the best-loved performer in Britain today

'Who does she think she is?' is something Martine has heard people say about her all her life. Born into the poorest and least-promising background and with only a loving mother's support to help her, Martine has dared to follow her dreams of stardom and has achieved more in her twenty-four years than most of those who turned their noses up at her achieve in a lifetime.

It's a story that includes a life on the run from a violent father, drink, drugs and even an attempted murder that filled her child-hood with fear; her early attempts at pop stardom and first loves, plus dates with Matt Goss and Mick Hucknall; her big break in *EastEnders*, and the shocking story of how she really came to leave the series.

Martine's story ends with today's triumphs over the tragedies of her life: the number one and patinum-selling singles and album, the starring roles in a new television series, a feature film and in *My Fair Lady* at The National Theatre.

The British public have taken Martine McCutcheon to their hearts – she is 'one of us' – and her life story is an inspiration to anyone born without any apparent advantages.

arrow books

Crying With Laughter

Bob Monkhouse

In this highly acclaimed autobiography Bob Monkhouse, one of Britain's most successful and enduring comedians, tells us in his own inimitable style the fascinating and often hilarious story of his life.

From disclosures of painful personal tragedies to uproarious anecdotes about the stars he has known, Bob's confessions are always blisteringly honest, touching – and often shocking.

Crying With Laughter combines heartache with hilarity, sexy showbiz revelations with genuinely moving tales of hard times, to create a passionate, witty and sparkling account of an extraordinary man's extraordinary life.

'An entertaining and abrasive canter through his up-and-down life . . . Witty, moving, candid – and very well written'
Sunday Express

'It makes a refreshing change to read some real revelations from the life of a true, old-fashioned star'
Daily Mirror

'Winning . . . genuinely funny'
Sunday Times

arrow books

Moab is My Washpot

Stephen Fry

'Stephen Fry is one of the great originals . . . This autobiography of his first twenty years is a pleasure to read, mixing outrageous acts with sensible opinions in bewildering confusion . . . That so much outward charm, self-awareness and intellect should exist alongside behaviour that threatened to ruin the lives of innocent victims, noble parents and Fry himself, gives the book a tragic grandeur that lifts it to classic status'
Financial Times

'Remarkable, perhaps even unique . . . that aroma of authenticity that is the point of all great autobiographies; of which this, I rather think, is one'
Evening Standard

'He writes superbly about his family, about his homosexuality, about the agonies of childhood . . . some of his bursts of simile take the breath away . . . his most satisfying and appealing book so far'
Observer

'This is one of the most extraordinary and affecting biographies I have read . . . painfully honest . . . and often, as you might expect, very funny . . . I hope to goodness there'll be a sequel. I can't wait for more'
Daily Mail

arrow books

My Turn

Norman Wisdom

The autobiography of one of Britain's best-loved comedians

Norman Wisdom's early years could easily have come straight from the pages of a Dickens novel. Left by their frightened mother, ill-treated by a brutal father, Norman and his brother were forced to fend for themselves, sleeping rough in London and stealing food to survive.

This is a rags to riches tale of the man Charlie Chaplin said would take his mantle and who went on to make millions laugh around the world for over five decades. Here are the hardships, tragedies and triumphs that gave him his inspiration.

From the days working the seasons at Scarborough, to the unforgettable and endearing character Norman Pitkin – the little man in a tight fitting suit, read of his rapid climb up the showbiz ladder.

'A classic rags-to-riches saga'
The Spectator

arrow books